Roughing It in the Suburbs
Reading *Chatelaine* Magazine in the Fifties and Sixties

Chatelaine, originally launched in 1928, had, by the fifties and sixties, nearly two million readers each month for its eclectic mix of traditional and surprisingly unconventional articles and editorials. At a time when the American women's magazine market began to flounder thanks to the advent of television, *Chatelaine*'s subscriptions expanded, as did the lively debate between its covers. Why?

In this exhilarating study of Canada's foremost women's publication at mid-century, Valerie Korinek shows that the magazine, though filled with advertisements that promoted household perfection through the endless expansion of consumer spending, contained fiction, feature articles, letters, and editorials that subversively complicated the simple recipes for affluent domesticity. Articles on abortion, spousal abuse, and poverty proliferated alongside explicitly feminist editorials. It was a potent mixture, and the mail poured in – both praising and criticizing the new directions at the magazine.

Chatelaine's highly interactive and participatory nature encouraged what Korinek calls 'a community of readers' – readers who, in their very response to the magazine, led to its success. *Chatelaine* did not cling to the stereotypical images of the era, but forged ahead, providing women with a variety of images, ideals, and critiques of women's role in society. The magazine's dissemination of feminist ideas laid the foundation for feminism in Canada in the 1970s and after.

Comprehensive, fascinating, and full of lively debate and history, *Roughing It in the Suburbs* provides a cultural study that weaves together a history of *Chatelaine*'s producers, consumers, and text. It illustrates how the structure of the magazine's production, and the composition of its editorial and business offices, allowed feminist material to infiltrate a mass-market women's monthly. In doing so, it offers a detailed analysis of the times, the issues, and the women and, sometimes, men who participated in the success of a Canadian cultural landmark.

Valerie J. Korinek is an associate professor in the Department of History at the University of Saskatchewan. She is a specialist in Canadian cultural and gender history, as well as in the history of Canada since the Second World War.

STUDIES IN GENDER AND HISTORY

General editors: Franca Iacovetta and Karen Dubinsky

Roughing It in the Suburbs

Reading *Chatelaine* Magazine
in the Fifties and Sixties

Valerie J. Korinek

UNIVERSITY OF TORONTO PRESS
Toronto   Buffalo   London

© University of Toronto Press Incorporated 2000
Toronto Buffalo London

Printed in Canada

ISBN 0-8020-4180-9 (cloth)
ISBN 0-8020-8041-3 (paper)

Printed on acid-free paper

Canadian Cataloguing in Publication Data

Korinek, Valerie Joyce, 1965–
    Roughing it in the suburbs : reading Chatelaine magazine in the
    fifties and sixties

(Studies in gender and history)
Includes bibliographical references and index.
ISBN 0-8020-4180-9 (bound)   ISBN 0-8020-8041-3 (pbk.)

1. Women – Press coverage – Canada – History – 20th century.
2. Chatelaine (Toronto, Ont.: 1928).   I. Title.   II. Series: Studies
in gender and history series.

PN4914.W6K67 2000   070.4'493054'0971   C00-931373-7

Every effort has been made to obtain permission to reproduce the illustrations that appear in this book. Any errors or omissions brought to our
attention will be corrected in future printings.

University of Toronto Press acknowledges the financial assistance to its
publishing program of the Canada Council for the Arts and the Ontario
Arts Council.

This book has been published with the help of a grant from the Humanities
and Social Sciences Federation of Canada, using funds provided by the
Social Sciences and Humanities Research Council of Canada.

University of Toronto Press acknowledges the financial support for its
publishing activities of the Government of Canada through the Book
Publishing Industry Development Program (BPIDP).

For my parents, Shirley and Fred Korinek

Contents

Illustrations   ix

Acknowledgments   xiii

1 'Lighting Up a Brush Fire'   3

Part One: Historicizing Production and Consumption

2 'A Closet Feminist Magazine': (Re)-Making *Chatelaine*   31
3 'A Faithful Friend and Tonic': Reading *Chatelaine*   71

Part Two: Traditional Fare?

4 'Your Best Medium to Sell Women': Covering and
   Advertising *Chatelaine*   105
5 'The Cinderella from Pugwash': Advice from the
   Chatelaine Institute   178
6 'Searching for a Plain Gold Band': *Chatelaine* Fiction   220

Part Three: Subverting the Standard

7 'How to Live in the Suburbs': Editorials and Articles
   in the Fifties   257
8 'Trying to Incite a Revolution': Editorials and Articles
   in the Sixties   308

9 'Here in the Lodge': *Chatelaine*'s Legacy   366

Notes   377

Select Bibliography   435

Index   447

Illustrations

1 *Chatelaine* cover, July 1960   39
  Reprinted with the permission of Maclean Hunter

2 *Chatelaine* cover, January 1957   112
  Reprinted with the permission of Maclean Hunter

3 *Chatelaine* cover, July 1962   115
  Reprinted with the permission of Maclean Hunter

4 *Chatelaine* cover, April 1960   117
  Reprinted with the permission of Maclean Hunter

5 *Chatelaine* cover, March 1960   119
  Reprinted with the permission of Maclean Hunter

6 'Her apron strings are "family ties,"' *Chatelaine*,
  November 1950   128
  Reprinted with the permission of Weston Bakeries Ltd

7 'One done, one to go,' *Chatelaine*, June 1954   130
  Reprinted with the permission of Weston Bakeries Ltd

8 'Freedom from Work on Washday,' *Chatelaine*, January 1953   132
  Reprinted with the permission of Westinghouse Canada

9 'G.E. Swivel-Top Cleaner,' *Chatelaine*, April 1954   134
  Reprinted with the permission of G.E. Canada

10 'She's in love ... and she loves Community,' *Chatelaine*,
   October 1953   136
   © Oneida Ltd. All rights reserved.

11 'Give the Bride a Bissell Sweeper!' *Chatelaine*, May 1954   137
   Reprinted with the permission of Bissell Ltd

12 'The Right Gift,' *Chatelaine*, May 1954   138
Reprinted with the permission of General Electric Canada

13 'Wake up, Henry,' *Chatelaine*, September 1958   140
Reprinted with the permission of The Quaker Oats Company of Canada

14 'Yardley Lavender,' *Chatelaine*, March 1958   142

15 'Only a Playtex Girdle,' *Chatelaine*, September 1953   143
Reprinted with the permission of Canadell Inc.

16 'For warmth and comfort,' *Chatelaine*, September 1958   145
Reprinted with the permission of Mary Maxim

17 'Why be a martyr,' *Chatelaine*, May 1967   149
The item is reproduced with the permission of Nabisco Ltd.
Aylmer Diet De Luxe® is a trade mark of Nabisco Ltd, © all rights reserved.

18 'Now Europe gives you a figure,' *Chatelaine*, October 1960   150
Reprinted with the permission of Triumph International, Germany

19 'Most English girls,' *Chatelaine*, September 1965   153

20 'Lo and behold,' *Chatelaine*, January 1963   154
Reprinted with the permission of Springs Canada

21 'Since the dawn of time,' *Chatelaine*, January 1966   156
Reprinted with the permission of Springs Canada

22 'For a bronze anniversary,' *Chatelaine*, May 1967   160

23 'Whoopee! He's off,' *Chatelaine*, September 1965   162

24 'On the double, Daddy,' *Chatelaine*, May 1961   164
Reprinted with the permission of Maple Leaf Meats

25 'Safest Gun in the west,' *Chatelaine*, September 1962   166
Reprinted with the permission of General Motors of Canada Limited, Oshawa, Ontario

26 *Chatelaine* cover, January 1952   188
Reprinted with the permission of Maclean Hunter

27 'Cinderella from Pugwash,' *Chatelaine*, April 1954   200
Reprinted with the permission of Maclean Hunter

28 'Chatelaine Beauty Clinic,' *Chatelaine*, November 1962   203
Reprinted with the permission of Maclean Hunter

29 'Five Rooms for Fun,' *Chatelaine*, August 1952   208–9
Reprinted with the permission of Maclean Hunter

30 '*Chatelaine* Expo Home,' *Chatelaine*, May 1967   211
Reprinted with the permission of Maclean Hunter

31 'The Wasted Years,' *Chatelaine*, September 1959   239
Reprinted with the permission of Maclean Hunter

32 'Sari in the Kitchen,' *Chatelaine*, September 1962   244
Reprinted with the permission of Maclean Hunter

33 'Common Law Wife,' *Chatelaine*, January 1952   278
Reprinted with the permission of Maclean Hunter

34 'Are Canadians Really Tolerant?' *Chatelaine*, September 1959   287
Reprinted with the permission of Maclean Hunter

35 'How to Live in the Suburbs,' *Chatelaine*, March 1955   292
Reprinted with the permission of Maclean Hunter

36 'Working Wives Are Here to Stay,' *Chatelaine*, September 1961   327
Reprinted with the permission of Maclean Hunter

37 'After Black Power, Woman Power,' *Chatelaine*,
September 1969   333
Reprinted with the permission of Maclean Hunter

38 'The Forgotten Canadians,' *Chatelaine*, June 1962   345
Reprinted with the permission of Maclean Hunter

39 *Chatelaine* cover, November 1968   346
Reprinted with the permission of Maclean Hunter

40 'The Real Poor in Canada Are Women,' *Chatelaine*, April 1969   350
Reprinted with the permission of Maclean Hunter

41 'The Good Life on $6500/Year,' *Chatelaine*, January 1968   360
Reprinted with the permission of Maclean Hunter

Acknowledgments

It is a pleasure to come to the end of this long process of writing a book and to reflect on those whose encouragement, expertise, and support made it possible.

Since the first version of *Roughing It in the Suburbs* appeared as a doctoral dissertation, my initial debt is to the graduate history program at the University of Toronto. My supervisor, Paul Rutherford, read innumerable drafts of the thesis and was, at times, my toughest critic. In post-critique lunches at the Faculty Club or in Chinese restaurants on Spadina, that criticism was always tempered with humour and comradeship, which made the process far more enjoyable. In the years since, he has continued to provide beneficial advice and encouragement. Sylvia Van Kirk and Laurel MacDowell both read numerous drafts and provided enthusiastic feedback about growing up female in the fifties and sixties. Other scholars, including Marlene Shore, Franca Iacovetta, and Ruth Roach Pierson, offered helpful suggestions and advice, and for that I am grateful. The financial support available at the University of Toronto was critically important to my graduate education: the University of Toronto doctoral fellowship, the Social Sciences and Humanities Doctoral Fellowship, and the Ontario Graduate Scholarship. My peers at the university – Elsbeth Heaman, Robin Brownlie, Chris Hull, Jane Harrison, Paul Deslandes, and Kari Bronaugh – all offered helpful commentary and a sense of scholarly solidarity. Finally, the conviviality and insanity of the 'bent historians' group, including Dan Healey, Blaine Chaisson, Stephen 'Dinny' Morrison, Chris Munn, Paul Deslandes, Robin Brownlie, and Carla Morse, put the process of writing and revising into perspective.

My second debt is to my colleagues in the Department of History at the University of Saskatchewan. I am fortunate to be with a generous group of scholars who have provided a congenial and supportive environment in which to work. In particular, the good-humoured and sage advice of Bill Waiser and Jim Miller has been critical to my successful navigation of the revision stage in publishing a book. They buoyed my spirits with their wry insights into the process of scholarly publishing and offered suggestions on the art of 'stealing time' for research. Thanks are also due to Larry Stewart, the current head of the department, who offered consistent support. The University of Saskatchewan also encouraged the publication of this book through the award of a publications grant, which assisted in the reproduction of the photographs. Finally, I wish to thank my colleagues and their partners for their warm hospitality in welcoming me to Saskatoon and their continued kindness during the writing of this book, especially Dave and Denise De Brou, Bill and Marley Waiser, Jim and Mary Miller, Gordon Desbrisay and Susan Blake, Martha Smith, Gary Hanson, and Dale and Pat Miquelon.

Other people who deserve recognition are those who assisted in the archival and oral research. I would like to thank Lee Simpson, group publisher and vice president of the Woman's Group at Maclean Hunter, for granting me permission to use the archival copies of *Chatelaine* at Maclean Hunter offices and for allowing me to reprint material from *Chatelaine*. I also thank the advertisers for their permission to reprint selected advertisements. Former editor Doris Anderson and former *Chatelaine* journalists June Callwood and Eileen Morris were generous with their time and provided me with oral histories of their days at *Chatelaine*. Similarly, I wish to thank those people who responded to my questionnaire about reading *Chatelaine*: Bette-Jo Baird, Jan Baldwin, June Ellis, Marjorie E. Hallman, Dorothy Marlow, Zena McLeod, Eileen Morris, Marjorie Prophet, Barbara Wellspring, as well as those who wished to remain anonymous. A well-deserved thanks to Albert A. Johnson, who scoured Nova Scotia in search of vintage copies of *Chatelaine* and found nearly a complete run. Ruth and Bob Morse acted as the brokers for these acquisitions. Most of my archival research was completed at the Thomas Fisher Rare Book Library at the University of Toronto and the Archives of Ontario, and I thank all staff members for their assistance.

During the manuscript revision process I incurred considerable debts to the University of Toronto Press. I wish to thank Bill Harnum for his initial and continued interest in this project. My editor, Gerry Hallowell, has always been enthusiastic about the project, and he generously offered his time to read the unrevised dissertation and offer shrewd advice for publication. The editorial staff, in particular Emily Andrew, Jill McConkey, and Frances Mundy, have provided ongoing assistance in navigating the process. Rosemary Shipton's skilful editing of the manuscript was of great help. I also thank Karen Dubinsky and Franca Iacovetta, the co-editors of the Studies in Gender and History series, for their insights and timely encouragement during the revision process. Elsbeth Heaman and Laura Macleod read the manuscript, as did three anonymous assessors: their comments and suggestions for revisions have made for a better book. In the end, of course, I am responsible for any errors or omissions that remain. I acknowledge the Aid to Scholar Publications Grant, which provided funds for publication.

Finally, I wish to thank my family and close friends. I am grateful for the support and friendship that Elsbeth Heaman and Robin Brownlie have offered over the years. Their intellectual curiosity, humour, and encouragement spurred me on during the revision process. Carla Morse's editorial advice, affection, and enthusiasm for the project were essential to the completion of the original dissertation. Although Penny Skilnik did not enter my life until the final stages of manuscript revision, she good-naturedly learned to accommodate my *Chatelaine* baggage (and clutter) and encouraged the endless hours spent revising the manuscript. Her companionship, wisdom, and diverting forays into western Canadian culture have been of incalculable value. The unsung heroine award goes to Ashley, formerly of Bloor West, now of Nutana, who has taken up faithful vigil wherever I set up my computer.

My sister, Kimberley Korinek, was my first and chief ally in the delights of popular culture and my childhood co-conspirator in 'thinking stupid thoughts' that, many years later, I managed to parlay into a career. Kim's sharp wit, critical intelligence, and indefatigable energy have cheered and encouraged me throughout the writing of this book. My parents, Shirley and Fred Korinek, have always supported my academic aspirations, and, from their example, I've learned the virtues of hard work, tenacity, and determination – all of which have been critically important throughout this process. Though neither of my parents was able to attend university, they were determined that their children would. Their constant financial and emotional support to 'keep well the road' has been an incredible gift. In gratitude, this book is dedicated to them.

Roughing It in the Suburbs

Reading *Chatelaine* Magazine in the Fifties and Sixties

Chapter 1

'Lighting Up a Brush Fire'

'It could sit on your coffee table and no one would think you had something subversive on it,' recalled journalist and contributor June Callwood, 'because everybody had *Chatelaine* and men thought it was harmless – all about Easter hats. It was far from that. It was like lighting up a brush fire. It was wonderful.'[1] This book explores the paradoxical and now forgotten world of *Chatelaine* magazine in the fifties and sixties. Naturally, the brush fires are the most intriguing – colourful, attractive, and, once begun, difficult to control – but the more banal aspects of the magazine also illuminate the collective concerns of Canadian women. Together, the incendiary, the traditional, and the commercial intrigued, infuriated, and inspired nearly two million readers to pick up *Chatelaine* each month.

The venerable doyenne of Canadian women's magazines, *Chatelaine* reached its prime in the fifties and sixties. Launched to great fanfare in March 1928, it has been a consistent performer over the seventy years of its existence – as an audience favourite and as a commercial success for Maclean Hunter. During the postwar years, the magazine's format was revitalized. Readership surged to unprecedented levels, and the periodical became a national voice and champion for Canadian women. Subsequently, in the eighties and nineties, it was retooled once again with the ascension of new editors, first Mildred Istona and later Rona Maynard. To recapture the market lost in the late seventies, both editors focused the magazine as a glossier, fashion-driven periodical. Given the long lives of magazines and newspapers, in comparison with television programs, movies, music, and other examples of popular culture, print media require periodic repositioning so they remain fresh and timely, representative of the concerns of their readers and the communities they serve.

Because of these inevitable adjustments, it is somewhat disingenuous to ask, 'Why isn't *Chatelaine* still feminist today?' By and large it is not because of a conspiracy on the part of the editors and publishers, but primarily because the feminist message that appeared innovative and radical in the sixties and seventies, when North American women were embracing second-wave feminism in a variety of local and national organizations or in consciousness-raising groups, is no longer avant-garde today. The reason for this change is debatable: some say we now live in a 'post-feminist' era; others believe that second-wave feminism has run its course and achieved many of its goals – in particular with respect to equity issues. Regardless, any mass-market periodical with feminism as one of its primary themes would be an anachronism today. The American women's magazine market offers a cautionary tale about the perils of selling feminism. *Ms.* magazine, once the American standard bearer of liberal feminism (although its circulation has always been a fraction of the traditional American women's magazines), gamely carried on through the eighties and nineties, though it faced a continual struggle for readers and advertisers.[2] No doubt it surprises people that *Chatelaine*, a seemingly mild-mannered Canadian women's magazine, has an activist past. However, it is far more noteworthy that *Chatelaine*'s editors combined commercial success with a feminist agenda in the fifties and sixties than that feminist content declined in the eighties and nineties, an era when feminism was under siege from the right-wing regimes of Margaret Thatcher, Ronald Reagan, and Brian Mulroney.[3]

Even more astonishing, the editors and publishers in the fifties and sixties accomplished this coup during a severe downswing in the fortunes of the North American periodical industry. This reversal was due to television. The novelty of the new national mass medium attracted record numbers of viewers, people who no longer had the time for general magazines.[4] Severely diminished subscription and newsstand sales resulted in declining advertising revenue, as red became the primary colour in the ledger books of North American magazine publishers – Maclean Hunter included. While some companies attempted to shore up the traditional formats (particularly those for American women's magazines), most publishers began to abandon their general-interest periodicals in favour of more specialized publications. If television offered a mass, undifferentiated market, magazine publishers realized they could offer advertisers exclusive markets through periodicals such as *Playboy* or *Cosmopolitan*, the two most popular magazines of the era. Those magazines targeted lucrative niche audiences – urbane, affluent, and seemingly primed for advertisers. *Chatelaine* took a different path, continuing to cater to a mass, national audience of women because television did not offer much programming specifi-cally devoted to women's issues. *Chatelaine*'s editors retooled their offerings to emphasize issues of concern to Canadian women.

Chatelaine's ability to buck a North American trend testifies to the success of the editorial team at Maclean Hunter. But commercial chal-lenges were not the only obstacles to be overcome. In addition, the editors had to contend with the change and turbulence of the era. The insecurity of living in the midst of Cold War propaganda and between Cold War adversaries provided a worrisome subcurrent throughout the fifties and sixties.[5] In hindsight, we know that this era would inaugu-rate nearly thirty years of economic prosperity for Canadians. At the time, however, people continued to fear the re-emergence of recession and depression, which had marked the end of the First World War and later traumatized the country throughout the thirties. It is against that economic and political backdrop, and its attendant fears, that the 'good life in the suburbs' supposedly played out across the country.

The first stage of the suburban drama involved decommissioned servicemen and women (whether war brides or hometown sweethearts) who headed to the new communities on the fringe of cities, where the purchase of new bungalows signified the beginning of their lives to-gether. Once the period of reconversion was over, many other newly married couples also headed to the suburbs, lured by dreams of afford-able home ownership and child rearing in a clean, safe, child-friendly environment. The means of entry into this familial paradise was not readily available to all Canadians, nor were all satisfied with the life-styles they found there. As with all myths, there are some truths to those images of the good life in the suburbs, but, as recent historical works make clear, many Canadian women and men did not embrace their redomestication in suburban bungalows uncritically or easily.[6] Despite government-secured mortgages from the Canada Mortgage and Housing Corporation and grants to ex-servicemen, many working-class and immigrant families could not afford to purchase new bunga-lows.[7] American and Canadian historians have begun to re-evaluate the fifties and sixties – to note instances of rebellion and resistance to the circumscribed roles of suburban women, as wives and mothers, that many contemporary media commentators, academic experts, and politicians heralded as the new standard in societal organization and child raising.[8] As historian Veronica Strong-Boag's work indicates, Canadian women were often ambivalent about their role in 'modern' Canada.[9] Interviews with former suburbanites reveal that equal numbers remember the new, child-friendly lifestyle fondly, while others chafed at their lack of amenities, opportunities for employment, and often cash-strapped existence.

Roughing It in the Suburbs is intended to contribute to this revisionist history of the fifties and sixties, and, in particular, of women's roles and opportunities as they played out in the pages of Canada's national women's magazine. Lest the title of this book mislead, it was intended not only as an ironic tribute to that classic piece of nineteenth-century Canadiana, Susanna Moodie's *Roughing It in the Bush*, but also as a playful means by which to question our enduring use of the suburbs as the symbolic icon of the era. The pioneering spirit with which many Canadian women responded to life in their new suburban bungalows, which were often poorly serviced, with little public transportation and few amenities in the first few years, had a precursor in Moodie's travails. For many Canadians, life in the suburbs was a much-cherished dream; for others, a prison they eagerly plotted to escape. Ultimately, the images, assessments, and revisions raised by a critical reading of *Chatelaine* indicate that, though not all its readers were suburban dwellers, 'the suburbs' functioned as a symbolic touchstone of modern Canada, complete with a gendered, racial, class, and region-specific ideology, to which editors, writers, and readers constantly referred.

Contrary to the misperception that a rising tide of affluence made the suburban life possible for the majority of Canadians, for many 'average' families it took tight budgeting and two jobs. The Canadian suburbs were not as homogeneous as their American counterparts, or as affluent, because the standard of living in Canada was lower.[10] Homes, cars, washing machines, small appliances, and a host of consumer durables flooded the market in the fifties and sixties, and Canadian consumers, fuelled by advertising fantasies, were just as eager to participate in this capitalist cornucopia as their American cousins. Canadians, however, had far less disposable income.[11] To accomplish their consumer dreams, they made ample use of credit purchases, instalment buying, and loans from the Canada Mortage and Housing Corporation, so consumer debt was common. Working wives were another strategy to increase family purchasing power. By the sixties, nearly 50 per cent of all Canadian women in the labour force were married. The participation of women in the workforce was problematic because it created tension between the valorization of the stay-at-home wife and mother and the new economic reality that saw waged work increasingly become the norm for women. Joan Sangster's oral histories of working women in Peterborough emphasize the internalized guilt, exhausting dual day, and societal approbation faced by many working mothers.[12]

Nostalgia for the fifties has left the impression that Canadians experienced an era of endless affluence and good times, of breadwinning dads and full-time moms, but the reality of the Canadian quest to live 'modern' in the fifties and sixties was the result of tremendous social and economic changes. Those developments, in tandem with the population explosion created by the surge of baby-boom births and the rapid increase in postwar immigration to Canada, meant that Canadian society was undergoing a remarkable change. The country that had endured ten years of economic depression, followed by six years of wartime social and economic sacrifice, emerged into a period where people had a modest level of affluence. Most significant, for the first time in many years, personal destinies and dreams took precedence over economic, political, and military tensions.

Changes in society and, in particular, in women's roles provided a challenge for *Chatelaine*: How to attract this new modern Canadian woman to the magazine? In sharp contrast to its American competitors' tendencies to celebrate the suburbs, *Chatelaine* did not trade on the stereotypes or uncritical portraits of domestic bliss. Instead, the editors, writers, and readers more often dealt with the difficulties in adjustment to modern living, and continually debated both the joys and the challenges of marriage and motherhood. This questioning led, in the pages of the magazine and in society in general, to the re-emergence of feminism in the sixties, in tandem with the politics of race, class, and, later, sexual orientation. Presumably, the relevance and importance of a 'traditional' woman's magazine would be diminished by such developments, but *Chatelaine* chose to confront the changes head on. The fact that the *Chatelaine* team maximized these challenges helps to explain its success. It offered a variety of material, and often unconventional fare, which explored diversity and addressed the changing times.

Roughing It in the Suburbs is not only a study of a shrewd editorial team, supported by a production staff that handled advertising and circulation demands, but also a detailed account of the readers and the text, and the relationships among them. Few historical cultural studies pay any attention to readers, undoubtedly because of a paucity of resources, and those that do merely offer an analysis of reader demographics. In this case, however, thanks to letters published in *Chatelaine*, the Maclean Hunter Papers at the Archives of Ontario, and advertising studies and demographic profiles, it was possible to offer a nuanced, historical portrait of the act of reading *Chatelaine*. By any measure, the historical portrait of *Chatelaine* is incomplete without an analysis of readers and reading. In the hands of readers, the text underwent a process of interpretation, revision, critique, and debate that put another layer of meaning on the product created by editors, writers, and advertisers. The writers and editors encouraged, educated, and entertained readers, but, most important, they responded to their demands. These readers were not passive consumers whose interaction with the magazine was limited to writing their yearly subscription cheque to Maclean Hunter, but an engaged, and engaging, group. As inveterate letter writers, they regularly wrote to the editors and authors to express their thoughts about the content of the magazine. Realizing that these responses were a gold-mine of information and evaluation, the editors read those letters closely, and each one received a personalized, though often brief, response. They published a representative sampling of readers' letters in each issue. 'The Last Word Is Yours,' the letters page, provided each individual with the perspective of the collective readership. Very quickly, this page became a 'must read' and, in an interesting twist, it often occasioned lively debate. Readers noted that the letters page frequently inspired them to reread and re-evaluate contentious articles, stories, or editorials. Letters were useful for editorial feedback, but they also taught other readers how to read the magazine critically. Restoring reader agency to the analysis here permits a number of important conclusions which are not possible in studies that concentrate solely on a textual analysis or a history of production.

In the end, the participatory nature of the magazine, the topics addressed, and the importance placed on reader input and suggestion, combined with the primarily female world of creation and consumption, resulted in the development of a national community of readers, writers, and editors. This *Chatelaine* community was primarily a 'community of discourse' or an 'imagined community,' but there were opportunities for personal connections to be made.[13] *Chatelaine* editors made frequent trips to give speeches across the country as a way to reach out to the readers, to meet them face to face, in an effort to discover what readers expected from 'their' magazine. Readers insisted that the editors remember to tailor the product for their audience. If not, they would complain – vociferously. Oftentimes, the letters page resembled a print precursor of e-mail correspondence, as women who had met only through letters responded to each other and, perhaps, took their relationship outside the magazine's perimeters. Highly participatory and at times creative, the letters page fostered a *Chatelaine* community of readers and strongly contributed to *Chatelaine*'s success.

Ironically, given the commercial and editorial success of *Chatelaine* in the fifties and sixties, few outside the former readership community or the editorial team are aware of the magazine's stature. This same indifference applies in general to Canadian popular culture, which until recently was dismissed as the detritus of advanced capitalism.[14] Although most of the history of Canadian popular culture remains to be written, *Chatelaine*'s history, along with that of other venerable Canadian periodicals, is long overdue.[15] Before we can address *Chatelaine*'s history, and its largely forgotten role in disseminating second-wave feminist messages to a mass audience of Canadian women, it is necessary to provide a brief overview of the variety of popular and academic perspectives on women's magazines. Given the interdisciplinary world of magazine scholarship and the important insights raised by this material, the remainder of this chapter addresses the lingering popular myths of women's magazines, international scholarship on women's magazines, the methodological approach used in this study, the theoretical apparatus, and the gendered cultural history in which this monograph is situated.

The Popular Myths about Women's Magazines

One of the reasons that *Chatelaine*, along with many cultural products addressed largely to women, has, until recently, been ignored by scholars is the disdain accorded to commercial women's magazines, both in Canada and elsewhere. The study of women's magazines has been hampered by the wholesale adoption of a number of myths and generalizations about these periodicals – their purpose, effect, and content.[16] These distortions arose out of the historical and popular literature on women's magazines. Within that literature there is an analytical continuum from Betty Friedan to Naomi Wolf which contends that women's magazines are 'bad.'[17] These authors claim that such magazines are pap for women, created by the machinations of male corporate executives, editors, and advertising executives. This masculine triumvirate supposedly operates one of the most widely known and oddly successful conspiracies of the twentieth century: it has encouraged millions of women to purchase or subscribe to magazines that advocate a narrow, purely domestic role. According to this theory, women's magazines create a state of unfulfilled desires or 'inarticulate longings.'[18] They foster insecurity about women's bodies, appearance, and relationships with husbands and children. Ultimately, all this insecurity is supposed to lead to increased consumption of the products advertised in the magazine and to the belief that women's fulfilment lies in the realm of domestic consumption, not in the workplace, higher education, or the public sphere. This is the myth of the women's magazine, one that informs many aspects of women's popular culture: soap operas, tabloid newspapers, and romance fiction.

Friedan's *Feminine Mystique*, published in 1963 to worldwide acclaim, is generally regarded as the book that launched second-wave feminism. Friedan's work is also the starting point for all researchers of women's magazines. Her exploration of advertisers, housewives, mass media, psychologists, and other influential commentators on women's identities in the post-1945 United States concluded that the problem with American women was the 'feminine mystique.' This mystique produced the nebulous sense of unease, fatigue, depression, and ennui that Friedan called the 'problem that has no name.'[19] Chief among the perpetrators of this crime were the women's magazines, which depicted a world of gleaming households, happy children, and attractive, contented wives and mothers. 'The image of woman that emerges from this big, pretty magazine,' Friedan wrote, 'is young and frivolous, almost childlike, fluffy and feminine; passive; gaily content in a world of bedroom and kitchen, sex, babies, and home. The magazine surely does not leave out sex; the only passion, the only pursuit, the only goal a woman is permitted is the pursuit of a man. It is crammed full of food, clothing, cosmetics, furniture, and the physical bodies of young women, but where is the world of thought and ideas, the life of the mind and spirit? In the magazine image, women do no work except housework and work to keep their bodies beautiful and to get and keep a man.'[20] Friedan's influential work was considerably more than an examination of women's magazines, but it is important that in building her argument about the feminine mystique, this former freelance journalist attacked her own previous clients. One of the difficulties with Friedan's research on American women's magazines was that she relied primarily on the fiction stories. A recent reappraisal of Friedan's work by historian Joanne Meyerowitz indicates that non-fiction articles in these same magazines sometimes encouraged women to participate in the workforce or politics and included profiles of women who had moved outside the domestic realm.[21] Although more research into American women's magazines in the postwar era is desirable, it is clear that historical revisionism is challenging Friedan's characterization of their content. At the very least, Meyerowitz's and Friedan's contradictory findings indicate the variety of material in women's magazines and serve as a caution to researchers to provide comprehensive portraits of this content.

This popular feminist critique of male-produced popular culture aimed at women, particularly Friedan's work, was an important starting point for an examination of what passes for 'normal discourse' about women's roles in society. It focused attention on a seemingly innocuous form of light entertainment for women and began to ask serious questions about popular culture, gender, consumption, and American society. It sought to answer questions about how femininity was constructed, or 'learned,' by reading women's magazines. Those valuable questions spawned a coterie of academic work, primarily in communications, sociology, and psychology, focused on charting the portraits of women in advertising and the media. At its peak in the seventies and early eighties, this analysis investigated cause and effect, equating these sexist representations with women's second-class status in society.[22] As with the studies of televised violence and its impact, however, these investigations of women and the media have not been able to make a conclusive link between image and behaviour.

In the years since the publication of *The Feminine Mystique*, this legacy has become extremely problematic. The first issue, one that researchers of women's magazines must confront, is the enduring nature of Friedan's thesis. It has become a truism that women's magazines are backward, ultra-conservative periodicals whose only function is to encourage consumption. But a critical appraisal of the myth of women's magazines raises questions about the assumptions and validity of that overarching generalization. From both a historical and a Canadian perspective, this myth, with respect to *Chatelaine* in the fifties and sixties, is completely inaccurate. It claims, or its adherents have claimed, that the American situation represents reality. It does not question whether women's magazines in other countries or in other time periods fit this analysis. The second issue, particularly from a feminist and cultural studies perspective, is that this myth entirely negates women's agency. It positions the readers as helpless pawns of the editors and, ultimately, of big business. It fails to acknowledge that reading a magazine, watching television, or consuming other types of popular culture involve the reader in making a series of choices. Readers choose to purchase or subscribe to a magazine, select what they read, and bring their own experiences and interests to interpreting the material. Furthermore, the myth does not question the presumption that readers of women's magazines are white, middle-class, suburban, heterosexual women, thereby negating the working-class, rural, male, homosexual, black, native, and immigrant experience with these magazines. Such determinism skews any analysis of the motives of the publishing companies, corporations, and advertisers. It assumes one large, monolithic motive behind these periodicals which, given the range of advertised products alone, is far too reductionist. For instance, although it is accepted as a matter of fact that commercial women's magazines are created to make money – for publishers, advertisers, and manufacturers – scholars seldom explore whether they actually do make money or are even consistent money makers.

Surveying the International Academic Perspective on Women's Magazines

Magazine research is an interdisciplinary pursuit, with scholars drawn from a variety of backgrounds including literary studies, women's studies, sociology, communications, journalism, commerce, history, and cultural studies. One of the weaknesses of this field is that work tends to be produced in disciplinary enclaves, with little interaction across fields or across linguistic or national boundaries. Within the past few years, a handful of new magazine studies have appeared in the United States and Britain.[23] All make advances in integrating the analysis of gender and commerce, and in offering more comprehensive portraits of magazine publishing and consumption. Though most of these studies refute, to varing degrees, the simplistic myths of women's magazines, their findings have not been integrated into public perception or other areas of feminist scholarship. The fact that their scholarly advances are so seldom recognized outside their own fields is evidence of the weakness of this small and relatively isolated community of scholars.

Work informed by the British cultural studies approach, and primarily written from the perspective of sociology and women's and cultural studies, are the most persuasive and sophisticated in their analysis of the women's magazine phenomenon. Janice Winship offered the first treatment of women's magazines that combined a Marxist feminist analysis of the text with an acknowledgment of the pleasure readers found in the products and the act of reading. Two groundbreaking books appeared in the early nineties which managed to merge the insights of critical theories with complex, well-integrated analyses. *Women's Worlds* summarized the variety of approaches to women's magazines and offered a new way forward: 'Within the literature, there are two primary scholarly approaches: the first represents the magazine as a bearer of pleasure, the second sees it as a purveyor of oppressive ideologies of sex, class and race difference. In academic criticism – literary, cultural, and sociological – these two alternative approaches are expounded by different theorists from different conceptual traditions, but of course for the actual reader of the magazine at the point of consumption, they can and do exist simultaneously.'[24] The role of the readers, or consumers, is strongest in the sociological literature, where scholars are keen to offer ethnographic data on how 'real' readers approach the magazines.[25] *Women's Worlds* offered a multi-pronged analysis of women's magazines from the eighteenth century through to the present. This model, combining cultural and feminist theories, history, and, within the analysis of contemporary magazines, reader responses, was tremendously helpful in constructing the methodological approach for this study. One weakness, the omission of economic analysis, was addressed in *Decoding Women's Magazines*, which emphatically urges that women's magazines be understood as both 'business enterprises and cultural texts.'[26]

One contemporary study, *Reading Women's Magazines*, is noteworthy for its detailed ethnographic analysis of 'average' readers. A worthwhile corrrective to the exuberance of other researchers, sociologist Joke Hermes discovered that, according to her eighty Dutch and British female readers of women's magazines, the convenience of the products, combined with the practical tips they offered, was the key reason for their popularity. Similarly, the recent work of Canadian sociologist Dawn Currie, *Girl Talk*, strives to combine analysis of the cultural text with the social process of reading teen magazines. Though Currie's work was released after this study was nearly complete, her 'critique of cultural studies, which simply reads the social off cultural texts, in isolation of any consideration of what makes these texts and their reading possible,' and her warning that scholars must not conflate images with either behaviour or ideology, concurs with this book's emphasis on the process of reading.[27] Despite the discoveries that contemporary ethnographic studies allow researchers, they are not overwhelmingly popular because of the magnitude of work required.

In the field of American studies and history, a number of studies have explored the creation of venerable American magazines – *Ladies' Home Journal*, *Saturday Evening Post*, and *Ms*. American historian Helen Damon-Moore, for instance, claims 'that the *Ladies' Home Journal* and the *Saturday Evening Post* were prototypes that aided in the creation, development, and sustaining of the commercializing of gender and the gendering of commerce. They were conveyors of both gender messages and commercial messages, serving a new and central function in American popular culture.'[28] Primarily, these historical works (*Magazines for the Millions*, *Inarticulate Longings*, and *The Adman in the Parlor*) are concerned with the intersection of gender and commerce; they are united in their fascination with the gendering of the editorial and advertising material in the magazines as well as their commercial imperative. These text-based studies focus on content, production, and academic 'readings' of the material, and seldom contain anything from readers. They all presume that the magazines were 'prescriptive' products that taught middle-class American women how to behave and, most important, how to consume brand-name products. In their failure to integrate readers, or even some of the British insights, into their analysis, they offer an overly deterministic analysis of the impact of magazine publishers and writers on readers. Rounding out the American school are celebratory works, such as Emily Farnham's recent book on *Ms.*, which offer a reappraisal of the goals of the creators and producers of the 'liberal feminist' mass-market magazine.[29]

The conclusions of the British and American magazine research have not been well integrated into the slim Canadian literature on magazines. With the exception of the recent publication of Currie's work, scholars searching for Canadian studies of mass-market magazines will be disappointed by both the dearth of material and, in many cases, its celebratory tone.[30] Fraser Sutherland's *Monthly Epic* provides a breezy, readable historical narrative of the magazine industry from its tentative beginnings in the late 1700s through to the 1980s.[31] Although one chapter and several smaller sections are devoted to *Chatelaine*, his attempt to survey the entire Canadian magazine publishing industry prevents sustained commentary about any particular magazine. In honour of its seventieth year of publication, *Chatelaine* released *A Woman's Place: Seventy Years in the Lives of Canadian Women*, edited by Sylvia Fraser.[32] In this handsome coffee-table book, Fraser reproduced excerpts from the *Chatelaine* opus. The other published works that include some analysis of *Chatelaine* in the twentieth century are articles by Mary

Vipond and Gertrude Joch Robinson. Most recently, sociologist Mary Louise Adams's study of prescriptive literature in the postwar era has made considerable, and effective, use of *Chatelaine* material.[33] However, her focus is primarily on a textual analysis, and her study offers scant evidence of how people responded to this material.

Compounding the fragmentary nature of magazine scholarship has been the tendency within the Canadian and American historical community to use products of popular culture without much engagement or awareness of the burgeoning literature in magazine or cultural studies. Instead, the popular feminist myths, if not actively cited, are implied in much of the work. According to Meyerowitz, American academics have 'adopted wholesale [Betty Friedan's] version of the postwar ideology.'[34] Much the same situation has prevailed in Canada, where *Chatelaine* is a convenient source for 'images' and 'ideas' about the experiences of Canadian women in the twentieth century. Both scholars and students make use of *Chatelaine* as a historical artifact, yet this sampling overlooks the fact that, as a cultural product, *Chatelaine* has a history of its own. The critical questions and commentary that scholars carefully offer to contextualize and qualify sources as varied and rich as census data, oral history, and legal history are often abandoned when it comes to periodicals. In the end, this sampling of *Chatelaine* leaves the impression that the magazine always presented a single dominant message, one that reinforced the hegemony of English-Canadian, suburban, middle-class women.[35] In articles and books by a number of Canadian historians, excerpts and articles from *Chatelaine* are used to illustrate the 'popular debate' on women's issues, the circumscribed roles available to women, or to indicate the conservative nature of the periodical.[36] Yet during the fifties and sixties *Chatelaine* was transformed from a thin magazine devoted primarily to fiction, departmental features, and cheerful editorials into an important resource for Canadian women which emphasized general feature articles, opinionated and often feminist editorial essays, and reader participation.

Given the range of material published in the magazine, it is possible to find *Chatelaine* articles, editorials, fiction, or advertising to support almost any argument. Yet these articles were conceived not to stand alone, but to function in a particular context, among other material, and often with reader commentary. As such, they produced a variety of possible interpretations beyond the most basic premise or preferred meaning of the article. Continuity or discontinuity with the collective memory of the readership community is also an important determinant of the material in a periodical. Successful magazines have their own personality or style – a world created by the distinctive graphics, shared experiences, buzzwords, and specialized language readily identifiable to regular readers. Most magazines offer readers clues about how they should be read, usually in the form of editorial asides and commentary, while readers' letters function in this same capacity too. All these elements add many layers to the experience of reading the periodical. Scholars who aim to understand these products and their readership communities need to be aware of the complexity of these worlds.

Methodology

To best understand the history and role of any magazine, one needs to examine how the periodical is constructed – the range of articles, fiction, advice, political commentary, and advertisements. As with woven cloth, it is possible up close to separate different strands of thread according to colour or texture, but, taken as a whole, the impression is quite different. There one discovers, quite quickly and often counter-intuitively, the recurring patterns and styles in the entire tapestry. In short, the tapestry is more powerful and meaningful than any individual thread.[37] British theorist Raymond Williams refers to this concept as the study of the 'flow' of mass culture. Given the scope of this book, to survey the flow of *Chatelaine* material, it was impossible to undertake a study of *Chatelaine*'s entire publishing history. Instead, the choice was made to examine closely two decades, the fifties and the sixties, when the magazine was at the height of its popularity and Canadian women's lives were in a state of flux. Although this book is primarily informed by a cultural studies perspective that prioritizes reader responses, historical context, and critical reading, a key component of the research methodology was a systematic content analysis designed to explore and manage the flow of the material over the twenty-year case study.

The sampling and content analysis of *Chatelaine* from 1950 through 1969 was conducted in two stages. The first stage, the general survey database, included all 240 issues of the magazine. Basic information for each issue was entered in this database, including price per copy and subscription price, editor's name, number of letters, page counts for the various components (advertising, fiction, articles, etc.), and information on the cover art. Finally, a section was available to make notes on the issue. If a particular issue was not included in the longer, second stage of database information, any salient notes were included here.

The second stage, the component databases (editorials, articles, letters, fiction, departments, and advertisements), was restricted to sixty issues. Each January, May, and September issue of the magazine was read closely and in its entirety, and all its components were entered into their respective databases.[38] Those months were selected to allow for seasonal differences in advertising and departmental content, without including major religious or public holidays. Of late, content analysis has fallen out of vogue with academics, but there is merit in including this analytical approach. First, it permits classification of material based on numerical percentages and forces an analytically rigorous method of researching the material. In this case, content analysis not only provided detailed statistical material about the prevalence of divergent themes and issues but also abolished a few myths about the images in the magazine.[39] Employing a content analysis imposed a rigour to the research, which meant that a vast amount of time was spent in critical, close reading of the periodical. Traditional historical archival research, oral histories, written questionnaires with former readers, and the use of published and unpublished readers' letters were also essential to the research approach. In the end, while content analysis provided a structure to handle the material, the research questions were not intended solely to quantify textual material, but emerged from a strong engagement with the field of cultural theories and studies.

Cultural Theories

One of the defining features of the academic landscape in the later half of the twentieth century has been the growing fascination with discourse theory, semiotics, cultural 'texts,' poststructuralism, and the art of 'deconstructing' or 'unpacking' meaning from multilayered, encoded, textual and visual materials. All these pursuits are an academic exercise to try to understand what the rest of North America, and oftentimes the world, refers to as popular culture or popular entertainment. This book is part of a growing body of work that seeks to understand why some forms of mass-produced culture become popular. This study marries three disparate, yet complimentary, analytical approaches to analyze *Chatelaine* effectively in the fifties and sixties: critical theories; feminist cultural analysis; and Canadian social, gender, and cultural history. Indeed, *Roughing It in the Suburbs* assumes that one cannot adequately understand the complex nature of cultural products without situating the product within its historical milieu. Nor can one overlook the competing elements involved in producing and consuming the product.

Given the burgeoning interest in cultural studies and its accompanying theoretical literature of critical analysis, numerous anthologies, articles, and monographs explain the art of 'doing' cultural studies.[40] The act of constructing an analytical framework for cultural studies has best been described as a 'bricolage.'[41] Thus, the overview that follows is not intended to summarize this amorphous field, but to provide an accessible guide to the theoretical framework of this study. Primarily, this book was informed by the theoretical work of Roland Barthes, Michel Foucault, and John Fiske. Barthes's essays on semiotics, in which he explains how language and illustrations function as textual and visual signs, are critical to any work in cultural analysis.[42] According to Barthes, signs have both a literal meaning and a mythological meaning. The mythological level of interpretation depends on the situation, the textual references, and, ultimately, on the person who views or reads the sign. The importance of this theory for our purposes is that semiotics liberates the analyses of cultural products from strictly deterministic interpretations, allowing that any given text can have multiple meanings and is open to interpretation. Furthermore, it prioritizes the act of reading, as opposed to the more traditional emphasis on the text and the creators. Thus, *Chatelaine* readers were considered active participants in constructing meaning as they read and interacted with the magazine.

The necessary counter to what, under Barthes, would be an unlimited number of interpretations of the magazine is the theory of power and knowledge formulated by Michel Foucault.[43] His emphasis on the relations of power, resistance, and the multiplicity of discourses informs the way that the analysis of *Chatelaine* has been framed in these pages. According to Foucault, 'power is not an institution, and not a structure; neither is it a certain strength we are endowed with; it is the name one attributes to a complex strategical situation in a particular society.'[44] It is 'a productive network which runs through the whole social body.'[45] To fully understand how power operates in a society, Foucault advocated studying the '"micropractices," the social practices that constitute everyday life in modern societies.'[46] In this way, a history of reading *Chatelaine* contributes to our understanding of feminine resistance and acquiescence to 'gendered norms' in the fifties and sixties. Where many American historians prioritized the power of advertisers and capitalism as the driving force behind the ideology and purpose of women's magazines, Foucauldian analysis encourages a reappraisal of the motivations, techniques, and tactics of all those involved in the process of production and consumption. Ultimately, 'it is misleading to think of power as a property that could be possessed by some persons or classes and not by others; power is better conceived as a complex, shifting field of relations in which everyone is an element.'[47] To Foucault, this sort of microanalysis is crucial if we are to understand the process by which societal norms are reinforced and normalized. At present, the scholarly debate rages over the degree of coercion within Foucault's theories, further problematized by his failure to provide a consistent position on the role of 'normative' powers, but that argument is beyond the scope of this book.[48]

'Where there is power, there is resistance,' Foucault wrote, and 'these points of resistance are present everywhere in the power network.'[49] Foucauldian analysis into the relational nature of power and the existence of a 'multiplicity of resistances' has informed the work of many recent social, and gender historians in their search to discover the agency of the marginalized, whether by class, race, sexual orientation, or region.[50] In tandem with other works in Canadian cultural, social, and gender history, this volume addresses the notion of resistance to the corporate and commercial intent of the magazine. As future chapters demonstrate, there was resistance to corporate agendas within both the editorial offices at *Chatelaine* and the homes of 'average' readers, as women rejected the portraits that glorified consumption or the perfect middle-class suburban existence. In the most famous case, the Mrs Chatelaine contest, a contest created by Maclean Hunter executives to celebrate homemaking skills, was co-opted by those who not only resisted this message but reformulated it as a celebration of 'slobs.' The resistance of readers from the margins – the working class, women from Atlantic Canada and the Prairies, and non-anglo women – developed as a recurrent event at *Chatelaine*. Their challenges encouraged 'rereading,' but also had an impact on editorial selection.

Poststructuralist analysis of discourse has been the greatest contribution that Foucault made to cultural studies scholars. 'We must not imagine a world of discourse divided between accepted discourse and excluded discourse, or between the dominant discourse and the dominated one; but as a multiplicity of discursive elements that can come into play in various strategies.'[51] Discoursive analysis liberates researchers to move beyond a focus primarily on the text and on the authorial, editorial, or commercial intent. 'Discourse transmits and produces power; it reinforces it, but also undermines and exposes it, renders it fragile and makes it possible to thwart.'[52] Although all components of the production and consumption chain have some degree of power and/or resistance, Foucault assumes that power is not dispersed equally.

Moving from high theory to applied theory, the work of Australian academic John Fiske, while often controversial, offers a useful example of how to apply the theoretical directives of Foucault, Barthes, and others. For Fiske, popular culture is a site of contested meanings or struggles between the producers of the products and their consumers.[53] It is a site in which the people or the consumers are not merely the acted upon, but the active participants. 'There can be no popular dominant culture, for popular culture is formed always in reaction to, and never as part of, the forces of domination.'[54] Where there has been a tendency to see *Chatelaine* as part of the structure from which Canadian women distilled gender prescriptions for their lives, the popularity of the magazine was often due, in contrast, to the oppositional or subversive material it published.

Two elements of Fiske's framework are particularly germane to the approach selected for this book. The first is the concept of the 'producerly text.' According to Fiske, and borrowing from Barthes, the producerly text is accessible and easy to read: 'It offers itself up to popular production; it exposes, however reluctantly, the vulnerabilities, limitations, and weaknesses of its preferred meanings; it contains, while attempting to repress them, voices that contradict the ones it prefers; it has loose ends that escape its control, its meanings exceed its own power to discipline them, its gaps are wide enough for whole new texts to be produced in them – it is, in a very real sense, beyond its own control.'[55] Systematic reading of the text, watching for preferred and non-preferred meanings and contradictions, are key to Fiske's methodology. Fiske presumes that popular culture cannot contain only the preferred reading desired by the advertisers or corporations because it cannot determine what the consumers will purchase, nor can it determine how they will interact with the product. He believes strongly in the notion of a preferred reading, regardless of how numerous the oppositional or non-preferred readings might be. As will become clearer in the chapters that follow, *Chatelaine* was a highly producerly text, and frequently the readers were beyond the control of the editors, writers, or advertisers.

Second, Fiske outlines a methodological approach to reading and understanding popular culture that integrates producers and consumers, texts and their readers. 'Analyzing popular texts ... requires a double focus. On the one hand we need to focus upon the deep structure of the text in the ways that ideological, psychoanalytic analyses and structural or semiotic analyses have proved so effective ... The complimentary focus is upon how the people cope with the system, how they read its texts, how they make popular culture out of its resources. It requires us to analyze texts in order to expose their contradictions, their meanings that escape control, their producerly invitations; to ask what it is within them that has attracted popular approval.'[56] Ultimately, *Chatelaine* readers were active readers, and their interaction with the variety of material published in the magazine provides a full portrait not only of the content of *Chatelaine* in the fifties and sixties but of the way in which the readership community negotiated these messages.

Largely absent from most of the critical analysis literature is the category of gender, and, since much of this work was developed in sociological, literary, and philosophical traditions, historical specificity is seldom present. Feminist cultural scholars are forging new paths in studying issues of gender. Tania Modleski reminds us that the introduction of gender to the field of inquiry can change the view of the reception and content of popular culture: 'that women exist in a contradictory relation to mass culture – as well as to its theories – suggests the importance of foregrounding the issue of sexual difference in our analyses.'[57] Two pioneering scholarly approaches, the work of Modleski and Janice Radway, provide some answers, but, most important, ways of thinking about women's cultural products which are critical to any study of gender and the media.[58]

Modleski's work examines the world of Harlequin romances.[59] Although critical of the subject matter and the repetitious narrative structure of these stories, Modleski claims 'that even the contemporary mass produced narratives for women contained elements of protest and resistance underneath highly "orthodox" plots.'[60] Similarly, in her conclusions, she resists criticizing the legions of female fans of such fiction, claiming instead: 'It would be pointless to end with a resounding denunciation of popular novels and their readers – a conclusion encountered all too often in studies of popular fiction. An understanding of Harlequin Romances should lead one less to condemn the novels than the conditions which have made them necessary. Even though the novels can be said to intensify female tensions and conflicts, on balance the contradictions in women's lives are more responsible for the existence of Harlequins than Harlequins are for the contradictions.'[61] Parallels are evident in the section addressing *Chatelaine* fiction, and indeed most of the 'traditional' material – the service departmental fare which assumes that women are responsible for houses, husbands, and children.

Radway's work, *Reading the Romance*, was a major departure from the traditional mode of feminist critical analysis when it was first published in 1984.[62] Radway's study of romance readers in the midwestern town of Smithton focused on a small group of devoted and articulate women, seventeen in total, who read romance novels on a daily basis. Although her small survey sample is a matter of some concern (and the conclusions she makes about the act of reading are entirely based on that limited group), Radway's work was, and continues to be, very influential.[63] Contrary to the way other academics have analyzed and scorned romance novels, particularly their perpetuation of patriarchal ideas of women's roles and romanticized views of gender relations, Radway's 'average readers' provided a different perspective and allowed her to conclude: 'Ethnographic investigation has led to the discovery that "such devoted fans" see the act of reading as combative and compensatory.'[64]

According to Radway, her sample group – all of whom worked in the home and most had children – claimed that reading romances provided a release from the pressures and strains in their daily lives. Reading, then, was an escape. 'It creates a time or space within which a woman can be entirely on her own, preoccupied with her personal needs, desires and pleasure.'[65] Her focus on how and why the women read was very instructive for this analysis of *Chatelaine* because the act of reading itself, regardless of the content, carried an ideological and social meaning of its own. Most of the women viewed reading novels as their time – time in which they did not have to nurture their families or attend to their husbands, and, by their admission, time that was 'taken' from doing something else. For many, this act of resistance, passive though it might appear, was not without commentary, and often criticism, from their husbands and children. Radway's focus on the reader – on her interpretation of what and why she read, on the interesting attention to the physical act of reading, and on the creation of an ad hoc female community when these women discussed their favourite novels and writers – provided important insights for this book. Through the letters written and published in *Chatelaine*, the sporadic visits of editors and writers, and the variety of contests run by the magazine, the editors, writers, and readers created and participated in a cultural community of Canadian women: something *Chatelaine*'s current editor, Rona Maynard, calls the 'the biggest kitchen table in the country.'[66]

Cultural and Gender History

Modeleski and Radway are both describing a cultural studies variation on the 'women's culture' theme in women's history. Studies of a distinctive 'women's culture' – whether the diaries and letters of colonial Nova Scotian women, the female world of consumption, or the private lives and political strategies of women in western Canada during the Depression – contribute to an analysis of the nature of women's experiences and the ways in which these experiences were differentiated from those of their male kin.[67] Clearly, a study of the 'magazine for Canadian women' contributes to this scholarship by demonstrating the value in studies of women's cultural products and the ways in which producers and writer sought to package and market a product aimed solely at Canadian women. Products of interest to women were not just the typical house and home features, but also political, legal, and feminist issues that would have resonance for Canadian women before and during the second wave of feminist activity in Canada. Although the magazine might presume that all women would share in household chores and child-rearing, it did not presume that these duties precluded work outside the home, activism, or equal participation in Canadian society. What Veronica Strong-Boag has referred to as the 'feminism of daily life' in her analysis of Prairie women during the thirties is also evident in *Chatelaine* during the fifties and sixties.[68] One might easily speculate that many of the women who subscribed to *Chatelaine* might well have demonstrated the internalized resistance and feminism of daily life described by letter writers and fictional heroines in the pages of the magazine, accompanied in the sixties by the more liberal feminist goals of the editorial essays. That example undoubtedly had an impact on their daughters, as these young women went off to university in the late sixties, at the height of feminist consciousness in North America, and began to found more activist organizations to attack sexism in society.

This book demonstrates the gendered tensions at work in the often idealized suburban consumer society and restores *Chatelaine*'s role in the growth of second-wave feminism in Canada. In both cases, the rich resources provided by the archival and published letters permit conclusions about the variety of ways Canadian women negotiated the competing demands and changing nature of their workday, and either criticized or embraced the new activism relating to women's roles in society.

Critics of a women's culture approach are right to point to the diversity and multiplicity of Canadian women's experiences, and to caution that such an approach often ignores differences among women in the attempt to prove gendered commonalties. Great care has been taken in this study to avoid that kind of essentializing and to highlight tensions, differences, and debates within the mass audience of Canadian women who were *Chatelaine* readers. In fact, there were repeated tensions in the readership community over representations of the ideal Canadian women, which, more often than not, provided readers with images of white, middle-class, urban women. Those debates over representation are illuminating about the paradoxes, tensions, and differences involved in producing, making, and reading a women's magazine. They demonstrate categorically that *Chatelaine* had a mass, national audience of women and men, from both working-class and middle-class backgrounds, who read the magazine. Unlike today, when readers might move on to another periodical if they found the content not to their taste, *Chatelaine* readers in the fifties and sixties were a tough audience to please. They demanded that the magazine be representative of their lives, particularly if the cover read 'for the Canadian woman.'

Although this book employs an interdisciplinary methodology, the possibilities and potential of critical and gender analysis fall short if they are not grounded in the reality of the historical perspective.[69] *Roughing It in the Suburbs* focuses closely on Canadian society during the two decades under review. It employs the convention, drawn from social history, of depicting history from the bottom up, as well as the more traditional 'top-down' approaches used in commercial and cultural histories.[70] Close attention is paid to the intersections and conflicts among race, class, and gender, and that troika in turn is expanded to include three other important categories of analysis: region, sexuality, and age. With respect to those categories of analysis, this study looks for inclusion and exclusion, drawing important conclusions about the material the editors saw fit to include as well as what they consistently avoided or minimized. For example, although the issue of sexual orientation is not one that occurs frequently in the magazine in those decades, this work questions its absence, pays attention to its infrequent mention, and critically examines how it is dealt with. It also employs the category of sexual orientation as a way to reread some of the fare in the magazine from an alternative perspective. Region is another important analytical category, not as an attempt to assuage the clarion calls of some historians for the return to national history, but because one of primary concerns of Maclean Hunter was to interpret Canada for Canadians.[71] That claim requires close evaluation. Did the magazine really accomplish that goal, or was there a persistent central Canadian bias implicit in its pages?

Finally, this book contributes to the new revisionist historiography that attempts to analyze, historically, our stereotypes and assumptions about the fifties and sixties.[72] Were the fifties really so affluent, conservative, and concerned with suburbia? Similarly, how radical and swinging were the sixties? While it would be dangerous to extrapolate generalizations about Canada from *Chatelaine*, it did provide startling contrasts with our myths of the postwar era of suburban affluence and contentment. The images presented in the pages of *Chatelaine* indicate that Canadians were better off in the fifties relative to pre-war Canada, but that universal, national affluence was a myth. Postwar affluence in Canada is much better understood as a sixties' phenomenon, when most areas of the country had modernized their houses and durables, and leisure pursuits and 'fashionable' spending were commonplace. Politically speaking, the activities that we associate with the sixties – student protest movements, sexual experimentation, and rock-and-roll crazes – did not manifest themselves until the end of the decade. Those differences from the prevailing myths will become clearer as we examine the magazine's articles, advertising, and editorials.

A Blueprint for the Book

This book is divided into three parts. Part One, 'Historicizing Production and Consumption,' provides detailed commentary about the history of *Chatelaine* and its editorial and production teams. Chapter 2 offers an exploration of the gendered division of production at Maclean Hunter and provides a behind-the-scenes portrait of the opportunity afforded to the editorial staff. Chapter 3 provides a demographic profile of the magazine's readers and a series of reader response case studies that illustrate the vital role readers played in 'consuming' the periodical. In fact, this material indicates not only that readers were active agents in 'making meaning' from the magazine but that their critiques of the content often aided in the production of the text.

Part Two, 'Traditional Fare?,' examines the standard material included within the genre called women's magazines, whether British, American, or Canadian. Clearly, this is the numerically significant material, yet the chapters on cover art and advertising, service material, and fiction indicate that there are opportunities, even in the most traditional material, for creative readers to read against the grain. What is fascinating here is not how much *Chatelaine* conforms to the conventions for the genre, but how often readers were critical of, or ignored, what the editors called 'the commercial package.' What does it mean if readers do not read the advertisements? What does it mean if fiction stories highlight traumas and conflicts within the suburban bungalow, rather than the joys of marital bliss? Those questions, and others, highlight the paradoxical nature of the product in question, as well as the importance of analyzing the reading of prescriptive material in evaluating its significance.

Finally, Part Three, 'Subverting the Standard,' offers two chapters that profile the most distinctive material in the magazine: the editorials and the articles. Although only a portion of the editorials and articles in the fifties and sixties were activist or feminist in orientation, the fact that a mass-market women's magazine had a consistent feminist agenda from the late fifties through to the seventies is nevertheless groundbreaking. Where American historians are quick to point to the novelty and prestige of *Ms.* magazine, Canadian women's historians have been far more circumspect about *Chatelaine.* In tandem with the material that disseminated second-wave feminist information, there were many articles that critiqued the nature of the genre and encouraged readers to be critically engaged with the material. Less frequently, some material directly contradicted other content in the periodical, particularly in the advertising and service department features. So, instead of providing an environment that supported and encouraged readers to consume the advertisers' products or to re-create themselves as the embodiment of the perfect Canadian housewife and mother, *Chatelaine* often, in a quietly subversive manner, encouraged Canadian women to think about other options for their lives. Chapters 7 and 8 explore this fascinatingly contradictory material and illustrate the changes and continuity between the fifties and the sixties. Though numerically less significant than the traditional fare, it was the editorials and articles that allowed

Chatelaine to command the authority, respect, and admiration that readers accorded the magazine. For this reason, in judging the entire impact of the magazine, this material is overweighted in importance. Although it is useful to demonstrate how unconventional *Chatelaine* could be, a number of readers resisted and criticized these changes. Ironically, then, while it is long overdue to claim *Chatelaine*'s place in the history of second-wave feminism in Canada, the inclusion of reader responses to this material indicates that not all readers embraced this feminist editorial agenda. Historians of second-wave feminism have not been inclined to spend much time researching the anti-feminists, but they did exist, and these letters provide insight into the tensions surrounding the often different desires of rural and urban women or stay-at-home mothers versus mothers who worked for pay.[73] Finally, chapter 9 offers conclusions about *Chatelaine*'s legacy.

It is for these many sparks and controversies that June Callwood called *Chatelaine* a brush fire. To fully appreciate the blaze, we first need to find out who set it, stoked it, and enjoyed it, so it is to both the producers and the consumers that we turn first in this analysis of *Chatelaine* in the fifties and sixties.

Part One

Historicizing Production and Consumption

Chapter 2

'A Closet Feminist Magazine': (Re)-Making *Chatelaine*

On the surface, the world of magazine production appears to be an arid topic, of interest only to journalism students or practitioners in the field. A study of the 'making' of a magazine, in contrast, has much to offer. A close exploration of the power relations at the periodical – the inherent conflicts and tensions between the editorial office and the business office, or within the corporation itself – offers behind-the-scenes insight into the way production itself is highly contested. Contrary to the impression that media producers have one agenda, or uniform goals about the product, it will become clear that, during the fifties and sixties, there was considerable jockeying in the *Chatelaine* offices over not only the content but the purpose of the magazine. A study of the 'micropractice' of cultural production dispels a number of enduring myths. First, the results indicate that the power of advertisers to determine content has, in many cases, been overstated. Commensurably, the power of readers to demand editorial changes has been underappreciated. It will also become apparent that, in contrast to the myth that the editors were all middle-class insiders from central Canada, they were, in fact, outsiders. Three of the four were from modest western Canadian backgrounds, and the fourth was a first-generation immigrant to Canada. Finally, an analysis of the process of production dispels the myths about circulation statistics. The presumption that the majority of subscribers were comfortable, middle-class urbanites is inaccurate. Instead, the majority of *Chatelaine* readers were working class, of average or less than average incomes, and from both rural and urban locations.

Chatelaine did not operate in a vacuum. Women's magazines stretch much further back than the creation of *Chatelaine* in 1928, and a history of the genre – and some of the British and American standard bearers – provides context for defining the term. It is against those international standards that *Chatelaine* was and continues to be judged. Any claims about the magazine's 'unconventional' content or activist role must be evaluated in the context of the genre and against the comparable American products. Ultimately, this material proves that *Chatelaine* offered Canadian women a unique product.

A Brief History of Women's Magazines

The first journal specifically addressed to women, *The Ladies Mercury*, originated in Britain in 1693, although the first publication to refer to itself officially as a women's magazine was *The Ladies Magazine*, which began in 1732.[1] American journals devoted to women commenced publication in the 1790s and, within a few years, readers could choose any number of products.[2] An ever increasing number of American women's magazines flourished in the early nineteenth century, but the grande dame of them all was *Godey's Ladies Book*, first published in 1830. Under the forty-year editorship of Mrs Sarah Josepha Hale (1837–77), whom magazine historian James P. Woods describes as a 'stalwart feminist,' *Godey's* became an American institution and was also popular north of the border.[3] It published 'fashions ... moral stories ... recipes, embroidery patterns and instructions, beauty and health hints, and elaborate illustrations.'[4] Although the precursor of the modern women's magazine formula is clear from this list, the magazine differed in two important ways from its later-day sisters. It did not have advertisements, so the full cost was borne by the subscription price. And the higher subscription cost meant that the magazine was reserved for the elite, not the masses. *Godey's* was eclipsed in its final years of publication as a more affordable group of magazines gained attention and made magazine readers of a mass audience of women.

The new format was created by Cyrus and Louisa Knapp Curtis, who in 1883 founded the *Ladies' Home Journal*. The secret of the *Journal*'s success was to forge what Helen Damon-Moore describes as 'a powerful and mutually reinforcing mix of gender and commerce.'[5] The Curtises combined editorial material of interest to women (food, fashions, fiction, advice columns) with national advertising for household products such as foodstuffs, cleaning supplies, and toiletries. At a time when national forums for advertisers were limited, the *Journal* provided an innovative way for business to target female consumers. Both James

McCall's *McCall's* magazine, which originated as an advertising flyer of his patterns, and Clark Bryan's *Good Housekeeping*, which was primarily a mail-order catalogue, soon followed the Curtises' lead.[6] What all these women's magazines shared, and continued to promote well into the twentieth century, was very affordable subscription or single copy prices, which resulted in a huge audience of women readers. The magazines recouped their costs and made healthy profits because of the large quantity of advertising included in the periodicals.

Canadian readers of women's magazines had to content themselves with the American and, less frequently, the British products until 1905. That year *The Canadian Home Journal* was founded, and it continued to serve a national audience of women readers until 1958.[7] Other entries included the short-lived *Everywoman's World* (1914–22), the upscale housing magazine *Canadian Homes and Gardens* (1925–62), and the society magazine *Mayfair* (1927–55). Both *Canadian Homes and Gardens* and *Mayfair* were Maclean Hunter magazines that catered to the upper and upper-middle urban audience.

Chatelaine's Debut

The first issue of *Chatelaine* magazine hit the newsstands, drugstores, and bookstores of the country in March 1928. The cover featured the title, *The Chatelaine – A Magazine for Canadian Women*, with an illustration of a lithe, elegantly dressed young mother reading to her two daughters. The woman's red evening dress, elaborate earrings, and well-coifed hair and the cherubic, strawberry-blonde children all indicated the publisher's intended audience: the affluent woman reader and her middle-class sisters. The gestation time for the magazine had been very short. Only seven months had elapsed since H.V. Tyrrell, vice-president and managing director of the Maclean Hunter Publishing Company, had drafted a report entitled 'General Plan for a Woman's Magazine of Large National Circulation.'[8] He perceived a 'logical opening' for a woman's magazine, since, in his estimation, *Western Home Monthly* and *Canadian Home Journal* did not fulfil their mandates as women's magazines and were really only 'second-rate Canadian magazines.' The motivations for the new magazine were strictly business: 'The more Canadian magazines there are of really creditable character, and the more magazine circulation there is available for advertisers, the more sure and rapid will be the growth of magazine advertising in this Country.' Tyrrell believed that the creation of the new woman's magazine would serve to increase the prominence of Maclean Hunter as a publisher of national magazines. It would also attract new customers by providing business with more options for advertising dollars. Tyrrell advised that the new periodical would not need a large influx of staff or capital expenditures, since the *Maclean's* staff 'should be able to launch and to handle such a woman's magazine with comparatively few additions to the present staff.'

Although financial considerations were the impetus for the creation of this new woman's magazine, Tyrrell proposed a mixture of offerings to attract the largest possible audience. 'The name to be selected,' he wrote, 'should be one that will indicate the distinctly feminine character of the magazine, and one that will appeal particularly to those interested in good housekeeping and home making. A well chosen name can have a strong appeal for reader and to advertisers alike. "Better Housekeeping" is one suggestion.' Tyrrell's suggestions were derivative: what he proposed emulated the format of successful American women's magazines. 'Better Housekeeping' was obviously an attempt to capitalize on the success of *Good Housekeeping*. Yet he was adamant that the new magazine should publish articles on Canadian women 'who have won prominence in various fields of endeavour such as politics, business, law, medicine, missions, domestic science, teaching, organizing, handling institutions and so on.' Tyrrell also indicated that 'one-fourth to one-third of the editorial matter should be fiction of the best quality obtainable. This measure of entertainment is necessary to provide variety and to widen the appeal of the publication.' Tyrrell's topics of interest were wide-ranging, including home service articles, fiction, and general articles about women in the public sphere. This last perspective was in keeping with the era. With the exception of Aboriginals, Asians, and Québécoise, the majority of Canadian women had received the suffrage only a decade before the launch of *Chatelaine*. Moreover, the Person's Case was being contested as the first issues came off the press; within two years, Canadian women had gained admission to the Senate of Canada. Every year a handful of exceptional, middle-class women entered the male-dominated professions: law, medicine, and politics.[9] It was in this climate of heady optimism about the potential of Canadian women that Maclean Hunter launched the new magazine. In the end, Tyrrell projected that Maclean Hunter should plan 'to print 60,000 copies right from the first issue.'

Canadian women were spared a generic title for the new periodical because, in an inspired twist of marketing savvy, Maclean Hunter decided to launch a national contest to name the magazine. Over 70,000 people responded to the *Maclean's* advertisement, hoping to win the $1000 prize. In the end a rancher's wife from Elbourne, British Columbia, Hilda Paine, pocketed the money for her suggestion 'The Chatelaine.'[10] The number of people anxious to win the prize money foretold the sales potential of the new magazine. From its December 1928 paid sales of slightly over 57,000, the magazine grew to boast an annual circulation of 378,866 in 1950. By the end of the decade this figure had almost doubled to 745,589.[11] In September 1958 *Chatelaine* purchased the subscription list of the *Canadian Home Journal* and officially became the only national Canadian women's magazine, until *Canadian Living* was launched in the seventies.

During the sixties, Maclean Hunter expanded *Chatelaine* into a series of products, and the division became known as the *Chatelaine* Group. In 1960, in response to fears that one of the American women's magazines would create a 'Canadian edition' and engage in direct competition with *Chatelaine*, Maclean Hunter bought the French-Canadian magazine *Revue Moderne* and launched *Châtelaine: La Revue Moderne*. This purchase enabled the company to offer advertisers a national market, one no American women's magazine would be able to match. Veteran editor Fernande Saint-Martin emphasized *Châtelaine*'s key selling feature – a French-Canadian identity – and employed French-Canadian journalists and fiction writers. In addition to Saint-Martin's editorial essay, the magazine included material modified and translated from the *Chatelaine* Institute in Toronto.[12] *Châtelaine*'s editorial office in Montreal employed a full, though smaller, editorial and support staff separate from the English-language Toronto headquarters. Both versions bought Canadian rights to the articles, so they could be printed in either periodical, and often articles originally published in *Chatelaine* were translated for *Châtelaine*. Although few articles originally published in the French edition made it into the English version, there was a large degree of overlap between the two publications.[13] Shared material aside, it would be incorrect to view *Châtelaine* as merely a translated version of the English magazine. The different editor, editorials, fiction, and, in many cases, general-interest articles created a different tone.

Miss Chatelaine, a separate magazine that grew out of the fifties' feature page called 'Teen Tempo,' was launched in 1964 to appeal to teenage girls and was extremely successful at attracting advertisers to its 'handy purse or pocket-size' format.[14] It was published between four and six times a year.[15] Publisher Lloyd M. Hodgkinson described it as a 'wholesome, constructive' magazine for 'young people.' Most issues included a mix of fashion, beauty tips, social pointers, and career information. According to Hodgkinson, *Miss Chatelaine* provided teenage girls with 'guidance.' 'It is basically a fashion magazine designed to give guidance and information on Canadian fashion,' he said, 'and through this service help give definition and growth to the fashion industry. In addition, *Miss Chatelaine* provides information on career opportunities, social situations important to the young, personalities, and educational developments. For entertainment, it carries regular fiction stories written by students in Canadian schools.' Maclean Hunter hoped that this combination of age-specific editorial content would wean Canadian girls off American teen magazines, promote the Canadian fashion industry, and, through this marriage of editorial and business goals, make a profit for the company. *Miss Chatelaine* was later rechristened *Flare* and repositioned as a Canadian fashion magazine.

Far less successful than either *Châtelaine* or *Miss Chatelaine* was *Hostess*, which Maclean Hunter launched in 1968 to compete with *Homemaker's Digest* in the controlled-circulation magazine category. The purpose of *Homemaker's Digest*, a new women's service magazine introduced in Toronto in October 1966, was to target 'prime homes.'[16] According to its marketers, a prime home was situated in one of the 53 Canadian cities of 25,000 population or more.'[17] Further exclusivity was achieved by restricting prime households to those in the 'top 75% socioeconomic' category, headed by breadwinning males under fifty-three years of age, living in a single-family dwelling, and with children. Adding insult to the injury that *Chatelaine* did not attract a 'prime' audience was the fact that the new editor, Jeannine Locke, was a former *Chatelaine* writer. In a defensive attempt to protect market share, Maclean Hunter hastily entered the controlled-circulation fray. Despite its determination to challenge the new competitor, it was at a disadvantage because it had to exercise caution when pitching *Hostess*. Maclean Hunter could not refer, as the *Homemaker's Digest* ads did, to 'waste circulation,' since *Homemaker's* applied the term to the bulk of *Chatelaine*'s audience. The advertisements for *Hostess* were therefore more understated, claiming that *Chatelaine* equalled women readers, while *Hostess* equalled homemaking readers.[18] Advertisers who wished to use the new periodical were required to place an ad of at least one half page in *Chatelaine*.

The promotion and marketing strategy of *Hostess* magazine raises many questions, from an advertising perspective, about the desirability of *Chatelaine*'s mass audience. Although it was often impossible to obtain evidence about the effectiveness of advertising, given the over-heated rhetoric of promotional material and research reports, the intro-duction of controlled-circulation magazines indicates that *Chatelaine's* audience and readers were not the prime audience that the company often touted, but a mass audience, one for which the purchase of advertised products was not a key priority. The commercial messages in *Chatelaine* often fell on blind eyes. The importance of the battle between *Homemaker's* and the short-lived *Hostess* was entirely due to the fact that *Homemaker's* attacked the seldom publicized weak spot at *Chatelaine* – the fact that it attracted a mass audience of Canadian women, not the primarily urban and affluent women advertisers cov-eted. What neither magazine had counted on was the increased postal rates in 1969 which drastically affected the viability of all periodicals, but particularly the controlled-circulation magazines. *Hostess* folded after only one year in operation, and Maclean Hunter forfeited a 'million-dollar investment.'[19] *Homemaker's* switched to a direct delivery system and survived.[20]

Alongside the implementation of three new periodicals, Maclean Hunter was busy making the *Chatelaine* Group more advertiser friendly. In 1960 the magazine began offering regional 'split-runs,' which ena-bled 'advertisers to introduce new products in one area while advertis-ing established products in other areas.'[21] Partial-page-size inserts were made available in 1962, which allowed advertisers to run special an-nual promotional advertising booklets. Finally, in 1967 the business department created '14 regional editions available to advertisers de-signed to suit their marketing areas.' These editions were implemented primarily to compete with television, so they could deliver a format suitable for both local and national advertising, specially targeted to female readers in urban areas.

According to a 1968 study, 'over a twelve-month period, the audience of *Chatelaine* combined editions increases to 51% of the total female population.'[22] By 1970 the circulation for the English version of *Chatelaine* stood at 980,000 copies, newsstand sales were 70,000, and, using Maclean Hunter's estimate of two women readers per copy, the magazine had 1,960,000 readers for each issue.[23] *Chatelaine's* market saturation and breadth was the envy of the U.S. women's magazines. Between the French and English editions, Maclean Hunter could authoritatively state that it addressed a vast, national audience of Canadian women. The product that kept Canadian women so enthused was a curious amalgam of feature articles, fiction, and departmental fare with a hefty dollop – slightly over 50 per cent – of advertising.

Browsing through *Chatelaine*

During the fifties and sixties, Canadian women could subscribe to *Chatelaine* for the affordable price of $1.50 per year, although during the lean years in the mid-fifties and at the end of the sixties the price rose to $2 annually. What arrived in mailboxes across the county was an oversized periodical, by contemporary standards, measuring eleven by fourteen inches and averaging between 90 to 110 pages. Awkward to hold, slimmer than the comparable American magazines, *Chatelaine* made its promise of Canadian content in reportage, fashion, food, and fiction its chief editorial hook. Browsing through a representative issue from 1960 provides an overview of the images, the variety of material in any given issue, and the experience of reading the magazine.

A smiling brunette and her Persian cat dominate the cover of the July 1960 issue as they gaze languidly out at the reader through the screen door of a fictitious cottage (illustration 1). These visual clues alerted readers to the fact that this was a summer issue, emblematic of the Canadian exodus from the cities to the country – to cottages, cabins, or camping. A muted orange colour scheme with two dramatic bands of black and white frame the photograph. On the black strip are the cover teasers: 'The Windsors – exclusive photo story'; 'Do the Gouzenkos regret their decision?' 'Women's great challenge – old age'; and 'We gave up our child.'

Immediately inside the front cover, the latest excerpt in Miss Clairol's famous ad campaign, 'Does she ... or doesn't she?' beguiled readers with a striking image of a big-haired blonde, with fetching dark-brown brows, and her child enjoying a day at the beach. Paradoxically, juxtaposed beside the ad was Doris Anderson's editorial, 'Let's have no child marriages here,' accompanied by the masthead and table of contents. *Chatelaine* editorials had a choice placement, which in modern magazines is reserved for advertisements, since this 'front of the book' location is always on view when the reader flips open the cover. Although this issue was slighter than average, as were all summer editions because of seasonal fluctuations in advertising, it mirrored the layout of most *Chatelaines* from the revamped 1958 issues through to the late sixties. Previously the magazine had been less consistent in column placement and in maintaining a consistent graphic image. In short, the early and mid-fifties' versions were more cluttered and visually chaotic, despite the similarities in content.

The first eighteen pages of the July 1960 issue were devoted to a

JULY 1960 15¢

The Windsors—exclusive photo story
Do the Gouzenkos regret their decision?
Women's great challenge—old age
"We gave up our child"

1 *Chatelaine* cover, July 1960

section called News and Views. These items included the editorial essay; the omnibus 'What's New' feature, which included a variety of anecdotes and information about the editors, contributors, and special features in this issue; and editorial endorsements for new consumer products – kitchen gadgets, toys, cosmetics, fashion, and furniture. All these pages were framed by half-page advertisements for a variety of products – perfume, insurance, tea, coffee, processed foods, *Maclean's* and Maclean Hunter products, linoleum, home improvement projects, paper products, feminine hygiene products, and cosmetics. Next, 'What's New with You' provided a collection of information on cross-country happenings and the editor's short profiles of 'exceptional' women – in the workforce, voluntary organizations, and education. 'What's New to See and Hear' usually profiled the latest Canadian cultural events – television programs, theatre, radio, and recordings. Also included in this information section was Lawrence Galton's 'Here's Health,' a page of late-breaking medical news culled from medical journals. The foreign affairs page, 'Your World Notebook,' gave 'a monthly background to the news headlines.' This month, Donald R. Gordon contributed 'What's Happening to Our Commonwealth.' Finally, 'Teen Tempo' provided an advice and fashion page for teens. In this instalment, Susan Cooper advised 'Mavis' that it probably wasn't a good idea to be in a 'constant twosome' with another teenage girl if she hoped to snag a boyfriend because 'shy boys ... will not approach two girls to ask one for a date.' Clearly, News and Views was interpreted very loosely and was, in fact, a potpourri of material geared to hold the attention of a mass audience of women and men.

Immediately after News and Views were the introductory pages (or 'starts') of all the feature articles and fiction stories. A dramatic exposé of the Gouzenkos, written by regular contributor Christina McCall Newman, was the lead article. The 1945 defection of Igor Gouzenko, a clerk in the Soviet Embassy in Ottawa, had created a scandal in Canada over national security issues and effectively launched Cold War fears in this country.[24] This article purported to bring readers abreast of the latest developments of the spy saga. To alert readers to the dark subject matter – communists in our midst and the Cold War in Canada – the graphic designer had opted for orange print on black, with a small grey silhouette of the mysterious, business-suited Igor Gouzenko. Perhaps it was an odd choice for a summer issue, but McCall Newman's article promised to bring home to readers that Dominion Day was not just 'a casual holiday' for Canadians. A flip of the page caused readers to jump from political intrigue to celebrity love-in, with photographer Roloff Beny's latest romp with royalty entitled '*Chatelaine* Calls on the Windsors' – a photo-profile of the misunderstood and, by then, rather aged Duke and Duchess of Windsor.

Following the Windsor piece were the fiction starts. 'The Inn of No Yesterdays' by N. Brysson Morrison, this month's *Chatelaine* Bonus Novel, promised readers a melodramatic romance full of passion and pathos: 'Vivian was pleading for the marriage she had abandoned. Now Dick had to choose.' In contrast, the next page proffered gentle summer fun in Nathan Kaplan's story 'How to Catch a Helpless Hero.' 'The trouble with Sydney, ' according to the story's introduction, 'was she was just too good at everything. The trouble with Greg Lundy was he wasn't good at anything. So she played dumb – and got the wackiest surprise of her life.' If none of those lines intrigued you, you could read the article 'How to Meet the Challenge of Old Age,' a collection of musings by *Chatelaine*'s experts, coordinated by staff writer Jessie London. Finally, 'Look Back for Tomorrow' by Katherine Marcuse promised a short story about an unfulfilled housewife and mother searching for the 'key to all her tomorrows.'

Following the third story were the *Chatelaine* department features. Given the emphasis on summer, this issue focused on the cottage theme with 'Quickies for Cottage Cooking,' featuring a selection of easy-to-prepare menus for the weekdays, when mother and the kids were at the cottage, and more sophisticated fare for the 'welcome-for-the-weekend supper for father.' Next, fodder for home-improvement dreams, came 'The Little House That Grew into a Gracious Home' by Olga Ann Ferda and Vera Jory, a quintessential *Chatelaine* do-it-yourself story about a couple who spent ten years painstakingly renovating and building a home on the 'outskirts of Toronto.' Finally, Ruth Doehler's '*Chatelaine* Personal Experience Story' entitled 'We Gave Up Our Child' profiled a couple's heart-wrenching decision to institutionalize their disabled daughter. After a few pages of ads for cameras, film, furniture, and diet products, the final departmental articles appeared. Both of them were classics from the *Chatelaine* Institute. 'How to Save Money on Food' informed readers that 'most families throw out three pounds a day. Here's how to buy and serve without waste.' Meanwhile, 'Shopping with *Chatelaine*' provided a survey of the institute's latest consumer evaluation – steam irons.

By now, readers were half way through the periodical. The primary visual appeal in the first half consisted of the full-colour illustrations that accompanied the fiction, the black-and-white photographs with the general features, and full-colour photos with the departmental fare. Ads were rare in the second quarter of the magazine, where all the features started, but subsequently grew more numerous and were the chief source of visual appeal. A large number of ads were either full colour or two colour and enlivened the never-ending black-and-white pages of editorial material. Structurally, *Chatelaine* was compiled so that most of the features, stories, and departmental articles would conclude at the back of the magazine. Full-page ads were more likely to appear in the first half, and, since the ads grew progressively smaller, the fourth quarter displayed a considerable number of very small ads for shoe polish, household cleansers, and over-the-counter drugs and remedies. Thus the layout of the periodical hooked the readers with compelling visuals and well-written one- or two-page starts, and then required them to turn to the back for the conclusions to the articles. The magazine's layout structured the readings in such a way that readers were exposed to the greatest amount of advertising material: ads framed most pages, and editorial content often consisted of one-quarter or one-half of each page, thus requiring six half pages to finish a feature or a piece of fiction.

The only new material to begin in the third and fourth quarters of the periodical was half-page, or smaller, *Chatelaine* departmental material or ads for *Chatelaine* crafts. For instance, 'Homemaker's Diary' offered tips on house cleaning and organization, while this month's '*Chatelaine* Crafts' promised 'Just two pairs of terry towels make this gay picnic foursome.' Departmental fare was simple stuff, to add excitement to tired suburban routines, and in this case it promised silly summer fun with patterns for a matching toga-style beach robe, 'outing kit,' 'wedge-shaped cushion,' and 'cutlery carry-all.' Such economical products were accessible for the limited budgets of *Chatelaine*'s readers. The long-time champion in this department was 'Meals of the Month,' which provided readers with a full menu plan for the period and one special recipe: 'Mexican Braised Short Ribs.' The last few pages of the magazine featured the 'Your Child' column, written by Elizabeth Chant Robinson, MD, who doled out such practical advice as 'Cool tips for baby's HOT-WEATHER COMFORT.' Surrounding this one-page article, which was normally printed on three successive pages, were the advertisements for children's products – baby food, drugs, powders, ointments, and clothes. Each issue of *Chatelaine* concluded with 'The Last Word Is Yours,' the regular letters page, and the full-colour cover advertisements, in this case for Dream Whip ('Strawberry days are here') and Red Rose 'Instant Tea.'

Reading or browsing *Chatelaine* required readers to switch gears quickly – from ads to features to fiction to departmental material and back to advertisements – in the space of a few pages at the beginning of the magazine, and often in composite jumbles at the back. Through these different components, readers negotiated a variety of messages about women's roles, desires, problems, and joys. The magazine did not promote 'one vision' of Canadian women, but a continuum that ranged from the stay-at-home mother with children through to the working wife, the childless couple, the single career woman, and even children. Meanwhile, ads pushed consumption for the family, home, and individual. The visual appeal of the magazine was primarily limited to the cover, the colour ads, and the few touches of colour applied to the stories and departmental features.

Editing *Chatelaine*

The person responsible for *Chatelaine*'s 'look' was the editor, and in the fifties and sixties the magazine had four editors and a host of managing, associate, and departmental editors. *Chatelaine* had always benefited from consistent editorial direction. Anne Elizabeth Wilson was the founding editor of *The Chatelaine*, but her double load of editing another Maclean Hunter publication, *Mayfair*, resulted in an editorial change before the first year was out, when Byrne Hope Sanders was hired to succeed her. As a child, Sanders and her family had emigrated from South Africa to settle in southwestern Ontario, and later she attended a Toronto private girls' school, St Mildred's College.[25] After graduation she started as a cub reporter for the *Sentinel Review* in Woodstock, Ontario, before switching gears to work for the T. Eaton Company as a member of the advertising staff. In 1926 she returned to journalism, as editor of *Business Woman*, before she assumed the position at *Chatelaine* in 1929. During the Second World War, Sanders was invited to head the Consumer Division of the Wartime Prices and Trade Board. As a 'dollar a year' woman, with the company paying her salary, she left the magazine in the hands of managing editor Mary Etta Macpherson. Once in Ottawa, Sanders created a consumer council of women and was responsible for overseeing the implementation of food rationing. The government selected her both for the leadership she had demonstrated as editor of *Chatelaine* and for the trust and confidence

Canadian women had in her. For her efforts, she was made a Commander of the British Empire in July 1946.[26] When she resumed her editorial responsibilities in 1947, she launched the *Chatelaine* Department of Consumer Relations, which consisted of 2000 '*Chatelaine* Councillors' from across the country who participated in a series of editorial surveys. In 1952 Sanders retired from the magazine, though there is some indication that she was 'encouraged' to resign so that Maclean Hunter could revamp it. She became the director of the Canadian Institute for Public Opinion (Gallop),[27] a move that reveals both the increasing popularity of polling in the postwar era and her own keen particiation in these new marketing strategies.[28]

By all accounts, Sanders's tenure as editor of the magazine was both long lived and successful. Doris Anderson, who was hired by Sanders, recalls her as a 'very ladylike' editor who 'would go around and look in everybody's office and make sure all of her children were there, smiling and happy.'[29] June Callwood remembers her as a women who wore a 'hat and gloves' and was 'regal, domineering and pretentious.'[30] Staffer Eileen Morris, later a freelance journalist, remembers that although Sanders projected a polished and professional image, she actually lived in straightened financial circumstances. Unbeknownst to *Chatelaine* readers, Sanders was the primary breadwinner in her family because her artist husband's income was erratic.[31]

In Sanders's farewell editorial in the January 1952 edition, she introduced the next editor of *Chatelaine*, Lotta Dempsey: 'Many of you know her well for she was a *Chatelaine* staffer for some time and has written often for the magazine. She's a fine person, a distinguished writer. She is what most of you are – a Canadian wife and mother.'[32] Dempsey was a reluctant conscript as editor, but Floyd Chalmers, vice-president of Maclean Hunter, was convinced she was both the logical and best successor to Sanders.[33] In her autobiography, *No Life for a Lady*, she described her experience at *Chatelaine* as follows: 'I defected for a considerable spell to a magazine, becoming for a stranger-than-fiction period editor-in-chief of *Chatelaine*.'[34] Originally from Alberta, Dempsey began her journalism career at the *Edmonton Journal* and the *Edmonton Bulletin*.[35] A freelance writer at *Chatelaine* since 1935, by her count she had published 316 articles at the time she moved into the editor's office.[36] Unlike Sanders, Dempsey's tenure at *Chatelaine* was brief, lasting less than a year. As is common in such abrupt departures, no formal explanation was printed in the magazine. Later, Dempsey claimed that she felt much more comfortable with the newspaper environment and that she 'preferred to do the writing herself to buying manuscripts from others.'[37] According to Anderson, there were other contributing factors. Not only did Dempsey dislike the administrative side of editing a major magazine but she suffered the animosity of her managing editor, Gerry Anglin, who had wanted the editorship for himself and was 'undermining' Dempsey.[38] After she left *Chatelaine*, Dempsey worked for a time at the *Globe and Mail* before settling in as a columnist with the *Toronto Star*.

Her successor, John Clare, was the only male editor of *Chatelaine* – a distinction he holds to this day.[39] Born in New Brunswick but raised in Saskatchewan, Clare attended the University of Saskatchewan.[40] After graduation he held a variety of newspaper positions at the *Saskatoon Star Phoenix*, the *Globe and Mail*, and the *Toronto Star*, and served as a war correspondent during the Second World War.[41] After the war, Clare joined the staff of *Maclean's* and, by 1952, had risen to managing editor. Chalmers brought Clare over to fill the void at *Chatelaine*, apparently promising him that once the magazine was in order, he could return to *Maclean's*.[42] Described as a 'good administrator and a good editor' who brought 'more polish to the writing' he 'was not interested in making [*Chatelaine*] a wonderful magazine.'[43] He rarely wrote any editorial essays and preferred to devote his space to wry anecdotes about the foibles of publishing a women's magazine, such as receiving letters addressed 'Dear Madam.'[44] According to Anderson and Callwood, Clare hated his time at *Chatelaine* and, when he developed high blood pressure, he returned to *Maclean's*.[45] Although Clare was listed as the editor, Anderson, a staff writer at *Chatelaine*, quickly moved up in the ranks, first to associate editor and, by 1956, to managing editor. Clare left the magazine as quietly as he arrived: all readers knew was that, in the September 1957 issue, Anderson was officially listed as managing editor in the masthead.[46]

Doris Anderson was born and raised in Calgary. Her mother ran a boarding house and, given the penurious and often turbulent family circumstances during her childhood, Anderson sought refuge in education and literature. Not uncommonly for this era, she raised her university tuition by teaching school in rural communities. After she graduated from the University of Alberta in 1945, according to a brief biography published in *Chatelaine*, 'she spent a year in Europe ... writing fiction on Paris' Left Bank and travelling through the British Isles on her thumb – and $46.'[47] Her autobiography, *Rebel Daughter*, paints a less romantic image of this time – one characterized by uneven employment and straitened economic circumstances.[48]

When she returned to Canada, Anderson worked at a number of

positions: editorial assistant with the *Star Weekly*, scriptwriter for the Claire Wallace radio program, and copywriter in Eaton's advertising department. In 1951 she joined the staff of *Chatelaine* as a promotional assistant and moved quickly to writing articles.[49] One of the key characteristics of her success was her ability to write with wit and knowledge about the travails of the 'average' woman. In 1977 Anderson retired as editor of *Chatelaine* to write novels and pursue other interests. Although she was not pushed, she recalls the period as a particularly difficult one. She was no longer enthusiastic about editing *Chatelaine* and wanted other challenges, particularly the editorship of *Maclean's*. Failing that, she was keen to try her hand at publishing periodicals, but both goals were nixed by the executives at Maclean Hunter. Anderson found this refusal a bitter pill to swallow after years of editorial and financial successes at *Chatelaine*, compared with the turbulence at *Maclean's*. Although *Maclean's* has yet to have a female editor, gender was not the only reason that Maclean Hunter refused to give Anderson the top position there or to make her *Chatelaine*'s publisher. She was not a skilled political player, and her often avant-garde views were considered too radical for *Chatelaine*, let alone other parts of the Maclean Hunter publishing empire.

Post-*Chatelaine*, Anderson has been involved in a variety of political, literary, and academic pursuits. A staunch feminist, she was president of the Canadian Advisory Council on the Status of Women from 1979 to 1981 and president of the National Action Committee on the Status of Women from 1982 to 1984. In addition to her autobiography, she has written two novels and one monograph on the international feminist movement. The recipient of many awards, medals, and honorary degrees, she was awarded the 'Officer of the Order of Canada' in 1984. Although now retired as chancellor of the University of Prince Edward Island, Anderson is still active both formally and informally in feminist networks and publishing circles.

In contrast to the numerous personnel changes during the fifties, in the sixties *Chatelaine*'s workforce remained fairly constant. On the managerial and business side, Lloyd M. Hodgkinson continued as publisher throughout the decade, as did Gordon Rumgay, the circulation manager, and A.B. Gardner, manager of advertising and sales. The sixties at *Chatelaine* were characterized by a great degree of continuity. Those who assumed senior positions had all worked their way up from within the organization and were familiar with the magazine's style and focus.

Biographies of *Chatelaine*'s editors, while interesting, serve an important purpose in understanding how the periodical was created. People often assume that the editors of women's magazines are from the 'chattering classes' – well-educated, affluent women and men. In the Canadian context, they presume that most people involved in national periodicals hail from central Canada, if not Toronto specifically, the centre of the periodical publishing industry. Clearly, that was not the case with *Chatelaine*. Sanders was the main breadwinner in her family, while the other three came from modest backgrounds. It is intriguing to speculate what impact their western Canadian upbringing might have had on their editorial vision. Perhaps it partly explains Dempsey's and Anderson's plain-spoken critique of government and the 'affluent' society. It is important that none of the editors belonged to the elite by birth or education, but had earned the position. They all believed in the liberal dream of individuals making the most of their opportunities. In addition, they introduced a national picture when their budgets permitted, avoiding the misconception that Toronto represents Canada.

Gendering Production

After her retirement from *Chatelaine*, Anderson tried her hand at writing fiction. *Rough Layout*, published in 1981, was dedicated 'To all the great people I worked with in the magazine business.' Jude, the protagonist, is the editor of a women's magazine entitled *Young Living* published by the fictitious Meridian Publishing Company of Toronto. The book is a humorous, often scathingly funny, account of the trials and tribulations of a women's magazine editor – a thinly veiled autobiography.[50] This excerpt, in which Jude defends the magazine to her feminist friend Lenore, provides insight into both the tensions of magazine production and the gender division of production at *Chatelaine*:

> 'Look, I push feminist articles as much as I can,' Jude protested. 'I've got a certain kind of magazine. It's not *Ms*. It's not *Branching Out*. It's not *Status of Women News*. But it does reach a lot of women and it can make an impact. Gradually. Bradbury [the publisher] would like to run a magazine only for affluent young couples living in penthouses. To him, women are technically dead after thirty-five, and they all belong to upper-class families. They own cottages, snowmobiles, cars. They travel constantly. They change their furnishings with every season. They use gallons and gallons of creams and bath lotions ... The reader is not a feminist, Lenore. She's a consumer – according to the people at Meridian.' In fact, Jude ignored, as

much as possible, the advertising department's view of the reader. She felt her audience was struggling with debts and personal problems. Far from being affluent, they were more likely pressed financially. The women worked because they had to. Most of them clung to polyester suits and easy-care hairstyles. Cooking was simple because recipes had to be made after they got home from work. Exotic cooking was something they liked to read about occasionally, and try on weekends. They were – especially the younger ones – intensely interested in keeping their marriages together, and caring for their children ... They were marginally interested in public issues such as ecology and nutrition. All these subjects Jude tackled; but for her own satisfaction, she laced the magazine with a strong dose of feminist articles.[51]

The sharp contrast between the advertising department's view of the readership and Jude's is obvious. The publisher's and advertising executives' focus on consumption emphasized the young, urban, affluent reader at the expense of the great majority of readers. That the ad men's grandiose impressions of the readership matched the overheated rhetoric of the consumer reports was not surprising. As urban professionals, resident in Toronto, the numbers and 'lifestyle' depicted confirmed their presumptions and validated their own sense of how Canadians lived. Conversely, the letters from readers were not glossy paeans to consumption, but at turns reflective, critical, or complimentary. The business executives and advertising department saw the numbers, read the figures, and calculated the circulation statistics, while Anderson and her departmental editors read the letters, met the readers at women's groups luncheons, tabulated their contest entries, and compiled the councillors' reports.

In a prepared statement read to the Royal Commission on Publications in 1960, Anderson explained the role of *Chatelaine*: 'First of all, *Chatelaine* is a kind of trade magazine for Canadian homemakers.'[52] However, she continued, 'the services and guidance that is one of the main jobs of a woman's service magazine is only half of the story because we devotedly believe that Canadian women have a wide and growing interest in matters outside the home.' Anderson's guarded brief was quite different from the more personal response she wrote to a dissatisfied subscriber the previous year: 'A magazine should have a purpose in publishing and that is to point out problems that should be brought to the attention of the public. This is our purpose in publishing articles on marriage, divorce, drug addiction, etc.'[53]

Before Anderson presented her brief to the commissioners, Blair Fraser, the editor of *Maclean's,* presented his statement. Although he sought to describe the role of his periodical within Canadian society and magazine publishing, his description of a typical *Maclean's* reader and the magazine was indicative of the difference between the two general-interest periodicals. 'We think of a *Maclean's* reader as an intelligent person in a relaxed mood, and a great deal of what we offer is intended only for his entertainment and not for his improvement. However, we have serious purposes. We want to report Canada and the world to Canadians through Canadian eyes.'[54] Fraser's goals were shared by all Canadian cultural industries and individuals alike because, in the aftermath of the Massey Commission Report on the Status of the Arts, Letters, and Sciences in Canaada, there was a heightened sense of the importance attached to creating, promoting, and popularizing 'Canadian culture.'[55] Within the Maclean Hunter Consumer Magazines Division, *Maclean's* and *Chatelaine* were regarded as sibling publications. Yet all the glamour, prestige, expensive talent, parental encouragement, and pride went to *Maclean's,* the first-born son. *Chatelaine,* as the younger sister, often got hand-me-down writers and one editor. She had to endure parental confusion about what she was doing and where she was going. More often, she suffered from a lack of attention. Anderson laments: 'We were always very much second fiddle to *Maclean's.* Much more money was spent on *Maclean's* and much more money was lost on *Maclean's.*'[56]

The structure of the magazine throughout the fifties and sixties remained fairly consistent, although in the later years of the decade a larger budget permitted the hiring of more staff. Magazine production at *Chatelaine,* as at most mass-market periodicals, was split into two different sections: the editorial and advertising (or business) departments. The editorial department included the editor, the managing editor (if any), the copy editor, the art director, the associate editors, staff writers, and freelance journalists. The business department included the publisher or manager (depending on the situation), the advertising manager, the circulation manager, and the sales staff. These two departments, through the attendance of the editor and the publisher (or manager) at Magazine Division meetings, reported to the director of the Magazine Division, who was responsible for approving budgets, general planning, and development. Anderson recalls what those meetings were like: 'I had to go to planning meetings, and these things were entirely male [except for her] with the chairman of the

board and the president, and the head of advertising, and the head of
magazine division, my publisher, and the Circulation Department.'
Within the male corporate hierarchy at Maclean Hunter, Anderson was
clearly an outsider.

The responsibilities of the business department were twofold: to sell
advertising space in the periodical and to handle the circulation promotions. Business imperatives were the order of the day: the constant
search for a higher circulation, for more advertisers, and for ways to
keep the current group of advertisers happy. The department ran various promotions, including discounting or the traditional special Christmas rates, to encourage as many people as possible to subscribe to the
magazine. Selling advertising was a similar process. The sales staff tried
to encourage new custom, maintain current accounts, and, if the circulation rose, raise the advertising rates. In addition, they worked on
ways to support their advertisers through billboards and in-store promotional material which reminded customers that the product was
'advertised in *Chatelaine* magazine.' The advertising department was
also responsible for commissioning the various market research reports. In contrast, the editorial department was concerned solely with
researching and writing editorial content. Its goal was to create exciting
copy for the readers. To this end, this department had regular editorial
meetings every couple of months. The editor was responsible for the
vision of the magazine. June Callwood recalls: 'The tone of the magazine is entirely hers. All those articles are her call.'[57] The managing
editor, concerned with schedules and production, vetted editorial copy
from the associate editors, selected letters from readers, and performed
the nuts-and-bolts jobs involved in putting out the magazine. It was the
job of the associate editors to oversee the service department and the
fiction components. They were responsible for generating ideas and
articles within their own sphere of influence and assigning staff writers
or freelance journalists to research and write these articles. The art
director and copy editors looked after the visual appearance of the
periodical, chose the layouts and art work, and proofed the finished
copy for errors.

Although the editor and the publisher met to discuss the magazine
and attended larger meetings within the Maclean Hunter company,
there was no contact between the editorial and the advertising departments. Both sides were often critical of the other – indeed, this sort of
binary organization created tensions. Further compounding the separa-

tion and difference of the two departments was a specific gender divide: the editorial department was primarily female, while the business department was primarily male (secretaries excepted). The work culture at Maclean Hunter, and in those days *Maclean's* was on the same floor as *Chatelaine*, was fraught with sexual tensions. According to Callwood, 'most of the women got hit on by the men ... There were affairs ... they didn't call them affairs, but they really were sexual harassment ... That was just how life was. You could say no, but you would be sure never to get any good assignments. I didn't get hit on because I was married and that protected me.' Callwood remembers that the female staff complained and that when the single staffers got married, they usually quit their jobs – a situation 'encouraged' by Maclean Hunter. When asked about the workplace culture at *Chatelaine*, Anderson responded: 'Well, we had a good time and, because we were women, we all worked very hard; most people really liked the job and they put a lot of themselves into the magazine.'[58] Problematic gender relations, competition between *Maclean's* and *Chatelaine*, and the division between the editorial and business sides of the periodical all worked to create a workplace culture in which the male editors and business staff occupied centre stage in the corporation's Magazine Division, while the largely female editorial staff at *Chatelaine* toiled away in obscurity and at what was regarded, in house, as a second-class periodical.

While *Chatelaine* was a commercial cultural product, created primarily to make money for the Maclean Hunter company by attracting a large number of advertisements to the magazine, the editors and their staff were concerned with producing material of interest to readers. Magazines always serve two masters – the advertisers and the readers. Admittedly, a large circulation and interested readers are not mutually exclusive concepts, but the difference in tone, content, and themes between the advertising copy and the editorial copy was often striking. The female editors serviced the readers, offering fact and fiction they thought would be of interest to them. They did not intentionally produce material that reflected the consumer ethos of the advertising department. They did not regard the readers as a vast audience ripe for commercial profit. In many cases they appear to have identified with their readership because they, too, were working women, experiencing the changes in the nature of women's roles and grappling with workplace challenges themselves.

In contrast, the advertising department was fixated on circulation figures, readership reports, advertising linage, and products consumed. Content was little more than the material between the advertisements. Not surprisingly, its main editorial focus was the service material – food, fashion, beauty, housekeeping, decorating, and child care. For the editorial department, the articles and editorials received more prominent attention, and the service department features rarely upstaged the general articles within the magazine. This paradoxical situation, where the business executives and Maclean Hunter directors had little knowledge of the material in the magazine, existed, according to Anderson, because 'the advertisers never read the magazine. They would look at the numbers, the number of readers, the circulation, the number of older women and younger women reading the magazine, the numbers game. I would get some complaints from the publisher and from the top brass on the ninth floor about turning this nice little women's magazine into a feminist rag. But as long as the circulation continued to go up and as long as the advertiser was there they couldn't argue with it very much ... They depended on those figures because they really didn't feel very secure themselves. They'd often quote their wives: "My wife didn't like this article" or "My wife wonders why you're doing this?"' The executives responsible for charting the magazine's advertising and business success seldom read the periodical because its 'feminine' content was of little interest. They had scant understanding or awareness of what the product they sold to advertisers offered Canadian women. The only male intervention into the editorial material of the magazine was the Dichter Study in 1958, which was commissioned primarily because of the falling ad revenue at the end of John Clare's tenure as editor.

The silver lining in this situation was that the female editors were accorded a level of autonomy and power that was unheard of at American women's magazines. Largely out of sight of the Maclean Hunter executives, Anderson was able to remake *Chatelaine*. Once the executives realized what she was doing, the increased circulation and advertising pages provided numerical proof that her new formula was a success. As long as the magazine continued to be commercially successful – increased subscription rates and increased advertising content – they did not question the format of the editorial material. It was easy for an innovative editor, like Anderson, to create a magazine that challenged the traditional women's magazine genre and offered readers considerably more than 'twelve different summer hairdos or fifteen ways to serve hamburger.'

Gendering Consumption

The advertising department's fixation on circulation figures and advertising pages caused it to regard *Chatelaine*'s readers as primarily 'consumer's in waiting' – waiting, that is, for the ad men to work their magic. Because all mass-market magazines are, in effect, sold twice – once to advertisers who purchase ads that support the periodical and once to subscribers – it is crucially important to examine the advertising discourse directed at the advertisers and advertising companies. This discourse illuminates the gendered world of consumption and provides a commercial assessment of the magazine's impact, role, and significance. This mandate is very different from the editorial goals because it is here that the glorification of commerce is celebrated and wildly optimistic. An excerpt from one such promotional advertisement about the power of *Chatelaine* is indicative of the genre: 'For 25 years *Chatelaine* has served the Canadian consumer, the retailer, and the advertiser. The consumer, by making a higher standard of living desirable. The retailer, by sound merchandising policies and the creation of a local demand for goods and services wherever he may be. The advertiser, by sparking reader ideas which create wants which can only be satisfied by sales.'[59] As a final encouragement, the ad ended with a provocative phrase: 'Advertise in *Chatelaine* ... be there when the sale is born.' The goal of advertising is to sell products, but, despite the claims of market research and pollsters, the methods are far from scientifically precise. Ads work by combining compelling, eye-catching images associated with moods and aspirations that are supposed to evoke desires in the reader, and then repeatedly publishing those images so that the widest possible audience is exposed to the material. Sow the seeds in *Chatelaine* and industry will reap the sales, went the standard refrain.

The manner in which Maclean Hunter executives advertised and described *Chatelaine* in the advertisers' rate guide, *Canadian Advertising Rates and Data* (*CARD*), differed considerably from the editors' vision. Although the advertisements for the magazine in *CARD* often repeated the line 'Please the reader first and serve the advertiser best!' it was clear that the business of *Chatelaine* was to promote consumption.[60] The plan was to present a nicely packaged periodical that caught and held the reader's attention while she flipped through the pages of advertising. The goal, outlined in countless ads in *CARD*, was Action: 'Chatelaine editors create the "mood to buy" by showing women *what to do*. Your advertising in Chatelaine shows them *what to do it with*. This combination 1–2 punch is a proven sales formula that gets consumer *action*! That's why we say ... if it's *action* you want, use *Chatelaine* (Canada's leading home service magazine).'[61] The language of these ads, because they were directed primarily to a male audience, often invoked sports or sexual metaphors to drive home the point about the power of advertising in *Chatelaine*. Lacking in subtlety, it was clear that the advertisers had the power and skill to seduce the consumer. They revelled in the machismo of the 'sure thing' secured by *Chatelaine* advertising.

To determine just how much action they were stimulating, *Chatelaine's* advertising department was constantly evaluating the magazine through reader surveys. Most of these surveys were done by the Gruneau Research Company of Canada. The reports, called Starch reports (named for their American creator, Daniel Starch), claimed to measure the amount of action generated by the ad and the editorial material. The following excerpt from a 1953 ad entitled 'If It's ACTION You Want ... Here It Is!' aptly conveyed the overheated rhetoric of the *CARD* ads and the Starch results. 'Thousands of women are spurred into Action with every issue of *Chatelaine*': for example, 'three editorials and nineteen advertisements on home appliances in November '52 got Action! Eighty percent said they took some action on one or more ... If all the Action could be visualized that *Chatelaine* starts in hundreds of thousands of homes across Canada, you would be convinced that advertising in *Chatelaine* produces the biggest return for your dollar. The only magazine on the continent demonstrating the Action resulting from its service articles and advertisements, *Chatelaine* Action Studies stand ready for your inspection. Advertise in *Chatelaine* for Action!'[62] 'Action' was defined as a purchase, an interest in the product or feature, or acting on the suggestions provided in the magazine, so action and purchase were not synonymous. Not surprisingly, Starch reports explained the finer details of what *action* meant in fine print at the top of the reports, but seldom printed this information in the *CARD* ads. When 80 per cent of respondents told Gruneau 'they took some action,' all this really meant was that the magazine had some impact on the reader. This simplistic relationship benefited the advertisers and was, as far as they were concerned, the purpose of the magazine. In practice, however, reader action could be entirely counter to the goals of the advertisers.

Along with the advertisements extolling the virtues of advertising in specific periodicals, there were general advertisements, placed by the Magazine Advertising Bureau of Canada (MAB), that offered information about the desirability of magazine advertising.[63] These ads usually took the form of a collection of vague phrases, such as 'Magazines, the good companions of the leisure hours, contribute to the better way of life, which is why they are popular with all members of the family.'[64] Other favourite tactics were to publish excerpts from the latest surveys of magazine readers. This one, based on audience surveys conducted in Toronto, Hamilton, London, and Ottawa, unequivocally stated the prescriptive effect magazines had on readers, and why magazine advertising was more effective than other forms. 'Magazine reading shows people how to act with others and teaches them what to expect.' Beyond instructions in the art of living, magazine 'reading permits people to get away temporarily from the anxieties, the provocations, and the problems of everyday life, and provides relaxing intervals when they are in a receptive frame of mind and can take the time to study advertising.'[65] According to the 'experts,' the market research people, magazines were both prescriptive literature and entertainment. Because the magazine was semipermanent, it lay around homes much longer than newspapers did. Each magazine was picked up numerous times and passed along to other family members or friends. The actual number of readers was much higher than the circulation sales figures. Just as *Chatelaine* ads trumpeted the action stimulated by reading the magazine, many of these studies confirmed what the magazine publishers wanted to hear or, more important, what they wanted to tell advertisers – that advertising in periodicals was a sure bet.

Some of the later MAB advertisements featured testimonials from satisfied companies. This representative example from the Jergens Lotion company again demonstrated the advertisers' faith in the power of their medium and the passivity of the reader. '"Magazines have always been our principal advertising medium. We value them because they are literally held in the hands we want to reach. When a magazine reader sees our advertisement – Jergens Lotion Stops Detergent Hands – she will glance at her own hands as she reads. She will make up her mind to replenish her stock of Jergens Lotion. Her own hands have become a part of our advertisement" ... Canadian magazine advertising sells in many ways: as a visitor to the home, with something new and vital to say each time it comes; as a companion for those quiet, receptive moments ... when most decisions to buy are made.'[66] Recent cultural studies of advertising are quick to dispute this simplistic cause-and-effect theory of advertising, but the rhetoric of ads directed at the advertisers indicates that they regarded female consumers as highly impressionable. The ad men saw clear demarcations of roles. They were the active agents who did things: created studies, developed ad campaigns, and, in effect, directed the action of the consumers. The consumers, always defined as female, were the 'acted upon.' In this discourse, men sold and women bought, or, more ominously, were bought. Advertisers were careful not to belittle the consumers or joke about their culpability, but the end result was the same: action. The acted upon had only a small role to play in the drama of consumption. Advertisers had the power to create the ads, structure their various meanings, and place them before a receptive audience. Readers were far less powerful in this equation, since they could exercise consumer choice or ignore the ads.

The irony, of course, was that the rhetoric used to woo the advertising agencies and their clients to *Chatelaine* often employed the same tactics that the advertising companies used on the readers of the magazine. In the end, this discourse cannot be accepted at face value as an indicator of a deterministic role played by magazines or of the cause-and-effect nature of magazine advertising. Instead, it reveals a gendered world of advertising directed at male advertising executives and corporations which promised fantastic results in an attempt to get them to 'buy' (place ads in) *Chatelaine*. The result, as the evidence of the reader demographics section, the *Hostess* experiment, and other marketing reports indicated, was seldom so successful because *Chatelaine*'s readers were not able to participate in the consumer society. All *Chatelaine* could deliver regularly was a mass audience of readers, not a 'better sort' of or 'affluent' reader, and that reality continually muted the advertisers' messages. Many commentators have speculated that advertising success must be judged both by sales and by the implementation of desires, wants, and moods in the readers. There is little ambiguity about the persuasive and the repetitious nature of advertising that constantly reinforced those messages. Yet the actual evidence from the readers – their letters – and the fact that *Chatelaine*'s audience was not the 'prime' consuming group desired by advertisers indicated that these readers were a tough sell. In letters, they indicated their displeasure not only with the affluence depicted in the ads or the overt commercialism of articles that pushed 'the good life,' but sometimes, too, with the number of pages devoted to ads.

The Balance Sheet

Ultimately, the advertising men at Maclean Hunter invested so much energy, money, and creativity in those industry advertisements because the advertising dollars were critical to *Chatelaine*'s financial health. The Canadian magazine industry has always been treacherous, given the relatively small, scattered population and the accessibility and affordability of American magazines. *Chatelaine*'s large circulation was an indicator of the popularity of the magazine, but not necessarily of financial prosperity. The true tests of commercial health were the advertising revenues and profit generated by the periodical. In terms of profit, *Chatelaine* was not overwhelmingly successful during the fifties and sixties – though there are some contradictions in the sources. The fifties proved to be a particularly trying decade, as split-run Canadian editions of *Time* and *Reader's Digest* appeared on Canadian newsstands and took close to 40 per cent of all advertising dollars spent on magazines in Canada.[67] The international trade drama in the waning years of the century and the threat of an American retaliatory cultural embargo if the magazine market is not opened up to more split-run products are indicative of what a difficult and enduring problem American publications have been for the Canadian periodical industry. Statistics available for the last five years of the fifties show that net advertising revenue accounted for 77 per cent of *Chatelaine*'s total revenue.[68] The gross advertising revenues for the magazine had increased from $1,336,970 in 1950 to $4,375,850 in 1959.[69] Yet despite this dramatic 227.3 per cent increase in advertising revenues, the magazine's balance sheet showed an overall loss for the ten-year period of $1,328,039.[70] The magazine had turned a small profit in 1951 and 1952, but sustained losses in all other years until it absorbed the *Canadian Home Journal* in 1958, resulting in a small profit in 1959. Interestingly, the losses of 1953–8 correspond with John Clare's tenure as *Chatelaine*'s editor.

According to the brief Maclean Hunter presented to the *Report of the Special Senate Committee on Mass Media* in 1970, the English and French versions of the magazine were 'profitable in some years (notably 1967, the year of Canada's centennial) but not in others.'[71] *Maclean's* fared even worse and turned a profit only in 1969. However, in an interview, Doris Anderson recalled that *Maclean's* drifted in the sixties, the victim of revolving editors, lack of direction, and numerous lawsuits, while *Chatelaine* continued to function as the 'milch cow ... working away ... always making a profit and never causing any trouble.'[72] The Maclean Hunter Budget Summary for 1961 shows a cash basis profit (before income taxes, donations, and other special charges) ranging from $11,952 to $118,892 for that year.[73] Ted Hart's 1971 speech draft for a Maclean

Hunter directors' meeting included impressive figures for net advertising revenues: $1,997,000 in 1958 to $4,040,000 in 1970.[74] It seemed likely that *Chatelaine* was a profitable enterprise in the sixties, though that success was overshadowed by the poor performance of the rest of the Maclean Hunter consumer magazines. Moreover, when the company made presentations to the Senate Committee, it was looking for government protection from U.S. magazines or favourable postal rates. It was thus inclined to present composite figures that showed blanket losses in the consumer magazine division. The published figures illustrated a 'laughable' profit margin: 'between 1905 and 1960, the company's consumer magazines collected nearly $130 million in revenues, and delivered a total profit, over the fifty-five year period, of precisely $410,604.'[75]

Many factors accounted for the problems faced by Maclean Hunter and other Canadian magazine publishers. The overflow circulation of American magazines was primarily to blame for the lack of advertiser interest in Canadian periodicals. In other words, national advertisers (many of whom were either American or multinational firms) had little desire, or reason, to advertise in Canadian periodicals when, for the price of advertising in the American magazines, they also gained entry to the Canadian market. Equally troubling was the realization that Canadians were far less likely to read magazines than were Americans. In general, Canadians were reading fewer magazines in 1969 than they had in 1959. 'In 1959 we bought 45 million copies of Canadian magazines. In 1969 we bought about 33.8 million copies.'[76] Another reason not addressed in the report, but mentioned in the Maclean Hunter archival papers, was the impact of urbanization on magazine advertising. According to Ted Hart, advertising manager of *Chatelaine* in the early seventies, 'the most significant change influencing the health of magazines in both the U.S. and Canada has been the migration of people to the cities.'[77] It was to recapture those lucrative urban markets that *Homemaker's* and *Hostess* were born. Although American magazines and urbanization were key factors, it was television that siphoned off the majority of magazine advertisers. In the words of the Senate report: 'Between 1954 and 1968, magazines' share of total advertising revenues dropped from 4.2% to 2.4 percent ... In the same period, radio's share increased slightly. But the big winner was television, whose share increased from 2.5% in 1954 to 12.9% in 1968.'[78] In light of all these depressing statistics about the state of the Canadian magazine industry, *Chatelaine*'s success at attracting readers and advertisers, as well as its modest profit margin, was an impressive feat.

Evaluating the Competition

While U.S. magazines are not a focal point of this study, they were the standard bearers of the women's magazine genre and were *Chatelaine*'s key competition. American women's magazines in the postwar era have been virtually ignored by historians. The summaries that follow are taken from my own sampling of these magazines, but primarily from the material available in journalism guidebooks and the memoirs of journalists and editors.[79] Brief by necessity, this overview of the American products nevertheless provides context by which to evaluate the claims of *Chatelaine*'s distinctiveness.[80] For starters, the big American women's magazines nicknamed the 'Seven Sisters' (*Good Housekeeping, Ladies' Home Journal, McCall's, Redbook, Woman's Day, Family Circle*, and *Better Homes and Gardens*) were all slicker, thicker, and more expensive than their Canadian rivals.

In 1960 a *Chatelaine* Consumer Council Survey reported that *Chatelaine* readers were also keen readers of U.S. women's magazines, primarily *Ladies' Home Journal* (39.4% of those surveyed read the magazine), *McCall's* (38.8%), and *Good Housekeeping* (27.8%).[81] Sixty per cent of *Chatelaine* Councillors read *Reader's Digest* Canadian edition, the most popular American magazine in Canada at that time. In 1968 the most popular American women's magazines in Canada were *Family Circle* (410,275 Canadian sales/issue), *Woman's Day* (252,898), *Ladies' Home Journal* (232,525), *Good Housekeeping* (184,549), *McCall's* (178,438), and *Redbook* (144,846).[82] On an individual basis, *Chatelaine*'s 900,000 plus circulation easily outnumbered any American rival, but the combined sales of U.S. women's magazines was huge. There were also other more specialized magazines for homemakers: the so-called shelter magazines such as *Better Homes and Gardens* and the Maclean Hunter *Canadian Homes and Gardens* tended to appeal to upper-middle-class and upper-class audiences with their features on interior design, home planning, and 'gracious living.'

There were key differences between *Chatelaine* and both the grocery store magazines (*Family Circle* and *Woman's Day*, which were primarily about food and could be purchased only in the grocery stores) and the other top American women's magazines. First, with two exceptions – editor Mabel Hille Souvaine at *Woman's Day* and Bruce and Beatrice Gould, the husband-and-wife editing team at *Ladies' Home Journal* – all the other American women's magazines were edited by men. Although most of the journalists and associate editors on these magazine were women, the final say rested with male editors-in-chief. Often these men had very conventional views of what was appropriate content for women's magazines.

Woman's Day and *Family Circle* were affordable magazines (10 cents per issue) and offered readers 'service' material. According to their statement to the Royal Commission on Publications, '*Family Circle* is not for entertainment or "escape" but a basic handbook on homemaking.'[83] The magazine concentrated on food, recipes, and affordable suggestions for homemakers. *Woman's Day* had a similar agenda. Ultimately, *Woman's Day* and *Family Circle* were modest, affordable magazines that offered thrifty menu plans, information on food preparation and purchase, and do-it-yourself tips for home improvement.

Ladies' Home Journal, *McCall's*, *Good Housekeeping*, and *Redbook* were bigger, glossier magazines, which cost 25–40 cents per issue. Although generally identified as 'women's magazines,' they all had slightly different styles and target audiences. *Ladies' Home Journal*, subtitled 'The Magazine Women Believe In,' was the front-runner in the fifties. Each issue contained between 130 and 300 pages (depending on the season) and offered women numerous fiction stories, a condensed novel, articles, and a variety of service material: food, fashion, beauty, interior design, architecture, and society news. As well, it had a number of regular departments: 'How America Lives,' 'Tell Me, Doctor,' 'Dr. Spock's Talks to Mothers,' and one of the most enduring features of all, 'Can This Marriage Be Saved?' (which is still published in each issue of the magazine).[84] It was aimed at upper-middle- and middle-class American women who enjoyed the opulent designs, dinner party menus, and fashion features. Service articles in *Ladies' Home Journal* were often multiple-page spreads featuring full-colour photographs of table settings, food, or interior design. The aspirational level of American women's magazine was much higher than the fare provided by *Chatelaine*. A Canadian reader, the wife of a construction worker from London, Ontario, explained the appeal of their service features: '*Ladies' Home Journal* fashions are very good – they are done in beautiful colour and show the right accessories with a dress or suit. The pictures of food are always shown with such lovely table appointments and flower arrangements.'[85] Asked to compare *Chatelaine* and *Ladies' Home Journal*, one reader stated: 'The *Chatelaine* is a nice little magazine. It is smaller and cheaper. It is quite satisfactory for regional matter. The *Ladies' Home Journal* is smoother, more sophisticated, shall I say, more comprehensive.'

Anderson offers a contrasting, though not surprising, view of the

American women's magazines. 'They were all still treating women as though all women were upper-middle-class women and they all had decorators,' she claimed. 'This was postwar, everyone was married and had young kids and lived in the suburbs. They were into a whole different way of life and I thought *Ladies' Home Journal* was out to lunch ... *McCall's* was glitzy. *Good Housekeeping* was recipes. And then the supermarket magazines were coming on fast with crafts.' 'I studied them like crazy,' she remembers. 'I took them very seriously.'[86] Not surprisingly, savvy editors on both sides of the border kept abreast of new developments by their competitors and either 'borrowed' them or developed strategies to keep up.

The elaborate production budgets of the American magazines were well beyond the budgets of Maclean Hunter. Anderson's strategy was to concentrate on the articles: 'There was a niche for us that was very, very clear to me,' she explained. 'You couldn't compete with *McCall's* because they had sixteen pages and we had at best four on a decorating feature. In other words, in all the service department features we were going to be beaten unless we found something special, so we tried to tailor all the articles in *Chatelaine* to be as Canadian as possible ... But we could certainly beat them on articles. I knew that. We could give Canadian women articles they couldn't get anywhere else that would deal with their lives and what was happening in this country. It was very deliberate.'

Along with expending more money on production, *McCall's* also attempted to transform its general features material. In the fifties *McCall's* underwent two editorial transformations to compete with the *Ladies' Home Journal*.[87] In 1956 the editors decided to market the periodical as a family magazine and promoted the theme 'Togetherness.' The aim was to attract male readers. Articles on sex and marriage, in addition to complete novels and the required fashions, recipes, and housekeeping articles rounded out the new package. The togetherness campaign received considerable criticism, and *McCall's* was mocked for the 'woefully sad expression, good only for wisecracks.' When the experiment failed to attract a sizable number of male readers, it was quickly abandoned. Herbert R. Mayes, the former editor of *Good Housekeeping*, was recruited in 1958 to give *McCall's* a new, bolder look that stressed photography, colour, fiction, and a new subtitle: 'The First Magazine for Women.'[88] It was this version that would eventually surpass the *Ladies' Home Journal* in circulation and advertising, making it the most popular American women's magazine in the 1960s.

Good Housekeeping, published by Hearst Magazines and edited by Herbert Mayes and later by Wade H. Nichols, billed itself as 'The Magazine America Lives By.' Similar to *Ladies' Home Journal*, and to a lesser degree *McCall's*, it was a thick magazine, running from 200 to 300 pages per issue. *Good Housekeeping's* editorial copy was fairly evenly divided between features, fiction, and the service material. Some of the regular features in the magazine were 'The Institute,' 'The Decorating Studio,' 'The Beauty Clinic,' 'The Baby Centre,' 'The Needlework Room,' 'The Bureau,' and 'A Page for Children.' In all, features and fiction were less sensational than either the *Journal* or *McCall's*.

In contrast, *Redbook*, edited by Wade Nicholls and later by Robert Stein, targeted young couples between the ages of eighteen and thirty-five with a mixture of feature articles, service articles, and fiction.[89] It began as a fiction magazine and, even through the fifties, when the fiction component of many mass-market magazines was in decline, continued to publish a novel or novella in each issue. It was published by McCall's Corporation, so one of the reasons for its younger audience profile was to prevent competition with *McCall's*. Given the younger demographics, the magazine often published more controversial material and, in 1954, was awarded the Benjamin Franklin Magazine Award 'for articles dealing with security risks, academic freedom and racial segregation.'

In contrast to *Chatelaine's* success and profitability in Canada, the American women's magazines found the sixties a more troublesome decade than the fifties as niche magazines began to chip away at the market for general (mass-market) women's magazines. 'Costs were soaring, competition from other magazines and television were increasing, and there was a tendency among advertisers to question how much they were getting for their dollars.'[90] According to Tebbel and Zuckerman, in 'the good year of 1960,' 40 per cent of mass-market magazines lost money, while 'in the bad year of 1961 a majority of magazines were operating in the red.' An indicator of the severity of financial losses at the American women's magazines was reflected in the Curtis Publishing Company's decision to sell the *Ladies' Home Journal*, along with another periodical, *American Home*, to the Downe Corporation for the 'distress merchandise' price of $5.4 million in August 1968. American women's magazines were generally slow to respond with new innovations, feverishly chased after new subscribers, though with little financial return, and in some cases hired a quick succession of editors in the hopes of reviving their fading fortunes.

McCall's rode the innovations of the late fifties into the sixties and then, under several different editors (including two women, Shauna Alexander and Patricia Carbine), found its circulation figures declining at the end of the decade. Under Carbine, who later participated in the founding of *Ms.*, Gloria Steinem was a regular contributor at *McCall's*. The only bona fide success in the American women's mass magazines in the sixties was the revamped version of *Cosmopolitan* under editor Helen Gurley Brown, author of the 1963 bestseller *Sex and the Single Girl*. *Cosmo* had nearly gone under, but Gurley Brown narrowed the magazine's focus to a new audience whom she affectionately called '"mouseburgers" – young women whose main interest lay in catching a man.'[91] This formula was a smash success and Gurley Brown, a former mouseburger herself, remained at *Cosmo*'s helm until January 1996, when she was replaced by the Canadian editor Bonnie Fuller.

The experiences of senior editor Lenore Hershey, first at *McCall's* and later as editor-in-chief at *Ladies' Home Journal*, were emblematic of the conservative, tradition-bound nature of the big American women's publications and stand in sharp contrast to the situation at *Chatelaine*. In 1968 Hershey went to Herb Mayer, the president of the company, and asked about her chances of promotion to the editorship of *McCall's*. Mayer's response was patronizing: 'He patted me on the head and said that despite my many talents, as far as he was concerned no women could ever edit a mass woman's magazine.'[92] So Hershey left to work at the *Ladies' Home Journal* under editor John Mack Carter, later editor of *Good Housekeeping*. She 'took it for granted that even on a woman's magazine, there would be few if any top women.' Her eyes were finally opened on the morning of March 18, 1970, 'the day on which 200 militant feminists walked into the office of John Mack Carter and staged the famous 11 hour *Ladies' Home Journal* sit-in.' By coincidence, Hershey was in Carter's office at the time, and her description of the events – complete with Carter's refusal to communicate directly with the protesters (he spoke to Hershey, who then addressed the group), and her plans to pull a 'dead faint' if it became 'any more violent' (the protesters shoved Carter's desk) – are both unintentionally hilarious and revealing. The protesters demanded that the *Journal* devote one entire issue to the feminist movement, but after exhaustive negotiations that demand was whittled down to an eight-page section with the following four article titles: 'Babies Are Born, Not Delivered,' 'Women Talk about Love and Sex,' 'Women and Work,' and 'How to Start Your Own Consciousness-Raising Group.' With the exception of the last article, the information provided in the *Journal's* pull-out feminism feature was already passé in *Chatelaine*. For her efforts and perseverance, Hershey was finally appointed editor of the magazine in 1973 – the first woman editor at *Ladies' Home Journal* since Louisa Knapp Curtis had edited the magazine in the late nineteenth century.

Another development within the field of American women's magazines, *Ms.* magazine, deserves mention, despite the fact that it was founded in 1972. Both Gloria Steinem and Patricia Carbine, the founders, had worked for traditional women's magazines – Steinem at *Seventeen, Ladies' Home Journal*, and *McCall's*, and Carbine at *McCall's* and *Look* (a general-interest magazine similar to *Life*).[93] They claimed that the sexist treatment they received at those publications, combined with the feminist movement of the late sixties, encouraged them to found an explicitly feminist women's magazine. *Ms.* eschewed the traditional women's magazine format – service material, fiction, and non-fiction pieces – for a mixture of feature articles with feminist topics and themes. When the editors abandoned the core of the women's magazine – the service department – that decision dramatically affected their advertising content. According to Amy Erdmann Farrell, Steinem repeatedly criticized the advertisers' demands that women's magazines (but not men's magazines) carry service material – a policy that penalized the unconventional format of *Ms.*, which had a strict policy against such material.[94] *Ms.* has alternatively been lauded as a feminist innovator or criticized for its liberal feminist perspective and tendency to trumpet 'women's culture' (sisterhood) at the expense of racial and class diversity. Despite its attempts to reach out to a variety of American women, it consistently drew subscribers from the ranks of the upper-middle-class, university-educated, female professionals. While the goals behind the creation of *Ms.* were noble, its 'success' is debatable, given its financial difficulties and relatively small circulation.

One thing is clear: *Chatelaine* was first to adopt a feminist message, and it did so subversively, packing feminism along with advertisements and service material. Although *Chatelaine* was not exclusively a feminist periodical, its wide variety of feature articles compare favourably with those considered advanced for a feminist publication in the seventies. It was also instructive that part of the impetus for the creation of *Ms.* was due to the male-dominated editorial departments and the glass ceilings in place at the traditional U.S. women's magazines. This contrast illustrated the rare opportunity that existed at Maclean Hunter, where women were the primary creators and editors of

Chatelaine's material. Maclean Hunter executives probably did not agree with these selections, but, given their penchant for hands-off management and their happiness with the ever-increasing circulation statistics, they usually did not or could not argue with the mixture of material.

In her written assessment of women's magazines, Anderson commented on *Chatelaine*'s feminism and compared the magazine with its American counterparts: In fact, now that I look back on the 1960s, I feel *Chatelaine* was a kind of closet feminist magazine. We had to be. We had a circulation of over a million women – the equivalent of 16 million in the U.S. (the top women's magazine there was *Ladies' Home Journal*, with a circulation of 7 million). *Chatelaine* had to appeal to all women in Canada. We also were frequently reminded through letters, of our middle-class, traditional audience ... For two years after we ran the first article urging that abortion be made legal in 1960, I was the target of a threatening letter-writing campaign aimed at closing the magazine and having me fired. But with the advent of the Women's Movement and the Royal Commission on the Status of Women, *Chatelaine* could be much more open in its feminism. In fact, by this time we were getting letters from women suggesting that we were too conservative and not feminist enough!'[95] Regardless of what Anderson could accomplish within the unique situation at Maclean Hunter, she was, ultimately, bound or prodded by the comments of readers.

Reader Profile

Chatelaine and Maclean Hunter were pleased that the magazine reached a large majority of Canadian women. The circulation figures were always a source of pride and were endlessly cited as proof not only that the company was delivering what Canadian woman wanted but, more important, that it understood its audience.[96] Although Maclean Hunter promotional material indicated that the readers of *Chatelaine* were largely urban, middle-class women with husbands and children, marketing surveys in the era portrayed a much less homogeneous audience.[97]

In 1969 the Canadian Media Directors Council published a study entitled *Canada's Magazine Audience: A Study from the Magazine Advertising Bureau of Canada* (CMA).[98] This work provided a detailed demographic profile of the readership of all the major Canadian magazines, the weekend supplements, and the most popular American magazines (*Saturday Evening Post, Time*, and *Reader's Digest*). During May and June 1968, 6000 Canadians from coast to coast were interviewed about their magazine-reading habits.[99] According to Raymond Kent, such reports and ratings figures 'constitute the currency for negotiating advertising space or time,' and their use as indicators of how people actually interact with media is of more limited value.[100] Their key importance lies in the demographic profiles of the readership and in the advertising department's belief that these reports were worthy of the time and money invested in generating them.

As in the fifties, the *CMA* reported that *Chatelaine* readers hailed from all regions of the country, included both men and women, and represented all major socioeconomic groups.[101] Ontario, the Prairies, British Columbia, and Atlantic Canada accounted for the vast majority of readers of both sexes, while the share of Quebec readers was much smaller.[102] The introduction of the French version, *Châtelaine*, in 1960 cut into the English version's readership in Quebec. In 1968 the total female audience of the magazine was estimated at 1,851,000 readers, while men accounted for 641,000 readers.[103] Thus, 23.2 per cent of all English-Canadian adults read *Chatelaine*, compared with 24.6 per cent of English-speaking adults who read *Maclean's* or 37.2 per cent who read *Reader's Digest*. In terms of households, other *Chatelaine* research reports claimed that in 1966 the magazine reached 37 per cent of all households in Canada.[104] While the magazine boasted of its younger audience and attempted to reach the young housewife, the figures generated by the *CMA* Report proved that it was not as successful as it would have liked.[105] For both sexes, readers were most likely to come from the 35–44-year-old age group, followed by the 55 and over age category, while the most desired age group, the 25–34 year olds, was in third place.[106]

With respect to education, *Chatelaine* readers were drawn from all educational levels, although women generally had more education than men. That characteristic was consistent with the Canadian population as a whole. The figures for the number of female readers who had attended or completed high school, as well as those who had taken advanced training, some university or college, or had completed degrees were higher than the English-speaking Canadian averages.[107] The vast majority of readers listed their marital status as married (67.9%), although the numbers of single readers (23.1%) and those who were widowed, divorced, or separated (8.3%) were higher than they had been a decade previously.[108]

The male readers surveyed, when questioned about their occupational status, were most likely to be employed as skilled or unskilled workers (23%), retired or unemployed (17.7%), or in the service industry (15.5%).[109] For women, the most common occupation listed was housewife (57.3%), followed by student (11.7%) or clerical/sales work (10.7%).[110] When readers were classified according to the occupation of household heads, the statistics revealed that the majority of readers were skilled or unskilled workers, service workers, or clerical or sales employees.[111]

To help their advertising and media clients put all the statistical data in perspective, the writers of the report included the appropriate statistical averages for English and French Canadians at the bottom of each table of information. It was simple, then, to contrast the magazine averages with the Canadian averages. For both male and female *Chatelaine* readers, their occupational categories mirrored the Canadian averages. There were no glaring discrepancies in terms of readers' occupations. Using the average figures provided for the number of female readers, and the number of English-Canadian women in general who were housewives, the survey illustrated that one out of every three Canadian housewives read the magazine.[112]

If the statistical information on occupation provided an imprecise picture of the majority of English-Canadian *Chatelaine* readers, the household income and principal wage earner's income clarified the situation. Although large groups of survey respondents did not report this information, the majority of *Chatelaine* households made less than $7000 per year in 1968.[113] According to the report, 44.3 per cent of *Chatelaine* reading households made less than $7000 per annum, which was the exact percentage of the English-speaking Canadian population that made less than $7000 per year. These statistics combined both male and female readers and are taken from the total audience statistics. Similarly, 52.5 per cent of *Chatelaine* readers listed the primary wage earner's income as less than $7000 per annum.[114] In comparison with the English-Canadian statistics, the readership of the magazine was average.

The vast majority of *Chatelaine* readers lived in single-family dwellings (79.2%). They were more likely to do so than the average English-Canadian family (74.1%), but not by a wide margin.[115] This fact was probably due to the larger number of rural and small-town dwellers among the *Chatelaine* readership, because homes (whether owned or rented) were the most common forms of accommodation in rural areas and small towns. One-third of all *Chatelaine* readers lived in a rural area – a number proportionately higher than the Canadian average.[116]

In contrast to the *CARD* advertisements, which often used terms like 'better sort,' 'quality,' and 'affluent' indiscriminately, and in comparison with the Canadian averages provided in the *CMA* study, it was clear that *Chatelaine* readers were average Canadians. Readers residing in homes were divided into four groups: Class A (Upper Group), Class B (Upper Middle Group), Class C (Lower Middle Group), and Class D (Lower Group). The classifications were based on factors such as wealth, type and style of home, neighbourhood, and standard of living. The Upper Group were 'wealthy' and had the 'best home in the area.' Equally easy to identify were the Lower Group, whose homes had a 'poor appearance,' with 'sparse worn furnishings,' and who often lived in the 'oldest and commercial districts.' The Upper Middle Group inhabited a 'fairly good home in or near an A district' or a 'suburban setting' and were 'above average in possessions and spending ability.' Finally, the Lower Middle Group was described as living in the 'older less prosperous sections or in newer low-priced housing developments.' These people could 'buy the necessities with little to spare' and had a 'fair standard of living, with few luxuries.' This last socioeconomic group represented 79.3 per cent, or 1,976,000, of the *Chatelaine* readers. *Chatelaine* had the lowest percentage of Upper and Upper Middle readers of any magazine in the survey.

One complete volume of the report was dedicated to a detailed analysis of the ownership and purchasing patterns of magazine readers. The relatively low level of discretionary spending enforces the conclusion that, regardless of the fantasy quotient involved in ad readership, for many readers the advertised products were well beyond their means. Over 80 per cent of readers had one or more cars, although they were just as likely to have purchased a used car as a new one.[117] The average weekly expenditure for groceries was $29. Family clothing expenditure for six months was, on average, $239. Cosmetics purchases were very low, the average amount spent was $4.35 per month, although 44 per cent of women claimed to spend less than $3 per month. In terms of even more discretionary spending or 'lifestyle' issues, most readers chose to consume very little alcohol, if any, preferred to vacation in Canada, and often spent less than $250 per annum on their vacations.[118]

In Section D, entitled 'Media Patterns,' the report attempted to quantify the act of reading magazines. By providing figures for frequency of use (number of times opened) and the amount of time spent with each periodical, the report gave the advertisers some sense of the readers' exposure to the material. It made no attempt to explore which parts of the magazines readers liked better, or how much time and attention they paid to advertising as opposed to editorial content. However, these figures, while less than adequate gauges of how readers read the periodicals, did give some sense of how much time they spent with the magazine. On average, male and female readers browsed through *Chatelaine* three times, spending a total of sixty-four minutes with each issue.[119]

Chatelaine's chief 'currency' was that it attracted a mass audience of average Canadian women, and some men, from all regions of the country. The readers lived primarily in single-family homes, but they were more likely to live in a rural area than most Canadians. In terms of occupation, education, income level, and household income they were fairly, sometimes slightly above, average. Certainly, the socioeconomic portrait illustrates convincingly that, in comparison with other periodicals and with the Canadian averages, the English-speaking *Chatelaine* community was most likely to come from the lower middle class. In other words, in terms of advertising priorities, readers represented women and families who had a small amount of discretionary spending and only a fair standard of living.

Conclusion

On the surface, the purpose of *Chatelaine*'s production seemed clear, but when one delves deeper the water muddies. The magazine was a commercial enterprise, created to enhance the company's role as a purveyor of national magazines and to increase advertising lineage in Maclean Hunter periodicals. Yet the magazine struggled in the fifties and turned a modest profit only in the sixties. The commercial messages and the editorial content were often at odds, owing to the parallel system of production in place at the magazine, as well as the separate spheres of production that gendered the editorial department female and the advertising department male. The female editors wrote for a like-minded audience. The male advertising executives were far too easily inclined to reduce the readers to one vast undifferentiated audience of consumers, for whom the advertising copy was supposed to create 'action.' While the advertising department wanted urban, affluent consumers, the editorial material seemed to attract more working-class, rural, retired, and unemployed readers. What the company had done was to create a magazine that a large number of Canadian women believed provided a forum of interest to them. It hired female editors with whom the readership identified, and, through the gendered nature of production, created a heterogeneous community of women (editors, writers, and readers) from varying classes, regions, and age groups. Their common bond was the editorial material. *Chatelaine* might best be understood as a magazine in which two languages were spoken: editorial and advertising. The language shared by the community of readers and creators was not the same as that used by the advertisers and the advertising executives.

Of equal importance to the internal dynamics of production at *Chatelaine*, the magazine's situation vis-à-vis its American competitors highlights the differences among mass-market women's magazines. Throughout the fifties and sixties, when television and the increasing specialization of the magazine market created difficulties for mass-market women's magazines, the big American periodicals continued to employ variations on their traditional format. Generally speaking, they did not embrace feminist material, nor did the organization of their editorial offices allow the female assistant editors and writers much role in constructing the final 'look' of the periodical. The fact that key women editors and writers from those magazines created a competing, feminist periodical for women is indicative of the glass ceilings and the stodgy editorial content at those periodicals. Within that context, the role accorded *Chatelaine*'s editors was unique. But that context, editorial climate, and system of cultural production are only half the story. The readers' role in consuming and reading the periodical, and the importance they accorded *Chatelaine*, contributed to the periodical's uniqueness. Despite the aims of the editors and producers to provide a forum for Canadian women, that goal would have remained stillborn if not for the participation and enthusiasm shown by readers.

Chapter 3

'A Faithful Friend and Tonic': Reading *Chatelaine*

Emma Davis, a Canadian citizen resident in Madras, India, wrote a letter to the editors of *Chatelaine* in early 1951 to describe the enjoyment she derived from reading the magazine. 'I can't count the times I have resolved to write you,' she said. 'My friends over the years have poked fun at me and *Chatelaine*. If I could not be found they would say, "Oh, she is at home with her *Chatelaine*!" During the war years I was stationed in England *Chatelaine* was a faithful friend and tonic, and it was handed around to lots of people. It would be a difficult task to say which article in the paper was appreciated most. As a matter of fact I myself start at the beginning and go right through to the end, then once again in case, when turning the leaves to read one of the stories I may have missed a page.'[1] Davis was an eager fan and close reader of the periodical, but similar sentiments were echoed in countless other letters from home and abroad. Canadian content was obviously a primary selling feature of the magazine, but equally important was Davis's description of *Chatelaine* as a friend. Within the pages of the magazine, Davis and others were able to reconnect with other Canadian women and participate in a community of fellow readers and letter writers. Davis's friend was also a commercial product, however, intended to produce a profit for Maclean Hunter and to stimulate consumption of the goods advertised in the magazine. The commercial imperative was something few readers noted when they described the act of 'reading' *Chatelaine*. This chapter explores the complex world of magazine consumption and indicates that, contrary to historical perceptions of how this 'prescriptive' material affected consumers, the addition of reader responses indicates that actual consumers, as opposed to the imagined consumers, exhibited a range of reactions to the material. Regardless of their level of engagement or their interests in certain components, none of the readers felt compelled to slavishly follow the magazine's suggestions – whether service features or feminism.

By 1959, one of every three English-speaking women in Canada, or a total of 1,650,000, read each issue of *Chatelaine*.[2] This section seeks to explore the variety of reasons women enjoyed, or disliked, reading the magazine. While academics are sensitive to the role of readers in refashioning the product, most have found it difficult to translate that interest into a sustained analysis of the consumers' motivations and interpretations.[3] This problem has been compounded by the lack of sources, particularly for historical cultural studies. Fortunately, this study of *Chatelaine* has been able to draw on numerous resources in an effort to examine the art of reading the magazine. These sources include the extensive letters printed in the magazine, the extant letters and behind-the-scenes editorial memos and notes in the Archives of Ontario, Starch figures, and the wealth of information contained in the 1958 Dichter Motivational Research Study on *Chatelaine* magazine. Although the statements in the *Chatelaine* material and the Dichter Study differed substantially, both demonstrate that *Chatelaine* (specifically the editors, authors, and readers) created a community, based on gender and nationalist markers, in which Canadian women shared ideas, dreams, recipes, personal stories, and information.

Throughout this book, the terms 'preferred meaning,' 'alternate meaning,' 'oppositional meaning,' and 'misreadings' are employed. 'Preferred meaning' is the one intended by the authors, editors, or ad makers.[4] Given the range of readers, their sociocultural backgrounds, their reasons for reading any particular text, and the open (or 'producerly') nature of pop cultural products, however, the preferred meaning is not the only interpretation readers may make of the material. While there are preferred meanings for each article, story, advertisement, or piece of cover art, there is not one, monolithic, preferred meaning for the entire magazine. The range of writers and departmental editors (the diversity of their backgrounds, interests, and purposes), coupled with the variety of components, made such a uniform meaning unlikely and virtually impossible. Instead, *Chatelaine* was a polysemic product – a magazine that contained a variety of messages and meanings for its readers. The active encouragement of writers and editors (and sometimes readers, through their published letters) to explore a variety of different angles invited readers to create their own alternate or oppositional readings of the material. I use the term 'alternate reading' to explain a meaning that the author or producers did not intend, while the term 'oppositional reading' is used to identify readers who were more actively 'reading against the grain' of the text. Alternate readings were more common than oppositional readings. 'Misreadings' refers to instances where readers have not understood the author's intent. They were most common in humorous pieces, where readers 'did not get' writers' attempts at irony, sarcasm, or subtlety. These distinctions will become clearer in future chapters that concentrate on the text, readers' responses, and the variety of available readings.

Magazines occupy an intriguing place within the mass media. Like newspapers, they are a print medium, but in composition they are equal parts print and illustration, editorial copy and advertising material. Subsidized by the hefty weight of advertisements, magazines are cheap compared with the costs of attending movies or buying a radio or television. Easily portable, they may be read anywhere: in the bath, on the living-room couch, or in the car. How they are read is determined by the reader: all at once, over the course of the month, for specific features, or quickly skimmed between chores. According to Janice Radway, readers of romance novels often claimed that their reading was both pleasurable and 'educational,' to deflect criticism from sceptical spouses. 'Romances are valuable according to this system because they enable the reader to accumulate information to add to her worth, and thus to better herself. In so justifying the act of reading,' Radway claims, the 'women affirm their adherence to traditional values and, at the same time, engage in a form of behaviour that is itself subversive of those values.'[5] Similar comments could be made for women's magazines, and *Chatelaine* in particular. June Callwood recollects that Doris Anderson was adept at creating an extremely eclectic mixture of material: 'She really snuck it in. She never wavered from her principles ... you never knew that you were picking up Marx's little Red Book and that was a very powerful mixture of messages. She wouldn't have succeeded if she had turned every article into a message.'[6]

Contemporary readers interviewed by Joke Hermes listed several reasons for reading women's magazines: 'easily put down and relaxation,' 'practical knowledge,' 'emotional learning,' and 'connected knowing.'[7] According to Hermes, 'practical knowledge does more than simply legitimate reading and buying women's magazines in terms of their practical use. It also furnishes the readers with a temporary fantasy of an ideal self. Depending upon one's background and upon context, one may fantasize oneself into someone who is up to date regarding new products, who knows a whole litany of small remedies.' Ultimately, 'reading about other people's experiences ratifies your own.' Magazines' ease of use, affordability, accessibility, and reliable household content, coupled with compelling articles and fiction, make them an irresistible form of popular culture for women. It is not surprising that some of the most enduring and popular magazines have been women's magazines or general-interest magazines with large audiences of female readers.

Studying Readers: The Dichter Study

In 1958 the *Chatelaine* advertising department commissioned the Motivational Research Institute in New York City to evaluate the magazine. Ernest Dichter, PhD, the American psychologist favoured by corporate America for his 'motivational research' fad, which promised to explain the ins and outs of consumer decision making, prepared the report.[8] Just one year previously, the grandiose claims of advertisers and their marketing people, including Dichter, had been profiled in American author Vance Packard's best-selling exposé, *The Hidden Persuaders*, which provided alarming images of the successful and subversive ways in which advertisements worked.[9] Part and parcel of the high-culture backlash against the success of commercial popular culture, and fuelled by Cold War fears about 'brainwashing,' the book and its message struck a chord with North Americans. In retrospect, Packard's book was an overstatement, for he gave the advertisers and their cronies far too much influence, while he portrayed the consumers as marionettes waiting for the advertisers to pull their strings. Nevertheless, for our purposes, what is important in this late fifties' skirmish between the glorification and the vilification of advertising is the degree to which the society of consumers was made aware of some of the methods and goals of the advertisers. In revealing the magicians' tricks and questioning the industry, *The Hidden Persuaders* exposed the means and the ends of advertising.

The businessmen in the Maclean Hunter offices were true believers in the abilities of Dr Dichter and his team to take the pulse of Canadian women. According to Noel Barbour, a former advertising manager at *Chatelaine*, the eight-month study and 210-page report (with the vaguely sinister title *A Motivational Research Study on* Chatelaine *Magazine*) was the 'largest motivational study for a publication ever done anywhere in the world.' It was also one of the major factors that, in the late fifties, convinced Maclean Hunter to take over the *Canadian Home Journal*.[10] Despite the fact that Barbour's description employs the marketing hyperbole endemic to the advertising department, the report is an important document. Because the researchers set out to discover the 'Canadian woman' – her reading expectations, impressions of *Chatelaine*, view of American women's magazines – and to learn how she reacted to promotional material in the periodical, their report illuminates the process of reading *Chatelaine*.[11] For the Maclean Hunter executives, the Dichter Study's startling conclusions served as a corporate wakeup call.

In the course of eight months, the research team interviewed 127 subscribers and non-subscribers from across Canada in three phases of interviews.[12] Women were recruited to mirror the demographics of the readership. Despite the limitations of the study, such as the overconcentration on urban readers and the fact that non-readers based their assessments on only a few copies of the magazine, the long, complex document is an extremely valuable resource for reconstructing the world of reading *Chatelaine* in the late fifties and provides extensive commentary about the 'nature' of women's roles in Canadian society. As well, it offers independent insight into women's perceptions of *Chatelaine*. Unlike the readers' letters, the excerpts published in the Dichter Study were from both *Chatelaine* subscribers and non-subscribers. All the women interviewed were given similar American magazines, either *Ladies' Home Journal* or *Woman's Day*, to compare with *Chatelaine*. One of the key findings indicates that subscribers were more likely to be fans of the magazine, happy with its current content. Those who seldom or never read *Chatelaine* felt that it was old-fashioned, dowdy in appearance, and not as pleasing as the American magazines. The publishers and editors took the findings very seriously, and the study provided the impetus for Maclean Hunter's revamping of the magazine in 1958.

The key findings were instructive. The Canadian woman, or, as she would later be called, the 'new Canadian woman,' was characterized as 'emerging rapidly into a state of social, economic and psychological independence as a woman and as a citizen.' Although the study did not use the term 'feminist' or embody feminist sensibilities, preferring the term 'progressive femininity,' researchers found that the Canadian woman was in a 'rapid thrust toward independence,' for which she needed 'guideposts to action, feeling, and world orientation.' Canadian women were attracted to American women's magazines, 'extract[ing] that which is useful and satisfying,' but ultimately they did 'not fulfill the Canadian woman's subjective and social ideals.' Dichter's study confirms what historians of postwar Canada have begun to chart: the increasing incidence of working wives; changes in the expectations of women's participation in society; and a sense that many women were no longer solely content with a narrowly defined existence. These changes, however progressive we might consider them in hindsight, were stressful, and what came through in the many printed comments from the participants was a sense that they were searching for direction, perhaps reassurance, about embarking on a new path.

The section in the Dichter Study entitled 'The Canadian Woman's Reading Expectations' assessed the women's answers to questions about the purpose of reading and concluded that readers were 'fundamentally acquisitive.' The researchers discovered that the Canadian woman had 'an aggressive desire to acquire knowledge, not for its own sake, but to assure her personal adequacy. Her needs appear to be less escapist or imaginative than here-and-now and practical.' The report writers were often vague when they used terms such as 'knowledge': it might refer to the informants' comments about political and practical material they gleaned from the magazine or to 'knowledge' about new consumer products. Years later, this thirst for knowledge was reconfirmed when a minor article about part-time university studies elicited a flood of mail both to *Chatelaine* and to several schools across the country. Similar views were expressed by the wife of a civil engineer from Toronto: 'I have gleaned information and facts that have helped in everyday life.' The report included a list of what readers expected a good women's magazine to be: 'future oriented; give guidance to behaviour and to performance; put new emphasis on the Canadian way of life; *address the modern woman who wishes to participate in Canada's economic, social and cultural growth; recognize a progressive femininity*; yield pleasure and satisfaction'; and, finally, 'offer attractive layout and art work' (emphasis added). A tall order for one affordable little periodical! Sixty-one per cent of those interviewed reported that they read 'magazines for the main purpose of acquiring new skills in the various phases of homemaking, and for simple suggestions of "how-to."' Other chief concerns were 'being modern,' 'assistance with child care,' and 'inter-family relationships,' in which Dr Marion Hilliard's articles (on women's sexuality, relationships, and life cycle) were frequently mentioned as outstanding examples of the type of information Canadian women needed.

Beyond the need for practical know-how and information about homemaking, nearly two-thirds of the respondents indicated that 'magazine reading enables them to meet the conversational demands that are made upon them.' Witness this comment from a Winnipeg woman, married to a lawyer: 'We'd be lost without magazines – we all love them! I'm always finding that they are wonderful as conversational bridges – when there is that lag in the conversation I can always think back to some article I have read and bring that up and usually someone else has read it too or has an opinion on it and away we go.' Her analysis of magazines as a common currency among women, or as a stimulus to conversations, was often repeated. Magazines served a social function and were not merely solitary pleasures.

Many of the women's comments suggested that magazines, or discussion about magazines, fostered a sense of identity or membership in a community. Participants claimed that magazine reading lessened their feelings of isolation. In fact, they drew solace and strength from their discovery, via magazine articles and letters, that other women across the country had experienced similar problems or crises. Some also believed that having magazines in the home fostered 'togetherness' among family members. The easy access to articles on family issues, teenage problems, and sexual matters often led to conversations about these topics. Without this stimulus, these issues might very well have remained dormant. Respondents specifically mentioned marital problems or problems in dealing with teenagers, and how the magazines had facilitated discussion or awareness of potential problems. Most participants were indifferent to the fiction included in the magazine, preferring that this space be used for more general-interest articles or service department fare. Finally, the report's authors provided short excerpts of readers' responses to questions about the effect of reading magazines. A Winnipeg resident, married to a district sales manager, reported: 'I have definite views on my own particular leanings – garnered strictly from magazines and books. I've had no political experience – so what I think or know is based on the written word.'

The manner in which the report identified the women interviewed in the survey clearly labels it as a commissioned product of the business and advertising departments: the names of the participants were not included, while their socioeconomic status and age were given. These participants were not providing scandalous information that required anonymity, yet the report writers determined that their individual identities lacked interest. What was critically important was their socioeconomic backgrounds – region, locale, and husband's occupation – all hallmarks of the advertisers' continual obsession with the 'prime' or 'better sort' of reading audience.

The variety of uses to which Canadian women put magazines was instructive and undoubtedly cheered Maclean Hunter executives. However, when asked to evaluate how well *Chatelaine* fulfilled their desires, most respondents reported that the magazine often left them unfulfilled, bored, and disappointed because of its dowdy and dated layout and design. Equally shocking for the Maclean Hunter personnel, the report found that *Chatelaine* was 'behind [the Canadian woman's] actual level of present development' and did not provide 'any yardsticks to the future.' Only in its 'implicit' nationalism did the periodical satisfy its readers. The group most satisfied with the magazine (only 25 per cent of those surveyed) were 'the French-speaking Canadian woman and the rural dweller,' and Dichter urged the company not to be satisfied with these 'most backward readers.' Instead, the Motivational Institute recommended that *Chatelaine* try to attract the more modern reader, 'lest it lose the most articulate and dynamic sectors of the female population.' An equal number of those interviewed, approximately 25 per cent, thought that American magazines were a much better product and, by comparison, that *Chatelaine* was inferior. The other 50 per cent were ambivalent towards *Chatelaine*, and the researchers concluded that the majority of Canadian women had 'fundamentally a *negative* loyalty to *Chatelaine*. As part and parcel of her new Canadian national consciousness, the Canadian woman feels that it is her duty to patronize a Canadian product and this in a large sense accounts for her subscription to *Chatelaine*.' Not surprisingly, the study recommended that the periodical upgrade its content, both qualitatively, and quantitatively, and improve the 'backward character of layout, art work, editing – ie., the old-fashionedness of its presentation factors.'

The contrast between American magazines and *Chatelaine* caused conflict for readers. On the one hand, most respondents commented on the greater visual appeal of the U.S. women's magazines – their larger content, variety of articles, timeliness, and 'glossy' nature – yet on the other hand they admitted to feeling guilty for consuming them. In some respects this quandary applies to all aspects of Canadian culture: the conflict between wanting to support the native product while simultaneously being seduced by the flashier, more colourful, more expensive American one. People explained that they would prefer Canadian magazines to emulate the style of American models, yet they preferred to read a magazine geared to their national interests and personality rather than to American women.

The Motivational Institute concluded that although the magazine had an important niche to fill, it must guard against complacency because its Canadian identity alone would not continue to guarantee subscribers and readers: 'Our findings are decisive regarding the need for a Canadian woman's publication. But it must be a publication that reflects the dynamism of the Canadian woman.' The report continued: 'Our belief is that when *Chatelaine* ultimately combines Canadian production, authorship and ownership with heightened style and vitality, neither the *Ladies' Home Journal* nor any other American publication will be able successfully to compete with it.' As the later increase in readers and advertisements illustrated, the implementation of the Dichter plan of action, along with the new editorial direction provided by Doris Anderson, proved successful for the magazine.

Writing to *Chatelaine*

The letters page, variously called 'Reader Takes Over,' 'You Were Asking *Chatelaine*,' or 'The Last Word Is Yours,' was a regular component of the magazine from the early years of the fifties. Given the importance attached to readers' letters, all letters, both those published in the magazine and those placed in the archival collections, were read thoroughly. The letters represent only a fraction of the magazine's readership, but they were the most effective means by which to judge the consumers' reactions to the material in *Chatelaine*. The statistical information in this book is taken from the letter database, which catalogued all the letters published in the January, May, and September issues during the fifties and sixties. In the general database of all issues in these two decades, only a running tally of letters per issue is included. Another key source for reader letters is the collection of letters to the editor from the year 1962, which is preserved at the Archives of Ontario.[13] While it is impossible to state with certainty that this group represents all the letters received during that year, it provides (as the only year with a file labelled January through December) an excellent sample from which to compare the database results and to assess how letters were chosen for inclusion in the magazine. Anderson claimed, in the magazine, in interviews, and in letters to readers, that 'The Last Word Is Yours' was both representative of reader concerns and an influential and popular component of the magazine. 'The Letters Page of *Chatelaine*,' Anderson wrote, 'is one of the best-read pages in the magazine. We receive many more letters than we publish, but we do try to give a fairly accurate representation of the many various opinions that are held by the people who write to us. Some of the letters we receive are constructive and very intelligent, and some are critical and often vicious. But since everyone who writes to our Letters Page wants to have his or her letter published, I feel we have a duty to print a representative selection of all types of letters.'[14]

To print a wide variety of responses in the magazine, the editors chose excerpts from an average of fifteen letters per issue.[15] The letters published in the magazine were most likely to come from female readers (82%), although men contributed their share (13%).[16] The writers were from all regions of the country, but were most likely to originate from Ontario (43%), the Prairies (24%), or British Columbia (14%).[17] The tone and purpose of their letters varied considerably. There was almost an equal weighting of positive (46%) and negative letters (40%). A particularly Canadian trait of neutrality or caution pervaded the remaining letters. The vast majority of letters were written in response to articles (71%). All the magazine's components received written commentary at some time during the decade, but, in comparison with articles, the responses to the other sections were considerably smaller.

The letters in the 1962 collection are numerous, long, and wide ranging. The vast majority address themselves to the articles, although this sample contains a great many angry letters in response to the 'blasphemous' nature of a fiction story run in the magazine. Using the two January 1962 files as comparison, of the 164 letters received, 93 (57%) were positive.[18] There were 71 negative letters (43%) and no neutral letters. Similarly, using the letters in the two September to December 1962 files, it was possible to profile the regional and national origin of the letter writers. All regions of the country were represented, but writers were more likely to come from Ontario (41%), the Prairies (22%), and British Columbia (14%).[19] Thus, a comparison of the published and unpublished letters reveals that the published letters page was representative of the letters received. There was no attempt to skew the selection in favour of positive mail (indeed, negative mail and the controversy it generated made for a livelier page) or to downplay representation from Ontario in favour of a greater national flavour. All regions of the country participated, as did a few readers from Britain and the United States.

Readers wrote freely about *Chatelaine* and its role in their lives. Frequently, their letters provided brief autobiographical material that illustrated an intense bond with the editors, the magazine, and the lives of other readers. In contrast to the advertising department's view that readers were merely consumers, these letters indicate that readers seldom defined themselves as such. Despite the large amount of correspondence received at *Chatelaine*'s offices, each reader received a personal, timely, reply. That fact alone indicates the value placed on readers' opinions and the editors' acknowledgment that their mass audience comprised real individuals, with real concerns. Clearly, readers were valued for much more than their decision to purchase the magazine. The sampling of letters to *Chatelaine* that follows surveys the distinctive letter genres and explores how women read the periodical. Other letters, addressed to various articles, fiction, or other components, are featured prominently later in this book.

For some women, the impetus to write to the magazine came from their desire to reach out to fellow readers. Many writers wrote to the editors asking that they publish their letters requesting pen pals from other parts of the country or from Britain. These letters provided a wealth of information about individual readers, since they described some of their favourite hobbies, gardens, religious affiliation, ethnicity, or geographical locale. This letter from Mrs Ada Reimer of Victoria was representative of the genre. 'I would very much like to have some Pen Pals from the Eastern part of Canada,' Reimer wrote, 'from places like Nova Scotia, Ottawa, Montreal, Toronto, Hamilton and all places across the border of the Eastern part of Canada. I would be glad to trade snap shots, also local papers, with any who care to write to me. One of my hobbies is collecting salt and pepper sets, I have about 75–80 sets now. My favourite flowers are Roses and Carnations. We attend United Church. I will try to answer all letters by return mail. Hope to be hearing from many of your readers in all parts of Canada.'[20] The isolation and loneliness in these letters requesting pen pals were often palpable. Although some Canadians were venturing onto the Trans-Canada Highway and travelling across the country on annual vacations, many readers could explore other regions of the country only through national magazines and television. The response to pen-pal requests was often overwhelming, as this letter from Muriel A. Jackson of Glasgow, Scotland, explains: 'The response to my request for a Canadian pen-pal which you so kindly published has been somewhat more than I can possibly cope with. From coast to coast literally, many wonderful people have written to me. Thank you.'[21]

Autobiographical letters often provided snapshots of the lives of 'average' readers and usually included information about how the magazine had helped, or perturbed them. As Mrs Roy Kittletz of Vimy,

Alberta, wrote: 'I am a farmer's wife with four children. I haven't even running water, but I do my work in clean pedal pushers and a clean shirt, my hair in a pretty net. I bake my own bread, keep a clean house, churn my own butter; I sew coats, dresses and embroider for the Women's Institute. We go to Church thirty miles away and I sing in the choir. In the summer the children and I play ball and go on picnics. If we go to Edmonton, which we do once a week or so, my husband takes me out to dinner and treats me as if I were still his bride. Happy? You bet I'm happy.' Finally, by way of explanation for her letter, she concluded, 'I have read *Chatelaine* since I was a little girl. I think I may say I am a better wife and mother for having read so many of your articles.'[22] Readers often employed an intimate or confessional style when they wrote to the magazine. The revelations and the language implied a friendship, or at least a belief on the part of the writer that the editors would be both interested and sympathetic. Readers like Kittletz were quick to criticize the editors for their Toronto-centric ideas or lack of awareness about living conditions throughout the country. Clearly, Kittletz was proud of her self-reliance and her family's 'standard of living,' which bore little resemblance to the way the term was used in the magazine. By the late fifties, the life described in her letter was out of step with the experiences of the majority of urban Canadians, particularly in central Canada and British Columbia. Readers on the Prairies and in Atlantic Canada were more familiar with the lagging 'modernization' in those regions.[23] But readers whose lives were often radically different from the majority wrote to the magazine to demand that, as Canadian women, *Chatelaine* be relevant to them. They made the periodical recognize that all its readers were not cut from the suburban mould and that their version of the 'better life,' in sharp contrast to the advertising content, was not driven by the purchase of consumer goods.

Still others wrote to request assistance, either from the editor or other readers, or to share advice. Mrs Delia Ash of Val d'Or, Quebec, trusted the *Chatelaine* community enough to send this poignant request: 'I've just received a letter from the Imperial War Graves Commission, Canadian Commission, announcing the unveiling of Groesbeek Memorial in the Netherlands on June 2, 1956. I would like to get in touch with other war mothers who are interested in taking the trip. If we travel together it will be so much nicer and not so lonely. I have my two sons' graves I want to visit over there, and surely there are others who will want to go. Won't you please write me?'[24] Unfortunately, it is impossible to know the result of Mrs Ash's request because follow-up letters were rarely printed. However, the archival letters permit a glimpse behind the scenes into the unpublished letters and responses to these requests for assistance.

Many women considered the editor, in particular, as their confidant or resource and turned to her for solutions to their problems. These concerns varied considerably. Letters requesting help or information on parenting issues, dietary requirements, marriage counselling, and sexual matters and health information were all included in the 1962 collection. Primarily, the letters indicate that the women felt they had nowhere else to turn. Or, conversely, they were embarrassed to seek help in their communities. As this letter from Newfoundland made clear, readers placed considerable trust in *Chatelaine* and in editor Doris Anderson. 'This month, for some reason my *Chatelaine* hasn't arrived and I'M LOST. I so do look forward to it. Although I do not agree with all of the articles I find it a lift to me in every way. Of special interest to me was an article awhile ago by Ron Kenyon – "The pill nobody talks about" ... Our religion forbids any birth control measures except the rhythm method and it was with great pleasure I read of the new discovery made by Fertility Tester Inc. of Illinois. However, I'm sure you realize that in this ... place these things are unavailable except by mail. Is it possible to advise me where they could be bought? I realize this is asking perhaps a great deal but as I've said I do look to *Chatelaine* for a great deal. Perhaps many women like me would like to know these things ... Thank you for the wonderful job you're doing. P.S. Do please look into my missing *Chatelaine*.'[25] Although the research of Angus McLaren and Arlene Tigar McLaren indicates that Canada's antiquated laws regarding the sale and distribution of birth control were sporadically, if seldom, enforced by the time this letter was written in the early sixties, this issue still remained a legal grey area until 1969, when the Criminal Code was amended.[26] Anderson's return letter sent the requested address and purchasing information, as well as her personal reassurance that postal delays were to blame for the late copy.

Other readers used the magazine's letters page as a forum for 'community' news – requests for information, jobs, and readers' advice. For instance, Mrs C.R. Van Dame of Toledo, Ohio, wrote: 'Two of my hobbies are favourite recipes and cookbooks. I am wondering if *Chatelaine* friends would care to exchange?'[27] Or consider this request from Clarence Gautreau from East Saint John, NB: 'I am a TB patient and have decided to take up watch repairing. I would appreciate it very much if I could receive any old ones to practice with. Thank you.'[28] The editors rarely provided any feedback about the outcome of such requests – even if they were aware of it. However, in rare cases where the replies were overwhelming, there would be follow-up information. That was certainly the case when Mrs Patricia Perron of Rawdon, Quebec, wrote her letter to the magazine. 'I wonder if your readers could help me out,' Perron began. 'I am expecting a baby this month. My husband and I have agreed on a boy's name but can't decide on a girl's. We like unusual names but not far-out ones. As we both have Irish ancestry, perhaps some of your readers could come up with something different from the current Irish names which are so popular.'[29] In the 'What's New' section of the October issue, the magazine brought the readers up to date on Mrs Perron's situation: 'Remember Pat Perron ... We were swamped – letters came from all over Canada and the United States and names such as Viva, Maeve, Moira ... delightedly awaited her baby daughter.'[30] Predictably, the editors informed readers that instead of the 'pixie-like little Irish Colleen,' Perron had given birth to a 'hefty ten pound, three ounce baby boy.' However, they were quick to add that the Perrons were keeping the list of names 'for future reference.'

Along with individual requests, readers' letters to the 'community' often included service notices or updates about their home towns for the benefit of far-flung former residents. Ethel Cameron, from East River, Pictou County, NS, wrote to the magazine (and other readers) to describe how she recycled her old issues; she sent *Chatelaine* 'to a hospital in India where the director Mary Nichol, a medical missionary, uses it to illustrate nutrition and baby care to nurses and expectant mothers.'[31] Afterwards, the used issues in these two decades, were sold to a local merchant for wrapping paper, and the proceeds went to defray part of the cost of the nurses' program. She provided the address so other women could direct their magazines towards this charitable enterprise, though this audience was not what advertisers expected when they praised the high 'pass along' readership of the magazine.

An exchange between an English and a Canadian reader indicates how *Chatelaine* could function as a balm for homesick Canadians abroad. In the December 1963 issue Mrs E. Spring of Harrow, Middlesex, England, wrote this poignant letter. 'How pleased I was to see Grand Pré mentioned in August. I used to live there and have many happy memories of the place,' she wrote. 'Often my sisters and I would go to the memorial park and see the statue of Evangeline and admire the lovely gardens. How well I remember the Apple-Blossom Festival. Although I have been living in England since 1947, I still long to see Grand Pré again at apple-blossom time.'[32] Mrs Spring was undoubtedly further saddened when this letter, from Mrs Kenneth Harris of Grand Pré, appeared in the February issue. Mrs Harris wrote, 'Sorry to disappoint Mrs. E. Spring but Grand Pré would never rate any special notice for its apple orchards today. The elaborate system of spraying, so necessary in recent years has made small orchards impractical. Today, one could almost count Grand Pré's orchards on the fingers of one hand ... They were, indeed, a beautiful sight, and we miss them too.'[33]

Despite the 'Canadian' content of the magazine, there were a handful of international readers – either Canadians abroad or tourists to Canada – who subscribed to the magazine. Many of these letters appear in later chapters because these 'outsiders' were particularly adept at explaining *Chatelaine*'s difference in comparison with the American magazines. However, two samples of the 'letter from abroad' deserve attention. The first, from Mrs Tsuyoshi Fujiwars of Sakai-City, Osaka, Japan, is a delightful example of 'Canadiana' fans who subscribed to the magazine because it reminded them of their travels in Canada. 'Hello from Japan,' she wrote. 'I am a Japanese housewife with two young sons. Every month something pleasant comes to our home all the way from Canada. Yes, it's *Chatelaine*. In 1962 we went over to Edmonton, Alberta, to stay one whole year on account of my husband's business. Everyone we met there was so kindly and friendly that we were able to enjoy our wonderful Canadian life to the full. Now, once the issue comes to our hands we make it a rule to see it by turns and to talk about our good days of Canada.'[34]

Other foreign readers commented on the role *Chatelaine* played in defining Canada and Canadians. Laura Faulkner of Staffordshire, England, wrote: 'For a long time I have intended saying how much I enjoy your magazine, which is subscribed by a friend ... It is by far the best present she could make me. I avidly read the stories, articles, and the ads, I like especially the stories of the Martin Family.' Of greater interest than her enjoyment of Canadian culture was Faulkner's explanation of how she equated Canadian women with *Chatelaine* readers, and how the magazine's message travelled around the globe. 'Your magazine,' Faulkner continued, 'even served as an introduction when I was in Ireland in June. I was 'sorting out' my fellow passengers on a Coach Tour, and finding that one was Canadian, I asked her if she read *Chatelaine*, and was delighted to hear that she did. As she had just returned from the Congo, I realized how it got around. This conversation took place while walking up the steps of Blarney Castle.'[35] Conversations about *Chatelaine* were not confined to suburban bungalows, but occurred in the most improbable locales. Just as at home, they served to stimulate family discussion and to establish instant familiarity among strangers.

The notion that readers, editors, and regular writers were friends was something that Anderson consciously attempted to foster: 'I always considered the readers my friends or that the magazine was their friend, and it came into their house and it had to be stimulating, something they couldn't wait to read, and also sometimes ... reassuring.'[36] Critics often dismiss the friendly tone of women's magazines as simply the commercial imperative of the genre.[37] But that is too simplistic a position, since many of the editors, Anderson included, were fans and readers of these periodicals long before they got that position. As a child, Anderson read *Chatelaine*, and her description of her memories of reading *Chatelaine* and her thoughts on editor Byrne Hope Sanders are instructive: 'I read the magazine all through the period she was editor in the 1930s because my mother got it. And I can remember some of those issues better than some of the issues that I edited, because magazines stuck around, you didn't throw them out. You used them for school projects and you'd go through them and cut things out ... And I read her editorials, and through reading her editorials you felt like you knew her and the magazine ... She sounded like a nice warm friendly person.'[38]

Readers felt similarly about Anderson, as this letter from Miss Fleurette Gagnon of Montreal indicates. 'Thank you for all the pleasure you have given me since I first subscribed to your magazine,' she wrote. 'It is most interesting and inspiring, and sometimes, lots of fun. I have been a subscriber for about seven years now, and have enjoyed every issue so much that I would not want to miss one.' Furthermore, she added, 'English is not my language, but through your magazine, I have learned a lot, underlining words I could not understand, so I could enrich my vocabulary. It is a real challenge and I enjoy every minute of it. Keep up the good work. It is wonderful! ... Please accept my best wishes for the New Year. Your faithful reader ...' [39] Gagnon was not the only writer to report using the magazine to learn English: in the sixties a number of European-Canadian women wrote to report that they, too, had improved their English skills by reading *Chatelaine*.

Chatelaine also functioned as an affordable gift that family members and friends gave to each other at birthdays or Christmas. Readers often had elaborate networks for exchanging magazines with friends and relatives. Gabrielle B. Griffiths, from Trenton, Ontario, wrote: 'I would like to take this opportunity to tell you how much I enjoy the magazine and each month I send a copy to my sister-in-law in North Borneo, from then on it finds its way to New Zealand.'[40] Moreover, appearing in *Chatelaine* was the easiest way to become a minor celebrity in towns and cities across the country. Miss Penny Morriss of Winnipeg, wrote: 'Thank you so very much for using the story of me in the Teens in the News section of the August issue. It was a real honour. *Chatelaine* has such a large circulation and so much influence in Winnipeg that it will give me a boost towards my goal of being a newspaperwoman when I graduate from university.'[41] The *Chatelaine* community existed outside the pages of the magazine because other media, along with local and community organizations, drew attention to the material in the magazine or praised their friends and members for their appearance in the periodical.

Another key link in the creation and sustenance of the *Chatelaine* community was the select group of readers known as the *Chatelaine* Councillors. In an editorial entitled 'Life Line from Women,' Byrne Hope Sanders reflected on the close association between the readers and the editors in *Chatelaine*'s history. Her description of the production of *Chatelaine* emphasized the women's world of the magazine: 'Most of our editorial staff are women, most of our contents are written by women ... We have no prejudice against men – on the contrary! But it is a woman's world we are interpreting.'[42] One of the main ways that the magazine kept in touch with and relevant to its readers was through the Consumer Council, which Sanders created in 1947. Composed of 2000 representatives from across Canada, these women were selected to mirror geographic and income levels of the readership and were the 'life line' for the editors. Sanders congratulated them for their work, which consisted of filling out questionnaires and responding to surveys, and reminded readers to 'remember the Councillors are there to bring the actual point of view of our women themselves into the magazine – and into your life. They are serving you, their sisters, by sharing their experiences and points of view.' Frequent reports from the councillors were staples of the magazine until well into the 1960s, making 2000 readers active participants in shaping and evaluating the periodical.

Slobs versus Perfectionists: The Mrs Chatelaine Case Study

In 1961 *Chatelaine* created the 'Mrs Chatelaine Contest,' an annual essay competition open to all Canadian homemakers. The preferred entrant was a married woman with children. Women who entered were required to answer questions about their families, thoughts about marriage and family issues, favourite recipes, and descriptions of their homes and their interior design. According to E.H. Gittings, assistant advertising sales manager for *Chatelaine*, the contest's popularity had exceeded Maclean Hunter's expectations: 'We received approximately 5,700 entries from our English edition and 400 entries from our French edition. Some of the entries were very elaborate indeed. They included such things as samples of pies, cookies, tape recordings of their voices, and in practically all cases, it was obvious that these readers had spent literally days preparing their entries. Mrs Saxton who won the contest last year, confessed after she had been selected that she had spent over 150 hours preparing her entry.'[43] By all accounts, both in the number of entries received and the amount of time contestants put into their entries, the contest was a success. Of course, the prizes were also very enticing. They included 'two first-class tickets via TCA DC-8 jet from Toronto to Paris; a ten-day stay in Paris with $1,000 to cover expenses, complete spring wardrobe in Easy Care Arnel, three piece set of ladies luggage; a Renault Dauphine car for your use during your stay in Paris.'[44] J.L. Adams, *Chatelaine* manager for Eastern Canada, wrote that the first winner, Mrs Joyce Saxton of Plenty, Saskatchewan, was a 'charming and delightful person,' even though in the course of the day she had remarked that 'although she read *Chatelaine* every month from cover to cover, her favourite magazine was *Reader's Digest* because it didn't flop around when she was reading it in bed.'[45] Over the course of the decade, attempts were made to ensure that women from all regions of the country were selected as grand prize winners. A farm wife and mother of three children, Mrs Saxton was an energetic housewife, as her published profile attests: 'She teaches swimming in the summer, is a member of or on the executive of nine clubs and community groups, preserved 140 quarts of fruit preserves last summer, 60 jars of jellies, 260 packs of frozen fruit and vegetables; sews most of her children's clothes and some of her own ... in the winter, with no farming chores, they work on remodeling the house.'[46] Contestants tended to be consummate wives and mothers and very service minded.

Such standards were not the case for all readers. For them, the Mrs Chatelaine Contest highlighted actual or imagined inadequacies in their various roles as wives, mothers, and, often, workers. One woman, Mrs Beatrice Maitland of Chatham, NB, took matters into her own hands and decided to write to the magazine and nominate herself for the

'Mrs Slob 1961' contest (Maitland's invention). The following excerpt from her first letter to Anderson provided her humorous critique of the standards required of 'Mrs Chatelaine' and makes a superb example of readers' creativity in fashioning 'oppositional' readings of *Chatelaine* material:

> Yesterday was the closing date for your Mrs. Chatelaine contest, but I didn't enter ... I wish someone, sometime, would have a competition for 'Mrs. Nothing!!' A person who isn't a perfect housekeeper, a faultless mother, a charming hostess, a loving wife, or a servant of the community. Besides being glamorous as a model, talented as a Broadway star and virtuous as a Saint. I have studied your questionnaire carefully but my replies are hopelessly inadequate ... To start with my appearance is absolutely fatal ... I am overweight, pear-shaped and bow legged. Consequently, not having much to work on I don't bother and cover it up with comfortable, warm old slacks ... Now, housework. Failure there too as I am a lousy housekeeper ... Entertaining? Practically never ... A game of cards or just talk with a few beers. No fancy food, drinks or entertainment ... Meals? ... We prefer plain meat and potato-vegetable meals with no frills. For birthdays our children choose the dinner. What's the menu? Usually hamburgers and chips. You can't win. Make a fancy meal from a magazine and they look like they are being poisoned ... The decor is middle English European junk shop, especially when the children start doing their homework. Community activities? I have always belonged to and worked with other organizations ... but I have become so sick of and bored with meetings I quit ... My philosophy as a home-maker – I guess that is, be happy, don't worry. You do what you can with what you've got when you feel like it. Consequently I'm never sick and I've got no nerves or fears. That is poor me ... So if you want to run a contest for 'Mrs. Slob 1961' I would be happy to apply and would probably win hands down. Thank you for your enjoyable magazine and my apologies for taking up your time.'[47]

Maitland's self-deprecatory style of humour and her parody of the conventions of the contest made for a witty letter. However, there was a considerable edge to her 'entry,' since she challenged the preferred reading of the contest – that all Canadian women aspired to or could afford the easy affluence of suburbia. The 'Mrs Chatelaine' mantle was awarded on the basis of family life, community volunteer work, philosophy of marriage and child rearing, interior design, and fashion sense. Many readers were quick to condemn articles that they felt were geared to 'higher-income' earners and not average Canadians. The tensions between the magazine's middle-class presumptions and the large number of working-class and rural readers were a constant source of friction. As an airforce wife with three kids, Maitland was clearly not part of the 'better-sort' of reader the magazine's advertisers and publisher sought.

Anderson's response praised Maitland's 'wit' and 'good humour' and acknowledged that the 'Mrs Chatelaine contest sets up pretty formidable rules but, in our defence, the woman who won it last year was a fairly average homemaker in Western Canada who lived on a farm.'[48] Neither Anderson nor Maitland anticipated the response that would follow the publication of her letter in the February 1962 issue. 'When I wrote that letter to you, back in the fall, I never dreamed that such a furore would ensue,' Maitland wrote. 'My stars! It's as good as having a best-seller! Strangers have shook my hand and said, "Welcome to the Club." And it's buzzing all over our P.M.Q. I have also had a lot of letters all very much in agreement. Who would have thought there were so many slobs in the country?'[49] Who would have guessed so many slobs read *Chatelaine*? Despite the magazine's attempts to encourage household perfection and reward the ideal Canadian homemaker, the Mrs Slobs refused to re-create themselves in that mould. With Maitland's treatise as their rallying cry, they wrote to her and to the magazine, professing support and encouragement to all the other Canadian slobs. Anderson's reply acknowledged that Maitland's letter and the ensuing letters in her support provided a wakeup call for the magazine: 'You certainly did stir up a furore. I for one found it extremely interesting to realize what a great load of guilt most of the housewives of this country carry around on their shoulders. It makes me a little guilty that women's magazines probably contribute as much as any medium to this feeling. Thank you for reminding us.'[50]

The letters professing solidarity with Mrs Maitland came from all regions of the country. This brief sampling captures the spirit of the letters.[51] Most continued Maitland's critique of the contest's middle-class bias and its limiting role prescribed for Canadian wives and mothers. Mrs F. Miller of New Westminister, BC, wrote: 'I received my issue of *Chatelaine* about one half hour ago and turned immediately to "The last word is yours." I say Three Cheers for Mrs Beatrice Maitland.'[52] Mrs C. Cserick of Ottawa deduced that the magazine was to blame for its unattainable style of homemaking and its focus on the suburban family. 'To be brutally frank I love *Chatelaine*,' Cserick wrote. 'But dear old *Chatelaine,* you write very little about us – don't you – we don't have a home of our own – 2 bedrooms is all, but we do like to read, listen to good music, watch good TV shows, take in a really excellent movie, drink gallons of coffee at odd hours, love our husband and kids, care for them and do 100 menial jobs a day.'[53] Interestingly, none of the readers who sympathized and identified with Maitland decided that the magazine was not for them. They considered the magazine a general Canadian woman's magazine, not one oriented to homemakers or urban middle-class women. Until Maitland's letter, many of these respondents remarked that they thought they alone had difficulties coping with the demands of homemaking in the sixties.

Perhaps the pithiest letter received was from grade 6 student Victoria M. Haliburton of Ville Lemoyre, Quebec, proving that readers of all ages considered themselves part of the *Chatelaine* community. 'I agree completely with Mrs. Maitland,' Haliburton wrote. 'The most common meal around our house is my father's specialty. Corn-and-tomato-york, he calls it, and it looks exactly what it is: namely, a mess of corn, tomatoes and bread crumbs. The same with most of our meals. No fancy French names for us. Macaroni and cheese sauce is macaroni and cheese.' She continued with this damning assessment of her mother's style of entertaining: 'Entertaining? The closest thing *we* have to that, except on rare occasions, is friends dropping in and out while my mother does the ironing or washing ... Housework? If my mother happens to be in the mood.' Ultimately, Haliburton promised Maitland a worthy competitor: 'If you ran a Mrs Slob contest, and my mother entered, there'd be some tough competition.'[54] Clearly, despite her age, Haliburton was familiar with the departmental fare and deduced that it was beyond her family both gastronomically and financially. If, from today's perspective, the departmental food material often appeared plain or uninspiring, these letters revealed that many readers were sceptical about the creations of the *Chatelaine* Institute kitchens. It would appear that the time requirement and the pseudo-sophisticated names, ingredients, and tastes were completely foreign and unenticing to many Canadian families. This letter from Greta Usenik of Paradise Hill, Saskatchewan, elaborated on the themes developed in Haliburton's letter when she challenged the *Chatelaine* editors to get out and visit 'average' Canadian housewives: 'Wish the entire *Chatelaine* staff could descend on me some afternoon and I'd show them how it's done. Our homes are modern, from plumbing to electric dryer, but no pile carpet or *glamour.* Also no patio, just the whole big outdoors.'[55] Clearly a little down-home western hospitality was what the citified, Toronto editors needed to get them back in touch with the lives of real readers.

All these letters illustrate that some readers were adept at providing oppositional and alternate interpretations of the magazine. They did not feel compelled to emulate the household perfectionism of the departmental material, nor did the contest encourage them to become super volunteers, homemakers, and wives. Rather, the magazine was construed as out of step with the average Canadian homemaker. One reader, Mrs W. Ockenden of Victoria, echoed Anderson's concerns about the amount of guilt the Mrs Chatelaine Contest induced in the readership: 'I am sure there are many more home-makers just like this except that many *do* worry because they can't be more like that perfect being so often portrayed in women's magazines.'[56]

Similarly, a letter from Mrs Neil Ferguson of Dutch Brook, Cape Breton, did not make specific reference to the 'Mrs. Slob' letters, but her critique of the contest and her comments about the classist nature of the magazine provided an important commentary about readers' class identifications. 'In the last two Mrs. Chatelaine contests it was quite well to do women that won. Do people from the middle-class income bracket ever enter these contests?' Ferguson wondered. 'There are a lot of women that would certainly enter if they could fill out the entry forms but how can they say how well they entertain when they are racking their brains as to what to cook up for their family for a hearty good meal when maybe there is very little pay coming in to provide the proper ingredients for a proper meal ... These women are the same ones that patch and do over the children's clothes from year to year to have their kiddies warm and presentable for school while the mothers themselves are likely wearing the same coat for the last five or six years.'[57] Clearly, many readers who identified themselves as average or middle-income families were not. Regardless of their income level, they believed that the magazine's contests and budget planning specials should be accessible to all readers. Anderson responded that the winners had both been in the $5000 income bracket, 'average' for Canadian families at that time, and not beyond the realm of the majority of readers. Mrs Ferguson probably thought that answer was a cop out.

Throughout the decade, the debate over the 'perfection' of Mrs Chatelaine was revisited yearly, after the publication of the winner and the regional runners-up. The oppositional and alternate readings, along with the large numbers of women who decoded the preferred meaning and honed their contest entries year after year, indicate the variety of ways Canadian women 'read' the periodical. Intended as a celebration of homemaking, it often became a celebration of slobs, the working-class, and regional difference. The editorial and advertising directives, which hoped that this feature would support the departmental features, and thus the advertisers products, fell on blind eyes because many Canadian women could not identify with its presumption of a middle-class, homemaking role for all women. These women offered oppositional readings, or alternate and critical commentary, about what they considered an 'unrepresentative' and unfair contest. They didn't meekly follow the prescription to become homemakers and they didn't cancel their subscriptions. Instead, they demanded that the magazine change. And *Chatelaine* did. By 1969 the contest was not afforded as prominent coverage in the periodical, and that year's winner was a working wife and mother who bluntly told readers she had no time for volunteer groups. In the seventies the contest was quietly abandoned.

'Reading' Remembered

Although relatively few in number, the twelve people who completed my questionnaire about reading *Chatelaine* provide additional commentary about their memories and thoughts on 'reading' the magazine. One respondent from London, Ontario, the mother of four children, recalls the role *Chatelaine* played in her adjustment to her new role as a stay-at-home mother and to the ways in which Canadian women were negotiating their changing status: 'It probably helped me cope with my stay-at-home family role and my community interests prior to returning to work on my profession in the mid 60s'[58]

Half the respondents reported reading other magazines as well as *Chatelaine*: *Maclean's, Reader's Digest, Time,* and the *United Church Observer,* along with the American women's magazines *Good Housekeeping* or *Redbook*. June Ellis, a homemaker and mother of six, recalls how she 'traded' her magazines with friends: 'I would look forward to trading my *Good Housekeeping* for her *Chatelaine* and we always told each other what we found most interesting ... Each magazine went through many hands before it arrived back home.'[59] Dorothy Marlow also passed her copies on to friends or donated them to the hospital.[60] June Ellis's description of 'trading' indicates that this practice was a means of economizing as well as a social event, as she compared notes with her friends about her favourite features. Other respondents, who did not report 'trading,' all mentioned that they talked about recipes, fashions, decorating tips and sometimes articles or editorials with their daughters, mothers, sisters, husbands, friends, and neighbours. Half the respondents purchased their own copy of the magazine, while the other half received gift subscriptions or borrowed others' copies.

According to respondents, *Chatelaine* offered practical material of use to homemakers, along with entertaining and educational articles. Many remembered the service material and how they looked forward to the 'new ideas' each month. Bette-Jo Baird recalled the competing demands between motherhood and career: 'I was a young mother who had given up an interesting career as an X-ray Technologist in a large hospital. I loved clothes – the latest in styles and make-up and hair-styles. I was interested in gardening and forever "doing-over" (on a limited scale!) our home while my husband was away on military duty. *Chatelaine* gave me information on all these interests and I read it from cover to cover each month.'[61] Asked to circle their favourite components of the magazine, most of the respondents circled a variety of service material, editorials, and articles: but in written reminiscence it was the service material that provoked most of the commentary. Although readers obviously enjoyed the service department material, there is another explanation for its popularity. After a passage of thirty to forty years, few readers could remember any details about articles, editorials, or fiction – except that they did or did not read those features – but, given the repetitious nature of service material and its readily identifiable content, correspondents could, realistically, remember using and enjoying those sections. The advertisements were the least favourite component.

Zena MacLeod, a teacher and a mother of four children, provided her definition of the 'typical' *Chatelaine* reader, along with her personal memories of reading the magazine: 'An average Canadian female who might have little time to read a lengthy novel but enjoyed light-reading, and those who like to keep up-to-date with fashions, etc. ... I know I found them pleasant to read and easy to pick-up. I do remember standing stirring food at the stove and reading *Chatelaine* at the same time!'[62] Other respondents also reported reading the magazine anywhere and everywhere – in the living-room, in bed, at the kitchen table, and, the classic, 'sometimes in the car while waiting for my husband.'[63]

A few of my respondents were new immigrants to Canada, and they spoke of the role *Chatelaine* played in their 'adjustments' to Canadian society. One recalled reading the magazine 'with morning or afternoon coffee to try to add interest to a deadly routine.'[64] And although she found the articles more interesting than American magazines, she reported being bored with the periodical in general. 'It helped to acculturate me to Canadian society. It taught me the role I had agreed to play by marrying a traditional man from Northern Ontario.' Conversely, a respondent who, at that time, was a teenage male in Cape Breton, described his experience with the magazine very differently: 'Light, interesting, fantasy, escapism from small town, straight, male-dominated, Catholic, Cape Breton.'[65] The comments of this male respondent, the only one in the survey, are indicative of the role *Chatelaine* may have played for younger gay men, particularly those in more isolated regions of the country. Although this letter is the only clear evidence of a gay male readership of *Chatelaine*, it should be stated that this informant, who wished to remain anonymous, was the only person who responded to my advertisements in the *Globe and Mail*. Clearly, he was determined that his experiences be retold, and this determination speaks volumes about others who chose to remain silent.

Given the modest sample, achieved primarily by the snowballing method, I cannot claim that these respondents were representative of how, why, and where other Canadians read *Chatelaine*. They indicate that there were a variety of reasons to read the periodical – for the service material, for articles, and for light reading. While the act of reading was a solitary one, wedged between work, housework, and child care, they all commented on the social aspect – trading magazines, clipping out recipes or articles, talking to family and friends, and, for a few, writing to the magazine or entering one of the contests (recipes and Mrs Chatelaine). They illustrate that many (in this case, half) *Chatelaine* readers were also inveterate consumers of other periodicals – both American and Canadian. Implicit in their comments was the belief that *Chatelaine* was *the* source for Canadian ideas, news, and views about Canadian women.

Critical Reading and Response: Ouida M. Wright's Case Study

Although it is clear from the Mrs Slob correspondence that readers were frequently critical of *Chatelaine*, studies of reader responses often fail to include negative commentary. Yet there were many negative letters to *Chatelaine*, largely in response to particular articles or stories. One general letter of critique came from Ouida M. Wright of Weston, Ontario. Wright's July 1962 letter was never published in the periodical, but the archival copy, and its three-page response from Anderson, permit further commentary about reader perceptions and editorial decision making. Wright wrote: 'I have received the August issue of *Chatelaine*, and that has been even more disappointing to me ... I believe that a woman's magazine should be of interest to any thinking human being, with, of course, the woman's point of view in mind – in other words, *Maclean's* magazine with a feminine viewpoint ... look back in your files to the magazine in which you had Madame Vanier on the cover. That's the best you've done yet. I think you have potential to be a fine magazine – your editorials suggest as much; yet the more glossy and attractive in appearance the magazine gets, the less stimulating it becomes.'[66]

Although Anderson was not in the habit of sending form letters to readers, most of her responses were, of necessity, brief. However, in this case Anderson crafted a three-page reply: 'Your letter depressed me considerably because you sound just like the sort of reader I feel I have been trying to reach and appeal to for the last five years.'[67] What follows was an explanation, and defence, of a general women's magazine. First off, she made clear the importance of advertising: 'We just simply can't ignore the facts of magazine life such as newsstand sales, advertising, and subscription sales. Our advertising, as you probably know, is our life-blood which pays for the editorial features.' Most important, for our purposes, was Anderson's outline of readership traffic through the magazine, and the varying appeal of the different components:

It's true that we try to include in every issue at least three or four articles which are more or less general and sometimes could easily appear in a magazine such as *Maclean's*, but the 'service' part of our magazine is very definitely wanted by women, and as a matter of fact the readership is usually higher in service articles than it is in general articles. I too would like to run pictures of prominent Canadian women on the cover, but the Madame Vaniers are fairly rare, and to be quite blunt with you, if we ran covers of secretaries, nurses etc., our newsstand sales would plummet. We know this because we tried this approach ... Even a cover of Madame Vanier – and I quite agree with all the things you have to say about her – sells far less successfully than a cover of Juliette or Toby Robbins, and it is way behind a newsstand sales compared to Elizabeth Taylor. I agree with you that Your World Notebook is a fine feature, and I assure you that we will continue to run it, but it's certainly not among the best read features of the magazine. It trails such regular features, for example, as Homemaker's Diary, Meals of the Month, etc.

Anderson's response was remarkably similar to the excerpt included earlier from her novel *Rough Layout*. Her response to Wright's critique exhibits the paradoxes and frustrations of editing the magazine. The pluses were the ability to reach a mass national audience of Canadian women and to offer educational and entertaining features. But that had to be accomplished without radically altering the 'genre' or format – the service material was non-negotiable, since that was the primary reason advertisers believed that women's magazines were such good places to situate their advertisements. The problem, which many critics of general women's magazines have overlooked, lay in the fact that the reader decided what they valued in the magazine and what they wanted to read. Traditionally, far too much emphasis has been placed on editorial and advertising intent, and not enough attention devoted to studying how actual readers respond to the material. If readers stop reading or, worse, stop subscribing, that is a serious problem. Magazine editors ignore readers at their peril. In the case of a mass-market periodical like *Chatelaine*, many women who subscribed did so for the features on homemaking. For them, the service material was as essential as a murder is to a mystery novel – a requisite of the genre.

Feminism 101: The Effects of Reading *Chatelaine*?

It is notoriously difficult to predict with any degree of authority the 'effect' of popular culture on its consumers. However, that does not stop speculation about the effect, nor academic attempts, usually via a labyrinthe of quantified studies of readers, to explain how the material affected people. On an individual basis, the letters, and the responses of the editors and readers alike, indicate some of the impact of reading the magazine. However, a brief comparison of two reader surveys provides some indication of how readers' views changed during the course of the sixties.[68] In March 1961 the magazine published 'The Canadian Homemaker: What You Think of Your Job – A Special *Chatelaine* Report.'[69] This report was the result of a three-month survey involving 250 'carefully selected representative housewives' from the ranks of the *Chatelaine* Councillors. The purpose was to 'find out whether the stereotype of the harassed North American housewife – tense, frantic, and frustrated – was fact or myth.' It is clear that although Betty Friedan is credited with 'discovering' suburban discontent, this historical 'fact' has been overstated. Other observers were also aware of these changes and were on the lookout for signs of morale problems. Their awareness is obvious from the way in which they framed their survey questions. The results, Jean Yack reported, revealed 'remarkably little evidence of "housewifeitis" ... no whining martyrs wailed on our shoulders.' She pronounced the councillors a 'a cheery lot.' In fact, a 'resounding' 86.7 per cent wanted their daughters 'to grow up to be housewives rather than working wives (4.9%) or unmarried career girls (1.8%).' When the surveyors asked women if their desire to work outside the home would change if they had affordable or adequate child care, only 6.3 per cent stated they would prefer to work, 47 per cent said no, and 43 per cent were in favour of part-time employment. According to this survey, the councillors, and therefore the readership, were depicted as happy Canadian housewives and mothers.

Astonishingly, this contented image had changed considerably by the end of the decade. In January 1968 the magazine published a long questionnaire that it presented to the Status of Women Commission. Over 11,000 women completed the three-hour questionnaire. They were from all regions of the country and from 'moderately comfortable financial circumstances.'[70] Even though the majority of the women who replied indicated that they did not work, they stated that if they could choose, 'marriage with children and a career' would be their preference.[71] They were in favour of government-supported daycare (72.7%); equal access to employment (80.5%); enforced equal-pay-for-equal work legislation (80.8%); government birth control clinics for women (74.8%); and wider grounds for abortion (55%) and divorce (94.5%). Based on this survey, it would appear that the majority of those who responded were not only aware but supportive of the key liberal feminist goals, centred primarily on equality of opportunity and equal participation in society.[72] By and large, according to Amy Farrell, those goals were the same as those of the editors and the editorial content in *Ms.* magazine from 1972 onward. By comparison, then *Chatelaine*'s 'subversive' feminism appears even more exceptional when judged against the open, or blatantly feminist, *Ms.* magazine. The Status of Women survey also revealed that the results from French-Canadian and English-Canadian women exhibited striking differences. The 3245 francophone women who answered the same questionnaire in *Châtelaine* showed 'a far stronger desire for independence as persons ... In almost every case, Quebeckers swing ten to twenty per cent higher in support of freedom of thought and action.' It was obvious from these answers and statistics that *Chatelaine* readers were not only well versed in women's political issues of the day but were very concerned that changes be made in Canadian laws and societal mores.

Although any overlap between the first survey group and the second seemed unlikely, both groups were deemed (in their respective years) to be representative of *Chatelaine* readers. Clearly it would be simplistic to attribute this transformation solely to *Chatelaine*, yet the magazine did play a role in this changing perception of the role of Canadian women. In light of the well-known place that *Ms.* occupies as a mass-market feminist beacon for American women, the evidence indicates that, in Canada, this role was incorporated into a mass-market women's magazine, where it reached a far larger audience and introduced the vast majority of Canadian women to the key liberal feminist demands. As future chapters will illustrate, this educational or activist role was successful. It took place within the confines of the women's magazine genre, and it attracted considerable reader commentary, both positive and negative. Based on this one study, it would appear that the vast majority of *Chatelaine* readers agreed with liberal feminist goals by the end of the sixties.

Conclusion

Once the reader had her copy of the magazine in her hands, she was in control. She selected what she wanted, she could read it anywhere she desired, and ultimately she interpreted the material based on her own frames of reference, regardless of the meaning the authors had intended. It was, to borrow John Fiske's terminology, a highly 'producerly' text. This interactive nature of *Chatelaine* was a large factor in its tremendous success. Readers felt encouraged to write to the magazine: to comment on the material, ask advice of the editors, follow the recipes, clip out the service department features to create scrapbooks of this material, frame the pictures of the queen, and respond to other readers or write to them directly as pen pals. Individual readers' suggestions, along with the recommendations of the *Chatelaine* Councillors, were incorporated into the magazine. Although *Chatelaine* often positioned itself as the expert and called on experts to write articles, it did not talk down to readers. The magazine apologized for mistakes, and the editors returned the readers' letters. In a word, they felt accountable to their readership.

The insights provided by the readers' letters stand in sharp contrast to traditional assessments of the effects of 'prescriptive' literature on consumers. It will be clearer in later sections just how varied (or polysemic) the messages and contents were. But regardless of the message – whether the conservative advertisements, the traditional service components, or the avant-garde editorials and articles – the readers did not meekly accept these components at face value. Many went beyond the preferred or intended meanings to invest the material with alternate or oppositional readings – to spoof the contests, to critique affluence, to challenge the 'universalism' of the portrait of 'the Canadian woman.' Perhaps the best example of the readers' refusal to be cowed by the experts was their responses to the Dichter professionals, where they offered brutally blunt assessments of how *Chatelaine* needed to improve itself if it were to remain representative of their 'modern' lives and to compete with glossy, American periodicals. If we return to Foucault's notion of the micropractices of power, it is clear that while editors, advertisers, and writers are clearly important in making the magazine, the ideological messages do not stop with 'making' a periodical. In the 'reading' stage, individual women brought their own critical skills to the material. They were far from powerless in this equation. And their comments demonstrate clearly that, regardless of the intent of the editors and advertisers (who did not speak with one voice, but had competing interests), once the issue was in the mail, their abilities to shape the meanings and messages gleaned were out of their control. At that stage, power shifted quite dramatically to the readers, who might or might not take the editoral clues, pick up the advertisers' seductive entreaties, read any or all of the periodical, or base their opinions on the letters of others within the readership community.

Power was not distributed evenly, but the readers had a strong role to play in the magazine because their views were solicited for readership studies, and their letters were read avidly by editors and other readers alike. Within the context of the time, the letters indicate that this community of women was going through growing pains – learning to be 'modern' and 'progressive,' to use the language of the Dichter Study. Some were beginning to re-enter the labour force and juggle the demands of children, homes, and husbands – and so were rethinking their traditional roles. Others were trying to emulate the suburban housewife model, prevalent in other North American media, and finding that a challenge. Far from our stereotypical view of *Chatelaine* and its readers as emblematic of affluent, happy, suburban households, the letters indicate that they were average Canadian women – primarily lower middle class and working class – from all regions of the country, who were pushing at boundaries, seeking social and economic emancipation, and hopeful that 'their' magazine would speak to these issues.

It is this extraordinary energy and activity generated by *Chatelaine*, combined with the nature and content of the material, that has allowed me to refer to *Chatelaine* as more than a magazine, to claim that it represented a community of readers, writers, and editors who formed a bond based on gender and nationality. Although they were not explicit about this sense of 'sisterhood,' as *Ms.* magazine would be, it was clear that they regarded the community as bonded and bounded by a Canadian 'women's culture.' Class, race, age, religion, and, less often, issues of sexual orientation would sometimes rock that community, and readers, writers, and editors were frequently not in agreement. There were conflicts and heated debates, but most members remained within the fold. When readers subscribed to the magazine, they often began a relationship that lasted for decades. The accomplished female editors, particularly Doris Anderson and her vision of what a woman's magazine should be, were important, but that importance has been overstated. The readers were also key contributors to making *Chatelaine* a Canadian periodical success story.

Part Two

Traditional Fare?

'Your Best Medium to Sell Women': Covering and Advertising *Chatelaine*

In September 1952 editor Lotta Dempsey informed *Chatelaine* readers that the magazine was launching a 'new cover girl series' that would profile 'tomorrow's stars.' These new Canadian stars were teenagers who the magazine predicted would 'one day set this country afire with their talent – perhaps their genius.' Because talent and genius are notoriously difficult to depict visually, Dempsey explained that the young women selected were also supposed to represent 'good-looking, wholesome young people with sound Canadian backgrounds. The kind you and I knew, growing up in Edmonton or Pictou or New Westminister.' Marilyn Young, a sixteen-year-old member of the corps de ballet of the Winnipeg Ballet, debuted on the September 1952 cover in a ballet pose against a yellow backdrop.

With such laudatory goals, one might suppose that *Chatelaine* readers would be eager to see these multitalented, home-grown teenagers, but reaction to the new initiative was mixed. Torontonian E.G. Reid was displeased, stating, 'I am not an old prude, and I enjoy *Chatelaine*, but the September cover is a disgusting spectacle for a respectable magazine. With all the beautiful flowers, fruits, and other subjects to choose from, all you have to offer is another leg show, on a scantily clad young woman. Will our sex never learn that we can't command respect if we do not respect ourselves? I would cancel my subscription, if it wasn't nearly out.'[1] Equally vexed was Mrs M. Earle of Winnipeg, who reported being 'shocked by the ungainly display of limbs on your September cover. Let's go back to pretty faces.' But other readers did not regard the cover as sexually exploitative: Gweneth Lloyd of Winnipeg thought the cover was 'nice,' while Katherine C. Houston from Toronto wrote that she 'was immediately impressed by your cover. It's attractive ... at the same time getting away from the average cover which merely looks like an ad for clothes.' Despite Dempsey's explanation of the goals of the new cover girl series, some readers reproached the editors for their lack of taste and respectability, while others were untroubled or cautiously congratulatory. *Chatelaine* readers did not let editorial directives colour their interpretation. Editors encouraged the participatory nature of the magazine by including a range of responses that tended to prolong these controversies and encourage readers to re-examine or reread contentious articles, editorials, or cover art. In this case, E. Wood from Saskatoon offered the last word on the September cover, stating: 'I was astounded when I read the criticism of E.G. Reid, Toronto. She may not be a prude, but she is certainly no artist. The graceful figure gave pleasure to many people of my age group, and I was brought up by Victorian parents.'[2]

For many reasons, it is apt to begin the analysis of *Chatelaine*'s components with cover art and advertising. Obviously, the cover was the first impression *Chatelaine* made. As the largest advertisement for the magazine, the cover art is indicative of how Maclean Hunter positioned the periodical, and how the readers wrangled over the difference between the company's ideal reader (presumed by the cover) and their own sense of themselves as the 'representative' reader. Equally compelling is the fact that the cover art and the advertisements are the most visually exciting, numerically dominant pages within the magazine's composition. From a financial point of view, these pages were the bread and butter of *Chatelaine*, the *raison d'être* for its creation, and the chief factor behind its continued viability. Finally, it is in these pages that all the stereotypes about the 'images' of women's magazines, and the images of the era, are confirmed. In the advertisements, and to a lesser degree the cover art, the world of consumption and affluence were queen (to use the more appropriate gender term). In an era where modernization was equated with a consumer paradise of products for home and family, the ad pages held the most persistent and seductive messages. Yet the variety of ways in which the corporations and their advertising agencies tried to sell a range of products – from linoleum flooring to mix-masters – offers intriguing insights into the dreams and aspirations of the readers.

As the opening anecdote illustrates, *Chatelaine* cover art was contested terrain during the magazine's heyday primarily because the photographs and layout had a dual and often conflicting purpose. According to Ellen McCracken, 'the visual images and headlines on a magazine cover offer a complex semiotic system, communication of primary and secondary meanings through language, photographs, images, colour and placement.'[3] Effective magazine design dictates that the cover should establish an identifiable face for the periodical and differentiate it from its competitors. Cover art is a magazine's advertisement for itself – an appealing, intriguing, entertaining picture to attract readers. But for longtime subscribers, the cover has an entirely different purpose. For them, the cover proclaims, from coffee tables, magazine racks, and night tables, that hundreds of thousands of Canadian households were *Chatelaine* households. The images that might captivate, jolt, or attract newsstand browsers away from the competition seldom satisfied the subscribers' desire for respectable, tasteful covers that would not clash with their decor. A letter from Mrs Alex Henry of Woodstock, Ontario, echoes the acute aesthetic sensibilities of some readers: 'Your covers often go so well with my living room décor, but why do you have to spoil the good-looking cover with that nasty-looking address tag?'[4]

Successive art directors had to negotiate the commercial imperative of production (to increase readership, advertising pages, and rates) against the editorial imperative of reader satisfaction (to offer readers 'representative' or aspirational images of themselves). This balance was a tall order and, unlike the other editorial components of the magazine, *Chatelaine*'s cover art catered to the commercial imperative. The cover was the editor's advertisement to the readers. In the cut-throat, competitive world of mass-market magazines, cover art positioned the periodical against its competition. Regardless of the disappointment of regular subscribers, it was one of the key ways to reinvigorate the subscriber base with new, younger women attracted by the youthful faces of *Chatelaine* cover girls. This tension would increase in the sixties, as the business department began a concerted effort to increase newsstand sales and maintain *Chatelaine*'s primacy in the Canadian marketplace. To that end the cover was made over, moving away from the dowdy, old-fashioned images of the fifties towards the multihued, visually exciting images of the sixties. Yet the competing visions between editorial and commercial imperatives were not the only tensions that surface in the cover images. Race, ethnicity, and Canadian nationalism would also prove difficult terrain to negotiate. With its consistent refrain, 'For the Canadian woman,' *Chatelaine* staked its image on being Canadian, and presumably attempted to appeal to all Canadian women – yet it consistently failed to provide portraits of diversity on the cover. An analysis of some controversial covers from the era indicate that there were deep fault lines in the reading community, lines that resulted every so often in tremors of dissension and the dispatch of critical letters to the editors.

During the fifties, *Chatelaine* had five art directors or art editors: Francis Crack, 1950–1; A. Stanley Furnival, 1952–3; Keith Scott, 1954–5; Ron Butler, 1956–8; and Joan Chalmers, 1959–62. This position was one of the few within the editorial department in which men figured prominently, although not exclusively, throughout the decade. The magazine's art directors favoured photographic images over illustrations; indeed, almost all cover art was one large photograph or a collage of smaller photos.[5] These photos were produced at various studios in Toronto. In select circumstances, celebrity photographers, such us Yousef Karsh, contributed seasonal or special covers for the periodical. Although newsstand sales increased throughout the decade, the percentage of single copies sold was never greater than 5.2 per cent.[6] Until the magazine was remodelled in September 1958, all versions of the *Chatelaine* cover featured the word CHATELAINE in large letters running across the top portion of the cover, with the subtitle 'For the Canadian woman' either above or below the title. The text used on the front cover made the preferred reading audience for the magazine very clear. The remaining three-quarters of the cover featured a photograph – a woman's face, young children, or the latest delicacy created by the *Chatelaine* Institute test-kitchen on a solid coloured background. The colours varied from bright Christmas reds to the more subtle pastel shades favoured on the spring issues. Although there were exceptions, the general impression of these early fifties' covers was of a dowdy, old-fashioned magazine. During the Sanders and Dempsey years, cover art design appeared stuck in an earlier era, with illustrations of dewy-eyed ingenues in their new Easter bonnets. Under John Clare's editorial direction between 1953 and 1957, Furnival, Scott, and Butler all implemented bolder colour schemes and often featured combinations of images, but these attempts to 'look modern' lacked both aesthetic sensibilities and themes to pull the various images together. In graphic terms, it seemed that the collective sigh the country breathed in the early fifties, when it became apparent that the postwar reconversion and economic boom were sustainable, was reflected in *Chatelaine* covers: they became more confidant, more colourful, with more upscale images. At the same time, the company spent more money on cover art and upgraded the paper stock. Yet some readers were often critical of these modern 'combination covers,' as this comment from WMP of Toronto indicated: 'Enjoy all the articles on the royal family, but the March cover is too much. Why mix our Queen's lovely face with fish and awning stripes?'[7]

In the Dichter-inspired cover that debuted in 1958, the title 'Chatelaine' had a vertical placement on the left side of the cover. The subtitle had been changed, to reflect Maclean Hunter's buyout of *Canadian Home Journal*, and was now 'The Canadian Home Journal.' This new layout displayed the title and subtitle in a bold colour on a white background. The remaining two-thirds of the cover featured photographs or illustrations on a black background. This white-and-black motif, along with the multicoloured text, made for a cleaner, more modern-looking cover. It was geared to attracting a younger reading audience, both single teenage girls and young married women.

The cover included blurbs or 'sell lines' (magazine production lingo for teasers that summarize contents) advertising each issue's featured articles. If the *Chatelaine* Institute produced a special food, decorating, or beauty feature, it too was advertised on the cover. Often the article titles on the cover were different from the actual titles inside the magazine. Editors tried to jazz up the subjects or provide suggestive titles that would lead the reader to search rapidly for the corresponding article inside the periodical. The size and number of these article titles varied, but they were usually used to frame the visual image selected as the major focus of the cover. A particularly important article, such as a piece by Dr Marion Hilliard or a new instalment on the queen, would merit a different-coloured banner to draw the reader's attention.

Regardless of the layout style, the use of colour, or the headlines and banners, the major focus of each *Chatelaine* cover throughout the decade remained fairly constant – a young, white, female face.[8] In some cases the magazine used children or babies, but they were almost always female (babies were wrapped in a pink blanket or some such identifier) to make it clear that the magazine was geared to female readers. Photos or illustrations of men, as husbands, teenage boys, or children, were notable for their rare appearances on the cover of the magazine. Royal and celebrity covers also concentrated on women – Queen Elizabeth II, the Queen Mother, Princess Margaret, or well-known Canadians such as Joyce Davidson or Charles Templeton and Sylvia Murray. The magazine also produced a number of covers without people, featuring food, flowers, or, rarely, art work.

Covers in the sixties stuck to a much narrower formula. Food was banished and, with a few exceptions, so were photographs or illustrations of babies and children. Maclean Hunter paid more attention to the cover and opted for a more sophisticated look, with a view to increasing newsstand sales. As Anderson commented to Lloyd Hodgkinson, 'The cover as it was designed three years ago has served us well, giving us a distinctive, different look from all other magazines on the news-stands.'[9] The typical sixties' cover featured a photograph of a woman's head and shoulders – usually a white model in her twenties.[10] All the covers featured glossy photographs on a variety of multicoloured backgrounds. Illustrations, either paintings or drawings, were abandoned. Besides female models, cover photographs of celebrities or royalty were increasingly popular. Featured celebrities were representatives from the world of Canadian television or popular music: Juliette Sysak, Fred Davis, Betty Kennedy, Marg Osborne, Adrienne Clarkson, Julie Christie, Ian and Sylvia Tyson, and Joni Mitchell. The American celebrities were Hollywood movie stars of the era, such as Elizabeth Taylor or Debbie Reynolds. Royal family covers were more popular in the sixties than the fifties. Male politicians also made infrequent appearances: first, Lester Pearson, accompanied by his daughter and grand-daughter; and then, while the country was in the throes of Trudeaumania, Pierre Elliott Trudeau – twice.

The selection of cover art, the preserve of the art director, was linked with a featured article or chosen to highlight departmental material. After Joan Chalmers left *Chatelaine*, cover art composition and design was the preserve of Kenneth Jobe, 1963–9, and later Keith Branscombe (1969). The few extant memos from the sixties illustrate the links between the cover art – the model, design, colours, and backdrop – and the magazine content: '*Cover*: Ties in with the article on femininity, shows head and shoulders of a pretty girl, pink predominates ... *Cover*: Mother and child looking at frosted cake, ties in with bonus cookbook. Colours mainly pink, accented in purple ... *Cover*: Head and shoulders of model, crossbeams of house in the background, tying in with Homes '60.'[11] The intended link between the cover art and the content was never very difficult to ascertain. Despite the above commentary, cover colours varied considerably and 'feminine' colours (pinks and other pastels) were used less frequently than bold, multicolured covers or singular, bold, background colours – black and white, blue, green, or red.[12]

Although *Chatelaine* was remodelled for the sixties, some readers found the continuity in *Chatelaine* cover art trying. Jean Young, an Edmonton reader, was critical of the sameness and banality of the covers when she wrote: 'Your cover designer is not in a rut – he is in a GORGE! I am so sick of the insipid females he has on the cover that I refuse to look at another one. The only cover that has been different in the last decade is the one with the stained-glass window. I intended to write and compliment you on it. If you can not find anything else to put on the cover just print the table of contents and the month in large letters so one can at least tell which issue is which.'[13] Nine days later, Anderson's reply sought to placate Young by stressing the commercial importance of the cover. 'I am sorry that you disagree with our Art Director on covers,' Anderson wrote. 'As a matter of fact you say "he," whereas our Art Director is Miss Joan Chalmers ... The reason we run so many large heads of young women on our covers is simply because from exhaustive surveys we find that these are the covers that sell best on the newsstands, and since we are in a very competitive business ... we just simply can't afford to deviate from what we know makes good business sense. However, I hope our readers like yourself will not judge us solely on our covers, but on our contents.'[14] Young was probably not impressed with this logic, since she was one of a number of readers who criticized the inconsistency between the ideals expressed in the editorials and the articles – Canadianism, pro-woman commentary, and intelligent journalism – and the obvious pandering to youthfulness, exaggerated femininity, and superficiality denoted by the magazine's cover.

Although it is true that *Chatelaine* covers lacked variety during the era, the fact that some readers were very resistant to change might help to explain this sameness. In the January 1957 issue the magazine published a Savignac drawing to highlight the travel feature it was promoting (illustration 2). In the introductory essay, Anderson explained the motivation for this different cover: 'Last summer when we were planning the January issue, we decided there was no better pickup for that after-Christmas slump you're probably going through right now than a travel issue. A travel-poster cover seemed only logical and one name came immediately to mind – Savignac. He is a dark, curly-haired Frenchman, internationally famous for his powerful, simple drawings. That's why our cover looks so different this month – it's a Paris import. Like it?'[15]

The cover's dark-blue background and whimsical drawing certainly made it stand out in a sea of female faces and staged shots of playful children. Ultimately, however, the cover had to appeal to the readers,' and not the editor's, artistic sensibilities. If the readers liked the new

2 *Chatelaine* cover, January 1957

approach to cover art, we will never know, since the only published response, from Mrs Campbell Humphries of Castleford, Ontario, was far from complimentary. 'What a horrid cover on your January issue! The colours are nauseating,' she wrote, ' the artistry [is] terrible; no proportion; no eyes; no tail end to the dachshund, if that is what the beast is supposed to be; measles on both characters' faces! I thought all this, then found you had imported it from Paris! Really! Whoever Mr Savignac is, he could take lessons in art from my four-year-old daughter.'[16] The fact that the monstrosity had been a Parisian import seems to have made the whole situation even worse. Perhaps she assumed they paid more for this cover than they were used to paying for their Canadian-produced artwork. It was clear from this experiment that the lack of innovation in cover design was not always attributable to the art director's lack of vision or the stinginess of the company, but stemmed from the readers' desire for the familiar.

During the era, cover controversies fell into four well-defined categories: sexually explicit or lewd covers; Canadian nationalism; depictions of racial 'difference'; and the ongoing demand for 'nice Canadian girls' to grace the cover. As the opening anecdote demonstrates, there was no consensus about what readers felt was appropriate for *Chatelaine*. Even male readers of *Chatelaine* waded into these discussions about gendered depictions and offered their conclusions – explicitly and implicitly – about cover material. F.W.L. of High Bluff, Manitoba, gave this thoughtful commentary in the early fifties: 'When I brought the July *Chatelaine* home, my wife looked at the cover and remarked, "What a vulgar picture!" Then I read the story of the teenagers in Kitchener and it occurred to me there might be a connection between pictures of that description and the rousing of the sex instinct.' In conclusion, he warned ominously, 'covers of this type will lessen your subscription list rather than increase it.'[17]

Floyd Allard, a teenager from Paddockwood, Saskatchewan, took an entirely different tack when he wrote to the editors to raise an innocent yet prescient question about the voyeuristic appeal of women 'looking' at other women on the covers: 'I like the cover picture on my mother's *Chatelaine*. But I wonder if girls enjoy looking at other girls – especially remodelled ones. Now take me. I'm not remodelled, just me. I'm not a man yet, but I'm getting there – and by golly I think the girls would like a picture of a man for a change. Personally, I think this one is pretty good. Of course if you don't, please return it as there are quite a few girls in school who wouldn't mind having it.'[18] Clare must have enjoyed a chuckle over Allard's question; he rewarded Allard's chutzpah by publishing the photograph in the editorial anecdotes inside the magazine.

Indicative of the changing times, male responses to *Chatelaine* covers in the sixties began to register disappointment, judging by this letter from Mrs Cynthia Ritchie of St John's: 'My husband is terribly disappointed with *Chatelaine* – to my amusement! Seeing "Prize-winning cheesecake" on the February cover, he quickly looked through the magazine. Almost as quickly he laid it down. "Wrong kind of cheesecake!" he grumpily commented.'[19]

The liveliest cover controversy involved *Chatelaine*'s decision to feature the infamous, scandal-plagued Hollywood actress Elizabeth Taylor on the cover of the July 1962 issue (illustration 3). Although tame by comparison with contemporary Hollywood imbroglios, Taylor's much-publicized affair with Debbie Reynolds's husband, Eddie Fisher, and the subsequent divorce and marriage, were considered scandalous. Readers from across the country were livid at *Chatelaine*'s decision to publish her photo on the front cover. From Moncton, Jennie L. Kennedy wrote: 'June Callwood's article on beauty ... is acceptable, but why did your magazine have to publish the cover picture of Elizabeth Taylor? This might be acceptable by readers of low-rated magazines, but adds no distinction to yours.'[20] The Taylor cover had debased the magazine, in Kennedy's opinion, from a respectable, middle-class journal to a 'low-rate' trashy tabloid. Others protested Taylor's Americanism and her failure to function as an appropriate role model for women. Mrs Elizabeth Saunders of Truro, NS, did not mince words: 'Surely there must be other subjects for the cover of a Canadian magazine than a homewrecker.'[21] From the west, Mrs T.H. Field of Edmonton pronounced the Taylor cover 'unworthy of your excellent magazine,'[22] while Mrs A.J. McDonald of Winnipeg concluded: 'She is a disgrace to womanhood.'[23] The most striking commentary about the 'values' behind the Taylor cover were expressed in a letter from 'A Shocked Reader,' who wrote: 'It was certainly in bad taste. Just when the old cow is moving for a fresh bull and stealing another woman's husband. It's too bad to condone legalized prostitution. Let her stay where she belongs.'[24] Mrs Eleanor M. Scott of Ottawa provides a valuable description of why she disliked this cover and how she resisted this case of editorial poor taste: 'I have subscribed to the *Chatelaine* since its earliest days ... But really, are you so hard up for covers as to sink so low as to have Elizabeth Taylor on the July issue!' As a concession to the demands of the market-

15¢

JULY 1962

CHATELAINE

Are you really a
good mother?

A NEW DIET
THAT W⊕RKS

Part II of the Eaton family's story

BEAUTY
does it always bring
UNHAPPINESS?

Elizabeth Taylor—typical of 11 unhappy

3 *Chatelaine* cover, July 1962

place, Scott offered a compromise. 'If you must have girls ... Think of all the nice looking, decent Canadian girls you could have or babies and children are always acceptable.' Her solution, she reported, was simple: 'I had to tear off the cover and put it in the waste basket and leave the magazine coverless, on the dining room table.'[25] Mrs Scott's age was undoubtedly a factor in her criticism, but other readers (who were either younger or did not identify their ages) also wanted the magazine to abandon its cover formula and to feature Canadians. The classist and nationalist tensions are evident – what might sell on the newsstands might shock subscribers. In the case of offensive material, readers could protest, but they could also physically remove the offending material or trash the magazine entirely. On the surface this act of resistance appears minor, yet Mrs Scott's action meant that the critically important advertising material was not reaching its audience.

While Elizabeth Taylor was an easy target, the challenges posed by depicting 'Canadian women' were a quagmire. In April 1960, for instance, *Chatelaine* featured a photo of a dramatically coifed and madeup brunette with the phrase, 'Is she a typical Canadian beauty?'[26] The photo was cropped so that only the head and shoulders of the naked model were visible, which made for a dramatic image (illustration 4). This portrait conveys a confidant female sexuality – the model looks directly at the reader instead of coyly averting her eyes. One can speculate about the degree to which art director Joan Chalmers's exposure to the artistic milieu her parents (Floyd and Jean Chalmers) supported and enjoyed, her training at the Ontario College of Art, and her lesbianism coalesced to produce this cover image.[27] It was supposed to highlight Eveleen Dollery's profile of a 'beauty' from each region of the country.

Reader commentary was scathing. Mrs Audrey Phillips of Ottawa wrote: 'If this cover appears outside Canada, the flow of immigrants to Canada will be set back fifty years. Can you honestly visualize the typical, average Canadian husband arriving home in suburbia and being met by this typical Canadian beauty, complete with rose?'[28] Mrs Guy Fortier of Montreal was even more outspoken: 'If looking like a squaw is your idea of looking Canadian, you have succeeded.'[29] The next month, A.I. Hainey of Beauharnois, Quebec, wrote: 'En garde! You have probably alienated all of your Quebec readers with that atrocious cover photo. We think you have depicted a really early-Quebec beauty – probably one of Pontiac's daughters.'[30] The racist tone of the negative letters are all the more disturbing because the 'elegant, femme du

4 *Chatelaine* cover, April 1960

monde' model was clearly identified within the text of the article as Jacqueline Gilbert, selected to 'epitomize French charm and glamour.'[31] In the fifties and sixties only three women who did not fit the racial stereotype of Anglo-Canadians, Americans, or British royalty made it onto the cover of the magazine (Gilbert, Native filmmaker Barbara Wilson in 1968, and Adrienne Clarkson in 1969), yet for many readers 'Canadian woman' was a narrowly defined category. Only two readers wrote supportive letters about the 1960 cover. Miss Ann Arthur Hitchcock of Cowansville, Quebec, wrote: 'Your Montreal reader ... has apparently forgotten that the true Canadian beauty would be an Indian.'[32] Meanwhile, pride was the motivating force from Mrs Henry Swig from Hagersville, Ontario: 'All she needs to do is come up to our Six Nations Reserve to see some of the best looking girls in Canada.'[33] Although a number of articles and editorials examined ethnic diversity in the country, or refugee issues, readers were not prepared to accept racial 'difference' as representative of Canadian beauty.[34] So, while the ethnic and racial composition of Canada was in the process of change owing to the waves of postwar immigration, most readers expected the editors to confirm their presumptions that the 'average' reader wanted an Anglo-Celtic female face on the cover.

Nationalism and pride in the Canadian landscape motivated some readers to request covers that profiled archetypal 'Canadian' scenes. This suggestion from J. Balint of Toronto was representative: 'Why, when you dare to be Canadian in content, when you stake your life as a publisher on the premise that Canadians care about themselves, do you continue to hide behind covers which, with their brassy and beatnicky wenches are about as Canadian as a herd of crocodiles? Give us our mountains and our forests, the light at Peggy's Cove, and the Peace Tower in Ottawa.'[35] Other readers wanted great Canadians and were most impressed when the magazine featured someone like Madame Vanier on the cover (illustration 5), but those issues were not commercial successes. Although the critics savaged the Taylor cover, the newsstand shoppers gobbled it up – an indication of the difficulty in creating, and successfully marketing, a mass-market women's magazine.

As the sixties reached its end, many readers criticized the models who, in retrospect, functioned as stereotypical icons of the decade with their mini dresses, hippie stylings, and 'mop' of tangled manes of hair. The magazine was obviously attempting to attract the youth market, and some of the established readers were resistant. Mrs J. MacArthur of Red Deer, Alberta, complained about the September 1969 cover, which

5 *Chatelaine* cover, March 1960

featured Joni Mitchell: 'September *Chatelaine* looks very good inside but the cover is nauseating. That mousy long hair is ugly and the girl herself is not even pretty. You should come west where there are really pretty girls.'[36] Mrs MacArthur was probably crestfallen when the editors pointed out that Mitchell was a westerner and she realized that her letter was published more for its unintentional humour than its criticism.

The controversies over *Chatelaine* covers illustrate the tensions between the commercial imperative to advertise the magazine to newsstand browsers and simultaneously to satisfy the long-time subscribers' demands for 'decent' Canadians. Covers were intended to be eye-catching advertisements for the magazine on the newsstands. They had to differentiate the magazine from American rivals and position it so that readers – Canadian women – knew it was a magazine for them. The emphasis on youthfulness and attractiveness had the primary goal of constantly refreshing the subscriber base with new, younger readers. The homogeneity of the cover models continued into the advertising pages, where images of young, suburban wives prevail.

The homogeneity of the images was carefully geared to attract the prime consumers because the commercial imperatives were the same: to sell magazines and, by extension, the products they advertised. In myriad ads that *Chatelaine* advertising executives placed in the Canadian advertising rate guide, *Canadian Advertising Rates and Data* (CARD), they consistently trumpeted the magazine's power to sell products. Although these advertisements were seldom subtle, the most blatant appeared in 1955, when Maclean Hunter announced, 'It's a fact *Chatelaine* Is Your *Best* Medium to Sell Women.' The text of the ad extolled the virtues of advertising in *Chatelaine*: 'More than three-quarters of a million women read *Chatelaine* for ideas on homemaking, cooking, grooming, and the answers to the many problems which homemakers face.' Commensurably, the ad reported, 'these women recognize that *Chatelaine* is designed for their needs and interests. They identify themselves with the material, both editorial and advertising, presented in *Chatelaine* ... When reading *Chatelaine*, they are keenly interested in products and services which can make them more efficient, more attractive, happier housewives. By advertising in *Chatelaine* you gain a select audience of alert, eager prospects who are interested and in the mood to buy ... and because of this they respond quickly to your sales message.'[37]

In the fifties, the *Chatelaine* CARD ads had promised advertisers that *Chatelaine* was the best medium 'to sell women.' A decade later, the advertising metaphors eschewed bold pronouncements in favour of more restrained, yet seductive, promises. In 1969, for instance, one advertisement in *CARD* teased, '*Chatelaine* is all woman: start an affair.' Instead of action and purchases, the advertisements began to stress the relationship between women and the magazine: '*Chatelaine* does more than reach a woman – it involves her. When a woman sits down to read *Chatelaine*, it's usually in a free moment when there are no demands on her time. It's a personal thing she doesn't have to share with the rest of her family. She's relaxed, receptive, in the right *frame of mind* to absorb information and new ideas ... *Chatelaine* touches every aspect of her life – from her point of view. We believe this environment, this rapport benefits advertisers. When a woman's in the right *frame of mind, share of mind*, and *share of market* can't help but follow' (emphasis in original).[38]

For all the advertising industry hype and hyperbole, the readers were often unimpressed. Reader Sheelage M. Sheeran, from Sherbrooke, Quebec, wrote to criticize the advertising and asked: 'Could you gloss things up just a little? On thumbing through this issue the advertisement for salmon is positively insipid – due entirely to poor colouring in the foreground. The setting is excellent. Libby's fruit cocktail is more attractive than is pictured here. Is the paper at fault? Is it not possible to make the coloured pictures more attractive?'[39]

The discrepancy between the confidant, seductive advertisements placed in *CARD* and the letter from Sheeran illustrates the difference between advertisement and reality, or between business exuberance and consumer shrewdness. Advertising copy writers who composed the *CARD* ads for *Chatelaine* began to use heterosexual metaphors to describe the relationship between advertiser and reader. Despite the men's club or locker-room bravado of some of the *CARD* advertisements – particularly apparent in their comments about the receptive and ready readers of *Chatelaine* – the heterosexual drama of the advertising pages is best understood not as conquest or defeat, but as seduction. The men had the financial and creative power to make and pay for the advertisements. Yet the women readers, accustomed to a constant barrage of attention, could avoid the ads, enjoy their visual and often humorous appeal, or plan future family purchases around them. The relationship was unequal, but it was not one sided. At some point, no matter how much attention, money, research, and planning went into an advertisement, it could still end up in the hands of an inattentive, uninterested reader who, for a variety of reasons, did not buy that product. Or, as Sheeran's letter indicates, it could easily be criticized and dismissed by the reader for its poor colouring, ugly presentation, and lack of verisimilitude. Scholars of advertising, both historical and contemporary, are divided about the effects of advertising, but all are unified in their belief that advertising promotes not reality, but a 'better world' for a 'better sort' of reader. According to advertising historian Roland Marchand, advertised images do not mirror reality, but offer consumers 'a Zerrspiegel, a distorting mirror,' that reflects the collective fantasies and dreams of the consumers rather than their day-to-day realities.[40]

In *Chatelaine* in this period, the language of advertising and the 'collective fantasies' uniformly depicted a comfortable world of middle-class consumption. The preferred image was that of the middle-class housewife who, in her role as the family's chief purchasing agent, bought, or influenced the purchase of, a vast number of consumer durables, food products, clothing, makeup, and children's supplies. Whatever the messages of other editorial sections of the magazine, the advertisements continued to depict women's roles very narrowly. Both Canadian and North American corporations used images to encourage women to consume their products. Since the importance and impact of the advertising lies not just in their attempts to sell products, but in the images they used to encourage consumption, a statistical and critical analysis of the advertising material found in *Chatelaine* magazine during the era will be the focal point of the section that follows. This decoding of ad content includes an examination of the major industries and brand names that advertised in *Chatelaine*; an analysis of the gendered images depicted; and the various themes, meanings, and codes that operated in the advertisements.[41]

Within the pages of *Chatelaine*, a wide array of products were advertised: food, children's merchandise, household cleansers, large and small appliances, clothing, beauty products, toiletries, cars, cigarettes, insurance, travel, drugs and medical products, stationery, and building and housing supplies, to name just a few of the most popular products on display. Of the products advertised, 91 per cent were nationally recognizable (although not always available) brand names. Some of the frequent advertisers in the magazine were Campbell's soups, Kraft food products, General Electric appliances, Swift's meat products, Noxzema skin cream, Heinz foods, Yardley fragrances and cosmetics, Avon cosmetics, Fleischmann's yeast, Listerine antiseptic, Simplicity patterns, Tex-made cottons, and Wabasso bedding. Despite the vast array of goods, products, and services advertised in the pages of

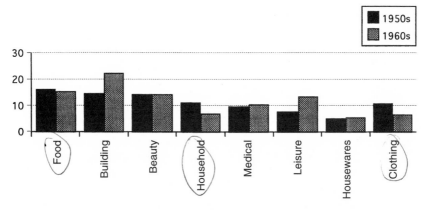

Figure 1   Products Advertised in *Chatelaine* in the 1950s and 1960s

Chatelaine, the vast majority of goods fell into the eight categories in figure 1.[42]

In addition to the shifts in the percentage of products advertised in the magazine, there were a number of differences between the fifties and the sixties. *Chatelaine* advertisements in the sixties had, to borrow a classic advertising cliché, a bold new look. They were larger, more colourful, and contained far fewer people than the comparable sample from the fifties. Advertisers may have believed that if no people were included in an advertisement, readers would be more inclined to insert themselves into the drama of consumption. The magazine continued to publish editorial and advertising material in what it referred to as a 50:50 ratio, though, in fact, 53 per cent of the periodical in both decades was devoted to advertising. The two most noticeable changes from one decade to the next were in the size of advertisements and in the greater use of colour. The number of full-page advertisements nearly doubled, to 30 per cent of all ads, while ads larger than one page accounted for a healthy 4 per cent.[43] There were considerably fewer one-eighth-page or smaller ads in the magazine.[44] Visually, this trend meant that the magazine was less claustrophobic. There were very few pages with numerous small ads, and lots of pages with only one advertisement. As advertisers spent more money to advertise in the periodical, it gained a more affluent look, for the smaller ads had always appeared thrifty and visually unappealing. The growth in full-colour advertisements (38%) and partial colour ads (10%) also added to the glossier, more affluent sixties' look. Even a black-and-white advertisement (52%) could appear more visually appealing if it was larger, more dramatic, or included more white space in its layout.

Layout of the ads also changed considerably, as the majority of advertisements were primarily graphics and illustrations (53%) or had an equal amount of graphics and text (26%).[45] The magazine altered the placement of ads, so that the first quarter of the magazine doubled the number of advertisements from its fifties' counterpart (18%), and the last quarter also had a greater number of ads (38%); the second quarter (13%) and third quarter (28%) had less advertising content than before. In other words, the magazine favoured a more modern type of ad placement – the majority of the ads appeared at the beginning and the end of the magazine, where the reader traffic was highest, while the least desirable advertising pages in the middle of the magazine were left for editorial. Finally, 48 per cent of the ads in the magazine contained no photographs or illustrations of people, but a variety of product shots.[46] These ads – usually just photographs or illustrations of the products or their packaging – were much less imaginative than those with people. Advertising studies of this era indicate that similar stylistic changes affected all periodical advertising in North America.[47]

Although the mixture of products was consistent throughout the era, noticeable changes in tone, cost, and reasons were touted for purchasing the products on display. The new products – in particular, diet products and pet food – and the increase in the number of ads for processed and convenience foods (11% of all ads in the magazine), wine and liqueurs (Canadian and foreign), British and European travel, European cheeses, and New Zealand lamb indicate that the magazine's advertising was moving upscale. Canadians had more discretionary income in the sixties. They were also more confidant that the economic boom would continue than they had been in the fifties, when fears of a postwar recession led to more cautious spending habits. Together, these factors were reflected in the greater range and cost of products advertised. In the *Chatelaine* ads, this affluence was linked with sophistication and greater leisure time.

The people who inhabited *Chatelaine*'s ad world remained remarkably consistent from one decade to the next. Most ads had only one (32%) or two (12%) people, although groups were not uncommon. Women – alone, in groups, and with children – were the stars of most *Chatelaine* advertisements. The popularity of male models increased, however, and they appeared with women, alone, or, less frequently, with children.[48] Youth, in this case interpreted as people in their twenties and late teens, were the select group, although the multigenerational grouping (predominantly parents with children) continued to be popular. Racially, the people depicted in advertisements continued to be very homogeneous (96% were white); only a handful of ads in either decade featured people of colour, and then they were usually trademarked product icons, such as Aunt Jemima. In terms of class, although there was a slight increase in the number of ads depicting working-class models (2.3%) and upper-class models (8.6%), the majority of people depicted in the *Chatelaine* ads were solidly middle class (73.26%). The majority of advertising dramas took place in the home, followed by 'play' or 'work' settings.

The narrow range of people represented in the advertisements – primarily white women (and men) in their twenties – was matched by their style of dress, appearance, mood, and body language. The clothing worn by advertising models in both decades tended to favour casual outfits, moderately dressy clothing, or business wear. However, there was a noticeable increase in the number of models wearing lingerie, or nothing at all, in the swinging sixties. Partially and totally nude models account for 13 per cent of all ads with people. Maternal images in advertisements dropped precipitously, while ads with sexual images (some quite graphic) increased.

In short, the ads featured in *Chatelaine* in the sixties were visually different from their dowdy predecessors in the fifties. The increased use of the full-page format, coupled with greater use of full-colour and partial-colour plates, resulted in a less parsimonious appearance. The ads were clustered at the front and back of the magazine, with far fewer sprinkled throughout the interior pages. Many featured only the product or its packaging. A far larger proportion of ads were for building supplies, while food advertisers were demoted to the second most popular product category advertised in the magazine. Likewise, leisure and travel products increased, while cosmetics, clothing, and housewares declined. The composition of ad-world people changed slightly to include more men, although they were most frequently accompanied by women, and sometimes children, but otherwise they were, as they had been in the fifties, mostly white, middle-class people. They were more sexual than they had been in the fifties, but in the campy, humorous, psychedelic way of the sixties: decorative blonde women, more stylish homes, or breezy, soft-focus shots of people at play or, less frequently, at work. The products, the campaigns, the models' clothing, and furnishings all bespoke greater affluence, more discretionary spending, and a desire to appear more sophisticated – capable of buying imported cheeses, making an 'ethnic' dish (from a pre-packaged mix, of course), serving an appropriate wine, or jetting off via Air Canada or Air Italia for a vacation in Europe. They were white, middle-class, Anglo-Canadians trying to live the *Chatelaine* version of 'the good life' – a Chef Boyardee spaghetti dinner, served with Bright's Manor St David's Claret, accompanied by a record from the Columbia Record Club, served on a linen tablecloth hand embroidered from a *Chatelaine* pattern.

The advertising statistics and summaries represent the overall trends in the era, but the trends obscure the numerous codes, messages, and images inherent in the individual ads. An analysis of some of the most compelling advertising fantasies points to issues that a pure content analysis often misses. The majority of ads were not worthy of distinction because they were straightforward, utilitarian presentations of products. Yet the more memorable ads were those that transcended the restrictions of the medium and grabbed the readers' attention, brought a smile to their faces, or lodged themselves in their memory. The examination of some of the ads that follows provides an analysis of their 'structure of meaning.'[49] According to Gillian Dyer, 'advertisements do not simply manipulate us, inculcate us or reduce us to the status of objects'; rather, 'they create structures of meaning which sell commodities not for themselves as useful objects but in terms of ourselves as social beings in our different social relationships.'[50] Through an examination of the various meanings, codes, dreams, and fantasies at work in these selected advertisements, we can better understand the world that confronted the *Chatelaine* reader and posit ways in which she mediated these messages.

'The Heart of the Home': Advertising the Fifties

Homemaker Supreme

One of the longest and most enduring ad campaigns to run in the magazine was a series from George Weston Ltd which paid tribute to 'the heart of the home.'[51] This distinctive series of advertisements ran from 1950 to 1954. These full-page, full-colour ads depicted various sentimental moments of the Canadian family, including daughter's graduation from high school, son's first job, and the Sunday family dinner. The second phase of this campaign, starting in 1954, depicted Canadian women outside the household. One ad featured women workers leaving the plant after their shift was over, while another featured a perky Atlantic Canadian wife, helping her husband haul in the fish nets. The illustrative style was reminiscent of Norman Rockwell's work. All the ads were bathed in warm tones, often pastel colours, denoting love, affection, and moments to remember. Although each ad had a different topic, the preferred message, which was explicitly stated in the ad copy, saluted Canadian women's work in the home with their husbands and family. A closer examination of two of these ads highlights the women's roles that Weston's felt compelled to salute.

'Her apron strings are "family ties"' featured an illustration of an attractive-looking woman, standing in her pink-and green kitchen, happily removing her apron before joining her family at the dining-room table (illustration 6).[52] The ad copy was extraordinary for its romantic ode to the Canadian wife and mother: 'Making her home a pleasant place to live is just one of many contributions made by the Canadian woman. For she is also a dietitian who plans good meals to keep her family fit for work or play ... a companion who shares in her family's pleasures and problems ... a nurse ever on call to care for her children's hurts ... a teacher who trains her children in good citizenship. In these and many other ways she is a one-woman business contributing vitally to the welfare of her family and the stability of Canada.' The preferred meaning, the meaning intended by the advertisers, could hardly be more overt. The Canadian woman's place was with her family.

Numerous covert codes were at work here: patriotism, the influence and importance of Canadian women, the professionalization of motherhood and housewifery, the business of the household, and, within the illustration, the codes of maternal love, family pride and happiness, and suburban contentedness. Everything would be all right if Mom was in the kitchen wearing her apron. This ad was a perfect example of the fifties' ad-world family: a middle-class suburban utopia with Mom in the kitchen, Dad carving the roast, and happy, well-adjusted Junior waiting for his dinner. This image is symbolic of much popular culture in the decade, and the preferred reading was intended to be positive.[53] This conception of women's roles was a good thing for women, their families, and the country. If one's family did not achieve this romanticized ideal, the tone of the ad copy, in particular, might have induced guilt in the wife and mother whose family did not fit this pattern. Whether one purchased Weston's products to reinforce a feeling of maternal pride or, conversely, to assuage maternal guilt, the ad was effective.

Her apron strings are "family ties"

The ties that hold a family together in loyalty
and affection start at a woman's "apron strings".

Yet making her home a pleasant place to live is just one
of many contributions made by the Canadian woman.

For she is also a dietitian who plans good meals to keep her family fit
for work or play . . . a companion who shares in her family's pleasures
and problems . . . a nurse ever on call to care for her children's hurts . . . a
teacher who trains her children in good citizenship.

In these and many other ways she is a one-woman business
contributing vitally to the welfare of her
family and the stability of Canada.

Weston's is proud that so many Canadian women are
valued Weston customers . . . . and that of its 5,025
shareholders about 45% are women.

And Weston's realizes that, to hold the confidence it has
enjoyed for over 65 years, it must constantly maintain the
highest quality in its products and so satisfy the exacting
standards of the Canadian woman.

"Always buy the best—buy Weston's"

G E O R G E   W E S T O N   L I M I T E D . . . C A N A D A

6 *Chatelaine*, November 1950

Superwoman

The second Weston's ad, 'One done ... One to go,' featured an illustration of women workers punching the time clock on their way home from work (illustration 7).[54] In this advertising fantasy, there were no tired, wornout workers. Their energy will stand them in good stead because, as the ad copy says, their family work day is just beginning: 'Five o'clock – one job done and one to go. Behind her is another day ... ahead is her home and family. For she is the modern wife whose skill and effort in office or plant is helping to build two big projects ... the Canadian Future and the Canadian Home.' Weston's has shrewdly tapped into and acknowledged women's increasing participation in the Canadian labour force from the mid-fifties onward. Again, the codes of patriotism, family, women's role, and women's service to the community ring loudly. But because she was modern, unlike our earlier woman who concerned herself only with her family, she gladly worked a double day. The staple of many ads to follow, particularly in the seventies, this Weston's ad portrayed the mythic superwoman, capable of handling all her family responsibilities as well as her job: 'Moments from now, the girl on the job will be transformed into the lady of the house. Out of the slacks or office suit ... and into a pretty house dress and fresh lipstick for a home-coming husband. These efficient hands will be flying in her very own kitchen, doing the jobs women love to do for their men ... fixing dinner ... picking up bits of mending ... whisking through a touch of ironing. And then ... the precious time of quiet sharing, as both dream of the future their present labours will make come true. The house they will own ... the garden they will tend ... the children they will educate and watch grow.'

According to Ellen McCracken, one of the typical techniques used by women's magazines, particularly in the advertising sections, was the 'transgressive and the forbidden, and then attempt to contain these elements by invoking dominant moral values.'[55] This ad fits her description perfectly, for it acknowledged women's work as something modern and different, and then incorporated it back into the familiar codes of household, family, marriage, and children. Women worked, according to Weston's, because they wanted consumer durables, the middle-class dream of a house, children, and a garden. Although not stated, the ad implied that married women's work was only temporary. As well, the code of femininity was particularly strong in this ad, assuring the reader that a woman who worked outside the home need

7 *Chatelaine,* June 1954

not be any less feminine than the housewife. Finally, the ad stressed that women's work, far from being personally fulfilling, emancipating, or necessary, was really in service of home and country: 'Canada is a working country ... and women stand side by side with their men to see that the work is done. It's a fine system, and a democratic one. And the not-so-silent partner helps her husband hold the line on both fronts. This is the way a family grows ... and with such families Canada reaches new horizons of happiness and achievement.'[56] Regardless of her working status, the wife was what she had always been – a help-mate to her husband. An alternate reading to this preferred meaning could make wives who did not work outside the home feel guilty about shirking their duty to family and country. Linking employment with democracy might have resulted in some very different interpretations of this ad.

The Mechanized Household

The various codes at work in these Weston's ads can be summarized as the super-motif of 'Mom Knows Best – and that's why she buys —.' It was a recurring motif in countless food ads, ranging from Kraft products, Campbell's soups, Ovaltine beverage, Coca-Cola, Sunkist oranges, and children's products. A large part of the advertising rhetoric of the fifties declared that the housewife and mother was proficient because the manufactured products she used had taken much of the labour and a large part of the guess-work out of running the household. Nowhere was this theme more apparent than in the ads for appliances and general household items. This code in the advertisements contrasted with the editorial service material (see chapter 5), which stressed the skill homemakers required to run their households effectively. The departmental features blended consumption and practical educational themes, while the ads emphasized solely the fulfilment and leisurely ease offered by purchasing a range of new appliances, cleansers, and convenience food products.

Canadian Westinghouse, in a garish, predominately blue, green, and purple advertisement, proclaimed in January 1953, 'You can enjoy Complete Freedom from Work on Washday' (illustration 8).[57] Once again, the advertisers portrayed the utopian middle-class household run by appliances, in which women were the monitors or 'bosses,' not the workers. This scenario made a very appealing fantasy for house-wives still stuck in the dark ages of laundry. However, another by-

8 *Chatelaine,* January 1953

product of this ad genre was the increased expectations and household or personal perfectionism that this freedom implied. If the family's laundry required little energy, then other uses could be made of the day – more house cleaning, more beauty regimes, or more volunteer work. Although the ad did not explicitly tell readers what they could do with their time, it was one of the few ads to link reduced hours spent in pursuit of a perfect house with leisure or relaxation. In most cases the found hours were linked to more time spent with children.

General Electric was also fond of this motif. Many of its ads for appliances, large and small, featured the theme of freedom from work through purchase of appliances. One particularly bizarre ad for a vacuum cleaner sported the subtitle, 'You do so little ... your G-E cleaner does so much' (illustration 9).[58] The graphic on this ad featured a large illustration of the vacuum. A typical suburban living room occupied the middle of the ad. The housewife was illustrated vacuuming the floor, and six cutouts indicated her vacuuming the curtains, the furniture, the paintings, the bookshelves, the tiles, and the lampshades. As was always the case with vacuums and floor polishers, the illustrations depicted a limp-wristed hold on the appliance, indicating either that the woman was floating along behind the cleaner or that it required little exertion. The startling part of this equation was that you could 'clean a whole room without once moving the cleaner!' While the preferred reading was freedom from work, or at least ease of use, this army of cutout and real women, tied to the vacuum cleaner, was also household perfectionism at its apex. This product that promised freedom from work actually encouraged vacuuming areas that, with other more cumbersome cleaners, would have been done only a few times a year. As readers of the *Chatelaine* service material well knew, this sort of fastidious house cleaning took a vast amount of time and energy.

Tools of Romance and Marital Bliss

By the end of the fifties there was an increasing emphasis on romance to sell a host of 'unromantic' products. As with all the ads in this genre, while the copy and graphics were confidently enthusiastic about the product and what it could do for the reader, they were also classic advertising fantasies. They created excitement about products in which the novelty quickly faded and the promise of revolutionized existence never materialized.

One of the most effective ways advertisers found to sell appliances

9 *Chatelaine*, April 1954

and housewares was to link them with weddings and bridal showers. Given the spate of young marriages, and the booming number of marriages in Canada, this was a timely motif for advertisers. In the world of these ads, love, marriage, and consumption were merged; many advertisements depicted wedding receptions where the wedding party stood blissfully, surrounded by the spoils of matrimony – the wedding gifts. Ads for Bissell sweepers, Community cutlery, and GE appliances aptly illustrated the code of marital consumption. A full-colour back-cover advertisement, 'She's in love ... and she loves Community,' featured a three-quarter-page illustration of a dreamy-looking brunette gazing out at the reader while visions of cutlery float through her head (illustration 10).[59] Employing an intimate, conversational tone, the ad confided: 'Ann's a lot like you. With a head full of dreams these days, but plenty of common sense, too. That's why she made up her mind to have all the silverware she needed, right from the start.' Oneida isn't selling just silverware here, but a dream of marital happiness, fantasies of the perfect life available to all young brides who 'buy all the silverware they need.' With names such as 'White Orchid,' 'Lady Hamilton,' and 'Coronation,' the ad made allusions to royalty, to a life of ease and happiness. Furthermore, many *Chatelaine* readers could afford the fantasy because this was affordable affluence – silver-plated flatware, not sterling silver.

Even more mundane household items, such as Bissell sweepers, used the marital, bridal, and love motifs to make their products seem an indispensable part of young marrieds' existence. In one ad a bride triumphantly holds her Bissell as her groom carries her over the threshold of their home (illustration 11). In addition, 'Give the Bride a Bissell Sweeper' featured a jaunty jingle to accentuate the value for money inherent in the product: 'Keeps rugs spick/Keeps home span/A Bissell helps her keep that man!'[60] The price – a mere $9.45 – was affordable for all but penurious budgets.

Perhaps the most glaring example of the bridal shower motif was the General Electric ad entitled 'The Right Gift for a Special Occasion' (illustration 12).[61] In this full-page black-and-white entry, the ad makers have presented an image of the wonders of marriage, all those new appliances that will 'make someone's life so much easier and happier – for years.' But look closely. Is the bride ecstatic or overwhelmed? Are those squeals of delight or a scream of terror? Are those shop window-panes or is our bride imprisoned behind a wall of appliances? The ridiculousness of many of these images, particularly for the large com-

10 *Chatelaine,* October 1953

11 *Chatelaine*, May 1954

12 *Chatelaine*, May 1954

ponent of *Chatelaine* readers who were already married, could readily undercut the romanticized version of marital happiness.

The Good Life in Suburbia

One overarching theme emerges from *Chatelaine* ads – the allure of the 'good life' in the suburbs. That drama was re-enacted in countless ads, but one Aunt Jemima ad is representative of the genre. 'Wake up, Henry! ... It's time for Sunday "Brunch"' showcased Dad's role in suburban family fun (illustration 13).[62] All the requirements are here: energetic kids, a dapper Dad, and a Mom prepared to orchestrate (and clean up) all the 'shakin' and flippin'.' In the *Chatelaine* ads, 'shaken not stirred' did not refer to the popular, macho film world of James Bond but to a domesticated dandy at ease with instant pancake mix. This family fun motif was employed quite often to jazz up otherwise basic products. The intended message was that the happy-looking housewife and mother bought not only the pancake mix but a weekly instalment of family playtime, a much-earned rest from meal preparation. Although Dads made infrequent appearances into the world of *Chatelaine* advertisements, when they did they were usually depicted as clean-cut, genial fellows who found delight in their families and their consumer durables.

Food manufacturers were not the only ones to sell their products by pushing suburban happiness. The manufacturers of building and decorating products employed this motif most of the time as well. However, they were also most likely to use affluent settings, imagery, or themes to sell their products. Home renovation and building were the ultimate dream or fantasy ads because they promised a perfect house and, when the husbands were included, passionate togetherness. The ad 'When a floor is Amtico Vinyl Flooring' featured a couple dressed in formal evening wear, dancing on their new product.[63] Half the ad was devoted to a full-colour photo of the flooring, but adjacent to the dancing couple, who were gazing rapturously into each other's eyes, were the words, 'A floor is moonlight ... and romance ... and beauty.' Other Amtico patterns, 'Renaissance' and 'Gleaming Stardust,' also promised to add romance to a marriage. The implied message was that any size of Amtico flooring in a house would be a ballroom inviting a wife and her husband out onto the dance floor. Interestingly, the production values in the building supplies' advertisements were usually higher than in many of the other products advertised. These advertisers most often

13 *Chatelaine,* September 1958

employed full-colour ads to make their products more appealing. Copper pipes, linoleum flooring, cedar shingles, and household furnaces were expensive and complicated products to buy, so advertisers strove to emotionalize them as much as possible. The reception of the Homes features in the late fifties and sixties, and the declining number of advertisers for these features, are evidence that the home and building product manufacturers were not getting a good response to their *Chatelaine* ads (see chapter 5).

The Craft of Femininity

While most of the products were pitched at women as consumers for the family, the ads for women's clothing, cosmetics, and toiletries were directed at the individual woman. These ads always employed the themes of self-improvement or the cult of youthfulness, and highlighted insecurities about body appearances or hygiene. These products used the hard sell: they told women they could not live without these products, or, if they did, their social lives, marriages, and self-worth would be jeopardized. Whether in the Noxzema ads ('Which of these skin problems spoils your *appearance*?'), the Listerine ads ('Why he left so early'), or Yardley's ('Makes you feel so fresh and feminine'), the code was feminine improvement (illustration 14). According to the ad makers, successful women (and success here was defined in terms of appearance, shape, youthfulness, and scent) owed their results to various perfumes, deodorants, soaps, or mouthwash.[64] Many of the ads for cosmetics and toiletries did not feature photographs of women, but included illustrations that were more easily manipulated to depict idealized versions of femininity. Most insidiously, the Yardley ads featured a china doll as their example of true femininity. The majority of the ads for women's clothing were advertisements for foundation garments, girdles, corsets, brassieres, and hosiery. In the fifties, the hourglass shape and cinched styles of women's clothes, made famous by Christian Dior, required most women to wear an assortment of uncomfortable products designed to shape, slim, 'lift and separate.' Readers knew from experience that these garments tended to be torturous, but the demands of 'the look' left them vulnerable to the unlikely claims of the designers' misogynistic vision of women's bodies. A leading male fashion designer promised that the 'invisible' girdles that 'let you feel ... *free*' allowed the natural you to shine while controlling or hiding other problem areas (illustration 15).[65]

14 *Chatelaine*, March 1958

15 *Chatelaine*, September 1953

The True North

Finally, one code, that of Canadian values or Canadiana, deserves mention. Many advertisements used photographs or illustrations of the outdoors, usually the domesticated view from the cottage, but often more rugged illustrations of mountains, rivers, and lakes, which linked products with the purity of the country. Similarly, there was a down-to-earth style to some of the ads that differentiated them from the more glossy, American images. This distinction was particularly clear in the ads for family clothing, featuring flannels, plaids, or printed cloth with outdoor motifs, or in ads where families cozily huddled around the recreation-room fireplace. One ad, for Mary Maxim hand-knit sweater patterns, proclaimed, 'For warmth and comfort there's nothing like a handknit ... sweater!' (see illustration 16).[66] The sweater names – Hoedown, Wolf, Fleur de lis, Oil Derrick, and Holstein Cow – identified the product as Canadian. Although improbably staged, the people in this ad looked more like genuine people than professional models. These products presumed that housewives and mothers had the skill, time, and free labour to create these affordable but labour-intensive garments. Such ads displayed an earnestness and lack of sophistication or artifice that seemed particularly Canadian. Of course, it may also have been an issue of finances and an inability to produce as slick an advertising campaign as the larger corporations. In the sixties, the ad-world image was slicker and more sophisticated.

'Does She or Doesn't She ...': Advertising the Sixties

Mom Knows Best

Food advertisers relied on two motifs to encourage consumption of their products: they linked the product with an emotional appeal to the housewife and mother about the importance of her role or they stressed the novelty of their product – its ease of use and quick preparation, or the latest solution for mealtime ennui. In 1965 Magic Baking Powder ran a simple yet powerful advertisement that featured a contented-looking blonde woman, half a page of text, and a mouth-watering chocolate cake sitting beside a tin of the product. The title read: 'Baking is a simple thing. Yet women who bake get three kinds of joy.'[67] The ad makers appealed to women's craft pride, their pleasure in preparing foods for their family, and their femininity: 'The joy of seeing how the

447 Hoedown   482 Outer Space   483 Choo-choo Train   449 Wolf   486 Fleur de lis   448 Golf   445 Oil Derrick   484 Hoedown   446 Holstein Cow

for warmth and comfort there's nothing like a handknit *Mary Maxim* sweater!

Striking, colorful design—wears beautifully—so reasonable in cost—that's a *Mary Maxim* sweater! You'll find the pattern grows under your fingers like magic—just a few rows work into inches of sweater. Perfect for winter sports and casual wear the year 'round. Knit these from *Mary Maxim* patterns specially created for *Mary Maxim* 4 ply Northland and Cloudspun wools.

Mary Maxim graph style patterns are so simple to follow! You see every stitch to be knit in all sizes. There are patterns for every member of the family from 4 to 44. Each pattern only 25c.

Miss Mary Maxim

Paris, Ontario
Dauphin, Manitoba

Send to your nearest branch for your FREE 24-page color catalogue TODAY!

Miss Mary Maxim   Dept. CH-4 \ Paris, Ontario
or
Dept. CH-4 \ Dauphin, Manitoba

Please send me your FREE NEW 24-page catalogue, wool samples, and information on knitting Mary Maxim sweaters.

Name (print)

Address

City _____ Zone ____ Prov. ____

American knitters send to
Dept. CH-4 \ Box 205, Port Huron, Michigan

16 *Chatelaine,* September 1958

family loves the good things you make. The pride when guests are frankly impressed. And a subtle, very feminine feeling ... something to do with a womanly art, a caring about people, a homeyness.' The 'feminine feeling' might be subtle, but advertisers were not as they went right for the emotional jugular vein. 'Baking is simple' creates the impression that women who did not bake were uncaring and unfeminine, and that their households lacked the warmth of a bake oven. In short, housewives who eschewed baking had not created homes. To help women get back into the swing of the 'womanly art,' they provided the recipe for Magic Mocha Cake – a tested recipe. Food, and its preparation, was equated with maternal love, pride, and nutritional concerns. There was little concern for the labour-intensiveness of cooking. Fleischmann's Yeast, for instance, regularly included recipes in its advertisements that required half a day to create. Despite the ever-increasing number of women entering the workforce, food advertisements stuck to their traditional version of Canadian women – the full-time, stay-at-home wife and mother who had both the time and the inclination to spend hours in the kitchen to demonstrate her love, abilities, and womanly arts for her family and friends.

The increase in the amount of processed food advertised in the magazine produced a contradictory message to the slogan 'Baking is simple.' Here the ads emphasized ease of use, speed of preparation, and guaranteed perfection. These advertisers also touted the nutritional value of their products to allay fears that they were not quite as good as meals made from scratch. Although it seems natural that advertisers would link these products with images of working women, particularly since this group was most in need of quick mealtime solutions, they never did. Instead, they linked processed food products with successful mothering, more time to spend with family, or standardized food that appealed to all members of the family. The mania for processed and ready-made food products was huge in this era – a time when Swanson TV dinners and an assortment of processed foods made their supermarket debut. Even though such foods were supposed to save women time, Kraft and other corporations presented recipes that included these products in casseroles, fondues, spaghetti dinners, cookies, and desserts. This alternative was suggested to assuage women's guilt for using processed food products, and not, as the Magic Baking Powder ad instructed, preparing their families' meals from scratch. Cake mixes, for instance, omitted dried egg powder from their ingredients to permit housewives to add a real egg to the mixture, thus preserving the impression that they were actually 'making' the product.[68] Women were 'creating' meals with these prepared products, though in far less time than they had from scratch. In 1968 Kraft ran a series of ads for Velveeta Cheese which touted its nutritional value by depicting young athletes and the woman behind their success – their mothers. One version of this ad deserves commentary for its unconventional imagery. The ad copy proclaimed, 'Behind every successful little girl is a mother who serves Velveeta,' accompanied by a photograph of a proud mother and daughter, dressed in her baseball uniform and holding her glove and bat.[69] Given the conservative nature of most advertising material, this untraditional image was guaranteed to catch the reader's eye. The rest of the ad featured the recipe entitled 'Big League Casserole' – Velveeta, milk, green pepper, Parkay Margarine, potatoes, and frankfurters – a quintessentially American meal calculated to appeal to children.

Dieting Dramas

The sixties ushered in a fixation with body image, weight, and fad diets. This obsession made way for a new product category that combined food producers with medical or chemical companies to create diet products. In the fifties, in contrast, *Chatelaine* beauty features had profiled women who 'cut back' to 1500 calories a day. The new ads were not coy. Slim-Mint Gum proclaimed 'Don't Be Fat!' while an ad for 'Miss C's Diet Book,' complete with dancing anorexic teenage girls on the cover, asked mothers, 'Is your daughter overweight?'[70] Metrecal, the new American diet drink, ran a series of ads in the early sixties. One featured a Toronto legal clerk named Hilda Lang, a former model, who was 'turning her dainty hand to such seemingly unglamourous chores as searching titles and serving writs.'[71] Few women worked in the *Chatelaine* advertisements, and those who did were usually in traditional female jobs. Still, the advertisers patronizingly applauded women like Lang, who toiled in the pink-collar clerical ghetto, for attempting what they labelled 'non-traditional' work. Although Lang was identified as slim (5 foot 5, 109 pounds), she was meticulous (today we would consider it obsessive) about keeping her weight down because she 'still knows the value of a slim figure. She knows she works better and feels better when she's not carrying any extra weight and an active social life makes it clear that her lack of excess pounds has the approval of a number of young men.' The link between thinness, greater sociability, better careers, and personal well-being was repeated in virtually all the diet-product advertisements.

Most diet advertisements used the dual prongs of wish fulfilment and scare tactics, offering readers images of the thin 'good life' or frightening phrases to propel the complacently overweight into a weight-loss regime. Some of the scare-tactic ads could rebound and offer readers silly and amusing ads. Ads featuring women enduring the drama of zipping up their too-small party dresses could be read as terrifying or as humorous foibles about human nature. Sometimes diet products offered readers intentionally funny ads, such as the one in 1967 for Aylmer Diet Fruit Cocktail which asked, 'Why be a martyr on cottage cheese?' (illustration 17).[72] The woebegone look on the model's face is meant to catch attention. The melodramatic expression, complete with mascara tear lines under her eyes, is hilarious – a spoof of the spartan regimes that encouraged women to eat cottage cheese salads at lunch hour. This ad, and others, mock diet advertisements and encourage readers to question both the practice and the products – the ridiculous toll effected by the starving, restrictive diets and fad products.

The clothing advertisement along with the fashion and beauty department features, also focused attention on body image, which in these ads meant the 'correct look.' Once again, the largest advertisers of women's clothing in *Chatelaine* were for foundation garments – bras and girdles – followed by Kitten and Acrilan sweaters (polyester clothing was one of the 'space age' discoveries of the sixties), dresses and pantsuits, and Jantzen swim and leisure wear. Unlike the fifties, which had offered fairly conventional, if silly, images of women in bras, girdles, and controlling underwear cavorting around, the sixties' ads were dramatic and overtly misogynistic. A 1960 'Distinction' ad, for instance, depicted a sexily clad model wearing a blue bra, girdle, and satin pumps standing surrounded by five other women dressed in full-length black negligees preparing to plunge swords into her back (illustration 18). The byline states: 'Now *Europe* gives you a figure so beautiful ... other women will hate you!'[73] Like many ads for food, cosmetics, furniture, and building supplies, the Distinction ad emphasized ethnicity as a way to make its product appear more sophisticated and appealing. The overt meaning of the ad used the sexist message that women are, by nature, competitors for the attention of men, and that body image, appearance, and male approval (unacknowledged but implied) are all important. In contrast to the feminism evident elsewhere in the

Why be a martyr on cottage cheese...

when you can have Diet De Luxe fruit meringues instead?

There's something pretty grim about making do with cottage cheese when your sweet tooth longs for something gooey. So why make yourself miserable when Aylmer Diet De Luxe allows you to have Fruit Cocktail meringues and cut calories too!

You see, Diet De Luxe packs Fruit Cocktail that contains one-half or less the calories of sugar-packed varieties (½ cup serving Diet De Luxe Fruit Cocktail—42 calories, regular—101) because Diet De Luxe is sweetened with Sucaryl® instead of sugar. Yet we're sure you'll love the fresh fruit taste! Diet De Luxe packs 36 kinds of fruit, fruit drinks, spreads, dessert toppings and pickles—all equally low in calories.

Just remember, to lose weight and keep it off, you'll really have to start a new calorie-reduced way of life. Diet De Luxe just helps you do it without giving up a lot of good food.

Diet De Luxe isn't magic, but it sure makes nice things, like Fruit Cocktail meringues possible. Give it a try!

Fruit Meringues
4 medium size meringue shells
1—15 fl. oz.* (or 14 fl. oz.*) can Diet De Luxe Fruit Cocktail, drained
½ pt. vanilla ice-milk dessert (calorie-reduced ice-cream)

Fill each meringue shell with ¼ cup vanilla ice-milk. Top with Diet De Luxe Fruit Cocktail. Serves 4. Calories per serving—approximately 221.

For free calorie-reduced recipes and menu suggestions, please write to: Canadian Canners Ltd., 44 Hughson St. S., Hamilton, Ont.

*There is no difference in can size. New Government regulations require minimum fluid ounces to be shown. This size of can may show either declaration for a time.

What a way to cut calories!

MAY 1967

17 *Chatelaine*, May 1967

18 *Chatelaine*, October 1960

periodical, or even the more general ethos of 'women's culture' at *Chatelaine*, appearance, in the clothing ads, is women's key asset in their predestined role – to find a man.

Blondes Have More Fun

Beauty products – cosmetics, toiletries, and depilatories – were dominated by hair-colouring products, dramatic new eye makeups, and depilatory creams. General cold creams, moisturized soaps, and moisturizing lotions were still advertised, but they were not as prominent as they were in the fifties. In the sixties, the inside front cover of almost every issue of *Chatelaine* was devoted to Miss Clairol products. These ads were remarkably consistent, and the May 1961 ad was representative. This full-page advertisement featured an attractive, well-coifed redhead and her baby lying on a blanket on the grass, presumably taking a nap after a picnic lunch. The photograph is cropped, so all that is visible are the woman's and the child's head. The trademark phrases of these advertisements in both the United States and Canada was the suggestive 'Does she or doesn't she?'[74] In this example, and in all cases in *Chatelaine*, the sexual pun of the phrase was undercut by the presence of children. So too was the intent – to make hair colour respectable, something that married, middle-class women might use, as opposed to the previous notion that only women of disrepute 'coloured' their hair. The ad copy explains why this young woman has decided to give herself a new look by changing her hair colour: 'Happy young mothers always look beautiful. But *she* has something special. A fresh, shining quality, an endearing warmth and radiance. See how her hair sparkles with life!'[75] The makeup and beauty products always promised that women would look younger and that they would improve on their natural assets. Month after month, these ads appeared beside Anderson's editorial essay, which this month was entitled 'Being feminine is not enough.' Reading *Chatelaine* meant learning to negotiate these jarring juxtapositions with ease, for the feminist or intellectually challenging articles were often surrounded or punctuated by ads that were the antithesis of everything they advocated.

Forever Young

Most of the ads for hair colouring and creams guaranteed to ward off the onset of wrinkles, and some forms of makeup repeatedly linked their products with youthfulness. The standout advertisement for Nivea Creme was a full-page ad featuring a naked, blonde baby girl smearing the product over her legs and stomach (illustration 19).[76] The phrase 'Most English girls start using Nivea at a very early age' drew the reader into the textual explanation about the famed English complexion. Doubtless the intention of the ad makers was for the advertisement to be decoded as cute – baby gets into mother's creme and makes a mess – but there is another, disturbing undertone. The phrase 'It can't work miracles' suggests that a woman is never too young to start protecting herself against the ravages of aging. Furthermore, by visually depicting the standard of youthfulness as the unwrinkled, perfect skin of an infant, the image was guaranteed to make even a teenager look 'old' and in need of commercial assistance. The definition of youth was a highly malleable one, ever changing to suit the needs of the advertisers, who portrayed younger women using creams, hair colourings, and makeup, and suggested that, by the mid-twenties, the battle against 'looking old' had begun in earnest. Whether women purchased these products or not, the message of the ads was clear – and constant repetition made them nearly impossible to avoid.

Sex Sells

Besides youthfulness, the beauty and toiletries ads placed considerable emphasis on sexuality. Although it is not surprising that cosmetics and beauty products would employ sexuality as a major theme in their advertisements, many other product areas also began, increasingly, to rely on the 'sexual sell' to hone their commercial message. Whereas advertisers in the fifties had portrayed the world of housewares as tantalizing products that signified marital happiness, in the sixties they adopted sexuality and affluence as their two chief advertising codes. Representative of this new-found emphasis were advertisements for Tex-Made sheets, which provide evocative examples of both codes, along with the peculiarly sixties' style of advertising with respect to colour and the use of fantastical images.

   In the fall of 1962 and the spring of 1963 the magazine ran a series of ads from Tex-Made called 'Lo and behold! Fashion invades your bedroom in Tex-Made Sheets!' (illustration 20).[77] These ads featured a sultry-looking brunette wrapped, ball-gown style, in a Tex-Made sheet that the ad copywriters had coyly called 'the evening dress of the year.' The ad and the copy seem most calculated to appeal to men. The

19 *Chatelaine*, September 1965

Lo and behold! Fashion invades your bedroom in Tex-Made Sheets!
(...it's the evening dress of the year for under $5)

Revealed...Tex-Made Sheets in new high-key colors! Eleven vivid colors including orchid, pumpkin, lemon, limelight and peacock! And the second most beautiful thing about Tex-Made Sheets is long wear! Each sheet has extra threads for strength, extra inches for length. That means after hundreds of washings (years and years of use) a Tex-Made still looks good as new. Wear the evening dress of the year for under $5. A Tex-Made Sheet in brilliant new high-key colors...made *right* here in Canada! Dominion Textile Co., Ltd., 1950 Sherbrooke St., W., Montreal, Quebec.

THE MOST FASHIONABLE BEDS IN CANADA WEAR

TEX-MADE
SHEETS

Chatelaine • January 1963

20 *Chatelaine,* January 1963

woman sports a seductive smile, but, perhaps most important, her 'gown' was both affordable and engineered to come off quickly. For heterosexual women readers, the ad's appeal lay in its fantasy value – imagining the impression they would make on their husbands or boy-friends when wrapped in Tex-Made's 'orchid, pumpkin, lemon, lime-light and peacock' sheets. The ad is also humorous, and readers un-doubtedly laughed at the absurdity of the woman's pose and predica-ment, perhaps imagining their own discomfiture in such an ensemble.

Biology is Destiny

At mid-decade, Tex-Made employed the codes of affluence and the biologically determined interests and passions of women in an eye-catching advertisement called 'Since the dawn of time' (illustration 21).[78] This dramatic ad, a series of photographs against a black backdrop, traced the evolution of women's bedrooms from the cave-dwelling era to the present. Although the bed furnishings evolve – the cave woman sleeps on fur, while the modern woman chooses Tex-Made – that is the only real change. 'Since the dawn of time, women have adorned the place they sleep in. Women haven't changed ... a bit. Bedrooms have. Thanks to Tex-Made, today's woman can adorn her bedroom in a thousand pretty ways.' Complementing the ahistorical nature of the advertisement, the ad's creators employed a Eurocentric gaze, so that the 'cave woman' and the 'modern woman' were both white-skinned brunettes. Finally, the company revealed that 'with Tex-Made, you can change your mind, change your mood, change your bedroom, week after week, after week.' This patronizing, sexist tone was often employed in *Chatelaine* ads in the sixties: women were por-trayed as gorgeous yet vacuous souls whose chief interests were fash-ion. Fashion became a catch-all phrase that had less to do with clothing styles and more with being up to date on the latest marketing crazes – colours, styles, decorations, makeup, hairstyle, and so on. 'Fashion' in bed linens and other household items was one of the ways that market-ers promoted conspicuous consumption. Planned obsolescence through 'fashion' changes taught consumers that they must never be satisfied, never rest, lest they or their houses appeared dated and unmodern. In striving to create visually appealing advertisements that would catch the reader's attention, the ad makers often offered vapid, sexist, patron-izing images of women.[79] This analysis is, of course, in retrospect. Given the images of the sixties – particularly from Hollywood – of the

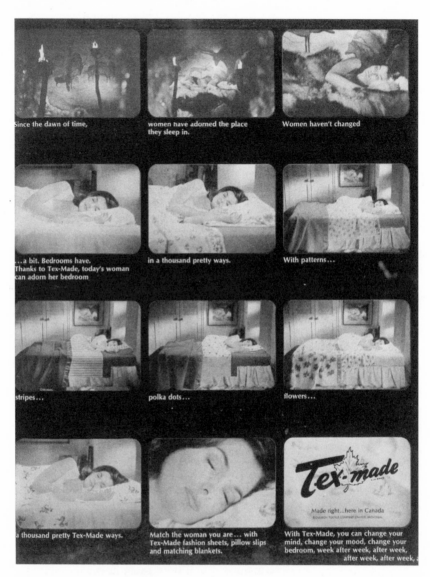

21 *Chatelaine,* January 1966

'dumb blonde' (Goldie Hawn on *Laugh-In*), the Bond girls from the movies, and the vacant-eyed look of the British fashion models Jean Shrimpton and Twiggy, the *Chatelaine* ads are in step with their cultural milieu.

'Husband-Coaxing' Ads

Similar in product type and nature to the housewares advertisements were the largest group of ads in the magazine – building supplies. These ads, for products as diverse as carpeting, copper pipe, air conditioners, paint, and other materials for home renovators, also employed the codes of affluence, sexuality, and fashion, and often included patronizing or sexist imagery and text to help 'sell' their products. In the sixties, as the Tex-Made advertisements illustrate, an explosion of colour, and fanciful names for those colours, really captured the enthusiasm of manufacturers and consumers alike. Avocado green bathroom fixtures, harvest gold washing machines, and mauve walls were all the rage. As the list from this McClary refrigerator ad for 'the Refrigerator of the Future' indicates, fashion colours were appearing everywhere: 'available in white, palomino, coppertone, avocado, and as illustrated, verd antique.'[80] These names and colours seemed new and exciting, and tapped into desires for a more affluent, cosmopolitan style of living.

All building supplies advertisements were targeted at couples. Even if the initial reader was a woman, the ad was structured in such a way that, when she 'showed it to him,' as countless ads instructed readers to do, he (the husband) would find the ad appealing. These advertisements usually depicted couples, if they featured any people, and often included some material of interest to men – humour, deprecatory remarks about women's passions for household renovation, or technical information about the type of product advertised. An ad for International Paints proclaimed: 'Behind every "Man in the Home" (the name of *Chatelaine*'s model house at Expo 67) there's a woman who has her heart set on Interlux paints.'[81] Since these were large-ticket items, or involved considerable work, women were expected to require their husband's agreement and his money, although the inspiration and influence of the purchase was hers alone. The central drama of many of these ads featured the poor, tired-out husband being pestered by his wife to renovate. Product manufacturers were in a dual role: to provide enough information and excitement about their products to get women interested, and to instruct them in the art of persuading recalcitrant hubbies to read the ad. At the same time, these ads managed to stress the things supposedly held dear by men – affordability, technical issues, design, and ease of installation or operation. Women had the influence and the persistence, while men were the arbitrators and holders of the cheque book.

A wonderful example of this often humorous style of advertising was the four-page, full-colour Domtar ad placed in the September 1965 issue of *Chatelaine*. The first page featured a photograph of a resigned husband, in his shirtsleeves, with the caption: 'Okay *Chatelaine*. I'm impressed. And so's the wife. But how can we fit that dream palace into our plans?'[82] The exasperated, grudging look on his face implied that the magazine's special Expo house and the advertising featured had worn him down. At long last, even he was interested in duplicating these new ideas at home. The next two pages featured the husband looking over a variety of Domtar products – tiling, wood panelling, brick work, and other supplies. By the last page of the ad the scepticism and grudging interest have metamorphosed into excitement: the husband is pictured smiling, while his ecstatic wife stands behind him. Beside the couple, the ad copy read: 'P.S. An aside to impatient wives. Need a little extra something to get that man of yours moving on these Domtar ideas for your home? Just mail the coupon and we'll speed back a package of colorful brochures ... that'll really get him off and running. Or our name isn't Domtar.' Women were, in many of the building supply ads, the manipulators behind their husband's wallets: they had the ideas and brought the ads to his attention, while he was the one who either purchased the product or not. By these means the company skilfully negotiated the often contradictory motives and interests ascribed to husbands and wives. In practice, this distinction often meant that women in the building ads were portrayed as overly excited housewives, eager dreamers who had little difficulty in conjuring up the latest 'fashions' in carpeting, wallpaper, or paint and in manipulating their husbands – in a good-natured way, of course, and with the company's assistance. Husbands were the repositories of common sense: they understood all the technical jargon and revelled in it as a display of machismo. They knew the importance of a dollar, of 'investing' in upgraded products, and ultimately they were the final arbiters.

The Good Life

Other building and supply advertisements took a different approach and employed codes of affluence – assurances that quality was worth the price and that 'success' increasingly meant upgrading to more opulent surroundings. Brinton carpets used an anniversary theme, coupled with male career success, to impart an affluent, exclusive aura to its carpets. In an ad titled 'For a bronze anniversary ... you deserve Brinton "Seigniory" carpet,' the company included this short essay about the dignified couple relaxing on their new carpet in front of the fireplace: 'It's a very special evening. Their eighth wedding anniversary and the first day with their new carpet. Last year, Blake was promoted to captain with the airline. Now he's flying the Bermuda run. Sally keeps busy with the local drama group, the hospital auxiliary and ... oh yes, their four children. Now that they can afford it they have decided to enjoy the finer things in life. That's why they chose a Brinton "Seigniory" carpet. "Seigniory" combines all their needs at once – soft and elegant to the touch and yet durable enough to hold its beauty long after the children have grown up' (illustration 22).[83]

This appealing advertising fantasy appears to cover all the angles of upper-middle-class success: excellent job, artistic-volunteerist wife who has time to mother her brood of four on the side, elegant home furnishings – and, to celebrate their eighth anniversary, they have donned evening wear to lounge in front of their fireplace. Yet many aspects of this ad fantasy are disturbing: the wife 'keeps busy,' but doesn't work outside the home; the amount of time and effort it takes to care for four children (presumably all under eight years of age) is casually dismissed; and it is really Blake whose success – career success – is reflected in the glow of their Brinton carpet. Where ads in the fifties were proud to portray the housewife in all her glory – and she was a force to be reckoned with – by the sixties, in many ads, the female characters were increasingly uncertain of how to define themselves, except in their role as chief consumer. Women's roles, as depicted in advertisements, were becoming increasingly negligible and fickle, as their only role became the selection of 'fashionable' products.

Leisure

Although products had often stressed the link between time spent on house cleaning or food preparation and leisure, the meaning of the term, and the sizable increase in leisure products advertised in the magazine, changed in the sixties. While in the ads of the fifties, families and housewives used leisure time with their children or husbands, usually within the home, leisure in the sixties became associated with

For a bronze anniversary . . . you deserve Brinton "Seigniory" carpet

It's a very special evening. Their eighth wedding anniversary and
the first day with their new carpet.
Last year, Blake was promoted to captain with the airline. Now he's flying the Bermuda run.
Sally keeps busy with the local drama group, the hospital auxiliary and
. . . oh yes, their four children.
Now that they can afford it they have decided to enjoy the finer things in life. That's
why they chose a Brinton "Seigniory" carpet. "Seigniory" combines all their needs
at once — soft and elegant to the touch and yet durable enough to hold its beauty
long after the children have grown up. The secret, of course, is Acrilan® acrylic fibre. Sally
realized as soon as the salesman showed her the label that her worries were over.
Blake loves the colour and deep velvet pile.
They both love the double security of Brinton and Acrilan.
Don't wait for your next anniversary to check on Brinton quality.

ACRILAN
Monsanto

BRINTON
CARPETS
BY
Armstrong

108   featured in "Man
in the Home" CHATELAINE EXPO67 PAVILION

22 *Chatelaine*, May 1967

life outside the home. Ads for Air Canada, Air Alitalia, the British Tourist Authority, and various Canadian provinces began to associate leisure with travel, certainly with an increase in air travel. And, because the travel and hobbies advertisements were for products to take people away from their humdrum existence, they addressed such issues as suburban ennui or sought to assuage people's boredom with their products – as in the advertisements for *Chatelaine* crafts, the Columbia Record Club, or Maclean Hunter books and records.

In 1965 Air Canada ran an advertisement with an ecstatic-looking housewife screaming 'Whoopee! He's off on another business trip!' – followed, in smaller print, by the phrase 'and I'm going with him' (illustration 23).[84] Initially, the humour plays on the women's evident liberation, soon replaced by the realization that she is going to accompany him. This ad is noteworthy, and enjoyable, on a number of levels. First off, and at its most overt, it serves up a classic advertising fantasy for the housewife reader: 'Suddenly, you're Alice in Wonderland – Queen of the May – Cleopatra. And AIR CANADA is your escape route to a holiday from apron strings – a change of scene … So, be prepared for a quick getaway. Get on the phone and ask your Mother to baby sit. Have your hair done. Pack for sight-seeing, shopping and, hopefully, a night on the town. One more thing. Give your husband a hero's welcome tonight. He deserves it.' Clearly, apron strings are not family ties in the sixties, and this ad readily acknowledges the drudgery of housework – for it promised a release from all mundane tasks. While they promise release, excitement, and new experiences, these ads also manage to conform, in some ways, to traditional (sexist) values. The sexual reward implied by the 'hero's welcome' was a characteristic of the more overtly sexual ads of the sixties (such as Tex-Made's 'evening dress of the year'), which often made links between the husband's income and the wife's sexuality – particularly as a form of repayment, reward, or tangible benefit (for men) of married life.

Ethnicity

Another extremely important thematic approach used in the *Chatelaine* advertisements was ethnicity. Food manufacturers were among the first to use this visual hook. Kraft foods provided 'an authentic Dutch dish using Velveeta,' Green Giant promoted 'Niblets Italiano,' while Uncle Ben's 'Spanish Rice' and Aylmer's 'Pea-ella' strove to link their products with Spanish cuisine.[85] Novelty, not authenticity, was the

Whoopee! He's off on another business trip!
(and I'm going with him by AIR CANADA)

Suddenly, you're Alice in Wonderland—Queen of the May—Cleopatra. And AIR CANADA is your escape route to a holiday from apron strings—a change of scene—a kind of no limit charge account for blue skies and happy times. So, be prepared for a quick getaway. Get on the phone and ask your Mother to baby sit. Have your hair done. Pack for sight-seeing, shopping and, hopefully, a night on the town. One more thing. Give your husband a hero's welcome tonight. He deserves it.

Ask your Travel Agent to tell you about AIR CANADA's economical Family Fare, exciting Package Tour and Fly Now — Pay Later Plans. Or just phone us.

AIR CANADA

ENJOY THESE AIR CANADA "NO CHARGE" EXTRAS: DELICIOUS MEALS & SNACKS—FRIENDLY, COURTEOUS, NO-TIP SERVICE—A COMFORTABLE, FAST JOURNEY

23 *Chatelaine*, September 1965

chief appeal, a little spice to break the monotony of the processed food products. The food manufacturers were not alone in these far-fetched attempts to provide an ethnic tie-in for products. Pond's Lipstick produced a line of makeup called 'Mexican Holiday Colours,' which it photographed on a blue-eyed blonde – either hesitant to use a Mexican woman in its advertisements or quick to illustrate how the makeup could provide Canadian women with an exotic new look. Similarly, Max Factor introduced a line of makeup called 'Pacific Sunset,' marketing its version of Hawaiian beauty.[86] Hair-colouring products, such as Max Factor's 'Coiffure Italienne,' also employed ethnicity as a marketing tool, as did some manufacturers of women's clothing.[87] Finally, while the house and building product manufacturers were most likely to emulate American stylings (the California look was increasingly popular), they occasionally ventured into more ethnic patterns or names – as when Domco Flooring promised that its new linoleum flooring would add a splash of 'La Dolce Vita' to life.[88] These attempts were not geared to attract ethnic and immigrant shoppers, as they were little more than promotional stunts. The recipes, cosmetics, flooring, and building supplies were all very 'North American' products to which their marketers had attached ethnic monikers in the hopes of making traditional products appear more novel or exciting. Increased travel and postwar immigration had promoted an interest in exotic products, but these goods were primarily ways in which Anglo-Canadians could safely experiment with diversity, not attempts to market products to newcomers in Canada.

Unlike the new-found fascination with ethnicity, the Canadian theme remained as popular as it had been in the fifties. Companies such as E.D. Smith, Gibbard Furniture, and Five Roses Flour, and marketing boards such as the Canadian Wood Council were quick to link their products with both the land or Canadian history. The historical link was new, inspired by Canada's Centennial in 1967. This celebration created a pride in and awareness of the Canadian heritage, thanks to federal, provincial, and regional funds earmarked for commemorations and civic buildings designed to fête the anniversary.

Masculinity

The increased use of male models in advertisements during the sixties was another departure from *Chatelaine* ads of the fifties. One of the major advertisers who consistently featured male models, and some-

On the double, Daddy! You've got to move fast to keep up with these dinner dates. Swift's Meats for Babies are on the menu! Mmmm, they taste so good. And their valuable nourishment is just what babies need for sturdy growth and glowing health. This is why so many mothers turn to Swift, the meat *specialist*—for the wealth of complete, high-quality protein fine meats provide. Babies especially share in the extra value, the extra goodness you always get when the label says. *Swift's Premium* ... the two most trusted words in meat.

24 *Chatelaine*, May 1961

times children, was Swift's meat products. In countless ads, men were depicted playing football, then eating steak; drooling while carving the roast beef; or biting into six-inch-thick sandwiches – all demonstrating the healthy appetites of Canadian men and the importance of meat on the housewives' shopping list. Other ads featured men sheepishly helping out around the house, humorously modelling underwear for over-weight men (a rare male entry in the body-shape ads), or ogling home building-supply products. The May 1961 Swift's Premium ad (this time for Swift's Meats for Babies) provides an excellent example of the typical *Chatelaine* man depicted in the advertisements (illustration 24).[89] Usually portrayed as a husband or dad, in this case the ruggedly handsome Dad is good-naturedly feeding his twin daughters. The daughters, like all women in *Chatelaine*, are getting the best of him ('On the double, Daddy! You've got to move fast to keep up with these dinner dates'), but he is a good sport. In short, whether in food, building supplies, clothing, medical, or leisure advertisements, *Chatelaine* ad men were handsome, well groomed, good natured, and helpful, providing perfect fantasy fodder for women readers. However, it is also clear from the ads that they were 'real men' – they liked sports, consumed considerable quantities of red meat, and were physically large and awkward around the home. These male models might be appearing in a woman's magazine, but all the advertisers took pains to ensure they were as heterosexual as possible. These gentle giants could help out in a pinch, but their sheepish looks made it clear that basic household tasks were not part of their regular routine.

Children: The Introduction of the Brat

Children were less popular in the sixties' ad world than they had been in the fifties, but they were still an important presence. In the fifties, most advertisements with children had played on their innocent and cute appearance. Ad makers believed, probably correctly, that they had tremendous visual appeal to all the young Canadian mothers of the baby-boom brood. The cute advertisements remained, but a new style – featuring 'the brat' – was inaugurated in the sixties. In general, boy models were more popular than they had been in the fifties. The dominance of boys as ad-world children was clear, although they were portrayed in a variety of ways: they were the more delicate children, in need of extra help with their schooling (educational products), more prone to illness (medical products), and the more needy beneficiaries of nutritional meals and supplements (food products and vitamins). Where beauty or decorative value was prized, girls were used, as in the Nivea ad. Not surprisingly, boys also had the starring role as the brat. In these ads, gender overrode their youth, and, like male advertisers and a few male models, they were allowed to patronize readers, to demand that readers purchase a product, or to behave badly in the ads. A General Motors ad featuring little Jimmy, the 'Safest Gun in the West,' illustrates how advertisements with male children were shockingly different from the innocent, cute images of the fifties (illustration 25).[90] Dressed in his western gear, and pointing his shiny six-shooter at the reader from the front seat of his father's new GM car, Jimmy is an arresting image. The ad copy, after requisite comments about Jimmy's cowboys-and-Indians role playing (no doubt an attempt to capitalize on the popularity of western movies and television programs), informs readers that Jimmy, like his father, understands quality: 'Jimmy and his Dad know that wherever they go in the West ... or East or North or South ... they travel safely with GM.' The implication, of course, is that female readers were ignorant of this information because the world of cars was a male preserve. Thankfully, Jimmy could point readers in the right direction.

SAFEST GUN IN THE WEST!

Our young buckaroo lives in an exciting world, packed with imaginary perils... make-believe gunslingers and Injuns springing up at every turn. In reality, though, young Jimmy rides the trail the safest way his Dad knows... in the solid dependability of a General Motors car. For Jimmy's Dad has learned over the years that GM means quality in motor cars, in trucks and buses, in famous Frigidaire appliances.

General Motors people achieve quality by using the finest materials with painstaking care and infinite attention to detail. The results are extra dependability, extra performance and extra beauty for you.

Jimmy and his Dad know that wherever they go in the West... or East or North or South... they travel safely with GM. They — and you — can take General Motors quality for granted because we don't!

GM IN CANADA

General Motors of Canada, Limited, Oshawa and Windsor
Cars and trucks

General Motors Diesel, Limited, London
Diesel locomotives, buses and Diesel engines

Frigidaire Products of Canada Limited, Toronto
Home appliances and commercial refrigeration

The McKinnon Industries, Limited, St. Catharines
Automotive parts and accessories

Chatelaine • September 1962

25 *Chatelaine*, September 1962

The brat appeared in wallpaper and carpet ads, as a destructive force, and as a know-it-all in china ads. While intended to be decoded as cute, these ads could easily be understood as patronizing, sexist, or annoying, as young males instructed, cajoled, and forced female adults to notice the ad and purchase the product.

Reader Response

One of the difficulties of advertising analysis is attempting to determine the intent and impact of the advertisements. Obviously, the advertisers' definition of success was a purchase, while the magazine's definition of success, judged by Starch figures, was readership. The readers' impressions are more difficult to ascertain. According to indicators in *CARD* and archival material, American and Canadian corporations were devoted advertisers in the periodical throughout the era, often according it the top spot for advertisements in the categories for food and food beverages, clothing and dry goods, drugs and toilet goods, furniture and furnishings, and soaps and housekeepers' supplies.[91] Furthermore, from 1960 to 1970, *Chatelaine* attracted between 23 and 28 per cent of all the magazine advertising placed in the country.[92] However, the magazine did not have a steady increase of advertising, and experienced a decline of 4 per cent in 1964, indicative of some advertising disfavour or lack of return from advertisements in the magazine.

Cultural experts eschew this simplistic economic determinism in favour of analysis of the myths that circulated in the advertising pages. Those arguments about consumer parables, and the implementation of desires and inchoate 'needs' fostered by ads, are compelling. Yet the money expended, exhaustive psychological study, and market research by advertising firms indicate the seriousness of their mission and intentions. While the advertising dreams are beguiling, however, we should not fall prey to the perception that readers were powerless to the seductive charms of advertising. *Chatelaine* readers did not lose their critical sensibilities when it came to this material. Further lessening the power of the ads were low readership statistics for them and the different manner in which readers approached this material. Few read the ads closely.

The Starch numbers, available only for the early seventies, indicate that 'noted' scores (women who remembered noting the ad, but could not identify the product) were very high for the four-page, full-colour inserts of advertisers like Kraft, Canada Packers, and the Dairy Foods Service Bureau, but that 'read-most' scores (where people read most of the advertisement) were much lower. For instance, a four-page advertisement for Kraft had a noted score of 73 per cent for June 1970 and a noted score of 60 per cent for December 1970, while the read-most scores were, respectively, 30 per cent and 11 per cent.[93] Each of those ads would have contained at least one Kraft recipe, which the Starch reports confirmed, and this addition increased the 'read-most' readership. Not all ad placements in the magazine were of this four-page, full-colour variety. The drop in readership, even to one-page, full-colour advertisements, was sizable. The average, of all the full-page, full-colour food ads Starched between 1966 and 1968, indicated that noted scores were 44 per cent for both recipe and non-recipe ads, but for read-most scores an ad with a recipe attracted a 21 per cent score, while an ad without a recipe attracted a meagre 11 per cent of those interviewed. Recipe booklets were another way that advertisers were able to attract reader attention, although for the cost involved in including tear-out booklets in the magazine, the 'readership return' was not much higher. A Canada Packers four-page, full-colour advertisement that included a sixteen-quarter-page booklet insert had a noted score of 78 per cent for the ad and booklet combined, and a read-most score of 38 per cent. The booklet was the more popular by far, as its read-most score was 38 per cent, while the ad garnered only 14 per cent. When asked by the Starch interviewers, however, 47 per cent of survey participants claimed to have kept the booklet (58 per cent kept it in their kitchen drawer), yet only 20 per cent had tried the recipes and 63 per cent 'intended to' try the recipes. The Starch scores indicate that readership – as opposed to noting the page – was quite low, considerably lower than any of the editorial components. Give-aways, such as booklets or coupons, increased reader participation, but in terms of product purchase (judged by those who tried the recipes) the results were mediocre.

Another indicator that the magazine's advertising was often not very effective was the amount of support given to advertisers' products by the magazine. Women's magazines were required to provide 'support' for the ads in the form of the regular service material that was printed in each issue. As chapter 5 indicates, the *Chatelaine* departments often failed to maximize advertising support. A few letters in the archival material relate to the 'advertising' value of departmental material and illustrate an interesting difference of opinion on the part of *Chatelaine* advertisers. A letter from a displeased advertiser, the Wabasso Cotton Company, which had complained that Wabasso sheets were not featured in a Homes special, prompted publisher L.M. Hodgkinson to send this apologetic reply: 'Thank you for your letter ... which clearly outlines your opinions regarding our use of Fieldcrest products in *Chatelaine* Homes 60. The points you make in this letter are very well taken and I know that you can appreciate the problem involved in trying to keep track of everything that our editors are doing. We do not like to place restrictions on them ... I will, however, review your feelings with Mrs. Reynolds and will make every effort to avoid duplication of the practice of *Chatelaine* featuring imported products when satisfactory Canadian products are available.'[94] While many Homes features did make use of products advertised in the magazine, long-time advertisers were not guaranteed a spot.

Similarly, new advertisers were keen to find out whether they would be given 'free' advertising in the pages of the departmental material or in-store promotional material ('As Advertised in *Chatelaine*' support). In 1960 Hodgkinson wrote to fashion editor Vivian Wilcox:

> They have contacted us with the hope that they can participate in some of our Editorial-Promotion Fashion Features. I do not know anything about their products and I am sure that you are qualified to assess them. However, I do know that they are an organization in Canada which is interested in establishing a brand name for their dress and they are planning to do this partly through advertising in *Chatelaine*. I pass the information on to you and hope that in your selection of fashion you will give consideration to this Company's product particularly when we have a feature which can be promoted and merchandised through the Department Stores across the country. Would you therefore, keep this in mind and if there are any reasons why we can't work with them will you let me know.[95]

Clearly, for many companies the difference between paid advertising and the departmental material was often indistinguishable. However, not all companies believed that this 'blurring' between paid advertisement and departmental material was to their advantage. In the opinion of the advertising manager of the Dominion Oilcloth and Linoleum Company, such tie-ins lessened the integrity of the departmental features:

> I am of mixed feelings about whether or not I want *Chatelaine* editorial material to be exactly the same as advertising. For special promotional features this is good. But for regular editorial it is bad and will, in the long run, create loss of faith in your editorials – as an advertiser that is important to me. Even if the ads appear after your editorial, which promotion wise is not as good as at the same time, this will still brand your future editorial material with commercialism. As I said, for special promotions only, this is not bad, because you are not implying a lie to your reader. You are coming right out and saying 'we worked with these advertisers – this is a dual concentrated educational-selling campaign directed by you.' But for regular features, no.[96]

Companies and their advertising executives had different approaches to the departmental and in-store promotions run by the magazine. Given the high number of dual campaigns, however, their concern was well placed that the reader might reach the saturation point.

Those joint initiatives were only part of the assistance *Chatelaine* advertisers received. They were also eligible to apply for the 'Chatelaine Seal of Approval.' Most issues of the magazine devoted a page to the seal and explained the lengthy process of assessment products underwent before recognition was granted (testing in the *Chatelaine* Institute, plant visits, and interviews with the manufacturers). This text encouraged readers to look for the seal on products they purchased, and provided a list of all the products that had been granted the seal. In effect, this endorsement provided free advertising. In 1961 the magazine's Consumer Council Survey 30 had questioned the *Chatelaine* Councillors, the 2000 readers from all demographic groups and regions, about the Seal of Approval.[97] Ninety per cent of the respondents claimed that seals of approval did have an 'influence on their choice, all other things being equal.' When questioned about what they thought the seal stood for, they selected a number of different definitions: 'It has been tested in the *Chatelaine* Institute (90%); Represents good value for price (21.7%); Best value available (7.1%); Advertised in *Chatelaine* (3.3%).' Finally, 46.9 per cent of the councillors reported that they had seen the seal on products when they were shopping. Ironically, many products that advertised in the magazine (particularly American companies) proudly displayed their *Good Housekeeping* Seal of Approval, and never applied to be evaluated for a *Chatelaine* seal.

Along with the seal, the Brand Names Foundation and the Magazine Advertising Bureau (MAB) both placed ads in the magazine which provided readers with explicit direction about the importance of the ads. The MAB advertisement, 'To anyone who has ever driven a car,' is representative of this genre and indicative of the advertisers' message. It was primarily a text-based advertisement, with a small inset photograph of a Model-A Ford. The message was simple: advertising was a progressive force in society: 'Somebody is always trying to get you to make a change. No sooner do you get a new dishwasher or clothes dryer or car than someone says, "Here's a newer and better one. Try it!" If you tried to buy everything that was offered, your money wouldn't last long. So, you become a smart shopper. You choose which things you are going to buy. Isn't it nice to have choice? Isn't it good to see so many people trying to please you by turning out ever-improving things? Of course, if it weren't for advertising, you wouldn't know what choices you had. As a matter of fact, if there weren't any advertising we might all still be driving Model-A's. And that was a fun car.'[98] Clearly, although the MAB was loath to mention capitalism by name, the ad alludes, through the use of the term 'choice,' to the joys of capitalism (the freedom to choose, and the freedom of the marketplace). The democracy of 'choice' had resonance with readers who were well aware of the cornucopia of goods available in the Western, democratic nations, in contrast to the Communist Bloc. One of the key planks in Cold War propaganda between the West and the East centred on the ideological meanings and values of consumer goods. It is no coincidence that Richard Nixon, vice president of the United States, engaged in heated debate with Soviet premier Nikita Khruschev in, and over, the replica American kitchen in the U.S. Exhibition in Moscow in 1959.[99] To consume was to be free – and ads such as the MAB insert offer readers reminders about the joys and responsibilities of 'freedom.'

The explicit nature of these advertisements raises questions about their inclusion in *Chatelaine*. One thing is certain, these ads were not just filler to increase the advertising content of any particular issue, but were clearly placed to assist advertisers. Ads such as this one encouraged readers to look at the ads closely (perhaps even to reread the magazine looking specifically for advertisements), to purchase the products advertised in magazines, to appreciate the power of advertising, and generally to reinforce the advertising component of the periodical. Ultimately, it seems unlikely that advertisements such as this would have been placed in the periodical unless the advertising manager and publisher felt that the magazine's advertisers required a more supportive environment. Or to use their rhetoric, that readers needed instruction about how to read and use *Chatelaine*'s advertisements.

While all these efforts point to the magazine's continued attempt to provide service to its advertisers, we may conclude that when the small Starch readership scores are factored into the analysis, the magazine was running an intensive campaign to bolster ad readership. This evidence suggests that the ads were not read as closely as advertisers might like, nor were they very successful at increasing sales of the products advertised. The ineffectiveness of advertising was not unique to *Chatelaine*, but a problem that plagued advertisers in various forums. Maclean Hunter had memberships, and thus subscriptions, to a number of advertising newsletters and reports (for instance, Dichter's *Motivations: Monthly Psychological Research Reports for Business*).[100] One report, 'The A.A.A.A. Study on Consumer Judgment of Advertising – Phase II,' undertaken by the American Association of Advertising Agencies in 1964 (and included in the Maclean Hunter archival material), concluded 'that advertising is not a central issue in the day to day lives of consumers.'[101] It included five reasons 'why people feel unfavourably toward advertising – Fake or misleading (21%); Too much advertising (19%); Interrupts entertainment (12%); It is repetitive (6%); High pressure advertising (6%).' Along with consumers' stated dislikes of advertising and the admission that they paid little attention to it, the association was forced to conclude (apparently without ironic intent) that 'a great many of the physical opportunities which consumers have for exposure to advertising pass them by.' Despite the barrage of ads, their colourful, bold style, and their eye-catching imagery, many consumers were resistant to or consciously ignored their messages.

Ultimately, one must consider how the *Chatelaine* readers responded to the products advertised in the magazine. Of the twelve respondents to my questionnaire about reading *Chatelaine*, nine stated that they disliked the advertisements, while three people stated that they enjoyed them.[102] In the letters to the editor, both those published in the magazine and those included in the archival papers, very few explicitly mentioned the advertisements. Ruby H. Bauer of Vermillion, Alberta, wrote, 'I thoroughly enjoy articles and advertisements of new products, fabrics and fibres, household appliances, and love new recipes that are different but practical enough for me to use.'[103] Mrs N.W.B. of Leaside, Ontario, seems to have tolerated the advertisements, but enjoyed the availability of products: 'All your reading material is worthwhile – nothing to be skipped or skimmed over, and when I see something advertised that suits my fancy I know it will be available to me.'[104] Meanwhile, Julia Mulligan from Langley, BC, told the editors how she had reviewed the magazine for her Women's Institute meeting: 'For the May meeting ... I reviewed the May issue of *Chatelaine*. I picked out the highlights, even commented on patterns and advertisements. I want to tell you how pleased my audience was. Some said, "Where did you find it all?"'[105] It would appear that most writers to the magazine did not feel it would be worthwhile to complain about the advertising material. However, one dissenting voice on advertisements did make it into the magazine. Mrs L.G. Henders of Elm Creek, Manitoba, wrote: 'I am somewhat disappointed. Although I recognize the value of advertisements to housewives and homemakers like myself, as well as their value to publishers in terms of dollars and cents, is it really necessary to have so many?'[106] The editors assured Mrs Henders that without the ads, they could not pay their bills.

In the sixties, a few letters were quick to criticize liquor advertisements. Mrs Harold Taylor of Truro, NS, wrote: 'One of the features of your publication which tempted me to subscribe in the first place – I was told it never had any liquor advertising. Was this statement ever true?'[107] Other 'anti-liquor' letters were received from Swift Current and Vancouver. Anderson replied that since the magazine began publishing recipes using wine, the staff had reconsidered the policy for wineries. However, she assured the readers that the magazine would never take 'hard liquor' or beer advertisements. Despite her critique of the liquor and tobacco ads, this letter from Mrs George Putnam of Vancouver indicated that she was a fan of the magazine's advertising: 'Am enjoying your new *Chatelaine* immensely – after a lapse of many years, it is new, and very much improved. Your advertisements are magnificent and I don't see how any one could ignore them! Especially do I enjoy there being no liquor advertisements, and no tobacco – hardly – would like to see none ... Again, your advertisements are most intriguing and compelling and beautiful material.'[108] Mrs Putnam's appreciation of the ads, primarily for their visual display, colour, and imagery, confirms the enjoyment some readers derived from the 'fantasy' component of the ads. Moreover, her comments about the omnipresent nature of the ads provides an interesting counterpoint to the often low Starch results.

A letter from Mrs Edna Hall of Ottawa made a link between the images of baby bottles and formulas pictured in some advertisements in the magazine and the decreasing number of young mothers who chose to breast-feed their infants. She wrote: 'In the past week I have seen advertisements for the following products – baby powder, soap powder, evaporated milk and refrigerators. These advertisements had one thing in common – all showed baby bottles filled with formula. It is advertising such as this which is largely responsible for the present-day attitude that bottle feeding is the "natural" thing to do and that breast feeding is old fashioned.'[109] Mrs Hall's comments were not restricted to baby-formula manufacturers, but to smaller images contained in ads for other products. Her letter confirms that some readers paid particularly close attention to the ads and made conclusions about the 'effect' of this material. Anderson replied: 'Your comment is a good one, and we will probably use your letter in our Letters Page.'[110]

Conclusion

When *Chatelaine* arrived in the reader's mailbox, her first impression of the magazine was the cover art. Once she opened the product, numerically speaking, the largest component was the advertisements. Given the strong visual pull of this material, it is obvious that the messages contained in these pages were significant.

Although the cover had a clear commercial mandate – to attract newsstand browsers – its chief goal was to lead readers into the magazine by providing visual clues to the issue's prominent feature or article, as well as a partial list of the top non-fiction articles. Finally, and seemingly in direct competition with the newsstand appeal of the magazine, the placement of *Chatelaine* on the tables or bed-stands of the nation sent a message to husbands, family, and friends, identifying readers as *Chatelaine* women. Women who commented on the at-home display value of the covers wanted a magazine that was attractive as well as respectable. They eschewed lurid covers, 'beatnicky wenches,' and discordant images in favour of appropriate seasonal covers, Canadian personalities (preferably as saintly and decent as possible), and positive reflections of Anglo-Canadian women. These women wanted the magazine to convey a certain status to all who would glance at it, pick it up, or borrow it. The last thing readers wanted was for friends and family to think they were reading a sensationalist, low-brow magazine.

Advertisements offered a seductive array of products to the readers and hoped, largely through a more affluent, sexual, and increasingly leisure-oriented approach, to get *Chatelaine* readers to part with some of their household and discretionary spending. While the evidence suggests that the advertisers were not as successful at selling the products displayed in the magazine as they would have liked, the images used to sell products, the 'structures of meaning,' were both pervasive and persuasive. The cumulative effect of the advertisements, not the readers' response to the individual ad, is where the real power of the advertising lay. As both the statistical and critical analyses makes clear, the preferred meaning of the advertising pages was, not surprisingly, consumption. In the fifties, consumption meant a suburban home, the 'traditional' family, the cult of youthfulness, the suburban utopia, passionate marriage, and fun times with the family. In some instances it could also reaffirm one's identity as a Canadian. For women, the images offered by the advertisers and corporations were as restrictive as they were seductive: the promise of perfection and purpose through purchase, whether in the household, child raising, marriage, or less frequently the larger community. With a little help from the advertisers, any *Chatelaine* reader could become a household dynamo – a master craftswoman on the cleaning, cooking, and purchasing frontier. Thus, while their roles were limited, the women depicted in the fifties' advertisements had purpose and drive, and were often portrayed – aided and abetted by the products and advertisers – as exceedingly competent.

Chatelaine advertising in the sixties was considerably different from the decade earlier. The advertising mix had changed slightly, with a rise in the number of household, furniture, and building supplies ads that demoted food advertisements into second place. Leisure and medical product ads increased, at the expense of cosmetics and clothing ads. The visual appeal of these pages was different, as the number of full-page, full-colour ads increased along with the decline in the number of small, text-heavy ads. In short, sixties' ads were more colourful, often had more sexual or fantastic imagery, featured fewer models (although more men), and consistently employed themes of affluence, ethnicity, sexuality, and less often Canadiana, to great effect. The bustling, efficient, well-coifed housewife of the fifties had been replaced by the vapid-looking, sexy young woman of the sixties, a woman who was often married, seldom employed, but equally unlikely to be pictured doing housework – a decorative sex symbol. Only the food advertisements stressed maternal, housewife, and craft pride in food preparation. At a time when many Canadian women were heading back to the workforce, the women of *Chatelaine*'s ad world were usually uncertain of any role beyond that of sex symbol or consumer. If the ad-world women were featured in a work setting (such as Metrecal's Hilda Lang), they were clerical workers or sales people. For the most part, ad-world women did not do anything except look alluring, worry about their figures, scheme how to influence their husbands to renovate the house, or colour their hair.

The larger number of men in the advertisements, particularly men who were depicted as the final arbitrators of product purchase, reduced the female role still further. Women were responsible for understanding the 'fashion' of cars, refrigerators, furnishings, and paint, while men were responsible for evaluating the technical information and approving the financial expenditure. Even children, particularly male children, instructed their hapless mothers in the art of consumption. Furthermore, the messages and codes of the advertisements were even more dramatically opposed to the messages contained in the editorials and advertising than had been the case in the fifties. If the ad-world housewife of the fifties conformed to the stereotypical image of that decade, she nevertheless demonstrated, in a variety of advertising dramas, her competency in the household, pride in her family, and security in her role; a decade later, the advertisers replaced her with an increasingly sexualized woman whose function, in most ads, was purely decorative.

The images provided in *Chatelaine* certainly confirmed Roland Marchand's claim that advertisements provide readers with a 'distorting mirror.' In the pages of *Chatelaine* ads, the portrait of 'Canadians' offered (white, middle-class, suburban women), along with the primary motif (the decorative consumer), do not reflect the varied realities of Canadian women during the sixties. Working mothers, newcomers, rural women, and working-class women do not appear in the fantasy ad world created in the pages of *Chatelaine*. Instead, readers were provided with fantasies of the decorative woman – as a symbol of increased sexual freedom for women, as an icon of affluence and increased leisure, and as a male plaything. In this seductive fantasy, advertisers offered Canadian women a release from the daily grind faced by the working women profiled in the feature articles. The fantasy was of an affluent lifestyle (purchased by the husband's professional wages, as in the Seigniory carpet ad) where women had the luxury of leisure time, the ability to spend money on a wide variety of household and personal items, and the freedom to transform themselves into more sensual, sexual beings. Paradoxically, this fantasy offered women a more liberated form of sexuality at the same time that the parameters were clearly defined. Heterosexual, marital sex was the only prevailing image presented in the ads, despite the sexual freedoms and experimentation unleashed by the sexual revolutions at the end of the sixties.

During a time of considerable flux in women's roles, the advertisers opted for safer images of women that were not restricted to the household or the office, but depicted the private world of sexuality, consumption, and affluence. These *Chatelaine* ads did not stand alone, but were part of the North American and European refashioning of women's images. Yet if the fantasy of a perfect life in the fifties rested on the shoulders of the super-housewife who cleaned, dusted, vacuumed, and cooked her way to happiness, the 'soft life' of the sixties' fantasy seduced women with dreams of wealthy (or at least comfortably middle-class) husbands who worked so that their wives and families might play and shop.

Given June Callwood's comment on the discordance among the cover art, the women's magazine genre, and *Chatelaine*'s content, perhaps the frothy, youthful covers and the pages of advertising that glorified an affluent, suburban lifestyle were manifestations of the ways in which *Chatelaine* could and did conform to the standards of the genre. Doris Anderson too has written about the negotiations involved in working within this format. She recognized that the advertisements paid the bills and that cover art was the magazine's own advertisement for itself, yet she hoped that they could co-exist with other more subversive material. The way to achieve this balance was to create a financially viable product. Rather subversively, then, those giddy, girlish *Chatelaine* covers and the mindless consumption encouraged by the advertisements both paid for and oftentimes masked the serious articles and editorials that made the magazine required reading in the fifties and sixties.

Chapter 5

'The Cinderella from Pugwash': Advice from the *Chatelaine* Institute

Women's magazines, like detective novels, soap operas, science fiction, and other pop culture formulas, are specific genres which, if they intend to keep and attract new fans, must follow certain conventions. One of the prime conventions of women's magazines is the inclusion of service department material. The departmental features – food, fashion, beauty, home design, housekeeping, gardening, children's pages, and children's health columns – offered readers the quintessential women's magazine fare. According to H.M. Pawley of Edmonton, these features influenced Canadian readers because they were first rate. 'I do think the recipes contained in *Chatelaine* are wonderful,' she wrote. 'I hear many women discussing them and the cookbook as if *Chatelaine* were the pillar of good housekeeping and food preparation.'[1] Conversely, other women found the didactic tone of the articles, and the incessant obsession with consumption (however low key compared with American magazines), an annoyance. 'When I settle down with my favourite magazine, I want to be entertained when I get the time to read,' wrote Mrs E. MacAlpine of Carbon, Alberta. 'I have no problem children, no old furniture, I'm living in a village and my housekeeping doesn't need changing ... I have taken *Chatelaine* most of the time for the thirty-five years I've been married and I don't like the changes.'[2]

Advertisers require women's magazines to carry this material because they believe it provides a 'supportive' environment for their advertisements. So, although not explicitly commercial in the way that advertisements and cover art are, this component of the magazine is associated with the goals of the advertisers and aims to offer women 'ideas' for the household which, they hope, will translate into sales. Through the inclusion of this material, *Chatelaine* conformed to the standards and offered 'typical' women's magazine fare. However, it would be reductionist to interpret the inclusion of 'ideas' for the household as a means by which Canadian women were encouraged to stay in their homes and content themselves solely with their housewifely role. Obviously, these sections were prescriptive literature. What they were teaching, however, merits careful analysis.

Staid and often dowdy in the fifties, with an emphasis on economical meals, modest renovations of suburban bungalows, and do-it-yourself sewing patterns, the departmental fare changed slightly in the sixties. In the later decade the service department writers made forays into previously uncharted territory by exploring such topics as ethnic and gourmet food delicacies, pop-art decorating schemes, beauty features for older women, and penny-pinching fashion articles. The editors hoped these novelty pieces would reinvigorate the departmental features, entice new readers, and create a devoted national following. However, despite the inclusion of these articles, the proportion of material that accepted the role of housewife and mother as the primary role of women was much higher in these sections than in other parts of the magazine.

Chatelaine service components allowed for diversity of experience while assuming that most readers were solely responsible for their family's welfare and household maintenance. This material speaks to an ahistorical generalization of the home and family as the 'women's world,' a common experience shared by all women regardless of class, race, sexual orientation, region, or age. In the sixties, increasing emphasis was placed on the working wife and, later, the working mother. Despite the changes, these features were still 'down to earth' compared with their American equivalent, as a number of corespondents, such as Mrs W.F. Bennett from Hutchinson, Kansas, indicated. 'Do you ever wonder why people in the United States subscribe to *Chatelaine*? I will tell you why I do,' wrote Bennett. 'I am fascinated by your recipes, they are so usable, so readable, and so uncluttered – and most of the recipes call for ingredients you have on hand. Congratulations to the editor; thought that you'd like a Yankee observation.'[3]

Other letters from international readers indicated that this material fostered the notion of a 'women's network' and a distinctive women's culture through the presumption of the commonality of women's experience. Women sent subscriptions to daughters, mothers, sisters, and friends for birthday and Christmas presents. They chatted with neighbours and acquaintances about the material and shared their recipes, diet plans, before-and-after photos, and housekeeping hints through the letters and departmental pages of the magazine. The editors shrewdly realized that reader participation was the key to continued success, but the intimate tone and participatory nature of the magazine should not be attributed solely to business acumen. While the participatory nature of *Chatelaine* attracted readers (and thus subscriptions or newsstand sales), the lack of a sustained consumptive or commercial ethos did little to encourage the purchase of products advertised in the magazine. The extant papers and memos of the magazine's editors illustrate a commitment to service. Their focus was definitely on the reader, not the advertiser. This fact was made clear by publisher Lloyd Hodgkinson's apologetic reply to an irate advertiser, explaining that he could not vet everything his departmental editors were doing.

Finally, the prescriptive nature of this material needs commentary. Although the departmental material was more prescriptive than other components of the magazine, readers were still free to implement these suggestions. Many readers' comments about departmental material illustrate what they preferred and what they did not find useful. Readers rejected styles of dressing, cuisine, or household maintenance that were too rich for their pocketbooks, that they did not enjoy, or that they found too onerous. Many of the comments of those who criticized the magazine's consumerist service department ethos came from those with lower incomes who felt excluded. By and large, they framed this issue not as personal failing, but as the magazine's inaccurate assessment of the class, or representative income level, of its readers. Given the prevailing uniformity and conformity during the fifties – part of the Cold War propaganda that linked 'difference' with disloyalty or defined democracy as exercising choices about consumer goods – tremendous pressure was placed on people to participate in this modern world and to 'keep up with the Jones.' *Chatelaine*, however, had regular readers who actively resisted this material, whether from an ideological perspective that was anti-consumerist; from a religious upbringing that stressed anti-consumerist beliefs; from rural locations and different value systems from those held by urbanites or suburbanites; or from nascent feminists and working wives who believed that the homemaking and cleaning articles were completely out of step with their lives. The letters and comments of these resisters, along with those from lower-income readers, provide an excellent vantage point from which to gauge how 'prescriptive' literature functions.

On average, about one-fifth of each issue was devoted to department features. Maclean Hunter's ads in *Canadian Advertising Rates and Data* (*CARD*) often described the primary role of the service department as dual purpose: it 'educated' Canadian women to a 'better standard of living' while it assisted advertisers by stimulating consumer demand for their products. This excerpt from a 1954 *Chatelaine* advertisement in *CARD* represents the perspective of the businessmen at *Chatelaine* and indicates how they believed the service department material functioned. 'Women's service magazines are close to the buyer. They focus the interest of your prospects on their pages in an atmosphere of "do something" ideas. Women read service magazines for ideas on how to improve their homes, their families, themselves.'[4] The phrases 'do something' and 'improvement' were key to much of the service department material, for it fostered an environment in which housewives were encouraged to seek new recipes, new decorating ideas, and innovative ways to solve housekeeping dilemmas. Neither perfection or contentment could ever be achieved, for there were always new trends, new colours, new types of foods, or changing cuisines with which to experiment.

Maclean Hunter was overconfident about the way the service department material supposedly worked. This excerpt from 1953 explained that 'tested recipes and menus from the *Chatelaine* Institute are read by some three-quarters of a million women. From *Chatelaine*'s service these same women get ideas that result in millions of wants that find their way onto millions of shopping lists for so-called "impulse" sales. Your advertising, run *with* those service articles and tied to this proven audience will produce the kind of action that means big, fast turnover to the grocery business ... Over the years *Chatelaine* has educated women to want more interesting, nutritious meals. It has been a big factor in raising the standard of living.'[5] To support this contention, the company marshalled the Starch figures to prove how many readers the departmental features regularly drew. Starch results for this material were mixed, but the percentages for readers who remembered 'noting' the material ranged from 55 per cent for 'Freeze Away' (a food feature) to 88 per cent and 80 per cent, respectively, for 'Cool in the Swim' (beauty) and 'Think Summer' (fashion).[6] However, the 'read-most' figures indicate that substantially fewer readers actually read these articles: obviously, the visual appeal of the sections made them highly recognizable, but most readers did little more than skim the photographs. The food features had the highest reading figures: 'Freeze Away' (43% of those 'Starched') and 'Stay Cool/Easy Party Menus' (47%). The fashion and beauty features had lower numbers: 'Cool in the Swim' (30%); 'Think Summer' (28%); and 'Real Cool – Tie and Dye Fashion' (28%). Impressive figures, but that was all – numbers that reflected how many women had 'noted' or 'read most,' not purchased or 'acted upon' the information.

Although the Starch figures were compiled by an independent firm and were the standards throughout the industry, where they served as the 'currency' of periodical popularity, there are additional ways of assessing the popularity of this material. First, the readers' letters to the magazine – judged primarily by those published in the magazine – paled in comparison with letters devoted to articles, editorials, and even fiction. The few letters received indicate that readers, their friends, and their family were fond of these features – particularly the food features – but they did not generate the interest that the feature articles did. Conversely, the variety of contests run by the various departments indicate that this material had a loyal following. The Family Favourites contest, and others for beauty makeovers, dieting transformations, and home design, were all more popular than the editors had expected. Family Favourites become a *Chatelaine* institution.[7] Contest entries peaked in 1956, when over 5000 entries were received. That tidal wave of entries delayed the results until the March issue because 'the Institute offices were almost adrift in recipes' and 'staff members all had to extend recipe reading to after hours at home.'[8]

Another important gauge of the popularity of the service departments was the phenomenal success of the *Chatelaine Cookbook*. Launched in 1965, it was a collection of the magazine's most popular recipes. The book sold for $6.95 in stores or, if ordered directly from the magazine, was available for $5.50. The *Chatelaine Cookbook* sold 110,000 copies.[9] At that time, any Canadian book that sold more than 10,000 copies was deemed a bestseller.[10]

Clearly, many readers demonstrated that they enjoyed this material, yet it is difficult to summarize why or to determine the effect, if any, of these articles. What the readers' commentary indicates is that very few readers enjoyed all the departmental material: some complained about food but loved crafts, or the food fans were not pleased by the fashion features. On a basic level, the departmental fare was supposed to create 'ideas' that advertisers and the business department at the magazine hoped would translate into sales. But this letter, from Mrs Ursula McGowan of Smiths Falls, Ontario, illustrates how 'reading' and 'consumer action' were two entirely different things:

My reasons for buying *Chatelaine* are varied. I enjoy the recipes even though I try only a few of them. I like the advertisements even though my income makes them only something to dream about in the far distant future. I like the health and advice columns – there is something to be learned from them. The stories are interesting and the illustrations delightful ... I buy for comfort and economy. If there is a harmony in the colours it is more accidental than intentional. As for favourite dishes, when there are seven people in a family there are seven favourite dishes and they all make their appearance at one time or another ... Sketching floor plans is fine for the amateur architect; for me, its a complete waste of time and effort. We push all the furniture back so the floor has the necessary space for assorted arms, legs, and paws watching TV.[11]

McGowan's letter indicates that while she enjoyed reading and fantasizing about some of the recipes and decorating features, she seldom used them. The decorating articles were hopelessly out of sync with her family's lifestyle and probably not an affordable option. For her, the realism of the material was not important – she wanted glossy images to fuel her fantasies. In contrast, Mrs Irene Makins of Ayr, Ontario, wrote to compliment the magazine on the practical nature of departmental features:

I have received my first copy of my subscription to *Chatelaine*, and am enjoying it from cover to cover – even the ads! I had always bought the occasional copy. But I decided it was time to give encouragement to a good Canadian magazine. I believe that Canada has a great many talented people in the arts ... Your magazine has articles which are of practical use to homemakers in almost every subject. Of special interest to our family in the May issue are: 1) Here's Health; 2) What's wrong with nursing 3) Homemaker's Diary 4) Food ideas 5) Accent on accessories 6) How to build your own patio 7) Let's not have a buffet supper. And of course the fiction. I can't say that I always enjoy them – but it takes all kinds to please all people ... best wishes for continued progress and growth. And may more Canadians as well as people of other countries grow to appreciate *Chatelaine*.[12]

Although her initial interests were the articles, the majority of her comments were about the departmental features – food, fashion, and home features were her favourites. Makins's letter illustrates that readers were very selective, customizing their reading to reflect their interests and tastes. If they disliked the rest of the magazine or did not find it applicable to their lives, they skimmed it or avoided it altogether.

The departmental material exposed two of the fissure lines within the magazine's community of readers – age and class. While most readers could be accommodated in the general articles, departments had a definite bias in favour of married, middle-class women. The material also presumed that women were the family's consumers and that a large degree of women's creativity and worth was predicated on buying and using products for themselves and their homes. In the case of fashion and beauty, youthfulness was the primary demarcater of interest, and teenagers and twentysomething women with sufficient disposable income were the preferred audience. One of the most persistent complaints about departmental fare, in particular interior design, fashion, and beauty, was that it catered only to affluent readers. This letter from an angry reader from Harris, Saskatchewan, illustrates the frustration many older, rural, working-class women felt when they read this material:

> I have been a subscriber to your magazine for many years. However, I doubt if I'll continue. I find that your magazine ... is not now as good as either our old *Chatelaine* or the *Canadian Home Journal* were. All the *Chatelaine* seems to contain is recipes of expensive fattening foods or pages of expensive furniture and houses. Gone is the old magazine we all went to, to relax and enjoy the reading ... What do I care about the furniture, houses and recipes you represent? How far would $225 a month go with a family of five in those mansions? Do come down to earth and remember that your readers are Common Canadians (We haven't even plumbing nor electricity and I know many more of your readers haven't). We are not rich enough for the *Chatelaine*'s ideas – Could you take a poll and find out what price range your ideas should follow ... I'd like to see a house – small compact – attractive enough for an older couple to build to retire to after spending years in company houses on small salaries and not going to have pensions or savings to bolster their old age pensions. Ask your staff. Are they all nobility to have such expensive ideas – what incomes do their parents have? We aren't bums – All around us are people in the same boat – young and old. What has *Chatelaine* to offer us?'[13]

Other readers, defining themselves primarily as older readers rather than 'Common Canadians,' criticized the ageist nature of the departmental material, particularly the beauty and fashion features. Miss Ruth C. Baxter, Annapolis Royal, NS, wondered where older women were supposed to get clothing and fashion information: 'I wish there were a magazine that would cater to the needs and interests of the older woman, say from fifty on. The most difficult problem for senior women is clothes. Is there any good reason why the older woman should be obliged to flaunt before the world her bony knees, her broad thickened thighs, her sagging upper-arm muscles? Wouldn't everybody feel a little happier to have those concealed?'[14] Similarly, a letter from Bertha Scott of Edgewood, BC, critiqued the lack of any departmental material for older women: 'I offer some constructive criticism. In most magazines of today, *Chatelaine* included, there are very few articles or stories written for the older woman by older women, therefore they are lacking for the older women's interests ... Take myself for instance, first I read your column, and the next few pages, then I turn to any helpful article, biography, travel, cooking, handicrafts, hints etc. and lastly I turn to the stories; should they please me I read them through, but more often I do not read them.'[15] Anderson's response acknowledged Scott's complaint, but did not promise that the magazine would rectify the situation: 'I realize that we carry a small amount of material addressed to the older woman, but the majority of our readers are mothers with young children ... with different problems of food preparation, child care, decorating their homes ... we naturally tend to cater to them.'[16] The concentration on younger women with children was due to the advertisers' and the business department's belief that those women were the prime consuming market in Canada. Older women, rural women, and lower-income women – consumers all – were not usually worth targeting with their own departmental material. 'Canadian woman' had a similarly narrow definition in the department material as it did in the commercial advertisements and cover art. She was defined as a young, married housewife and mother, with the purchasing power of a middle-income family or higher, and presumably from an urban or suburban locale. For 'Common Canadians,' to borrow the phrase from the critic from Saskatchewan, it was not impossible for women outside the preferred reading audience to read, use, or enjoy the departmental features, but they often had to work to tailor the service material to their own situations. Frequently, reading such material exacerbated class, regional, and ageist differences within the readership.

'Dollar Meals That Taste Like a Million': *Chatelaine* Food

The food articles and monthly menu plans were the cornerstone of the service department material. During the era there were two primary food writers, Marie Holmes and Elaine Collett, both directors of the *Chatelaine* Institute. According to Holmes, the role of the institute was 'to keep our fingers on Mrs Homemaker's pulse ... We try to give her news of all the latest developments that will make her housekeeping easier and her meals more attractive; we find out her problems and the answers to them.'[17] According to the editors, the institute was able to accomplish this goal through 'letters and telephone calls, from *Chatelaine*'s own two thousand strong Consumer Council, surveys and via the country-wide trips and meetings where women can meet Institute representatives personally.' Sometimes, the readers went to the magazine directly, as in 1957 when 'thirty-six members of Women's Institutes in Halton County, Ontario, boarded a bus for Toronto. They toured our kitchens, laundry, and editorial offices and then settled down in the *Chatelaine* Institute for a cup of tea and a chat.'[18] Although the company and the advertisers' perception of the service department material was to sell products, the women who worked in the institute and the readers regarded it differently. These staff members were professionally trained as home economists and dietitians, and their advice reflected that training, whether administered through the magazine or in person. In an era where professional 'experts' of all stripes were widely regarded as 'leading authorities,' the expertise of the women in the *Chatelaine* Institute gave the magazine an important aura of legitimacy. They were the bourgeois experts to whom novice and experienced housewives could turn for advice, and many readers seemed to have relied on their services extensively. The middle-class ethos that ran throughout the material produced in the institute always stressed planning, budgets, schedules, and routines – in a word, efficiency.

Although the food articles generated by the institute during the fifties covered a wide range of topics, from preserves to breakfast menus to tentative forays into ethnic fare (anglicized versions of Italian and Chinese food), the majority of recipes provided in the magazine were for standard Anglo-Saxon Canadian dinner ideas or desserts. Food articles followed four formats: the Family Favourite feature in January or March; the regular monthly page Meals of the Month; special features throughout the year; and, from the middle of the decade onwards, the Name Brand recipes feature each October. Surprisingly, a sampling of recipe ingredients revealed that 53 per cent of recipes printed in the magazine did not make use of convenience foods in the finished product; rather, they featured products made from scratch, even though the makers of processed food products were the primary advertisers in the food category.[19] This statistic illustrates that the service department features were not simply free advertising for *Chatelaine*'s advertisers. Similarly, while the *CARD* ads and Maclean Hunter stressed consumption, the overwhelming theme of fifties' food articles was thrift. Whether it was 'Penny Wise Meat Loaf Dinners in Company Dress' or 'Dollar Meals That Taste Like a Million,' thrifty, affordable family meals were the star attraction of the food articles.[20] According to Anderson, part of the reason for the institute's focus on realistic or budget meals, in sharp contrast to the lavish, full-colour spreads of the American women's magazines, was that the organization itself was on a strict budget from Maclean Hunter and many of the departmental features were accomplished economically.[21] The Dichter Study, however, recommended that the magazine gloss these features up to build interest in the magazine, and these suggestions were implemented in the sixties. Although it was accurate to claim that the food features created ideas and sparked sales, they did not spark any conspicuous consumption of processed food products or gourmet-style seasonings or accessories. The 47 per cent of food articles in which processed foods were used almost always featured canned soups (Campbell's advertised in every issue of the magazine) or tinned vegetables in such features as 'Drama from a Can,' yet seldom required any of the new frozen food products.

In the January 1951 issue the magazine launched what was to become a much-anticipated yearly feature of the magazine: 'Fifty Family Favourites.'[22] The institute sent a letter to each *Chatelaine* Councillor requesting her family's favourite recipes. The councillors responded by sending in 1500 recipes, and it was from this huge source that the magazine selected the best fifty. Often the January cover featured one of the recipes, and this feature became a popular new year's issue (illustration 26). Institute staff encouraged the readers, too: 'Stop wracking your tired brain and add these 50 favourite recipes to your favorites, and coast along for a few months on someone else's discoveries. You will find among them some specially tasty supper dishes such as barbecued spare ribs, economical ham and egg pie and an Italian spaghetti with a particularly piquant sauce.' The recipes came from all across the country and, because they were approved by ordinary people (many

26 *Chatelaine* cover, January 1952

recipes were accompanied by a photo of the councill/
well consider these dishes sure-fire winners for the
the lucky councillors in 1952, Mrs J.D. Gillespie of
BC, wrote that her recipe for Graham Wafer Cake was ꜜ
like everyone to enjoy it. I tried nearly all the recipes you pᵣₙ.
year. We did so enjoy the change of diet.' Special departmental articles
such as this one brought readers together and literally had them swap-
ping recipes with one another as if they were neighbours.

Contests and reader input were key to the success of the food section
in the magazine. The readers responding to the contests came from
across the country, many from suburban, rural areas or small towns.
Women from the big cities did not fare as well in these cooking compe-
titions and were more likely to participate in fashion and beauty com-
petitions. A profile provided of the winner of 1951's 'Salad Contest' is
representative of the biographies that accompanied winning entries.
Doreen Ohlman of Plevna, Ontario ('150 miles northeast of Peterborough'), a twenty-five-year-old mother of five children under the age of
six, was the grand prize winner.[23] According to the editors, Ohlman
lacked 'many of the conveniences many urban dwellers take for granted.
She, her husband and their five children live in the wilds of Ontario,
eight torturous miles from the small hamlet of Plevna. Without super-
markets and departmental stores Mrs. Ohlman must shop the hard way
... Mrs. Ohlman tells us that her copy of *Chatelaine* comes to her via train
and "stage" and is pretty used up after it has been passed around from
home to home in the Land O'Lakes district.' Entries such as Ohlman's
were selected both for the quality of their product as well as the desire
to include readers from more remote areas of the country. Although we
have a tendency to believe that all Canadians shared in the modern
consumer society of the fifties and sixties, it must be remembered that
modernization did not arrive at the same time in all regions of the
country. A number of Dominion Bureau of Statistics reports indicated
that rural areas, and the Prairies in particular, had few of the 'modern
conveniences' that central Canadians took for granted. Rural women
like Mrs Ohlman continued to read the magazine and participate in its
contests despite the overt difference between her 'pioneering ways'
and the suburban lifestyle often on display in the advertisements or
depicted in the home-planning features.

In 1954 the magazine decided to open up the Family Favourites
contest to all readers, making it a bona fide national recipe contest. It
was a much-anticipated annual feature until 1967, when it was aban-

recipes were accompanied by a photo of the councill'
well consider these dishes sure-fire winners for the
the lucky councillors in 1952, Mrs J.D. Gillespie of
BC, wrote that her recipe for Graham Wafer Cake was _
like everyone to enjoy it. I tried nearly all the recipes you pᵢ.ᵢ.
year. We did so enjoy the change of diet.' Special departmental articles
such as this one brought readers together and literally had them swap-
ping recipes with one another as if they were neighbours.

Contests and reader input were key to the success of the food section
in the magazine. The readers responding to the contests came from
across the country, many from suburban, rural areas or small towns.
Women from the big cities did not fare as well in these cooking compe-
titions and were more likely to participate in fashion and beauty com-
petitions. A profile provided of the winner of 1951's 'Salad Contest' is
representative of the biographies that accompanied winning entries.
Doreen Ohlman of Plevna, Ontario ('150 miles northeast of Peterborough'), a twenty-five-year-old mother of five children under the age of
six, was the grand prize winner.[23] According to the editors, Ohlman
lacked 'many of the conveniences many urban dwellers take for granted.
She, her husband and their five children live in the wilds of Ontario,
eight torturous miles from the small hamlet of Plevna. Without super-
markets and departmental stores Mrs. Ohlman must shop the hard way
... Mrs. Ohlman tells us that her copy of *Chatelaine* comes to her via train
and "stage" and is pretty used up after it has been passed around from
home to home in the Land O'Lakes district.' Entries such as Ohlman's
were selected both for the quality of their product as well as the desire
to include readers from more remote areas of the country. Although we
have a tendency to believe that all Canadians shared in the modern
consumer society of the fifties and sixties, it must be remembered that
modernization did not arrive at the same time in all regions of the
country. A number of Dominion Bureau of Statistics reports indicated
that rural areas, and the Prairies in particular, had few of the 'modern
conveniences' that central Canadians took for granted. Rural women
like Mrs Ohlman continued to read the magazine and participate in its
contests despite the overt difference between her 'pioneering ways'
and the suburban lifestyle often on display in the advertisements or
depicted in the home-planning features.

In 1954 the magazine decided to open up the Family Favourites
contest to all readers, making it a bona fide national recipe contest. It
was a much-anticipated annual feature until 1967, when it was aban-

oned because it was too successful – primarily because the institute staff found it too time-consuming to read and evaluate the entries. Most letters received from entrants in the contest were effusive in their praise for the feature. Often readers commented that they had kept their issues for reference. Mrs Roy McNichol of Dundee, Quebec, explained, 'I've kept the January issue of Chatelaine for the past three years.'[24] Similarly, Mrs E.G. Sundquist from Nanaimo, BC, wrote: 'Never having entered a contest of any kind before, I am not quite sure just how to go about it ... I trust you may be able to use them even if they are not good enough to win a prize, so that others may enjoy a taste pleasure we have enjoyed for many years. Besides I rather feel that I owe *Chatelaine* something in exchange for all the perfectly grand recipes it has given me through the years.'[25] While winning the contest was clearly the entrant's intent, it appears that the recipe forum and exchange was also pleasurable. According to readers, the contest's popularity was due to the realistic nature of the recipes. Most demanded that the recipes meet their daily requirements, as this letter from Margaret Rasmussen of Vancouver illustrates: 'Your contest has interested me very much, mainly because of the request for family recipes. Other homemakers like myself who have children ... are mainly interested in reliable, simple-to-prepare items which are not too rich or costly. It's not that we wouldn't all like to be able to make chiffon cakes, etc., but we just can't afford to at the rate food we prepare is devoured. You are probably aware of this situation but perhaps like to be reassured by your readers from time to time on what they want and why.'[26]

The Meals of the Month menu page was another popular *Chatelaine* food feature, judged by the fact that whenever this page of detailed meal plans was omitted, readers wrote to complain. Mrs E.H. Donnelly of Windsor, Ontario, wrote: 'I would very much like to know why you discontinued those Meals of the Month. I was just lost without them and as that was the main reason I bought your magazine you can imagine how disappointed I was. I keep hoping each time I get a new magazine that you will again be planning all my menus for me. I am sure that many others must have found that as helpful as I did.'[27] Mrs Grace DeJong from Montreal agreed with Donnelly, commenting that the 'new setup of the daily menus page' was 'such a boon for a housewife especially these days – to be able to get an idea for the next day's or week's meals.'[28] Even a cursory glance at these meal plans confirmed that considerable time was spent in the kitchen by the many Canadian women who followed the institute's style of meal preparation. These were labour-intensive meals. *Chatelaine's* meal plans advocated hot lunches for children, and dinner meals always included a meat entrée or casserole, vegetables (often creamed or scalloped), a fancy rice or potato side dish, and dessert.

Other features represented the special type of food article featured in the magazine. Whether profiling food that men liked to eat, planning meals for the calorie conscious, or encouraging picky children to tuck into well-balanced meals, the *Chatelaine* Institute tried to respond to the many demands placed on the fifties' kitchen and the resident house-wife short-order cook, chef, baker, and dietitian. Articles such as Elaine Collett's 'Food Fit for a Queen' (hamburgers, apple pie, roast chicken with mushroom stuffing, herbed new potatoes, minted new green peas, garden salad, and thick western sirloin) in the June 1959 issue were representative of most of the food features.[29] The emphasis was on 'Canadian' food, either contemporary or old-fashioned favourites, which used ingredients that would be available all across the country, were not very expensive, and appealed to all ages and appetites. As the menu makes very apparent, the difference between American and Ca-nadian foods was often negligible. What the magazine did was create names, such as Western Sirloin, that reflected regional diversity. The more 'realistic' or 'thrifty' (depending on the readers' perceptions) menus also created a 'Canadian' image. This image was less affluent and more practical compared with the lavish American features.

The fourth type of food feature was the National Brands recipe collection printed in each October issue from the mid-fifties on. These were huge, forty-page collections of recipes, complete with corporate identification. Not surprisingly, they made specific and extensive use of the sponsors' products. Accompanying this yearly feature was an in-creased amount of food advertising, usually from products included in the recipe collection, which was the point in the first place. Some readers were fond of this supplement: Mrs Lois Browett of Hamilton wrote to Anderson to request another copy of this much-cherished issue. 'Would you possibly have a "back issue" of *Chatelaine* dated October 1957 that I could purchase?' she asked. 'I know this request sounds a little strange but I was keeping that particular copy as it had some nice recipes (over 200) called "Cookbook of Thirty Minute Spe-cials." Unfortunately, my youngest child cut up pages 60–73 and 78 to 81 and the pieces are missing.'[30] Yet Mrs Browett's letter was an anomaly in the extant letters about these National Brands features. Most of the readers did not appreciate the two hundred 'free' recipes. Mary G.

Wark of Owen Sound, Ontario, complained that there were 'far too many of these self-improvement articles now – housewives can't be bothered reading that – all those thousands of recipes – I never used one of them – and I do love to cook.'[31] Mrs Beryl Haslam of Pointe Claire, Quebec, voiced a similar complaint about those October issues with the huge recipe content: 'The fact is, I find your magazine rather dull! So much advertising ... However, I am not too interested in such an amount of recipes.'[32]

In contrast to the success of the Family Favourite's issues, which each had fifty recipes, these National Brand features were not as successful for two reasons. First, the magazine simply overwhelmed the reader with far too many recipes. Equally important was the clearly commercial component of this feature. A large part of the success and the charm of the Family feature was that the recipes came from other women. Readers found them interesting because they provided a glimpse into how other Canadian housewives fed their families or entertained. The recipes from corporations lacked the authenticity and 'genuine'ness of those from fellow readers plus they so evidently pushed their own products in contrast to the recipes from readers which were regarded as more economical or practical.

In the sixties, under the continuing direction of Elaine Collett and her institute staff, the format of the food articles changed slightly. The family food contest remained until 1967, famous Name Brand recipe features were dropped in favour of inserts or booklets full of recipes featuring advertisers' food products, and the Meals of the Month page continued, but most food articles were the stand-alone features in each issue.

Critics continued to assail the 'affluence' depicted in the pages. Mrs John Enslen of Seven Persons, Alberta, enumerated her reasons for cancelling her subscription: 'I find the magazine becoming most uninteresting ... who is interested in how some very wealthy lady spends her leisure time and how she arranges her expensive clothing budget ... The recipes may be good (many are), but must one continuously buy canned goods to make a satisfactory meal?'[33] Despite Enslen's concerns about affluence in the pages of the departmental features, the predominant theme in the food features continued to be thrift, in articles entitled '98 Cent January Specials,' 'Ten New Ways with a Pound of Hamburg,' or 'Eat Thrifty Meals.'[34] Many of these features were part of the January family budget specials, although a concern with thriftiness permeated most of the food articles. The key, as Collett repeatedly informed readers, was planning: weekly menus and shopping lists were completed only after women consulted the weekly supermarket specials. The casserole and other meatless or meat-extending meals were the focal point of many economical food articles. This excerpt from 'How to Eat Better and Save $200' is a good example of Collett's style of writing and some of the issues she addressed:

> Even a good manager like Rita Rose (and you) can learn new moneysaving cooking habits without sacrificing one ounce of taste appeal or sound nutrition. She was providing simple, fairly economical and nutritionally balanced meals for her family. But because she'd kept certain cooking habits she'd developed as a working wife in her early marriage, Rita was spending more than she needed to. We showed her how to achieve the same result – tasty meals and balanced nutrition – on $3.85 less a week ... Because as a working wife she had come home late and put dinner on the table in a hurry, Rita relied on the convenience foods (cake, pie, pudding mixes, canned soups and vegetables, heat-and-serve meat pies) and on meats that could be fried or broiled – usually the expensive cuts.[35]

Although the primary food advertisers in *Chatelaine* were processed food producers – prepared meats, canned soups, processed cheese, and some cake mixes – the magazine did not wholeheartedly endorse this material in its food features.

Reader Donna Atcheson of Saint John, NB, a fan of such features, offered this commentary: 'What are women most interested in? MONEY! How to make it spread around one's rent, food, clothing etc., and still come out on top. Articles on this subject have intimate and universal appeal. We are all interested in how other women meet these same problems and master them or go under, and we are always willing and even eager for helpful advice on the subject ... In January 1962 an equally interesting article "101 Ways to Save Money" told us how Stan and Rita Rose and we too could eat better, dress better, live better!'[36] Similarly, Mrs Margaret N. Davies of Cobourg, Ontario, attributed *Chatelaine*'s attention to thrift to its Canadian values: '"102 Ways to Save Money" – your January issue is a gem. There is another way to save money – buy *Chatelaine*! I have purchased various American publications through the years but it is no longer necessary to part with 35 or 50 cents per month in order to have the latest in good living and variety of reading. *Chatelaine* is geared to the Canadian Way of Life and Miss Collett's recipes are in line with Canadian tastes and economy.'[37] By the sixties, 'Canadian tastes' had begun to shift away from the traditional meat and two veg anglophone meals.

Affordable meals in the sixties were slightly more glamorous than their fifties' counterparts. The magazine strove to present more novel food ideas to its readers, such as 'Try These Strange Fruits,' which introduced readers to the joys of ugli fruit, persimmons, and mangoes.[38] One of the quickest ways to bring novelty into the food pages was to feature 'ethnic' food and, in the sixties, the number of ethnic food features were five times higher than the corresponding fifties' sample.[39] Anglo-Canadian housewives were urged to incorporate 'ethnic' recipes (Italian, Chinese, Spanish, and other European) into their family's diet as a way to provide diversity and new twists on economical eating. The ubiquitous tuna casserole was replaced by lasagna or curried chicken dishes. In features such as 'South Seas Foods to Enchant Your Natives,' which included recipes for 'Native Drums Barbecued Chicken,' 'Yams Tahiti,' 'Montezuma Casserole,' and 'Muu-Muu Punch,' the magazine combined ethnic food (or at least *Chatelaine*'s version of it) with affluence and an increasing interest in gourmet cuisine.[40] Multiculturalism and the desire to appear more cosmopolitan encouraged this interest in different cuisines, particularly for parties and special occasions. A synopsis of the types of food submitted for the 1965 Family Favourites Contest revealed that many Canadian housewives were incorporating ethnic cuisine into their meal plans: 'Chinese food is the most popular foreign dish, followed by Italian.'[41]

Another major thematic shift in the sixties was the emphasis placed on speed of preparation – acknowledgment that working wives did not have time for elaborate meal preparation and intricate recipes. 'Thirty Dinner Menus' or 'Quick Casseroles from Cans' promised meals that women could prepare – although they were little more than combinations of canned products – and serve within thirty minutes.[42] Even though the magazine encouraged and touted the value of processed food products for its simple and quick recipes, it criticized their cost. Year after year, in every budget article, Collett meticulously pared away all the processed and deli-counter foods from the women's grocery lists, stating: 'Save money by doing food-preparation work yourself. Every added convenience provided in foods you buy – or in the packaging of them – increases the costs.'[43] There was no indication what advertisers thought of this message, one so at odds with their reasons for buying space in *Chatelaine*.

The food section provided for wives – both those in paid employment and those at home – with a variety of different meals that were economical or fast or different. The large readership of these features is reflected in this letter from Ruth E. Moyle, director, Consumer Section, Department of Agriculture and Food for Ontario: 'On my return from the CAC Convention in Ottawa, I learned what a readership *Chatelaine* has. Our mailbag has been bulging with requests for our "Mail-a-Menu"! ... Regretfully, due to the overwhelming response we have reached our quota and have been forced to close our mailing list until further notice. Even in our wildest dream we didn't picture the project becoming so popular.'[44] Meanwhile, letters from readers indicate their appreciation. Mrs K. Norman, Islington, Ontario, wrote: 'For many months I have been meaning to thank you for Meals of the Month. They are a great inspiration for what could be a tedious job of meal planning, 365 days of the year.'[45] Readers complimented the individual features and recounted their successful use of the recipes. Mrs Jean Rousseau of Ste Foy, Quebec, wrote: 'Your recipes are interesting, easy to follow, and the approximate price and calorie value are a great help. I tried your Chicken Gruyere Tarte ... as a late-evening hot buffet and was voted a wonder cook by friends. Bravo for *Chatelaine*.'[46] Pat Ferguson of Camp Wainwright, Alberta, was eager to share with other readers how she had customized *Chatelaine* recipes to meet her circumstances: 'The article on freezer management and accompanying recipes ... were very good. As the wife of a "great white hunter" I found the Braised Beef recipe good, but substituting moose for beef, it was superb. I hope you'll pass along my suggestion to hunting widows who find themselves with hundreds of pounds of "free" meat to prepare.'[47]

'*Chatelaine* Takes a Fresh Look at Housecleaning': Cleaning Regimes

The articles on housekeeping were another major component within the *Chatelaine* departmental features and the magazine's most repetitious fare. Although it was possible to put different spins on meal preparation or decorating, housecleaning by its very nature was tiresome both to read about and to do. However, in their many series on how to 'modernize' homecleaning, the *Chatelaine* Institute attempted to provide different, usually quicker, ways to accomplish the household tasks. The home economist training was most evident in these pieces because the writers insisted on a 'planned' approach to household cleaning regimes. More could be accomplished in less time if housewives had a system, stuck to it, and then (particularly in the later years of the decade) rewarded themselves with time off for good behaviour. Whether it was 'Plan Your Housekeeping', 'Streamlined Homemaking for the Career Woman,' or '*Chatelaine* Takes a Fresh Look at Housecleaning,' the presumptions, and advice, were almost always the same. An analysis of the 1959 series provides a taste of these articles.

In March the magazine launched the '*Chatelaine* Takes a Fresh Look at Housecleaning' series, which stated: 'We'd rather see a clean untidy house than a frantic you.'[48] That phrase 'clean untidy' summarized perfectly how the institute had shaved time off the housework regime. Cleanliness was still important, but fastidious rules about tidiness were relaxed. This eight-page article provided housewives with a strict schedule, one worthy of examination for the level of detail in these housework articles and for their instruction into how housework should be performed. The daily list of chores to be performed gave some indication of the high standards expected even in an article purportedly about 'clean untidiness.' Each morning the housewife was advised to 'throw bedclothes back and open window wide' and to 'make-up and dress becomingly for your homemaking role' in 'slacks and a gay shirt, or a pretty housedress. Morale is half the battle here.' From there it was on to breakfast, and then the breakfast dishes, which one was supposed to 'drain dry' to save time. After that there was room for a 'small job,' which the magazine translated as 'handwash a fragile blouse, bath the baby, play with your preschooler or give yourself your weekly shampoo and pin-up.' Next was the living room, dining room, and hall area of the house, where the housewife was instructed to 'tidy, dust once over lightly as you go with a treated cloth, carpet sweep, dust mop, and finish a room at a time.' These tasks, unless stated otherwise, were to be performed every day. After a brief break for morning coffee, a 'phone call, the paper or a magazine,' it was into the bedrooms to 'make beds, tidy bedrooms, dust, and dust-mop,' again a room at a time, and then into the bathroom to 'tidy, clean basin and replace any soiled towels.' Later, it was back to the kitchen to start the dinner – vegetables to 'peel and wash' for storage and to 'prepare dessert.' After this work had been completed, Mrs Housewife could finally take her lunch. In the afternoon, there were more dishes to wash, another 'special job' which, depending on the day, could be ironing or an intensive spot clean of some part of the house, then a tea break. By this point the children were home from school and it was time to set the table (or ask the children to do it), make dinner, and do the dinner dishes. The final chores of the day were to set out the breakfast dishes and cereal, and to put the water in the coffee pot so that everything would be ready for the next day.

The institute's vision of clean untidiness was still rigidly structured and fastidious. By the time the special jobs had been done (and, on Fridays, extra tasks were taken on to free up time on the weekend), it was an intensive, exhausting schedule. Noticeably absent from all these instructions was any indication that husbands or children (other than setting the table) should perform any tasks in the house. Although they provided hints to assist the working wife, there was no suggestion that husbands share any of the household chores. Proving the adage that 'work expands to fill the time available,' other than those two coffee breaks and lunch time, the housewife's day was consumed by cleaning, tidying, grocery shopping, and clothes washing. Once her children and husband returned home, her remaining hours awake were largely spent catering to their needs. If this article was taken seriously, and housewives tried to emulate the institute's advice, they need never have worried of having 'nothing to do.' Three letters were printed in the June issue, two negative and one in praise of the article. Audrey Singer of Port Credit, Ontario, wrote: 'Having read Elaine Collett's "Fresh Look ..." I feel the need to cry out with an "everywoman's" voice. I have tried to follow her routine, and it has left me exhausted. Would you ask a maid to do all these things in one week?'[49] Mrs D. Robinson of Greenwood, NS, appreciated the article, saying she had 'picked up some very helpful hints.'[50] Finally, N. Smith provided a rather terse commentary: 'Altogether, I think your suggestions are maddening.'[51]

In the sixties the magazine featured a series of regular columns on housekeeping and household matters: Una Abrahamson's 'Homemaker's Diary,' which was later replaced by 'Of Consuming Interest' and Carol Taylor's 'Shopping with Chatelaine' and the 'Seal of Approval' features. These half to one-page articles provided collections of hints about household maintenance or advice on how to purchase products for the home – linens, appliances, clothing – under the 'Shopping' and 'Seal of Approval' banners. These two columns combined educational features and advice with subtle product endorsements.

Chatelaine included a few pieces on housework in the sixties. One, 'A Streamlined System for Housekeeping' by Una Abrahamson, was part of the 'Mother Who Works' special feature, geared to assist working mothers plan their housekeeping. 'Are you aware of the revolution that has taken place in housekeeping?' the article asked readers.[52] Unfortunately, the revolution did not involve a challenge to the almost exclusive relegation of housework to women. Instead, it advocated that women simplify their routines – eliminating overly fastidious routines, purchasing upgraded appliances, and implementing planned shopping and menu plans. These were practical suggestions (although clearly limited to middle-class readers with the means to follow them), yet they failed to address the basic inequity of unpaid household work. Husbands could help with the yard work, take out the garbage, and, if they were very helpful, assist with childcare. Children did not take an active role in the household, although the article urged that they should be responsible for their own rooms and for simple chores like setting the table. Although this article did not advocate the extremely time-consuming, perfectionist style of housework that had been recommended in the fifties, it was still a conservative reappraisal of housework and did not recommend any revolutionary solutions to the drudgery of household maintenance.

Housework articles were some of the most traditional fare included in the magazine, yet readers were prepared to critique this literature and felt free to ignore its prescriptions. Where Elaine Collett and her crew were so successful in their food articles, these housekeeping articles often fell on blind eyes. Many readers, in different contexts, wrote to express their joy and delight about their haphazard days, lack of strict scheduling, and, at times, more slothful habits. They were not prepared to clean house in this manner just because *Chatelaine* said so. These housework articles, like the Homes features, were not successful because they were too didactic. There was too much expert guidance and advice, and not enough input from the readership. Significantly, although the magazine responded to letters from readers who requested advice with their decorating or beauty regimes, never once did it print a request for another housekeeping article.

'Whatever Happened to the Homely Girl?'
Fashion and Beauty Features

Although a staple of women's magazine departments, fashion and beauty features waxed and waned throughout the years, appearing prominently in the April beauty issue and the September fashion issue, which featured back-to-school clothing for teenagers and university 'girls.' Like fashion and beauty features today, many of these articles were merely collections of photos or illustrations of various designers' clothing, shoes and accessories, undergarments, makeup and cleansing creams, complete with price and the stores in which the products could be purchased. By and large, under the editorial imprint of Eileen Morris (1950–2), Rosemary Boxer (1952–6), and Vivian Wilcox (1956–69), these pages showcased different products and taught readers the annual 'new' look.

Nothing brought beauty to the masses better than the annual makeover contests. One in particular, 'The Cinderella from Pugwash,' promised that readers could learn from the transformation of Marion Clarke described in 'Clerk to Cover Girl: Her Beauty Story Can Help You Too' (illustration 27).[53] This article told a twentieth-century fairytale about a young woman from a small community in northeastern Nova Scotia whose entry into the *Chatelaine* contest became the 'magic wand' that whisked her to Ontario, where 'her Prince Charming – the TV camera ... wooed and won our makeover girl.'[54] While in Toronto being styled, introduced at various parties, and photographed for the cover, Clarke appeared on the CBC show *Tabloid*. The producers were so impressed by her that she was asked back for a second appearance and eventually given a job contract. The story of Clarke's transformation was framed in black-and-white photos depicting the various stages of her *Chatelaine* experience. Even Boxer was astonished by the changes winning a *Chatelaine* contest could make in someone's life: 'We certainly had no idea that we were going to see Marion change from a clerk with Imperial Oil to a television performer when we met her the day she got off the plane and we began to plan our beauty makeover of her. We did see great possibilities, though, in this poised brunette with the wide-spaced intelligent blue eyes and the fresh complexion so many Maritime women have.'

Of course, the magazine could hardly have hoped for a better ending for this story, which proved the importance of eye makeup, foundation cream, and a good haircut. The patronizing tone evident in Boxer's comment about Clarke's features, and the regional stereotype of the fresh-faced Maritimer, were part of her style of writing. She was the 'expert' who brought makeup to the ignorant and innocent, transforming them into women of beauty and presence. Similarly, while most of the women who entered these contests were from cities, there was great appeal in selecting someone provincial, for whom the trip to Toronto would be a big adventure and the transformation very dramatic. While reference was made to Clarke's personality, the makeover, Boxer's expertise, and the prestige of winning a *Chatelaine* contest were clearly the

SPRING BEAUTY SECTION

Chatelaine

Cinderella from Pugwash

BY ROSEMARY BOXER
Fashion and Beauty Editor

The magic wand was a letter to Chatelaine's Spring Beauty Contest. Her coach — a shining North Star whisking her to wonderland. Her Prince Charming — the TV camera that wooed and won our makeover girl

Here's the picture I sent along with my entry to the Spring Beauty Week Contest

ONE SATURDAY last September Marion Clarke, a tall brown-haired girl of twenty-one, came home from her job in Halifax to spend the week end with her family in the nearby village of Pugwash. Her reading that week end included Chatelaine and when she saw the announcement of our Spring Beauty Week Contest, Marion showed it to her mother and remarked, "Guess I'll send in an entry and win that trip to Toronto."

She was smiling when she said it, mocking her own air of casual confidence she did not feel, but when the hundreds of entries from all parts of Canada were sorted, judged and judged again, Marion was one of the finalists. And in the final judging she was the one we chose to fly to Toronto by TCA for a week in November as our guest at the Royal York Hotel. She was the girl who got, in addition, a hundred dollars for her Christmas shopping and was given a complete

Good-by to our TCA stewardess . . .

I tell fashion models about Pugwash . . .

Later Hy Rossman fits my new evening gown.

27 *Chatelaine*, April 1954

chief reasons for Clarke's new life in Upper Canada. Clarke's return to Nova Scotia, particularly her family's reaction, provided a nice contrast to Boxer's fashion-speak prose, but even they eventually came around to the 'new look.' 'Back home, not even her sister, Eleanor, recognized her with her new hairdo ... The first thing her brother Joe said at the airport when she came home was, "What did they do to your hair?" Her mother sadly observed, "They've plucked your eyebrows." But everyone, when they became accustomed to the new Marion, liked the way she looked.' The meaning was obvious in this piece: style and glamour triumphed over down-home values and the natural look. How did readers respond to this Cinderella story?

Two lengthy letters were printed in the June 1954 issue in response to Clarke's makeover, one negative and one positive. The first, from D.I. Langley of Prairie, BC, criticized the changes wrought in Clarke: 'Ugh! If that is what your beauty experts turn out ... how glad I am that I did not enter your Spring Beauty Week Contest – not that I stood a chance of winning. I like the sweet unsophisticated look of the pre-treated Miss Clarke. But, oh, the after effects! She looks like a water-soaked poodle.'[55] Another letter, from Mrs Murray Smith of Pugwash, took an entirely different approach: 'I have known Marion Clarke since she was a wee girl – a girl to whom fame has come overnight. We in Pugwash and surrounding countryside are most appreciative of *Chatelaine*'s interest shown her, an interest which will have such far-reaching effects on her future life and career.'[56] The story of Marion Clarke may have touched many Canadian women, particularly those who envied her success and vowed to enter the next contest. For the winner's community, regardless of the nature of the contest, the publicity from the *Chatelaine* exposure regularly created Andy Warhol's 'fifteen minutes of fame.' *Chatelaine* was a prestigious magazine, and those who were fortunate to be published or to appear in the periodical, particularly contest winners, never seemed to forget the thrill of national exposure.

These makeover contests, like the recipe contests, were instrumental in creating interest in the magazine, increasing the readership, and getting women across the country interacting with the periodical and talking among themselves about the latest *Chatelaine*-induced craze. The fashion features differed from the food contests in that they attracted younger women to the magazine. Most manufacturers and corporations strive to get consumers young, hoping they will remain loyal consumers as they age, and *Chatelaine* seems to have made an effort to attract younger women to the magazine. Once they came to regard it as an authority on Canadian fashions, it was not a large jump to regard it as expert on food and nutrition, parenting, or household planning. In this way, the magazine became part of the currency of conversations among women, part of their lives, and, for some, part of their dreams.

Makeover mania hit a fever pitch in the sixties under *Chatelaine's* reigning doyenne of beauty, Eveleen Dollery. As beauty editor, Dollery wrote all the copy for the magazine's makeovers and regular articles. Her advice was almost always the same: women should maximize their appearance through good haircuts, effective makeup, and exercise and toning regimes. These short articles were mostly illustrations or photos with minimal text. In the November 1960 'What's New with Us' column, Dollery and her 'expertise' were profiled. 'In her career as a beauty editor Eveleen Dollery has "made over" – personally and through *Chatelaine's* Beauty Clinic – about fifty thousand women. This month, for the first time in her life, she made over four men, and proved they really are the weaker sex. (In the excitement of being photographed, one of them fainted!) Eveleen also noted that men are more adventure-some. Not one of our models balked at suggested changes in clothing or haircuts. But women often have to be coaxed and wheedled into new colours and hairstyles. Final conclusion: "Men, poor things," says Eveleen sadly, "have a lot less scope about changing their appearance than we have."'[57] Poor Dollery was often thwarted in her makeover attempts by women who feared radical transformations. But being beautiful was hard work, and Dollery was ruthless in her determination to remodel candidates – in spite of their reluctance. Part of the appeal of the beauty makeovers for readers was the fantasy of transformation. In the capable hands of the *Chatelaine* beauty expert, a 'homely girl' could be transformed into a chic, fashionable woman. The most consistent theme in all this material was that girls' and women's 'natural assets' were all visual – skin, face, posture, figure – and the tools of maximizing these assets were makeup, exercises, and beauty regimes (creams, hair colouring, astringents). Intellect and education were not part of the beauty equation.

One of the services Dollery provided readers was the '*Chatelaine* Beauty Clinic' (illustration 28). Participants received a beauty question-naire which, once completed and returned, was analyzed by Dollery and her staff. In short order the reader received her own, individual 'beauty analysis' in the mail. The service cost women one dollar. This advertisement for the service, 'Which half of your face is more beauti-

"Which half of your face is more beautiful?"

Eveleen Dollery
Chatelaine Beauty Editor

WHEN you next look into a mirror, hold a piece of paper so that it divides your face in two, brow to neck. Study this half of your features. Good? Move the paper over and examine the other half. Better or not so good? Is one eyebrow crooked, the other smoothly arched? Are the lashes of one eye more luxurious than of the other? Is the right side of your upper lip thinner than the left? It is true that every face has one side in better proportion than the other. So use the better side of each feature as a guide to shape the other not-so-well-shaped half.

For useful picture guides to help you enhance all your features write to Chatelaine Beauty Clinic for a personal beauty analysis. It includes up-to-date information on make-up changes and beauty products. We show you how to care for your hair and style it to suit your face. If you have a figure problem, we'll send along diet and exercise sheets, also a calorie chart. Send us the coupon below. We will mail you a questionnaire. Then fill in the questionnaire and return it to us with $1 for a complete beauty analysis.

- -

CHATELAINE BEAUTY CLINIC, 481 UNIVERSITY AVENUE, TORONTO 2

Please send me a beauty questionnaire to complete for my beauty analysis.

NAME ....

STREET ....

CITY .... PROVINCE ....

ful?' illustrates the narcissistic and exceedingly detailed examinations Dollery encouraged readers to perform. 'When you next look into a mirror, hold a piece of paper so that it divides your face in two, brow to neck. Study this half of your features.'[58] It is this sort of material for which women's and fashion magazines have been routinely criticized – and with good reason – because few women will emerge unscathed from such a study. The purpose, naturally, was to encourage product purchases to 'fix' the newly discovered 'flaws.' To help readers, the return beauty analysis included 'up-to-date' information on beauty products and their application. Cosmetics and toiletries advertisers in the magazine got a tremendous boost from this material. Although the magazine usually refrained from explicit recommendations of a specific product, the 'beauty analysis' undoubtedly contained considerable product endorsement and information.

One major difference in the sixties was the increased emphasis on dieting. Metrical, the first liquid diet product, was introduced to American consumers in 1959–60 and, by 1961, it and other copycat products were selling $350 million worth of dieting products annually.[59] The use of ever thinner models – British model Twiggy was the fashion star of the late sixties – valorized thinness. *Chatelaine* began to feature an increasing number of dieting features, with titles such as 'Three Dazzling Diet Successes,' 'Three Diet Winners Discover New Beauty,' or 'A 212 Pound Girl Becomes a Hundred Pound Bride,' all written by Dollery.[60] Women submitted their personal 'diet-success stories' to the magazine, and the winners (the women with the most dramatic weight loss) were featured in the April issue. Naturally, the articles included the requisite before-and-after photos. Dollery's commentary concentrated on the women's diet secrets and invariably contained patronizing words about how they had discovered their 'inner beauty' during the process. With such stock phrases as 'Tired of looking far older than her years, Dawn lost 123 pounds' and 'revealed her hidden prettiness,' the message was clear that, whatever the circumstances, large women were unattractive.[61] Often, part of the vibrant new life awaiting the recently reduced were dating opportunities. In one article, weight loss brought a marriage proposal: 'Here's the Cinderella story of Barbara Diamond who once wore size 42 dresses, avoided mirrors, and was frustrated with loneliness. Today this pert schoolteacher picks her dresses off the size eight rack, enjoys her new good looks and is happily engaged to be married this August.'[62] It was a simplistic yet compelling message, but, given the enormous amount of weight these women were said to have lost, readers were sceptical about the articles' authenticity. Mrs Ronald Hatch Sr of Red Head Cove, Newfoundland, asked: 'Did this really happen to Dawn and Nina? Did they really lose this much weight [123 and 146 pounds, respectively]? It's really unbelievable. A doctor gave me these pages from *Chatelaine* and says that I too can be like Dawn, I weigh 196.'[63] The editors assured Mrs Hatch that it was possible: after all, Dawn and Nina had done it, why couldn't she?

To assist *Chatelaine* readers battle bulges and to compete with other North American products, the magazine endorsed two diet programs: 'Chatelaine's MM Diet' in 1962 and the 'LP Diet,' a liquid diet program, in 1966.[64] It was a compromise, according to the editors, born of the realization that dieting was here to stay and that the magazine should do its part by providing a safe diet for readers: 'If dieting's here to stay – and in our affluent North American society it begins to look that way – the best diet is one that's nutritionally sound, shows results fast enough to be encouraging and teaches us the kind of food we should eat for the rest of our lives if we want to stay slim.' Canadian and international readers were enthusiastic about the results possible on the LP diet. According to Mrs Margaret Devine of Ballycastle, Northern Ireland, the diet was effortless: 'Thanks for a diet that works. I didn't need even to apply will-power.'[65] Others, such as Mrs B. Eugenie Terrell of Mallorytown, Ontario, were quick to report how many pounds they had lost: 'I have been on the LP diet for two weeks and have lost ten pounds.'[66] To paraphrase Susie Orbach's famous phrase of the seventies, fat was not yet a feminist issue in *Chatelaine*.[67]

Like many of the other 'experts' who wrote *Chatelaine*'s departmental material, fashion editor Vivian Wilcox was an industry award winner. In 1963 she was honoured at the Garment Salesman of Ontario Market Banquet for her work in the fashion industry and presented with the 'Judy Award.'[68] In keeping with the magazine's glossier appearance in the sixties, the fashions became more adventurous – and more expensive. Wilcox attended the European fashion shows and wrote reports, profiled new fashions available in the stores, pinpointed each season's 'in look,' and instructed readers about ways to build their fashion wardrobes. Despite a few articles with such titles as 'Fashions for Your Golden Years,' teenagers and women in their twenties were the primary focus of the articles.[69] The aim was identical to the beauty material – in this case, the transformative power of fashionable clothing. Being in and being thin were important: the right clothes could translate into better career and personal opportunities, and ultimately unlimited happiness. For example, in 'Whatever Happened to the Homely Girl?' Eveleen Dollery and Vivian Wilcox combined forces, writing: 'She's vanished into prettiness, thanks to make-up and clothes magic! Here's how three smart working girls use modern beauty and fashion knowledge to turn their average faces and figures into above-average good looks.'[70]

Chatelaine received few letters about the fashion material. Some readers were enthusiastic about the fashion pages. Audrey Vogt of Quesnel, BC, wrote: 'Just to let you know we keep up with fashions in the Cariboo. My sister bought her New Year's dress in Prince George last year. It was featured in your December issue of that year. I meant to write this letter last year, but it got sidetracked.'[71] Another fan was Mrs Phyllis Poulter of Montreal, who noted: 'The fashion pages keep me aware of the latest style trends.'[72] Most readers, however, were critical, and those criticisms indicate the regional, class, and ageist tensions at play within the community of readers. For instance, Mrs A.F. Pearce of Colfax, Saskatchewan, complained: 'Having just finished "Five Smart Girls Who Sew" I can't for the life of me figure out just what is so smart about them. There are thousands of women who make their own clothes, so it can't be that. You show one that must be at least twenty-five with a skirt about three inches above her knees. Aren't there any bricks in Ontario you can tie to the bottom to bring it down? If these women want to dress like teenagers, why not send them back to high school, but please don't try to shove them down our throats as "smart women." They're anything but. If this is considered "smart" in the east, I am glad I am a plain old westerner.'[73] Similarly, Mrs P. Allen of Moose Jaw, Saskatchewan, wrote: 'I feel Vivian Wilcox, your fashion editor, is talking out of turn in "worst mistakes" ... if Miss Wilcox lived in Saskatchewan in the winters of 30 and 40 degrees below zero, I'm afraid even she would wear slims, carcoat and kerchief for shopping.'[74] Meanwhile, Mrs Dorothy Brown cautioned the magazine not to forget the budgetary restrictions of most readers:

> I have one complaint, that is in regard to the teen aged clothes advertised. They are much too expensive ... As a mother of three girls in high school and two younger children also, I cannot afford ten or fifteen dollars for a sweater ... and neither can most of my friends, and certainly the girls themselves do not earn enough to buy such items. The clothes selected are attractive but I have noticed for quite some time that the price quoted are far more than what most white collar families can afford, and I should

imagine most of your readers would be in this class. This is not merely my opinion but have heard it from other women as well ... A recent copy had a budget wardrobe for an adult which was excellent.[75]

Home Decorating and Design

Over the years, the turnover in the position of home design editor, later renamed home editor, was quite rapid: John Caulfield Smith, Catherine Fraser (mother of former *Saturday Night* editor John Fraser), Doris Thistlewood, Barbara Reynolds, Alain Campaigne, and Annabelle King all held the position during the fifties and sixties. Home editor was a demanding job, as this description of Thistlewood's responsibilities indicates: 'Being *Chatelaine*'s home planning editor ... involves much more than writing one or two features a month for the magazine. Only a small part of her work gets into print. Hour-long speeches to women's clubs, radio interviews, visits to designers, architects, and decorators somehow all get wedged into her workday. Then there are the letters from readers with decorating problems. She's delighted to help them and generous with ideas on everything from how to spend wedding present money to building brighter bazaar displays. After hours she gives us advice.'[76] The description of Thistlewood's multifaceted role as a liaison with designers, disseminator of 'new ideas' through the magazine, presenter to women's groups, expert adviser to readers, and staff counsellor in her 'off hours' illustrated yet another forum in which the magazine transcended the print format. These visits from the *Chatelaine* experts were highlights in many communities, and cross-country trips were frequent. *Chatelaine* staff were emissaries who brought a personal message to communities, attracted new readers, and touched base with readers.

The articles on home planning fell into three categories: the *Chatelaine* Home Decorating series in 1952 and 1953; the single features on topics such as renovating, painting, suburban building, and architectural houses; and, starting in 1958, the yearly 'homes' feature, in which the magazine built and furnished model homes in various regions of the country, as a promotional showcase for advertisers and an 'idea book' for readers. In 1952 the magazine launched 'The Course in Home Decorating,' written by Catherine Fraser ('an outstanding authority'). This course was intended 'to help you give your home more charm, more beauty ... You will want to read, study and save all seven issues.'[77] The magazine often suggested that readers should cut out the service de-

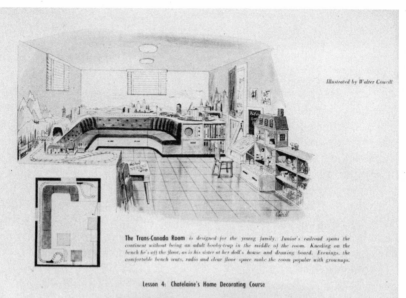

Illustrated by Walter Cowell

The Trans-Canada Room *is designed for the young family. Junior's railroad spans the continent without being an adult booby-trap in the middle of the room. Kneeling on the bench he's off the floor, as is his sister at her doll's house and drawing board. Evenings, the comfortable bench seats, radio and clear floor space make the room popular with grownups.*

Lesson 4: Chatelaine's Home Decorating Course

5 ROOMS FOR FUN

By Catherine Fraser, *Chatelaine Home Decorating Consultant*

See Canada first—in your own basement. These "coast-to-coast" recreation rooms are keyed to the play-and-party needs of your young fry, but grownups will enjoy relaxing here, too.

A recreation room should be chiefly for young fry, from toddlers to twenties, but it should be prepared to accommodate adults on occasion, too.

It isn't a substitute for the living room; but it will save the living room from suffering too much wear and tear, so that this can remain a place where grownups and young folks feeling grown-up may read and talk and visit without volcanic interruptions.

It should be a place for play and fun, and the fun should start with planning and building the recreation room. There'll be more fun if the whole family's in on the project—and more still if it's built around the theme of a family hobby or a trip to some favorite part of the country . . . even if it's a trip you haven't taken yet.

These are some of the considerations we had in mind in planning this fourth lesson in Chatelaine's Home Decorating Course, but as we have stressed since the beginning, the basic consideration in planning any room must be usefulness.

We had seen many recreation rooms in which Junior's trains had to be dismantled before his parents could play a game of ping-pong, before we visited a home where trestles of planks and orange crates carried the tracks around the walls where they weren't in anybody's way. That useful idea became the basis of our Trans-Canada Room, pictured above.

In another home we know, the modest-sized L-shaped living room seemed to bulge at the seams because it just wasn't built to accommodate an outsize upright piano. The idea of moving the piano to the recreation room was the spark that exploded into our Stampede Room (opposite page)—and then we were away.

We said, "These are Canadian basements we are planning for, basements that will serve their main purpose through eight cold months." So we went to work to create rooms with an atmosphere of coziness and warmth, and which derive their design from any Canadian child's knowledge of, and interest in, his or her own country. We left Mexican motifs and Hawaiian designs to the Mexicans and the Hawaiians and we stayed happy at home in our own country—but we weren't content until we had covered its whole breadth from the soft, shrouded slopes of the Pacific to the salty cragginess of our Atlantic shore. We amused ourselves thinking of inexpensive ways to furnish and decorate these rooms in keeping with the regional theme of each one—amusement, we think, long outlasts the corny jokes carved on wooden plaques and the midway kewpie dolls that some people put in their basements instead of the garbage.

We never missed a chance to make these "all-Canadian basements" Continued on page 58

20   CHATELAINE—AUGUST, 1952

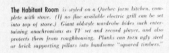

The **Totem Room,** *like all four on this page, is designed for the teen-age family. Totem figures and Indian masks can be copied from real thing in books and museums, and painted on plywood. Drumheads for stool and end table are of leather.*

The **Habitant Room** *is styled on a Quebec farm kitchen, complete with stove. (If no flue available electric grill can be set into top of stove.) Giant oldstyle wardrobe hides such entertaining anachronisms as TV set and record player, and also protects them from roughhousing. Planks can turn ugly steel or brick supporting pillars into handsome "squared timbers."*

The **Stampede Room** *grew around an upright piano which, while still a good instrument, crowded a small living room. The back covered with rodeo or travel posters, it creates an attractive wall break, and is equally handy for afternoon piano practice or evening singsongs when the cowhands hit town.*

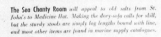

The **Sea Chanty Room** *will appeal to old salts from St. John's to Medicine Hat. Making the dory-sofa calls for skill, but the sturdy stools are simply log lengths bound with line, and most other items are found in marine supply catalogues.*

partment material to compile a reference scrapbook. Some women believed that other readers were taking 'the course' and they derived enjoyment from this knowledge, as this letter from Mrs R. Dowson of Nemiskam, Alberta, explained: 'Your course in home decorating was a most effective way of reaching busy housewives. It's much easier to study when one knows thousands of women are in the class.'[78] The course was viewed as an affordable way of obtaining some decorating expertise, and the younger readers were appreciative. Mrs E. Dodds of Montreal wrote: 'Your lessons on home decorating are wonderful! I've started my scrapbook for we have bought a duplex and will move next May. That will give me plenty of time to read your seven lessons, benefit by them and put them to use in our own home.'[79] These articles were clearly written for younger women who would be decorating their first homes, since they stressed planned buying and economizing on a budget, and dealt with issues for which new houseowners needed assistance. In keeping with the magazine's *raison d'être*, the Canadian angle was constantly stressed, in the use of colour to match the local flora and fauna and in Canadian theme rooms, such as the August 1952 article 'Five Rooms for Fun' with the line 'See Canada first – in your own basement' (illustration 29). The suggested recreation room themes were 'the totem room, the habitant room, the stampede room, the sea chanty room and the trans-Canada room,' and all were outfitted in the stereotypical furnishings and accessories that those terms bring to mind.[80]

The decorating course and other singular features received very positive letters from readers, indicative of both their enjoyment and the fact that the material attracted their attention and was actually read. Articles such as 'How to Buy More with Your Home Furnishing Dollar' were always popular, according to Marion Downton of St John's: 'This kind of article is just what we "first time furnishers" need and eagerly look forward to more of the same in future *Chatelaines*.'[81] The most appreciative devotees of *Chatelaine*'s service material were skilled in the 'art of making do,' stretching their decorating and grocery dollars, and they responded to articles that reflected that reality.

By the sixties, Canadian design (as illustrated in the magazine) had become more sophisticated, incorporating antiques and collectibles in design plans. This was also another indicator of the up-market shift suggested by the Dichter Study as a way to attract the more affluent or 'progressive' market. In the sixties, the big feature of the year was the homes annual, which was a long special (10–15 pages) covering the

The Man in the Home Pavilion at Expo 67 is the prizewinning architectural design in a contest sponsored by the Canadian Lumbermen's Association. We built and furnished it as the

**CHATELAINE
EXPO
HOME**

30 *Chatelaine*, May 1967

latest household and interior design. If readers commented in the fifties that many of the homes features were far too affluent and well beyond their means, this gap was even more so for the sixties. The homes produced were larger (one had over 4000 square feet of living space), featured opulent furnishings, and were geared not to the average first-time buyer, but to the upper-middle-class family or the mature home purchaser in search of a grander home. Only those groups would have the necessary income to buy a 'Design Home.' In May 1967, for example, the magazine profiled its *'Chatelaine* Expo Home' (illustration 30).[82] The house was the 'prize-winning architectural design' from a contest sponsored by the Canadian Lumbermen's Association. It was built on the Expo site, then decorated and furnished by *Chatelaine.* According to the rules of the Lumbermen's Association, the house was designed for an average Canadian family – 'a couple with a son, fifteen, and two daughters, ten and five' – and, in the words of Alain Campaigne, it possessed a 'serene dignity.' However, the magazine's definition of 'average' was quite exclusive. The house included a fully equipped workroom for the man of the house, an intercom, formal dining room, three bedrooms, and a den. Undoubtedly, it was meant to be a show-case for Canadian manufacturers, the magazine, and Canadian designers. Still, the magazine's implication that average Canadians could afford to live this way was a bias that ran through much of the homes and interior design material.

All visitors to the Expo site were given a raffle ticket to win the house and a car; if the winner lived outside Montreal, he or she would receive $30,000 and the blueprints to replicate the house elsewhere. In the January 1968 issue the winner was announced: 'Before it was too late, 17 year old Douglas McEachen, a grade 12 student at Sheldon Williams Collegiate in Regina, dug into his savings and flew down, alone, for his first look at Expo the weekend before it closed. He visited Chatelaine's Man in the Home Pavilion, deposited his ticket on the house draw – and won ... Doug received $30,000 cash in lieu of the house. The money went straight to an investment agency, and eventually will finance Doug's university music studies.'[83] McEachen's win is more than just another interesting anecdote about the magazine; it illustrates the wide range of people attracted by the variety of the magazine's content and its external promotions. This letter from Saul Field of Willowdale, Ontario, also confirms that interest and provides commentary about the perceptiveness of the visitors: 'Shortly after the opening of Expo 67, our postman began to bring us a steady stream of inquiries from all over the world from people who had visited the Chatelaine Expo Home. The reason? Our colour engravings decorated the interior – my wife Jean's, in the bedrooms, and six-year-old daughter Martina's, in the child's room. My own prints hung in the living room, foyers, basement and stairwells. We would like to express our heartfelt thanks for their interest. Most of the letters inquired whether the work was for sale. The answer is "no" for Martina's prints, but "yes" for Jean's and my prints.'[84] Each year, visitors, in the cities in which the design homes were located, were able to walk through the fully furnished houses and see, in detail, the latest trends in Canadian design, furniture, and decorations.[85] However, the location of the design homes was limited to suburban areas in British Columbia, the Prairies, Manitoba, Ontario, and Quebec. The Atlantic provinces and the North were completely ignored. Chatelaine spent a considerable amount of money producing these features, but readership lagged and advertising followed. By the end of the sixties and into the seventies, the number of editorial pages outnumbered those for advertising. The purpose of the model homes – to provide a conducive environment for home building supplies and manufacturers to advertise in Chatelaine – failed.

An additional service provided by the homes department was the

'*Chatelaine* Decorator Service.' Barbara MacLennan, decorator service consultant, was responsible for providing readers with individual 'interior design' advice. This service worked on the same premise as the beauty consultant – only in this instance readers submitted their room plans, sketches of their present furniture and design problems, and awaited MacLennan's assessment. According to Mrs E. Armstrong of Etobicoke, Ontario, the service worked very well. 'Since 1957 I have used *Chatelaine* Decorator Service for our various apartments and houses, always with pleasing results, but never as outstanding a plan as Barbara MacLennan recently did for our living-room. The first time my husband looked at the plans he exclaimed that the high-back swivel chair was exactly what he wanted.'[86] It was a very affordable way to get a 'customized' design plan (it cost one dollar), and for the magazine it was a way to promote its service department features and provide greater exposure to its advertisers.

Gardening

In contrast to the home design features, the gardening columns were one of the most popular departmental features. Helen O'Reilly's gardening column ran regularly in the magazine during the fifties. According to editor Lotta Dempsey's introduction, O'Reilly, a former law student and publishing firm employee, had shifted her attention to gardening and 'she and a friend raise delphiniums, and other valuable flowers, like sweet peas' on a 'wonderful country project just outside Toronto.'[87] The photo accompanying Dempsey's description showed an older woman clad in denim overalls happily shovelling manure into a wheel barrow. Hardly the typical glamorous portrait of the expert, but it complemented the down-to-earth manner of O'Reilly's writing style. She wrote informative, no-nonsense articles on a variety of gardening conundrums – perennials, lawn maintenance, growing strawberries. Her articles were usually informative full-page essays that provided the Latin name, detailed growing instructions, germination requirements if using seeds, and instructions on how to buy economically at the local nursery. Mrs D. McCowan of Burrows, Saskatchewan, noted her appreciation for the gardening columns: 'We get so many good hints from your magazine. *Chatelaine*'s Garden Chart was worth all we paid for it as peonies are our special flower and we have to transplant them this fall, and did not know how. I will be glad of any advice you can give on home economics as it helps our clubs so much. We are all rural women, and the club is The Great West Homemaker.'[88] Ironically, for a magazine that tried to attract the urban reader, rural readers were more apt to find the magazine indispensable – a result of sparser resources, fewer sources of information, and less access to groups and available 'experts.'

After O'Reilly left the magazine (no explanation was forthcoming), the position of garden editor remained vacant until 1964, when horticultural writer Lois Wilson was hired. She continued on in the same spirit as O'Reilly, producing sophisticated articles on a wide variety of gardening issues – fall gardening preparations, winter indoor gardens, landscaping and fence construction, and Canadian wildflowers. Enthusiasts were ecstatic that gardening had returned and that it reestablished the high standard set by O'Reilly. Mrs G.S. Morris of Victoria, BC, commented: 'About a year ago I wrote to you requesting an article on African violets. I have just received my November issue and must tell you how delighted I am with it.'[89] Mrs Louise Johnson of Hudson, Quebec, another of the legion of African violet fans in Canada, wrote: 'As I belong to the class of super enthusiasts I might as well confess: African violets have become a way of life for me. May I congratulate Lois Wilson for such an excellent article ... and you for publishing it.'[90] Wilson was recognized by professional organizations and horticultural professionals for her work. According to the magazine, 'she recently served as one of the three judges of Bermuda's Floral Pageant ... Also this year, the National Council of State Garden Clubs, with a total of half a million members in the U.S. and other countries, presented Lois with a Certificate for Horticultural Literature "in recognition of the distinguished service in literary effort of horticultural interest."'[91] The following year, Chatelaine published a letter from Leslie Laking, director of the Royal Botanical Gardens in Hamilton, praising Wilson's work: 'I have just read Lois Wilson's article, "Our Centennial Heritage of Canadian Garden Plants" ... It is a magnificently produced article which will be appreciated by every horticultural-minded person in Canada. Congratulations. The results are exciting magazine fare.'[92] Eventually, Wilson would produce a Chatelaine gardening book.

Crafts

The position of Chatelaine's craft editor was created during the sixties and held by writer Wanda Nelles. In contrast to the American magazines, which often printed a sewing or knitting pattern, Chatelaine published a small, usually quarter-page, advertisement for a craft kit or pattern. Readers had to send away for the pattern or kit, and prices ranged from 50 cents to $3.00. Several readers' letters commented on the absence of (free) craft material in the magazine, including M. Siemienska of Montreal: 'I think your magazine is wonderful BUT – every issue contains pages of recipes, and absolutely no knitting. I am not much of a cook, but I love knitting which I find very relaxing. Please do something.'[93] For many, such as this reader from Prince Rupert, BC, pleasurable departmental material meant craft ideas and projects, not recipes:

> When one tries to buy *McCall's Needlework* magazine, one is told, 'that came out last week and we are all sold out.' We pay from thirty-five cents to five dollars for petit point charts, knitting books etc. One year's subscription to certain English and American magazines may produce one usable idea, we keep buying them. Some of them have neither stories or recipes. Why can't we have Canadian ideas? Your petit point picture of Halifax Clock Tower deserves more space in your magazine ... If you run a Mrs Chatelaine contest and judge it from a hobby angle, you might find the results most interesting. Most women of my acquaintance are not too interested in recipes because they come in every magazine, and cooking is not a hobby to us at all. If we ever managed to make something look like the picture, our husbands would still demand a square meal on the side. The pretty pictures are fine to look at but how about some good old fashioned tips. Weights, measure and substitutions for cooking. Changes in recipes for sea level dwellers and etc. We live with modern conveniences but still have old fashioned troubles ... *No faults to find with Chatelaine but give us more to chew on. Make it a magazine we can refer to, not one we read and discard.*[94]

Although the letter was addressed to Anderson, it was Jean Yack who underlined the sentence and wrote in the margin 'good point.' Also noteworthy was the importance the reader placed on 'Canadian' crafts and affordability. Once again, 'Canadian' meant identifiable motifs, buildings, flora and fauna or scenes – which were then featured on a variety of needlework patterns. Undoubtedly the letter from Prince Rupert played a role in the magazine's decision to start a craft contest the following year. The winners received a prize, and their craft was not only featured in the magazine but turned into a *Chatelaine* pattern. This letter from English reader M. Mawson describes the excitement created in her community by the winning *Chatelaine* entry: 'The interest in the toy is quite personal as it was at my suggestion the entry came to your competition – the result of which gave so much pleasure over here. Miss Irving's vicar congratulated her in the Church Magazines notes and very soon the local press paid her a visit and took photographs for a splendid article in the *Gazette*. Your magazine is gifted to me by a friend in Kentucky, U.S.A ... Pardon an old person (I'm 73) for intruding on your valuable time.'[95]

Children

Another regular feature was the column entitled 'Young Parents' or 'Your Child.' This section usually contained only one article, 'Child Health Clinic,' which was surrounded (or 'supported,' in the parlance of the advertising department) by advertisements for baby formula, children's medical products, and children's clothing. 'Clinic' was written by Dr Elizabeth Chant Robertson, a nutritional researcher at the Hospital for Sick Children in Toronto. The focus of the column was decidedly medical, as most columns featured very specific information about childhood diseases, growth and development, disciplinary matters, and nutrition and dietary requirements. They were informative, without ladling guilt onto mothers or talking down to them. In keeping with the era, 'Young Parents,' regardless of this column's title, was intended for mothers. Fathers were rarely addressed, and though the term *parent* was often used, it was employed as a synonym for mothers. Interestingly, despite the challenges of raising all those baby-boom families, the magazine devoted little space to children or their concerns. It was rare to receive any letters in response to these articles, particularly Robertson's columns, so it does not appear to have been a popular section. In contrast, the same amount of space devoted to Helen O'Reilly's gardening columns resulted in far more letters of praise.

One of the irregular features in the magazine throughout the fifties was the children's page called 'Chatty Chipmunk.' 'Chatty' (his formal name was Chatsworth) was written by Laura Aliman, wife of Gene Aliman, the *Maclean's* art director.[96] Aliman's daughters – Susie, aged 11, and Jenny, aged 4 – were consultants for this page of children's games, brain teasers, and do-it-yourself craft ideas. The feature started in 1955 and continued into 1957, though it was soon eclipsed by the Teen Tempo page (the precursor to *Miss Chatelaine*, which later was rechristened *Flare*) and quietly dropped from the magazine. While it ran in the magazine, the column attracted letters from boys and girls, from Canada and the United States, who wrote to thank 'Chatty' for the fun games and puzzles. Even adults wrote to commend the magazine for the section, since it provided an added resource for children's entertainment. This letter, from Mrs Robert Edmonds of Kaipokok Bay, Labrador, was representative: '*Chatelaine* is a must among my collection of magazines. I look forward to every mail I receive it. Mail comes to us every six weeks. As the community teacher and nurse, I often use Chatty Chipmunk's page in school. The children are delighted with Chatty's ideas and he has become much loved by the boys and girls.'[97] The children's page was often a staple in American women's magazines. Still, as letters from readers made clear, regardless of whether there was a separate child's page, children used the magazines to do school projects or to cut and paste colourful images for their own amusement.

After Robertson retired in 1964, the magazine featured a series of 'experts' who, with the exception of Dr Johanne Bentzon and Marguerite W. Brown of the Institute for Child Study, contributed only a few articles each for this column. Brown's articles examined child psychology, particularly issues of development and parenting: praising children, disciplining, temperament problems, the role of parents and of fathers. Although few letters were specifically about the 'Your Child' column, many readers included this column in their list of what they enjoyed in the magazine. This letter, from Vancouver doctor Gladys Story Cunningham, indicates her pleasure with the contents of this column: 'It is such a satisfaction to read an article on Sex Education which asserts that sex education is really part of the education of the person as a whole; that sex is a part of the personality and not a "thing apart." Marguerite Brown's article ... is a fine contribution to the thinking of many parents and others associated with growing people.'[98]

Conclusion

The importance of the expert writers for *Chatelaine* department fare cannot be overestimated, since they gave readers confidence in the legitimacy and accuracy of this material. Not only were experts a staple of women's magazines, but suburban North American women were becoming increasingly reliant on them as replacements for the more traditional familial guides. Although the departmental features were supposed to encourage readers to take action – to buy flower bulbs, dresses, food, furnishings, or baby food – the experts gave the material integrity and distinguished it from the advertisements. Equally important was the nature of the advice, information, or 'ideas' conveyed to the readers. The most successful service material – food, gardening, household advice, and the parenting column – provided readers with practical information. In those features, the commercial nature of the material was often subtle. These departments also acknowledged that women's roles were changing, and some effort was put into changing the most traditional of the components. Although these articles link gender and consumption, most of the suggestions, recipes, or garden plans called for affordable products. The least successful features – fashion, beauty, and homes pieces – were those that featured persistent middle- and upper-middle-class biases and presumed that all readers were urban or suburban dwellers with considerable disposable incomes. The commercial ethos was strongest in these features.

Resistance to such messages was hard work, despite the modest audience *Chatelaine* attracted. Many revisionist historians of postwar North America note the agency of consumers and, at times, their resistance to the status quo. But those moments have been celebrated far more often than the costs have been detailed. 'Opting out' of the consumer-driven society attracted attention, in an era when the capitalist system and the 'choices' available were regarded as one of the primary hallmarks of the democratic way of life. In many cases, the resisters were not opposed to consumption per se, but came from more modest backgrounds. They praised the traditional values of thrift and making do, and a philosophy that did not prioritize conspicuous consumption. They were usually rural or small-town folk, or often from the Prairies or Atlantic Canada; they might be older; and they frequently expressed a strong religious commitment. In contrast to the 'ideal' reader of this material, these resisters identified themselves as 'Common Canadians' and, in many respects, they were. Census statistics and economists indicate that Canadians did not have the disposable wealth of Americans until well into the sixties, although the gap in earnings between the two countries was always in evidence. More modest, less glamorous than the American women's magazines, *Chatelaine* employed a softer sell. Thanks to its own budget restrictions, it could not emulate the high gloss of the American women's magazines even if it desired to. Even so, many readers criticized the affluence. They told tales of 'making do with less' which, if not antithetical to these articles and the advertising they supported, indicate they did not embrace the consumer ethos uncritically or without reservations. Rather subversively, the departmental editors often aided the readers – such as by tailoring articles to modest budgets. Finally, as we shall see, the messages in the fiction, but primarily in the editorials and articles, provided other strategies for living that did not highlight the virtues of consumption or the importance of appearance. Those alternative images challenged, and sometimes implicitly criticized, the images in the service department pages. In the end, those contradictions within the readership and within the editorial content meant that this service material could not have been digested easily or uncritically.

Chapter 6

'Searching for a Plain Gold Band': *Chatelaine* Fiction

Like service material, formula fiction has long been a staple of women's magazines. Recently, academics have turned their attention to this previously dismissed form of popular fiction, realizing that the stories' simple plot lines and readily discernible themes and symbolism make excellent sources from which to understand the concerns of a given society.[1] According to John Cawelti, formula fiction is popular because it serves four purposes within society: it affirms 'existing interests and attitudes'; resolves 'tensions and ambiguities' within the culture; enables 'the audience to explore in fantasy the boundary between the permitted and the forbidden and to experience in a carefully controlled way the possibility of stepping across that boundary'; and assists 'in the process of assimilating changes in values.'[2] This letter from reader Dorothy Paga of San Martin, Peru, confirms Cawelti's conjectures. 'Thanks to my mother-in-law my copies of *Chatelaine* arrive fairly often out here in the Jungles of Peru,' she wrote. 'Although I do not agree with some of the stories it still is excellent reading. I have enjoyed the "Last Word Is Yours" and feel a lot of Canadians have little to do when an article in a magazine will cause them to write some of the remarks they do but it does add for good reading ... I am sorry to say that I like Sheila MacKay Russell's stories. Maybe some of them are a little far fetched but still good reading and think how much fun it would be to live like that.'[3] Clearly, reader fantasies were relative; most *Chatelaine* readers would find Paga's lifestyle more exotic than the western Canada of MacKay Russell's fiction. Plots and characters might change, but the formula was timeless: romance fiction. It featured characters and settings that the readers were familiar with, as the drama often took place in suburbia, and all the stories had the requisite happy ending. But in working towards the resolution, the characters often grappled with tensions, emotions, and issues that threatened to disrupt or prevent the happy ending. It was these fissures in the plotlines that made the stories compelling, for they illustrated the paradoxes and ambiguities faced by women readers in the era.

Romance fiction has been the fiction of choice for many women, according to Janice Radway, because it is 'compensatory literature.' It 'supplies them with an important emotional release that is proscribed in daily life because the social role with which they identify themselves leaves little room for guiltless, self-interested pursuit of individual pleasure.'[4] Radway contends that through romance reading, women create a community for themselves, albeit one mediated by the mass media, in which they seek comfort, support, and relaxation. Readers confirmed Radway's assessment in their letters. Mrs M.A.E. McLeod of West Hill, Ontario, commented: 'We housewives like a story as a pick-me-up while resting the arches and getting ready to tackle the next job. A laugh over a cartoon or a cry over a piece of fiction is to my mind what I hope to find when I pick up a magazine.'[5] In contrast to the editorials and the articles, which provided thought-provoking pieces along with entertainment, the short stories had a different dynamic: they provided fantasy or escapism, although some were thinly veiled morality tales. In all cases, they did not overtask the reader, but provided a source of relaxation. The fissures permitted readers to interpret the stories differently and to identify with the heroine's problems, but they seldom provided resolutions in which the heroine opted out of the status quo.

Chatelaine had always published fiction, but during the fifties and sixties the fiction component of the magazine was under attack and in decline.[6] It limped along throughout the fifties, growing progressively smaller, until the Dichter Study recommended that it be jettisoned entirely. Many devoted readers disagreed with these findings and wrote to voice their complaints. Elizabeth Hammond, director of the Shoe Information Bureau of Canada, expressed the betrayal fiction's fans felt in this decision: 'Funnily enough it's been on the tip of my "typewriter finger" for several months to send you a scrawl saying, "wherethehellisthefiction" ... BUT – when I opened my February *Chatelaine*, I felt I must speak my piece. Not only was there fiction – but GOOD fiction ... I felt really cheated when *Chat* dropped fiction – in fact I lost considerable interest in the magazine, although I did skip through it.'[7] Anderson's reply acknowledged that Hammond had not been alone in her disappointment: 'I have to admit that we goofed in the first few issues of the combined magazine last fall. We had just finished a fairly extensive survey about what readers wanted and it seemed to prove that they were fairly indifferent to fiction. However, surveys, like everything else, can be quite wrong, as we realized several hundred letters later!'[8] Although fiction was brought back, in overall terms the amount of space devoted to this component declined from 11 per cent in the fifties to 9 per cent in the sixties.[9] In most cases the magazine published two stories per issue, and a few times a year included a fiction bonus, which was printed on newsprint at the back. These bonuses usually contained three short stories or a complete serialized novel.

During the era, a number of prominent Canadian authors wrote for *Chatelaine*, including Morley Callaghan, Hugh Garner, Gabrielle Roy, Hugh MacLennan, Mazo de la Roche, Ernest Buckler, Alice Munro, Margaret Laurence, Roger Fournier, Yves Thériault, Ethel Wilson, and Jane Rule. The magazine also published a previously undiscovered George Bernard Shaw, and in the sixties a story by Pearl S. Buck, then a phenomenally popular American author. Highbrows within the *Chatelaine* reading audience might have enjoyed these stories, but readers like Verna Vanmeer of Burnaby, BC, protested: 'How about a simple, uncomplicated love story? Morley Callaghan is all right for the smart set, but he and his kind of writer are not for us simple souls.'[10] Vanmeer probably enjoyed the work of Edmonton writer Sheila MacKay Russell, the author of the best-selling novel *The Lamp Is Heavy* (later made into a film), who contributed two series exclusive to *Chatelaine*. The first, 'The Martins of Alberta,' was a saga about the trials and tribulations of a 'Master Farm Family,' and the second, 'Drama in a Hospital,' was a nursing series.' Altogether, Canadians contributed a quarter of the fiction published in the sixties, an increase of 10 per cent from the previous decade.[11]

The fiction editor, Almeda Glassey, was based in New York City. She made frequent trips to Toronto, but her main job was to read through the 'thousands of manuscripts' the magazine received each year.[12] Here *Chatelaine* was at a disadvantage, since it was competing with American magazines and the editors could not pay comparable rates. For their efforts, writers were paid $400 for short stories and up to $1000 for condensed novels.[13] In comparison, an American magazine like the *Ladies Home Journal* could afford to offer $10,000 for a serialized novel or monograph, depending on its popularity.[14] Thus, other than works by Canadian authors (who were often delighted to have the opportunity to write for the magazine), the majority of the imported fiction paled in comparison with the stories in American magazines. This fact was often noted by the readers. Miss K. Murphy of Grimsby, Ontario, wrote: 'At one time you could count on *Chatelaine* for interesting fiction ... Now, the fiction is strictly second class ... I wonder why *Chatelaine* does not take a tip from the prosperous American magazines and follow their set-up and spread on articles. Why do we not see more articles and stories by Canadians?'[15] Regardless of nationality, most of the authors were women – or adopted female pseudonyms.[16]

The type of fiction published in the magazine was primarily formula fiction: romance, melodrama, and mystery. To aid prospective writers, the magazine published this short description of its requirements in *Writer's Digest*: 'Stories of 3,000 to 4,000 words are most in demand. Canadian settings are preferred. A story's dominant character should be a woman, involved in a situation which Canadian women can readily recognize and with which they can feel identification.'[17] Stories selected for publication in the magazine came through the Toronto office, and less frequently the *Châtelaine* office in Montreal, or via Almeda Glassey in New York. The composite portrait, taken from the formal sampling of stories, confirmed the description printed in *Writer's Digest*. As letters and commentary indicate, however, there was considerable disagreement, both within *Chatelaine* and among readers, over how many women 'identified' with either the protagonists or the plots of some *Chatelaine* fiction.

Throughout the era, most fiction stories in the magazine were romances – either the traditional format or the marital/family romance in which the characters are already married and, in essence, fall back in love rather than consummate a new love affair.[18] The family or marital romances were fascinating because those plots tended to focus on marital dissatisfaction and problems, which, by the end of the tale, were favourably resolved. They provide intriguing vantage points on marriage and life in the suburbs, although this category also included teen romances, questions about when to have children, or employment concerns. In essence, they focused on a variety of romantic and interpersonal tensions or difficulties. In comparison to the fifties, the percentage of romance (both categories) fell dramatically in the sixties from 88 per cent of all fiction to 61 per cent. Part of this decline was due to the decreased space allotted to fiction, but there was also an increase in the number of mystery fiction and protagonist's quest storylines.[19] The quest plot lines involved the heroine in some sort of search, usually personal, which did not include a romantic involvement. According to Cawelti's analysis, these stories would be classified as melodrama, a fantasy world 'that operates according to our heart's desires' and bears out 'the audience's traditional patterns of right and wrong, good and evil.'[20]

Most fiction was set in Canada, although the percentage of stories with Canadian settings was lower in the sixties.[21] These romances, mysteries, and dramas unfolded in urban, rural, and suburban settings.[22] The high number of stories with rural locales stood in striking contrast to the relatively few articles that featured rural issues or topics, though they mirrored the continuing popularity of the rural and small-town setting in Canadian literature. For rural readers, the fiction component was the most reliable source for material that depicted a version of rural life. The majority of all *Chatelaine* protagonists were Anglo-Canadian women in their twenties. They were equally likely to be married or single, and the majority of them were wives and mothers, or, if unmarried, students, nurses, or writers. Of the married female protagonists, only 25 per cent worked outside of the home. Generally speaking, most fiction stories focused on a small group of characters and, after the protagonist, the two other most prominent characters were Anglo-Canadian men. Even though both these secondary characters were usually white males, their ages, marital status, and occupations differed. The alpha male was usually in his thirties, married, and working in either the corporate sector or as a professional. The beta male was younger (usually in his twenties), single, and employed in corporate, agricultural, or blue-collar jobs. Most plots focused on some sort of triangle or tension between a lead female character and her interactions with two male characters – husband, suitor, father, brother, or friend. For all these characters, regardless of gender or occupation, home and family were the primary concerns. The gendered construction of male and female characters' personalities were varied: women characters were more likely to have dominant personalities and to exercise agency than male characters; women were far more emotional; male characters were slightly more aggressive than women; and, interestingly, both women and men had an almost equal chance of being weak or submissive, and being victimized.

Women were not cowering victims in this fiction. Female characters were usually the protagonists, which meant they were more likely to exercise their agency and to determine the resolution of the story. These gendered relations of power illustrate an almost contradictory combination of female autonomy within a seemingly traditional genre: in *Chatelaine* romance stories, the woman almost always got her man. Overall, in the fiction sample, the female characters determined the resolution in 60 per cent of stories, while both men and women equally determined the outcome in 3 per cent of cases. These findings parallel the conclusions of Alison Light's work on British women's magazine fiction in the 1950s. 'They all offer their women readers symbolic landscapes of lost and found identities,' Light wrote, 'of simultaneous rebellion and submission, an exploration of social constraints and often a deeply pleasurable resolution of them which is – often impossibly – both individual and fully social.'[23] In other words, fictional heroines had autonomy and exercised their own agency in the majority of these stories; paradoxically, however, they chose the socially respectable and expected position for women: marriage and the home. Female characters were often the more powerful characters in the stories, but they were equally likely to achieve this power through feminine wiles (crying, scheming, overemotional displays intended to manipulate), through exploiting their sexuality, or because they were mothers, wives, or daughters (family role). Female power deriving from feminism (either liberal or maternal) was rare. In stories where the male characters had power, they relied on patriarchal privileges, institutional reasons (business, medical, and legal expertise), or, very rarely, sexuality.

Whatever the plot or genre, the primary focus was on gender relations. Most writers employed gender issues in their works of fiction, and a large number also addressed class and age.[24] These were stories concerned with the individual and her personal dramas (much like televised soap operas, where the interior world of emotions and relationships takes precedence over the corporate or professional workplaces of the characters), and far less with geographical, political, or international events. The lack of defined Canadian locations and settings did not matter because this was an interior world of emotions, feelings, personal identity, and class consciousness. Characters were evaluated in the course of most stories by personal, often biological, categories (gender, appearance, family connections, and class) rather than more public or meritocractic issues (educational attainments, employment, or knowledge). The discourse employed in *Chatelaine* fiction was that of personal identity and the private world of gender, emotions, and class. Although themes varied, the most popular were dating/marital problems, family issues, conflict in gender roles, and violence or class stratification. Binary conventions or oppositional pairings were conventions easily and readily used in formula fiction, since they provided a readily accessible framework of interpretation. Indeed, much character and plot development was so explicit as to need no interpretation. *Chatelaine* stories portrayed three binaries repeatedly: feminine/masculine, adult/child, and hero/villain.

Although information on the editorial selection process, for fiction or for any of the article components, is limited, these excerpts from the archival papers for 1962 provide insight into the editorial decision-making process. They also reveal a certain editorial disdain for the 'commercial' stories published in the magazine. In a memo to editor Doris Anderson, managing editor Keith Knowlton wrote: 'Fiction. Another story by Mary Jane Rolfs whose stuff we've bought before. Like the others of her kind, she writes a good commercial package, with all the right elements and all the correct stops pulled ... the outcome is predictable from the word go. If it were not angled to a specific season, I'd pass it up without hesitation. As it is, though I'm not enthusiastic, I wouldn't be inclined to dismiss it too quickly: it's built for the Christmas issue and, no matter what my own views of it are, I know it would have appeal for many of our fiction readers. Worth considering on a strictly business basis.'[25] Gender played a role in Knowlton's critique, for his statement about Rolfs's story implied that it would appeal to female readers, though not to him. *Chatelaine*'s requirements were for saleable fiction, not necessarily 'good' fiction.

A letter from Anderson to W.O. Mitchell confirms that good stories submitted to the magazine were not necessarily published: 'Dear Bill, Thank you very much for letting us see the enclosed story, but I'm afraid we are going to have to turn it down since we have a very limited amount of space we can devote to this kind of story even from such well-known writers as yourself. Right now, we have a bit of an oversupply, and for this reason I am returning the enclosed story.'[26] No extant letter expresses how Mitchell felt about being declined by *Chatelaine*, one of the few Canadian outlets for short fiction.

The archival records contain a letter of protest from one angry Canadian author, Jane Van Every of Waterloo, Ontario, who criticized both the editor's judgment and her perception of what readers liked to read:

Dear Miss Glassey: Re your letter of November 6th.
    How do you aim at a market? Read all that has been written in that magazine, and then try to write the same old thing? But I am bored with most of the stories in *Chatelaine*. Usually, I can't force myself to finish them.

Edna [Staebler, an occasional correspondent for the magazine] tells me that they are mostly American stuff that can't find a market. There are no good Canadian writers. My God, why don't you give us a chance? Just for fun I have conducted a campaign to find out how other people like your stories. I have been asking people of all mentalities for a long time, and I have yet to find one who likes them. They read *Chatelaine* for the other stuff, and they are getting tired of that too. Too much sameness. The illustrations are the only things that really thrill. In that quarter *Chatelaine* beats them all, and for that reason alone I send my stories to you ... How about a story set in a famous old Canadian House? No, it's *New Yorker* style makes it unsuitable for mass-circulation. But that is what's wrong with *Chatelaine*. They have a poor opinion of their reader's mentality, so don't blame readers if they have a poor opinion of *Chatelaine*. The *New Yorker* does not have to send all sorts of people to your door, asking for subscriptions in the name of charity. You send your money and that's it. You don't even mind sending a few extra dollars exchange. With the *New Yorker* and the *Atlantic Monthly* there is no circulation race, because they give you something worth reading. They do not look down on their readers. They lift them up, and not with a new way to paint your face or do your hair, or even a fancy recipe.[27]

Van Every was obviously bitter about her rejection – apparently not the first – from the magazine, but her critique of the fiction component was a fair one. There was a great amount of repetition within genres. Glassey was 'furious' with Van Every, but wrote, in an internal memo, that she did not believe there was 'much point in getting down to her level of name calling.'[28] Her formal response encouraged Van Every not to place all the blame for her rejection letters on the editor and highlighted the differences between *Chatelaine* and the American literary magazines: 'It's impossible to compare *Chatelaine* with the *Atlantic* and the *New Yorker*. Both of these magazines aim at a small "class" market, the former heavily subsidized by its book publishing house, the latter mining a restricted and lucrative market. It would be nice to see the struggling literary magazines in this country get as much support from Canadian readers.'[29]

The editorial commentary about another story again stressed the importance of a 'commercial' vehicle – not experimental fiction or 'quality' short fiction, but a genre-driven story which, the editors thought, had appeal for their fiction readers. In a memo to Knowlton, Anderson wrote: 'Fiction. Woman ill, gets a crush on her doctor, later (to her relief?) it's all one-sided. A very likely item, I think – hospital atmosphere, illness (our readers dote on it), handsome doctor, and a situation with which many could identify.'[30] In summary, a good commercial *Chatelaine* story delivered identifiable plots and escapades (preferably with a little romance), user-friendly texts that were open enough to allow readers to participate in the process of 'making meaning,' and a happy ending. After all, Anderson's comment revealed that even she was not 'sure' about the protagonist's feelings. Many readers wanted 'clean' fiction – no affairs, pre-marital sex, or explicit sexuality. Mrs James Hoult of Montreal wrote: 'May I congratulate you on having dared to publish such a refreshing and wholesome story as "The New Woman," by Harriet Frank, Jr. In this day of so-called sophisticated fiction – which to me means only one thing, unadulterated smut – it's a nice change to read so charming a piece.'[31] This expectation posed some limitations on Glassey, as this letter to Mrs Sewell Haggard at the Curtis Brown publishing company in New York illustrates: 'I simply hate to keep sending stories back to you, but in spite of the charming French setting I'm afraid we can't use this one. The heroine on the brink of an illicit affair is still an unsympathetic subject for our readers.'[32]

A key component of the stories' appeal was their illustrations. All fiction illustrations were full-page, multicoloured drawings depicting the story's climactic moments, and they provided much-needed visual appeal in the magazine. Mrs L. Muise of Welland, Ontario, would second Van Every's assessment of the enjoyment some readers derived from these illustrations: 'I have for a number of years been an ardent reader of your *Chatelaine* magazine and especially enjoy your short stories. Both my friends and I agree that the illustration of a story plays an important part in attracting the reader's interest. This clever job we have noted was very well done in the past by a Mr Wes Chapman. It would be interesting to see more of his fine work. Many thanks for a fine magazine.'[33] Mrs Muise was an especially close reader to notice the illustrator's name, since it was hidden, in very tiny print, somewhere within the illustration.

Although an assessment of the readers' views of *Chatelaine* fiction is made difficult by the infrequency of published or archival letters that specifically commented on particular works of fiction, it is clear that some 'average' readers or writers were disenchanted with the editorial selection. Anderson herself, a self-confessed 'fiction addict,' waded into the controversy when she published an editorial about the unreal world of women's fiction: 'We need some new models and, believe it or not, real people are living great dramas everyday all around us ... Anyone can be a heroine with tawny hair, green eyes and a thirty-nine inch bust. But it takes a real heroine to mouth classic clichés with all the confidence of Elizabeth Taylor, when her nose shines and her health shoes are double tied. Take your tawny haired heroines. I want to read about her.'[34] Writer and reader Brigitte Sagmeister of Downsview, Ontario, disagreed with Anderson's critique of readers' preference for the tawny-haired heroine over 'real' women. In a letter strikingly similar to Van Every's, Sagmeister wrote: 'I very much enjoyed "Confessions of a Fiction Addict" ... However, it seems to me that this salvo in honour of the shiny-nosed should have been directed, not at the general public, but at the publishers. I know, because I've been trying to sell stories to them that didn't feature tawny-haired, thirty-nine-inch bust heroines ... But they feel they're not of enough general interest. Wouldn't it be interesting to take a fiction-taste poll among women?'[35]

Despite such criticisms of the fiction – the repetitious nature, the 'commercial package' or formulaic structure of most of the stories, and the low readership – some women (and men) did read the stories. Much of the fiction component offered traditional fare – judged by plot structure, genre, or themes – but some did not, and a representative sampling of this material allows for a less-jaundiced perspective on *Chatelaine*'s fiction. Although the overview of the characteristics and repetitive nature of *Chatelaine* fiction might paint a conservative picture, a wide-ranging number of themes were included – housewife unrest, masculinity, working women, heterosexuality, lesbianism, adultery, feminism, ethnicity, class, and suburban ennui. These fissures are indicators of the tensions, conflicts, and anxiety in suburbia. American historian Wini Breines has remarked on the paradox of the era, the prescribed world of women, and the 'cultural discontent and resistance' beneath the stereotypical facade of the fifties.[36] This same paradox characterizes the dynamics at work in the fiction component of *Chatelaine*: many of the stories vividly illustrate social fissures and discontent as the female characters strain against and question the prescribed limits of their world and engage in moderate rebellion (most often within their own minds), only to accept the slightly modified or rethought status quo at the end. The short stories illustrated that progress towards the resolution – marriage and a perfect life in suburbia – was not without its problems, and there were various turns in the road where the characters could have made detours.

Searching for a 'Plain Gold Band'

A substantial part of the romance fiction followed a format I have chosen to call 'fluffy' or 'fluffs.' In these light, insubstantial, inconsequential stories, women met men, had some sort of conflict (most commonly the eternal love triangle), and, once the problem was resolved, they lived happily ever after – which invariably meant they married or made plans to marry. The appeal of stories of this nature resides with women seeking light, escapist fare. Some romance fiction, while still written in the breezy style that characterizes this genre, also addressed complex issues. For example, Eileen Jensen's 1961 story, 'Who's Afraid of Love?' promised a romance with this opening caption: 'Take one bewitching island, add a handsome man who wants to forget, a beautiful girl who wants to escape. Mix under a sunny sky ... and see what happens.'[37] Perfect spring fare.

However, as the story unfolds and we are introduced to the 'girl' in question, we discover that she is not a bubble-headed teenager but a thirty-year-old fashion editor at a woman's magazine. The conflict in this story was between her professional success and her personal life: 'The hat, like her apartment and the corner office with the window, was Harriet's badge of success – visible proof that a bright, ambitious small-town girl with no one to lean on could come to Toronto, work hard, concentrate on her job, and achieve success. Now she was bucking for that other badge of a successful woman – a plain gold band. She had discovered to her dismay that she was a little late. Most of the eligible men are picked off by the time they're thirty.' Years before social scientists reported that women over thirty were losers in the marital sweepstakes, *Chatelaine*'s career woman had ruefully discovered the high price of professional success.

Naturally, the search for the plain gold band forms a major theme of all *Chatelaine* romance fiction, and female characters were eager to obtain that status symbol. The romance genre demands a happy ending, which Harriet achieves: invited to her friends' summer cottage (Muskoka, naturally), she meets a biology professor from the University of Western Ontario and love blossoms. While this story encourages women to view marriage as their ultimate goal, Jensen's story provides a more complex piece of romance fiction. It features an 'older woman' who has achieved professional success on her own merit. Her definition of success is two-pronged, career and mate, not the singular focus on marriage. Similarly, while the goal is achieved, and it is clear at times that she would give up all her professional success for the right man, there is no commentary, either between the characters or in Harriet's mind, that marriage will unequivocally mean the termination of her career. The ending is ambiguous and resists the assumption that she will give up her career to grab the gold ring.

Marital Bliss?

Although the goal of most romance fiction was marriage, in 'Regret' this resolution came as a bittersweet conclusion.[38] This pattern was amplified in all the family/marital type of romance, as most plots revealed the difficulties in keeping a marriage afloat. The preferred audience for this story, according to the editors, was 'every woman and especially the bright young glowing girl,' who, they promised, 'will find a part of herself and her life in this love story of today.' Assuming that was the case, the message they were given was exceedingly bleak. Our heroine, Bea, aged twenty-nine, returns from an exciting life touring and working in European cities to Toronto, where she settles into a good job and a comfortable apartment. She starts dating Larry, the epitome of respectable middle-class values. Yet a phone call from Val, her European boyfriend, forces a reappraisal of her new life, and she realizes that life with Larry is terrifically dull – no spontaneous adventures, no parties, no excitement. Had this been fantasy, Bea would have ditched Larry and jumped on the first jet back to Europe. But heroines in *Chatelaine* fiction took a different tack, well illustrated by the epiphanous moment in this story.

While dining out in a restaurant, Bea is overcome with regret about lost friends, faded memories, and growing old. Meanwhile, poor Larry is plodding along asking her to marry him: 'Larry's voice came toward her with the hesitant words she had been hurrying toward all day. "... a good life," he was saying softly, his hand covering hers. "Not as exciting as you've been used to but ... you and I ... so wonderful to be with. Bea, don't cry. Why are you crying?" And her voice, with a new timbre she did not recognize, with a tired tenderness that coupled the sweetness of acceptance and the inevitability of regret, saying, "It's nothing – it's because I'm so happy." She watched the young couple leave, the girl's eyes anxiously searching the faces in the bar, and sighed with relief and recognition.' As many a *Chatelaine* heroine before her, Bea makes what she considers to be the right decision as she opts for security and stability, not passion or excitement. For stories within a romance genre, these outcomes were depressingly unromantic. A good marriage, according to many authors, was one in which the heroine realized that her best option for a mate lay in selecting a mature, dependable candidate – in essence, the selection of a 'good provider.' These women followed their heads, not their hearts. The moral of Goldreich's story, and one endorsed by the editors of the magazine in their introductory comment, was that regret was an inevitable component of marriage. Bea trades the excitement (and instability) of single life for the security of marriage. One reader, Mrs E. Carnochan of New Westminister, BC, was pleased with the story: 'I have read with a very great deal of pleasure your story "Regret." The other story, "No Strings Attached," was not worth reading.'[39] For Mrs Carnochan, security was preferable to freedom.

Housewives' Lament

Once married, women often entered that contested terrain of the suburban bungalow, and *Chatelaine* published a number of stories which explored that phenomenon. The housewife tales were very interesting, both for their discussion of the dissatisfaction experienced by the heroines and for the ways, often very superficially, that the authors reconciled this discontent.[40] 'This Is Life,' by Sylvia Shirley, put the moral of the story right up front, under the title, to catch the reader's attention: 'Home is more than a shelter. It's a haven created by the warmth and tenderness of a woman's heart.'[41] The heroine, Ruth, a stay-at-home housewife and mother, her husband, Sam, and her pre-school daughter, Debbi, are the main characters. In contrast to most stories that took place in suburbia, or at least the private family home, this story was set in a small, third-floor apartment. A minor family crisis – a broken fishbowl – precipitates Ruth's soliloquy about her life. 'Afraid to use the precious new vacuum cleaner, Ruth ran the carpet sweeper back and forth, carefully collecting the debris and just as carefully collecting her anger. Nobody showed any respect for her work. It simply had no value to anyone. How did women stand it? It was impossible to simply go on being a cow and a third-rate menial. How many women were institutionalized every year because they couldn't take it. Homemaking was not the glamorous adventure the magazines painted. You couldn't go backward, women must have some other place, some other rights. Who had made this a man's world anyway, and if it was, why had they bothered to educate women, show them that there could be freedom?'

This passage provides a trenchant critique of the prescribed roles offered women in the fifties, as well as the impossibly high standards often set by the service material and advertisements in women's magazines. It is instructive that, instead of 'ease of use' or 'freedom from worry' portrayed in the appliance advertisements, Ruth worries about wear and tear on the machine – hardly the image of carefree, conspicuous consumption. Stories such as this one illustrate the polysemic nature of the magazine – the inclusion of a wide variety of often conflicting material. This acknowledgment of ambiguity resulted in greater reader identification, since it recognized, and mimicked, the actual inconsistencies in women's lives. However, one limitation in many stories that featured this theme was that the female characters rarely uttered this critical commentary; rather, it was kept as an internal dialogue between the reader and the character. Ruth's reconciliation to her lot comes after an evening out with Sam, breakfast in bed (prepared by Sam and Debbi) the next day, and the clichéd discovery that her 'helpers' had used all the dishes in the house. After her fury abates, and while cleaning up, she reflects on the situation and realizes that her husband and daughter would be lost without her. 'She took a deep shivering breath. How near the edge of darkness they lived, and how much depended on her! Dear God, if she ever let go her end ... Ruth took a quick look around the shining kitchen, breathed deep the good warm smell of the meat in the oven, remembered her mother-in-law with no real place to feel wanted on Sunday, heard Debbi's child-song from the next room, saw her husband's tender uncertainty and blinked. This was life, quick with warmth and love, red-blooded, sure and sane!'

The moral was obvious. All women must shoulder their family burdens and bear their responsibilities. Accepting their role as wives and mothers provided happiness, or, at the very least, contentment. The ending affirmed the belief that all women had a common lot in life, as the title suggested: 'This Is Life.' But no matter how neat and pat the ending of this story, real readers could have interpreted this tale of housewife's lament differently. Ruth's questioning had opened a door for the readers to take a different path. Although this protagonist opts for the status quo, her critical analysis of her life serves as a form of empowerment. She realizes that as discontented as she often was, her role in the family was paramount. This story exemplifies that paradoxical situation in which the female character has agency, yet opts for the status quo.

'A Family Tool, a Mommy': The Working Wife and Mother

Unlike fiction in the fifties, where married women often lamented their homekeeping roles, in the sixties many fictional heroines agonized over other complications: whether to work or have children, and how to acclimatize to married life. Two stories, 'The Best Wife in the World' and 'Couldn't Any Mother?' illustrate both sides of the working-wife conundrum as well as the strikingly different and contradictory messages in the magazine's fiction. Barbara Holland's story published in January 1965 is an interesting one about a woman's determination to be 'the best wife in the world,' although she makes clear from the start that that 'was exactly the kind of woman Andy didn't want.'[42] The protagonist, Dinah Belknapp, is a biologist who works for the Department of Lands and Forests, studying the effect of suburban developments on wildlife. Ironically, she will soon be suffering from her own case of overexposure to suburban life, for she quits her job as soon as she marries Andy Tomlinson. His effort to dissuade her fails, as this exchange illustrates: '"I stick to my guns," said Dinah ... "Nobody can do a really good job on two jobs at once." "And I'm you're new job?" "Of course. I'm going to be a wife. A housewife."'

While still on their honeymoon in Jamaica, Dinah starts buying an assortment of women's magazines to educate herself about her new job. With her scissors and paste pot at her side, she cuts out pertinent information from these magazines, pasting the columns in one of four scrapbooks with such titles as 'Entertaining' or 'Love and Marriage Relations.' Beneath this gentle spoof of the art of reading women's magazines is an important critique of the purpose and effect of this prescriptive literature. Very simply, Dinah's constant attempts to 'be perfect' result in her own, and her husband's, unhappiness. Once back in suburbia, her days revolve around meals and housework. Liberation comes in the unlikely form of an orphaned baby raccoon, who turns up at her friend's back door. Having volunteered to raise it, she quickly realizes the folly of her ways. Yet it falls to Andy to voice this realization and encourage her return to work: '"You know what would make me happy? If you'd go back to work" "But Andy, what about the house? What about the cooking?" He laughed, and ... kissed her. "The house will be a terrible mess, I hope. And we'll send out for corned-beef specials, with coleslaw. We'll have a standing order, two corned-beef specials every night. And a great big basket of fresh fish, for the fattest raccoon in Canada. And you'll be the worst wife in the world, and I'll be the happiest man in town!"'

The wish-fulfilment nature of this story is apparent: many readers could only dream that their husbands would be happy married to 'the worst wife in the world' or that they would encourage them back into the paid workforce. Still, it illustrates an issue that was increasingly familiar to many readers as married women's workforce participation expanded in the sixties. Much of the contemporary commentary encouraged women to view work and marriage as undesirable, if not incompatible. Had this story taken a more traditional format, Dinah's experience with the baby raccoon would not have prompted a return to work, but the determination to have a child. Consequently, in many ways this unconventional story – in topic, themes, meaning, and resolution – turned the tables on readers expecting a light-hearted romance.

A year later, Barnett Kleiman's 'Couldn't Any Mother?' covered the same territory: the role played by women's magazines and the difficulty in balancing paid work with family life.[43] The key difference here was that Kleiman's heroine, Jan, was not only married but also a mother. The story emphasized the disorienting effect feminism, or women's liberation, had on women like Jan who were happy, contented, stay-at-home wives and mothers. This passage illustrates the destabilizing effects of 'liberated' women's magazines articles: 'The world, however, kept stirring her up. The TV forums on wasted intellect, the latest books on feminine potential, the magazines ... "Who Am I?" one magazine article demanded. "Look in the mirror and ask yourself honestly: Who am I? The tragedy of the wife and mother is her Lost Identity. You have a right to be a person," the article said ... She often slapped the magazines shut by way of rebuke, but the words kept thumping around in her mind, and she began casting uneasy glances into the mirror. Maybe the real me is buried, after all, she began to worry. Maybe it isn't enough to be content. What good are needle-point chair seats to the world?'

Predictably, the protagonist, Janice Ann Mason, gets a job as a nurse in a doctor's office because the magazine articles, the television, and her next-door-neighbour Doris (a liberated instigator) think she should, now that all her children are school age. Naturally, it does not work: Janice 'mothers' people at the office, her kids get sick, and she has no time to host spontaneous dinner parties on week-day evenings or to keep her house immaculate. All those events overwhelm her and un-

dermine her determination to work to 'improve her mind.' The solution – and only one is advanced – is simple. The story ends with Janice
happily telling her husband, Ken, that she has been fired: '"Darling,
darling, don't you understand?" Jan held out her arms as though to
encompass the house and everything in it. "I've got a job!" "Yes, but
women these days are entitled ..." Ken persisted, "My girl Wilma keeps
saying ..." Jan faced him squarely. "Good for Wilma!" she said, her eyes
flashing. "And Miss Knox and millions of other women! I know who I
am, I'm Janice Ann Mason! I'm all the terrible things writers scorn: a
family tool, a mommy. And you know what? I love it." ... Jan had never
felt so over-flowing with satisfaction. If Doris were here she'd tell her a
thing or two about fulfilment.' The next-door neighbour with the same
uncommon name as *Chatelaine*'s feminist editor was a none-too-subtle
rib on the part of Kleiman or *Chatelaine* staffers!

Two competing issues are at work in this story. The first, with which
many historians of second-wave feminism would agree, is that wom-
en's liberation of the sixties and seventies ignored and derided the stay-
at-home wife and mother – a situation feminists from the eighties and
nineties tried to remedy. Many women were, as the articles about
feminism and feminist issues in the editorials and articles indicate,
feeling unsure of a world where being 'just a housewife' or, in this case,
'a family tool, a mommy,' were terms of derision. However, this unease
is also skilfully, and not too subtly, manipulated by the author of this
story. Male characters pay lip service to liberation while referring to
women, even married women in their thirties, as 'girls.' Janice is an
insecure heroine, one who is quickly influenced by what she reads or
watches on television, yet letters from readers to *Chatelaine* indicate that
they were not gullible, mindless vessels into which *Chatelaine* poured
information. This story reads more like a married male fantasy: give
your wife the freedom to explore the workaday world, and she will
soon head back to the homefront. Most married women who resumed
working in the sixties did so because they had to, or because they
wanted to increase their families' standard of living, and not for their
own personal fulfilment. Finally, had the character really wanted to
develop her mind – instead of serving the devices of a writer out to
illustrate how unhappy 'liberation' made women feel – she would not
have taken the job she did. Kleiman's description of her work portrayed it as purely clerical in nature. Surely, suburban wives and mothers could handle telephone calls, appointment books, and scheduling –
after all, those were the tools of their trade.

Male Angst: Trapped Men and Suburban Ennui

Sandwiched among the housewife discontent tales was a unique collection of stories – more prevalent in the fifties than the sixties – that featured trapped, bitter husbands. Julie Prise's 'The Dark Hall' was representative of this troubling genre: a somber tale, told from a male protagonist's vantage point, about the stifling nature of marriage and work as a white-collar drone at the firm of Wellington and Sanders.[44] The interior monologue, a regular plot device, was featured in this story as our unnamed husband reflected, while he rode home on the streetcar, on his life, marriage, and wife, who was seated at the front: 'It would be interesting to watch a woman who hadn't the remotest idea her husband wanted a divorce. She was so safe in her busy unfledged existence, bounded by the price of carrots, a weekly pamphlet on how to bring up her children and a yen for crackpot lectures. Scrambling little Libby. She seemed inexhaustible in her energy for the unimportant.'[45] This indictment of the typical housewife and mother seems quite out of place for a woman's magazine. Our backseat philosopher was the stereotypically 'trapped man,' tethered to a wife and two kids, a sick mother, and an uninspiring job, all of which he detested and resented.[46] In sharp contrast to the way reconciliation is achieved in the housewife tales (resignation and responsibilities), trapped men needed to reassert their dominance and virility. In this case, once they alighted from the streetcar, he 'stalks' his wife down the street:

Two blocks they went, and three ... An overhanging branch hit him in the face and the tingling sensation was pleasant. He was surprised to discover he was enjoying himself. Every time he put his foot down, she listened. She felt. The heart inside the little green jacket was beginning to thump. And he was doing it. She was not thinking of anything in the world but him. He was adventure, a stranger in the night, bringing excitement to Libby. When they were not more than two arms' length apart, he whistled to her softly. She broke into a run. With the swiftness of fright, with both hands out, she pushed at the gate of the iron fence, swung it open. And he wheeled her around against the open gate and imprisoned her in his arms. He thrust his hands through her hair and jerked her hair back. He could see her face, flung up to him, a pale blur in the night, her mouth rounded to scream, her eyes big with shock. And he saw the shock leap to fury when her eyes met his. She lashed out at him with her fist. He laughed, brought his mouth down hard on hers and held her close while the wind blew her hair against his cheek. Abruptly her struggling ceased.[47]

The sadomasochistic imagery, the pursuit, and Libby's terror at an impending assault all served to reinvigorate the husband's attraction to his wife. Instead of a divorce, they plan a vacation. This story was troubling and perplexing from a number of perspectives, not least the questions it raised of the readers' reaction. Did women find such tales appealing? Was there a sufficiently large male audience for *Chatelaine* fiction to warrant such stories?

An important subtheme in this story, and many others, was the way the author dealt with heterosexuality. *Chatelaine* stories were never explicit – in fact, most readers complimented the editors for the 'clean' fiction. The sensual culmination of most tales was the kiss and 'tender embrace.' Male characters initiated these moments of abandon, but to reassure themselves and the readers that they were 'real men,' it was common for the adjectives 'hard,' 'forceful,' and 'skilful' to be used. These terms were code words for manliness and a powerful male heterosexuality. In turn, the women who were the beneficiaries of these kisses often expressed their sexuality as a concession: they went limp, ceased struggling, or gave in to their partner's skilfulness. In *Chatelaine* fiction, sexuality was something only men possessed and could, at their own convenience, turn on or off in their partners. Passion, as defined by this story and countless others, was male controlled, often included violence or mind games, and occurred and finished swiftly. In contrast to the male characters and their passion, the female characters seemed dazed by the force and the pace; before they were aware of what was happening, it was over.

The link between trapped men and violence, fairly common in fiction of the early fifties, was abandoned by the end of the decade and never reappeared in the sixties. However, the notion that men were also trapped in suburban hells was a recurrent theme. One of the best examples of the suburban discontent told from a male point of view was Hugh Garner's 'The Wasted Years' (illustration 31). This late-fifties' story of suburban angst and anger was directed at the jailer, his wife: 'This is about Dorothy and me and the fourteen years we'd been married and why, as I looked at her across the room that night, I thought, "I hate her." It's about something else, too ... A story every married couple should read.'[48] The unnamed protagonist explains his discontent:

31 *Chatelaine*, September 1959

'Dorothy is a fine wife and mother, and I guess I'm lucky she isn't lazy or dirty like some wives I've met. My sudden hatred for her was quite impersonal, as is the hate of the convict for the prison guard. I had suddenly realized that thanks to her I'd become one of the married prisoners that inhabit every suburb like ours in the country. I'd become a Dagwood Bumstead almost without knowing it, a guy who was fenced in by habit and custom, and by marriage. I looked back over the years and thought of all the things I'd once planned on doing, and how I'd given them all up in exchange for a twenty-year mortgage on the bungalow, a car still owned by the finance company, and a house full of instalment furniture and gadgets.

Garner's indictment of the culture of consumption implicitly contradicts and critiques the messages provided by the advertising material in the magazine. The freedom promised in the advertisements had proved illusive as well as ironic, as the protagonist laments the constrictions of suburban marriage and the accompanying entanglement – life on the instalment plan. Given the misogyny in this piece, and the bitter, resentful mood of the protagonist, it is difficult to anticipate the resolution. Determined to head out on his own, our hero makes it as far as a downtown bar, where, drink in hand, he surveys the room. The bar functions as a locale for society's undesirables – and as the antithesis of the safe, middle-class existence. Projecting all sorts of classist assumptions onto his fellow 'drinkers' – that they are pitiful and pathetic – he quickly decides to return home. Once home, Dorothy informs him that, in his absence, their son broke a window, effectively restoring the focus to the minutiae of everyday life. 'She got up to go to the kitchen, and I grabbed her and kissed her. "What brought this on, the drinks?" "No, I just felt like it, that's all." ... What was a seven dollar window compared with living like all those people I had seen downtown? I knew I didn't hate Dorothy.'

The difference between downtown and suburbia was stark. Suburbia represented family, contentment, security, and safety, while downtown represented the dismal lives of the working class. Our bourgeois male protagonist had a boring job as a cost accountant, yet at night he could return to the kids and wife on Rosemary Lane. The moral, uttered by the protagonist in the concluding sentence, was that 'contentment is the reward of virtue.'

Although still married, all the men in these stories experience some epiphanous event which, intellectually at least, undomesticates them. The stories end with the reassertion of their manliness. These characters serve notice that they intend to reassert their privilege as 'men of the house,' and, in most cases, the women accept this role with gratitude. The restoration of order in these trapped-men marital dramas revolves around a new-found appreciation of their wives, but also a definite determination to take back the control they had abdicated. For women readers, the misogynistic themes in all these stories could not have been more overt. If they read oppositionally, they could take some interest in the male perspective of marital life, but their sympathies could hardly lie with female characters that are bullied, stalked, and forced back into more circumscribed roles.

The Morality Tale: Young Marriage

If mature adults found marriage trying, then youngsters were bound to flounder. Young-marriage stories, like housewife-discontent and trapped-male tales, also highlight difficulties in adaptation to societal expectations, and to conventional gender roles in particular. The story that generated the most interest in the sixties, as judged by reader letters to the editor, was Alec Rackowe's novel 'Trial Marriage.'[49] It followed the family/marital romance genre, complete with happy ending, with a teenaged romance at the centre. Employing a didactic and moralistic style of writing, Rackowe's tale follows the relationship between eighteen-year-old Arlene Reeder, the privileged daughter of a bank manager, and her twenty-one-year-old boyfriend, Jeremy Banks. This working-class, former high school football hero was ambitious to scrape together enough money, working at a gas station, to take an engineering degree at college. Set in the fictional suburban community of Claremont in the northeastern United States, the plot is simple. An ultimatum from Arlene's father that she must stop dating Banks while living 'in his household' propels the headstrong, sullen teenager into a hasty marriage with Banks. From there, the tale becomes predictable: life in a rooming house proves far from ideal; penury and immaturity cause a rift between Jeremy and Arlene; they separate; find strength and maturity in adversity; and reconcile to attend college together.

As the synopsis makes clear, 'Trial Marriage' was not a romanticized view of young love, but a thinly disguised morality play that illustrated the difficulties faced by those who married young – before their education was completed and they could support themselves – and to people below their class status. Although the outcome and much of the plot were not surprising – particularly in a magazine where premarital sex and divorce were virtually unknown – the rigid gender stereotypes forced Arlene and Jeremy into foreign, uncomfortable roles. Shortly after hearing of her daughter's marriage, for example, Arlene's mother counsels her: 'We're not just mother and daughter any more. We're two married women. We can talk to each other on that level.'[50] For Jeremy, the changes are equally stark: 'You're a married man now. You've got obligations, bills to meet. It creeps up on you. Suddenly all the ropes are in place and you're tied down. Maybe you better think of a permanent job.' Individuality is subsumed beneath the traditional categories of 'wife' and 'husband.' The story's resolution depends not on Arlene and Jeremy's challenging the gender categories – making them more flexible – but on 'maturing,' on realizing that their lives are eradicably changed and they must give up much of the excitement and the dreams of youth in exchange for the conventions of marriage.

The published reactions to Rackowe's story were favourable. According to the editors, 'We usually don't hear much from you about fiction, but Alec Rackowe's novel of young love, "Trial Marriage," touched the heart of a current and not uncommon problem, judging from your many letters.'[51] What the majority of readers praised was the moral of the story, not the fiction itself. Dr B.F. Nixon of Moose Jaw, Saskatchewan, wrote: 'I wish to commend Alec Rackowe for writing such a fine story and *Chatelaine* for publishing it. We badly need such stories, pointing out in readable and plausible form the grief and disillusionment of early marriages. In this excellent story, sex isn't even mentioned, which alone makes it unusual and outstanding.'[52] Outstanding and also unrealistic, since surely one of the primary motivations for early marriages was the inherent conflict between teenage hormones and pronouncements against premarital sex. A good story, according to these readers, was one with a message, not necessarily a piece of entertainment or an engaging work of fiction. Another reader, whose name the editors withheld, identified with the plot too well: 'It points out two things wrong with today's teen-age society – the attitude of "going steady" with one person throughout the teen years, and the mistaken idea that marriage works miracles. I, myself, made these two mistakes – but with no happy ending. Throughout my teen years I dated only one boy. Our parents tried to break us up for our own good, but we rebelled and got married, thinking this would end our problems. Reality set in, and my husband of three months enlisted in the forces. I am still legally married to him, and, at twenty, wish I had listened to my parents.'[53] While it is interesting that the reader wished she had listened to her parents, she provides no indication that reading stories like 'Trial Marriage' would have averted her situation. Only Mrs W. Hingston of Cawell, Saskatchewan, commented on the characterization, as well as applauding the moral to be learned: 'Regarding your fiction, I fluctuate from very pleased to disgusted and back again. But I must write to you now to tell you how touched and thrilled I was with ... "Trial Marriage." It is refreshing to find a story whose characters have real depth of character, and yet are human. Would like to see all young people and parents of young people read it, for I'm sure many would receive courage and comfort from it.'[54] In her reply Anderson confirms that others were equally impressed by the story: 'We rarely get comments from our readers about fiction stories, but this particular story seems to have struck a responsive chord with many women.'[55] For these readers, fiction serves as a sugar-coated format to convey important messages: they are more enjoyable and more readable than a non-fiction article on the same topic, but still worthwhile and educational.

A discordant note came from an Edmonton reader, who wrote to criticize a story in the September issue ('Good-bye, My Darling Daughter') that had also focused on young marriages. The criticism highlights the views of a reader who was not delighted at the preachy tone of some stories, the repetitive nature of *Chatelaine* fiction, or the fact that some of the fiction was aimed at younger readers:

> Please do not print this letter in your letters column. (That only serves to convince me that most of your readers are idiots who want to see their names in print. You must have some intelligent readers.) I just feel a trifle annoyed about your last issue and the story (I have forgotten the name) about the young kids who eloped and then decided to strike out on their own ... I am heartily sick of young marriage stories ... There are other people in the world who deserve attention ... surely other adult situations that are amusing (Oh, how I long for a cute, sophisticated story in your sometimes very ponderous 'educational' magazine) ... or adult stories that are profound. This was nothing ... Please, something, else! By the way ... by educational I mean I get the impression that the Good Ladies of *Chatelaine* (and men, of course) are setting out to inform and educate and 'help' the poor little average Canadian woman. Oh well, small wonder you feel like that. Look at the letters you receive. Ever read any of the stories in *McCall's* or *Good Housekeeping*? For women's magazines they are unusually good.[56]

Although it is impossible to know whether the low readership of the fiction components was attributable to criteria mentioned in this critique – the didactic nature of much of the fiction and the accusation that the magazine's 'commercial package' catered to the lowest intellect of their mass audience – it provides some indication that, beneath the indifference and the silence, lay considerable frustration with the quality and content of that fiction.

The Martins of Bright Hills, Alberta: Class and Race

While the romance stories and family/marital romance subgenre examined love, dating, marriage, and the joys and difficulties of married life, most of the protagonist quest stories (which often had romance subplots) were issue driven. Nowhere was this more apparent than in the work of Sheila MacKay Russell's hospital stories or her 'Martin Family' series. The protagonists were not necessarily feminists, although in all cases their abilities to think for themselves, and to stand up for what they believed in, meant they were assertive women. These women were usually the dominant characters in the stories, the characters with

SARI
in
the
kitchen

A NEW CHAPTER IN THE STORY OF
THE MARTINS OF ALBERTA

By SHEILA MacKAY RUSSELL

Milly drifted into the room, and the Martins suddenly realized they were facing a crisis.

The day Milly Schmidt first wore a sari to prepare breakfast in their kitchen, the Martins were stunned but not immediately alarmed. In the initial paralysis of their amazement, they assumed that there was a logical explanation, such as, (a) they were suffering from hallucinations, (b) she was trying on a Hallowe'en costume, or (c) she had gone temporarily out of her mind. That she was wearing it because she preferred it to the dowdy house dresses she had worn for fifteen years as their hired girl was too incredible to occur to them.

Accustomed to her solid jarring tread, they were subconsciously aware of something amiss when she floated into the dining room on noiseless feet, deposited the toast and floated out again to the whispered accompaniment of ankle-length garments. Gripped by early morning lethargy however, no one looked up until she had repeated the performance with the boiled eggs. Then, one by one, Nan Martin, Harvey Martin and each of their two sons and one daughter who remained at home, raised their eyes to

32 *Chatelaine*, September 1962

agency, and the characters who affected change. Two of Russell's stories that proved most controversial with readers, 'Sari in the Kitchen' (illustration 32) and 'The Hutterites,' examined racial issues and, specifically, the prejudicial attitudes of Canadians.[57] Additionally, 'Sari' contains a persistently classist commentary which, despite the obvious concern for valuing ethnic diversity, was completely acceptable.

The plot of 'Sari,' published in 1962, concerns the decision of Milly Schmidt, the Martin's live-in maid, to wear the saris given to her by acquaintances who had recently returned from India. This decision causes considerable upset within the family and forces the Martins to undertake some painful self-examination of their hypocritical attitudes towards ethnic difference. This excerpt provides a sample of Russell's writing style and illustrates the Martin family's first encounter with the saried maid:

Accustomed to her solid jarring tread, they were subconsciously aware of something amiss when she floated into the dining room on noiseless feet, deposited her toast and floated out again to the whispered accompaniments of ankle-length garments ... For a moment the room was pregnant with silence as one of Alberta's more prominent Master Farm families digested the fact that it was facing a crisis. Then ... four pairs of eyes swivelled to Nan Martin, who looked back at her family with an expression of strained concentration on her patrician features ... Such an exotic getup had its place, Nan conceded, but that place wasn't on their hired girl.[58]

The entire story is consumed with the Martins' soul searching on how best to handle the situation. Although the family decides to support Milly's unconventional behaviour, the maid's victory is short-lived because of the apoplectic reaction of the townspeople of Bright Hills, Alberta. Milly's major concern is that the 'Master Farm Family' not suffer further embarrassment or find themselves the butt of community chin-wagging by the townspeople, whom she calls the 'crumbs in town,' and so she decides to remove the garments. While it is clear that Russell intended 'Sari' to function as a cautionary tale about the range of bigotry and prejudiced behaviour that existed in all strata of the community of Bright Hills (a good stand-in for Canada), the unexamined classist commentary proves much more troubling. It is the proud, vain Nan Martin (described as 'the daughter of an English remittance man whose attempts to transfer British social strata to Canadian soil had been met with good-natured ridicule') who must wage a battle of wills with her hired maid from Muscrat Crick, as well as preserve her family's dignity and social position as Master Farmers. Nan and the family conquer their bigotry, but they do not reconsider their classist beliefs. Even as unlikely a candidate as Milly sides with the Martins over the 'town crumbs.'

Reader commentary was divided. The letter published in the magazine from Mrs Janet Campbell of London, Ontario, explicitly critiqued the classist nature of the Martin stories:

How much longer must we be subjected to the insane fiction of Sheila MacKay Russell ... I was born and raised on an Alberta farm and lived on a farm for twenty years, and I must say that the Martins do not even remotely resemble any farm family I have ever seen or known. To me the Martins are snobbish, pretentious, ridiculous, non-people with non-problems, who look down on and snicker at their poor, dumb, ignorant, foreign hired-maid – all of which is as hilarious as thalidomide. Mrs Russell would do us all a favour if, in her next installment, she has the Martins nominated as Master Canadian Farm Family, and then as they fly to Ottawa in their private plane to accept their award, the plane crashes in the northern wilderness. Exit the Martins. R.I.P. No one will mourn.[59]

Campbell's letter is similar to the Mrs Slob correspondence, although she is far angrier. Once again, it illustrates vividly how some readers read oppositionally – in this case offering a plausible and, for some weary readers, fitting ending to the Martin series. However, Mrs B. Larsen of Edmonton disagreed, and her letter to Doris Anderson, and Anderson's response, provide the preferred meaning of 'Sari':

> It is to be hoped that all your readers do not exhibit the inability of Mrs Janet Campbell to see below the surface of a gentle and intelligent satire ... I think she has entirely missed the point of Sheila MacKay Russell's story, 'Sari in the Kitchen.' It was my impression that Mrs Russell did not intend us to laugh at Milly and her harmless desire to wear out her saris but at ourselves and our horrified rejection of anything that violates our slavish need for conformity. I'm sure that no one but a superficial reader would find the Martin stories inane. Their thoughtful themes show the author's deep understanding of life and human nature. I'm delighted that we're to see more of her work with the new hospital series. I enjoyed the first story immensely ... I do hope that you will give us more for the thinking woman in your magazine, not less, as Mrs Campbell would seem to suggest.[60]

Reader commentary about *Chatelaine* components certainly proves the subjective nature of 'interpretation.' Although Mrs Larsen's letter indicates that she is not a 'surface reader,' the fact she ignores the classist commentary in the work illustrates that not all 'thinking' women readers commented on all aspects of a piece of fiction. In her response, Anderson praised Larsen's 'excellent letter' and her 'thoughtful comments.'[61] She continued: 'I believe that you interpreted the story "Sari in the Kitchen" correctly, and Mrs Campbell did not ... your letters, and letters like yours are a welcome encouragement in our efforts.' Class was a persistent blind spot in the magazine. Unless articles were specifically about poverty, or lower-income women, *Chatelaine* failed to deal adequately with the fact that not all readers identified with the persistent middle-class emphasis that masqueraded as classlessness.

Lesbianism?

One story, 'Vixen in the Snow,' proved to be an exception to all others in
the romance genre because it was a fantastic story of imaginary friends
and 'true love' imagery that featured a chaste lesbian plotline.[62] From
the suggestive title and the story's opening teaser, 'The story of an elfin
girl and a love that knew neither time nor age,' it is clearly not a
standard piece of romance fiction. The illustration that accompanies
this story is drawn in a shade of blue-gray and features a fox and a
bright-eyed young woman caught in a blinding snow storm. 'Vixen in
the Snow' contains a veritable treasure trove of suggestive imagery. The
author's choice of a fantasy or fairytale genre allows her greater lati-
tude in character development, plotting, and motivation.

The setting is Hazen's Hollow, an isolated location, seven miles from
the village where the protagonist's family lives. This 'queer place,' as
the Hollow was identified, was formerly inhabited by the Hazen family, who have long since abandoned their farm. The Hollow has returned to its natural state – a rustic garden of Eden. It is a fertile and
enchanted place where weeds, wild flowers, animals, and two young
girls cavort among the tangle of shrubs, grasses, overgrown fruit trees –
apples, naturally – and abandoned cottages.

The narrator and protagonist of this story is the aptly named Ivy
Frazier. Throughout the course of the story she ages from ten to nine-
teen, and the plot follows her weekly visits to her elderly Uncle Ira, the
Hollow's only remaining resident. On her first solo journey to the
Hollow, at the age of ten, she immediately falls in love with the place
and meets the mysterious Mattie Hazen:

> This morning, though, as I was passing the old Hazen cemetery, I caught a
> flash among the tipsy headstones ... and turned to investigate it, I saw,
> stretched out in the sun on a fallen moss-covered slate marker surrounded
> by patches of pink and white ground phlox, a mother fox. Her ears were
> alert, but her pointed face was placid and pleased ... with infinite care I
> lowered myself until I lay flat on my stomach in the tall weeds and gave
> myself up to the pure pleasure of watching them play. They were so pretty
> and graceful and unconscious of being observed that I laughed aloud ...
> 'Now you've done it,' said a voice in my ear, and I turned my head quickly
> ... A little girl was lying prone beside me, her slanting yellowish eyes
> laughing at my discomfort ... She had a pointed little face, and her remark-
> able eyes were fringed with long black lashes, but her hair was the pecu-

liar thing about her – reddish, with a queer dark gloss to it. It was the sort of hair you wanted to stroke. She said, 'I'm Mattie Hazen. What shall we play?'

And so the love that knew 'neither time nor age' begins. Rich's use of the word *queer* is worth mentioning, particularly because of its absence from most other works of fiction in *Chatelaine* and Rich's repeated use of the term. The other story that used that word – 'Mr Nightingale,' by Sheila MacKay Russell – was about a presumably homosexual nurse. Rich's use of 'queer,' then, could be understood as a code word for lesbian readers or those familiar with the multiple meanings of the term. Naturally, Mattie and Ivy become fast friends and their weekly rendezvous by the Hazen cemetery becomes the focus of the story. The imagery and the intense friendship between the two girls is reminiscent of Lucy Maud Montgomery's *Anne of Green Gables*. Given the popularity of that work and the similarities between the texts, it would appear that Rich was familiar with Montgomery's novel.

When Ivy returns to her uncle's home, she is quick to tell him about her new friend and 'breathlessly' tells him that she 'loves her.' Ira, the stereotypically laconic, unflappable farmer, advises her to 'keep your tongue between your teeth' and not to tell her family or friends. Ivy's visits continue and, throughout the summer, she is able to spend more time in the Hollow than during the school year. Notably, while Mattie and Ivy's relationship blossoms easily and becomes a source of great joy to both of them, Ivy's relationships with other girls are an entirely different matter: 'None of the other girls were like her, and their silly chatter and budding interest in the boys and bewildering habit of being Best Friends one day and Not Speaking the next left me uneasy and unhappy.'

Threats to Mattie and Ivy's relationship come from two fronts: teenage boys and Ivy's mother. The most troubling threat to Ivy and Mattie's relationship is Ivy's persistent suitor, Fred Ellis. When Ivy turns sixteen, her mother comments on her unhealthy attachment to the Hollow and her misguided priorities: '"I've just about reached the limit of my patience with you, Ivy," she announced. "And the first thing you know, Fred will stop asking you. He'll get as sick as I am of hearing nothing but the Hollow, the Hollow, the Hollow. You're going on 17 and it's time you grew up. You act like a child, always running to the Hollow to *play!*" Oh, the scorn she put into that word, and I suppose she was right. I'd been so wrapped up in the Hollow and Mattie for so many years that my emotional development hadn't kept pace with my age.' This emotional immaturity implied by the bond with a female, as opposed to a male, parallels the psychiatric descriptions of female homosexuals.[63] It is not beyond the bounds of interpretation to posit that the Hollow is much more than a geographical location, particularly given Ivy's mother's concern about how much time she spends there. The Hollow's fecund and particularly female imagery easily invokes sexual imagery. Although psychiatrists were quick to condemn sex deviates (one of the terms for homosexuals in the era) for their immature expressions of their sexuality, they were also quick to impress on parents that masturbation was another form of juvenile or immature sexuality that required vigilance. Playing in the Hollow could be a metaphor for masturbation just as easily as it could for lesbianism or intense same-sex bonding. More explicitly, Ivy's mother is concerned that her daughter is not maturing properly. Fred is not her primary focus, nor does she seem to respond to this relationship properly. Although the mother is not aware of Mattie, Ivy immediately makes the connection between her relationship with Mattie and her immaturity. Fred symbolizes more than just marriage and the normal life: he is Ivy's future. If she spurns him, she will jeopardize an ordered, comfortable life for a tenuous, insecure one.

Attempting another tactic, Ivy's mother warns her that Uncle Ira ruined his life by pining away for a young woman who had died of pneumonia. This serves as the climactic moment of the story, as Ivy's mother reveals the name of Ira's long-lost love: Mattie Hazen. Interestingly, when her mother mentions Mattie's name, Ivy's face 'went stiff and queer' and her father, on hearing the conversation, remarked that Mattie was a 'queer looking girl.' In an attempt to rationalize the relationship, Ivy decides that her Mattie must be the deceased woman's namesake. Shortly after this discussion, Ivy makes one last, tragic trip to the Hollow, where she discovers Uncle Ira dying of pneumonia. She races to find Mattie, but while running in the now-raging snowstorm, she trips over a headstone – Mattie's headstone – and promptly passes out. Her family, and the ever-loyal Fred, find her lying in the snow.

After weeks of bed rest she is finally able to tell Fred what happened, and this concluding paragraph completes the story for the readers as well:

I told him a little of all this, because I thought he should know why I couldn't marry him. He refused to understand, or perhaps he couldn't.

'Ivy, darling,' he said, 'you've been very sick. You had a terrible shock, finding your uncle dying, and then lying out there in the snow all that while until we found you. No wonder you're all mixed up and upset. That little girl you say you used to play with – all children go through that, you know ... You'll forget about it when you're stronger.' I closed my eyes, pretending to be even more tired than I was, and after a while Fred went away. For just a moment I was sorry and a little lonely. But I'd get used to loneliness, I thought, as I began the long wait for the kind of love that I knew now could exist – the kind of love that refused to surrender to death, the kind of love that I might never find, but for which I could never, now, accept a substitute.

Perhaps it is unreasonable to wish that Rich had provided a better definition of 'the kind of love' to which Ivy refers, but the imagery and intensity of the relationship, coupled with the decisive dismissal of Fred, permits one to conclude that this 'fairytale' is really about the 'love that dare not speak its name.' The ending of 'Vixen in the Snow' is remarkably different from the conventions of *Chatelaine* romance. Few stories ever focused on female friendship as the major plot device. If female friendships occurred in the stories, they were almost always secondary to the love interest. Very few romances, and few fiction stories in general, included such open-ended resolutions. The reader can conclude Ivy's tale according to her perception of what the story had been about. Was the unrequited, intense love Ira's for Mattie, or was it Ivy's for Mattie? Those readers who believe in an afterlife can imagine Ira and Mattie happily reunited, but there is no authoritative direction for that conclusion. More important, Ivy is the protagonist; it is her story that occupies centre stage; and the outcome for her resists closure. Ultimately, Rich's use of the fantasy or fairytale genre permits two very different interpretations of this story. On the one hand it is a mystical story of undying love between Mattie and Ira, and of a passionate friendship between Ivy and Mattie; on the other hand, if readers follow the suggestive language, the code words, and the metaphors for female sexuality, it is a love story between two teenage girls, complete with an affirmative ending in which the remaining character expresses her determination to seek out that sort of love again.[64]

'Drama in a Hospital': Queerness

The issue of homosexuality was addressed more explicitly in one of Sheila MacKay Russell's morality tales, 'Mr Nightingale,' where she turned her attention to queerness. Although this story is the only overt example of homosexuality in sixties' fiction, *Chatelaine* did publish a story by Jane Rule on non-lesbian themes and, in that same issue, publicized the release of Rule's lesbian novel, *Desert of the Heart*. 'Mr Nightingale' was considerably different from 'Vixen in the Snow,' although it mirrors the use of 'queerness' as a novel topic – one sure to attract even the most jaded readers. The author's use of the term *queer* is deliberate, for the story explores the character and background of Leslie Norland, a male nurse: 'A man nurse? Obviously, he had to be a weirdo, and obviously, Karen (another nurse) had to let him know it.'[65] Russell uses an androgynous name, a little ambiguity about his sexuality and appearance (he is slight and very attractive), along with the adjective *queer* to get readers speculating about Norland's sexual orientation. Not surprisingly, he is not gay, and the story turns into a case study about gender stereotypes and reverse discrimination. By story's end, he and Karen have shared a kiss meant to prove his heterosexuality. Similarly, his life story has been fully revealed – his previous job as a hospital orderly, his lack of money to finance a medical career and hence his decision to study nursing, and his determination to support his younger brothers and sisters – all of which add up to a saintly portrait of a misunderstood man. Some readers expressed their frustration with these 'issue' stories, as this letter, received the previous April from B. Millway of Burnaby, BC, indicates: 'Many thanks for Frances McCormick's "The Countess Asked Us to Tea." May we expect to have more such bright intervals in the overall gloom of health and social problems thinly disguised as fiction?'[66]

Mysteries

Although less popular in the fifties, mysteries were a staple in *Chatelaine*. Frequently, the bonus novel was a mystery, as the two-part structure was particularly suited to that genre: readers anxious to discover 'whodunit' would be quick to purchase the next issue of the magazine or make sure their subscriptions were up to date. Mysteries published in the magazine tended to be melodramatic tales, jam-packed with terrifying experiences for the protagonist – murder, kidnapping, automobile accidents, mysterious deaths and disappearances, and family intrigue. They were often set in exotic or dangerous locales, and the mood of these pieces was meant to be dark and terrifying.[67] The following two excerpts illustrate the tone, language, and the nature of these tales. Mignon G. Eberhart's introduction to his story, 'Speak of Love and

Murder,' reads: 'Maggy's marriage to Kirk was just days away, when out of the past came Josh – with a kiss and a warning. Now two mysterious deaths had loosed dread whispers in the night-filled corridors.'[68] Similarly, Jacquelyn Humble's 'Ominous Stranger' tantalizes readers with this introductory sentence: 'She had learned to live with her own frailty, but why did this man terrify her so much?'[69] To generalize, the protagonist (almost always a woman) endured one spectacularly horrendous event after another. She was the archetypal vulnerable innocent, perpetually terrified and dependent on men – boyfriends, husbands, or the police – to protect her and solve the crime(s). At the end, she usually 'melted' into the arms of her protector. Unlike the romances, women in mysteries were victims, and men fell into two categories: protectors and tormentors. It is possible that readers enjoyed the thriller aspect of these stories, much as modern readers flock to the Stephen King genre of thriller fiction (although these stories were considerably less violent than King's). However, one trusts that very few readers could identify with the fantastic plots or the perpetually terrified, helpless, overwrought protagonists. A letter from Cecile E. Leslie of Chilliwack, BC, explained why older readers, and some women in general, may not have cared for this type of fiction: 'I dislike "horror" stories, and you have had too many of them lately. Most women living in lonely parts of Canada have their own experiences of terror or horror. We relive them too thoroughly in stories like "Murder in Muskoka" (a hideous title), and that one of the nice girl lured to a lonely house for marriage. Life for a woman can be thrilling enough and troubled enough without murders and murderers – stories, too.'[70]

Conclusion

Fiction readers received a hefty dose of moralism, some fantasy, a little humour, and, sometimes, depictions of the upset of suburban husbands and frustrated homemakers. Although the romance fiction often provided escapist moments of entertainment and relaxation, many of the stories were also didactic. Frequently these stories were morality tales, laced with a little bit of romance or romantic tension, a narrative hook to hold the reader while the lesson was taught. The chief lesson *Chatelaine* fiction taught readers was that, while life for women could be trying, frustrating, or even deeply disturbing, a good marriage and a happy family life could provide the necessary antidote to a harsh world. The greatest discontent expressed in the *Chatelaine* stories came from male protagonists. The connection between male frustration and violence was a disturbing theme in far too many tales. It serves as a caution about the happy world of suburbia, as well as an indication that not all of *Chatelaine*'s fiction readers were women. The large number of family and marital dramas reflected the majority of the magazine's readership, who were married and for whom such fictional stories would have great appeal. Family and marital dramas in particular highlighted the joys and frustrations married couples faced on a daily basis, along with the reassurance that a happy resolution would be found. Conventional romance stories pointed young women towards the right man, defined as one with education, good career prospects, and, more than likely, a similar (middle-class) background. Although the material presumed that, for many women, marriage and the household were their lot, a number of conflicting issues – paid employment, workplace harassment, feminism, and even the difficulties in adjusting (or reconciling oneself) to married life – indicate that the stories attempted to cover some controversial topics. In addition, many stories provided instruction and critiques of women's magazines, their 'stereotypical' content, and the ways in which readers used them.

The endings were always happy, because that is a standard convention of formula fiction. But they were never so iron-clad that readers were prevented from imagining and formulating their own alternative conclusions. Letters from readers, particularly the intense and detailed commentary about Sheila MacKay Russell's Martin series, verify that many readers were attentive and capable of sophisticated commentary about character motivations, plot structure, and the author's purpose in writing the stories. The fiction component had a lower readership than the general feature articles owing to the uneven and often repetitious character of the stories, and perhaps to the editor's decision to opt for 'commercial' packages – complete with happy endings and identifiable situations rather than more challenging works of fiction.

The more sophisticated and appealing stories made effective use of humour, but the resolutions were often the same. The handful of stories with feminist plots or quest plotlines (which did not necessarily involve romantic liaisons) were the only stories which broached conventions, and in which the status quo was not reaffirmed in the resolution. Fantasy 'romances' like 'Vixen in the Snow,' for example, offered readers an interesting departure from the norm. However, while the resolution almost always reinforced the status quo, the twists and turns in plot development highlighted many different options for the protagonists and readers alike. For readers whose lives were not as perfect as those of the heroes and heroines of these stories, those moments of conflict, anxiety, confusion, and reappraisal provided readers with the resources to change, interpret, or rewrite the endings in their own imaginations or life situations.

Part Three

Subverting the Standard

'How to Live in the Suburbs': Editorials and Articles in the Fifties

Although it is clear that the traditional fare in *Chatelaine*, in particular the fiction, could contain messages that critiqued the affluence and consumerism displayed in the advertisements or highlighted tensions in producing and consuming 'women's magazines,' it was in the articles and editorials that *Chatelaine* dared to deviate dramatically from the genre. During the fifties, *Chatelaine* began to offer a range of material that was noticeably different from the features in American women's magazines. In a decade noted for a plethora of popular culture odes to the suburban housewife and mother, *Chatelaine* began, quietly yet subversively, to include feminist content. The fifties mark a transitional phase for *Chatelaine*, as the editorial disruptions created an ever changing mixture of material, and as Doris Anderson's confidence – both as an editor and a feminist – began to grow. In the sixties these changes would be realized, with a more politicized, activist, 'closet' feminist magazine. Through it all, the readers were an active part of this process – urging the editors and writers onwards or criticizing the rapid changes. Once again, the wealth of information contained in the reader responses to editorial policy and changing content mitigates against any simplistic assessment of the goals and accomplishments of the magazine. Although the vast majority of *Chatelaine* readers were housewives, it would be inaccurate to assume that, because of this occupational similarity, they all wished to read genteel articles about life in suburbia. In fact, many of them applauded the controversy occasioned by the editorials and articles, as this letter from Mrs Doris Gehman of Cultus Lake, BC, reveals:

I must write to you or break a blood vessel. Please! Please! Do not pay too much attention to the funny little people who want you to print only what they wish to read and what they agree with. Please go on printing articles that keep us thinking and occasionally step on our toes a bit. When I read a magazine I want to have something to think about. What if I am mad with the author – I have a good argument with him while I wash dishes and make beds. Makes me prove to myself I'm right or maybe I'm just a wee bit wrong ... The work flies fast as my thoughts and I come out of it with the house tidy and my ideas more firmly planted than ever or perhaps my thinking has been a bit tight fitting and I've had to let it out at the seams. Anyway I hope you are making money and can stand the cancelled subscriptions. I'll never cancel mine until you start filling your good magazine with nothing but taffy recipes and a bunch of sweet stuff! Long life![1]

Her description of why she read magazines and how she used them in her daily routine no doubt summarized a familiar situation to many housebound Canadian housewives. Mrs Gehman's letter sheds light on the 'internal resistance' experienced by many readers and echoes the resistance of fictional heroines as well. This discontinuity between outwardly appearing to conform to the status quo, yet inwardly experiencing reservations, has begun to appear in historians' accounts of the fifties and helps explain why second-wave feminism emerged so quickly and forcefully in the sixties.[2] Equally, it points to the centrality of the editorials and articles in the magazine.

Editorials and articles were the most lively and consistently appealing pages in *Chatelaine* in both the fifties and the sixties. The secret to this appeal was the rich mixture of unconventional, challenging, thought-provoking, and traditional material that editors and writers provided for the readers. The editors presumed that the readers were intelligent and seldom patronized them. The editorials and articles fostered the 'community' of *Chatelaine* readers by encouraging reader participation, offering a variety of texts that were open to alternate or oppositional readings and misreadings, and using an intimate tone in the editorial essays.

Editorials

The lively editorial essay, written in turn by Byrne Hope Sanders, Lotta Dempsey, and Doris Anderson, was a staple in the magazine during the fifties and functioned as the gateway into the periodical. Sanders and

Anderson worked the genre into an art form. Owing to her short tenure at the magazine, Dempsey wrote only a few editorials, but even this small sample indicates that her essays would have found her a similarly dedicated following. Only John Clare eschewed the editorial format. The editorials in each issue of *Chatelaine*, except during Clare's tenure in the mid-fifties, were written in an intimate, woman-to-woman tone. Located on the first page of the magazine, these half-page essays were intended to be thought-provoking and stimulating. Because of their tone, prominent placement, and subject matter, readers seemed to take these editorials very seriously, whether or not they agreed with the editor's perspective, and this section increased their confidence in the integrity of the magazine and the editor. The editorials also played a major role in distinguishing *Chatelaine* from American women's magazines. American magazines did not offer editorial essays; instead, they offered commentary about the magazine or editorial notes that glorified the era and women's suburban roles. Readers noted this difference. Agnes L. Honey of Salmon Arm, BC, wrote to commend the magazine for its stance on nuclear testing: 'Thank you for your editorial, "Let's Not Guess about Fallout." I am so glad *Chatelaine* had the gumption to call for action and "not sit and wait for something to happen."'[3] Time and again, readers commented on the persuasive power of the *Chatelaine* editorial to publicize issues and to affect change. Those readers who were critical of editorial commentary, a much less frequent occurrence, also believed in the power of the editor's pen. According to G.L., from Galt, Ontario, 'Your editorial "Honesty and High Prices" is one of those propaganda yarns that gets me all het up.'[4] Whether thought provoking or irritating, these editorials were one of the linchpins of the *Chatelaine* community. The editors shared their personal thoughts on a variety of issues, and the readers felt they were taken into the editor's confidence, thereby creating a bond between the readers and the editors. In addition, it was through this format that many 'hot topics' of the day – feminist, educational, cultural, and political – were disseminated to the readers. Ultimately, the editorials fostered a feeling of collectivity and solidarity among the readers and editors of the magazine.

To provide a context for the textual analysis and readers' analysis that follows, a brief summary of the editorial results provides a general overview of the editorial writers, themes, and topics during the decade.[5] Sanders, Dempsey, and Anderson were the primary editorial essay writers. John Clare preferred to compile a feature entitled 'Chatelaine Centre' (one originally inaugurated by Lotta Dempsey), a page of anecdotes about contributors, producers, and readers of the periodical. He contributed two editorial essays and commissioned two guest editorialists. Editorial topics varied, but the most common topics concerned *Chatelaine*, philosophy of life, travel, marriage, motherhood and family, women's issues, current events, and feminism. The most popular themes favoured *Chatelaine*'s importance, family, professional issues, and culture. The editorials explored the private world of women (the home and family), along with the public sphere (women in the media and wide-ranging gender and political issues). Although all the editors had different styles, during Clare's tenure as editor there was a noticeably different tone in his essays. His dissatisfaction and frustration with the job were only partly to blame. Because he made little effort to find out what readers were interested in, his essays or Chatelaine Centre pieces often were at odds with the other editorial components of the magazine.[6] Unlike the other editors, he did not understand his audience of female readers. This is not to say that a male editor could not interpret the 'Chatelaine ethos' to the readers; rather, the criticism is that an uninterested male editor, with no desire to learn about or interact with the readers, could not create editorial material that had as much resonance with them.

Readers connected to editorials in which the editors confided their personal views, thoughts, or insights about their roles, the magazine, or Canada during the fifties. An examination of each editor, in turn, illustrates the differing nature of the *Chatelaine* editorial and provides insight into the readers' reaction to each editorial perspective.

Byrne Hope Sanders: Maternal Feminist

Byrne Hope Sanders was in a reflective mood in her farewell editorial in 1952 as she reminisced about her tenure at the magazine. 'I remember writing my first editorial for *Chatelaine* in 1929 when the magazine was a few months old and I was in my mid-twenties,' she wrote. 'Since then thousands of you have had the same experiences that I have, been married, raised a family, lived through a depression and terrible war. But in spite of all the difficulties, life has been full and good, hasn't it?'[7] This excerpt epitomized the Sanders's style of editorial writing. As the well-meaning 'big sister,' she doled out encouragement, praise, and timely advice based on her own experiences. The few readers' letters that commented on her editorials exhibited both admiration and frustration with her patronizing tone of noblesse oblige. She always knew better than the readers, and, because their only voice lay in writing her a letter, one she could discard or publish at will, the relationship was one sided. In Sanders's defence, she would claim that the readers were her first concern and, embued with a strong sense of social reform uplift, that she cared deeply for them. Her ideology and personality were best suited to the type of work she had performed in the war effort: encouraging team spirit, hard work, and dedication to a greater good. She was a maternal feminist, convinced that the power of the household should have an impact on the nation and that wives and mothers were a force to be reckoned with: 'It's been enlightening over the years to read your letters and to try to reflect your development as women in a magazine. It's been exhilarating to watch your growing pride in your works as homemakers and in an understanding of the vital roles we play in the nation's life as wives and mothers.' Consistent with her maternal feminism, she rarely paid any attention to issues of class or race, assuming that her readers shared her racial, class, and ethnic background.

In the final two years of her editorials she covered many topics, with essays entitled 'Working Wives Outside the Home' (July 1950), 'Lilacs in the Rain' (May 1951), 'Honesty and High Prices' (June 1951), and 'What Do You Think of *Chatelaine* Magazine?' (September 1951). From the title through to the last paragraph, Sanders's editorial on working wives was full of contradictions and ambiguity. 'It's a situation which is obviously going to bring about many heartaches – and many triumphs. The heartaches for those who have keyed their standard of living to a double pay envelope, who are weary of working – but can't stop. The triumphs will come for professional women, and women who want to earn their own money, for their own perfectly good reasons – and who will have an increasing opportunity to do so.' Rising to a crescendo in her concluding comments, she wrote: 'For good or ill, mankind is pressing forward to some unknown goal. Somewhere in that progress, surely, lies the principle of the right to earn money – provided one can, and provided one wants to.'[8] The essay's feminist language was forward thinking, and she cast her vote, shakily, in favour of women's choice about paid employment. Noticeably absent were any references to the large numbers of Canadian women forced to work for more immediate concerns than their standard of living or the type of car they drove. Even though she had been married, raised a son, and handled a Herculean work load, particularly during the war, she fretted about the women 'who are weary of working.' Her classist assumptions and cautious tone made it evident that Sanders was not wildly optimistic about what the future held for working women.

Sanders was adept at penning 'philosophy of life' editorials, such as her 'Lilacs in the Rain.' Written for the May 1951 issue, it was a romantic piece about the beauty of spring. While lamenting that the hectic pace of daily life kept many people from enjoying simple pleasures, Saunders admonished housewives to forsake their daily grind, to 'leave the floors, and the dishes, and the darning, and hurry, hurry out into the garden!' Like most of her editorials, this one did not question the bourgeois values reflected in her instructions, such as her perceptions of beauty, or admit that her readers might lack a private garden in which to commune with nature. However, editorials such as this compel a re-evaluation of the assumptions and purposes for a women's magazine. In a format that has been widely criticized as merely a vehicle to sell household cleansers, this advice ran counter to the advertisers' goals and questioned the household perfectionism of the advertisements. How would readers evaluate the advertising dramas or the service fare in that issue, after reading those instructions from the editor?

One of the most consistent themes throughout *Chatelaine*, including the editorials, was the magazine's Canadian origin. The administrators responsible for marketing *Chatelaine* constantly wrapped themselves in the flag as the primary means of distinguishing the product from American women's magazines. The content, tone, editorial leadership, and price also differed, but the powerful identification of nationalism was always a key factor in selling the magazine. Letters, questionnaires, and interviews with readers about why they read the periodical almost always started with the refrain that they preferred to read 'our own' *Chatelaine* instead of one of those 'other' magazines. The Dichter Study also confirmed the importance of the magazine's nationalism. Not surprisingly, the editors often asked the readers to write to tell them what they liked or disliked about the magazine. Sanders was no exception, and in September 1951 she exclaimed: 'My job as editor of *Chatelaine* is an enthralling one.' 'I believe all Canadian editors feel that sense of excitement and growth – because our magazines are key to the expansion of Canada itself. Our country is developing a mind of its own, a national consciousness, a vital personality. It's stimulating just trying to keep up with it.'[9] As her editorial continued, it became apparent that one of her main concerns was not fostering Canadian nationalism, but stemming a tidal wave of American culture that freely entered the country. Sanders ended with a plea for readers to write to tell her 'the changes you'd like to see' and 'the new features you'd introduce if you yourself were editor.' The backdrop to Sanders's appeal was the increasing popularity of American magazines, and more seriously the appearance of split-run periodicals like *Time* and *Reader's Digest* that syphoned off Canadian advertising to American publications, creating a potentially dire situation for Canadian periodicals. Equally important was the early fifties' obsession with defining, finding, and creating Canadian 'culture,' thanks largely to the media coverage accorded the Massey Commission study and report.

Two months later, in the November 1951 issue, the letters section contained excerpts from fourteen letters responding to Sanders's request. According to Mrs W.R. Pringle of Headlingly, Manitoba: 'Your editorial acted on me like bait to a fish.'[10] A self-proclaimed 'purse pinching joe,' she reported that she liked everything but the fashions, because they were too impractical. The letters arrived from across the country, from married and single women, and from male readers. Arthur Hanna of Montreal wrote that he was 'in complete accord with the theme of your editorial ... More power to you.'[11] Ron de Armand from Vancouver wrote expressing his surprise that he enjoyed reading *Chatelaine*: 'Your magazine has been coming to our office for quite some time now, and up until today I've just glanced through it. Today I had nothing to do ... so I sat down and started to read *Chatelaine*. I must say I was a bit surprised that its contents were of great interest. *Chatelaine* is supposed to be a woman's magazine, but I'm sure that just about as many men read it.'[12] De Armand's decision to preface his comments with the statement that he had 'nothing else to do,' so he read *Chatelaine*, was common among male readers. Entering this women's territory, even if only to 'glance' through it, required a plausible excuse lest male readers cast aspersions on their masculinity.

Unlike these two male readers, the majority of the female readers were not so complimentary. While most writers did find something they liked in the magazine, quite often the 'excellent' (their words) editorials, many expressed varying levels of dissatisfaction with the magazine. The most dissatisfied was Mrs N. Schurko of Gatehill, Ontario, who wrote:

For some time now I have been deliberating with myself whether your magazine is worth getting or not. Your editorial in the September issue, however, rouses me to some hope. With the exception of some articles, the stories have been insipid, the exclusive fashions of no use to me, and the recipes too extravagant. All in all, your publication is lacking in originality ... Why not endeavour to make it more truly Canadian? ... Consider the national groups in Canada – the Germans, Italians, Finns, Poles, Mennonites, Doukhobors, Ukrainians, Yugoslavs, even the Eskimos and Indians. Instead of a laissez faire attitude toward them, why not sponsor each group in a way which will make other Canadians understand and accept them as fellow citizens? Not only would your magazine prove more interesting, but it would become more popular, particularly with all the groups involved ... Your magazine is too self-centred. It should open up its vistas and broaden its horizons.[13]

Noticeably absent from Schurko's list of Canadian groups were the predominant English and French Canadians. Hers was a request for a more inclusive, relevant magazine for all Canadian women, regardless of ethnicity or class. It is worth emphasizing that Schurko's request for refocusing the magazine addressed the editorals and articles, not the service material or the advertisements, which she clearly realized were necessary and relatively inflexible components of *Chatelaine*. Her commentary on Sanders's vision of the magazine forms an appropriate conclusion to this section. What we now refer to as feminist commentary was not prevalent in the early fifties, and Sanders's editorials were progressive and atypical by comparison with other periodicals. Clearly written from a maternal feminist perspective, they feature a celebration of women's culture and commonalities. The lack of attention to issues of class, ethnicity, and race is not surprising. That few readers thought to question their absence was probably indicative of *Chatelaine*'s smaller readership among non-English speakers and a lack of awareness of their absence on the part of English-Canadian readers (although at odds with the influx of newcomers, or New Canadians, after the Second World War). Class issues, always phrased in terms of 'affordability' of the products advertised and promoted in the magazine, were often criticized by the readers. Sanders had a middle-class blindspot that grouped readers as essentially the same, or striving for upward mobility. Dempsey and Anderson soon abandoned this perspective.

Lotta Dempsey: Feisty Outsider

Readers were quick to comment on the different tone of the magazine under Dempsey. Mrs F.C. Knight from Burlington, Ontario, wrote: 'How much I enjoy Lotta Dempsey's Chatelaine Centre, and how very lively and peppy the whole magazine is lately.'[14] The editorial section was revamped into the Chatelaine Centre, subtitled 'A Meeting Place for People Who Are Doing Things around Canada.'[15] The format was changed to include a smaller, usually quarter-page, editorial column and little anecdotes about the exploits of Canadian women or *Chatelaine*. When the urge struck her, Dempsey wrote full-length editorials, such as the one on Agnes Macphail.

Dempsey's editorial on Macphail, Canada's first female member of parliament, chronicled the injustices in the political system, particularly the patronage system, which had left the recently defeated Ontario MPP without any income or pension and reduced her to a state of proud poverty.[16] Dempsey called on the readers of *Chatelaine*, and the Canadian government, to recognize Macphail's plight and reward her for twenty years of 'courage and integrity' with an appointment to the Senate:

> If every one of the more than a million readers of, say, this magazine alone stopped thinking of this as a 'political' or 'club woman's' question, and lined up her neighbour, her dentist, her best friend, her groceryman, her golf club, her grandmother, her son-in-law and her milkman to sign a letter to the Prime Minister (no stamp required), that would make quite a backlog of nonpartisan rooters. If this particular Government of this Dominion had the courage to fly in the face of ancient tradition ... Agnes Macphail could be a member of the Upper House ... If all these quite plausible things happened, Agnes Macphail might feel called upon to graciously decline ... the one post ... which has been offered to her in tribute to three decades of national service – That of matron of a mental institution.[17]

The difference in Dempsey's tone from that of Sanders was readily apparent. Dempsey recognized the influential role that her position as *Chatelaine* editor accorded her, and the readers responded to her encouragement, although not all with the intended results. A Montreal subscriber wrote: 'Congratulations on your request regarding Agnes Macphail. It is delightful to realize that a magazine for Canadian women is at last loyally supporting one. My letter to the PM is in the mail.'[18] From conservative Toronto and a self-proclaimed 'former admirer' of Dempsey came this response: 'I am disillusioned regarding your astuteness, ability and common sense. Your editorial re Agnes and the Senate nauseated me. The CCF have always advocated abolishing the

Senate, none more so than A.M.'[19] Dempsey's editorials, selection of articles, and *bon mots* in Chatelaine Centre won her both fans and enemies: many letters received threatened to cancel subscriptions or promised to renew subscriptions, based on her editorial direction. In hindsight, it would have been interesting to watch her progress over the course of some years at the helm of the magazine. It appears, too, that her style may have made some people at Maclean Hunter nervous, though no hard evidence exists to back up this presumption.

Another noteworthy Dempsey editorial appeared in the August 1952 issue. The summer issues of the magazine usually contained happy, feel-good stories to accompany Canadians at the cottage or on vacation. Dempsey broke from this mould to question the comfortable shallowness of many Canadians. 'En route across Canada: At every station people look prosperous. Men in sport shirts, women in slacks and bright summer dresses, children burdened with little beyond an aura of well-being,' Dempsey wrote. 'I keep remembering a similar journey of less than two decades ago. Then there were brave but beaten men and women in the parched prairie droughtlands. Children of Alberta mining towns peering hungrily into the glowing windows of half-empty dining cars ... I listen to conversations of well-fed, well-dressed people enjoying the ease and luxury of modern trains and planes. They seem to have everything ... everything except some indefinable inner security ... and faith.'[20] The contrast to Sanders was apparent: there were no 'times are good' sentiments in this piece. Dempsey urged readers to re-examine their well-being, to anchor their sense of self-worth in something more than material affluence. Essays such as this were oppositional to the consumer ethos of the advertising content and some of the service department material. They explicitly encouraged readers to undertake critical and, ultimately, oppositional readings.

The letters section of the same issue included excerpts from twelve letters – the usual mix of complimentary, critical, and negative opinions. Most of them complained about some aspect of the magazine while praising others. It was a rarity in the fifties and sixties for two letters to be published from the same author, but, in this issue, Sanders's harsh critic returned. Mrs Schurko had continued to read the magazine and felt compelled to write an appraisal of Dempsey's *Chatelaine*: 'Your editorials are highly controversial, but precise and happily reach into the very heart of the Canadian people. Good luck to you.'[21] Unfortunately, within one month of Schurko's letter, Dempsey had left the magazine.

John Clare: Champion of the Status Quo

John Clare continued Dempsey's Chatelaine Centre format for the editorial page. Unlike Dempsey, he rarely wrote any editorial columns,
preferring anecdotal information and previews of the features in each
issue. There were two noteworthy exceptions: 'It's a Tough Time to Be
in Love' in May 1954, and his only signed editorial in October 1957,
'One Man's Opinion: The Unsimple Truth about Why Husbands Never
Phone Home,' published, ironically, after Anderson had become managing editor and his name was no longer listed in the masthead. He
favoured a gently deprecatory sense of humour and his tone was that
of a sheepish, misunderstood male in a female world. Given his
background as a war correspondent, *Maclean's* writer, associate editor,
and reluctant conscript to the *Chatelaine* editorship, this position was
justified.

   'It's a Tough Time to Be in Love' described newlyweds, the recently
opened Toronto subway, and the besieged state of marriage, circa 1954.
Readers who might be anticipating an essay about Cold War politics or
the prevailing ethos were disappointed. Instead, this editorial served to
discredit the naysayers who viewed marriage as under siege from two
modern developments: young marriages and working wives. However, the editorial also had undertones of romanticism, paternalism,
and a decidedly heterosexist, bourgeois view of what constituted a
normal individual. Clare wrote: 'Fortunately there continues to be something within all normal people which makes them feel that marriage is
good and meant for them. They experience the romance and drive of
young love. They want a house of their own; they want children; they
want security; and above all they want the comradeship and affection
that marriage alone can provide. And they want it to last.'[22] Clare went
on to list books and a variety of courses offered at Toronto churches to
prepare young couples for marriage; he also encouraged them to read
Chatelaine's articles on marriage in the issue. The editorial ended on a
note strikingly familiar to Sanders's final piece. 'Don't take marriage
too seriously, because it always was a tough time to fall in love. Wars,
depressions, economic booms and atomic bombs will always be incidentals compared to such fundamentals as love, marriage and the
raising of families. So get a ring, a license, two tokens for the subway –
and hang on.' Obviously, Clare's vision of the world of *Chatelaine* was
one set apart from the political reality of life during the Cold War – the
incidentals, as he so delicately termed them. The primary focus of

women's lives was the private realm of love, marriage, and raising families. Clare's commentary was self-centred, patronizing, and sexist, although not atypical for the era. His ideas and essays were representative of the prevailing images from the popular culture of the fifties, whether magazines or television programs (*Father Knows Best* or *Leave It to Beaver*). Dissatisfaction with the status quo, apparent in the work of Dempsey and Anderson, and in some pockets of cultural activity – the Beat poets, Canadian poet Irving Layton, *Peyton Place*, and liberal questions about 'progress' – were not in evidence here. Clare was a supporter of hegemonic values, and his work demonstrates a certain self-satisfied complacency, not the counter-hegemonic questioning of society.

Some readers were not pleased with the direction *Chatelaine* had taken under Clare's editorial guidance, particularly in 1953, when the contrast with Dempsey and Sanders would have been most pronounced. D.A. Robertson from Lethbridge, Alberta, wrote to voice her complaint in the March issue: 'After your most successful 1952, it was a great surprise that I read the new February issue – alas, the mid-winter doldrums seem to have hit your staff. Sorry to blow off like this, in my first and only letter to any magazine, but are all the improvements in *Chatelaine* during the past two years going to come tumbling down in one issue? I hope this relapse is only temporary.'[23] As the type of articles published in the magazine continued to improve, these critical letters diminished. It should be restated, however, that the mid-fifties was the only time that *Chatelaine's* circulation lagged behind its Canadian competitor, *Canadian Home Journal*, and that the periodical failed to turn a profit.[24]

Doris Anderson: 'Emerging' Feminist

In September 1958 the new and improved version of *Chatelaine*, subtitled 'The Canadian Home Journal,' debuted.[25] In the revised version, Doris Anderson reinstated the editorial essay with a piece on Dr Marion Hilliard, a popular *Chatelaine* contributor, who had died suddenly that year. The response to that editorial was phenomenal, and Anderson never looked back. After a hiatus of roughly five years, the editorial essay, as opposed to the Chatelaine Centre collection of anecdotes, returned as a regular feature of the magazine. Anderson wrote with conviction on many topics: some of her recurrent themes were educational issues, current events, politics, and Canadian nationalism. The vast majority of the editorials were feminist in orientation, concerned with gender inequity and hopeful of improving the status of Canadian women.

When Anderson appeared at the Special Senate Committee on the Mass Media in 1971, she was asked why she included a personalized editorial essay in the magazine. Her reply is illuminating: 'I think every editor has to edit a magazine the way he sees it. I find the editorial, the personalized editorial form, a very useful device for covering sharp controversial issues very quickly, and I would hate to give it up. I cannot see that I am going to give it up. I can't see that I am going to run out of topics, or that the country is going to have all its problems so beautifully solved that I am going to have nothing to say.'[26] Most of the sharp, controversial issues that Anderson addressed were feminist issues. A representative sampling from the last two years of the fifties attests to the feminist content of Anderson's editorials: 'We've Been Emerging Long Enough,' 'We Need More Women Scientists,' 'Clichés We Can Do Without,' 'Are Ladies Obsolete?' 'Do Women Really Dominate Men?' and 'Let's Stop Acting Like a Minority Group.' The October 1958 editorial, 'Emerging Long Enough,' questioned why, so many years after the first-wave feminists had broken through numerous gender barriers (in particular the achievement of suffrage), Canadian women were 'still emerging.'[27] She criticized the token inclusion of women on various councils, in municipal, provincial, and federal politics, and blamed this scant representation for the perception that women were part of the decision-making process, thereby retarding numerical equality in the corridors of power. Women were not spared in Anderson's editorials. She often criticized them for being complacent – and this editorial was no exception.

In 'We Need More Women Scientists' in April 1959, Anderson took a different approach. She considered the growing North American fear of being scientifically eclipsed by the Soviet Union and argued that one of the great untapped resources was the 50 per cent of the students left out of the Space Age scientific race – the girls. Anderson shrewdly constructed her argument to focus on the best interests of the nation, not women. 'Almost from the time a little girl picks up a toy in her playpen, she is taught that mechanical matters and scientific affairs are the province of boys and men; this subtle propaganda is continued through high school and university.' Providing an international point of comparison, she continued that, 'in Russia, seventy-five to eighty percent of doctors and engineers are women. But at the University of Toronto, for example, out of 1,974 engineering students, only twelve are women ... Our female brain power is presently one of our richest untapped reservoirs. The longer we fail to make use of it, the less chance we have for survival in the Space Age.'[28] These editorials were created to get readers, female and male, thinking and talking about these issues. For the marketers they were also pure gold; they created 'good word of mouth commentary' about *Chatelaine*, one of the Dichter recommendations to increase circulation.

One of Anderson's favourite styles of editorializing was to take an isolated incident of sexist behaviour or language, tell her readers about it, and then, with heavy doses of sarcasm and thinly suppressed anger, criticize the behaviour or the language. In May 1959 she wrote an editorial entitled 'Clichés We Can Do Without' which set out to challenge the commonplace phrases of North American society, circa 1959, such as 'In spite of everything she is utterly feminine'; 'She thinks like a man,' or, conversely, 'What she needs is a man.'[29] Her criticism of the last phrase was vintage Anderson: 'Well it may surprise the complacent person who says this, but a man is, quite often, just what she doesn't need. Perhaps what she needs much more is a good holiday, or a little more money, or a little less worry, or just someone, male or female, to listen to her.'

Finally, in her September 1959 piece, entitled 'Do Women Really Dominate Men?' Anderson unleashed a hard-hitting feminist critique that would become her signature in the sixties. She revealed that, at one of the many luncheons she had attended, the guest speaker had, in the course of his speech, told the almost solely female audience, 'Of course, North American men are dominated by their women.'[30] The speaker was merely paraphrasing the popular thesis advanced by Phillip Wylie's best-selling book, *Generation of Vipers*, which criticized, among other things, the impact of 'Momism' on American men. Wylie maintained that the overwhelming attachment of suburban males to their mothers resulted in their emasculation (figuratively speaking) as adult men. The suburban world, according to Wylie and other popularizers of this canard, was a matriarchy in which women dominated their husbands and sons. Anderson reported that only a flutter of protest was heard in the auditorium, and she attacked this misperception:

The Canadian husband is still the kingpin of his own particular split-level. Occasionally he may change a diaper or wash some dishes, but he expects to come home to a nourishing dinner, clean socks, tidy living room, fresh smelling babies and to receive, as well, a reasonable amount of cherishing of his own ego. Most women are delighted to provide these services and have no desire to run the household themselves. And let's be logical – if we really were the dominant sex, would we continue to do (more or less cheerfully) such monotonous and repetitious tasks as making beds, dusting ... and picking up after the whole family day after day? Are these the tasks the Super Sex would choose for itself? Let's not confuse having some voice about family finances, occasionally going out to work while married, making tiny inroads into some traditionally male professions, having three women in the House of Commons and an imperceptible sprinkling of women on civic boards with domination of men. We're still a long, long way from equality with men – and a thousand light years from domination.

This editorial provided a taste of what was to come in the sixties, when Anderson became more confident of her editorial voice and moved on to criticize divorce laws, abortion laws, and other gender inequities in a more hard-hitting fashion. Editorials such as these were what Canadian women came to expect from her. It is this type of discourse for which the magazine was known during the sixties and seventies. These editorials elicited praise and created a forum in which women's voices (whether writers or readers) could overcome their isolated, insular worlds. Furthermore, although Anderson's editorial position gave her a prominent place from which to write about these issues, as her autobiography and experience at Maclean Hunter make clear, she too was just as bound, and frustrated, by the conventions of the day as the 'average' reader. For their part, the readers were very complimentary regarding her editorials, although they often voiced complaints over the articles they thought were too strident, too far fetched, or simply un-Canadian.

Articles

In the mid-fifties, Mrs H. McMaster of Orangeville, Ontario, wrote a mildly sarcastic and pointed letter to the editor, questioning him about the side effects of reading *Chatelaine*: 'I have just finished reading the April number of *Chatelaine* and am feeling sorry for myself as I picture my mental upheaval when I discover a lump in my breast. I am afraid my children are all sex deviates and I must learn the address of that mental health clinic in Toronto so that I will lose no time in hastening there the next time one of my family has a fit of blues or shows signs of a temper tantrum. Do you think you might be putting ideas in our heads?'[31]

Every month Mrs McMaster, and many other readers, took the baited hooks that the *Chatelaine* editors and writers dangled in front of them in the form of lively and controversial feature articles. These articles served as the primary means of attracting new readers while keeping loyal readers renewing their subscriptions. Each month the article titles, often employing puns or sensational prose such as 'A Mother Inferior,' 'Canadian Women Are Suckers,' or 'My Daughter Married a Negro,' were advertised on the cover of the magazine. If readers' responses are any gauge, the editors were successful – most letters were provoked by feature articles.[32] By emphasizing Canadian topics and locales, the editors of *Chatelaine* and Maclean Hunter created a unique niche in the women's magazine market. *Chatelaine* offered lively, opinionated pieces that generated discussion, controversy, and interest across the country, and often beyond. The purpose of the articles was to bring novelty to each issue, 'something to look forward to,' to get women talking about the magazine, and to broaden the readership. The articles were a way to reach out not only to the housewives and mothers but also to working women, single women, and teenage girls, for whom the departmental material often had less appeal.

An overview of the articles of the decade reveals a remarkable range of topics and writers. The articles also reflected the time in which they were written, although caution should be used in extrapolating the everyday concerns of Canadian women from the pages of *Chatelaine*. The most popular series was written by Dr Marion Hilliard: actually, these articles were dictated by Hilliard and ghost written into article format by freelance journalist June Callwood. Dr Hilliard was chief of gynecology and obstetrics at Women's College Hospital in Toronto. Her articles were groundbreaking and extremely popular because she wrote with authority, verve, and candour about women's medical issues – primarily sexuality, childbirth, and menopause. Another popular topic was Britain's Royal Family. The June 1953 issue, for instance, was a special commemorative issue devoted to Elizabeth II's coronation. Throughout the decade, articles by Marion 'Crawfie' Crawford, Elizabeth's nanny, kept *Chatelaine* readers enthralled with stories of the young princesses' early years, the older members of the family, and the personality of the young queen. Other writers also tackled royal topics, but, lacking Crawford's intimate connection, they were not as successful. Theme issues were rare: the only other one during the decade was the March 1955 issue entitled 'How to Live in the Suburbs.' There were the requisite stories of celebrities, but *Chatelaine* put a different spin on this genre by featuring Canadians. Readers were introduced to Barbara Ann Scott's life after figure skating, Juliette, Gordie Tapp, Ma Murray, Don Messer and his Jubilee family, Marilyn Bell, and others. Rarely did the magazine cover the Hollywood or Broadway beat, unless the featured actor or performer was Canadian. Occasionally American stars were chronicled, but these items were not as successful. Finally, a series started by Anderson in the mid-fifties, 'The Women of –' profiled influential women in cities across the country.

Always eager to please readers, and on the advice of the Dichter Study, the magazine inaugurated three monthly columns towards the end of the decade: 'What's New in the Arts,' 'Your World Notebook,' and 'Here's Health.' According to Anderson, these columns responded to weekly letters that complained: 'I'm tired of recipes and advice about burping the baby. When I sit down with a magazine I want to get away from housework. Why don't you run something on theatre, poetry and books?'[33] The arts column, originally written by Robert Fulford, was a page of paragraph-length reviews about books, television shows, new plays, or Canadian writers. After one year, Fulford gave up the column and Edna May took over. The current affairs column was often written by a political insider, later by journalist Christina McCall, and provided a brief, but detailed synopsis of international and Canadian political news. The health column was written by a U.S. medical writer, Lawrence Galton, and offered a compendium of late-breaking news from medical journals. Many readers, including Mrs P.J. Kennedy from East Chezzetcook, Halifax County, thanked the magazine for Galton's column: 'I am a constant reader of your health column. It has helped many in the community.'[34] The only other long-running featured column was for teenagers. The 'Teen Tempo' page, started in the late fifties, was directed at teenage girls, and concentrated on dating, clothing, summer jobs, and bedroom decoration.

Despite this turn towards regular featured columns, the vast majority of *Chatelaine* articles, and certainly the most popular ones, were the big features: the exposés on marriage, voyeuristic tales of the life of the Royal Family, personal experience stories written by *Chatelaine* readers and usually ghosted into final form by a staff writer, or some examination of sociocultural changes in the 'Canadian way of life.'

Although articles accounted for only 15 per cent of the magazine's content in the decade, their importance, prime location, and novelty proved key to the magazine's success.[35] Some of the articles received additional publicity on the radio or in newspapers because of their controversial subject matter. Others garnered praise from business groups or manufacturers for presenting their product or service in a complimentary light. One such consumer affairs article, 'Insurance for Wives – Who Wants It?' by Mary Jukes, 'resulted in requests for 27,225 reprints,' and officials from the insurance companies wrote 'letters of commendation on Miss Jukes' handling of the article.'[36] In the early fifties, there were often only two or three articles per issue, but, by the end of the decade, the magazine usually offered seven to eight articles, and sometimes over ten. Articles tended to be short: most were less than three pages long. The vast majority (70%) were written by women.[37]

Chatelaine published an equal number of articles from freelance writers and staff writers. A list of writers whose work appeared in the magazine in this decade reads like a who's who of Canadian publishing, along with prominent Canadian and American writers, politicians, members of the news media, doctors, and academics.[38] Most article topics were assigned by the editors and bore his or her imprint, as June Callwood explains: 'I never had ideas. Everything I got was an assignment ... Doris would call in that dry voice of hers and say, "How do you feel about doing a piece about sex and married women?" And I'd say "Sure, what's it supposed to be about?" and she'd say, "Well, look at it this way ..." she would just block it out and always by telephone.'[39] Within a couple of days, she received Anderson's feedback and suggestions, if any, for revisions. The whole process, from the phone call to finished article, took Callwood 'three weeks if you didn't do anything else.' Whether the author was an 'expert' by profession or from research and interviews, the authorial voice was assured. Expert commentary was one of the magazine's selling points, mentioned in advertising directed towards readers, in briefs to the royal commissions, and in the advertisements aimed at attracting new advertising clients.

Although always presumed to focus solely on women's domestic exploits, Chatelaine articles in the fifties were considerably more diverse topically and thematically. The three most popular topics for articles in the fifties were women's private lives, medical issues, and women's public lives. Thematically, family, culture, and class stratification were the most prevalent.[40] In contrast, the geographic locale of the articles was consistent: general Canadian settings predominated – that is, articles that mentioned more than one province or region – followed by provincial or regional settings. Of the provincial settings, Ontario proved the most popular, followed by the Prairies, Quebec, and British Columbia. This bias towards articles set in Ontario can be attributed to the fact that the magazine's offices were located in Toronto, and the freelancers who appeared most often were from the Toronto area. The editors made a genuine effort, particularly in later years, to inject more regional and national flavour in the articles and were prepared to pay for writers' travel expenses. Articles with international perspective, primarily American, British, and European, were rare. Although an effort was made to represent regional diversity in the magazine, the writers and editors consistently favoured urban and suburban topics over rural or northern ones.

The focus of articles, regardless of their topic, was on gender and, less frequently, on class. Even though the magazine covered numerous topics – the arts, politics, Britain's Royal Family, nuclear war, or traffic accidents – they were usually written from a woman's perspective and pitched to female readers. For this reason they concentrated on marriage and children, issues that women were deemed to have in common. Most articles either presumed a middle-class, or higher, standard of living or regarded middle-class ideals as the norm to which everyone should and did aspire – a suburban home, an employed husband, a stay-at-home wife and mother with children.

The sampling of articles that follows was selected for a variety of reasons, primarily because these pieces indicate the role of the readership community, the distinctive nature of Chatelaine articles, and the articles that were the most popular during the decade – judged by letters, Starch reports, and other indicators. The large number of articles, and their inherent interest to cultural and social historians, made selection a daunting task. These articles were grouped into six categories, four of which cover specific topical and temporal categories: marriage and women's issues 1950–3; marriage and women's issues, 1957–9; Dr Marion Hilliard's medical columns, 1954–6; and humour, 1954–9. The other two categories span the decade and are devoted to examinations of two types of articles: ethnicity and race, and class. Although the articles have been classified and grouped according to their predominant topical reference, there is considerable overlap of themes and secondary issues, in keeping with the Chatelaine style of making articles relevant to their major readership group of married women.

'Housewives Are a Sorry Lot': Marriage and Women's Issues, 1950–3

In March 1950 journalist Beverley Grey, a self-proclaimed business girl, 'looks over her married friends, shudders, takes a reef in her girdle and strikes out with these observations' in the inflammatory article entitled 'Housewives Are a Sorry Lot.'[41] Part of what made *Chatelaine* magazine so popular was its self-parody and literary attacks on 'women's roles,' which other women's magazines held as sacrosanct territory. 'Housewives' was a direct hit on the magazine's target audience. Grey wrote that 'marriage brings a full stop to mental development' and that, 'as soon as the wedding is over, a woman drops phony interests in such things as sports, politics, and world events.' If the synopsis at the beginning of the article was not enough to inflame the readership, Grey's vitriolic analysis of the modern housewife would. 'The truth is, most housewives are lazy. They are too lazy to put down their magazine and write the story they think they could; too lazy to walk a block to do their shopping in person; too lazy to learn to sew if they can't afford new underwear. They cover up for their laziness with monologues on their backaches and the cost of meat ... if the individual housewife is saddening, housewives in the mass are appalling.' Controversial articles like this one sold partly because it was different and, ultimately, because it touched a raw nerve for many married women.

Until 1952, the magazine did not publish readers' letters regularly. However, if a particular article generated a large amount of mail, it would feature a representative selection of letters. Owing to the volume of mail received over the Grey article, the headline article in the June 1950 issue, 'Housewives Blast Business Girl,' was a composite essay of readers' letters to the magazine. According to the editors, over five hundred housewives had written to criticize Grey's article: 'The three things which most of them resented were the attacks on their happiness, their mental status, and their laziness.'[42] These letters, and their insights, are invaluable. Not only do they illustrate how a seemingly hostile article could alienate some readers while serving as a vehicle of self-examination for others, but they provide some indication of who read the magazine, and why, and offer perceptive comments about Canadian housewives during the fifties. One reader wrote: 'When we're poking about the kitchen with runs in our nylons, hair in wisps, we don't look like your Marie Holmes illustrating how to make marmalade (who does?).' Another took Grey herself to task. 'Whatever is the matter with you, Beverley Grey – I hope it is curable. Stop being a sour puss and you will find that married women are people too ... In our village the women are clever and kind, some more efficient than others. Our children are healthy and usually very happy. We like our husbands. We give service to the community. We understand municipal affairs and work to improve them. We have political opinions and we don't fight over disagreements. When we are in trouble we help one another.' In an editorial aside, the editors printed a box with the caption 'Who Is Beverley Grey,' accompanied by a picture of the hapless newspaper journalist. For her part, Grey was quoted as saying: 'I was amazed at the commotion I caused ... my telephone hasn't stopped ringing. And I've learned a lot more things about housewives I didn't know before.'[43] Many writers who published articles in *Chatelaine* achieved instant fame, with the accompanying praise, or, as in Grey's case, felt the censorious blast of notoriety.

As this article revealed, readers read beyond the preferred meaning. Judging by later letters, it could have been read as a piece of sarcasm, or as the cynical, bitter musings of a spinster. The artwork that accompanied the piece was a cartoon of a disenchanted housewife, implying a light-heartedness that was absent from the written text. Artwork was an important, and often overlooked, part of 'reading' *Chatelaine*, since it strove not only to attract the reader but to introduce, summarize, or depict the major themes of the articles as well. While many exposés featured stark black-and-white photos, the use of colourful cartoon drawings was intended to lighten this article's tone and encourage readers to interpret Grey's text as a work of black humour, rather than an attack. Grey's article epitomized *Chatelaine*'s method of using inflammatory articles to generate controversy and excitement among its key reading audience.

Another type of article favoured by the magazine throughout the period was the exposé. Morgan Winter's 'Common Law Wife' featured the classic conventions of this genre, complete with melodramatic photograph (illustration 33). It tackled a sensitive, previously taboo subject matter. The sensationalist or overly dramatic style of writing usually brought a quick response from the 'shocked and appalled' readership.[44] The teaser, or opening blurb, claimed: 'She may live in a suburban bungalow, pack her youngsters off to school and join the girls for coffee – but she can never forget that a common law marriage is no marriage at all.' The article explained how unjust Canadian divorce laws were greatly to blame for the increase in common law marriages. Winter also revealed the classist nature of what was then a derogatory term. 'To

THE
COMMON
LAW
WIFE

By MORGAN WINTER

She defies convention for a chance at happiness. She may live in

a suburban bungalow, pack her youngsters off

to school and join the girls for coffee — but she can

never forget that a common law marriage is no marriage at all

33 *Chatelaine,* January 1952

most people the phrase is familiar only in police court news – "the dead man and his common law wife were said to have been drinking heavily before the fight started." But common law wives – women who are "married but not churched" – represent a surprising cross-section of the Canadian housewife population and a surprising percentage of it too, although their numbers are impossible to more than guess at.' Throughout the article, readers learned of the legal vulnerabilities of these women and the daily shame they endured. Although this exposé was not intended to glorify a particular 'lifestyle,' the article did not moralize or condemn such unions. Ultimately, *Chatelaine* did not try to invoke closure at the end, but left it to the reader to decide how such a thorny issue of legal, religious, and moral conventions should be solved.

Reader response, as always, was mixed. M.F. Walpole of Hamilton, Ontario, wrote: 'We appreciate such articles as "Common Law Wife" ... With a little soul searching these articles can be gathered into a useful supply of information on which to guide a rocky marriage such as many of us women face today.'[45] As an aside, Walpole told the editors that she had also renewed her subscription because she didn't 'want to miss an issue or any additional articles.' Other readers were far from sympathetic. Many did not accept the article's preferred meaning that common law wives were victimized by the outdated Canadian legal situation and came from all classes. Mrs L. Hosie from Regina had the 'urge to write' and provides this alternate reading of the article: 'I consider that paying allowances to a common law wife tends to encourage immorality.'[46] Interestingly, Mrs L.M. from Winnipeg offered an oppositional reading of the article and of the lifestyle promoted by it: 'How many real marriages besides mine do you think the January publication of "Common Law Wife" will finish? For the sake of our seven children I was fighting to hold our home together, but I lose – the common law wife, with the help of *Chatelaine*, emerges the winner. Thank you.'[47] Intended to publicize the plight of common law wives, the article was interpreted by readers like Mrs L.M. as a celebration of adultery and explicit permission for husbands to leave their wives for the 'other woman.' Over the course of the decade, a few readers commented on the power of *Chatelaine* articles to harm (or 'set back') the women of Canada. As these two letters indicated, many readers saw a simple cause-and-effect relationship between reading about taboo subjects and their incorporation into Canadian society.

Another popular genre within the marriage and women's issues field were those about the Canadian family. Two different stories published in early 1952 garnered a large number of letters to the editor and featured two distinct types of families. In the same issue as 'Common Law Wife,' Blanche Gunton, a novice freelance writer and housewife, contributed 'We Drove the Kids to Alaska.'[48] This story typified the fifties' concerns of family, finances, and happy times. The article chronicled the exploits of the author's family as they made their pilgrimage from Aurora, Ontario, to Alaska and back. Gunton wrote: 'We drove 11,000 miles, five-in-a-car, heard wolves howl by night, threw snowballs on a glacier and came home better friends than we'd ever been – and all for $465.' To make their trip so economically, they slept in their car – the boys in a plywood box, complete with cover, which they placed on top of the roof; daughter, Rosemary, in the front seat; and Blanche and husband, Claude, on a mattress in the modified back seat and trunk. Although meals were home cooked every night, it had been decided that 'Dad and the boys would ... shop' while 'Mom was to have a vacation.' This story captured the do-it-yourself rage of the fifties, the increasing popularity of camping throughout the decade (an affordable holiday for large families), and the myth of the happy, suburban family playing together. The Guntons' experiences, encounters with nature, and good-natured manner in which they all got along made for wonderful escapist reading in this winter issue, just as the editors had intended. This was a endearing piece, but not so fantastic that it was beyond the realms of most readers. The writer, married to a dentist, went to great pains to play down her upper-middle-class status, taking pride in how affordably the trip was accomplished.

Stories like this one always garnered favourable responses, but Gunton's tale proved especially captivating. Many readers wrote to *Chatelaine* requesting exact descriptions of the sleeping compartments designed by her husband. Mrs E.A. Scully of Lethbridge, Alberta, wrote: 'As a word picture of a most interesting and educational holiday this story can't be beaten.'[49] A year later, the Chatelaine Centre informed readers about a family that had been inspired by the Gunton article: 'After reading *Chatelaine*'s story ... last year, the Carmans (of Welland, Ontario) took to the road too and drove all around the Gaspé and the eastern United States. Mother and daughter slept curled up on the car seats. Father and son slept on a collapsible table with their heads in the trunk. The trip was such a success they are planning to go to the Rockies this summer.'[50] Clearly, some *Chatelaine* content did create 'action' among the readers, but often it did not tie in with the advertising material at all.

'All One Big Happy Family,' by Marjorie Wilkins Campbell, profiled an entirely different sort of family, the Winterburns, a large farm family from the Haliburton region of Ontario.[51] The opening teaser prompted, 'If you're going crazy with two kids in a bungalow on a busy street, come down to the farm and meet the thirteen Winterburns.' The magazine 'discovered' the family when Norma Winterburn wrote a letter to the staff, enclosing her favourite maple syrup recipes and a short description of her large household. In a noticeable display of urbanism and Toronto-centrism, the editors claimed to be amazed that a family like this still existed and set out to probe how it was possible. Among other things, readers learned that the Winterburns farmed on land cleared by Fred Winterburn's grandfather and that this land was central to their identity. 'The other important character in the Winterburn story is the two-hundred acre farm itself – forty acres cleared, the rest rough bush and grazing land – for the Winterburns literally live off it. Fred Winterburn built their home from its limestone, oak and birch; he builds five or six punts each year from its pine to sell to summer tourists; and the boys help harvest its cedar for Dad's shingle mill. The Winterburns eat its vegetables, beef, milk and butter. The farm's blueberries (523 baskets last year), strawberries (900 quarts), its shingles, boats, maple syrup and surplus steers, hogs and chickens provide the Winterburns' $2,500 annual cash income – to which family allowance for six of the children adds $432.'

The Winterburns' mode of living was dissected, respectfully, as if they were residents of another land. In a manner reminiscent of *National Geographic*'s treatment of the exotic 'other,' *Chatelaine* editors substituted big-city bias and bourgeois presumptions. The class-based differences were readily apparent: the Winterburns ate at a 'linoleum-covered table' laden with 'good, plain food,' around which 'everything is shared.' In a magazine full of consumer durables, processed foods, and fashion sections, this piece was opposed to the pace and purpose of the commercial material and the 'representative' life it depicted. Norma Winterburn bought flour and sugar in hundred-pound bags, her tinned vegetables in flats of tins, and preserved or made much of the food the family consumed. Pictures of the interior of the cabin, and of the fortyish Winterburn parents with their children, bore testimony to their difficult livelihood and rustic living conditions. The romance of this piece, like the later seventies' television show *The Walton's* (about a rural Virginia family during the Depression), glorified the simple, agrarian life. 'And then, one evening soon, the Winterburns will all gather round the big table, reach for crisp brown pancakes and one of the large pitchers of new maple syrup, and count up the latest sugaring-off as the best ever.' The seasonality of rural life, the family-based economy, the gentler pace of life, and the hardships endured – all of which form lasting bonds of family – were stressed in this article.

Post publication, the family reported 'receiving orders from all over Canada' for their maple syrup.[52] For M.M. Storey of Grandview, Manitoba, the Winterburn article proved enjoyable, but not for the preferred meaning that depicted them as the antithesis of the nuclear, suburban families. 'I enjoy reading *Chatelaine* and articles like "One Big Happy Family" in March are tops with me. Not because of the family angle, for big families were commonplace when I was young, but because I was born in Norland and this story took me back to my childhood. Those Winterburns are a fine-healthy looking bunch and no wonder they learned to work hard early in life – that land is very stony and it was hard to make a living. Do I remember the maple syrup! We never get any half as good now. Thanks for Nora Winterburn's recipes.'[53] Storey's comment that it wasn't the 'family angle' that made the article enjoyable, but the 'nostalgia angle,' illustrates how readers' own personal resources colour their interpretations. Interestingly, unlike magazines today, with their rigid boundaries among writers, editors, readers, and participants, the *Chatelaine* community was very fluid: article suggestions often came from readers; participants in the articles found themselves at the centre of attention for a short while after they appeared; and keen readers often wrote directly to the participants rather than the editors.

One of the key identifications for this community was Canadian nationalism. In the early years of the decade, no article created more fuss than 'Canadian Women Are Suckers,' written by two American women and published anonymously.[54] Given a prominent cover advertisement, this article informed the readership: 'You are suckers about men in general and husbands in particular because you let them live in another world, a masculine world where there is no place for you.' The American critics informed Canadian women that their own husbands assisted them around the house, including child care. They talked to them about current events and issues other than the home and household; they did not take fishing and hunting vacations with the boys; and they vacationed as families in the United States. The article ended with this encouragement to Canadian women to get jobs: 'Taking a job should not be thought of as proof that your husband can't support you, but looked upon as a fulfillment of your talents and capabilities. Neither does it mean that you are being unfeminine and neglecting your family. Instead of spending spare time at teas and bridge parties, concentrate your interests and enthusiasms. When your family no longer needs all your time you will find that a career will help you to be a fascinating personality rather than just "the wife."' Although this article overlooks the fact that many North American women were taking jobs to supplement the family income, it appeared a decade ahead of the same commentary in Betty Friedan's *Feminine Mystique*.

The headline of the May 1952 letters section needed no interpretation: 'Suckers is a fighting word: So say hundreds of Canadian women who saw red at the observations of two American wives in March *Chatelaine*.'[55] The letters that month represented excerpts from twenty-four of the hundreds of letters received. Mrs L.A. Pecker of Port Credit, Ontario, wondered: 'Why we have to tolerate this type of article in a Canadian magazine?'[56] Another group of women from Antigonish, NS, responded with this criticism of Americans: 'We have often wondered why American men have a world-wide reputation for being wolves. Now we know. They are so seldom unleashed that they run wild as soon as they can pry their wives' arms from around their necks.'[57] And from V.W. in Vancouver came this analytical reply: 'I think it is very clever of *Chatelaine* (tongue in cheek) to encourage you to be so brave and brash ... *Chatelaine* knows people will get up on their ears and the result may be a bit of useful heart and mind searching.'[58] This article proved so incendiary that the magazine received letters in response to the previous letters published in the May issue. Mrs R. May of Strathcona, Manitoba, contributed a common-sense analysis of this tempest: 'There was a lot of truth and a lot of nonsense in the article ... but I was pleased that you stood your ground and said that *Chatelaine* published the article as opinion, not advice. My opinion is you should publish more such articles and really wake people up ... All power to your magazine.'[59]

The final article in this section returns to the exposé genre for Gerald Anglin's 1953 piece, 'The Pill That Could Shake the World.'[60] Although the birth control pill was 'discovered' in the fifties, it would not be on the market until the early sixties. Accompanied by a dramatic black-and-white photograph featuring the profile of a woman's face, her one visible eye open wide while she opened her mouth to swallow a capsule, this article was meant to attract attention and generate discussion, if not controversy. Anglin investigated the scientific developments of the pill, along with a condensed history of the birth control movement in Canada and the United States, and commentary about the application of such a pill in controlling world population. 'A simple and economical birth control pill which was easy to buy obviously could influence greatly the sex life and the marital happiness of many Canadian families. Some thoughtful men believe, moreover, that such a pill could save the world from a threat they consider greater than the atomic bomb – the threat of over-population which is already taking a staggering toll in human life and misery.' Maclean Hunter and *Chatelaine* personnel consider Anglin's article as one of the groundbreaking pieces published in the magazine, years before American magazines were publishing similar ones. Even though the article was meant to excite, it was a fairly straightforward piece of liberal reportage, concentrating on facts, scientific developments, history, and implications for the future.

For many women, articles in *Chatelaine* were one of their few sources of information, often the only one they could obtain without fear of embarrassment or chastisement. The letter from Mrs Margaret Sorhus of Kindersley, Saskatchewan, epitomized those readers for whom these articles were a 'godsend': 'After reading your article I feel compelled to write and congratulate you for it. Here in Canada we may as well be living in the middle ages as far as birth control goes. I have several friends as well as myself wondering why sterilization is not legal in Canada. If it were it would certainly solve the problem for those of us who have four or five children and cannot afford any more.'[61] Conversely, readers like Madeleine Waldron from Montreal were outraged about *Chatelaine*'s endorsement of birth control: 'If you intend printing anything again like "The Pill That Could Shake the World," consider my subscription cancelled. Yes, I am a Roman Catholic, and I do believe that the Dr Henshaws and the Margaret Sangers do immeasurable harm. You, as a publisher, share responsibility for placing such ideas before a public already very selfish and materialistic.'[62] Articles published in the early years of the decade within the large category of marriage and women's issues ran the gamut of styles, topics, and themes.

'Are Canadians Racial Bigots?' Race and Ethnicity

Throughout the decade, although they were more prevalent in the later years of the fifties, some articles explored issues of race and ethnicity. All the pieces were sympathetic to new immigrants to the country and often celebrated cultural highlights (particularly cuisine and household customs), yet their tone changed noticeably. The issue of immigration surfaced in 1957 as the focus of Jeannine Locke's piece, 'Can the Hungarians Fit In?'[63] It followed a young Hungarian immigrant couple, Frank and Katey Mayer, from their arrival in Canada in search of 'the good life.' The plight of Hungarians had captured the attention of Canadians when a large number of refugees emigrated, so *Chatelaine*'s article was a timely examination of this phenomenon. Locke's feature detailed the Mayers' flight from Hungary and subsequent arrival in Canada: 'Only six months ago in the darkness of an early November morning, she and her twenty-seven-year-old husband, Frank, were crouched in a ditch a few yards from the border between Hungary and Austria ... Sixteen days later, Katey and Frank Mayer were in Canada.' The article was obviously intended to put a more humanistic spin on the large numbers of postwar immigrants flocking to Canada. It detailed both the Mayers' impression of North America, along with the more traditional voyeuristic impressions of the immigrants, particularly their struggles to overcome language difficulties, find lodgings, and get their first jobs. Their accommodation to the ways of the country were detailed, in 'Hungarian English,' along with the story of how their names were Canadianized. 'While Frank was being "operationed" (Katey's word) ... Katey went to work "cleanering" in St Joseph's Hospital ... It was there that she got the name Katey. Her name at home had been Katarin. On her first day at work in the Hamilton hospital, an orderly told her, "Your name here is Katey" ... On the advice of Canadian Hungarians that "Francis is not so good a name in Canada as Frank," Ferenc promptly became Frank.' Locke was quick to include Hungarianisms in the article, from Katey's speech to her discovery of the wonders of the supermarket, marking them as humorous and photogenic objects of fascination for Canadian readers. Articles such as this one, and the piece about the Winterburns, presumed that they were speaking to the normative group – white, urban, Anglo-Canadian, middle-class readers. They freely positioned both the Mayers and the Winterburns as 'others,' 'not us.' Yet the responses indicated that many 'others' were included among the *Chatelaine* audience.

The article also paid tribute to the commercialized 'good life' available in Canada and equated freedom and democracy with the plentitude of goods available in the West. According to the article, many Canadians were eager to assist in housing the new immigrants, and the Mayers were fortunate to find accommodation with a surgeon's family in Toronto who had specifically requested a refugee couple to live in their furnished flat. It was there, amidst the 'nine children ... three dogs, two fish, a pussycat, a skating rink, an English cook and a grandmother from Scotland,' that Katey was introduced to the wonders of the grocery store: 'She came home staggering under a load of sardines, instant coffee, canned soups, ham and chicken legs – all newly discovered delicacies. She brought home so much ice cream that they used it in great scoops even in their coffee.' Although the middle-class experts in the *Chatelaine* Institute would have been appalled by such nutritional heresy for the advertisers, this sort of feature was pure gold because Katey Mayer's description of a democratic consumer paradise was the sort of vision they pushed in the advertisements.

Locke's article romanticized the Mayers (and, by implications, all postwar newcomers), profiling a couple who described their reception in Canada as 'a fairy story.' Canadians were depicted as warm-hearted, friendly, and often wealthy people who vied for the chance to host newcomers and help them acclimatize to 'Canadian ways.' In an era in which immigrants were called New Canadians and multiculturalism was unheard of, the decision to emigrate to Canada meant integration. In essence, *Chatelaine's* article conveyed the impression that immigration was about learning the language, getting a job, and discovering the joys of Canadian life: grocery stores, high-heeled shoes, and planning for their own home in suburbia and their first car. The onus was on the immigrant to adapt to Canadian life. In this article, the immigrants in question, Katey and Frank, were all too eager to get jobs, learn English, and get retraining at the university, which they deduced was the key to participating in the good life in North America. It both romanticized the immigrant experience, glossing over or neglecting the indecision and fear that accompanied such a momentous change, and congratulated Canadians for a job well done in welcoming the new immigrants. The article ended with Locke's patronizing expression of praise: 'But like most of their countrymen, they're integrating nicely.'

Letters received about this article were favourable, though for a variety of reasons, as this one from Mrs M. Filwood from Toronto illustrated: 'I enjoyed [the article] ... This Hungarian woman ironed clothes for the doctor's wife and, I gathered, did other helpful duties for her, just out of sheer enjoyment of helping. If this article states the whole truth it does give me hope that all is not lost in this cold, calculating world.'[64] Other readers were more sensitive to the experience of the émigrés than to their usefulness to their hosts. A Nova Scotia reader commented: 'I was impressed by the article ... Although I've never met any Hungarians, I am sure they would make better Canadians than some of us born in Canada if they were given the time and opportunity by us ... Hoping to read more on our fellow Canadians.'[65] Rev. G. Simor, who was affiliated with a Hungarian relocation group, wanted the article to serve as inspirational literature to others: 'I hope many people will read this article, especially immigrants, and that they too will be encouraged by the wonderful successes and achievements of this couple.'[66]

At the end of the decade the self-congratulatory tone was replaced by concern, as the September 1959 cover asked, 'Are Canadians Racial Bigots?' The actual title, 'Are Canadians *Really* Tolerant,' was co-written by Yvonne Bobb, a West Indian immigrant to Canada, and Jeannine Locke. The dramatic title and opening teaser – 'We smugly boast that we have no racial barriers, but, says this young West Indian, in practice we're just as prejudiced as any nation. We just dodge the issue by keeping the colored people out' – made it perfectly clear that this article was not about to pull any punches (illustration 34).[67] Bobb's experi-

CHATELAINE • SEPTEMBER 1959

Are Canadians really tolerant?

We smugly boast that we have no racial barriers, but, says this young West Indian, in practice we're as prejudiced as any nation. We just dodge the issue by keeping the colored people out

By YVONNE BOBB

as told to Jeannine Locke

WHITE CANADIANS are smug about their record of untroubled relations with colored people. But I believe that they have simply side-stepped trouble, by keeping all but a very few colored people out of the country. Most Canadians are, in fact, no friendlier toward people whose color and customs differ from their own than are those residents of Little Rock or London's Notting Hill whose behavior white Canadians loudly deplore. It's easier for Canadians to conceal their unfriendliness; that's the difference.

After three years in this country I can see an advantage in the kind of discrimination practised in the southern United States—it is at least forthright. In Canada, where there are no apparent restrictions on my freedom, I'm allowed to stumble into barriers —prejudices against my color which, although subtly applied, are nonetheless real.

I came to Canada from Trinidad to continue my studies as a librarian, though to enter the country I had to serve a year as a domestic. Since my arrival I have formed very few friendships with white Canadians. I have tried. I was told that the YWCA was the place to meet other strangers in Toronto. I went to the YWCA, where I was Continued on page 64

27

ences – her inability to meet other Canadians, the subtle yet systemic racism she encountered, her difficulty in finding an apartment, and her simmering resentment – were all dealt with matter of factly and without any sugar coating to make the article more palatable for readers. This was a tough, angry article, and many of her statements illuminated Canadians' hypocritical analysis of racial integration: 'Most Canadians are, in fact, no friendlier toward people whose colour and customs differ from their own than are those residents of Little Rock or London's Notting Hill whose behaviour white Canadians loudly deplore.'[68]

Not surprisingly, letters in response to Bobb's article were the most numerous in the November 1959 issue. The editors felt compelled to provide this introduction to the letters: 'From the replies to Yvonne Bobb's outspoken comments on colour prejudice in this country, we can take some heart ... Not one writer thought intolerance was good or even a necessary evil. All looked forward to the day when we shall have One World, with all its children truly brothers. One sidelight: many readers remind us sadly that intolerance often occurs, too, between white and white.'[69] This statement, and some of the featured letters, ran counter to *Chatelaine*'s earlier pieces that had glorified ethnicity and the way in which Canadians had welcomed European immigrants. Mrs Helen Ostapec of Thamesville, Ontario, wrote: 'I am a native of Czechoslovakia and our skin may not be quite as dark as that of a West Indian or Negro, but our name is foreign and most of the Canadians hold it against us as though we were freaks of nature. Thanks to Yvonne Bobb for writing her story.'[70] Mrs M. Ferrare of Toronto provided an interesting simile about how the magazine had effected her: 'The article was like a shot in the arm, and I take the injection gladly.'[71] It was rare for readers to identify their ethnicity or age when they responded to articles, but in commenting on articles about ethnicity it became important for letter writers to identify themselves to the other readers, as partial explanation of their perspective. The comments from Helen Kent of Richmond Hill, Ontario, criticized Bobb's article because it did not mirror her own experiences. 'Yvonne Bobb forgets that most immigrants feel strange and unwanted for several months after their arrival here. Undoubtedly, her colour adds another dimension to the situation, which white immigrants do not have to deal with, but, as a coloured Jamaican who came here eight years ago, I cannot permit your magazine to think that all coloured people think or react as she does ... If we show as much patience and tolerance as we possibly can, some time in the distant future there may be real understanding. We are the ones who have to teach (Canadians) that we are acceptable, so we might as well face up to that fact and responsibility.'[72] This long letter illustrated not only the importance *Chatelaine* articles were accorded (and her concern about the impact the article could have on other West Indian immigrants) but the fact that readers used the letters section as a forum in which to address other Canadian women. Although Bobb's article had demanded change, the letter writers all preferred slow, evolutionary change rather than anything dramatic.

Articles on race and ethnicity demonstrate the changes in the magazine, and its readership, through the decade. The earlier concentration on romantic, voyeuristic pieces about the Hungarians gave way to critical articles about the hypocrisy of Canada's treatment of new immigrants. Because later articles were written from personal experience, rather than the perspective of Anglo-Canadian journalists, they seemed more authentic and encouraged readers to be more honest in their replies. Articles on non–Anglo Canadians also demonstrated that *Chatelaine*'s reader transcended racial and ethnic barriers. It was a forum for Canadian women, one that immigrants were quick to realize existed for them as well as the native born. Articles such as these gave the impression that *Chatelaine* was a leader in social issues reportage.

'Is the Coffee Party a Menace or a Must': Middle-Class Concerns

While articles on race and ethnicity were easily earmarked, articles focusing on class issues were more subtle, eschewing the term *class* in favour of phrases such as *standard of living*. Blatant use of the word *class*, or references to any class other than the presumed (and desired) middle-class reader, would not appear in the magazine until the sixties, when the magazine published articles on poverty, life in the inner cities, and single mothers.

One of the most popular series of articles in the mid-fifties, 'We Sent an Expert to Help This Family Make Both Ends Meet,' was written by Sidney Margolius.[73] The author of a best-selling book, *How to Buy More with Your Money*, Margolius helped members of the Woods family of Riverside, Ontario, work out their financial problems. Readers of *Chatelaine* were able to follow their progress in a series of three articles. The Woods, Russ and Joie and their two children, were described as a typical, white-collar family. Russ, the sole wage earner, worked as a music teacher for the Windsor public school system, earning $4450 per year. Margolius paternalistically described the reason for their problems, and how they represented the majority of Canadian families. 'Theirs is the struggle of many young white-collar families as they strive to participate in Canada's climb toward a higher standard of living while fighting the inroads of a cost of living that has bounced up sixteen percent in just three years. More than twice as many Canadian families have mechanical refrigerators and vacuum cleaners as had them ten years ago. But more than half our families are still without even these basic amenities, and the drive to own them and sewing and washing machines and other equipment for more comfortable living is causing much midnight budget juggling.' It quickly became apparent that this was not a family with serious economic problems. Russ's salary was comfortably middle class, slightly higher than the statistical average of the day, and the family's true problem was impulse spending, particularly on items they bought on instalment plans. Margolius put them on a budget, telling readers: 'The budget is like a muscle: the more they use it, the more effective it will become. They'll accumulate the money to buy in larger quantities, save instalment fees, anticipate their needs when cut-price buying opportunities arise.' He stressed buying effectively, as opposed to saving money, paying down their mortgage, or investing for their future. According to *Chatelaine*, this was the typical family struggling to make ends meet, not the rural, immigrant, or working-class family. Canada was portrayed as a sort of classless world of conspicuous consumption, and family budgeting was construed as temporary belt tightening before the next wave of planned purchasing.

Readers were swift to critique this article and, as all the correspondence indicated, they examined the family budget in minute detail. One of the chief criticisms of the budget was the absence of a category for regular church contributions. Rev. W.B. Macodrum from Geraldton, Ontario, responded: 'That Margolius budget rather disturbed me. It is the first I have studied where no mention is made of religious support.'[74] All the other letters printed questioned why such a relatively comfortable family should have been profiled. This letter from Mrs D. Milner of Winnipeg highlighted her frustration and anger: 'I'd like to see the Woods family try to buy a house (not new), carry insurance, and raise a family on considerably less than $4,450 as we are doing. We pay as we go or do without. And we enjoy life. Let's be honest: they are living way beyond their means. On $4,450 we could bank $1,000 a year and still feel that we were living like kings.'[75] In response to an update on the Woods's situation, this compelling letter from Mrs Lillian Tustin of Aldergrove, BC, appeared in the letters section: 'I was quite appalled ... at the thought that there were those who could not raise two children and keep out of debt on nearly $300 a month. I would be in heaven on this income, as I am at present bringing up six children, all under fifteen years and the oldest a spastic, on a hundred and forty dollars and this is the most we have handled in six years. Most years our income has been less than $1000 ... Even a load of wood extra can throw our own buying out of kilter ... going into debt is entirely out of the question as we could never get along at all if we did.'[76] These readers did not realize that the magazine was aimed at more affluent readers than they, so they thought that the editors and Margolius had erred in selecting an unrepresentative family. Lower-income readers of *Chatelaine*, often, though not always, from rural areas of the country, would voice these complaints about articles focusing on what they considered suburban issues or, according to Mrs W.J. Henley of Huntsville, Ontario, 'selfish' families like the Woods and their 'pagan' lifestyle.[77]

In 1955 the magazine devoted an entire issue to an examination of the suburban phenomenon (illustration 35). 'How to Live in the Suburbs' was brimming with information on ways to deal with such vexing issues as 'There's a Problem Child Next Door' and 'How to Furnish a New Home without Panic Buying,' or philosophical issues such as 'Is the Coffee Party a Menace or a Must?'[78] The departmental editors had also joined in the fun by staging a fashion show. Included in the group of glamorous young wives modelling the latest suburban fashions was a future mayor of the City of Toronto – June Rowlands. In the Chatelaine Centre piece at the front of the magazine, the editors explained the purpose of the issue: '*Chatelaine* explores this expanding horizon, discussing the customs, reporting the problems of suburban living and suggesting some of the answers. Our coverage of this big story began way back last August and before it was concluded had drawn in nearly every member of the staff. We chose Don Mills, near Toronto, for a close look, partly because it contained families whose incomes, problems and outlook represented a fairly average cross-section of this part of national life and partly because it was one of the most modern, planned suburbs in Canada.'[79]

The centre-piece of the issue was Doris Anderson's 'How to Live in a Suburb,' complete with a black-and-white photo of a morning coffee klatch. This article employed all the trademarks of the *Chatelaine*

35 *Chatelaine* cover, March 1955

article – research, interviews, information garnered from academics and academic journals – along with Anderson's pithy observations and witticisms: 'Suburbia is the friendliest community in North America since the days of the stockade and Indian raids.'[80] This was not a self-congratulatory article about the joys of living in the middle-class enclave. Gender, race, and class were analyzed in her portrait of the 'white man's white-collar community.' 'The main patterns of conformity are fairly rigidly laid out right from the start. Most of the people in any given suburb fall into the same income group. They often have the same kinds of jobs. They're roughly in the same age group. Old people and teenagers are rare. There are no Negroes, no Chinese. Non-English speaking families are the exceptions. There are no slums, no "big" houses, no wrong side of the tracks.' The promised 'solutions' were not very helpful. Not surprisingly, the onus was on the individual woman to create the suburban life she wanted (whether to be a joiner or an iconoclast was up to her), but systemic changes such as moving to the city were out. Suburbia was founded, after all, on the availability of affordable housing and the belief it was a good place to raise children. As for class and ethnic differences, Anderson suggested women 'point out to both Mary and Bill that the rest of the world who don't live in Sunnyvale Acres are not inferior or funny but merely different, and there's nothing terribly wrong with being different.'

From a nineties' perspective, Anderson's and *Chatelaine*'s analyses of life in suburbia leave major issues unexamined, particularly the affluence of the community and the lack of 'representativeness' of the community. This planned suburb was well established by the time of this profile, in contrast to the majority of suburban experiences.[81] Yet, for a women's magazine, this article was heretical, particularly for its critique of the lack of intellectual stimulation for women in the 'burbs.' 'You may discover that you are unconsciously playing down your education, taste and opinions that might mark you as different. One young suburban housewife told me: "You've got to be mediocre or you become as big an oddity as the emu ... I buried the fact that I had an M.A. degree in English under the sod of our new front lawn."' Anderson touched a nerve for residents of Don Mills 'concerned about the impression we may make all over the country,'[82] and the magazine published two letters from residents complaining about the article. 'The coverage given our homes and the fashion show (March) was a great compliment, but we take exception to the article, "How to Live in Suburbia" ... In our neighbourhood there are eight university-trained wives; not only have they not had to "bury their degree under the sod of their front lawn," but they have been asked to utilize their knowledge in the growth of our community organizations. We agree that suburban housewives, isolated from the mainstream of life, can easily become narrow in their outlook and thinking. We, in Don Mills, are endeavouring to see that this situation does not arise.'[83] Another resident of Don Mills wrote to complain about the article: 'Some of the things you mention aren't necessarily done ... 1. No coffee parties in the mornings. Mornings are for housework. 2. Racial intolerance – a lot of people in Don Mills look different from everybody else – this is Canada!'[84] Neither letter was concerned that other Canadian women would interpret their lives as particularly charmed or affluent. Readers who did not reside in Don Mills wrote congratulatory letters about the article, yet only this letter from Kay Parley of Toronto pointedly complimented Anderson for her direct analysis:

> The isolationist attitude setting apart a clique of thinkalikes, lookalikes, talk-alikes, who want to raise their children in a narrow rut, seems nothing short of a tragedy. Some lucky providence got me born on a Saskatchewan farm where the nearest neighbours were a large family of Polish immigrants ... The girls became my friends, I visited in their home ... I am glad I live now where everything from Yiddish to Dutch is spoken in the stores and a Hindu woman in a silk sari with a diamond in her nose shops beside me at the freezer. Children need the chance. They should know that these are the people they have studied about in school, the people the artists painted, the people who composed the music they hear, the people who make up the rest of the human family ... Doris McCubbin must be congratulated for pointing up the situation so cleverly.[85]

The last years of the decade witnessed a departure from the often solipsistic articles on the classless middle class of Canadians. Lorraine Porter's 'We Found Fun and Freedom on $2,100 a Year' profiled two ex-Torontonians who had chucked their city jobs, retired to their six-room cottage, and were eking out a comfortable existence north of the city.[86] Unlike the Winterburns, this couple was decidedly middle class, owning land in Pickering and Richmond Hill which they planned to sell to finance their retirement years. Yet they had opted out of keeping up with couples like the Woods. Instead, the Porters described life on two acres of land, the seasonal joys of rural life, travel to Mexico via bus to save wear and tear on their car, and the joys of fresh food. Porter's comments about their food buying was, presumably unintentionally, a direct assault on the food manufacturers and advertisers whose ads subsidized the magazine each month. 'Our food is tastier and more nutritious now than four years ago when we spent twice as much on groceries. With both of us working at that time, I shopped hurriedly, and bought "quickies," such as frozen foods, store pies and cakes, and delicatessen delicacies. With a monthly budget of $58.51 for groceries, we buy carefully these days. And I have only half as much to buy now – for instance, I buy flour to bake pie crusts, but the fillings come from our orchard.' The contrast between this excerpt and the article on the Woods was striking. Although the vast majority of the articles that made explicit reference to class issues depicted the middle-income level, occasionally an article such as this one made it into the magazine. While not the gritty portraits of poverty the magazine would highlight in the sixties, such articles provided a very different overt meaning: they spoke to a lasting tradition of anti-consumerism (which might be dated to the Depression-era *Chatelaine* and the magazine's role as a right-hand helper to the rationing and conservation campaign during the Second World War) and, as such, provided a counter to the messages of the advertisements.

'Fatigue' – The Problem That Has No Name:
Dr Marion Hilliard's Articles

The articles that most captivated the readers' attention were the medical series written by the team of Dr Marion Hilliard and June Callwood. Hilliard's sudden death in 1958 brought an end to the series, but her brief biography, written by Clare four years earlier, should have piqued the interest of even jaded readers. 'Dr Hilliard has an insatiable appetite for life. She's Chief of Staff at Women's College Hospital, Toronto, is a practicing surgeon and women's doctor, and acts as marriage counsellor on the National Committees of the Church of England and the United Church of Canada. She has such variously assorted interests as hockey, Beethoven, the theatre, trout fishing, Chinese food and liberal causes.'[87] Not mentioned in the biography, though not surprising for the era, was the fact that Hilliard lived with a female partner and was, among her friends and some colleagues, quite candid about their relationship.[88] It is, of course, yet another of the ironies of *Chatelaine* in this era that the most respected, and beloved, expert on women's heterosexuality and health was herself a middle-class, closeted lesbian professional. With Callwood's ghost-writing assistance, Hilliard was able to convey her unique perspective and personality to the readers. Above all, her articles were written in a plain, common-sense style. Her medical training gave her the authority to write about these issues, but her pieces were free of medical jargon and accessible to all readers. She did not patronize the reader; instead, the reader was treated to a conversational, personalized approach. In an era that did not favour blunt, direct talk about such 'private matters' as sexuality, menopause, menstruation, or childbirth, Hilliard's articles were exceptional for their explicit and calm manner. Most important, this information was readily available to all Canadian women in an easily obtained and very respectable format – their own women's magazine.

'Woman's Greatest Enemy Is Fatigue' was the first essay in the series. The opening blurb explained why such an innocuous subject had been Hilliard's choice for her first essay: 'Because fatigue strikes every woman during the three most critical periods of her life. Because fatigue is often a tragic mask for boredom, fear or selfishness. Because fatigue can break up your marriage, bring on mental illness or shorten your life.'[89] Hilliard's definition of fatigue included perpetual tiredness, but also 'a state of apathy toward tomorrow, of headaches, backaches, crying spells, heaviness of body and mind,' all of which sounds remarkably similar to something American feminist Betty Friedan would later call 'the problem that has no name.'[90] Although Hilliard's three most critical phases of women's lives were defined as pregnancy, the first few months after childbirth, and menopause, she did not exclude unmarried women or married career women from her advice. All women were told to make time for themselves and to get proper rest; that housework could wait; and, in the case of new mothers, that fathers should be called into service. Hilliard's reward for women whose exhaustion was caused by overly fastidious housework regimes was a 'dunce cap.'[91] For those with a bad case of ennui, Hilliard advocated work. 'I wish I had kept records of the number of times I have found that the solution for fatigue is part-time work. Housewives who are lonely and frustrated by the repetitive tasks of cleaning a home; women in the grip of the menopause who are frightened and upset; women living with older people who rasp on their nerves – all can be helped by getting out into another world. As you can see, some fatigue is caused by too much to do and some by too little; some is a by-product of a glandular change and some is the result of monotony or pure selfishness. Fatigue is such a common occurrence that it has been called the Great North American Disease.'

Notably absent was any reference to medication, psychological assessments, or women's victimization. Hilliard was an optimist: she encouraged her readers to help themselves and to acquire a sense of self-esteem as individuals, not just as wives or mothers.

Letters such as this excerpt from Mrs E.F. Hartwick of Arvida, Quebec, illustrate the reaction the article elicited: 'I feel I must write to thank you on behalf of all your readers and particularly the thousands of harassed mothers of pre-school age children for your wonderful article ... I had practically convinced myself I must be neurotic with my chronic weariness, and lack of energy ... This is the kind of article that should be spread far and wide for its outstanding contribution to the well-being of all women.'[92] Older readers like Mrs Louise Sandvold of Crystal Springs, Saskatchewan, wrote: 'How I wish I had read it years ago. As it is, it will be a great help in the years to come.'[93] The magazine did not receive any negative letters about the Hilliard articles – at least, it did not publish any in the letters column – until the series had run for a few years and the good doctor had ventured into more psychosocial pronouncements.

Perhaps one of the most controversial Hilliard articles published was 'Woman's Greatest Hazard – Sex,' which the magazine ran in the January 1956 issue. Realizing this was a sure-fire hit, the editors chose not to spend any money on cover art. Instead, they centred the title 'Woman's Greatest Hazard: Another Challenging Article,' minus the word sex, in the middle of the cover and framed it with a yellow border. This was the only instance in the fifties and sixties of a *Chatelaine* cover with no illustrations. The blurb was a subtle, decorous, yet no less effective teaser for the article: 'A reluctance to talk about this basic personal problem has caused confusion and unhappiness to countless women. This is why *Chatelaine* presents this frank, intelligent article ...'[94] Although the magazine went to great pains to present the article in as unsensational a style as possible, this issue proved to be extremely popular. It sold out within days of hitting the newsstand. Hilliard's article was not a technical how-to piece; she presumed a basic knowledge among her readers. Instead, it systematically abolished several sexual shibboleths: women's unresponsiveness, seniors' asexuality, romantic versions of sexuality, and male prowess about all things sexual. Passages such as the following, in which Hilliard explained the difference between male and female responses to sex, undoubtedly reassured many readers: 'The male inevitably arrives at marriage with the conviction that love-making is a straightforward simple pursuit with certain fulfillment. He is so constructed that, while the atmosphere of love-making may vary considerably, his own enjoyment is relatively constant. Women, on the other hand, are deeply dependent for their enjoyment on the atmosphere. It must be just so, with no distractions, no jarring moments, no annoyances, or else she is incapable of genuine response.'[95] Hilliard was quick to advocate that married couples 'need experience and practice,' but she also made it perfectly clear that though women's responses to lovemaking were different from men's, women could, should, and did respond to sex: 'The same woman can experience the whole galaxy of climaxes, from the top to the bottom, depending on her mood.' One of her concluding comments was that 'love-making is a human need, a comfort for the body, a soother for nerves and brightening influence on the spirit.'

Although not the first article to mention women's sexual capacity, this article (as well as the Kinsey publications in the late forties and fifties) broke the silence that still hindered the public discussion of sex: it talked openly of sexual adjustment after marriage, advised couples to maintain a sense of humour, and stated unequivocally that women could and should find sex pleasurable.[96] The absence of moralizing – Hilliard promised to examine unmarried women's sexuality in the next issue – clearly marked the essay as something most Canadian women had not seen before. If they had, it was not in a mass-circulation women's magazine. Readers' reactions were mixed. Some like Mrs John A. Brown of Toronto were 'disgusted and horrified ... Is nothing sacred and personal any more? ... I think you should know how articles of that sort appear to women of my sort – the better educated, more carefully brought-up sort – in other words (old fashioned but true) a lady.'[97] E.M.K. from Halifax was equally chagrined: 'If women want this sort of information, let them ask for it in private – I would blush to think my daughter of fifteen would get this article and read it.'[98] But others, in remarkably candid letters, told how pleased they had been to read the essay. R.H. in Edmonton responded: 'I feel compelled to write and thank you for it. If I had been able to read such an article twenty-five years ago I should be a much happier woman today.'[99] Another reader from Campbellton, NB, 'only wished there had been such plain truthful articles written twenty-five years ago.'[100] The most original letter came from Owen J. Bennett of Abbotsford, BC: 'It should be required reading for all couples who intend to marry. After seventy years of living I feel sure it would save millions of lives from being tainted with the nasty grey shade of misconception and vulgarity regarding one of God's most beautiful and useful gifts.'[101] It was articles such as this that set the magazine apart from the American women's magazines, got people talking and writing, sold copy, and ultimately made *Chatelaine* a household word. In the words of Mrs Hilda Carscallen of Whitby, Ontario, 'one of Dr Hilliard's articles is worth the whole subscription price for a year.'[102] An American reader, Bonnie Lee McCubbins Adams of Fayetteville, Arkansas, praised *Chatelaine* for its 'honesty in dealing with a vital subject' and noted, with some consternation, that the Hilliard pieces were 'franker than even our most popular magazines would dare publish.'[103]

Although most Hilliard articles contained medical information, or were premised on Hilliard's expertise as a gynecologist, she also branched out into more psychosocial articles. One of the first of this new thematic approach, 'How to Stop Being Just a Housewife' in the September 1956 issue, was another ground-breaking article. Hilliard was quick to condemn the idealized version of women promulgated by the media and, in particular, advertisers: 'There is a prevailing image of womanhood, slightly plump in a cotton print dress, surrounded by adoring golden-haired children as she bends over an oven door to take out a pan of biscuits. In this pink picture, the woman's face is brimming with contentment, tears of tender joy stand in her eyes and she is bathed in a glow of fulfilled femininity. She's wonderful all right, but she's no more real than the fantasy image millions of men have of themselves.'[104] Hilliard argued that 'women need to work to gain confidence in themselves. Women need to work in order to know achievement. Women need to work to escape loneliness. Women need to work to avoid feeling like demihumans, half woman and half sloth.' Finally, she critiqued the misguided focus on beauty and catching a husband at the expense of getting an education or training for some sort of employment:

> The married woman is fooled, into believing that she can spend her whole life without acquiring a single skill. This is the deep dark water under the thin ice of a married woman's composure. Frittering away the scant years before she marries, she learns no trade. She comes to marriage with little ability beyond a certain flair for looking attractive in strong sunlight. On this house of cards, she builds her self-assurance. She rises in the morning full of the delight of greeting her young loveliness in a mirror. But time won't hold still and this butterfly reaches her mid-thirties, when her children are almost independent and her one small talent is beginning to

weather. The change in her appearance, which had counted for so much, makes her unsure. She is now ready, with her family nearly grown, to take part in the bustle outside her home, but she is newly timid and has no training. Unskilled occupations look wearying, unworthy and dull; so she sits at home and becomes more despondent with each empty, wasted day.

This trenchant critique of women's roles before and after marriage, seven years before Betty Friedan made the same observations, ran completely counter to the received wisdom about the content of women's magazines. However, the Hilliard pieces had proved themselves very popular. Maclean Hunter and the editors of *Chatelaine* wanted to increase and keep the circulation. Increased circulation meant higher rates for advertising copy, which meant a greater chance of profit. Content mattered, but, from a business perspective, anything that would guarantee sellout issues was assured of a place in the magazine. Thus Hilliard's articles, while running counter to much conventional material published in American women's magazine, made it into the periodical. Such articles make it clear that *Chatelaine*'s agenda was to publish a wide variety of material. It was not merely a 'feel good' periodical for housewives, but it encouraged them to question the status quo and, at the very least, stimulated readers to think.

Readers like Mrs Z.W. Dean of Calgary were quick to pick up on the surprising variety in the magazine: 'Just a line to say how much I have enjoyed Dr Hilliard's fine, sensible articles. She must be a wonderful woman and I'd love to meet her! Congratulations too on your many varieties of writing – I like your magazine.'[105] Other readers took offence at Hillard's article and wrote in defence of the profession 'unlike any other.' A.B. from Ontario claimed that the article 'made my good Scotch blood run cold ... "Just a Housewife" doesn't do me justice and I'm not bragging. No other job in the world gives a person the chance to use their abilities in so many different ways for the betterment of mankind and the world in general.'[106] Mrs R.B. from Alberta concurred, adding: 'If anything, so far from hunting for more work, most women I know would give anything to just have one afternoon a week off.'[107]

Humour

While articles like Hilliard's offered critiques of Canadian housewives and clearly contradicted the rosy world of the advertisements, *Chatelaine* also occasionally used humorous articles to parody itself and to ease the seriousness of the feature articles. All the articles were in the genre made famous by the American humourist Erma Bombeck – wry mother / housewife observations about the foibles of everyday life. Many readers failed to see the humour in these pieces, but, for some women, they provided moments of release and proved to be just the tonic they needed to get through the day. Phyllis Lee Peterson's 'Don't Educate Your Daughters' pithily dissected the folly of the university-educated housewife and mother. In the following excerpt, Peterson contrasts the two types of housewives – the educated and the uneducated – toting up their relative merits and general happiness:

> I have reached the inescapable conclusion that the happiest women are those who have to take off their shoes to count up to ten. If you don't believe me, look around you. Look at Dora B., for instance, the dumb little blond who never got through high school. Everyone felt sorry for Dora when she went out to work while the others went to college, but Dora knew her own career. By the time the rest of you emerged into reality with heads stuffed full of biology and eugenics, Dora'd put them into practice. Now the young husband she helped get started is a ball of fire and her four children are full-grown while you're still pushing a baby around the chain store. Dora knew by instinct what you lost through education, that a woman's real job is a man and the sooner you get behind him and push, the better.[108]

Self-deprecating styles of humour were one of the foundations on which housewife humour was based, but there was also an edge to these pieces, part anger and part frustration, about society's expectations for women. Humour such as this found the readers nodding in agreement or, for those who read it as a non-humorous article, filled with indignation. One of the reasons that readers so frequently misread these articles was that they very successfully mocked the earnest tone of the advice articles in the magazine, and women's magazines in general. Some readers were not keen about the self-parody of either the magazine or their roles, displaying an insecurity and sensitivity about 'being just housewives.'

Under the title 'Do Educate Your Daughter,' the magazine printed responses from readers. Of the eight letters to the editor reprinted in the magazine, most were critical of the article, illustrating vividly how ironic, satirical essays clearly intended to be interpreted as humorous could so easily be misread. Respondents were quick to enumerate their educational accomplishments or to list their degrees, as in a letter signed by six university-educated Saskatoon women: 'We the undersigned, are completely disgusted with the article ... Dullness and frustration may be found in marriage by every woman, regardless of her education. The truly educated woman ... will make something more of her marriage.'[109] Mrs Joan Arkett of Parry Sound, Ontario, was also not amused: 'My daughter goes to college!'[110] Interpreting the article as a straightforward piece of advice to mothers, Mrs James French of Whalley, BC, claimed, 'Never have I read such a narrow-minded article.'[111] Only one letter, from Mr and Mrs P. Grant of Agincourt, Ontario, interpreted the piece as a work of humour and predicted that a literal interpretation would be all too common: 'We enjoyed your humorous article, "Don't Educate Your Daughter" ... While amused at the irony of its reverse logic, we were sobered by the thought that many people actually think this way ... Doubtless, there are men who prefer wives too ignorant to argue or too simple to see through them. If an education can keep our daughter from marrying one it will be an excellent investment.'[112] Doris Anderson admitted that although the editors wanted to include more humorous pieces in the magazine, it did not seem worth the effort of writing letters to those readers who had misinterpreted the comical intent and been offended.[113]

'The Sickness in Our Suburbs': Marriage and Women's Issues in the Late Fifties

By the end of the decade, the tone of the articles on marriage and women's issues had changed. *Chatelaine*, under Anderson's editorship, featured more articles on controversial topics – abortion, suicide, and teenage delinquents – as well as articles that depicted more balanced assessments of women's roles. In short, the magazine articles indicated that women could lead fulfilling lives outside the household. In the October 1958 issue, Dr Alastair MacLeod, assistant director of the Mental Hygiene Institute in Montreal, contributed an article ominously entitled 'The Sickness in Our Suburbs.'[114] In this update to the 1955 special feature, the 'eminent psychiatrist' warned that 'suburbia is a growing threat to our mental health ... It breeds boredom, suspicion and loneliness and disrupts family life by confusing the roles of the sexes. Here's where we've gone wrong – and what we can do about it.' Most of the article was devoted to MacLeod's thesis that the major problem in the suburbs was 'the blurring between the roles of the sexes,' which created 'matriarchies' or 'manless territory where women cannot be feminine because expediency demands that they control the finances and fix the drains and where ... men cannot be masculine because their traditional function of ruler and protector has been usurped.' According to MacLeod, this lack of a clear separation of gendered roles left suburban children 'bewildered.' The article did not suggest practical ways in which to overcome the suburban dilemma, other than that humans are highly adaptive. Although MacLeod's article condemned the mutable gender roles he purportedly discovered among suburban women in Montreal, he did not place the blame for this situation, or the demands for change, on women. 'I am strongly against trying to cure them by attaching blame to women. Women have already an almost insupportable load of guilt. They feel guiltily responsible for their sense of harassment, they blame themselves for any turmoil in marriage, they feel guilt when children misbehave, more guilt if they miss a home-and-school meeting, guilt if they can't grow roses or make garlic salad dressing. Women cannot bear much more guilt; they are already ill with it.'

How did the objects of such academic analysis and angst react to this article about the ills of suburbia? One thing was perfectly clear from the letters *Chatelaine* printed in the January 1959 issue: the MacLeod article touched a nerve all across the country and, at the time of publication, over three hundred letters had arrived.[115] According to the calculations of the editors, 42 per cent of the respondents supported the suburban way of life and disagreed with MacLeod's findings, 39 per cent agreed generally, and 11 per cent looked elsewhere for the troubles with suburbia. Expert or not, many women were not about to swallow MacLeod's theories about the importance of strict gender roles and the primacy of the male. From Mrs Vera Fiddler of Ottawa came this response: 'I was mad when I read Dr MacLeod's remarks ... Dr MacLeod is apparently in favour of women acting as servants.'[116] This letter, from Mrs Irene Craig Neil of Port Stanley, Ontario, contradicted MacLeod's findings about the 'matriarchy' of suburbia with a pithy retort: 'I left the suburbs because I was in danger of getting just too itsy bitsy feminine. I know of nowhere in Canada that the male ego receives as much flattery as it does in suburbia ... The modern rebel soon feels a sense of smothering in the male prestige and dominance of suburbia.'[117] Overall, readers thought the psychiatrist's analysis missed many of the nuances of suburban life, such as its affordability and the desire on the part of many women and men to work together to share their duties. Instead, they pointed to such factors as the lack of culture, the dearth of shops within walking distance, and the constant microscopic gaze of academe as undermining life in the suburbs. The inclusion of readers' responses about this article critically demonstrates how historians must be wary of extrapolating concerns and 'ideals' from some of the conventional material in *Chatelaine*. Readers' comments indicate that they were not about to swallow the eminent psychiatrist's diagnosis of their maladies. They were highly resistant, quick to fire off a missive to the editors about their concerns, and ready to teach others to read critically and not accept the advice of the 'experts' as gospel.[118]

The MacLeod article, like the Grey, Anderson, and Hilliard pieces before it, was not the only one to criticize the situation of the stay-at-home housewife. In an article entitled 'How Much Are You Worth to Your Husband,' writer Cynthia Steers examined the value of women's unpaid work in the home.[119] She advanced a key component of feminist ideology – that the unpaid work of women in the home subsidized the economy and put women at a distinct disadvantage. By her calculations, she figured that housewives saved their husbands $257.65 per month, assuming that the average 'middle-income' family ($5000–$8000 range) with three children would have to employ eleven people to replace the housewife: a housekeeper, cleaning woman, laundress, home economist and shopper, chauffeur, baby sitter, handyman, seamstress, cleaner, hostess, and gardener. In addition, the husband would lose his $1000 tax deduction for a stay-at-home wife. While *Chatelaine* obviously thought this sort of fiscal enlightenment would be thought-provoking reading for its subscribers, many of the readers were disgusted that a monetary value could be placed on their job as spouse, housewife, and mother. Of the three letters printed, all were critical of the thesis and tone of the article. Mrs Anna Tennenhaus of Bathurst, NB, wrote: 'Cynthia Steers article ... is appalling and asinine. She lists chores performed "for the husband," when in reality they are performed for HER home and herself. Most North American wives are sheltered in superior homes, fed excellent food, dressed in pretty clothes, driving nice cars, enjoying much social life, protected for the eventuality of widowhood, all by one man who usually struggles much harder than she does to obtain these amenities for THEIR families.'[120] Reader Tom Richardson of Kindersley, Saskatchewan, thought, 'Now would be a good time to have an article on how much is the husband worth to the wife.'[121] Clearly feeling that men had been unjustly accused, Mrs D.T. Vanstone of Beaconsfield,

Quebec, claimed: 'I feel I receive every cent of the hypothetical amount in the pleasure of living with a husband who excels in assisting with the tedious tasks, and in the care of two wonderful children.'[122]

Two very disparate articles published in the August 1959 issue generated voluminous mailbags of letters to the editors. 'How to Go to University at Home,' by Eileen Morris, was a straightforward piece about options for part-time enrolment in undergraduate university programs, as well as information about correspondence university courses. According to the article, 'some twenty-five Canadian universities offer courses especially designed for even the busiest homemaker.'[123] Interested homemakers were advised to contact the magazine for more information, which was available free, though they had to include a stamped, self-addressed envelope. *Chatelaine* made frequent use of such services to readers; they were further links that connected the readers with the periodical, and informal reader surveys to test which articles and items had more appeal. Non-commercial services such as these were impressive, since they indicated to readers that the magazine took them seriously, and also established *Chatelaine*'s authority and integrity on a variety of issues. The October issue of the magazine included this editorial report: 'Within three weeks an unpretentious August feature had drawn the biggest *Chatelaine* mail of the month ... The response: more than one thousand letters as we go to press. Every one of the twenty-five universities offering courses received inquiries from potential scholars. Front runners were: University of Toronto, University of British Columbia, University of Alberta, McMaster and Western, in that order.'[124] The response to the article had been both staggering and completely unexpected. Anderson wrote a letter to Morris to let her know of the response and to encourage her to write another article for the magazine: 'The response to your story ... is practically swamping us. By rough calculation almost every woman in Canada has now been inspired to go back to University.'[125]

Although *Chatelaine* editors prided themselves on having their fingers on the pulse of Canadian women, they were never entirely sure which articles would be critical successes and which would be too controversial, boring, or uninspiring. Further evidence of the enduring impact some articles had on readers was this poignant letter written to Anderson in 1962 by Mrs Phyllis Bentley: 'I have been cherishing a clipping from your magazine dated August 1959 in the hope that one day I might see my way clear to begin studying. I wonder if I might still be able to get information about a homemakers degree course in my city Montreal? I would be most interested to know whether Loyola University offers such a course leading to a B.A. degree.'[126]

The other article in the August 1959 issue that attracted attention, this time of a critical nature, was Joan Finnigan's 'Should Canada Change Its Abortion Law?'[127] The preface indicated that it would be a critical examination of a controversial topic: 'It's among the world's harshest – and critics charge most backward. By recognizing only one reason for abortion, it forces desperate women to seek help from a vicious back-room racket that often deals in death.' Finnigan went on to quote statistics of back-room abortions and provided reasons why the law should be changed. 'The very narrowness and inflexibility of this law does not stop abortion, but drives it underground into comparatively dangerous channels where Canadian women every year lose their lives.' This article is one of the progressive pieces of social criticism for which the magazine would be even more visibly identified throughout the sixties. Later, the editors acknowledged that they 'knew we were heading into controversial waters,' but after reading the letters, reported that responses were 'split evenly for and against abortion.'[128] Mrs H.C. Walshaw of Calgary wrote that the article 'was excellent and has occasioned some thoughtful discussion among my own friends and acquaintances.'[129] V. Leclair of Ottawa agreed with the need for change and proposed women's activism: 'Let us stop pretending that we have religious freedom. Since the medical profession seems disinclined to help, it is up to women's groups to act. Thanks for a wonderful article.'[130] Negative letters employed moral and religious arguments in their criticism of Finnigan's suggestions. This letter from Mrs R.S. Ricciotti of Wallaceburg, Quebec, was representative of these letters: 'Your article should have been titled Should Canada Legalize Murder?'[131] Only this letter from Mrs K. Kirkpatrick of Duncan, BC, argued for legalized abortion as a method of family planning: 'At twenty-nine I am one of the "worn-out" mothers, having had seven children in less than nine years. We need help – the Swedish way.'[132]

Conclusion

By and large, *Chatelaine*'s editorials were not just introductions to the magazine or light-hearted essays addressed to affluent, happy, suburban women. Instead, they were timely, concise, issue-driven essays. Articles, particularly those by Hilliard and Callwood, indicate that *Chatelaine* published material that was thought provoking and implored readers to question the status quo. Under another name, Betty Friedan's problem without a name was Hilliard's 'fatigue.' Friedan was vocal about the fact that American women's magazine editors would not publish excerpts of her book, even though she had worked for them as a freelance journalist.[133] It was only after *The Feminine Mystique* topped the best-seller list (1963) that the women's magazines sought her for articles and featured her in numerous personality profiles. In contrast, *Chatelaine* published the Hilliard articles in the mid-to-late fifties, and it would publish even more overtly feminist articles, by Christina McCall, in the early sixties.

Articles and editorials published in *Chatelaine* were different from the American competitors – a fact that was noted time and again in readers' letters. Canadian writers, topics, locales, and subjects, coupled with the different tone and content mix, made *Chatelaine* unique. Equally important, these articles generated interest, commentary, criticism, and suggestions from readers. Readers' letters indicate that the *Chatelaine* community was active in interpreting the offerings and that the 'preferred meanings' of these components were often ignored, misinterpreted, or opposed by readers who were clearly engaged by the material.

Regardless of the variety of the magazine, or whether the article, topic was an entertainment feature, a medical article or one devoted to marriage and children, these articles formed a common currency among Canadian women. In an era in which only women's pages in newspapers or American women's magazines might cover these issues, *Chatelaine* provided a unique medium for Canadian women. It educated, entertained, criticized, and encouraged its readers, and the readers responded with letters of their own in which they took the editors to task or commended them for particular features. Readers responded to other letters and, in turn, the editors often pursued article topics that had originally been suggested by the readers. Beyond reading the magazine, readers clipped many articles for future reference. Regularly, the topics and issues discussed in the magazine made their way into countless conversations across the country – at coffee klatches and cocktail parties, over supper with the family, and among female family members.

Chapter 8

'Trying to Incite a Revolution':
Editorials and Articles in the Sixties

In the sixties, the tone and the content of *Chatelaine* editorials and articles changed. They were more edgy, more political, and less complacent than they had been in the previous decade. One of the many readers to comment on this shift was Mrs Edith Sacker, a recent German immigrant to Vancouver, who wrote: 'It has been a long time since I enjoyed any article as much as your October editorial ... I came to Canada from Germany eight years ago where my sister and her friends are just as engaged as we are here in questions such as, "Should married women work outside their homes? in politics? etc." Really women don't have a choice any longer. Whether we want to or not, we have to go beyond the limits of our houses if we don't want to sink into apathy or be reduced to mere machines. A magazine like yours is so very important in giving moral support to those still intimidated by former generations who, after all, didn't have to live in our times.'[1]

Chatelaine's tradition of thought-provoking, informative journalism continued while its campaign to educate women about second-wave feminism expanded considerably. No subject matter was considered taboo. Articles and editorials that addressed abortion, divorce, battered children, incest, drug abuse, interracial marriage, lesbianism, sexuality, and poverty all appeared. In the editorials, readers came to expect thoughtful essays from Doris Anderson that probed issues of concern to Canadian women. Most frequently, she highlighted feminist and political issues. The general feature articles were different because they were written by a cadre of talented staff and freelance writers. Among the journalistic luminaries who wrote for the periodical in the sixties were Christina McCall, Adrienne Clarkson, June Callwood, Barbara Frum, Jack Batten, Mordecai Richler and, occasionally, Doris Anderson herself.

Editorials

'I've just finished reading this month's editorial,' wrote Phyllis H. Meeks of Georgetown, Ontario, 'and as always I felt prompted to write and tell you how much I enjoyed it. Well, why not? For a periodical which offers so much to its readers for so little, in my opinion the editor's column is the cream on the top. I start with this page – and always return to read it over!'[2] Meeks's words were representative of the majority of letters received about the editorial essays during the sixties. The importance of the editorials outweighed the fact that they were only a half page long. As the magazine's opening salvo, they offered important, authoritative commentary about issues of concern to Canadian women. Many women took inspiration from these essays to lobby their politicians, get involved in women's groups, or rethink a contentious matter. Others, like Dora Flagg of Wainfleet, Ontario, were inspired to try their hand at new things or to reactivate long-forgotten aspirations. 'While reading the editorial today,' Flagg wrote, 'I had the urge to write to you. Is it possible for a woman who has lived just a simple life on the farm to ever write for a magazine? I have written poems, true stories for my own pleasure. Just to send to the waste basket. I am 53 years of age the children grown.'[3] Overall, the vast majority of letters written about the editorials were positive and supportive of Anderson's essays. Those perturbed readers who wrote letters of complaint about the editorial content were critical of the changing nature of women's lives during the decade or felt threatened by feminism's impact on their own lives.

Although the Canadian feminist movement during the sixties was neither as organized nor as large as those words suggest, it had an unofficial leader in Doris Anderson. Through her monthly editorials, readers across the country were given an education on all the key issues of second-wave feminism: equal work legislation, birth control, abortion, divorce legislation reform, working wives and mothers, the hardships felt by working-class women, and the high degree of sexism that pervaded politics, the workplace, and society during the era. For variety, she also included a number of articles on other injustices within Canadian society – child abuse, single mothers, and racism, to name but a few. Although anger and determination characterized the tenor of most editorials, a few times each year Anderson included humorous editorials, usually self-deprecatory in nature, in which she poked fun at popular culture, images of women in media and culture, and her at-home persona. Clearly, the editorials published during the sixties were substantially different from those the magazine had published a decade earlier. Most of the difference can be attributed to the fact that there were four different editorial styles during the fifties.

In the sixties, the most popular editorial topics were women's political issues, current affairs, women's issues, feminism, and mothering.[4] Classified thematically, the most consistent theme throughout the decade was feminism, followed closely by politics, conflict in gender roles, women and the media, family and international issues.[5] These results differed substantially from the fifties, when both the subject matter and the main thematic issue of editorials was *Chatelaine* and *Chatelaine*'s importance, as well as the family, cultural, and professional issues. And, to judge from their letters, most readers were very fond of the editorial essays. The available Starch material claimed that 73 per cent of *Chatelaine*'s readers noted the editorial essay, and 43 per cent read most of each editorial.[6]

According to Anderson, the publisher and corporate brass were not aware of the changing editorial content and tone until well into the decade – at which point the magazine's success, in terms of circulation, could not be questioned. Even that notoriously conservative component, advertising, was able to put a positive spin on Anderson's feminist editorials, as these excerpts from Ted Hart's presentation outline for both the Yardley Sales Meeting and the Proctor and Gamble Meeting illustrate: 'Doris Anderson's regular preface is concerned with the feminist movement. You will agree that *women's* battle for equal status could affect not only her *lifestyle* ... but that of us *all*.'[7] Feminism was presented as just another 'lifestyle' choice and, of course, another way to sell advertising. However, Hart's interpretation was clear: this 'lifestyle' was one that savvy advertisers and companies would exploit, and conservative ones would ignore at their peril.

Editorial inspiration came from many places – current events and other news media, academic journals and American newspapers, interactions Anderson had with the public and with magazine readers, Anderson's own personal experiences, or the response in letters from readers. One such letter, from a North Vancouver reader, described her family's experiences with the drug thalidomide in the early sixties. Anderson's reply gives an excellent indication of the process of editorial inspiration and how, in this case, one reader's letter resulted in an editorial essay: 'Words cannot express my sympathy for you in the situation you describe in your letter. I was so disturbed by the newspaper reports and then by your letter that I have written an editorial for our June issue on thalidomide ... Thank you again for writing to us and providing the final stimulus that prompted me to write the editorial.'[8] Readers' input, while often not directly acknowledged in the published magazine, was an important part of editorial conception.

'Let's Have Action!' Feminist Editorials

An analysis of a number of these feminist editorials illustrates Anderson's increasing confidence with both her editorial voice and the readers' response. The February 1960 editorial, 'We'll Do Our Own Censoring, Thank You Very Much,' critiqued the CBC's decision to censor its interview with French feminist and philosopher Simone de Beauvoir. In a cogent defence of freedom of expression, Anderson listed the points of view expressed by de Beauvoir in the cancelled show and critiqued the standardization of North American thought:

> According to the producer of the show, Miss de Beauvoir said North American women have only a superficial freedom, that marriage in a way is obscene because couples are tied together and sometimes have to live in hell ... she was in favour of divorce because she thought marriage archaic in the twentieth century. She said women were equal to men and that the idea that women were only good for childbearing was a throwback to the Middle Ages. When asked about her religion, she said she was an atheist and that nobody had proved the existence of God ... the fact that some viewers – or even a majority of viewers – might not agree with her, is the best possible reason for giving her a hearing. In this standardized world of ours where so many things are pre-prepared and pre-digested, surely we should be allowed to do our own censoring in our own living rooms – with a snappy little twist of the dial ... Leave us this small decision, please.[9]

Anderson's preferred editorial style was to grab a contentious issue, briefly explain the circumstances and substance of the debate, then offer a critique. Here, while never stating whether she agreed with the views expressed by de Beauvoir, she communicates de Beauvoir's views to a mass audience of Canadian women. Ironically, the audience of *Chatelaine* readers was much larger than the CBC would have reached with its francophone talk show. Anderson's contempt for the usual offerings of North American popular culture was clear, as was *Chatelaine*'s different path. Anderson quickly, and authoritatively, carved out the editorial space at *Chatelaine* as a page for critical thinking, feminist analysis, and commentary about social mores.

However, readers were not cowed by Anderson's position or her valorization of de Beauvoir's writings. The majority, 'three to one,' agreed with the CBC.[10] The magazine published six letters, five negative, about the de Beauvoir editorial. Margaret Sluth of Ste-Therese, Quebec, summarized the tone and content of the 'no' side: 'I heartily agree with the CBC. You state that network time should not be given to irresponsible crackpots, etc. How can a woman of your supposed intelligence feel that anyone who denies the existence of God, and who thinks marriage in a way obscene, can be anything but a crackpot?'[11] Other critical commentary was received from readers in British Columbia and Ontario. This lone letter of agreement, from Mr B.E. Field of Flesherton, Ontario, took a congratulatory stance: 'Your editorial was the most courageous and intelligent item I have read in a long time.'[12]

In response to this angry outpouring of mail, in her next editorial, 'A Timid Defence of Feminists,' Anderson wrote: 'From time to time in conversation with a male friend or business acquaintance, my companion will recoil and with mingled shock and deep hurt exclaim: "Why you're a feminist!" Actually, I am – and then I'm not. But since at least half the world are masculinists, I really can't see why there isn't at least a surface tolerance of us poor, lone, on again–off again feminists.'[13] Equating a 'true' feminist with the radical first-wave British feminists who had chained themselves to buildings, Anderson preferred in 1960 to define an 'on again–off again feminist' as one who wants 'a better and fuller life for women' – and not, as she hastened to add, at the expense of men. In short, the demand was for equality. Her semantic game of calling men *masculinists* diffused the ire raised by the term *feminist*. Anderson enumerated some of the tactics used by the masculinists throughout the world, and, in comparison with these crimes (which range from foot binding in China to the deprivation of legal rights in North America), the demands of liberal feminism seemed mild.

As the decade progressed and readers became more accustomed and more receptive to editorials on feminism and women's rights, Anderson began to stake out a more aggressive position against women's oppression and demanded parliamentary and legal reforms. 'Women: A Chance for Change,' printed in 1969, highlighted the statements of American psychologist Dr Richard E. Farson, who was convinced that a women's rebellion was imminent: '"I think we will see within the next two years a massive rebellion of women that is at least comparable in magnitude to the black revolution or the student protest," says Dr Richard E. Farson. Bluntly, Farson stated, "women are oppressed." His prognosis for the future was dire: "Revolution always comes as the result of the work of a very small minority of the people affected. The rebellion is not only going to be women against men, it's going to be women against everyone who holds women back – including women who discriminate even worse against women than men do. I think we'll call the Uncle Toms of the women's revolution 'Doris Days.'"'[14]

The comparison with 'A Timid Defence of Feminists' was startling. Even compared with the de Beauvoir editorial, this one packed a considerable wallop. Rebellion, revolution, and the implication of the term 'Doris Days' were aggressive, radical words for any publication. For a mass-market women's magazine, they are astonishing. By the end of the decade any regular reader of *Chatelaine*'s editorial pages had matriculated through a steady course of feminism and was fully versed in the feminist critique of North American society. Many were not convinced, although their letters of protest astutely recycled the key words used by feminists to critique the feminist agenda, such as this letter from Mrs G. Baiton of Swift Current, Saskatchewan: 'We hear and read a lot about the status of women. I consider myself to have a "special" status, that of being a mother. The "now" generation is blaming society for caring for maternal things ... I sat behind a desk once. That desk never once said, "Hey Mom, I love you."'[15] Similarly, Margee Hughes of London, Ontario, made it clear that she was not in favour of revolution: 'I would never presume to disagree with a great authority such as Dr. Richard E. Farson ... But women in the majority seem more than content, even complacent, to carry on the old traditional custom in carrying out the king's smallest command ... Once married we tend to walk a pace behind.'[16]

It was for writers like Hughes that Anderson often penned editorials which criticized the backwardness of some women. Thus, while she frequently educated readers about feminism, lobbied politicians about women's issues, and censured chauvinistic men about their views on women, she also critiqued the complacency of women. In her May 1968 editorial, 'Not Chattels – But Chattel-Like Minds?' Anderson bemoaned the apathy of many women and many readers:

One of the most discouraging 'dead weight' factors in changing any law concerning women is the apathetic attitude of many women themselves. Even though we no longer live in a simple society, their attitude seems to be 'My man, my child, my cave.' Every week I receive, for example, letters from women who are bitterly opposed to some of the laws regarding women that are already on our statute books. 'Why should a woman receive equal pay with my husband?' they ask. Why? If for no other reason (such as fair play and human dignity), because if an employer can hire a woman to do the same job at lower pay than a man, they quite likely will hire a woman and that would put men at a disadvantage ... if married women working in the labour force aren't concerned about their own problems, why should legislators be? ... sometimes I think many of us, though enjoying all the freedoms other women and men have fought for, still have chattel-like minds. Or else, why the apathy?[17]

Her frustration was palpable. Clearly, the subtext of Anderson's editorial decried the magazine's lack of impact. After the numerous editorials and articles detailing the mistreatment of women in the law, workplace, and society in general, many women were blithely content with their own personal situation. Any sense of solidarity or sisterhood with other less-fortunate women was lacking. Published letters regarding this editorial were all complimentary. Mrs V. Musgrave of Willowdale, Ontario, wrote: 'Bravo! If every woman in this country who shares your views ... were to write to her members of parliament in Ottawa, then the legislators might be concerned enough to see that the necessary laws are passed. I shall write asking for laws such as abortion, and divorce reform, expansion of public day-care centres, and broader civil rights for women. I thank you for your article in favour of woman, the individual.'[18] Mrs Leona A. Graham of Saint John, NB, concurred, adding: 'Since *Chatelaine* is so widely read by Canadian women of all ages, I am sure the thought-provoking editorials will have considerable impact especially among the young married women who will keep on working and campaigning for equality of status and wages. Please keep writing.'[19] Noticeably, neither writer mentioned women's groups or organizations. Their preference was for individual action.

Some of Anderson's frustration came from her increasing realization of the limitations of a medium like *Chatelaine* for affecting change. Two editorials published in 1967 examined the purpose and limitations of women's magazines. The first, 'All Hair Combed and No Knotty Laces,' attacked the critics who claimed that women's magazines instilled a perfectionist ethos of mothering, household maintenance, and marriage:

Women's magazines are often accused of setting all kinds of unattainable goals of perfection. We're told we advocate perfect houses, perfect children, perfect meals which are perfectly served at perfectly appointed tables ... But that isn't the way life is at all. For myself, as a far from perfect cook, mother, interior decorator, hostess and conversationalist, I would happily settle for a lot less. In fact, perfection for me is ... sending the children to school with their buttons on, hair combed and no knots in their laces ... arriving home from a once weekly shopping marathon and not discovering within an hour that I'm out of sugar or salt or peanut butter ... checking the children after lights out and finding them – well, now, that is my idea of perfection.[20]

Clearly, the editor would never have won her magazine's Mrs Chatelaine Contest. It was in editorials such as this, together with some humorous ones, that the bond between editor and readers was obvious. Regardless of her position as editor, Anderson was 'everywoman' in her off hours. The self-deprecating humour did not set *Chatelaine* apart from American women's magazines, but its overt rebuttal of the often 'perfect' world constructed by women's magazines certainly did. *Chatelaine*'s willingness to poke fun at itself, or to lampoon its genre, encouraged readers not to take the magazine too seriously. Editorials such as these encouraged readers' critiques, stimulated alternate readings, and mocked the self-importance of many women's magazines.

Taking a completely opposite approach, Anderson's editorial 'The Snail-like Battle for Progress' bemoaned the magazine's lack of success in encouraging legal and parliamentary reforms for women:

This magazine has often been accused of being a national nag harping on the ills that need to be changed in our society. Rightly or wrongly we consider this prodding a part of our job. (And we hardly have been alone in the task). For over twenty years we have been trying to push our stagecoach era divorce laws into the twentieth century ... Back in the fifties we started advocating reform of Canada's rigid abortion law ... For almost twenty years we have been advocating that Canadian laws about abortion be changed. In 1960, this magazine came out with one of the first articles about baby beating ... These are just a few of the major issues we have tackled again and again. At times I've wondered what good we were doing. Nothing ever happened. Our legislators move with such Ice-Age slowness ... Apparently nothing happens in this democracy until everyone is in favour of it.[21]

Anderson would eventually cite, as one of her reasons for retiring in

1977, her belief that she had taken the women's magazine as far as it could go. After all, to paraphrase her commentary in *Rough Layout*, the mass-market magazine was not the *Status of Women News*. On the other hand, there was a tone of resignation, which indicated that Anderson wished the magazine's educational campaigns had been more effective. Her faith in the power of a national women's magazine to effect change, particularly legislative change, seems naive. The editor believed that one of the purposes of the magazine was to act as a mouthpiece, or champion, for Canadian women's concerns and as a leader in the fight for equality for Canadian women. On an individual level, the editorial content affected women greatly. In interviews, Anderson revealed that 'women keep coming to me to this day, one came up to me last night and said, you have no idea how you influenced my life.'[22]

The politicized editorials that appeared with great frequency throughout the decade also demanded a royal commission on women's issues. In a 1964 editorial entitled 'We've Had All the Studies of the Problems of Women We Need. Let's Have Action!' Anderson proposed that 'we call a sit-down strike on all committees about women until something is done about the problems we know all too well about.'[23] Reluctantly, in 1966 she changed tracks and called for 'a forward-looking commission composed equally of impartial men and women, prepared to take a cool twentieth-century approach to our problems. Because these questions affect us all – men, women and children – and for our own collective good, we should set about getting some answers.'[24] The Pearson government's refusal to grant a commission in November 1966 was derided, in a classically sardonic style of writing, in Anderson's February 1967 editorial:

> Finally, the setback ... The brief calling for a Royal Commission on the Status of Women in Canada, which was taken with high hopes to Ottawa last November and had the backing of thirty-two women's organizations, got as much attention at our nation's capital as if we had asked to have all the postboxes painted shocking pink ... in the last ten years in Canada we've held thirty-one royal commissions on such subjects as Gerda Munsinger and freshwater fishing. Half the population of this country – the female half – is undergoing great change. The effect of this change will influence the family, the economy, and all of our lives for the next century. Yet we're told the subject of women in Canada today doesn't warrant a royal commission. If this is the final decision, it's a setback to the nation – not just its women.[25]

Clearly, *Chatelaine* editorials were not prepared to back away from controversy or from harsh criticism of government neglect. Finally, in March 1968 Anderson wrote her last editorial on the commission, hopeful that the report would not become just another 'dusty report on a shelf in Ottawa.'[26] Anderson and *Chatelaine*'s role in calling for a royal commission on women has been noted elsewhere, but it should be stressed that the magazine was often very critical of political waffling and quick to call for action, not merely study.[27]

'Here's Dirt in Your Eye, House': Poking Fun at Women's Magazines

Interspersed among editorials on feminism, politics, women's issues, and the role of popular culture were humorous articles in which Anderson poked fun at herself, the magazine, and the expectations placed on women. In lifting the serious tone that often hung over the editorial page, Anderson demonstrated that she was a feminist with a well-honed sense of humour. In 'A Summer's Day Confession,' she wrote about the contrast between the perfectionist view of women expounded by the media and her own slothful ways: 'As I go through life taut of throat, slack of muscle, my cupboards not partitioned, my plants unpolished, my sheets unclassified, trailing a trunkful of recipes that should be made, photographs that should be sorted, does it bother me? ... I'll settle for being a happy summer idler.'[28] In response, reader Murial Kerr of Ottawa wrote: 'I retired from teaching June 28. I've lived thirty years in this apartment and had set my alarm for 9 am., preparing to attack with vigour and ruthlessness some big walk-in cupboards. Well, bless you! I'm just going to "leave em lay," put on some old clothes and drive out into the country to pick raspberries.'[29] Permission from Anderson to revel in relaxation was always greeted ecstatically by the readers.

Perhaps the most engaging, and subversive, entry in this genre was the editorial entitled 'Here's Dirt in Your Eye, House.' Running counter to the advice printed in the departmental features in the magazine, Anderson confided that household maintenance was a never-ending burden, one to which women should allot only a certain portion of time and then do something more relaxing, fulfilling, or stimulating. The essay concluded with this statement: 'Here's dirt in your eye, house! I've got a book to read, a poem to write, a thought to think.'[30] Readers were in complete agreement, as this letter from Mrs Margaret Reynolds of Edmonton illustrated: 'Your June editorial, "Here's Dirt in Your Eye,

House," pleased me to no end. Who dictates that a home must be shining clean and dust free at the expense of all other more worthwhile activities? A moment taken from a busy life can be better spent in a few lines penned to an absent friend with a message of cheer, congratulation or sympathy, rather than wasted on chasing dust which will only return anyway ... I do try to establish reasonable priorities and housecleaning comes low on the list.'[31] One wonders what Elaine Collett and the *Chatelaine* Institute staff, chief supporters of perfectionist housewifery, thought of such editorials. More important, what did *Chatelaine* advertisers think of material that challenged household perfectionism and their corporate profits?

Articles

Reader commentary in the magazine continued to be as lively, and as varied, as the general feature articles themselves. Complainants such as Phyllis M. Hodgson of Gibsons, BC, wrote: '*Chatelaine* used to be a wholesome family magazine, so why did you have to spoil it by riding the bandwagon of sex, sex and more sex? I'll venture to say that the majority of your articles are medical. When I have the urge to read detailed medical history, then I'll subscribe to a medical journal. Yours in disgust.'[32] Defenders such as Mrs Ilse Levi of Edmonton were quick to reply: 'What on earth gives Phyllis Hodgson the idea that *Chatelaine* is becoming a sex magazine? What's wrong with a few love stories or articles on women and sex? *Chatelaine* does not contain much sex and the little it does contain would not be anything to start blushing about and feeling disgusted over.'[33] And then there were the closet fans, such us Bernard E. Morin of Ottawa, who wrote: 'Being a male member of the "under twenty-five swing set," I admit to a rather negative, satirical attitude when, out of sheer boredom, I picked up September *Chatelaine*. Wow! Jack Batten's article on Can. Pop was excellent, I then happened upon Annabelle King's decorating article, Condominium. Her ability to effect total environment in limited space decorating ... completely blew my mind.'[34] Clearly, the sixties had come to *Chatelaine*, and the result was a bubbling cauldron of commentary on the letters page about the diverse, bizarre, disgusting, and controversial articles the magazine published. In fact, according to Doris Anderson, criticism and commentary often did not stop there, since readers regularly approached her at luncheons and dinner speeches to criticize the articles.[35] Although articles had a prestigious place in the magazine during both decades, the greater space devoted to this material in the sixties allowed the magazine to publish a broader range of material. On average, each issue had ten articles, ranging in size from a half page to more than five pages in length.[36]

Unlike fiction, the vast majority of articles were written by Canadian women.[37] Many were experts in their fields or had completed a prodigious amount of research to qualify as experts for the purpose of the article. Payments for articles varied. Contributors of the short 'What's New' features were paid $100, while those amateur writers who sent in 'Personal Experience' articles received $250.[38] Otherwise, first-time authors were paid $300, and $400 for a second article. Regular contributors such as Eileen Morris were paid $500, while 'big names' – for example, like Margaret Mead – got $600. Given *Chatelaine*'s emphasis on Canadian authors and photographers, most articles were set in Canada and concerned issues of interest to Canadian readers. At times, American, British, or European issues or locations made their way into the general feature articles (particularly 'Your World Notebook'), but they were always linked with the Canadian scene. The articles, like their fifties' counterparts, aimed for national coverage. It was far less common for articles to focus on one particular province or city. When limited in this way, the bias of the magazine's production base and authors quickly became apparent: articles with an Ontario-centric locale were paramount.

The magazine printed an assortment of article topics, though the favourite topics bore a striking similarity to those in the previous decade. The most popular topic category continued to be women's private lives.[39] However, even with the inclusion of articles on the Mrs Chatelaine Contest winners, this category declined from that of the fifties. The number of articles devoted to political issues and current affairs, as well as women's public lives (particularly career and educational articles), increased considerably. Figure 2 illustrates these and other changing trends in *Chatelaine* article topics. The jump in articles devoted to history can be explained by the Centennial celebrations and the interest in historical articles generated by the nation's birthday. To appeal to a mass audience of Canadian readers, the editor opted for a mix that contained educational, informative, and entertaining articles in every issue. The Starch results indicated that article readership was quite high. Although the figures varied, the general range for most

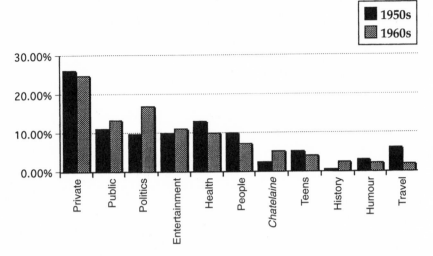

Figure 2   Articles Published in *Chatelaine*, by Topic, in the 1950s and 1960s

feature articles revealed that approximately 82 per cent of readers noticed the articles, while the range for those who read most of the articles
was from 36 to 53 per cent of those surveyed.[41]

Thematically, the sixties differed from the fifties in two important
ways: a greater emphasis on money (or the lack of it) and the increasing
emphasis on women's employment. Any regular reader of the magazine in the sixties was inundated with articles about wives and mothers
returning to work, the importance of education for young women, and
the increasing likelihood of dual-wage earning couples. Far less emphasis was placed on marriage and issues of class stratification. Figure
3 lists the top themes in each decade and the changing focus from the
fifties to the sixties. The primary factor that accounted for the rise in
familial themes was the Mrs Chatelaine Contest features, which had
not existed a decade earlier. The greater emphasis on cultural issues,
feminism, and politics in the sixties mirrors changes in article topics.
International themes declined, mostly due to the decline in the number
of travel articles. While figure 2 illustrates that the largest percentage of
general feature articles in the magazine was devoted to women's private lives, it would be wrong to construe that *Chatelaine* presented the
stay-at-home mother and housewife as the ideal Canadian woman or
that it was uncritical of the status quo. Changing times brought different topics to the forefront, even within the articles on women's private

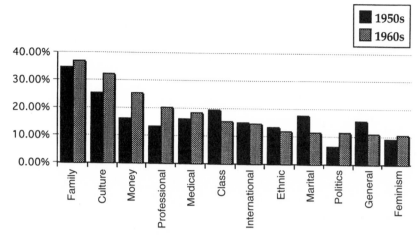

Figure 3   Articles Published in *Chatelaine*, by Theme, in the 1950s and 1960s

lives. Eventually, even the Mrs Chatelaine Contest had to change with the times. In 1969 the headline announcing the winner proclaimed: 'I Was a Working Mother When That Term Was a Dirty Word.'[42]

'What's New'

The first articles in each issue were the short (half- to one-page) columns in the 'What's New' section, which regularly featured a potpourri of information on health, political events, the arts, and the *Chatelaine* community. The short section allotted to the magazine allowed readers to glimpse the work culture at *Chatelaine* offices. Frequently, this section was devoted to short biographies of contributing writers, updates on the staff's personal lives, or comments on the magazine's role in Canada. These brief, gossipy tidbits usually strengthened the bond between the magazine and its readers. Regular readers regarded the magazine writers and staff as friends, as they became well acquainted with their passions and the process of magazine production. In at least one instance, however, the breezy nature of these revelatory comments about *Chatelaine* staff provoked an angry response from a reader. Mr H.C. Stratton of Windsor, Ontario, wrote to complain about the editorial staff's double standard: 'For a magazine that's always crying for sympathy against American periodicals swamping the Canadian people, this article really takes the cake. Also our government giving support to

see "Canada First," spend money at home etc. Then a prominent leading Canadian magazine boasting about their staff spending their money
travelling abroad – now this is a free country and you can spend your
money where you like and by the same token we can buy magazines
where we like. We did like to believe you people were consistent.'[43]
Stratton's complaint indicated that readers could, and did, resent the
lifestyle of the staff represented in the magazine ('career girls,' as they
were wont to call them in critical letters), and that many readers scruti-
nized the magazine closely. This section also included directions on
how readers were supposed to read the magazine.

The regular feature 'What's New with You' highlighted the varied
lives of average Canadian women, as opposed to celebrities or politicians. It often profiled women engaged in non-traditional jobs or volunteer projects. One excerpt describes how the column was compiled
each month: 'Jessie London, who has been editing the column, writes
about thirty letters each month to check facts and fill in details. Among
her forty correspondents scattered across Canada from Newfoundland
to British Columbia are housewives, alert secretaries of women's clubs,
schoolteachers, newspaper reporters, and two male free lancers.'[44]
'What's New with You' featured an assortment of items with novelty,
national appeal, and women's lives as the prime criteria for inclusion.
This column preferred to feature women outside urban areas, focusing
on rural dwellers and residents of small towns.

The cultural feature, 'What's New in the Arts' with Edna May, highlighted developments in Canadian theatre, television, publishing, and
radio. Her mandate was to review or interview Canadian celebrities,
but items about American celebrities, movies, or television frequently
crept into the column. May resigned in mid-decade and the task of
writing the column fell to *Chatelaine* insiders. Its purpose was twofold:
to showcase Canadian talent and to provide a space for high-brow and
middle-brow culture within a mass-market periodical. Surprisingly for
a women's magazine, the column often featured only male actors,
writers, producers, or singers. Although the magazine published articles on culture, as opposed to the entertainment industry (Hollywood)
or celebrity profiles, only infrequently, when it did there was an implicit link between masculinity and high- or middle-brow culture. One
feature article in 1961 by Claude Bissell, 'The Intelligent Woman's Guide
to Books' (which, according to the author, he had selected specially
with *Chatelaine*'s readers in mind), did not contain one female author in
his collection of the best twenty books of the century.[45]

'Shopping with *Chatelaine*' was also included in the 'What's New' section. It was a basic overview of the latest consumer goodies, ranging in price from small-ticket cosmetic, food, and clothing items to the more expensive appliances and home entertainment products. The final component, 'Here's Health,' 'Your Health,' or 'What's New in Health,' continued throughout the decade, although Lawrence Galton stopped writing the article in the mid-sixties. Thereafter, the article was rarely signed, so it was probably compiled by the staff writers. The format did not change from the fifties, and presented six to eight new medical developments gleaned from academic journals each month. Letters received in the *Chatelaine* offices indicated that 'Your Health' was a popular feature and that many writers believed that Galton would be able to assist them with their medical problems, however complex. Surprisingly, another group of Galton fans were medical doctors. They regularly wrote to *Chatelaine* to request the medical journal sources for his information. The importance of Galton's column, particularly for residents of smaller communities, cannot be overestimated, for it provided a regular source of medical information on the common ailments of North Americans.

Another regular feature included in the introductory shorts at the front of the magazine, although not formally included in the 'What's New' section, was the political and foreign affairs page. Before the magazine officially changed the name of this page from 'It's Your World' to 'Your World Notebook' in February 1961, a coterie of journalists offered their perspectives. Whether it was René Lévesque's 'Where Does Quebec Go from Here?' or Eric Sevareid's 'What Will Happen in 1960?' the purpose was to present concise background information on the news headlines.[46] Under assistant editor Christina McCall, the page kept its original mandate to provide interpretative essays on current events, as well as statistical analysis, maps, and supplementary historical background for interested readers. Her initial columns, 'Our Stubborn Stand on China,' 'Nuclear Weapons: Why Can't Canada Make Up Her Mind?' and 'Our Troubled Dollar: What the Crisis Means,' were representative of the diverse subject matter, as well as the focus on both national and international events.[47] The brief statement about the new column on the 'What's New with Us' page notified readers of the purpose for the name change: 'The Column's name has been changed to Your World Notebook for a very good reason, because we hope you will cut the page out and keep it in a scrapbook.'[48] Patronizingly, the page came complete with a dotted line as a cutting guide. Many letter writers mentioned keeping scrapbooks of this and other material, and it was a common hobby during the era.

While evidence is slim, it would appear that although 'Your World Notebook' had fans and regular readers, those who clipped the articles were primarily high school students working on geography or history projects.[49] Adult clippers, as this letter from Mrs D. Ross MacDonald of Hensall, Ontario, indicated, were more inclined to keep the recipes and articles of more immediate concern than foreign affairs and politics: 'I have been a subscriber to *Chatelaine* for a few years. I eagerly look forward to it each month. My husband tells me I devour every page, because I really do enjoy each and every article. When I'm finished with the magazine it looks slightly moth-eaten by scissor clipping of your wonderful articles on child care, teens and their problems, recipes, meal planning, home care. Many times articles appear on my husband's study desk for his files (my better half is a minister).'[50] Mrs MacDonald was not the only writer to comment on the magazine's appeal or usefulness to men. Many wives ran clipping services or highlighted important articles for their busy spouses to read.

As the years progressed, the infrequency of the 'Your World Note-book' page and its eventual demise indicated that it was not a popular feature. It was succeeded by the 'Booksbooksbooks' page of book reviews, written by Christina McCall Newman and then Adrienne Clarkson, which profiled Canadian books, with a particular emphasis on popular academic works, novels, and best-selling non-fiction. This full-page, regular stand-alone feature was, by 1969, included with the other 'What's New' columns.

'Woman Power': Changes in the Private and Public Realms

The innovation that marked the 'What's New' features – their concentration on average women, general medical information, and Canadian entertainment and cultural topics – was mirrored in the longer stand-alone general features each month. One of the most contentious articles published in the magazine during the decade exemplified the provocative style of writing used by the writers of women's private lives. In 'Housework Is a Part-Time Job,' Eileen Morris probed the numerous canards about housework, the role of the housewife, and the expectations fostered by women's magazines.[51] She eschewed the victim model of housewifery. Quoting from studies conducted in the United States which reported that the average housewife devoted '82 hours of household labour' each week to maintain her home and family, Morris provided her own 'part-time' solution to this taxing issue.[52] The article was accompanied by a detailed time breakdown of all household tasks – food preparation, child care, cleaning, and shopping – as well as a photo-essay. Peppered throughout the article were sarcastic quips about the perceptions of the housewife fostered by the media and advertising:

> My philosophy is that housework is work – but work to be finished. It must be done automatically ... I would never coo over my freshly ironed wash and murmur at its polished whiteness. I just don't happen to have that kind of mind. There was a time when women took pride in being martyrs to their houses. The model homemaker then worked until she collapsed ... With young children you have to face reality. You live each day in a cluttered setting. With two small boys, our home has all the serenity of a sand and gravel pit. You can fight this and eventually be carried off in a straight-jacket. Or you can accept it and do your best ... Here in the lodge let's admit it – you have but one left arm and one right arm, and you want time to use both for something more significant than scrubbing away at the pattern on the kitchen linoleum. This is the housewife's moment of truth.

Her comment 'here in the lodge,' was a particularly apt description of the world of *Chatelaine*. Despite the fact that Morris's definition of 'part-time' work was a ten-hour day, the readers responded vociferously to what many perceived as an abdication of her maternal and wifely roles. According to the editorial commentary that preceded the letters, 'never, but never, has an article drawn more mail in the past year.'[53] Fifteen of the twenty-two letters published in the May issue were devoted to this article, as were seven of the twenty letters in the June issue. In a rare instance in which the editors invoked closure, they announced that the June letters were the 'final resounding chorus on the rights and wrongs of Eileen Morris' Part-Time Housework.'[54]

Mrs Myrtle Gallup of Danville, Quebec, expressed the frustrations of many working-class readers when she wrote: 'Having just completed a fifteen-hour day when I sat down to devour my *Chatelaine*, the article was maddening. Lucky Eileen Morris – never mends anything, just throws the worn article out. Lucky, E.M. – never washes windows or curtains. Lucky E.M. never has to bake a cake or make an apron for a church sale.'[55] Morris's solutions were geared to a suburban, middle-class perspective, and for many lower-income, small-town, or rural inhabitants they were neither desirable nor possible. Others, like Mrs J.B. Hughes of Calgary, bragged of their hours on the job as indications of their dedication and prowess: 'Fiddlesticks! ... Yours till 8 pm.'[56] Mrs F. Weeks of London, Ontario, shrewdly observed the discrepancy between Morris's article, the *Chatelaine* department fare, and the nature of many women's magazines: 'Since Eileen Morris has so much time on her hands I suggest she obtain a position as a saleswoman. Anybody who could sell a woman's magazine that line could sell bathing suits to Eskimos.'[57] Only Estelle Cooper of Red Deer, Alberta, noticed the amount of work required even of Morris's revised housework schedule: 'I admit this schedule can be done – so can the four-minute mile if you have the energy!'[58] Those in agreement with Morris's schedule, such as Mary Daniluk of Windsor, Ontario, wrote in her defence. Daniluk's commentary about why she believed other women were so vehemently opposed to the article was also instructive: 'Any mother of two and housekeeper of a normal home who bristled angrily at this article should check her motives for two reasons: either the truth hurts or she is afraid of spare time, not knowing how to use it. We often hear reference to man hours, lost through illness and accident, but never of women hours lost over coffee, cigarettes, TV, idle complaining and sleeping in. I have practised Eileen's method for a year and a half now and I certainly verify her article.'[59] Ruffled feathers and disgruntled readers aside, the magazine was making a statement about the changing nature of women's roles within the home and attempting to provoke Canadian homemakers to rethink their household regimes. That many clung tenaciously to working until 8 p.m., or much later, was not as surprising as the publication during the decade of a number of housework articles similar in tone and content to Morris's piece. Those articles did not glorify the house beautiful; rather, they attempted to advance the thesis that housework should be disposed of quickly and efficiently, so that women would have time for other endeavours. That was not standard fare for a woman's magazine to promulgate.

Commensurate with Morris's housework article were articles on marriage and the roles of wives and mothers which, in a similar vein, were not paeans to marital bliss, but critical assessments of married women's status. A series of three articles, all written by Christina McCall in 1961 and 1962 (before Friedan's 1963 bestseller), combined discussions of women's private lives, particularly marriage, with a cogent feminist critique.[60] In a biographical aside in her 'Booksbooksbooks' column in 1966, McCall referred to herself as 'a onetime militant, sometime waver-

36 *Chatelaine*, September 1961

ing feminist.'[61] No time-lines were proffered, but presumably her feminism was well entrenched when she produced this series of articles.
'Working Wives Are Here to Stay' began with this provocative blurb:
'They're labelled luxury-mad materialists. They're blamed for delin-
quency and divorce. They're accused of throwing men onto breadlines.
But the fact is Canada's 700,000 working wives are merely unrecog-
nized pioneers in a social revolution.'[62] Employing a historical and
sociological perspective and supported by Dominion Bureau of Statistics information, the author explained the increasing entry of married
women into the workforce in Canada, the United States, and Britain as
a result of financial need, not as a matter of personal fulfilment. The
article was accompanied by a gritty, black-and-white photo-essay of a
'typical' working wife and mother, bookkeeper Gertrude Carpenter of
Scarborough, Ontario (illustration 36). Readers learned that Mrs Carpenter was the major wage earner in her family of five because her
husband was on partial disability. The photo-essay depicted Carpen-

ter's dual workday (family and job demands kept her occupied from 7 a.m. to 11:45 p.m. Monday through Friday), her determination, and the decidedly unglamorous, exhausting nature of her existence. There was absolutely no glorification of the 'super-mom' of seventies and eighties fame who, so the media would have us believe, combined corporate jobs with child care, gourmet dining, and conspicuous leisure. According to Mrs Carpenter, she worked 'not for glamour and stimulus of a career, but to meet medical expenses and mortgage payments.'

Reader commentary was not favourable. One reader, Mrs Mike Levin of Selkirk, Manitoba, was angered by the feminist agenda of the *Chatelaine* writers: 'A slop-pail full of sickening, conscience-lulling hogwash, cooked up by *Chatelaine* and a crew of two-faced social workers, eagerly devoured by those who put the Joneses ahead of their children – like the Carpenters. Poor babies! You career girls at *Chatelaine* are trying to incite a revolution that will end forever a happy childhood in the kind of home God meant them to have. From the nursery in the hospital, to the nursery down the street! Moms with a college degree or some kind of training belong in the outside world, not to baby!'[63] Mrs Levin's interpretation of the article, regardless of the apparent lack of glamorization of the Carpenter's life style, brought the voice of child welfare (that traditional concern raised by those opposed to working mothers), anti-feminism, and the rural woman's voice to the letters page. Of course, it was clear that Mrs Levin perceived the valorization of the working mother to be a threat and an insult to her way of life. As a recurrent topic of interest, the world of the working wife and mother merited numerous investigations throughout the decade. The magazine consistently attempted to direct women towards interesting and accommodating jobs (both part time and full time), offered suggestions about how women could reorient themselves to the demands of the workplace, and profiled successful working mothers and various career women.[64] Indicative of the vast numbers of wives and mothers who were returning to the workforce, virtually every year the magazine devoted at least one article, usually a special pullout feature or a comprehensive article, to various facets of women's employment.

Despite critical commentary, McCall followed up 'Working Wives' with 'All Canadians are Equal – except Women,' an astute and pithy commentary about the ineffective equal pay legislation on the books in most Canadian provinces and at the federal level. According to the author, 'part of the fault lies in the innocuous wording of the legislation, but even more to blame are prevailing social attitudes and the general weak-kneed refusal by women to test the laws.'[65] How did readers respond to another figurative call to arms? Reactions were mixed. Mrs Eldon Finnell of Ponteix, Saskatchewan, thought it was 'a wonderful article, but how much more effective if written by a man.'[66] Conversely, Mrs Eugenie Ross of Don Mills complained that she did not 'know of any force that does more to encourage the attitude women have toward themselves as being sub-standard than trashy magazines like yours ... [the] greatest service you could do Canadian womanhood would be to cease publication.'[67] Conversely, Mrs Berchtold of North Vancouver applauded the magazine's stand on contentious issues, although she did not formally state her agreement with McCall's article: 'Every so often letters appear in your magazine with instructions to cancel subscriptions as the writers have found a certain article or story "offensive." In other words, they didn't agree with the opinion of that particular author. If *Chatelaine* is going to print only articles that they feel sure will offend no one, I will cancel my subscription as this would result in nothing but pap. Reading material with which one agrees is neither educational nor stimulating. Surely one's convictions should be strong enough to take a bit of a jar ... How can we learn anything if we are afraid to examine new ideas?'[68] The magazine offered its tacit agreement with Mrs Berchtold by publishing the final instalment of the feminist trilogy in the same issue as her letter.

'Why Can't We Treat Married Women like People?' made the earlier articles seem mild by comparison. Based on McCall's own frustration about the changed nature of her status after two years of marriage, she took umbrage at the stereotypical portrait of the married woman and the docile reaction of married women to the derogatory comments. According to her, 'before marriage you are regarded as a reasoning, responsible individual. After the wedding you are pigeonholed as an empty-headed, witless dummy, scarcely able to comment on the weather.'[69] She was fed up with hearing the constant refrain 'I'm just a housewife,' which McCall decoded, rightly, as 'I'm just a nothing.' The fault lay, in large part, with Canadian society: 'The social attitude we seem to be stuck with: that every girl should find herself a husband as soon as possible after she reaches the age of eighteen. In meek compliance most Canadian girls tend to do just that. More and more of them marry at nineteen, have their first child at twenty, and are caught, all during what should be their years of self-discovery, in a round of housekeeping and childbearing. Then at age of thirty or thirty-five ...

they suddenly come to, to find that the world has gone right by and left them chronically bored and hopelessly fumbling.' McCall's solution was not for women to leave their kitchens and homes en mass to enter the workforce. Instead, she recommended that 'we try to instill both in ourselves and our children the belief that girls have as much responsibility to grow into fully formed opinionated adults as do boys.' To accomplish that she proposed that 'we try to stave off the urgency to marry at least until the middle twenties and give girls time to work at something which they can either return to when their children are grown or that will, at very least, bolster their self-respect through the years when they're wholly domesticated.' Though these articles presumed that women were responsible for the household, they urged women not to limit themselves to the housewife role. One of the fundamental credos of many *Chatelaine* feature articles, and editorials, during the sixties was that there was life beyond dishpan hands and ennui.

The authors continued to advance this agenda even when responses from readers were often critical, angry, or bemused about the unhappiness of some married women. In what she probably considered the worst fate possible, Mrs Maxine La Croix of Montreal decided that 'Christina McCall ... doesn't deserve to be married or have the title of Mrs.'[70] Conversely, Mr Fred Olsen of Cumberland, BC, claimed that the 'article really "sent" me. Please write a book along the lines of your article and I'll peddle two hundred copies personally.'[71] According to Mrs Helen Max-Duca of Vancouver, the blame for this situation should be attributed primarily to women: 'Married women don't want to be treated like people. They like to be treated like women. It gives them a sense of security to hide behind the excuse men so generously give them, pampered and irresponsible, therefore dumb. We should not blame men for it – very few women desire to get out of this comfortable situation.'[72]

One indicator of the feminist commitment of the editorial staff was an internal memo declining the publication of an article proffered by Rabbi Abraham Feinberg of Holy Blossom Temple in Toronto entitled '1962 Woman and Her World.'[73] In her evaluative memo about Feinberg's submission, associate editor Jean Yack wrote:

This is so much nonsense ... I am sik sik sik (sic) of jerks telling women 'it's all your problem dearie ... now go home and think yourself into a better frame of mind and some worthwhile tasks.' e.g. say 100 times daily: doing dishes is GOOD for the world...blah. He says females should stay home and make it lovely...admits papa won't spend much time there ... suggests absolutely no help will be forthcoming from papa, mentally or physically ... then says, but to stop war women maybe should take over government ... Really, how naive ... Also, I wonder what these guys think will happen if educated, and well-educated, women stay home, raise kids and, as these guys suggest, do study and think etc., to enrich and ennoble their minds ... they'd soon outstrip their husbands who haven't the time for self-enrichment and discovery, that's what ... so we'd have another problem: male worker bonehead drones, and charming, intelligent, noble, cultivated wives ... Ha! p.s. I don't think much of this piece.[74]

By no means were all the general feature pieces in the magazine feminist articles. Despite the staff's own personal politics, they were cognizant of the fact that they were editing a women's magazine and had to include a variety of material. It was this concern for the general reader that resulted in their now-famous decision not to publish advance drafts of Betty Friedan's *Feminine Mystique.*

Much has been made of the fact that *Chatelaine* passed up the opportunity to publish chapters from Friedan's book. At the time, the editors explained that the topic was well covered elsewhere and that to print Friedan would be repetitious. The extant editorial correspondence about this work provides a different reason, however, one concerned with the style of writing and the content. Jean Yack's commentary was succinct: 'This is a little too heavy for us ... though some of the subject matter is interesting. On the whole, I'd skip.'[75] Keith Knowlton pronounced it 'heavy-footed' and asked, 'Anyone interested in a treatise on feminism and feminists?'[76] After their editorial meeting, Knowlton wrote this brief note to Almeda Glassey, the fiction editor: 'Thanks for letting us see this [*Feminine Mystique*] but we find it a bit too heavy-footed. Good material, but a little turgid in style for a general audience.'[77] A large number of American and Canadian women soon proved otherwise, sending Friedan's book onto the bestseller list. Charting a course to keep a mass audience of Canadian women reading the magazine meant that the editorial staff frequently opted for 'commercial' packages rather than challenging works, so as not to offend, intimidate, or overwhelm the average reader.

Despite its refusal to publish excerpts from *The Feminine Mystique,* *Chatelaine*'s role as Canada's feminism primer continued throughout the decade, reaching its climax in Jack Batten's article 'After black power, Women Power,' published in the September 1969 issue (illustration 37).[78] The anti-feminist side continued to send missives to the editors. Lia Lafontaine of Ville de Laval, Quebec, pleaded: 'Please stop brainwashing every educated woman out of her home!'[79] Accompanied by a dramatic photo of a female demonstrator, the article's subtitle declared: 'A new breed of female: mainly young, brainy and North American, is calling for a new revolution. The goal: to free women from second-class status and sexual slavery.'[80] Batten's article, despite his concerns about representing 'the enemy,' provided readers with a history of feminist literature and the link between women's liberation (as it was then called) and black and student protest groups in the United States. It also summarized the tenets of feminism according to each organization, presented short interviews with key feminist personnel in the United States and Canada, and recounted a visit to the offices of the National Organization for Women (NOW) in New York City. Batten analyzed the demands of both the radical women's libbers and the centrist, mainstream feminist groups and concluded that they all had the same focus: power and equality. All groups shared a determination to remake society, not, as he had assumed, to dominate men. Included in Batten's article was this quote from the Female Liberation Movement about the 'purpose' of the mass media: 'The Female Liberation Movement (FLM) shares with most women radicals a streak of suspicion of the mass media. "We must enter communities, not use the political platform or the MEDIA," Roxanne Dunbar recently wrote in the FLM newsletter. "The people do not believe anything they hear through these organs." Ti-Grace Atkinson of The Feminists, another New York–based group, feels the same way about newspapers and magazines, *men's* media' (emphasis in original). Although many radical, and not so radical feminists had branded American women's magazines as organs of oppression, *Chatelaine* was one of the most consistent disseminators of feminist ideology, history, and information to a mass audience of Canadian girls and women. Reader responses, whether vociferous or congratulatory, indicated that 'the people' believed that the information presented in the magazine was accurate. Naturally, agreement and action did not necessarily follow from reading articles like 'Woman Power.'

The enthusiastic letter from sixteen-year-old Marie Kiciuk of Winnipeg was representative of the letters in favour of feminist articles: '"Woman Power" was one of the best articles I have read in your magazine. I have been interested in the Feminist movement for a long time. Unfortunately, living in the "wilds" of Manitoba, literature is

37 *Chatelaine,* September 1969

scarce and I would like to find out more.'[81] Colleen Fitzpatrick of Burnaby, BC, was perplexed about the magazine's choice of a male writer for such an important piece on women's liberation.[82] Other readers, however, were angry and appalled by Batten's article. The revulsion described by Mrs Aileen Sivell of Oakville, Ontario, provided graphic insight into her 'feelings' as she read the piece:

> That article made my flesh crawl in horror and revulsion ... The picture emerged of a hard-core group of emotionally crippled, spiritually sterile and physically barren ... (I hate to use the word) women. Dropouts, all, from their respective roles as women, wives and mothers, consumed with a hatred and bitterness and desire for revenge against men and society (for their own stupidity and ineptness), they now in their extreme frustration seek to deny, discredit and denigrate the unchangeable fact of their own biological functions and responsibilities in the cycle of life. I could pity more these wretchedly unhappy creatures were it not for their ruthless determination to sacrifice on the altar of their own wounded ego, husbands, homes and children, guilty and innocent alike.[83]

Mrs Sivell's letter attracted considerable attention and, in the January issue, two women responded to her criticism. Mrs Hazel Vogan of Bath, Ontario, applauded her efforts: 'Cheers for Mrs Aileen Sivell ... I, too, have become more and more repulsed by the Feminist Movement. I hope we will hear from more women, like Mrs Sivell and myself, who still champion "husbands, home and children."'[84] Feminist issues were not anathema to all the correspondents from Ontario, however, as this excerpt from an 'open letter' from Marily Jones of Ottawa to Mrs Sivell indicates: 'Had you read the article more closely, you would have become aware that the Feminists "don't make the mistake of naming man as the enemy" ... I can only shake my head sadly and quote Juliet Mitchell: "Women have to find their chains before they lose them." You seem to refuse to acknowledge their very existence.'[85] The battle continued on the letters page between women who welcomed a changing role for women and those who, whether defensive or proud of their maternal and homemaking status, supported women's traditional roles. Amid the clamour, it is important to remember that the feminist groups Batten chose to explore had far more radical agendas than the more prevalent liberal feminist message that usually found voice in *Chatelaine*. Historians of second-wave feminism have shown that radical feminist groups in Canada were restricted to the seventies, for the most part, and were far less popular than either liberal or social feminism.[86] The two camps cannot be differentiated by marital status, region, or class, for pro-feminist commentary came from rural women, and married women, middle- and working-class women. Only women with younger children seemed more likely to advocate the status quo.

Conventional Fare

The paramount article in favour of women's traditional roles was Marta Wasserman's 1962 article, 'How Mothers Mix Up Daughters for Love and Marriage.'[87] Printed in the same year as the McCall articles, it offers an interesting comparison to this feminist series, particularly since McCall was Wasserman's ghost writer. Wasserman, 'an eminent Ottawa psychoanalyst,' urged women to be happy with the status quo. In this excerpt she describes the primary reasons behind women's unhappiness: 'One of the most blatant and most widely perpetuated social lies of our time is the flat statement that women are equal to men. This just isn't so. Of course women have as much value as human beings as men do ... Women aren't free to pursue self-centred lives. They *have* to do the drudgery. But the drudgery could be made bearable, in fact even prideful, if only young girls were taught to look on it as part of their privileges as women, to realize that a country cannot do without capable mothers and wives [emphasis in original].' A modest proposal? A gender turncoat? Given the tone of the article it could have been read as satire, but readers took it at face value.

The Wasserman article had fans like Mrs D. Desmond of Vancouver, who wrote: 'Perhaps the best article ever printed by a woman's magazine, so packed with truth and help for women of all ages that it should be printed, over and over again.'[88] Or Mrs C. Munson of Terrace, BC, who found it 'the wisest and truest piece I have read on the subject. Every word is a gem.'[89] However, Mrs Ellenmie Melcher from Rockyford, Alberta, thought Wasserman was wrong to blame mothers: 'Mothers don't deserve all the blame. How many men make their wives feel like partners and recognize their efforts?'[90] Whatever the editors' motivations for publishing Wasserman's article, it was revealing that they chose this long, angry letter from J.S. Cameron of Etobicoke, Ontario, as the lead letter on the page:

> Marta Wasserman's article left me more than a little baffled. Apparently she would have all mothers lie to their daughters by telling them what a

grand and noble profession homemaking is. I have a daughter ... but she will certainly know all the facts of marriage and everything that goes with it before she marries, not after. Come down to earth, dear editors – look around you. Take a jaunt to the supermarket some morning. Take a look at the poor specimens of human faces and see if you see anything noble in them. I don't know of one intelligent woman who is happily married, not one. Marta says women have to be drudges. How true. In most cases, if they marry they most certainly will be drudges and worse. If you really want to do a service to Canadian women, why don't you do a series of articles on 'How to Escape Marriage' for girls who are not the maternal, homemaking type? To me the average woman wastes most of her life in stupid and senseless activity. Please do not tell us to lie to our daughters. Give them a chance to make a better life for themselves than most of us have had.[91]

Later, other readers wrote to criticize Cameron's analysis of the Wasserman article. Mrs Jean Griffin of Ottawa wrote: 'I simply cannot agree with J.S. Cameron ... I am happily married and gave up a career as a chemist with no misgivings whatsoever ... I trust Mrs Cameron's letter was written on a "blue" day.'[92] The Wasserman article and the reader feedback indicated that many readers were proud housewives and mothers, while others railed at the limitations of their domestic role. In the end, while *Chatelaine* played an important role in increasing knowledge about feminist issues, the magazine continued to include articles that served as a counter-balance, glorifying the status quo or, ironically, advocating a more narrowly defined role for the majority of women. As a career woman, after all, Wasserman was disregarding her own advice.

Brave New World: Birth Control and Sexualities

Among the chains that held women back in the sixties was the lack of access to reproductive information and contraceptives – the pill – and draconian abortion legislation. The campaign for greater access to birth control and safe, legal abortions was one of the causes *Chatelaine* supported. Although reproductive rights were clearly part of the 'feminist agenda,' the magazine structured the articles – their content, tone, and purpose – as medical articles, thereby linking reproductive rights to women's health, the population crisis, and new medical trends. It was difficult to discern whether the magazine's policy was pragmatic or prudish. The numerous articles on abortion, the pill, and other forms of birth control, including vasectomy and even test tube babies, all eschewed sustained commentary about freedom of sexual expression for women or the feminist campaign behind such medical news.[93] At a time when many medical practitioners were reticent about providing their patients with contraceptive information, when the criminal code prevented access to legal abortions for victims of rape, sexual abuse, incest, or as a birth control measure (it was legal only if the mother's life was endangered), *Chatelaine's* campaign was noteworthy.

Women's sexuality, of varying types, did make its entry into the magazine. This area had not been neglected in the fifties, thanks to the cogent essays produced by the team of Dr Marion Hilliard and June Callwood. The sixties articles mirrored the increased sexual freedom and sexual awareness in that decade. Articles on children's sexuality dealt frankly with the issues of masturbation, how parents should explain sex and 'proper' sexual behaviour to children, molestation, incest, and, infrequently, concerns about homosexuality.[94] If the Hilliard and Callwood pieces were startlingly open about sexuality, particularly the acknowledgment that women should experience sexual pleasure, then the articles in the sixties opened the remaining Pandora's boxes about sexuality – the criminal kind and the deviant kind (as homosexuality was construed throughout the articles).[95] Clearly, the articles in the sixties were more inclusive about the variety of sexual experience – children's, heterosexual women's, lesbian, gay male, and men's sexuality. Two articles merit closer attention, Renate Wilson's 'What Turns Women to Lesbianism?' and June Callwood's 'Sex and the Married Woman.'[96]

According to Wilson, 'unlike male homosexuality, there was far less fact and more myth about the causes and frequency of this sexual deviation among females.'[97] The opening paragraphs introduced us to Jane, 'a slim, quiet spoken' twenty-six-year-old salesgirl, and her partner, Teresa, a thirty-year-old 'somewhat stocky figure' who 'drives a delivery truck.' We learn that they have lived together for four years in their own apartment, that they love each other, 'share the double bed' (*Chatelaine's* genteel euphemism for sex), and 'look forward to spending the rest of their lives together.' To make the situation perfectly clear, Wilson, as the expert, made this authoritative statement: 'Jane and Teresa are lesbians – homosexual females. They are attracted only to women and find the idea of lovemaking with a man repulsive. On the surface this is all that distinguishes them from heterosexual, or normal, women. The real differences lie deep and concern both their evolution and evaluation of themselves as women.' Having clarified that hetero-sexuality was normal and lesbianism was abnormal, the rest of the article set out Wilson's research findings, her interviews with North American psychiatrists and Canadian religious groups, and her discussions with Teresa and Jane's friends from Vancouver. Although the article aimed not to be merely sensationalistic, covering historical, medical, religious, and personal issues, the emphasis was on the causes of lesbianism and how it could be avoided or treated. Jane and Theresa's friends and, ironically, the religious groups, advocated acceptance, thereby criticizing and coun-tering the dominant psychiatric angle of the piece.

Despite Wilson's incessant question 'Why?' the article was thorough and informative for lesbians, people unsure of their sexuality, or those interested in what a lesbian was. Wilson provided a definition of the term: 'The word *lesbian* is derived from the Greek island of Lesbos, where poetess Sappho enjoyed and sang the praises of such relation-ships with women. Lesbians come in all ages and nationalities, profes-sions and social classes. They can be married, single, childless or mothers of several children. They can hang out on skid row or live respectively in suburbia. They may never advance their sexual longings beyond an affectionate hug and kiss, or they may take part with another woman in sexual activity leading to orgasm.' It was an inclusive, if classist, defini-tion of the lesbian. She hesitated to state the sexual nature of the relationship, but admitted that, for many women, lesbianism went beyond a passionate friendship. She borrowed the statistics of the Ameri-can expert, Dr A.C. Kinsey, whose report estimated that 2 per cent of women were exclusively lesbian, and 15 per cent partially so. Wilson knew the terms used in the community and in psychiatric literature, but she revealed her bias by listing them in the order of: 'gay,' 'deviant,' 'invert,' 'homophile,' 'butch,' and 'femme,' and by stating that the women she met in Teresa and Jane's apartment were not 'distinguish-able by appearance.' Her description of these women stressed, except for one butch, their normality or their ability to pass as normal in society. Ultimately, the emphasis in Wilson's article was on the homosociability of their world (their friendships and relationships with other lesbians) and the legal, religious, and social pronouncements against lesbianism. No letters were published in the magazine about this article, so it is difficult to gauge how readers, both heterosexual and homosexual, responded to it.

In contrast, Callwood's piece on married women's sexuality provoked a maelstrom of letters to the editor which condemned the subject matter, with a special opprobrium saved for the author. Setting the tone quickly, the opening blurb promised a provocative article: 'One in four wives (and that's a low estimate) finds marriage is not a gateway to sexual joy – in fact, it may even decrease it. What goes wrong for women in sex and marriage?'[98] Quoting Masters and Johnson, along with other experts, Callwood surveyed the theories of why so many couples had difficulty with sex, the conflicting advice on how women could attain orgasm, and the role sex played in marriage. Part of the problem with marital sex was familiarity. One housewife who had requested anonymity stated: 'Sex with your husband is comfortable, like house slippers, because he knows what to do ... But for that sense of intense and delicious excitement that you once enjoyed when sex was new, you have to look outside of marriage.' Ultimately, Callwood wrote that women's delivery from the 'century of frigidity' into the age of 'sexual revolution' was 'marvellous.' Unlike all the articles on birth control and reproductive issues, she was clearly championing the idea that non-procreative sex was a normal, desirable part of marriage. The article also acknowledged the existence of premarital and extramarital sex, although Callwood did not endorse either option. Today these statements appear far from incendiary, yet in the late sixties they provoked an eye-popping reaction in most readers, particularly in the context of the hippie life style and its free-love mantra of the decade.

For the most part, readers criticized the author and the magazine for printing 'smut.' A few indignant readers, such as Mrs J. Barkaman of Steinbach, Manitoba, cancelled their subscriptions: 'Do you realize that the article "Sex and the Married Woman" contained some dangerous half-truths? For instance, the idea that sex is unsatisfying because a couple is married could be misinterpreted by unwary people. Many deep thinkers believe that the indiscriminate search for sexual pleasure is the beginning of the downfall of the family, and society. In view of that fact, I could not allow my teenage daughters to read this suggestive, half-truthful article, and believe you have forgotten your responsibility of honest journalism, I regretfully ask that you take my name off the subscriber's list.'[99] Audrey L. Wosley of Chilliwack, BC, also felt the need to keep the magazine away from her teenagers, although she took extreme measures to protect impressionable young minds: '*Chatelaine* really scraped the bottom of the barrel when you printed "Sex and the Married Woman" ... This is the first time I have had to burn my copy before my three children were able to read it.'[100]

As was often the case with such brouhahas, some readers went back to reread the offending article to re-evaluate whether the fuss was merited. Mrs P.A. Robinson of Regina was one of those who wrote to complain about the negative commentary the article received. Her analysis of why the article infuriated so many readers was suggestive: 'I decided I just had to read "Sex and the Married Woman" again to find out what all that howling was about. I found it very interesting. It's time someone woke the sexually frigid woman – apparently there are many, according to those who have written to criticize. Guess they don't like the truth. I think there should be more free and open discussions about sex, and I pat *Chatelaine* on the back for publishing June Callwood's article.'[101] Meanwhile, Barbara B. Duncan of Markham, Ontario, interpreted the venomous letters as an indication of readers' jealousy: 'I suppose there will always be those who hate success. But can't any of your readers say a kind word about June Callwood? I've seldom read such venom poured forth against anyone.'[102] As many controversial articles indicated, and this was certainly no exception, the commentary in the readers' page became an intrinsic part of reading the article – half the fun was comparing your viewpoint with the plucky souls who had written to the magazine.

'Why Men Want Out of Marriage?' Exploring Masculinity

Other infrequent topics of discussion and controversy were men, masculinity, and the differences between the sexes.[103] In particular, the differences between masculinity and femininity were familiar ground because they appeared in virtually all articles on marriage, marital problems, dating, and relationships. Two articles, presenting both the positive and the negative images of masculinity and the relationship between the sexes, were representative of those devoted to this topic. The first, 'A Husband and Wife Change Jobs,' provided a reassuring article for housewives about the demanding nature of their job. As an added bonus, the husband's inability to perform his wife's role and the ease with which the woman reintegrated herself into the workforce gave stay-at-home wives and mothers validation and inspiration. The article employed a 'he said–she said' format, allowing the aptly named Copes – Michael and Pam – to tell their stories. Michael's two weeks as a househusband proved revelatory: 'For the first time I comprehended the really hard work involved in keeping up a house and family. The job is fraught with hazards.'[104] Most of Michael's hazards were moving objects – Mark (2), Jane (5), and Richard (8) – and their diapering, feeding, and bathing regimes. His description of the first morning on the job was priceless and undoubtedly brought tears of laughter to the housewives who read the magazine: 'It all began at 6.30 on the Monday morning Pam started as a filing clerk in a downtown Toronto office, fourteen miles from our home. No sooner had I donned my house-working uniform – wash and wear casual slacks, sport shirt and sandals – than young Mark woke up with a dirty diaper. I nearly gagged on an empty stomach. It was four diapers later that I learned to hold my breath. And it was only at the end of the week that I became sufficiently proficient.' Despite his determination to be organized, to provide basic meat-and-potato meals, and to stick to a schedule, Michael discovered that, even with half days on the weekends, he still worked an eighty-seven-hour week. Exhaustion, boredom, and frustration quickly wore him down. By the end of the experiment he was glad to go back to work, raised the housekeeping budget (since he found it inadequate), purchased a new iron for his wife (to replace the faulty one he couldn't master), and voluntarily did the dishes each evening to ease Pam's workload and his guilt. His relief at the end of the role reversals was palpable. Pam's story was different. She enjoyed working in the office, and when she returned home at night she could read the paper, watch television, or unwind, free from the demands of child care. She wrote: 'I didn't work as long, nor think as hard, as I work running a home and bringing up a family; but because of the commuting I found it equally exhausting.'

Readers were quick to add their two cents' worth, and all of them enjoyed the article, although for very different reasons. Mrs F.W. Barret of Botwood, Newfoundland, complimented the article's authenticity: 'It was so true to life. I didn't realize just how hectic and demanding keeping a home in running order really was.'[105] Mrs Bonnie Heath of Stratford, Ontario, enjoyed sharing the article with friends: 'My January issue is pretty well worn out after all my friends finished borrowing it.'[106] Conversely, other female readers believed that articles such as this were part of a sinister agenda on the part of the *Chatelaine* editors. Carmen Bernard of Weston, Ontario, complained: 'Now *Chatelaine* has reached, I hope, the culmination of the new feminist campaign. What about some other topics for a change?'[107] The only published letter from a male reader came from house-husband Gerald L. Morris of Stavely, Alberta: 'My wife started a hairdressing course last July,' he reported. 'In turn, I am househusband as well as breadwinner for our family of five, ranging in age from 10 down to 1½. Fortunately, my office is off the living quarters. My wife comes home Saturday nights and returns Monday morning. I cook, wash, scrub, wax, clean house etc. My hours are usually 7 am to midnight, and I'll gladly throw my vote with the ladies – a woman's work is never done!'[108] Reader responses provided rare glimpses into the way 'average' Canadians negotiated work and family demands. Ironically, they also illustrated the entrenched nature of gender role division in the home. Both Michael Cope and Gerald Morris describe 'doing women's work,' even though, in Morris's case, he had been performing the household maintenance and child care for ten months. Men might have participated in household chores in rare instances, but they interpreted such work as 'helping out.'

The articles on masculinity frequently elicited negative commentary from both male and female readers. Male readers most often responded to what they perceived as an anti-male agenda, whereas women readers criticized the high-octane testosterone behaviour trumpeted in these articles. Mollie Gillen's 'Why Men Want Out of Marriage' proved too candid for readers' liking. The problem, according to men like Gil Morrison and Eddy Harbett, was that Canadian men were chafed by too much togetherness in marriage. The theme of overdomestication ran, subliminally, through this description of Morrison's difficult life. 'Gil Morrison is a Toronto advertising executive, aged thirty-five, with a split-level house in the suburbs, two children ... and a wife who has kept her figure. The family four-door sedan is left for his wife's daytime use: Gil drives a Jaguar XKE in and out of town. His wife is popular with the neighbours, noted for her charm, her efficient management of home and children, her tasteful, well-planned dinners, at which Gil is a smiling, genial host. And Gil wishes he never had to see her again ... here lies the crux of the problem for men like Gil. Have we put so much togetherness into marriage that it runs counter to a man's basic instinct?'[109] Should readers have missed the problems, this statement from Eddy Harbett offered a red flag to the problems of Canadian men: 'A man wants a comfortable home, nice kids – and let's be frank – available sex in a socially acceptable way. But it isn't his whole life.' Readers were equally frank in their comments.

Mrs Marion Schaffer of Sudbury, Ontario, reported that she had recommended the article to her minister as reading material for the church's pre-marriage courses. Furthermore, she wrote: 'Many thanks for the perceptive article ... It seems that fewer girls marry under the influence of rose-coloured romanticism nowadays, but it would be wonderful to set straight any girls who still harboured those ideas.'[110] In a letter positively dripping with sarcasm and thinly veiled anger, Mrs Hazel Norrish of Thornhill, Ontario, adopted an alternate reading by claiming the wife as an endangered species:

> We women have to face the fact that wives are fast becoming obsolete! The only function they can perform that other women cannot (or will not) is to work 18 hours a day, 365 days of the year for no pay! Think about it. A man can live in an apartment, eat well-balanced meals from the frozen food counter while the corner laundrette and dry-cleaning establishment attend his laundry. Pretty girls are a dime a dozen: now he can even have sex and respectability with the use of birth control pills ... For slathering day-in-and-day-out devotion he can get a dog. For dignified, aloof and high bred love, a cat – they are quite content to be thrown out of the house and left alone for hours on end with nothing to do ... Yes girls, it is becoming quite clear that dull well-behaved wives who love their husbands are a crashing bore. The emotions of love, trust and companionship that marriage entails are just a drag to the average man. Well, if they don't like us that way – fine, there must be hundreds of better places to be than behind that eternally dirty sink![111]

Whether Norrish's feminist edge had been sharpened by the magazine, her experience as a suburban wife, or that particular article was not clear. Whatever reaction the magazine hoped to provoke with this article's indictment of the suburban housewife, readers like Norrish were quick to see through it and to use it as a sarcastic call to arms.

Whatever Happened to Chatelaine Left Hand? Race and Ethnicity

The magazine had a penchant for exploratory articles about those groups defined as 'other' – men, people from diverse ethnic backgrounds, immigrants, the working class, and the poor. The purposes behind such articles were multiple: to offer readers insight into how other Canadians lived their lives, to provide a wider base of interest from which to encourage subscriptions and readers, and to highlight issues in need of social redress. Readers' images of themselves, as not-men, not-ethnic, or not-poor, were also reinforced. Articles on race and ethnicity in the sixties took two forms. Stories of race expanded from their fifties' emphasis solely on black Canadians to offer recurring analyses of the situation facing Aboriginal Canadians.[112] Meanwhile, ethnicity was divided into examinations of individual immigrants or their families in Canada, occasional articles on the French-Canadian situation, or articles that glorified multiculturalism – particularly in the Christmas issue in a format such as 'Christmas around the world.'[113]

Unlike the fifties, when Native Canadian issues were never raised in the magazine, the sixties witnessed numerous articles devoted to analyses of the plight of the First Nations.[114] This new-found interest in Aboriginal women was part of the general surge of interest in Aboriginal issues sparked, in no small measure, by increasing Aboriginal activism (then referred to as 'red power'). In 1962 Anderson sent writer Frances McNab and a photographer to the Stony Indian reserve to interview the Poucettes and report on their living conditions. The Poucettes were pleased to be interviewed and photographed by the magazine; in fact, the 'What's New with Us' column reported on the unusual circumstances that occurred while the *Chatelaine* team were at the reserve. 'It's not every day that a baby is named after a magazine, but *Chatelaine* has been so honoured. When photographer Jack Long and writer Frances McNab ... went out to the Stony Indian reservation at Morley, just west of Calgary, to photograph the Poucette family, they discovered that a new member had been born to one of the Poucette daughters, Mina Left Hand. As a matter of fact, there hadn't been time to go to the Calgary hospital and Mrs Poucette had delivered her own grandchild. In honour of their visitors the Poucettes decided to call their new baby girl Chatelaine Left Hand – Laine for short.'[115] McNab was appalled by the living conditions on the reserve and her article, 'The Forgotten Canadians,' provided a stinging indictment of Canada's policy with respect to First Nations people (illustration 38). 'We self-righteously denounce nations that repress their native peoples,' she wrote, 'yet we force some 200,000 Canadians – our Indians – to live in segregation to preserve their rights, deny them control of their own affairs, do little to help them from near poverty.'[116] This article passed without commentary, at least judging by the letters published in the magazine.

By decade's end the approach was more ambitious, as the magazine devoted a special feature to 'Canadian Indians, 1968,' complete with photographs and a long, hard-hitting article from Barbara Frum. Although not mentioned in the article, Frum and her husband had adopted an Aboriginal child. To support the feature, the cover photo was devoted to a portrait of a Native Canadian woman – filmmaker Barbara Wilson (illustration 39). Inside, Frum's article was framed by seven

38 *Chatelaine*, June 1962

pages of black-and-white photographs of successful Native Canadians (from a white, middle-class perspective – upwardly mobile professionals and university students), along with those who preferred a more traditional life style on the land. Whatever the case, even in pictures depicting bleak conditions on reserves, the images attested to Native Canadian pride and tenacity and provided evidence of the feature's subtitle: 'Playing the white game is out, being proudly Indian is in. This warmly perceptive series tells why Indians are angry, what they believe in, what they seek.'[117] The title of the article, 'How Ottawa (and We) Slept,' set the tone for the issue, as Frum angrily denounced white Canadians' treatment of Native people: 'The Indians of Canada are conquered people. Force this fact up out of your subliminal into your conscious mind and you will be ready to grasp what four hundred years of Indian policy has been about. We've ghettoized Indian people on special lands not of their own choosing, forced Indian religion underground, outlawed the speaking of native languages in Indian

39 *Chatelaine* cover, November 1968

schools, attacked Indian culture, overruled honourable treaties in our courts of law.'[118] Colonization and assimilation – Frum stopped short of calling it genocide – were the two prongs of the Canadian Indian policy. The argument, the compelling photographs, and the cover photo combined to make this feature a 'must read.'

The editors reported that Frum's article had elicited 'raves.'[119] W.J. Wacko, research and training officer with the Community Development Branch in Alberta, sent his congratulations and assessment of the impact of such an article: 'These well-documented and up-to-date articles will make a significant contribution in educating the Canadian public.'[120] Mrs B. Spence of Saskatoon was also delighted by the article: 'I am a treaty Indian by marriage and was extremely pleased to see a positive article ... I am glad *Chatelaine* took the initiative.'[121] 'Just a note to say Kuyanamik (a great large thank you),' wrote David C. Ward, the president and managing director of Team Products based in Edmonton. 'Having lived with this all my life, reading your article among all the negative stories on Canada's Native People is like a breath of fresh air and a flash of sunlight to one trapped in a cave. I feel positive that this article will be a great inspiration to many Indian people. We at TEAM have been fighting a battle for three years to stress the positive side of the Indian situation, and it is gratifying to see someone else, not only understand, but do something about it.'[122] Because of the positive portrait in *Chatelaine* and the perceptive, analytical commentary of Frum's article, many people were prepared to believe that this exposure would create some momentum on Native Canadian issues in the country. Only one dissenting voice was registered about the article, and the magazine published a long excerpt of that letter – possibly to illustrate some of the differing approaches within the Native community. Native activist Kahn-Tineta Horn of Caughnawaga, Quebec, criticized Frum and the magazine for not going far enough in their analysis of the problems and the possible solutions. 'I am a Mohawk of the Six Nations Iroquois Confederacy and the only free Indian engaged in continuous welfare work for my people,' Horn wrote. 'There are some 250,000 Indians in Canada, but in your article there are only twelve Indians referred to ... I find an article like this is amusing but confusing. The article was particularly successful in such wide views as the love of the land, which is the fundamental foundation of the whole Indian existence and culture ... That is why such an article must not be construed to encourage a change at this time in the Indian Act, because the first thing that the politicians will do is to find some phony excuse to change the

Indian Act to the extent of stealing the precious land of Caughnawaga away.'[123] Although *Chatelaine* was an unlikely locus for such an argument, it is noteworthy that the magazine did provide a national forum to debate some of the pressing issues of Canadian society.

'The Real Poor in Canada Are Women': Class Issues

In addition to articles on Native Canadians, *Chatelaine* published an increasing number devoted to poverty in Canada.[124] Poverty didn't just happen to other people, it stressed; it happened to *Chatelaine* readers. With the exception of a series of articles in 1969 written by Ian Adams, these articles favoured terms such as *poverty, welfare,* or *public housing* and avoided the vocabulary of class. For some, the startling portraits of poverty, complete with dollar figures for annual income, shattered the mythology of a middle-class existence in Canada. Christina McCall Newman's introduction to her 1965 article claimed: 'They don't starve, but they merely exist in an affluent society where the gap between them and the average middle-class Canadians gets wider and harder to bridge.'[125] For reader Bonnie Lee Morris of 100 Mile House, BC, the article proved profoundly upsetting:

> I am horrified to learn that our family are among the invisible poor spoken about in your magazine of April 1965. I had always believed we were average in income and in the way we live. Only a short time ago I contemplated entering your Mrs Chatelaine contest: I was proud of our status in life and what we are accomplishing. We are a family of five. The oldest boy just turned seven. Last year, our income was just barely over the $3,000 mark. I canned 400 jars of fruit and vegetables. I also made 54 jars of jams and jellies. I feel we are well dressed. I sew, making 99 percent of my clothes, including suits and coats. I make all our curtains, drapes, breadspreads, flannelette sheets. We were able to purchase crown land and have built our own home. It is not a shack, but a well-built three bedroom home. We have several electrical appliances, and are purchasing a 1965 pick-up and TV. As I stated before, I was proud of the job we were doing on our income. Now I find myself wringing my hands, saying 'My stars, we're poor. We are so poor.' At first I wished I hadn't read this article, I almost decided to quit in despair. Now, I am determined to try harder.[126]

By any definition an industrious housewife, Morris identified the power of the *Chatelaine* article. Her letter illustrates the self-loathing placed on those who 'discovered,' regardless of how many appliances they owned, that they were not 'average,' not middle class. Although regional differences and the cost of living made her family's annual income go farther than it would have in the urban areas of central Ontario, nevertheless, according to the bald, statistical data presented in the article, hers was a working-class family. The article had clearly stated that poverty, or the gap between the middle class, the working class, and the unemployed, was not a matter of individual gumption and determination (as Morris believed), but was systemic. In her defence, other readers had also formulated that opinion, as this letter from Mrs Patricia Stitson of Gravenhurst, Ontario, illustrates: 'I don't think it's quite fair to put Mr Poulin in with the Indians of Hornepayne. If the Indians of Hornepayne spent a little less on taxis and liquor, they would not have to pick in the garbage dump. Mr Poulin and a great many like him are hindered by ill luck and lack of training, not ambition.'[127] Bad luck and race, according to Stitson, separate the poor from the middle classes. What angered her most about the piece was *Chatelaine*'s grouping of Aboriginal and white poor together, the supposedly undeserving with the deserving.

The series on poverty – 'The Real Poor in Canada Are Women,' 'Life on Welfare Is Hell,' and 'Can Anything Be Done about the Poor?' did not use the semantic dance so common in other articles on this topic (illustration 40). In the first article of the series, Ian Adams was unequivocal about his particular bias and about the correlation between class and gender. 'If you came out of the slums, as I did, you know all the jargon really means is that for a woman with three kids on welfare, a man is only a sometime thing ... when all those nice middle-class ladies with their association and service clubs pressured the government into the appointment of a Royal Commission on the Status of Women, they never thought for a moment that everywhere they went they would be hit by the simple fact: the real problem women in this country have is that they are poor.'[128] He assumed the position of the angry journalist – a confrontational style full of moral outrage – to shatter some of the myths about poverty. Adams pointed to racial inequity as a further delineator of poverty: he indicated that the earnings of Indian women were 'non-existent.'

The next instalment provided an insider's perspective of the welfare life style. As the title suggested, it was not an article about pulling oneself up by the bootstraps, but a blistering indictment of systemic poverty and the inability of many well-meaning do-gooders to fully

THE POOR
LIFE '69
PART TWO

The real poor in Canada are women

Three million women in Canada – one half of all the women in Canada –
are poor. Maybe it's time they stopped taking their economic beatings with
a sweet feminine smile, and started to fight back   by Ian Adams

CHATELAINE

comprehend the situation, much less make improvements: 'I don't profess to know about solutions. Euthanasia? Overdramatic maybe in this big, gorgeous "buy now, pay later" society. But sometimes you wonder if just "existing" really is worth the tremendous effort involved. When there is no hope, only grim reality left, oblivion can seem like bliss.' The conclusion was intended as both a challenge and a calculated insult: 'For God's sake, do something! Don't sit there on your Christian rear ends and mouth pious, meaningless platitudes! "They never had it so good." "Damn abuses of welfare these days." "Can't get them lazy bums to work no matter how you try." Fiddlesticks! Balderdash! Go to hell. Do what you want, but I repeat, please do something.'[129] These articles served numerous purposes. They were exposé articles calculated to be shocking (in this case, both language and content provide the readers with numerous jolts) and to peel back the layer of silence shrouding a contentious issue. The educational and informational value, as Bonnie Lee Morris's letter indicated, were another key purpose. They struck at the assumption of universal middle-classness in their attempt to enlighten and energize readers. To that end, the final instalment was the most successful. Adams's sights were set on exploding 'the myth that Canada is a middle-class country.'[130] Citing government surveys, statistical reports, and the Hellyer Task Force on Housing, Adams wrote: 'If you take the $8,000 a year figure of 1961 as where the idealized middle-class Canadian family-life begins ... then you are confronted with the inescapable conclusion that in 1965 more than 60 per cent of Canadian families lived below the economic level where middle-class life begins.' Affluence, according to Adams, was chimerical. Most Canadians had to go into debt to participate in the 'good life,' and, for some, life on the instalment plan was beyond reach. Faithful reader, these articles screamed, you are part of the silent majority of working-class and poor Canadians. That articles so clearly at odds with the advertising would be a featured series in separate issues clearly refuted *Chatelaine*'s position as a primer on the good life in Canada.

Readers' reactions to these bleak, gritty portraits were mixed and the article about the welfare mother elicited little sympathy. Mrs K.M. McNeil of Mabou, NS, wrote: 'I certainly didn't "enjoy" "The Real Poor in Canada Are Women" but I am glad you printed it. It needs to be shouted from the rooftops!'[131] Nina Leclerc of West Hill, Ontario, thought it would have achieved greater effectiveness if it had been published in the business press. 'Once again a heartrending feature on the plight of so many Canadian mothers in a woman's magazine and once again the usual advice: Women will have to ... etc. Organizing takes time and strength; where will those overburdened and defeated women find either? The strong must take care of the weak, or what are men all about otherwise? If an article of such overwhelming importance were printed in the business sections of our papers ... it might arouse some action.'[132] Her assessment that *Chatelaine* was preaching to the converted was one that many readers would make, but other evidence suggested that these articles did make their way through the system, ending up in university classes, government offices, and on ministers' desks, all through the informal network of shared magazines, magazine clippers, and letter writers. Miriam Hutton of Winnipeg assured the magazine, 'I am going to make your article required reading for all the social work students I teach ... I wish it could be required reading for every women's group in the country.'[133] Conversely, Mrs Gary W. Phillips of Creston, BC, was affronted by the article and complained: 'If your purpose was to turn the public even more against welfare recipients, then I'm sure you succeeded. The one and only question that woman should be asking herself is, Does any man or woman have the right to lay claim to the pay cheque of another? The answer is no!'[134] However, Joan Gagnon of Ottawa wrote to attest to the accuracy of the piece: 'This is one of the most interesting and factual pieces of literature written. As a recipient of Mother's Allowance I agree wholeheartedly. One interesting thing she failed to mention is the fact that there are a number of recipients, such as myself, who were taxpayers for over fifteen years.'[135] Only Mrs D.C. Kerr of Chatham, Ontario, noticed the contradictions implied by the publication of such an article in a general interest women's magazine as well as the jarring juxtaposition so common in popular culture between totally divergent articles and advertising content: '*Chatelaine* always provides food for thought, but the May issue gave me indigestion with the combination of "Does the Queen Need a Raise?" and "It's Hell on Welfare: A Mother's Story." I just couldn't work up much pity for the Queen after reading about a mother and seven children living on $70 a week. Dignity is something every human needs. Why does it mean castles and servants for one and a washing machine that works for another? Both women are supported by taxes. I'm not against royalty – just for ordinary people.'[136] Wisely, the magazine refrained from trying to answer Mrs Kerr's question.

'Women in Canada': Regional Snapshots

In a similar vein, the magazine also probed the nature of regional difference and disparity.[137] The featured series 'Women in Canada,' which began in 1966, focused the journalistic gaze on a region or province every few months. Writer Catherine Breslin made an effort to meet and interview a diverse assortment of women for each region, both urban and rural dwellers, and representatives of upper, middle, and working classes (though they were not referred to as such). The articles were usually popular outside of the region, but those from the featured region were highly critical. For instance, in the 'Women of Nova Scotia,' Breslin profiled seven women: Laney Kohler of Lunenburg, whose husband was a sea captain; teenager Sharon Warner of Port Hawksbury, whose father worked as a toll collector on the Canso Causeway; Teresa McNeil, a home economist at St Francis Xavier University in Antigonish; Ivy Bower of Upper Ohio, a single senior who worked as a licensed hunting guide; Elizabeth Reddick and Maxine Gough from Halifax, who were both schoolteachers and, as black Nova Scotians, told a tale of bigotry and prejudice; and Catherine McKinnon, a Halifax swinger and singer.[138] This excerpt, complete with statements from Bower, gives an indication of Breslin's style as well as the 'characters' she interviewed. 'Ivy Bower laid down the rifle she had been cleaning and slid a pan of biscuits into the oven. "I'm one of those that always loved the woods," she said. "But there ain't no sport left to it." ... Bower belongs to a vanishing breed too: the kind of Nova Scotian who has been called "hard as nails, soft as butter, and independent as pigs on ice." At 68, she is still scratching out a living as a licensed guide. "I don't like the cities and I don't like the towns and I don't like anybody that does. But up here we got a lot of friends, and there's always the open door."'

Outside Nova Scotia, Bower and the others made for fascinating, if voyeuristic, reading. The women profiled did not conform to the traditional style for this sort of regional piece (respectable housewives, volunteer workers, and wealthy elderly ladies of stature), but were individuals, characters even, who represented a diverse group of Nova Scotian women. Joyce E. McElroy of Calgary wrote, 'I am especially enjoying your women of Canada series,' undoubtedly because Breslin had not arrived in Alberta at the time McElroy posted her letter.[139] For Brenda Bravery of West Ewell, Surrey, England, the feature on Nova Scotia reminded her of her summer vacation and summoned up wonderful memories: 'I was fortunate enough to visit Nova Scotia last year, and it was truly beautiful, and the women were incredible, wonderful hostesses, cooks, and homemakers.'[140] Apparently she was not troubled by the discrepancy between the women she met and those she read about in the article.

Readers from Nova Scotia, however, were horrified. This letter from Marie Woodworth of Berwick, NS, enumerated their complaints:

> Catherine Breslin did a very poor job of representing the women of Nova Scotia. Tourists planning to visit our fair province may expect to see elderly ladies running around the woods with rifles, teen-agers hanging around corners with nothing to do, few young people with fewer dates, small fishing and steel-working villages, only one city, excuse the expression, Halifax, and lonely wives waiting at home for their husbands to return from sea. What of the other areas of the province: Annapolis Valley, Cabot Trail, South Shore, and the rising areas of the province? We are intelligent, happy, successful people with modern living facilities as other parts of Canada. I can't wait to read your future articles on Canada. I won't know whether to believe them or not.[141]

She felt the magazine made them look foolish, less 'modern' and 'developed' than they really were, and that the profiles of unique individuals were unrepresentative of Nova Scotian women.[142] Another reader, P. MacKenzie Campbell of Sydney, NS, complained of the stereotypical portrait: 'Why do writers harp on such exaggerated phrases as "the barren coal-and-steel stretches of Cape Breton Island?" I have seen more scars along the Toronto waterfront adjoining the highway leading from the main city to Scarborough, and I don't mean this as a pun.'[143] One of the special Centennial series quickly turned into a exercise in letter writing in defence of the reader's region against the Upper Canadian *Chatelaine* reporter who had 'got it wrong.' What could be more quintessentially Canadian?

The other articles continued in the same style and usually elicited nothing but derision from the profiled province. The most vociferous commentary came after the publication of 'The Women of British Columbia' in February 1968.[144] The subtitle, 'On this beautiful last frontier, there's often hardship and loneliness – but the reward is a free and individual life,' was a fitting summation of six of the seven women profiled. It did not prepare readers for the seventh, Georgina Archie, a Native Canadian resident of 'Skid Row' in Vancouver: 'At 21 ... Archie can summarize her life with a small but appalling collection of statistics. She's borne and lost three sons. She's been arrested 25 times "by rough guess," jailed about a dozen. She's cut her wrists three times, once collapsed from an overdose of drugs. Angry, turbulent, compassionate, Georgina stands as a living indictment of the double bind of poverty and racism in Canada.' Undoubtedly, the magazine's purpose in including Archie was to highlight the plight of Native Canadians, not to pillory them, nor to suggest that Archie was representative of all Native Canadian women, yet Aboriginal and white readers alike were angered by the negative portrait. Ethel Brant Monture of Middleport, Ontario, complained: 'The article "Women of British Columbia" was a sadness to us Indian readers. Why was such a pitiful creature chosen to represent us when B.C. has many Indian women we could view with pride? The article was not a dissertation on prostitution in B.C., which "vocation" has many other than Indian there. We continue to wonder why the Canadian news media deny us the racial courtesy given to other citizens.'[145] The magazine's goal of presenting diverse portraits of Canadian womanhood had backfired completely: each region (or in this case, race) wanted the article to present a positive, glowing assessment of women in the region, as befitted a special series inaugurated as part of the Centennial celebrations. Miss Pearl Williams wrote to complain on behalf of the B.C. Conference Sub-Committee of the United Church of Canada: 'Surely Catherine Breslin knows that many Indian women are doing well in society and are making a fine contribution to Canadian life. To be fair, why did she not portray one of these?'[146] One reader, Mrs Beatrice Carroll of Wisteria, BC, was angered by immigrant groups in British Columbia, who were, in sixties' parlance, 'living the good life,' in contrast to Native Canadians: 'The plight of Georgina Archie typifies the plight of many of our native women in beautiful British Columbia, where women from Germany, and China live the good life. "A log cabin out in the woods away from everybody" ... Bless her, the dream of thousands the world over. I hope she attains it, it should be hers by legacy.'[147]

In defence of their series, the editors printed this afterword under the last letter: 'The Women of Canada ... has featured three Indian women: Phyllis Gibson of Regina, a part-time nurse and mother ... Barbara Stevenson of Winnipeg, a high school graduate with a commercial art diploma ... However, not all Indian women have happy stories to tell, and with Georgina Archie we presented the other side.'[148] As these excerpts from the series and reader commentary indicated, the articles on region and on Canada in general were seldom puff pieces that glorified the status quo unconditionally or presented idealized versions of Canadian womanhood. They epitomized the peculiarly Canadian trait of taking pride in diversity and difficulty, and were not merely hagiographic articles about the bounty, beauty, or people of the nation. But for many readers, they failed to present air-brushed portraits of their region, as they wished to see them presented to other readers across the country – as modern, prosperous, safe, congenial, and, ultimately, as good places to live.

'Why I Left Canada': Canadiana and Canadian Nationalism

One place readers were usually assured of a 'positive' piece of Canadiana was in the historical articles. Profiles of famous families of Canada such as the Molsons, Eatons, and Dunsmuirs, or of Canadian women such as Susanna Moodie and Catherine Parr Traill, delivered the type of articles readers demanded: positive, affirming articles that glorified individuals and families, and paid tribute to Canada's past.[149]

The magazine resisted publishing articles on modern Canada that were purely complimentary or without critical commentary about improvements, whether political, cultural, economic, or social. One of the most controversial articles published on Canada, written by a young Canadian author named Mordecai Richler, was entitled simply 'Why I Left Canada.'[150] Both the bombast and sarcasm typical of Richler's later essays are present as he decried the 'cultural and political backwater' where theatre and novels were classified as 'amateurish' or 'unspeakably bad,' 'mistrust' prevailed, and 'prosperity on the installment plan ... seems to be the norm.' His parting blow was reserved for the state of mind and the growing similarities between Canada and the United States. 'Look here, it's indisputable that Canadians on all levels are better off materially than people are in Europe but they also seem less happy, more incomplete. Leisure is a chore. The people I know go about their pleasure with a dreary obligatory air. It appears to me that in America today, and in this instance (and indeed in many others) the difference between American and Canadian is negligible, everything must be good for you ... It seems that little is done for its own sake or simply because it's enjoyable.' Vintage Richler, the essay was intended to rile feathers and to get Canadians thinking about their national self-absorption and smugness.

Not surprisingly, some readers were irate, others were bemused, and still others, although they represented the minority opinion, heartily agreed. Donna E. Gerlach of Regina, in an unintentionally ironic yet no less delightful response, asked, 'Who is he, anyway?'[151] Miss K.M. Graws of Sydney, NS, had a similar question: 'Why did he come back, and when may we have the pleasure of his leaving again?'[152] Mrs K.A. Godenir of Ponteix, Saskatchewan, attributed Richler's dyspeptic essay to his lack of awareness of other regions and her belief that 'perhaps, to date, he has met and mingled with the wrong people.'[153] No one was more affronted or disturbed by Richler's article than Mrs A. Hanley of White Rock, BC, whose passionate, angry letter threatened: 'If someone does not asphyxiate Mordecai Richler soon, I shall probably be forced to do it myself ... When I consider how five generations of my family worked and suffered to make Canada a great country, I know just how the Congolese feel. The least you can do is protect your country from the insults of others.'[154] Semantically at least, Mrs Hanley stripped Richler of his citizenship for his blasphemous article. However, sprinkled among the anti-Richler letters were some complimentary ones. These were readers who, while not necessarily in agreement with all his comments, recognized the satirical nature and the purpose of such articles. Mrs R.E. Clubbe of Ottawa sent this assessment: 'I heartily congratulate you on a most amusingly written and very, very true insight into the Canadian way of life. I, a backward European (English), have lived here for five years, and if I had the gift of expressing my thoughts as you have, I would have written exactly the same.'[155] Similarly, Mrs J. Wiszniowski of St Catharines wrote: 'Bravo! Many, many thanks for that genuine article. It was the most daring lecture and how very, very real.'[156] In a mass-circulation periodical it was impossible to satisfy all readers and, as controversial articles attested, a little controversy was good for business – it drew in new readers, got faithful readers fired up, made the magazine a lively read, and the letters page an even livelier forum of correspondence. The magazine often embraced this tactic with respect to the country, whether to get readers to think critically about the nation's attributes and problems or to provide jolts to readers – many of whom were devoted nationalists – which then reverberated onto the letters page. Just because one of *Chatelaine's* key selling features was its Canadian origin, it did not necessarily follow that all articles reflected the country to the readers through rose-coloured glasses.

'The Good Life on $6500 a Year': Suburbia and Slobs Revisited

Although the magazine strove to push the Canadian angle in the majority of its feature articles, the annual family budgeting specials published each January and the Mrs Chatelaine articles published each May also permitted readers a view of how women and families in different regions lived. One of the consistent complaints about the family budget special was that the families selected from requests in the mail bag had higher incomes than the majority of Canadian families. Even when the magazine paid close attention to selecting families with the median Canadian income, a large portion of the readers were disgusted that such 'high-income' Canadians were selected. This letter from an Ottawa reader, Mrs J.C. Bradley, represents many of those critical readers who remembered another time and place when the values of thrift, and not conspicuous consumption, carried the day. 'In January I was amazed that you spent nine pages on a family that rushed blindly into debt. In my neighbourhood when I was a child, the families had a cow, chickens, a garden and the mothers always baked their bread and cake, pies, etc. The clothes were always sewn by the mothers. Not so much money, but wisely used and planned.' The retort from the associate editor, Jean Yack, while polite, illustrates the tensions that surfaced each year around the popular, yet problematic, feature: 'Today's urban middle-class families don't have cows, face stronger social pressures to own more, achieve more (hence spend – and sometimes borrow – more). The Daubenys, we felt, were typical of such families, and our suggestions for them would help many Canadians.'[157] Older readers, and readers from rural areas of the country, were most likely to criticize the income levels and 'planned consumption' that often categorized these features. They felt little compassion for those pressured into debt by their penchant for pacing the neighbours purchase for purchase.

In 1968 the Craig family of Brampton, Ontario, was in the budget spotlight. Grace Craig wrote to the magazine after reading about the 1967 budget family, the Beausejours of Toronto, because her husband's detailed analysis of the Beausejours's budget and spending plans revealed that the Craig family of six ate for substantially less per week than the Beausejours family of four. In this update letter to the *Chatelaine* staff in 1969, Grace Craig provided insight into the fishbowl that budget families were thrust into and the unreal nature of the experience:

Doing the story was like a trip to a different planet where ordinary words no longer have the same meaning. Ask my husband. He's the one who noticed our food costs were just half of those of the previous budget family. We wrote to *Chatelaine*, and were chosen for the feature. The strangest day was spent taking fashion pictures. There was no one there I knew, not even myself transformed by a two-hour makeup job, radically new glasses, and a professional hairdo. We were amazed at the variety of response to the article. We had inquiries about the procedure for overseas adoptions, exchange of ideas of coeliac diets, requests for knitting patterns used for my red dress. The funniest reaction was that of the people who said flatly we did not exist! We still feed our growing family of six for $75 a month ... I revamped my whole wardrobe: five new knitted dresses, two new pairs of high boots, and a new winter coat ... The children needed many new things and Alan needed new lab coats and trousers for school. Our total clothing bill last year for the six of us was exactly $373.37.[158]

The Craigs' experience was typical of many budget families, Mrs Chatelaine winners, and others accorded featured status in the magazine. Years later they were still writing update letters to the editors or dropping by to see them, an obvious indication of their continuing delight with their own personal *Chatelaine* moment. Craig's brief commentary about the experience indicated that, although many of the photos of real people (as opposed to models) were seemingly 'natural' or 'down to earth,' they were still creations of the art director, photographers, and departmental editors.

Alan and Grace Craig, as Grace's commentary hinted, were a very different budget family (illustration 41). They met as students at the University of Toronto. They bought their first 'cash book' for logging all family expenses at the University of Toronto Bookstore; appropriately enough, it was on sale, and ten years later they were still using that system. Along with their own biological children, Shelagh (8) and Geordie (6), the couple had adopted two more: Anitra (4), a refugee from Hong Kong, and Theo (2), a 'mixed-racial child.'[159] Although they were currently living in Brampton, Alan had held pastorates in Hardisty, Alberta, Toronto, and rural Ontario. The blurb for the story – 'Alan and Grace Craig live the good life by ignoring status symbols for the things they really want, and make more meaningful investments, such as an education for their children' – prepared readers for a budget couple with different goals from most. Quite simply, where other families were

41 *Chatelaine*, January 1968

caught up on the consumption treadmill, the Craigs preferred to steer their own course. They believed in saving up for purchases and not buying on instalment plans; purchased much of their food in bulk or at discounted or sale prices; had simple tastes in home furnishings, clothing, hobbies, and leisure (predominantly books, music, and crafts); and tithed a whopping 11.2 per cent each month to the church and other charitable organizations. The editors undoubtedly believed that finally – after two decades' worth of criticism from readers about the profligate ways of budget families – they had found the perfect couple.

Most readers agreed. Mrs Elisabeth Harding of Nipigon, Ontario, was delighted with the choice of the Craigs. 'Congratulations. At last you have published a "how to live" article on a family, earning less than $8,000, that actually believes in giving to church and charities. I had wondered how many people, like ourselves, believed in sharing what they had. The Craigs have other similarities to our family also, in that they grow and freeze their own produce where possible.'[160] One of the chief criteria employed by Mrs Harding in her evaluation of the budget family's 'representativeness' was its similarity, in income and beliefs, to her own family. Mrs Etta L. van Nostrad of Gormley, Ontario, hailed the Craigs as 'a breath of fresh air' and concluded that there was 'still some hope for the human race.'[161] However, for Mrs Edward Hiebert of Cloverdale, BC, the Craigs were just too perfect: 'It is pure fiction, and I can't think of many housewives that will back up this statement.'[162] Although the editor was usually good about leaving 'the last word' to the readers, in this case she quickly jumped in lest other readers accept Mrs Hiebert's alternate reading of the Craig budget article. 'The Craig story is fact, not fiction. Four *Chatelaine* editors interviewed the Craigs and personally checked their statements and account books. A consulting nutritionist double-checked their menus and found them nutritionally sound. The Craigs do not regard themselves as, nor did we say they were, "modern Canadians." In fact they abhor the food waste so prevalent in developed countries ... While not all of us may prefer to live as economically as the Craigs, it can be done. They do it – and that was the point of telling their story.'[163] Although the *Chatelaine* editors rarely invoked closure on letters page debates, in this case they were not prepared to tolerate any hint of alternate or negative commentary. A family like the Craigs seldom ever came along, and the editor wanted to bask in this moderate, cautious approach to budgeting a little longer.

The Mrs Chatelaine winners, as the Mrs Slob letters in chapter 3 indicated, also suffered from questions of 'representation.' Of course, one housewife and her family could hardly be expected to represent the goals, ideals, styles, and dreams of all the readers, but many readers compared Mrs Chatelaine to themselves and often found her perfection repellent. Great care was taken in the selection of the winner and of the runners-up to avoid slighting one particular region or province. The winners came from almost all parts of the country – only British Columbia and the Territories did not have a grand prize winner during the decade, although they did have runners-up each year. The first winner, Mrs Joyce Saxton, hailed from the farming community of Plenty, Saskatchewan. She was followed by Josephine Ouellet of Sillery, Quebec; Florence E. Holt of Regina; Ethelyn Mosher of Middleton, NS; Leone Ross of Charlottetown; Elsie Lee Fraser of Calgary; Eva Hammond of St-Hilaire, Quebec; Diane McLeod of Toronto; and Bettie Hall of Montreal. All of them had a number of children and, with the exception of Bettie Hall, were active in community, church, and cultural events in their respective communities. According to the supplementary information the editor provided each year, the contest continued to be extremely popular and many women entered in multiple years. For example, Mrs Henriette Van Der Bregen of Weyburn, Saskatchewan, was selected as provincial runner-up three years in a row.[164] For the winners, the Mrs Chatelaine experience proved very enjoyable. This letter, from winner Ethelyn Mosher of Nova Scotia gave some indication of the prestige, interest, and even international acclaim accorded the winners. 'Being Mrs Chatelaine is one of the nicest things that has ever happened to me. When the excitement has died down, I know the memory of this happy time will give pleasure to my family and to me for many years to come. There have been letters, cards, and telegrams from every province in Canada, with the exception of Newfoundland, and many from the United States and Brazil.'[165] One of the runners-up, Mrs Marjorie E. Hallman of Pictou, NS (Nova Scotia's runner-up for 1963), had fond recollections, stating: '*Chatelaine* has been resource, teacher, companion and friend. Also has reinforced my self-esteem when I made it as runner up in the "Mrs Chatelaine Contest."'[166] For each Ethelyn Mosher and Marjorie Hallman, of course, there were plenty of sore losers and proud slobs who continued to share their views each year in the letters page of the magazine.

One reader, Marianne Fenton-Marr, nominated herself as 'Mrs Chatelaine' in her letter to the editors. 'I hereby appoint myself *Chatelaine* woman of the year,' she wrote. 'I live in an ordinary bungalow. I have one child and two foster children. I bake all my own bread, cakes, pies and cookies. I make good nourishing soups. I make all the clothes. I make my husband's shirts. I knit sweaters, make hats for myself. I do all my own washing and ironing. I take my boy to hockey, baseball and lacrosse. In summer holidays we go camping. I do lots of gardening, make fruit into jams and jellies. Oh, I almost forgot. I teach my children and several neighbours' children the violin. Will you ever publish this letter? Of course not, but I got it off my chest.'[167] Obviously a human dynamo around the home, either Fenton-Marr was a disconsolate loser in the contest or never entered, believing that her chances of winning were not good because she was not actively involved in volunteer or community projects. Another reader, Mrs Houston of Bowmanville, Ontario, complained: 'How sweet, goody, goody and religious do you have to become to be able to measure up to your average Mrs Chatelaine winner? How original, they all are, with their Home and School, Scouts and Guides, Sunday schools, etc. ... Well then, a big handshake to lousy housekeepers like me, who reads a book while she should be waxing floors.'[168] Fenton-Marr got a response, although not the one she was looking for, from Mrs John Barrett of Hearts Delight, Newfoundland, who wrote: 'Here's happy reading to Mrs G. Houston of Bowmanville, Ontario, from one lousy housekeeper to another. Long may she wave her book, and I don't care if Marianne Fenton-Marr drowns in her good nourishing soups and balls herself up in her hand-knitted sweaters. Here's to our side.'[169] The perfectionists might have won the contest, but it certainly appeared that those who sided with the 'slobs' took just as much pleasure, perhaps more, in ridiculing it and sanctimonious writers like Fenton-Marr. The success of the contest had less to do with the number of entrants or the calibre of the winners, but with the substantial amount of interest it generated in the magazine. Certainly, it fostered a sense of community among entrants and letter writers alike. We will never know whether Mrs Houston wrote to Mrs Barrett personally after her letter appeared in the magazine, but it was clear that theirs was a friendship or alliance formed in response to and aided by the magazine. As Mrs Mosher's commentary made clear, many readers, having been introduced to other readers through the pages of the magazine, felt free to write personal letters to them.

Contested Celebrity: Regions v. the Centre

If several average Canadian women were made into celebrities by their inclusion in various *Chatelaine* feature or departmental articles, it was equally clear that many Canadian celebrities shared their personal lives, goals, and sometimes autobiographies with the *Chatelaine* community. There were profiles of American celebrities – Elizabeth Taylor, that sixties' 'vixen,' was featured in two articles – but the majority were Canadians. Juliette, Marg Osbourne, Don Messer, Fred Davis, Gordon Sinclair, Pierre Berton, Tommy Hunter, and others all had their day in the magazine, usually accompanied by a cover photo. Other than the glamorous Juliette or the blustery portraits of Sinclair and Berton, the majority of articles on Canadian celebrities stressed their quintessentially down-to-earth qualities. Jas. I. Allen of Bechard, Saskatchewan, wrote: 'My heartfelt appreciation to Christina McCall for her fine and appropriate write-up on Don Messer. Everyone in Messer's outfit are real humans, no skittish malarkey or wisecracks to mar the human touch.'[170] Even those who were not able to watch the show on television were able to appreciate Messer and his Islanders on the radio, so also enjoyed the article. One such reader, Mrs Henry MacArthur of Bonilla Island Light Station, Prince Rupert, BC, wrote to thank the magazine: 'Enjoyed your article on Don Messer. Have listened to the islanders on radio for years and agree they are tops. The program is often interrupted here ... I can imagine the consternation of some opera-loving fans if their favourite program were interrupted.'[171] Her criticism of the CBC's programming, the divide between high-brow and popular culture, was reflected in the letter of another reader. However, Mrs Dennis Bude of Alma, Saskatchewan, spoke to the prevalent urban bias in the article and the magazine: 'I wondered at the lack of consideration of the rural woman in so many of your leading articles. I don't after this article. First of all, the music of Don Messer is not country corn. It is the very music of the pioneers. The country music which is on the hit parade may be called corn. The old reels and waltzes which Messer plays are not. Perhaps if *Chatelaine* were to delve more deeply into the countrywoman's life, it would find less rubbish than it thinks ... We are homemakers before we are rubes.'[172] Like so many others before her, Mrs Bude believed that the magazine should be aiming for readers just like her. When the magazine missed the mark, these subscribers were quick to write, claiming that the periodical was not representative of Canadian women. In the case of rural women, this criticism was often true: they rarely appeared in the magazine articles despite their continued presence on the letters page.

Conclusion

As in the previous decade, the editorials and articles printed in *Chatelaine* during the sixties were wide ranging in their examination and critique of the roles of Canadian women. Still, there was a noticeable shift to more explicit feminism in the editorials and, in the general feature articles, towards a more activist stance. Via the editorial pages, feminist ideas were disseminated to a mass audience of girls, women, and men. By the end of the decade, all regular readers were conversant with the goals of second-wave feminism and many seemed to have become converts, particularly to issues such as pay equity, changes in women's legal status, and the importance of the women's voice in politics and the workplace. While some readers welcomed this new direction, others were tired of the magazine's 'inciting revolutions.' Without doubt, the inclusion of an editorial, and particularly the feminist subject matter, differentiated *Chatelaine* from its American competitors. Although feminist ideas were prioritized in the editorial essays, they formed only one of a number of issues and topics for the general feature articles. Similarly, the general feature articles educated and entertained readers on a vast number of topics – illicit drugs, sexuality, gender roles, employment opportunities for women, poverty, racism, reproductive issues, and the less contentious issues of national history, Canadian identity, regional differences, Canadian and American celebrities, and changes in the private world of the household. The articles gave *Chatelaine* a breadth of appeal quite astonishing for a woman's magazine.

Divergent content is only half the story. The responses of readers to this material indicate that, while many people applauded this new activist direction, an equal number of critics frowned on the changes both in the magazine and, more pointedly, in women's lives. The debates carried out on the letters page of the magazine (a precursor of e-mail bulletin boards) demonstrate that the community of readers was far from unified. Age, class, region, race, and ideological perspective often caused rifts within the readership, yet these readers generally stuck with the magazine. Today, critics would be quick to bail out in search of other more amenable reads.

The unheralded role that *Chatelaine* played as a disseminator of second-wave feminist ideas is important to the march of feminist awareness and organizing in Canada. Clearly, many readers cut their feminist teeth on the *Chatelaine* articles and editorials. Although it is easy to celebrate this unconventional role that *Chatelaine* performed, it is important to remember that there were resisters to this message. *Chatelaine* deserves its place in the history of the second-wave feminist campaign in Canada, but many readers were not amused by this ideological shift. 'Closet feminism,' as Doris Anderson has referred to this shift, was not without risks, and the greatest risk of all was that the editor might take the campaign too far and alienate a core of readers. Although editorial fatigue and renewal are cited as the primary reasons for the change in the late seventies from Anderson's 'closet feminism' to Mildred Istona's glossy fashion magazine, another important reason was reader fatigue. Circulation statistics had begun to fall as some readers tired of activism and longed for a return to a more entertaining tone.

Chapter 9

'Here in the Lodge':
Chatelaine's Legacy

In the fifties and sixties, during *Chatelaine*'s heyday, the magazine created a community of readers, writers, and editors who explored the changing nature of women's lives. Canadian women's lives were in flux, and the editors and writers experienced this transition period – from the stay-at-home world of the suburbs to the world of working wives and mothers – along with their readers. The novelty of the situation, the isolation of suburbia, and rapid-paced changes in living all heightened the importance of *Chatelaine*. The paradoxical material and polysemic messages in the magazine were due to the challenges and uncertainties of the new roles and options facing women and to the editor's determination to make the material appealing to a mass audience of readers. Whether women agreed or disagreed with the magazine's coverage of feminism, employment opportunities, or the latest pseudo-scientific study of how best to clean their suburban bungalow, it was clear that in the 'lodge,' or women's club atmosphere created in the pages of *Chatelaine*, a wide variety of women's issues and experiences were discussed and debated. Entry into this national forum for women was economical and accessible, and a cross-section of women from all regions of the country, from rural and urban areas, from the middle and working classes, participated in the magazine.

This cultural history of *Chatelaine* in the fifties and sixties permits a number of conclusions about the process of production and consumption. First, incorporating the methodological insights of cultural studies and international magazine studies into the Canadian context provides conclusive proof that readers exercised a degree of control and power over this cultural product. The messages sent to readers by the various components of *Chatelaine* provided them with a complex portrait of

Canadian women. However, the readers were able to ignore the material (the low Starch scores for ad readership), resist the information (responses to the house-cleaning service features), reinterpret the components (the letters about Russell's fiction), enjoy the material (articles), criticize the ideology (editorials), or remove or destroy irritating images (cover art, articles). They did not passively accept the ideas, themes, suggestions for living, ideology, or entertainment aspects of the magazine. Power was not solely vested in the hands of the Maclean Hunter executives or editors, nor with the advertisers. Maclean Hunter's image of the magazine, as a profit generator and as a vehicle for advertisers, was not strong enough to overpower the agenda of the female editors and writers or to negate the readers' power. Despite the commercial messages of the advertisements and the tacit support given to advertisers by the departmental material, for example, those advertisers were never able to prevent the editors from removing all processed food products from the annual family budget specials. If the advertisers and business staff had exercised complete control over the messages in *Chatelaine*, they would have vetted all the material for messages that ran counter to their commercial ethos.

Ultimately, *Chatelaine* was a 'producerly text': it contained within its pages diverse ideas, opinions, and messages.[1] It encouraged readers to think about, and not just absorb, the material. It often offered 'clues' on how to read the magazine, such as 'Ten Fiction Plots We Can Do Without' or 'Here's Dirt in Your Eye, House,' which parodied the women's magazine genre. Articles and editorials such as those, or letters from readers, exposed contradictions in the material and actively encouraged readers to think critically and carefully about what they read. Furthermore, the community created by the magazine was based on gender, nationality, and readership – it transcended, but did not obliterate, differences of class, age, region, or race. Those demarcators, particularly class and age, would repeatedly expose fissures in the community and result in differing interpretations of the material, its purpose, and its effectiveness. With such a heterogeneous, mass audience, the magazine was unable to invoke closure over the multiple meanings and interpretations of its editorial pages. This study of *Chatelaine* has illustrated the vital importance of including reader responses to popular culture, particularly as a means of analyzing the popularity of the product and demonstrating the variety of ways in which consumers respond to prescriptive literature.

Another important theme in this study has been the tension between the competing and often contradictory commercial and editorial imperatives that characterize mass-magazine production. When Maclean Hunter created a commercial package to provide Canadian and North American advertisers with another vehicle to reach consumers, it did so to make a profit. From H.V. Tyrrell's first memo to Colonel Maclean about the financial feasibility of a new Canadian women's magazine, particularly its attractiveness to advertisers, the company's and the business department's ethos was clear. The publisher, the Maclean Hunter company, and the men who worked in the business department all sought to maximize returns at the magazine. To that end, they solicited as much advertising as possible and offered advertisers a variety of services to improve their chances of selling their products in the magazine. As well, the circulation department aggressively marketed subscriptions to the magazine to increase the number of readers. They also commissioned several studies of the magazine and paid for it to be 'Starched.' The commercial imperative was evident in the cover art and the ads, and it sometimes crept into the editors' commentary about fiction stories. The business department focused on the bottom line and concerned itself with the numbers – advertising pages, circulation statistics, Starch figures, and readership surveys. When those numbers were good, the publisher, the business staff, and Maclean Hunter executives were happy.

In contrast, the editorial imperative was not solely about numbers but also about people – the editors, the writers, and the readers. It would be far too deterministic to dismiss women's magazines, and *Chatelaine* in particular, simply because they were commercial products intended to produce a profit. That is only half the story. The other half is that the editors had their own agenda – to interest and speak to readers – which meant they were committed to creating a magazine that had the broadest possible appeal for Canadian women. There was some interaction between the publisher and the editor, and even some of the departmental editors, but, as archival letters indicate, the editors' authority in their realm was secure. The editorial and business staff were separated from each other by convention – business and editorial are two distinct and often antagonistic divisions within commercial magazines – and by gender. The result was a segregated and largely autonomous cadre of female editors and writers at Maclean Hunter who were pretty much left to their own devices when it came to planning, creating, and commissioning editorial material.

This situation was not the case at *Chatelaine*'s chief competitors, the

American mass-market women's magazines – *Ladies' Home Journal*, *McCall's*, *Good Housekeeping*, and *Redbook*. There female editors were the exception to the rule and, as the experience of Lenore Hershey indicated, men were in the top positions at most of these magazines. The frustration with the glass ceiling and editorial practices at the mass-market women's magazines formed part of the impetus for the creation of *Ms.* magazine. With huge subscription bases, and backed by the deep pockets of their corporations, the big American women's magazines, and their editors, created glossy, affluent periodicals geared to upper-middle-class American housewives and mothers. *Family Circle* and *Woman's Day* (the supermarket magazines) were smaller, more affordable periodicals that offered readers feasible family dinners, craft ideas, and a few feature articles. These general-interest women's magazines were in trouble in the fifties and sixties as television syphoned away advertisers. Equally important, the mass-market magazines had difficulty adjusting to the times and began to lose readers to more narrowly focused competitors. Two of the most popular magazines of the era, *Playboy* (launched in 1953) and *Cosmopolitan* (remodeled in 1965), did not attempt to be mass-market magazines but successfully marketed their periodical for a specific and limited demographic group. Niche marketing, not mass marketing, became one of the chief criteria for the commercial success of most American magazines – a situation that is even more true of the magazine publishing industry today.

In contrast, Maclean Hunter's commitment to hiring strong female editors (Sanders, Dempsey, and most particularly Anderson) created a magazine that was attuned to Canadian women and felt itself responsible to them. It was also, unlike its American competition, a commercial success. Only during the John Clare era at the magazine did the circulation and advertising numbers falter. This pattern indicates that a committed female editor played a key role in *Chatelaine*'s success. As well, the editorial vision is chiefly responsible for the tone of the magazine – the conservative, more traditional, ideology apparent in the magazine in both the pre- and post-Anderson eras indicates that the editor's vision was very important to *Chatelaine*'s tone and content.[2] Buttressed by the findings of the Dichter Study, which encouraged Maclean Hunter to make the magazine more pro-active and not reactive, Doris Anderson reformulated the periodical into one that combined a wide variety of material – one Anderson herself later called a 'closet feminist magazine.'

The legacy of *Chatelaine*'s decision to include feminist articles and editorials, as well as the other general feature articles on topics such as birth control, abortion, lesbianism, menopause, and women's sexuality, should not be underestimated. *Chatelaine* reached a mass audience of women and disseminated its mixed messages far more effectively, respectably, and affordably than any other format could or did. As well, for women outside urban areas, where access to libraries, social services, and other resources was limited, the magazine provided them with the 'new' information. *Chatelaine* played a unique role in cultivating a mass-market audience for second-wave feminist ideas, worked as a champion for women (lobbying for the Status of Women Commission), and educated readers about the discriminatory nature of Canadian society. No American women's magazines were in the forefront of the feminist movement there, nor did they consistently illuminate and popularize feminist ideas.

June Callwood has stated, as have other commentators and academics, that Doris Anderson must be given considerable credit for the service her editorials and article selection had upon the promulgation of feminist ideas in Canada during the late fifties, sixties, and seventies.[3] Of course, *Chatelaine* was not the only source for feminist ideas in the sixties – television, radio, and newspapers would offer sporadic coverage of these issues. But, given *Chatelaine*'s large national audience, its commitment to publicizing feminist ideas, the dearth of Canadian or American feminist magazines, the lack of attention to feminist issues in mass-market U.S. women's magazines, and the small number of women's organizations until the mid to late sixties, *Chatelaine* performed an important role.

The Hilliard/Callwood articles of the mid to late fifties, along with Anderson's editorials and the articles written by Christina McCall in the early sixties, all predate the publication of Betty Friedan's *Feminine Mystique*. Those articles and editorials anticipate and enumerate much of Friedan's thesis, clearly claiming a spot for *Chatelaine* in the history of second-wave feminism in Canada. By the end of the sixties, readers had matriculated through a course of feminism that included such issues as legislative inequity, birth control and abortion information, equal pay for equal work, the systemic sexism of Canadian society, and the valorization of women's sexuality. The inclusion of feminist material was not always appreciated and sometimes vociferously criticized, but it led to an atmosphere of anticipation about the magazine and to a spirit of discovery and growth. The progression in the articles and in Anderson's editorials indicates that this was a journey undertaken by the writers, editors, and readers which strengthened the spirit of community.

In comparison to the heady days of the sixties and early seventies, when regular instalments of feminist articles and editorials created an aura of excitement about *Chatelaine*, the magazine changed considerably after Anderson's retirement in 1977. Even the most casual conversation about this study inevitably leads to the question, 'Well what happened to *Chatelaine*?' The first and easiest answer is that the magazine has changed and, rightly or wrongly, *Chatelaine* now offer readers a more fashion-driven periodical where political or feminist issues appear infrequently. Another answer might be that feminist issues are not part of the 'agenda' of the current editors. Yet a simplistic answer like that overlooks the inevitability of change – in the world of magazines and in the lives of Canadian women. When *Chatelaine* included feminist material in the fifties and sixties, that was noteworthy, and clearly atypical for women's magazines. *Chatelaine* was also riding a wave of interest in the political excitement and potential of second-wave feminism. It did not create a movement, but savily responded to changes in women's lives and the tenor of the times.

What was new and exciting in the fifties and sixties, however, appeared dated by the late seventies. Anderson herself admitted that she had lost interest in the message and the magazine, and, having covered most of the issues of second-wave feminism, that that focus was stale. Advertisers and readers were also dropping off, so a repositioning or a face lift was necessary. Mildred Istona, Anderson's successor, deserves credit for turning the periodical around – but to do so, she went in the opposite direction, emphasizing fashion and entertainment. Most recently, Rona Maynard has attempted to nudge the magazine in a slightly different direction – towards the community aspect of old, with more emphasis on articles and issues – though she has not abandoned the fashion and 'youthful' appeal of the Istona days. What should be clear, both from this study and from the subsequent situation, is that editing a mass-market women's magazine is not about an editor setting a course, then dragging the readers along in her wake. The readers must find the messages compelling and interesting, or they will leave in search of other options. Regardless of how many might long for a return to *Chatelaine*'s heyday, the feminist movement and feminism is no longer newsworthy or exciting for the vast majority of women. In these post-feminist days, a magazine with a predominantly feminist message will be a tough sell – witness the challenges at *Ms.*, where making feminism appealing to a mass audience of readers is an ongoing struggle.[4] Equally overlooked in the commentary about the 'decline' of *Chatelaine* are the strides made by television, the creation of other Canadian women's magazines (*Homemakers* and *Canadian Living* in particular), and the move towards more specialized magazines, all of which have eroded the importance and prestige once accorded to *Chatelaine* in the fifties and sixties.

The second important legacy of the magazine in the fifties and sixties was the significance of the *Chatelaine* community in providing a sense of connection for many Canadian women. The letters to the magazine, the contests, the kinship subscription base, the appreciation of Canadians abroad, the community recognition, the *Chatelaine* Councillors, and the cross-country visits of writers and editors all indicate the prestige attached to reading the magazine and participating in the community. This aspect of a women's pop cultural product, and the community of users and creators who sustained it, is one that has been overlooked in the past. Despite the fact that the magazine's content was routinely mentioned on radio shows, in newspapers, in schools, and social service departments, and sometimes made its way, via industrious clippers, to ministers and politicians, it is *Maclean's* which has been accorded the position of the prestigious, important magazine of the era. Historians have neglected *Chatelaine*, much as the Maclean Hunter executives did, because they have not realized that, beneath its conventional cover and format, lurked an unconventional women's magazine. Interspersed among articles on dieting, fashion, child care, and casserole recipes were articles, editorials, and even some fiction that succinctly and consistently questioned the status quo of Canadian women.

Letters printed in the magazine and in archival collections enumerate how important the magazine was to its readers. It was a magazine to be read, in the evocative phrase of Grace A. Bontaine, in 'that precious hour of peace and afternoon tea, when all the troublesome tasks are done – the children are not yet home from school – and it's too early to think about dinner.'[5] Readers wrote to the magazine to suggest article topics and to critique or praise articles, editorials, fiction, departmental fare, and, far less often, the cover art or advertisements. Those letters, in turn, often encouraged others to reread the controversial articles or reexamine a cover photo. Readers' letters shaped the art of reading the magazine and were the major means of communication among members of the community. They also provided the inspiration for some articles and service department material, and played a role in 'creating' or 'inspiring' material in the magazine. The letters page functioned like a print precursor of e-mail and indicated a high level of interaction and enjoyment of the comments, criticisms, and thoughts of other readers. Starch figures show that it was an eagerly read component of the magazine.

However, the letters page was not the only manifestation of the *Chatelaine* community in action. *Chatelaine* material was used by social services and educational departments across the country. Previews of the new issues and household tips were provided on women's radio chat shows. Sometimes women's groups visited the *Chatelaine* offices in Toronto. More often, the editors or writers made trips across the country, talking and meeting with readers in their own communities. All these interactions strengthened the bond between readers and the magazine. In addition, the 2000-strong group of *Chatelaine* Councillors regularly responded to surveys and questionnaires from the magazine which sought to evaluate the material, discern life-style trends, and provide future editorial suggestions.

Chatelaine contests (Family Favourites, Mrs Chatelaine, and others) were extremely popular, and they, too, encouraged reader participation. Even those who did not enter the contests enjoyed using other readers' recipes or reading about the winners. The more creative and critical readers – such as 'Mrs. Slob' Beatrice Maitland – created anti-contests, much to the delight of the other 'slobs' across the country. The Mrs Chatelaine Contest is an excellent example of how the preferred meaning – the valorization of the perfect housekeeper and community volunteer – was given an alternate interpretation by the dedicated group of slobs. Thus, a contest dedicated to rewarding a very traditional view of women's roles backfired as it quickly became more popular to be a part of the slob team that mocked the contest and ridiculed the winners' middle-class perfectionism. These contests brought the 'real' women into the magazine and, whether accompanied by before-and-after pictures, or makeover essays, shrewdly allowed readers to participate in 'making the periodical.' Women who were featured in the magazine invariably described the experience as a memorable one and reported that other readers from all over the country had written to congratulate them on their success. The hometowns of the winners also lauded and celebrated their success. Taken together, the contests and the contestants are proof of the prestige that was accorded to *Chatelaine* at the time and the enthusiasm for participation in the community created by the magazine.

Another more informal indication of the *Chatelaine* community was the process by which new members were brought into the fold. Many letters from readers suggest that subscriptions to the magazine were common presents in female kinship networks (mothers, daughters, grand-daughters, sisters, and cousins) or among friends. The letters from foreign readers or from Canadians living abroad always detailed how their family or friends provided them with a gift subscription. For them, the magazine was 'a little of home.' Other letters, and the *CARD* data, provide evidence of a sizable pass-along audience of readers. The original subscriber often had networks of friends with whom she exchanged magazines and, in the case of magazines going overseas, these networks were often elaborate. The final destination of some of these well-travelled, well-read issues was as donations to hospital waiting rooms, doctors' offices, or volunteer agencies, where popular reading material was at a premium.

Another distinctive aspect of the *Chatelaine* community was its heterogeneity. Despite the fact that the magazine was produced in Toronto, its appeal was nationwide. Most of the readers were anglophones, but a goodly number of francophones, First Nations people, and newcomers were also reading the magazine. Critics of women's magazines have depicted the readership as largely middle-class, suburban readers, but, in the case of *Chatelaine*, this generalization was inaccurate. In the fifties, the reader surveys indicated that the magazine had a large proportion of working-class, unemployed, and retired readers, as well as dedicated rural subscribers. In the sixties, the numbers of more affluent readers increased, paralleling the general rise in Canadian incomes in the decade, but 79.3 per cent of all *Chatelaine* readers still came from the lower-middle-class group and, in regional breakdowns, rural readers still represented 30 per cent of all subscribers. Time and again, comparisons to statistical averages for the era prove that readers were average, not affluent, Canadians.

'In the lodge,' as journalist Eileen Morris described *Chatelaine* magazine, Canadian women were writing, reading, and grappling with many important (and many not-so-important) issues.[6] Those issues changed the way many women regarded their roles, their aspirations, and their dreams for their daughters. Arguably, *Chatelaine* had more of an impact on Canadian women in the fifties and sixties than previously credited. A historical microstudy of consumers, creators, and producers of *Chatelaine* demonstrates the historical importance of the text, particularly the magazine's role as a forum for feminist ideas. It also provides a detailed portrait of the conjuncture of events that allowed the editors so great a degree of editorial autonomy. But most important, this study offers a detailed portrait of a cultural community of Canadian women. The 'women's culture' in evidence in *Chatelaine* presumed a commonality of gender interests, which was often contested by readers' letters. Despite stereotypes about women's cultural products and the era, the material in *Chatelaine* refutes the notion, beloved by advertisers, that Canadian women were complacently content with the status quo symbolized by the image of a happy, carefree, suburban mother. Instead, they were critically engaged in discussion and debate about women's changing roles. The energy and drive evident in the letters to the editor indicate a strong commitment to women's activism and increased participation in Canadian society. The application of the insights of cultural studies – particularly reader responses – to this historical study permits a more sophisticated analysis of the ways in which historical readers 'read' a periodical. The wealth of information contained in readers' letters indicates how average readers reacted to the product. The energy, wit, and creativity demonstrated by *Chatelaine* readers conclusively refutes the perception that consumers merely absorbed the messages within the magazine. In contrast, their active negotiations with the product demonstrate that the agency of the consumers of cultural products must be restored to our analysis of their impact. Without the readers, the participatory world of 'reading' *Chatelaine* in the fifties and sixties would be lost. The community of *Chatelaine* readers provides historians with a rare vantage point into the ways average Canadian women negotiated their changing roles during the rise of second-wave feminism in the postwar years.

Notes

Chapter 1: 'Lighting Up a Brush Fire'

1 June Callwood, interview by author, 23 May 1995.
2 See Amy Erman Farrell, *Yours in Sisterhood: Ms. Magazine and the Promise of Popular Feminism* (Chapel Hill, 1998).
3 See Sylvia Bashevkin, *Women on the Defensive: Living through Conservative Times* (Toronto, 1998), for a comparative analysis of the fate of feminism and feminists in the seventies, eighties, and nineties.
4 For an analysis of the impact of television in Canada, see Paul Rutherford, *When Television Was Young: Primetime Canada, 1952–1967* (Toronto, 1990).
5 Reg Whitaker and Gary Marcuse, *Cold War Canada: The Making of a National Insecurity State, 1945–1957* (Toronto, 1994).
6 A number of new historical studies about the postwar experience in Canada temper the overriding myth of easy-going suburban affluence. See Veronica Strong-Boag, 'Home Dreams: Women and the Suburban Experiment in Canada,' *Canadian Historical Review* 72, 4 (1991), and '"Their Side of the Story": Women's Voices from Ontario Suburbs,' in Joy Parr, ed., *A Diversity of Women: Ontario, 1945–1980* (Toronto: 1995); Joanne Meyerowitz, ed., *Not June Cleaver: Women and Gender in Postwar America, 1945–1960* (Philadelphia, 1994); Elaine Tyler May, *Homeward Bound: American Families in the Cold War Era* (New York, 1988); Wini Breines, *Young, White and Miserable: Growing Up Female in the Fifties* (Boston, 1992); Franca Iacovetta, *Such Hardworking People: Italian Immigrants in Postwar Toronto* (Montreal and Kingston, 1992); Douglas Owram, *Born at the Right Time: A History of the Baby Boom Generation* (Toronto, 1996); Annalee Golz, 'Family Matters: The Canadian Family and the State in Postwar Canada,' *left history* 1, 2 (1993); Mona Gleason, 'Psychology and the Construction of the

Normal Family in Postwar Canada, 1945–1960,' *Canadian Historical Review* 78, 3 (1997); Mary Louise Adams, *The Trouble with Normal: Postwar Youth and the Making of Heterosexuality* (Toronto, 1997); and Lorraine Blashill, *Remembering the Fifties: Growing Up in Western Canada* (Vancouver, 1997).

7 See John R. Miron, ed., *House, Home and Community: Progress in Housing Canadians, 1945–1986* (Montreal and Kingston, 1993), for more detail on the changes in patterns of housing in Canada and access to single-family dwellings.

8 Other useful surveys of Canadian history and society in the fifties and sixties are Alvin Finkel, *Our Lives: Canada after 1945* (Toronto, 1997); Robert Bothwell, Ian Drummond, and John English, *Canada since 1945*, rev. ed. (Toronto, 1989). For the United States, see David Halberstam, *The Fifties* (New York, 1993).

9 See Strong-Boag, 'Home Dreams, ' and 'Their Side of the Story.'

10 See John Porter, *The Vertical Mosaic* (Toronto, 1965), for a comparison of the difference between the Canadian and the American 'middle class.' Porter's famous study indicated that the majority of Canadians in the fifties were in the lower-middle class and working-class economic categories.

11 For an analysis of consumer goods and consumers, see Joy Parr, *Domestic Goods: The Material, the Moral, and the Economic in the Postwar Years* (Toronto, 1999).

12 Joan Sangster, *Earning Respect: The Lives of Working Women in Small-Town Ontario, 1920–1960* (Toronto, 1995).

13 Those terms are borrowed from Roland Marchand, *Advertising the American Dream* (Berkley, 1985), and Benedict Anderson, *Imagined Communities* (London, 1983), respectively.

14 One recent, and extremely worthwhile, exception is Geoff Pevere and Greig Dymond, *Mondo Canuck* (Scarborough, 1996), which explores the delicious irony and insanity of Canadian telvision, radio, and movies of the past thirty years. There are, however, no references to popular magazines.

15 David Abrahamson describes the current state of American magazine research as 'brilliant fragments,' because most practitioners of cultural studies, cultural history, communications studies, or journalism prefer to concentrate on the other mass media – television, movies, newspapers, radio – and only rarely on magazines. For some examples of British and American research on women's magazines and magazines in general, see David Abrahamson, ed., *The American Magazine: Research Perspectives and Prospects* (Ames, IA, 1995); Joan Barrel and Brian Braithwaite, *The Business of Women's Magazines* (London, 1988); Brian Braithwaite, *Women's Maga-*

zines: The First 300 Years (London, 1995); Irene Dancyger, *A World of Women: An Illustrated History of Women's Magazines* (Dublin, 1978); L. Ann Geise, 'The Female Role in Middle-Class Women's Magazines from 1955–1976: A Content Analysis of Nonfiction Selections, ' *Sex Roles* 5, 1 (1979); Lee Jolliffe and Terri Catlett, 'Women Editors at the "Seven Sisters" Magazines, 1965–1985: Did They Make a Difference?' *Journalism Quarterly* 71, 4 (1994); Alan Nourie and Barbara Nourie, eds., *American Mass Market Magazines* (New York, 1990); Kate Peirce, 'A Feminist Theoretical Perspective on the Socialization of Teenage Girls through *Seventeen* Magazine,' *Sex Roles* 23, 9/10 (1990); David Reed, *The Popular Magazine in Britain and the United States, 1880–1960* (Toronto, 1997); John Tebbel and Mary Ellen Zuckerman, *The Magazine in America, 1741–1990* (New York, 1991); and James P. Wood, *Magazines in the United States* (New York, 1971).

16   For the most recent assessment of the literature on women's magazines, see Dawn Currie, *Girl Talk: Adolescent Magazines and Their Readers* (Toronto, 1999).

17   Betty Friedan, *The Feminine Mystique* (New York, 1963), 19. These books cover both American and British women's magazines and appear in order of publication. Cynthia White, *Women's Magazines, 1693–1968* (London, 1970); Gaye Tuchman, Arlene Kaplan Daniels, and James Bennet, eds., *Hearth and Home: Images of Women in the Mass Media* (New York, 1978); Kathryn Weibel, *Mirror, Mirror: Images of Women Reflected in Popular Culture* (New York, 1977); Katherine Fishburn, *Women in Popular Culture: A Reference Guide* (Westport, CT, 1982); Marjorie Ferguson, *Forever Feminine: Women's Magazines and the Cult of Femininity* (London, 1983); Naomi Wolf, *The Beauty Myth* (New York, 1990); and Susan Faludi, *Backlash: The Undeclared War against American Women* (New York, 1991).

18   Jennifer Scanlon, *Inarticulate Longings: The Ladies Home Journal, Gender, and the Promises of Consumer Culture* (New York, 1995).

19   Friedan, *The Feminine Mystique*, 19.

20   Ibid., 36.

21   Joanne Meyerowitz, 'Beyond the Feminine Mystique: A Reassessment of Postwar Mass Culture, 1946–1958,' in Meyerowitz, ed., *Not June Cleaver.*

22   For a sampling of this material, see Alice E. Courtney and Thomas W. Whipple, *Sex Stereotyping in Advertising* (Lexington, MA, 1983); Alice E. Courtney and Sara Wernick Lockertz, 'A Woman's Place: An Analysis of the Roles Portrayed by Women in Magazine Advertising, ' *Journal of Marketing Research* 8 (February 1971); Geise, 'The Female Role in Middle-Class Women's Magazines'; Yvonne Mathews-Kline, 'How They Saw Us: Images of Women in National Film Board Films of the 1940s and 1950s,'

Atlantis 14 (spring 1979); Carol Moog, *'Are They Selling Her Lips?' Advertising and Identity* (New York, 1990); Andrea Nugent, 'Canada's Silenced Communicators: A Report on Women in Journalism and Public Relations, ' *Atlantis* 2 (spring 1982); Gertrude Joch Robinson, 'The Media and Social Change: Thirty Years of Magazine Coverage of Women and Work, 1950–1977,' *Atlantis* 8 (spring 1983); and Task Force on Women and Advertising, *Women and Advertising: Today's Messages—Yesterday's Images* (Toronto, 1977).

23 See Helen Damon-Moore, *Magazines for the Millions* (Albany, 1994); Jennifer Scanlon, *Inarticulate Longings: The Ladies' Home Journal, Gender, and the Promises of Consumer Culture* (London, 1995); Joke Hermes, *Reading Women's Magazines: An Analysis of Everyday Media Use* (Cambridge, 1995); Ellen Gruber Garvey, *The Adman in the Parlor* (Oxford, 1996); Richard Ohmann, *Selling Culture: Magazines, Markets and Class at the Turn of the Century* (London, 1996); Richard Ohmann, ed., *Making and Selling Culture* (Hanover, NH 1996); Mary Thom, *Inside Ms.: 25 Years of the Magazine and the Feminist Movement* (New York, 1997); Amy Erdmann Farrell, *Yours in Sisterhood: Ms. Magazine and the Promise of Popular Feminism* (Chapel Hill, NC, 1998); Currie, *Girl Talk*.

24 Ros Ballaster, Margaret Beetham, Elizabeth Fraser, and Sandra Hebron, *Women's Worlds: Ideology, Feminism and Women's Magazines* (London, 1991), 2.

25 See Currie, *Girl Talk*, and Joke Hermes, *Reading Women's Magazines*, for further commentary on the ethnography of such forms of popular culture.

26 Ellen McCracken, *Decoding Women's Magazines: From Mademoiselle to Ms.* (London, 1993), 3.

27 Currie, *Girl Talk*, 284.

28 Damon-Moore, *Magazines for the Millions*, 3.

29 Readers interested in a more detailed overview of the historiography of British and American women's magazines should consult V.J. Korinek, 'Roughing It in Suburbia: Reading *Chatelaine* Magazine, 1950–1969' (PhD dissertation, University of Toronto, 1996).

30 Currie, *Girl Talk*.

31 Fraser Sutherland, *The Monthly Epic: A History of Canadian Magazines* (Markham, ON, 1989).

32 Sylvia Fraser, ed., *Chatelaine – A Woman's Place: Seventy Years in the Lives of Canadian Women* (Toronto, 1997).

33 Mary Vipond, 'The Image of Women in Mass Circulation Magazines in the 1920s,' in Susan Mann Trofimenkoff and Alison Prentice, eds. *The Neglected Majority: Essays in Canadian's Women History* (Toronto, 1977); Gertrude Joch

Robinson, 'The Media and Social Change: Thirty Years of Magazine Coverage of Women and Work, 1950–1977,' *Atlantis* 8 (spring 1983). Both these articles merit attention. They contend that the maternal emphasis in Canadian and American women's magazines reigned supreme, regardless of the era or the changing nature of women's roles. However, Robinson does distinguish Doris Anderson's *Chatelaine* from the rest of the women's periodicals at the time, noting that coverage of working women in *Chatelaine* was often quite enlightened. Two other graduate theses, one of which focuses partially on *Chatelaine*, while the other examines only one component of the magazine, offer analyses of *Chatelaine*: Susannah Jane Foster Wilson, 'The Relationship between Mass Media Content and Social Change in Canada: An Examination of the Image of Women in Mass Circulating Canadian Magazines, 1930–1970' (PhD dissertation, University of Toronto, 1977), and Inez Houlihan, 'The Image of Women in *Chatelaine* Editorials: March 1928–September 1977' (MA thesis, OISE, University of Toronto, 1984). See also Adams, *The Trouble with Normal*.

34 Meyerowitz, 'Beyond the Feminine Mystique,' 230.

35 A number of factors account for this situation, the absence, except for the Robinson article mentioned above, of any work related to the images, themes, production, or readership of *Chatelaine* in the postwar era. Second, the legacy of Friedan's influential book, *The Feminine Mystique*, which provided a damning portrait of American women's magazines in the postwar era. Finally, Canadian historians have only recently begun to publish articles and monographs about Canadian social history in the fifties and sixties. Useful though these works are, they make ample use of the more 'traditional' articles from *Chatelaine*, without providing much, if any, commentary or context about the diversity of material printed in the magazine.

36 For examples of the ways in which material from *Chatelaine* has been used in women's and social histories of Canada in the postwar era, see Joan Sangster, 'Doing Two Jobs: The Wage-Earning Mother, 1945–1970,' in Parr, ed., *A Diversity of Women*, 102–5. In a section in this article entitled 'The Popular Debate,' Sangster describes a host of American and Canadian media portraits of middle-class, suburban women's lives. She notes that *Chatelaine*, under Anderson, was a trailblazer in the seventies, but this comment omits Anderson's work in the late fifties and sixties. Other examples may be found in Sangster, *Earning Respect*; Owram, *Born at the Right Time*; Adams, *The Trouble with Normal*. Veronica Strong-Boag's use of material from *Chatelaine* includes references to readers' letters and debate within the magazine, but her work tends to use some of the most conserva-

tive material from the periodical: 'Home Dreams' and 'Their Side of the Story.' A more balanced view is presented in Beth Light and Ruth Roach Pierson, eds., *No Easy Road: Women in Canada, 1920s to 1960s* (Toronto, 1990), which offers excerpts from both the traditional and the unconventional material in *Chatelaine*. Ironically, in an earlier work, *'They're Still Women After All': The Second World War and Canadian Womanhood* (Toronto, 1986), historian Ruth Roach Pierson cited numerous examples of conservative material from *Canadian Home Journal* (which would be purchased by Maclean Hunter and amalgamated into *Chatelaine* in 1958), as well as from *Saturday Night* and other Canadian periodicals to support her case about women's experiences during the Second World War and beyond. Little attention was paid to *Chatelaine*.

37 British theorist Raymond Williams was the first to offer a cautionary warning about the effects of studying the individual threads instead of the entire weaving. He recommended that scholars study the 'flow' of material, instead of 'the discrete single work,' because scholars were in 'danger of narrowing our notion of text too much ... and by doing so missing the normal characteristic of mass culture ... one of "flow."' Raymond Williams, *Culture* (London, 1981).

38 Those readers who are interested in this material, along with a more detailed description of methodology, categories of analysis, and the database structure, should consult the appendix in my thesis, 'Roughing It in Suburbia.'

39 For instance, although one of the defining hallmarks of the era was the increased birth rate and an emphasis on child rearing, within the pages of *Chatelaine* maternal images, themes, and issues were not as numerous as expected. This was particularly true in the advertisements, where neither maternalism nor sexism appeared often. Space constraints preclude reproducing a detailed summary of the database material here. Readers interested in this material, and in a more detailed description of the methodology, categories of analysis, and database structure, should consult the appendix in my thesis, 'Roughing It in Suburbia.'

40 Those interested in reviewing the development of the field and reading a brief introductory article on the key historiographical developments should see Cary Nelson, Paula A. Treichler, and Lawrence Grossberg, 'Cultural Studies: An Introduction,' in *Cultural Studies*, edited by the same authors (New York, 1992), 1–16. The bibliography in this anthology is an excellent source of critical and cultural analysis works. Michael Gurevitch, Tony Bennett, James Curran, and Janet Woollacott, eds., *Culture, Society and the Media* (London, 1982), is also useful, although not as current as the

previous article. Another valuable, although idiosyncratic, source is John
Fiske, *Power Plays, Power Works* (London, 1993). Of specific interests to
feminist academics is Sarah Franklin, Celia Lury, and Jackie Stacey, 'Introduction 1: Feminism and Cultural Studies: Pasts, Presents, Futures,' in *Off-
Centre: Feminism and Cultural Studies*, edited by the same authors (London,
1991), as well as Tania Modleski, ed., *Studies in Entertainment: Critical
Approaches to Mass Culture* (Bloomington, 1986).

41 Nelson, Treichler, and Grossberg, 'Cultural Studies,' 2.
42 Roland Barthes, 'Myth Today,' in R. Barthes, *Mythologies* (London, 1973), is
   a fine essay for those interested in an introduction to the art of semiotics.
43 Michel Foucault's work forms an extremely important component of
   modern critical analysis. A good introduction to the main components of
   his theoretical work can be obtained from the anthology *Power/Knowledge:
   Selected Interviews and Other Writings, 1972–1977* (Brighton, 1980), and in
   his more accessible work, *The History of Sexuality, 1: An Introduction* (New
   York, 1978). Another useful introduction is the anthology edited by Paul
   Rabinow, *The Foucault Reader* (New York, 1984). Finally, a feminist analysis
   of Foucault's work, Nancy Fraser, *Unruly Practices: Power, Discourse and
   Gender in Contemporary Social Theory* (Minneapolis, 1989), offers a critique
   of the absence of gender analysis in Foucault's work.
44 Foucault, *The History of Sexuality*, 93.
45 Michel Foucault, 'Truth and Power,' in *Power/Knowledge*, 119.
46 Nancy Fraser, 'Foucault on Modern Power: Empirical Insights and Normative Confusions,' in *Unruly Practices*, 18.
47 Foucault, *Power/Knowledge*, 29.
48 Fraser has written extensively on the 'confusion' in Foucault's conceptions
   of power; see *Unruly Practices*. For more information into the 'liberal'
   Foucault, see David Hoy, *Foucault: A Critical Reader* (London, 1986);
   Graham Burchell, Colin Gordon, and Peter Miller, eds., *The Foucault Effect:
   Studies in Governmentality* (Hemel Hempstead, 1991); and Andrew Barry,
   Thomas Osborne, and Nikolas Rose, eds., *Foucault and Political Reason:
   Liberalism, Neo-Liberalism and Rationalities of Government* (Chicago, 1996).
   My thanks to Elsbeth Heaman for suggesting these sources.
49 Foucault, *The History of Sexuality*, 95.
50 For recent examples of the use of a poststructuralist or Foucauldian analy-
   sis in Canadian history, see Elsbeth Heaman, *The Inglorious Arts of Peace:
   Exhibitions in Canadian Society during the Nineteenth Century* (Toronto, 1999);
   Kathryn McPherson, Cecilia Morgan, and Nancy M. Forestell, 'Introduction: Conceptualizing Canada's Gendered Pasts,' in *Gendered Pasts: Historical Essays in Feminity and Masculinity in Canada*, edited by the same authors

(Don Mills, ON, 1999); Franca Iacovetta and Wendy Mitchinson, eds., *On the Case: Explorations in Social History* (Toronto, 1998); Carolyn Strange, *Toronto's Girl Problem* (Toronto, 1995); Joy Parr, 'Gender History and Historical Practice,' *Canadian Historical Review* 76, 3 (1995); Lykke de la Cour, Cecilia Morgan, and Mariana Valverde, 'Regulation and State Formation in Nineteenth-Century Canada,' in Alan Greer and Ian Radforth, eds., *Colonial Leviathan: State Formation in Mid-Nineteenth Century Canada* (Toronto, 1992); Mariana Valverde, *The Age of Light, Soap and Water: Moral Reform in English Canada, 1885–1925* (Toronto, 1991).

51 Foucault, *The History of Sexuality*, 100.

52 Ibid., 101.

53 The most useful of Fiske's works are *Reading the Popular* (London, 1989) and *Understanding Popular Culture* (London, 1989). Also of interest, although more specialized in focus, is John Fiske and John Hartley, *Reading Television* (London, 1978). Fiske's more recent work is *Power Plays, Power Works*.

54 Fiske, *Understanding Popular Culture*, 43.

55 Ibid., 104.

56 Ibid., 105.

57 Modleski, 'Introduction,' in *Studies in Entertainment*, xvi.

58 As in the brief survey provided of critical theory, this review of the work of two feminist popular cultural critics / academics is not meant to provide an overview of the now considerable historiography. Interested readers should turn to Franklin, Lury and Stacey, *Off-Centre*; Angela McRobbie, *Feminism and Youth Culture: From Jackie to Just Seventeen* (London, 1991); Helen Taylor, *Scarlett's Women:* Gone with the Wind *and Its Female Fans* (London, 1989); Leslie G. Roman and Linda K. Christian-Smith, *Becoming Feminine: The Politics of Popular Culture* (London, 1988); Lorraine Gamman and Margaret Marshment, eds., *The Female Gaze: Women as Viewers of Popular Culture* (London, 1988); and Annette Kuhn, *The Power of the Image: Essays on Representation and Sexuality* (London, 1985).

59 Tania Modleski, *Loving with a Vengeance: Mass-Produced Fantasies for Women* (New York, 1984).

60 Ibid., 25.

61 Ibid., 57.

62 Janice A. Radway, *Reading the Romance: Women, Patriarchy, and Popular Literature* (Chapel Hill, NC, 1984).

63 This study continues to be lauded as a critically important work in American studies of popular culture; a second edition was printed in 1991.

64 Ibid., 211.

65 Ibid., 61.

66 The participatory pleasure fans derived from interacting with popular culture texts has been enumerated most recently in the work of Henry Jenkins and Lisa Lewis. See Henry Jenkins, *Textual Poachers: Television Fans and Participatory Culture* (New York, 1992), and Lisa A. Lewis, ed., *The Adoring Audience: Fan Culture and Popular Media* (New York, 1992).

67 For some examples of the women's culture approach in women's history, see Margaret Conrad, '"Sundays Always Make Me Think of Home": Time and Place in Canadian Women's History, ' in Veronica Strong-Boag and Anita Clair Fellman, eds., *Rethinking Canada: The Promise of Women's History* (Toronto, 1986); Susan Porter Benson, *Counter Cultures: Saleswomen, Managers, and Customers in American Department Stores, 1890–1940* (Urbana, IL1986); Veronica Strong-Boag, 'Pulling in Double Harness or Hauling a Double Load: Women, Work and Feminism on the Canadian Prairie, ' in R. Douglas Francis and Howard Palmer, eds., *The Prairie West: Historical Readings* (Edmonton, 1992).

68 Strong-Boag, 'Pulling in Double Harness or Hauling a Double Load.'

69 Much of the work in cultural analysis examines contemporary cultural products and assumes that readers will understand the social / contextual situation in which the product is produced and consumed. Hence many 'textual analyses' offer little sociohistorical commentary. Recently, a few academics have begun to call for a closer attention to this contextualizing. See Damon-Moore, 'Introduction, ' in *Magazines for the Millions*, 1–13; and Angela McRobbie, 'New Times in Cultural Studies, ' in Angela McRobbie, ed., *PostModernism and Popular Culture* (London, 1994). For an example of a cultural history article that offers a firm sociohistorical context to situate the 'reading,' see Joy Parr, 'Shopping for a Good Stove: A Parable about Gender, Design, and the Market,' in Parr, ed., *A Diversity of Women*.

70 Of course, these terms, and the ideology of social history, owe a tremendous debt to their early practitioners and popularizers. See E.P. Thompson, *The Making of the English Working Class* (London, 1963); Herbert Gutman, 'Work, Culture, and Society in Industrializing America, 1815–1919,' *American Historical Review* 78 (1973); Herbert Gutman, *Power and Culture: Essays on the American Working Class*, edited by Ira Berlin (New York, 1987).

71 For examples of the new nationalism in Canadian history, see J.L. Granatstein, *Who Killed Canadian History?* (Toronto, 1998), and Michael Bliss, 'Privatizing the Mind: The Sundering of Canadian History, the Sundering of Canada, ' *Journal of Canadian Studies* 26, 4 (1991–2).

72 For a good overview, see Owram, *Born at the Right Time;* Adams, *The Trouble with Normal;* and Parr, ed., *A Diversity of Women*.

73 For historical commentary on the routes of anti-feminism in Canada, see
Veronica Strong-Boag, *Independent Women, Problematic Men: First and
Second Wave Antifeminism in Canada from Goldwin Smith to Betty Steele*,
Occasional Working Papers 2 (Vancouver, 1993), and Karen Dubinsky,
*Lament for a 'Patriarchy Lost'? Antifeminism, Anti-abortion and R.E.A.L
Women in Canada*, Feminist Perspectives 1 (Ottawa, 1985).

Chapter 2: 'A Closet Feminist Magazine': (Re)-Making *Chatelaine*

1 Irene Dancyger, *A World of Women: An Illustrated History of Women's Magazines* (Dublin, 1978), 13–17. For additional sources of information for the
early history of British women's magazines, see Brian Braithwaite, *Wom-
en's Magazines: The First 300 Years* (London, 1995); Cynthia L. White,
Women's Magazines, 1693–1968 (London, 1970).
2 John Tebbel and Mary-Ellen Zuckerman, *The Magazine in America, 1741–
1990* (New York, 1991), 27.
3 James P. Wood, *Magazines in the United States* (New York, 1971), 51.
4 Ibid., 51–2.
5 Helen Damon-Moore, *Magazines for the Millions: Gender and Commerce in the
Ladies Home Journal and the Saturday Evening Post, 1880–1910* (Albany,
1994), 2.
6 Tebbel and Zuckerman. *The Magazine in America*, 99 and 102.
7 For more information on the *Canadian Home Journal*, see Fraser Sutherland,
The Monthly Epic (Markham, 1989), 156–7.
8 Archives of Ontario (AO), Maclean Hunter Record Series (MHRS) A-4-1,
box 38, Report by H.V. Tyrell, 'General Plan for a Woman's Magazine of
Large National Circulation,' 25 August 1927.
9 Readers interested in the accomplishments of first-wave feminism in
Canada, and women's lives during the interwar period, should see Carol
Lee Bachi, *Liberation Deferred?* (Toronto, 1983), and Veronica Strong-Boag,
The New Day Recalled: Lives of Girls and Women in English Canada, 1919–1939
(Toronto, 1988).
10 Lotta Dempsey, 'When We Were Very Young,' *Chatelaine*, March 1948,
20–1.
11 Maclean Hunter photocopy, 'Annual Circulation – June; December,'
undated, but presumably from 1986, judging by the most recent figures
included.
12 Neither the French nor English version of *Chatelaine* has attracted much
academic or analytical attention, but the historiography on the French
version is much more comprehensive than the English version. Readers

interested in an analysis of the role and content of *Châtelaine* should see
Marie-José Des Rivières, *Châtelaine et la littérature (1960–1975)* (Montreal,
1992); Jocelyne Valois, 'La press féminine et le rôle social de la femme, '
Recherches sociographiques 3, 5 (1967); Claire Choquette, 'L'évolution du
discours critique de la chronique "Lectures" de la revue *Châtelaine* (1960–
1980)' (MA thèse, Université de Sherbrooke, 1983); and Mary Jane Green,
'Popular Fiction: Changing Images of Quebec Women in the Short Stories
of *Châtelaine,' Journal of Popular Culture* 2, 2 (1985).

13 Dean Walker, 'Magazines in Canada,' in *Good, Bad or Simply Inevitable:
Report of the Special Senate Committee on Mass Media*, volume 3 (Ottawa,
1970), 229.

14 Miss Chatelaine ad, *Chatelaine*, February 1964, 74.

15 'Chatelaine Magazine Group: Submission to the Special Senate Committee
on Mass Media,' 18 February 1970, 1.

16 Walker, 'Magazines in Canada,' 221.

17 Ad for *Homemaker's Digest, CARD*, January 1968, 133.

18 *Chatelaine* and *Hostess* ad, *CARD*, February 1968, 117.

19 Walker, 'Magazines in Canada,' 230.

20 Once the startup difficulties were surmounted, *Homemaker's* proved a very
popular periodical, one that inspired advertiser and consumer confidence.
It is still in publication today.

21 AO, MHRS F-4-5-a, box 449, Ted Hart Papers, 'Hart Speech to Directors,
Draft 1971' (delivered early 1971).

22 'Chatelaine Magazine Group,' presented by Lloyd M. Hodgkinson, publisher; Submission to the Special Senate Committee on Mass Media, February 18, 1970, 1–2.

23 'Chatelaine Advertisement,' *Canadian Advertising Rates and Data*, April
1970, 69.

24 See Reg Whitaker and Gary Marcuse, *Cold War Canada: The Making of a
National Insecurity State, 1945–1957* (Toronto, 1994), for more detail about
the 'mythology' surrounding Gouzenko and Canadian reaction to it.

25 'Byrne Hope, Sanders, CBE,' in *Canadian Who's Who, 1981* (Toronto, 1981),
876.

26 H. Napier Moore, 'Welcome Home,' *Chatelaine*, January 1947, 56.

27 This is a common fate of long-tenured magazine editors, regardless of the
success necessary to achieve a multiple-year run as editor of a mass-
market magazine. Most recently, Condé Nast incurred considerable bad
publicity for its decision to 'encourage' Helen Gurley Brown, the woman
credited with turning around the fortunes of *Cosmopolitan* in the sixties, to
retire. Only in the last few years was Brown's thirty-year run at *Cosmo*

beginning to show in flagging circulation and advertising numbers. She was replaced by the Canadian Bonnie Fuller. However traumatic these changes, 'change' is not possible if the old editor remains in charge. Magazines are frequently remade to tap into new interests and audiences and to satisfy advertiser preferences.

28 For an overview of the history of polling in Canada, see Daniel J. Robinson, *The Measure of Democracy: Polling, Research, and Public Life, 1930–1945* (Toronto, 1999).

29 Anderson interview, 1994.

30 Callwood interview, 1995.

31 Eileen Morris interview, 1996.

32 Byrne Hope Sanders, 'Goodbye and Good Luck,' *Chatelaine*, January 1952, 3.

33 Anderson interview, 1994.

34 Lotta Dempsey, *No Life for a Lady* (Don Mills, ON, 1976).

35 'Lotta Dempsey,' in *Canadian Who's Who, 1984* (Toronto, 1984), 297.

36 Lotta Dempsey, 'New Editor, New Friend,' *Chatelaine*, February 1952, 3.

37 Noel Robert Barbour, *Those Amazing People! The Story of the Canadian Magazine Industry, 1778–1967* (Toronto, 1982), 161.

38 Anderson interview, 1994.

39 Lee Jolliffe and Terri Catlett, 'Women Editors at the Seven Sisters Magazines, 1965–1985: Did They Make a Difference?' *Journalism Quarterly* 71, 4 (1994). In their content analysis of American women's magazines from 1965 to 1985, Jolliffe and Catlett found 'that the presence of women editors did not reduce stereotypical portrayals in the magazines studied, but did increase positive portrayals of women.' *Chatelaine* was more conservative in the Clare years, but it is debatable to what extent that stemmed from gender or from neglect and indifference to the women's magazine format.

40 'John P. Clare,' in *Canadian Who's Who, 1973–1975* (Toronto, 1975), 187.

41 David MacKenzie, *Arthur Irwin: A Biography* (Toronto, 1993), 188.

42 Anderson interview, 1994.

43 Callwood interview, 1995.

44 John Clare, 'Five Men, All Writers, Move into the World of Women,' *Chatelaine*, May 1957, 1.

45 Anderson interview, 1994, and Callwood interview, 1995.

46 Doris Anderson and Floyd Chalmers dispute Anderson's hiring, but, according to Anderson, Chalmers wanted to hire Gerry Anglin as *Chatelaine* editor, since Anderson was due to get married. She threatened to quit the magazine and was ultimately given the job. See Sutherland, *The Monthly Epic*, 249–50.

47 Lotta Dempsey, 'Behind the Scenes at *Chatelaine*,' *Chatelaine*, April 1952, 80.

48 Doris Anderson, *Rebel Daughter* (Toronto, 1996).

49 'Doris Hilda Anderson,' in *Canadian Who's Who, 1993* (Toronto, 1993), 17.

50 Anderson interview, 1994.

51 Doris Anderson, *Rough Layout* (Toronto, 1981), 56–7.

52 'Joint Submission of *Maclean's* Magazine, *Chatelaine* and *Canadian Homes*: Blair Fraser (editor of *Maclean's*) Doris Anderson (editor of *Chatelaine*) and Mr. Gerry Anglin (editor of *Canadian Home*),' *Report of the Royal Commission on Publications: Hearings*, volume 21, Toronto, 14 December 1960, 25–6.

53 AO, MHRS F-4-4-a, box 426, Doris Anderson to Mrs Mary Bordewick, Vancouver, 3 September 1959.

54 'Joint Submission,' 16.

55 See Paul Litt, *The Muses, the Masseys, and the Massey Commission* (Toronto, 1992), for an overview of the significance of the Massey Report. For evidence that culture existed before the Massey Commission, see Maria Tippett, *Making Culture: English-Canadian Institutions and the Arts before the Massey Commission* (Toronto, 1990).

56 Anderson interview, 1994.

57 Callwood interview, 1995.

58 Anderson interview, 1994.

59 '*Chatelaine* Ad: Twenty-Five Years of Service,' *Canadian Advertising*, March–April 1953, 102.

60 '*Chatelaine* Ad: Ideas, Wants, Sales!' *Canadian Advertising*, May–June 1953, 100.

61 '*Chatelaine* Ad,' *Canadian Advertising: Canadian Media Authority*, January/February 1955, 102.

62 '*Chatelaine* Ad: If It's ACTION You Want ... Here It Is!' *Canadian Advertising*, November/December 1953, 104.

63 The Magazine Advertising Bureau was an organization independent of Maclean Hunter, but largely dominated by their personnel.

64 'Magazine Advertising Bureau of Canada: Make Your Advertising a Family Affair,' *Canadian Advertising*, January/February 1955, 92.

65 'Magazine Advertising Bureau of Canada Ad,' *Canadian Advertising*, September/October 1955, 98.

66 'Magazine Advertising Bureau of Canada Ad: Canadian Magazines Are Held in the Hands We Want to Reach,' *Canadian Advertising*, January/February 1958, 114.

67 *Report of the Royal Commission on Publications* (Ottawa, 1961), 16. The term *split run* refers to the practice of producing various copies of mass-market magazines so as to attract local advertising. American periodicals, most notably *Time* and *Reader's Digest*, produced a 'Canadian split-run' for sale

and distribution in Canada which contained Canadian advertising, effectively siphoning advertising away from the Canadian periodicals.

68 Schedule 2, Consumer Magazine Division of Maclean Hunter Publishing Company, from Appendix F, 'Report of the Financial Consultant,' in *Report of the Royal Commission on Publications*, 177.

69 *Report of the Royal Commission on Publications*, 19.

70 'Report of the Financial Consultant,' *Report of the Royal Commission on Publications*, 161.

71 *The Uncertain Mirror: Report of the Special Senate Committee on Mass Media*, volume 1 (Ottawa, 1970), 154. It is impossible to locate the actual figures for advertising revenue in the 1960s as the company was not required to release this information. Even when it did, for the Senate Committee, it was assured that those numbers would remain confidential.

72 Anderson interview, 1994.

73 AO, MHRS F-1-2, box 391, 'Maclean Hunter Publishing Company Ltd., Budget Summary for Year Ending December 31, 1961.'

74 AO, MHRS F-4-5-a, box 449, Ted Hart Papers, 'Speech to Directors, Draft 1971.'

75 *The Uncertain Mirror*, 154.

76 Ibid.

77 OA, MHRS F-4-5-a, box 449, 'Ted Hart Speech to the Directors, Draft 1971.'

78 *The Uncertain Mirror*, 157.

79 Amy Erdmann Farrel, *Yours in Sisterhood: Ms. Magazine and the Promise of Popular Feminism* (Chapel Hill, North Carolina, 1998), and Joanne Meyerowitz, 'Beyond the Feminine Mystique: A Reassessment of Postwar Mass Culture, 1946–1958,' in *Not June Cleaver: Women and Gender in Postwar America, 1945–1960* (Philadelphia, 1994), are the only revisionist works on women's magazines specifically. Other sources on women's magazines may be found within journalism studies, communications, and magazine histories. See Mary Ellen Zuckerman, *Sources on the History of Women's Magazines, 1792–1960: An Annotated Bibliography* (New York, 1991); Tebbel and Zuckerman, *The Magazine in America*; Alan Nourie and Barbara Nourie, eds., *American Mass-Market Magazines* (New York, 1990); and Barbara Ehrenreich and Deirdre English, *For Her Own Good: 150 Years of the Experts' Advice to Women* (New York, 1978). In addition, see memoirs from advertising executives and journalists from the era: Helen Woodward, *The Lady Persuaders* (New York, 1960); Mary Thom, *Inside Ms.: 25 Years of the Magazine and the Feminist Movement* (New York, 1997); Fredelle Bruser, *The Tree of Life* (Markham, ON, 1988); Lenore Hershey, *Between the Covers: The Lady's Own Journal* (New York, 1983); and Carolyn G.

Heilbrun, *The Education of a Woman: The Life of Gloria Steinem* (New York, 1995).

80 The Dichter Study reported that 'the major competition for Chatelaine is in women's magazines from the States. We found, neither in depth interviews, nor in the personality profiles of the *Star Weekly* or *Canadian Home Journal* that emerged from our projective tests, any substantial competitive reader interest ... As a matter of fact, other Canadian publications appear from our material to suffer from the same general weaknesses attributed by our respondents to Chatelaine ... *Maclean's*, apparently a more popular magazine than *Chatelaine*, is nevertheless considered less interesting and desirable than the *Saturday Evening Post*, *Time*, *Life* and other general U.S. publications with which it competes.' Ernest Dichter, Ph.D., 'A Motivational Research Study on Chatelaine Magazine,' conducted for Maclean-Hunter Publishing Co. [Dichter Study] (New York, 1958), 147.

81 AO, MHRS F-4-1-a, box 430, R.G. Scott to L.M. Hodgkinson, re Weekend's Report on *Chatelaine*'s Consumer Council, 19 December 1960. The questionnaire was completed by 1048 readers.

82 Lloyd M. Hodgkinson, publisher and director of Maclean-Hunter Limited, 'Chatelaine Magazine Group: Submission to the Special Senate Committee on Mass Media,' 18 February 1970. The statistics on the Canadian circulation of U.S. women's magazines are taken from the appendix, dated 1968.

83 Chairman J.B. Scarborough, vice president of Family Circle, Inc., 'Submission of Family Circle Incorporated,' *Royal Commission on Publications: Hearings, volume 24*, Ottawa, 20 December 1960, 128.

84 Wood, *Magazines in the United States*, 113–14.

85 Dichter Study, 115.

86 Anderson interview, 1994.

87 Woodward, *The Lady Persuaders*, 139.

88 Wood, *Magazines in the United States*, 121.

89 Ronnie W. Faulkner, 'Redbook,' in *American Mass Market Magazines*, ed., Alan Nourie and Barbara Nourie (New York, 1990), 432.

90 Tebbel and Zuckerman, *The Magazine in American*, 246.

91 Stephanie Childs Sigala, 'Cosmopolitan,' in Nourie and Nourie, eds., *American Mass Market Magazines*, 80.

92 Hershy, *Between the Covers*, 44.

93 Sandra Werner, '*Ms.*,' in Nourie and Nourie, eds., *American Mass Market Magazines*, 267.

94 Farrell, *Yours in Sisterhood*, 193.

95 Doris Anderson, 'Women's Magazines in the 1970s,' *Canadian Woman Studies* 11, 2 (1980): 16.

96 This theme was repeated constantly in all the promotional advertising in *Canadian Advertising Rates and Data (CARD)*, in the magazine, and in the briefs Maclean Hunter and *Chatelaine* made to the Royal Commission on Publications in 1961 and the Special Senate Committee on Mass Media in 1970.

97 Their were small differences in the audience composition in both decades. Those interested in detailed information specifically about fifties' readers should consult Valerie J. Korinek, 'Roughing it in Suburbia: Reading *Chatelaine* in the Fifties and Sixties' (PhD dissertation, University of Toronto, 1996).

98 *Canada's Magazine Audience: A Study from the Magazine Advertising Bureau of Canada, 1: Profile of Readers [CMA]*. Originated by the Canadian Media Directors Council, validated by the Canadian Advertising Research Foundation, conducted by ORC International Limited, 1969). Studies such as this one are extremely difficult to locate because few of them were ever purchased by libraries and most corporations have long since discarded them. This study is available at the National Library in Ottawa.

99 Ibid., 202–3. The country was split into five regions: Atlantic, Quebec, Ontario, Prairies, and British Columbia. However, 'the Yukon, N.W.T., institutions, Indian reserves and RCMP areas and other remote and sparsely populated northern areas were excluded at the outset.'

100 Raymond Kent, ed., *Measuring Media Audiences* (London, 1994), xi.

101 *CMA*. It should be noted that all statistics reported, unless stated otherwise, refer to the English version of the magazine and do not include readership figures for *Châtelaine*.

102 Ibid., 63. The statistical totals by region were Ontario (48.5%), Prairies (23.8%), British Columbia (13.3%), Atlantic Canada (10%), and Quebec (4.4%). For comparison, the regional population percentages for all Canadian adults were Ontario (36.1%), Quebec (28.7%), the Prairies (16%), British Columbia (10%), and Atlantic Canada (9.2%).

103 Ibid., 12 and 10. Most of the male readers of *Chatelaine* read the periodical because their wives or mothers were subscribers. However, that was not always the case, as this letter from J.J. Way of Wooler, Ontario, to Doris Anderson attests: 'I am sending back the June *Chatelaine* as I will not be taking it any longer. Not until I get a wife to read it as it is more for a woman than a man. I did have a lovely Christian wife, and she enjoyed reading *Chatelaine* but she passed away nearly 10 years ago and I have lived here in my nice home all alone for all that time. I can say that I am tired of trying to keep batch and keep house. I often looked at the nice cakes and things cooked and often wished that I had someone to try the

recipes ... Thank you for your past years of service.' AO, MHRS F-4-4-b, box 446, J.J. Way, Wooler, Ontario, to Doris Anderson, 14 June 1962.

104 '*Chatelaine* Advertisement,' *Canadian Advertising: The Media Rate and Data Authority*, January/February 1966, 108.

105 Claims about the youthfulness, above-average income, and urban nature of *Chatelaine*'s audience were all trumpeted in the *CARD* advertisements throughout the sixties. Only with the introduction of *Hostess* magazine in 1968 did the advertisements in *CARD* acknowledge that the *Chatelaine* audience did not reach as many urban, affluent women as they would have liked.

106 *CMA*, 10 and 12. Of the total *male* audience of the magazine, the age breakdown was as follows: over 55 years old (21.9%); 35–44 years (20.8%); 25–34 years (16.7%); 45–54 years (15.1%); 15–17 years (10.8%); 20–24 years (7.7%); and 18–19 years (6.9%). For *women*, the age breakdown was slightly different: 35–44 years (22.7%); 55 and older (17.6%); 25–34 years (16.8%); 45–54 years (16.5%); 15–17 years (10.8%); 20–24 years (10.5%); and 18–19 years (5.1%).

107 Ibid., 18. Female *Chatelaine* readers were most likely to have some high school education (36.8%), or had completed high school (22.6%), completed public school (14.6%), special training (no university) (7.1%), graduated from university or done postgraduate work (5.8%), some elementary school (5.7%), or some college or university (5.2%). In comparison, the English-speaking general female population of Canada was statistically most likely to have some high school (36.4%), or had completed high school (19.5%), completed public school (16.9%), some elementary school (11.0%), some special training after high school (5.3%), some college/university (4.1%), or graduated from university or done postgraduate work (4.1%).

108 Ibid., 20.

109 Ibid., 28. After the top three categories (determined by the surveys), the remaining male occupations were clerical or sales (11.1%), students (10.2%), professional or technical (9.6%), farmers (6.1%), manageral (5.4%), or housekeepers (2.4%). These figures refer to the total male reading audience, not the primary male reading audience.

110 Ibid., 30. Once again, using figures from the total female audience, after the three top occupational categories the remaining female occupations were service (8.2%), retired or unemployed (5.2%), professional or technical (5%), skilled or unskilled (1.5%), or managerial (0.4%). No female readers listed their occupational category as farmer.

111 Ibid., 54. The figures were skilled and unskilled workers (24.9%), service workers (15.7%), clerical and sales workers (13.2%), professional and

technical (10.9%), retired and unemployed (10.5%), farmers (8.9%), managerial (8.2%), housewives (6.7%), and students (1.0%).

112 Ibid., 30. The figure for English-Canadian housewife readers of the magazine were listed as 1,061,000 of the total female audience. The comparable English-Canadian average was 3,257,000 women who listed their occupation as housewife.

113 Ibid., 34 and 38. For 'household income,' 16.1 per cent of respondents declined to report their annual income, whereas for the category of 'principal wage earner's income,' 18.8 per cent declined to report the amount.

114 Ibid., 38.

115 Ibid., 55. For the total audience figures, while most preferred single family homes, 12.2 per cent of *Chatelaine* readers lived in multiple family housing (defined to include semi-detached and duplexes) or apartments, flats, or rooms (7.8%). In comparison, English-Canadian averages were 14.4 per cent for multiple family housing or 9.8 per cent for apartments, etc.

116 Ibid., 106. Total readers by community size were as follows: farm, rural, non-farm (30.1%); 1000–29,999 (17.8%); 30,000–99,999 (6.1%); 100,000–349,000 (11.5%); 350,000 and over (34.5%). Only 25 per cent of all Canadians lived in a rural or farming community.

117 *Canada's Magazine Audience*, 3: *Ownership and Purchase Patterns* (a Study from the Magazine Advertising Bureau of Canada, 1969), 2 and 8. The exact figures on car ownership were as follows: 85.6 per cent of the total male and female audience owned one or more cars; 14.4 per cent did not own any cars.

118 Ibid., 47, 33, and 31. Monthly expenditure on liquor from the primary male and female audience of *Chatelaine* was as follows: under $5 (27.3%); do not purchase (24.8%); not reported (21.3%); $5–9 (13.5%); $10–14 (6.1%). Travel destinations were listed as United States (34.2%); continental Europe (3.8%); British Isles (3.3%); Caribbean, Bermuda (2.4%); none of these (Canada?) (58.8%). Primary audience expenditure on vacation travel in the last twelve months was under $250 (39.4%); $250–499 (21.5%); $0 (15.8%); $500–999 (11.2%); not reported (6.4%); $1000–1499 (2.1%); $1500–1999 (1.2%); $2000 and over (2.4%).

119 'Section D: Media Patterns,' in *Canada's Magazine Audience*, volume 1, 152 and 153.

Chapter 3: 'A Faithful Friend and Tonic': Reading *Chatelaine*

1 Emma Davis to editor, 'Reader Takes Over,' *Chatelaine*, March 1951, 90.

2 '*Chatelaine* ad,' *Canadian Advertising: Canadian Media Authority*, January /
February 1959, 118.

3 Rosalind Brunt has criticized cultural studies' practitioners for their use of
'imagined communities' or audiences instead of concentrating on 'actual
beings living in a material world.' She claims: 'By not asking merely, What
do people do with the text? (stop) but, What do they do with the text *in the
real world*? a way is offered for "audience" to mean more than merely
receiver or reader of others' encodings.' Ballaster et al. also critique the use
of the 'implied reader' in magazine research and the 'little attention paid to
"her" relation to the historical reader.' See Rosalind Brunt, 'Engaging with
the Popular: Audiences for Mass Culture and What to Say about Them,' in
Cultural Studies, ed., Lawrence Grossberg, Cary Nelson, and Paula
Treichler (New York, 1992): 69–80, and Ros Ballaster, Margaret Beetham,
Elizabeth Fraser, and Sandra Hebron, *Women's Worlds: Ideology, Feminism
and the Women's Magazine* (London, 1991), 2.

4 These terms originate in the work of Stuart Hall, one of the founders of the
British Cultural Studies School and a member of the Birmingham Centre
for Studies in Cultural Studies. They have been 'imported' to North
America and popularized by John Fiske (see chapter 1 for more details).
See also Hanno Hardt, *Critical Communication Studies: Communication,
History and Theory in America* (London, 1992), 185–92.

5 Janice Radway, *Reading the Romance: Women, Patriarchy and Popular Literature* (Chapel Hill, NC, 1991), 118.

6 Callwood interview, 1995.

7 Joke Hermes, *Reading Women's Magazines: An Analysis of Everyday Media
Use* (Cambridge, UK, 1995), 31, 36, and 41.

8 Dichter's Motivational Institute and its goals (to help advertisers and
cultural producers discover ways to 'motivate' people to increase their
consumption) had pride of place in Vance Packard's bestselling jermiad
about the American advertising industry, *The Hidden Persuaders* (New
York, 1957). Despite Packard's fears that people like Dichter would discover how to 'manipulate' people into consumer binges, all he was ever
able to do was to demonstrate how people used products, not how to give
advertisers a guaranteed formula to sell products to the gullible.

9 See Packard, *The Hidden Persuaders*.

10 Noel Robert Barbour, *Those Amazing People! The Story of the Canadian
Magazine Industry, 1778–1967* (Toronto, 1982), 171.

11 *Chatelaine* was not forthcoming about this report, claiming that all copies
had been burnt in a warehouse fire. Perhaps that is not surprising, given
some of its negative commentary. Marketing research reports such as the
Dichter Study offer important and useful sources for social historians of

modern North America, particularly historians of culture and consumption. This information appears here courtesy of Dr Ernest Dichter's widow, Hedy Dichter, who manages the remaining archives of Dichter's institute near New York City.

12 Dichter Study, 4–6.

13 This collection of letters is part of the Maclean Hunter Collection at the Archives of Ontario. Despite the title, the company did not donate all its documents to the archives, so the records are fragmentary.

14 Archives of Ontario (AO), Maclean Hunder Record Series (MHRS) F-4-3-a, box 434, Doris Anderson to Mrs M.K. Paul, Caledon, Ontario, 7 March 1962.

15 Chatelaine General Survey Database. Altogether, 1778 letters were published between January 1960 and December 1969. The average, for the 120 issues, is 14.8 letters per issue. This figure obscures a range of from 8 to 23 letters per issue over the period. Unlike the fifties, in the sixties the letters column was never omitted from the periodical.

16 The statistics are generated from the Chatelaine Letters 1960s Database, which includes 446 letters – all those published in the January, May, and September issues from 1960 to 1969. In 5 per cent of the letters analyzed, the writer's gender was unclear.

17 A smaller proportion of letter writers were from Quebec (7.5%) and Atlantic Canada (7.2%). Very few letters were received from outside the country. Those that did were, with rare exceptions, from Britain (1.8%) or the United States (1.3%).

18 AO, MHRS F-4-3-a, box 434, Files: 'Letters to the Editor: January 1962' and 'Letters to the Editor: January 1962, File 2.' The letters were counted and the tone of each letter was categorized as negative, positive, or neutral.

19 Ibid., box 435, Files: 'Letters to the Editor: Sept–Dec., 1962 File 1' and 'Letters to the Editor: Sept–Dec., 1962 File 2.' The letters were counted (total number is 169) and the region or country of origin was noted. The remaining results were Atlantic Canada (6.5%), Quebec (5.9%), Canadian but with no address (3.5%), Britain (2.9%), United States (1.7%), Other (1.1%), Europe (0.5%).

20 AO, MHRS F-4-4-a, box 441, Mrs Ada Reimer, Victoria, BC, to Doris Anderson, October 1959.

21 Muriel A. Jackson, Glasgow, Scotland, to editors, 'Letters to Chatelaine,' Chatelaine November 1956, 3.

22 Mrs. Roy Kittletz, Vimy, Alberta, to editors, 'Letters to Chatelaine,' Chatelaine, June 1957, 2.

23 Although rather slim on analysis, this collection of memories about grow-

ing up in western Canada (primarily the Prairies) during the fifties indicates that, for many families, modernization – defined as electricity, indoor plumbing, and the use of electrical appliances – did not appear until the late forties and fifties. See Lorraine Blashill, ed., *Remembering the Fifties: Growing up in Western Canada* (Vancouver, 1997).

24 Mrs Delia Ash, Val d'Or, Quebec, to editors, 'You Were Asking *Chatelaine*,' *Chatelaine*, March 1956, 3–4.

25 AO, MHRS F-4-4-b, box 445, Newfoundland reader to Doris Anderson, January 1962.

26 Angus McLaren and Arlene Tigar McLaren, *The Bedroom and the State: The Changing Practices and Politics of Contraception and Abortion in Canada, 1880–1997* (Don Mills, 1997), 132.

27 Mrs C.R. Van Dame, Toledo, Ohio, to Doris Anderson, 'The Last Word Is Yours,' *Chatelaine*, March 1961, 154.

28 Mr Clarence Gautreau, TB Hospital, East Saint John, NB, to editors, 'The Last Word is Yours,' *Chatelaine*, March 1964, 90.

29 Mrs Patricia Perron, Rawdon, Quebec, to editors, 'The Last Word Is Yours,' *Chatelaine*, April 1965, 108.

30 'What's New,' *Chatelaine*, October 1965, 2.

31 Ibid.

32 Mrs E. Spring, Harrow, Middlesex, England, to editors, 'The Last Word Is Yours,' *Chatelaine*, December 1963, 84.

33 Mrs Kenneth Harris, Grand Pré, NS, to editors, 'The Last Word Is Yours, ' *Chatelaine*, February 1964, 76.

34 Mrs Tsuyoshi Fujiwars, Sakai-City, Osaka, Japan, to editors, 'The Last Word Is Yours,' *Chatelaine*, October 1967, 132.

35 AO, MHRS F-4-3-a, box 435, Laura Faulkner, Staffordshire, England, to Doris Anderson, 27 September 1962.

36 Anderson interview, 1994.

37 Joy Lehman, '"The Advice of a Real Friend": Codes of Intimacy and Oppression in Women's Magazines, 1937–1955,' *Women's Studies International Quarterly* 3 (1980): 63–78.

38 Anderson interview, 1994.

39 AO, MHRS F-4-4-a, box 438, Fleurette Gagnon, Montreal, to Doris Anderson, 2 January 1958.

40 Ibid., Gabrielle B. Griffiths, Trenton, Ontario, to Doris Anderson, 5 November 1959.

41 Ibid., box 440, Miss Penny Morriss, Winnipeg, to Doris Anderson, 22 July 1959.

42 Byrne Hope Sanders, 'Life Line from Women,' *Chatelaine*, January 1951, 3.

43 AO, MHRS F-4-a-b, box 431, E.H. Gittings, assistant advertising sales manager for *Chatelaine*, to Mr F.D. Adams, 22 June 1961.

44 'Mrs Chatelaine Contest Advertisement,' *Chatelaine*, December 1960, 15.

45 AO, MHRS F-4-1-b, box 431, J.L. Adams, manager for Eastern Canada (*Chatelaine*), to L.M. Hodgkinson, 14 February 1961.

46 'Meet Mrs. Chatelaine,' *Chatelaine*, April 1961, 111.

47 AO, MHRS F-4-3-a, box 434, Mrs Beatrice Maitland, Chatham, NB, to Doris Anderson, 1 November 1961.

48 Ibid., Doris Anderson to Mrs Beatrice Maitland, 10 November 1961.

49 Ibid., Mrs Beatrice Maitland to Doris Anderson, 2 February 1962.

50 Ibid., Doris Anderson to Beatrice Maitland, 12 February 1962.

51 Readers interested in an extended commentary about the Mrs Chatelaine correspondance should consult Valerie J. Korinek, 'Mrs Chatelaine versus the Slobs,' *Journal of the Canadian Historical Association*, new series, 7 (1966).

52 AO, MHRS F-4-3-a, box 434, Mrs F. Miller, New Westminister, BC, to Doris Anderson, 12 January 1962.

53 Ibid., Clara Cserick, 'Slob par excellence,' Ottawa, to Doris Anderson, 27 January 1962.

54 Ibid., Victoria M. Haliburton, Ville Lemoyre, Quebec, to Doris Anderson, 24 January 1962.

55 Ibid., Mrs Greta Usenik, Paradise Hill, Saskatchewan, to Doris Anderson, 19 January 1962.

56 Ibid., Mrs W. Ockenden, Victoria, to Doris Anderson, 16 January 1962.

57 Ibid., box 435, Mrs Neil Ferguson, Dutch Brook, Cape Breton, to Doris Anderson, 25 September 1962.

58 Anonymous questionnaire, London, Ontario, completed 28 December 1993.

59 Questionnaire of Mrs June Ellis, Brookfield, NS, completed 16 July 1993.

60 Questionnaire of Mrs Dorothy Marlow, Middleton, NS, completed 29 June 1993.

61 Questionnaire of Mrs Bette-Jo Baird, Comox, BC, completed 22 July 1993.

62 Questionnaire of Mrs Zena MacLeod, Scotsburn, NS, completed 28 October 1993.

63 Marjorie Hallman, questionnaire completed 18 January 1994.

64 Anonymous questionnaire, Scarborough, Ontario, completed 2 July 1993.

65 Anonymous questionnaire, Halifax, completed 8 June 1993.

66 AO, MHRS F-4-4-b, box 446, Ouida M. Wright, Weston, Ontario, to Doris Anderson, 22 July 1962.

67 Ibid., Doris Anderson to Ouida M. Wright, 14 August 1962.

68 Unfortunately, I did not find any comparable questionnaire material from the fifties, so the 'effects' on the readers must be gauged by the two sixties'

surveys. Maclean Hunter did not include the councillors' reports in the archival material, so I had to rely on published surveys or summaries of surveys. Studies of popular culture are frequently hampered by the lack of material in archives.

69 Jean Yack, 'The Canadian Homemaker: What You Think of Your Job – A Special Report,' *Chatelaine*, March 1961, 54–5.

70 Brief 346: Brief of the Readers of *Chatelaine* Magazine to the Royal Commission on the Status of Women, presented by Doris Anderson, editor, June 1968, 2.

71 Ibid. In response to the question 'Are you a working wife?' 53.82 per cent answered no, 22.93 per cent worked full time, and 19.36 per cent worked part-time. If they could choose freely, 53.99 per cent would opt for marriage, children, and career, compared with 32.62 per cent who would choose marriage with children and no career.

72 See Nancy Adamson, '"Feminists, Libbers, Lefties and Radicals": The Emergence of the Women's Liberation Movement,' in *A Diversity of Women: Ontario, 1945–80* (Toronto, 1995); Nancy Adamson, Linda Briskin, and Margaret McPhail, *Feminist Organizing for Change: The Contemporary Women's Movement in Canada* (Toronto, 1988); Constance Backhouse and David H. Flaherty, eds., *Challenging Times: The Women's Movement in Canada and the United States* (Montreal and Kingston, 1992).

Chapter 4: 'Your Best Medium to Sell Women': Covering and Advertising *Chatelaine*

1 E.G. Reid, Toronto, to editors, 'Reader Takes Over,' *Chatelaine*, November 1952.

2 E.Wood, Saskatoon, to editors, 'Reader Takes Over,' *Chatelaine*, December 1952, 72.

3 Ellen McCracken, *Decoding Women's Magazines: From Mademoiselle to Ms.* (London, 1993), 13.

4 Mrs Alex Henry, Woodstock, Ontario, to the editors, 'The Last Word Is Yours,' *Chatelaine*, September 1960, 154.

5 Statistics from the General Survey Database, which includes all 240 issues published from January 1950 to December 1969.

6 Based on the figures for 1950, 1955, and 1959, the percentage of net single copies sold was calculated using the figures for net single copy and total net paid copies. See *Canadian Advertising Rates and Data*, Fourth Quarter 1950, 120; *Canadian Advertising: Canadian Media Authority*, May–June issue 1955, 100; *Canadian Advertising: The Media Rate and Data Authority*, January/ February 1960, 116.

7 W.M.P., Toronto, to editor, 'Reader Takes Over,' *Chatelaine*, May 1953.

8 Statistics from the General Survey Database.

9 AO, MHRS F-4-1-b, box 431, Doris Anderson to Lloyd M. Hodgkinson, 'Re 1962,' 10 November 1961.

10 Statistics compiled from the Chatelaine Survey Database.

11 Archives of Ontario (AO), Maclean Hunter Record Series (MHRS) F-4-1-a, box 429, series of memos from Joan Meredith to L. Hodgkinson: 19 December, 16 August, and 19 July 1960 .

12 From the Sixties Chatelaine Survey Database, the predominant cover colours in the decade were multicoloured primary/bold colours (30 covers); black and white (14); multicoloured pastel colours (12).

13 AO, MHRS F-4-3-a, box 435, Jean Young, Edmonton, to Doris Anderson, 20 June 1962.

14 Ibid., Doris Anderson to Jean Young, Edmonton, 29 June 1962.

15 'Chatelaine Centre,' *Chatelaine*, January 1957, 1.

16 Mrs Campbell Humphries, Castleford, Ontario, to editors, 'Letters to *Chatelaine*,' March 1957, 2.

17 F.W.L., High Bluff, Manitoba, to editors, 'Reader Takes Over,' *Chatelaine*, September 1951, 72.

18 Floyd Allard, Paddockwood, Saskatchewan, to editors, 'Reader Takes Over,' *Chatelaine*, June 1954, 3.

19 Mrs Cynthia Ritchie, St John's, to editors, 'The Last Word Is Yours,' *Chatelaine*, April 1963, 120.

20 Mrs Jennie L. Kennedy, Moncton, NB, to editors, 'The Last Word Is Yours,' *Chatelaine*, September 1962, 144.

21 Mrs Elizabeth Saunders, Truro, NS, to editors, ibid.

22 Mrs T.H. Field, Edmonton, to editors, ibid.

23 Mrs A.J. McDonald, Winnipeg, to editors, ibid.

24 AO, MHRS F-4-3-a, box 435, 'A Shocked Reader' to Doris Anderson, July 1962.

25 Ibid., Mrs Eleanor M. Scott, Ottawa, to Doris Anderson, 7 July 1962.

26 Cover, *Chatelaine*, April 1960.

27 See Veronica Cusack, 'Patron Saint,' *Toronto Life*, January 1995, 46–52. Although Chalmers reluctantly agreed to be interviewed by Cusack, she refused to comment 'on many aspects of her life: her nine-year relationship with lover Barbara Amesbury, her spell in England in the fifties and her career as an art director' (49). During her tenure at *Chatelaine* she was closeted, as were virtually all gay and lesbian professionals in the era. Although readers were never privy to this information about Chalmers, from a modern perspective it factors into an evaluation of the covers she designed for the magazine – particularly since most of her covers fea-

tured assertive female models and artistic compositions, and differed considerably from the male cover designers who preceded and followed her.

28 Mrs Audrey W. Phillips, Ottawa, to editors, 'The Last Word Is Yours,' *Chatelaine*, June 1960, 136.

29 Mrs Guy Fortier, Montreal, to editors, ibid.

30 A.I. Hainey, Beauharnois, Quebec, to editors, 'The Last Word Is Yours,' *Chatelaine*, July 1960, 84.

31 Eveleen Dollery, 'Is There a Typical Canadian Beauty?' *Chatelaine*, April 1960, 115.

32 Miss Ann Arthur Hitchock, Cowansville, Quebec, to editors, 'The Last Word Is Yours,' *Chatelaine*, August 1960, 112.

33 Mrs Henry Swig, Hagersville, Ontario, to editors, ibid.

34 A few readers, such as Mrs Archer Hay-Roe, were supportive of racial diversity in *Chatelaine*'s models (a tactic the magazine used very infrequently): 'It was a joy to see the little Oriental baby modeling the baby set in Crafts (February). What a sweetheart! Such a friendly gesture toward the kind of cooperation we want in this world. Why should all our models have white skins?' Mrs Archer Hay-Roe, Edmonton, to editors, 'The Last Word Is Yours,' *Chatelaine*, April 1961, 156.

35 J. Balint, Toronto, to editors, 'The Last Word Is Yours,' *Chatelaine*, December 1960, 116.

36 Mrs J. McArthur, Red Deer, Alberta, to editors, 'The Last Word Is Yours,' *Chatelaine*, October 1969, 120.

37 'Chatelaine Advertisement,' *Canadian Advertising: Canadian Media Authority*, September–October 1955, 106.

38 '*Chatelaine*, Advertisement,' *Canadian Advertising Rates and Data*, October 1969, 75–7.

39 AO, MHRS F-4-1-b, box 431, Sheelage M. Sheeran, Sherbrooke, Quebec, to Doris Anderson, 28 August 1961.

40 Roland Marchand, *Advertising the American Dream: Making Way for Modernity, 1920–1940* (Berkeley, CA, 1985), xvii. For other useful scholarship on the ways in which advertisements operate, see Jackson Lears, *Fables of Abundance: A Cultural History of Advertising in America* (New York, 1994); Raymond Williams, 'Advertising the Magic System,' in *Problems in Materialism and Culture* (London, 1980); Judith Williamson, *Decoding Advertisement: Ideology and Meaning in Advertising* (London, 1978); Gillian Dyer, *Advertising as Communication* (London, 1982); William Leiss, Stephen Kline, and Sut Jhally, *Social Communication in Advertising: Persons, Products and Images of Well Being* (Toronto, 1986); John Berger, *Ways of Seeing* (New York, 1973); William M. O'Barr, *Culture and the Ad: Exploring Otherness in the*

World of Advertising (Boulder, CO, 1994); and Paul Rutherford, *The New Icons? The Art of Television Advertising* (Toronto, 1994).

41 There were 1007 advertisements in the Fifties Ad Database. Given the large number of ads published in each issue, a decision was made to sample one issue per year, instead of the three issues used for the other component databases. The Fifties Ad Database includes all the ads from the January 1950, May 1951, September 1952, January 1953, May 1954, September 1955, January 1956, May 1957, September 1958, and January 1959 issues.

42 'Food,' represents general food products, processed food, baby food, baking supplies, and soft drinks. 'Household appliances, furniture, and building supplies' include all home furnishings, appliances (both large and small), home entertainment, paint, wallpaper, and anything connected with repairing, remodelling, or building a home – copper tubing, roofing shingles, furnaces, and the like. 'Beauty and toiletries' include all cosmetics, shampoos, soaps, depilatories, hair colouring, mouthwash, and so on. 'General household products' include household cleansers and general items for the home, such as paper products, light bulbs, and aluminum foil. 'Clothing' is self-explanatory, except that it includes all family members, and both ready-to-wear garments and the notions, patterns, and material needed for sewing at home. 'Medical products and feminine hygiene,' include medical products for the entire family. 'Leisure, hobbies, and crafts' include all travel advertisements, knitting, and sewing patterns that were not clothing, book clubs, record clubs, and do-it-yourself manuals. 'Housewares' include linens, towels, bedding, china, silverware, pots and pans, and so on.

43 The Sixties Ads Database has 998 advertisements (9 less than its comparable fifties database). In the fifties, only 18 per cent of advertisements were a full page and very few (1.1%) were larger than one page. Unless otherwise identified, all statistics about advertising in *Chatelaine*, are taken from this sampling.

44 The number of half-page ads (sixties figure/fifties figure) (21%/29%) declined slightly, but the number of quarter-page advertisements was fairly consistent (22%/21%); the largest declines were in the eighth-page category (10%/13%) and under (7%/12%).

45 In the fifties, most ads had an equal amount of text and graphics (41%); other categories were as follows: mostly graphics (38%); mostly text (18%); or no graphics (3%). The sixties were more visual: ads with mostly text (15%) were less common, although the number of ads without graphics (6%) doubled.

46 In comparison, only 33 per cent of the fifties' ads did not have any people

in them. Although all types of products used ads without people, the majority of ads without people came from these six product categories: building supplies, appliances, and furniture (26%); food products (21%); leisure – including travel, hobbies, and crafts (14%); medical (11%); general household (8%); and housewares (7%).

47 William Leiss, Stephen Kline, and Sut Jhally, *Social Communication in Advertising: Persons, Products and Images of Well-Being* (Toronto, 1986); Richard W. Pollay, 'The Subsidizing Sizzle: A Descriptive History of Print Advertising, 1900–1980,' *Journal of Marketing* 49 (summer 1985).

48 In the sixties, the gender breakdown for advertisements (with people) were women alone (51.6%); women and men (14.2%); men alone (7.8%); mother and children (7.6%); parents and children (2.8%); boys and girls (2.6%); boys alone (2.6%); girls alone (2.4%); unrelated adults and kids (2.4%); unidentifiable gender (2.3%); teenage girls (2.1); fathers and children (0.5%); teenage couples (0.1%); and teenage boys (0.1%). In the fifties, the order was women alone (56.5%); women and men (14.7%); mothers and children (6.8%); girls alone (3.8%); unidentifiable (3.2%); and men alone (3.13%).

49 Both Judith Williamson, *Decoding Advertisements: Ideology and Meaning in Advertising* (London, 1978), 12, and Gillian Dyer, *Advertising as Communication* (London, 1982), 116, use this term to describe the advertisement's effect on the viewer.

50 Dyer, *Advertising as Communication*, 116.

51 'A Vice President Comes to Dinner,' Weston's advertisement, *Chatelaine*, August 1951, inside back cover.

52 'Her apron strings are family ties,' Weston's, *Chatelaine*, November 1950, 56.

53 For further examples and analysis of the discontinuity between popular culture and 'reality' for many North Americans (women in particular), see Karal Ann Marling, *As Seen on TV: The Visual Culture of Everyday Life in the 1950s* (Cambridge, MA, 1994); Susan J. Douglas, *Where the Girls Are: Growing Up Female with the Mass Media* (New York, 1994); and Stephanie Coontz, *The Way We Never Were: American Families and the Nostalgia Trap* (New York, 1992).

54 'One done ... One to go,' Weston's, *Chatelaine*, June 1954, 75.

55 McCracken, *Decoding Women's Magazines*, 2.

56 'One done ... One to go.'

57 'Complete Freedom from Work on Washday,' Canadian Westinghouse Company Ltd., *Chatelaine*, January 1953, back cover.

58 'Enjoy Easier Cleaning with the new G-E Swivel Top Cleaner,' Canadian General Electric Company Ltd., *Chatelaine*, April 1954, 92.

59 'She's in love ... and she loves Community,' Oneida Community Ltd., *Chatelaine*, October 1953, back cover.

60 'Give the Bride a Bissell Sweeper,' Bissell Carpet Sweeper Co. of Canada Ltd., *Chatelaine*, May 1954, 46.

61 'The Right Gift for the Right Occasion,' Canadian GE Appliances, *Chatelaine*, May 1954, 93.

62 'Wake Up Henry – It's Time for Sunday Brunch,' Aunt Jemima Ad, *Chatelaine*, September 1958, 43.

63 'When a floor is Amtico Vinyl Flooring,' American Biltrite Rubber Company, Ltd., *Chatelaine*, September 1959, 77.

64 'Look Lovelier in 10 Days,' Noxzema, and 'Why He Left So Early,' Listerine Antiseptic, *Chatelaine*, January 1953, 47 and 2; 'Makes You Feel So Fresh and Feminine,' Yardley Lavender, *Chatelaine*, March 1958, 4.

65 'Lets You Feel So Free,' Playtex Girdle, *Chatelaine*, January 1953, 57; 'Magic Controller,' Playtex Girdle,' *Chatelaine*, September 1953, 5.

66 'For warmth and comfort, there's nothing like a handknit Mary Maxim sweater!' Miss Mary Maxim, *Chatelaine*, September 1958, 49.

67 'Baking Is a Simple Thing,' Magic Baking Powder, *Chatelaine*, September 1965, 61.

68 Marling, *As Seen on TV*, 227.

69 'Behind every successful little girl is a mother who serves Velveeta,' Kraft, *Chatelaine*, September 1968, 21.

70 'Don't Be Fat,' Slim-Mint Gum, *Chatelaine*, May 1967, 169; 'Miss C Diet Book,' *Chatelaine*, September 1968, 104.

71 'Staying Slim – Is it worth the trouble?' Metrecal, *Chatelaine*, May 1961, 4–5.

72 'Why be a martyr on cottage cheese ... when you can have Diet De Luxe fruit meringues instead?' Aylmer Diet De Luxe Fruit Cocktail, *Chatelaine*, May 1967, 19.

73 'Now *Europe* gives you a figure so beautiful ... other women will hate you!' Distinction by Triumph of Europe, *Chatelaine*, October 1960, inside back cover.

74 For a fascinating history of this historic campaign, see Malcolm Gladwell, 'Annals of Advertising – True Colours: Hair Dye and the Hidden History of Postwar America,' *The New Yorker*, 22 March 1999, 70–81. My thanks to Ben Redekop for sending me a copy of this article.

75 'Does she or Doesn't She?' Miss Clairol, *Chatelaine*, May 1961, inside front cover.

76 'Most English Girls Start Using Nivea at a Very Early Age,' Nivea, *Chatelaine*, September 1965, 3.

77 Tex-Made advertisement, *Chatelaine*, January 1963, 71.

78 Ibid., January 1966, 15.

79 There were a number of blatantly patronizing, sexist advertisements that portrayed women as fickle, fashion-driven consumers. Ads for Chevrolet Camaro, 'Go ahead. Let him drive it once in a while,' *Chatelaine*, May 1967, 138, ecstatically promised, 'Colours? Emphatically yes! To provide a contrast with your favourite outfit or to match your favourite hair colour!' Or ads featuring long-suffering men (usually husbands), such as this ad for Femcin tablets with the phrase: 'I used to suffer from menstrual cramps.' After explaining how much his wife, and thus he, suffered from her 'black moods,' depression, and complaining, the ad ends with this relieved note: 'Well, life has been different for my wife, and for me, ever since she first used FEMCIN ... she now acts like the woman I married every day of the month.' *Chatelaine*, September 1968, 82.

80 McClary advertisement, *Chatelaine*, May 1967, 17.

81 International Paints advertisement, ibid., 113.

82 Domtar advertisement, ibid., 99.

83 Brinton advertisement, ibid., 108.

84 Air Canada advertisement, *Chatelaine*, September 1965, 63.

85 'Velveeta – Dutch children thrive on it ... so can yours!' Kraft, *Chatelaine*, September 1965, 15; 'Niblets Italiano,' Green Giant, *Chatelaine*, January 1963, 15; 'How to be famous for your Spanish Rice!' Uncle Ben's, *Chatelaine*, May 1964, 71; 'Buena! Aylmer **Pea**ella,' Aylmer's, *Chatelaine*, May 1961, 63.

86 'Mexican Holiday Colours,' Pond's High Lustre Lipstick, *Chatelaine*, May 1961, 115; and 'Pacific Sunset,' Max Factor, *Chatelaine*, May 1964, 5.

87 'New! Coiffure Italienne Color Highlight Shampoo by Max Factor,' Max Factor, *Chatelaine*, September 1965, 19.

88 'Tomorrow you can whoop it up in Cherokee Territory ... Tomorrow you can entertain in Spain ... Tomorrow you can splash à la Dolce Vita ... because today you discovered Domco Solid Vinyl Tile,' Domco, *Chatelaine*, September 1968, 106–7.

89 'Swift's Premium' advertisement, *Chatelaine*, May 1961, 22–3.

90 'The Safest Gun in the West!' GM, *Chatelaine*, September 1962, 130–1.

91 'Chatelaine Ad,' *Canadian Advertiser: The Media Rate and Data Authority*, May/June 1961, 103: 'The MAB [Magazine Advertising Bureau] Revenue Summary for the first quarter of 1961 shows *Chatelaine*, ahead of all magazines in Canada in the following major advertising classifications: Clothing and Dry Goods: Combined revenue $107,041; Drugs and Toilet Goods: Combined Revenue: $299,989; Food and Food Beverages: Combine Revenue: $569,464; Furniture and Furnishings: Combined Revenue: $111,237; Soaps and Housekeepers' Supplies: Combined Revenue: $42, 605.'

92 AO, MHRS F-4-5-a, box 449, Ted Hart, 'Hart Speech to Directors, Draft

1971,' 5. The share of market varied during the decade. According to the Hart document, the numbers were '1958 – 12%; 1960 – 23%; 1962 – 27%; 1964 – 23%; 1966 – 28%; 1968 – 28%; 1970 – 29%.'

93 AO, MHRS F-4-5-a, box 448, Ted Hart, 'Report Prepared for Kraft Foods Limited,' 10.

94 AO, MHRS F-4-1-a, box 430, Lloyd M. Hodgkinson to Mr H.T. Markey, advertising manager, Wabasso Cotton Company, 23 June 1960.

95 Ibid., Lloyd M. Hodgkinson to Vivian Wilcox, 18 August 1960.

96 Ibid., Militza Anich, advertising manager, Dominion Oilcloth and Lino-leum Co. Limited, Montreal, to Barbara Reynolds, home editor, 18 April 1960.

97 AO, MHRS F-4-1-b, box 431, Lloyd M. Hodgkinson to J.E. McDougall, Cockfield, Brown and Company Ltd., Montreal, 24 March 1961. Cockfield, Brown was an advertising firm.

98 'To anyone who has ever driven a car – The Magazine Advertising Bu-reau of Canada Advertisement,' advertisement for MAB, *Chatelaine*, September 1968, 102.

99 For an expanded analysis of the Cold War propaganda over consumer goods, see Marling, *As Seen on TV*, 243.

100 AO, MHRS E-2-3-e, box 336. A collection of these reports, all from the fifties, is in this box.

101 Ibid., box 339, American Association of Advertising Agencies, 'The A.A.A.A. Study on Consumer Judgement of Advertising – Phase II,' 28 October 1964, 2.

102 The twelve participants were from Nova Scotia, Ontario, and British Columbia. They were almost entirely female, 11 to 1, largely from rural areas, and represent an age range of early forties to early eighties.

103 Ruby H. Bauer to editors, 'Reader Takes Over,' *Chatelaine*, May 1958, 8.

104 Mrs N.W.B. to editors, *Chatelaine*, September 1951, 72.

105 Julia Mulligan, home economics convener, Langley Women's Institute, to editors, *Chatelaine*, August 1956 2.

106 Mrs L.G. Henders, Elm Creek, Manitoba, to editors, *Chatelaine*, November 1958, 116.

107 AO, MHRS F-4-3-a, box 435, Mrs Harold Taylor, Truro, NS, to Doris Anderson, 30 November 1962.

108 Ibid., Mrs George Putnam, Vancouver, to Doris Anderson, 16 October 1962.

109 Ibid., box 434, Mrs Edna Hall, Ottawa, to Doris Anderson, 18 August 1962.

110 Ibid., Doris Anderson to Mrs Edna Hall, Ottawa, 27 August 1962.

Chapter 5: 'The Cinderella from Pugwash': Advice from the *Chatelaine* Institute

1 H.M. Pawley, Edmonton to editors, 'Letters to Chatelaine,' *Chatelaine,* June 1956, 3.
2 Mrs E. MacAlpine, Carbon, Alberta, to editors, 'You Were Asking *Chatelaine?' Chatelaine,* May 1955, 4.
3 Mrs W.F. Bennett, Hutchinson, Kansas, to editors, 'The Last Word Is Yours,' *Chatelaine,* July 1964, 74.
4 '*Chatelaine* ad,' *Canadian Advertising: Canadian Media Authority,* September–October 1954, 114–15.
5 '*Chatelaine* ad,' *Canadian Advertising: Canadian Media Authority,* September–October 1953, 104.
6 Archives of Ontario (AO), Maclean Hunder Record Series (MHRS) F-4-5-a, box 448, 'Readership June 70 Issue,' quoted in Ted Hart, 'Report Prepared for Kraft Foods Limited 1970–1971,' 26.
7 'Fifty Favourite Family Recipes,' *Chatelaine,* January 1954, 22.
8 'Chatelaine Centre,' *Chatelaine,* February 1956, 1.
9 AO, MHRS F-4-5-a, box 449, Ted Hart, 'General Presentation – Script October 14, 1971,' 3.
10 'Chatelaine and Hostess household coverage,' advertisement, *Canadian Advertising Rates and Data,* 1969.
11 AO, MHRS F-4-3-a, box 435, Mrs Ursula McGowan, Smiths Falls, Ontario, to Doris Anderson, 27 October 1962.
12 Ibid., Mrs Irene Makins, Ayr, Ontario, to Doris Anderson, 12 May 1962.
13 Ibid., box 434, A Subscriber, Harris, Saskatchewan, 5 March 1962.
14 Miss Ruth C. Baxter, Annapolis Royal, NS, to editors, 'The Last Word Is Yours,' *Chatelaine,* May 1966, 106.
15 AO, MHRS F-4-4-b, box 446, Bertha E. Scott, Edgewood, BC, to Doris Anderson, 8 June 1962.
16 Ibid., Doris Anderson to Bertha E. Scott, 29 June 1962.
17 'Chatelaine Centre,' *Chatelaine,* March 1954, 1.
18 'Chatelaine for the Canadian Woman,' *Chatelaine,* October 1957, 1.
19 In the Food Database, lists of Chatelaine Institute recipes were scanned for ingredients, in particular the use of convenience foods, such as canned soups, cake mixes, tinned vegetables, and pre-made pastry dough, to guage whether the magazine made a conscious attempt to promote processed and convenience foods. Processed food advertising accounted for 9 per cent of all food advertising in the magazine, while unprocessed food and baking supplies accounted for 4.75 per cent of food advertisements.

20 'Penny Wise Meat Loaf Dinners in Company Dress,' *Chatelaine*, April 1953, 20–1, and 'Dollar Meals That Taste like a Million,' *Chatelaine*, January 1959, 18–19.
21 Anderson interview, 1994.
22 'Fifty Family Favourites,' *Chatelaine*, January 1951, 25.
23 'Prize Winning Salads,' *Chatelaine*, August 1951, 19 and 21.
24 Mrs Roy McNichol, Dundee, Quebec, to editors, 'Letters to *Chatelaine*,' *Chatelaine*, January 1954.
25 Mrs E.G. Sundquist, Nanaimo, BC to editors, ibid.
26 Margaret Rasmussen, Vancouver, to editors, 'You Were Asking *Chatelaine*?' *Chatelaine*, February 1955, 4.
27 Mrs E.H. Donnelly, Windsor, Ontario, to editors, 'Reader Takes Over,' *Chatelaine*, November 1952, 3.
28 Mrs Grace E. DeJong, Montreal, to Editors, 'Reader Takes Over,' *Chatelaine*, July 1954, 3.
29 Elaine Collett, director of the *Chatelaine* Institute, 'Food Fit for a Queen,' *Chatelaine*, June 1959, 24–5.
30 AO, MHRS F-4-4-b, box 442, Mrs Lois Browett, Hamilton, to Doris Anderson, 30 June 1962.
31 Mrs Mary G. Wark, Owen Sound, Ontario, to editors, 'Letters to *Chatelaine*,' *Chatelaine*, March 1957, 2.
32 Beryl Haslam, Pointe Claire, Quebec, to editors, 'The Last Word Is Yours,' *Chatelaine*, December 1959, 116.
33 AO, MHRS F-4-3-a, box 434, memo from J.M. Donovan to Chatelaine Editorial Department, 19 January 1962: 'Mrs John Enslen, Box 23, Seven Persons, Alberta, requested cancellation of her subscription and refund of remaining portion. She has some comments in her letter concerning the contents of *Chatelaine* which we thought you might find interesting.'
34 Elaine Collett, '98 Cent January Specials,' *Chatelaine*, January 1960, 26–7; 'Ten New Ways with a Pound of Hamburg,' *Chatelaine*, September 1961, 47; and 'Eat Thrifty Meals,' *Chatelaine*, September 1967, 46–7.
35 Elaine Collett, 'How to Eat Better and Save $200,' *Chatelaine*, January 1962, 40.
36 AO, MHRS F-4-4-b, box 442, Donna Atcheson, Saint John, NB, to Doris Anderson, December 1962.
37 AO, MHRS F-4-3-a, box 434, Mrs Margaret N. Davies, Cobourg, Ontario, to Anderson, 10 January 1962.
38 Una Abrahamson, 'Try These Strange Fruits,' *Chatelaine*, February 1964, 68.
39 Ethnic cuisine, as a theme of food features, accounted for 15 per cent of all sixties' food articles. It ranked third behind thrift (26%) and new and

improved (21%). In the fifties, ethnic cuisine was ranked in eighth spot (2.6%) of all food articles, behind thrift, traditional values, new and improved, entertainment, special, speed of preparation, and ease of preparation. Sixties Food Database and Fifties Food Database.

40 Elaine Collett, 'South Seas Foods to Enchant Your Natives,' *Chatelaine*, May 1963, 46–7.

41 Editors, 'What's New with Us,' *Chatelaine*, March 1965, 2.

42 Elaine Collett, 'Thirty Minute Dinners,' *Chatelaine*, September 1960, 42; and 'Quick Casseroles from Cans,' *Chatelaine*, May 1968, 48.

43 Elaine Collett, 'Feed a Family of Five for $22 a Week,' *Chatelaine*, January 1961, 54.

44 Ruth E. Moyle, director, Consumer Section of the Department of Agriculture and Food, Ontario, to editors, 'The Last Word Is Yours,' *Chatelaine*, September 1969, 124.

45 Mrs K. Norman, Islington, Ontario, to editors, 'The Last Word Is Yours,' *Chatelaine*, January 1960, 80.

46 Mrs Jean Rousseau, Ste-Foy, Quebec, to editors, 'The Last Word Is Yours,' *Chatelaine*, May 1964, 86.

47 Pat Ferguson, Camp Wainwright, Alberta, to editors, 'The Last Word Is Yours,' *Chatelaine*, January 1967, 72.

48 'Chatelaine Takes a Fresh Look at House Cleaning,' *Chatelaine*, March 1959, 63–70.

49 Audrey Singer, Port Credit, Ontario, to editors, 'The Last Word Is Yours,' *Chatelaine*, June 1959, 110.

50 Mrs D. Robinson, Greenwood, NS, to editors, ibid.

51 N. Smith, Scarborough, Ontario, to editors, ibid.

52 Una Abrahamson, 'A Streamlined System for Housekeeping,' *Chatelaine*, January 1965, 25.

53 Cover, *Chatelaine*, April 1954.

54 Rosemary Boxer, 'Cinderella from Pugwash,' ibid., 31.

55 D.I. Langley, Prairie, BC, to editors, 'Reader Takes Over,' *Chatelaine*, June 1954, 3.

56 Mrs Murray Smith, Pugwash, NS, to editors, ibid.

57 Editors, 'What's New with Us,' *Chatelaine*, November 1960, 2.

58 Eveleen Dollery advertisement, 'Which Half of Your Face Is More Beautiful?' *Chatelaine*, November 1962, 90.

59 Harvey Levenstein, *Paradox of Plenty: A Social History of Eating in America* (New York, 1993), 137.

60 Eveleen Dollery, 'Three Dazzling Diet Successes,' *Chatelaine*, April 1963, 40–5; Eveleen Dollery, 'Three Diet Winners Discover New Beauty,'

Chatelaine, April 1964, 30–5; and Eveleen Dollery, 'A 212 Pound Girl Becomes a 100 Pound Bride,' *Chatelaine*, April 1966, 56–7.

61 Dollery, 'Three Diet Winners Discover New Beauty,' 32, and Dollery, 'Three Dazzling Diet Successes,' 42.

62 Dollery, 'A 212 Pound Girl Becomes a 100 Pound Bride,' 56.

63 Mrs Ronald Hatch Sr, Red Head Cove, Newfoundland, to editors, 'The Last Word Is Yours,' *Chatelaine*, July 1964, 74.

64 '*Chatelaine*'s MM Diet,' *Chatelaine*, July 1962, 26–7; and 'A New Way to Lose Weight: LP Diet,' *Chatelaine*, February 1966, 17–19.

65 Mrs Margaret Devine, Ballycastle, Northern Ireland, to editors, 'The Last Word Is Yours,' *Chatelaine*, May 1966, 106.

66 Mrs B. Eugenie Terrell, Mallorytown, Ontario, to editors, ibid.

67 Susie Orbach, *Fat Is a Feminist Issue* (New York, 1979).

68 Editors, 'What's New with Us,' *Chatelaine*, April 1963, 3.

69 Vivian Wilcox, 'Fashions for Your Golden Years,' *Chatelaine*, April 1961, 46–7.

70 Eveleen Dollery and Vivian Wilcox, 'Whatever Happened to the Homely Girl?' *Chatelaine*, October 1963, 42–5.

71 Audrey Vogt, Quesnel, BC, to editors, 'The Last Word Is Yours,' *Chatelaine*, March 1960, 148.

72 Mrs Phyllis Poulter, Montreal, to editors, 'The Last Word Is Yours,' *Chatelaine*, February 1966, 90.

73 Mrs A.F. Pearce, Colfax, Saskatchewan, to editors, 'The Last Word Is Yours,' *Chatelaine*, October 1965, 164.

74 Mrs P. Allen, Moose Jaw, Saskatchewan, to editors, 'The Last Word Is Yours,' *Chatelaine*, January 1965, 72.

75 AO, MHRS F-4-3-a, box 434, Mrs Dorothy Brown, to Doris Anderson, 3 November 1961.

76 'Chatelaine Centre,' *Chatelaine*, April 1956, 1.

77 Catherine Fraser, 'Course in Home Decorating: Lesson One,' *Chatelaine*, May 1952, 21.

78 Mrs R. Dowson, Nemiskam, Alberta, to editors, 'Reader Takes Over,' *Chatelaine*, January 1953, 3.

79 Mrs E. Dodds, Montreal, Quebec, to editors, 'Reader Takes Over,' *Chatelaine*, July 1952, 4.

80 Catherine Fraser, 'Five Rooms for Fun – See Canada First in Your Own Basement,' *Chatelaine*, August 1952, 20–1.

81 Marion Downton, St John's, to editors, 'Reader Takes Over,' *Chatelaine*, March 1958, 6.

82 Alain Campagne, 'Chatelaine Expo Home,' *Chatelaine*, May 1967, 89.

83 Jean Wright, 'What's New at *Chatelaine*,' *Chatelaine*, January 1968, 3.

84 Saul Field, Willowdale, Ontario, to editors, 'The Last Word Is Yours,' *Chatelaine*, January 1968, 68.

85 In 1998, a house listed on the resale market in Saskatoon was characterized as a 'Chatelaine Design Home,' so clearly the status of these homes is still apparent to some.

86 Mrs E. Armstrong, Etobicoke, Ontario, to editors, 'The Last Word Is Yours,' *Chatelaine*, February 1964, 76.

87 'Chatelaine Centre,' *Chatelaine*, April 1952, 1.

88 Mrs D. McCowan, Burrows, Saskatchewan, to editors, 'Reader Takes Over,' *Chatelaine*, October 1954, 3.

89 Mrs G.S. Morris, Victoria, BC, to editors, 'The Last Word Is Yours,' *Chatelaine*, January 1966, 80.

90 Mrs Louise Johnson, Hudson, Quebec, to editors, ibid.

91 Editors, 'Honeybees on Bikes in What's New with Us,' *Chatelaine*, September 1966, 2.

92 Leslie Laking, director of the Royal Botannical Gardens, Hamilton, Ontario, to editors, 'The Last Word Is Yours,' *Chatelaine*, May 1967, 184.

93 M. Siemienska, Montreal, to editors, 'The Last Word Is Yours,' *Chatelaine*, July 1961, 88.

94 AO, MHRS F-4-4-b, box 444, anonymous writer, – Lighthouse Station, Prince Rupert, BC, to Doris Anderson, 3 May 1962.

95 Ibid., M. Mawson to Jean Yack, 8 April 1963.

96 'Chatelaine Centre,' *Chatelaine*, January 1956, 1.

97 Mrs Robert Edmonds, Kaipokok Bay, Labrador, to editors, 'Letters to Chatelaine,' *Chatelaine*, July 1956, 2.

98 Gladys Story Cunningham, MD, Vancouver, to editors, 'The Last Word Is Yours,' *Chatelaine*, January 1967, 72.

Chapter 6: 'Searching for a Plain Gold Band': *Chatelaine* Fiction

1 See Maureen Honey, ed., *Breaking the Ties That Bind: Popular Stories of the New Woman, 1915–1930* (Norman, OK, and London, 1992); Jean Radford, ed., *The Progress of Romance: The Politics of Popular Fiction* (London, 1986); Janice A. Radway, *Reading the Romance: Women, Patriarchy, and Popular Literature* (Chapel Hill, NC, 1991). For an interesting case study that examines the quintessential formula magazine, *Reader's Digest*, see John Heidenry, *Theirs Was the Kingdom: Lila and DeWitt Wallace and the Story of the Reader's Digest* (New York, 1993).

2 John G. Cawelti, *Adventure, Mystery and Romance: Formula Stories as Art and Popular Culture* (Chicago 1976), 35.

3 Archives on Ontario (AO), Maclean Hunter Records Series (MHRS) F-4-3-a, box 435, Dorothy Paga, San Martin, Peru, to Doris Anderson, 12 December 1962.

4 Radway, *Reading the Romance*, 95.

5 Mrs M.A.E. McLeod, West Hill, Ontario, to editor, 'Reader Takes Over,' *Chatelaine*, November 1951, 114.

6 Statistics are taken from the General Survey Database, which includes all 240 issues published from January 1950 to December 1969.

7 AO, MHRS F-4-4-a, box 438, Mrs Elizabeth Hammond, director of the Shoe Information Bureau of Canada, to Doris Anderson, 30 January 1959.

8 Ibid., Doris Anderson to Mrs Elizabeth Hammond, 6 February 1959.

9 General Survey Database figures, based on total page fiction and total magazine page counts for 1950–9 and 1960–9.

10 Verna Vanmeer, Burnaby, BC, to the editor, 'The Last Word Is Yours,' *Chatelaine*, October 1958, 136.

11 The editors provided biographical information only on authors who were Canadian or were prominent writers. They identified the authors as Canadian by virtue of their birthplace, citizenship, or primary residence. Statistics are taken from the Sixties Fiction Database, which includes all the fiction stories published in the January, May, and September issues from January 1960 to September 1969. Of the fifty-nine stories in the sample, fifteen were written by Canadian authors.

12 AO, MHRS F-4-4-a, box 440, Almeda Glassey to Mrs C.K. Potter, Saskatoon, 5 January 1959.

13 The Chatelaine, Correspondents Inventory – December 31, 1961; lists the amount paid for articles, photographs, and fiction. Stories 4413: Fiction: Easy as Pie, and 4450: Fiction: The Big Mouth, were each worth $400. The condensed novel 'The Spanish House,' or 5713 on the inventory list, cost $1000. AO, MHRS F-4-1-b, box 432.

14 AO, MHRS F-4-4-a, box 438, Almeda Glassey to Keith A. Knowlton, 23 June 1959.

15 Miss K. Murphy, Grimsby, Ontario, to editors, 'The Last Word Is Yours,' *Chatelaine*, November 1961, 134.

16 Of the sixty authors who wrote the stories in the Sixties Fiction Database (one was co-authored), forty-nine were women, ten were men, and one androgynous name could not be classified. Thus, 82 per cent of the stories were written by female authors. The Chatelaine Correspondents Inventory dated December 31, 1961, lists the author for item 4450 as Susan Seavey= John Schaffner. AO, MHRS F-4-1-b, box 432.

17 AO, MHRS F-4-4-b, box 446, Keith A. Knowlton to Elizabeth Stewart, editorial assistant of *Writer's Digest*, 31 October 1961.

18 The breakdown for the fiction database was traditional romance, 18 out of 59 stories; family/marital romance, 18 stories; protagonist's quest (melodrama, see fifties fiction), 15 stories; mystery, 7 stories; and medical drama, 1 story.

19 In the fifties, stories in the genre 'protagonist's quest' accounted for 7.3 per cent of all fiction, and mysteries represented a negligible 1.47 per cent. A decade later, the number of stories published from each genre increased: 'quest' stories represented 25.4 per cent, while mysteries represented 11.8 per cent of all *Chatelaine*, fiction.

20 Cawelti, *Adventure, Mystery and Romance*, 45.

21 Canadian settings account for 66 per cent of all the sixties' fiction (it was 83 per cent in the fifties). Generally, while the locale was 'Canadian' (22.8% of all stories), it was really meant to be 'anywhere' – and hence accessible to readers across the country. The specific settings were quite different from the fifties. Western Canada was most popular (21%), followed by Ontario (12%), Quebec (5%), and the Maritimes (5%). The large number of Sheila MacKay Russell stories – all set in and around Edmonton – account for this shift to western settings. After the Canadian locales, American settings were most popular (22.8%), followed by Europe (7%), the Middle East (1.7%), and Australia (1.7%).

22 Characters were equally likely to live in urban (37.5%) and rural areas (37.5%), while less likely to live in suburbia (25%).

23 Alison Light, 'Writing Fictions: Femininity and the 1950s,' in Radford, ed., *The Progress of Romance*, 162.

24 Results are taken from the Fifties Fiction Database, which includes all stories published in the January, May, and September issues from January 1950 to September 1959.

25 AO, MHRS F-4-4-b, box 443, Keith A. Knowlton to Doris H. Anderson, 23 April 1962.

26 Ibid., box 445, Doris H. Anderson to W.O. Mitchell, 25 June 1962.

27 Ibid., box 446, Mrs Jane Van Every, Waterloo, Ontario, to Miss Almeda Glassey, *Chatelaine*, fiction editor, 9 November 1962.

28 Ibid., Almeda Glassey to Doris Anderson, undated.

29 AO, MHRS F-4-4-b, box 446, Almeda Glassey to Mrs Jane Van Every, 22 December 1962.

30 Ibid., box 443, Doris H. Anderson to Keith A. Knowlton, no date.

31 Mrs James Hoult, Montreal, to editors, 'The Last Word Is Yours,' *Chatelaine*, July 1963, 84.

32 AO, MHRS F-4-4-b, box 443, Almeda Glassey to Mrs Sewell Haggard, Curtis Brown Ltd, New York, 23 August 1962.

33 AO, MHRS F-4-3-a, box 435, Mrs L. Muise to Doris Anderson, 29 October 1962.

34 Doris Anderson, Editorial: 'Confessions of a Fiction Addict,' *Chatelaine*, July 1965, 1.
35 Brigitte Sagmeister, Downsview, Ontario, to Doris Anderson, 'The Last Word Is Yours,' *Chatelaine*, September 1965, 170.
36 Wini Breines, *Young, White and Miserable: Growing Up Female in the Fifties*, (Boston, 1992), xi.
37 Eileen Jensen, 'Whose Afraid of Love?' *Chatelaine*, May 1961, 33.
38 Gloria Goldreich, 'Regret,' *Chatelaine*, September 1965, 28.
39 Mrs E. Carnochan, New Westminister, BC, to editors, 'The Last Word Is Yours,' *Chatelaine*, December 1965, 88.
40 For another good example of the housewife theme, see Ruth Henning, 'Some Nights I Could Scream,' *Chatelaine*, January 1958, 13.
41 Sylvia Shirley, 'This Is Life,' *Chatelaine*, May 1950, 30.
42 Barbara Holland, 'The Best Wife in the World,' *Chatelaine*, January 1965, 18.
43 Barnett Kleiman, 'Couldn't Any Mother?' *Chatelaine*, January 1966, 23.
44 For examples of other trapped men, see Frances Malm, 'The Millionth Man,' *Chatelaine*, September 1951, 88; Lucia Mason, 'What Does She See in Him?' *Chatelaine*, January 1952, 10; Julie Prise, 'The Fishy Mr Kessinger,' *Chatelaine*, May 1952, 19; and Hugh Garner, 'The Wasted Years,' *Chatelaine*, September 1959, 33.
45 Julie Prise, 'The Dark Hall,' Chatelaine May 1951, 71.
46 See Barbara Ehrenreich, *The Hearts of Men: American Dreams and the Flight from Commitment* (New York, 1983), for a discussion of this phenomenon.
47 Prise, 'The Dark Hall,' 75 and 77.
48 Garner, 'The Wasted Years,' 33.
49 Alec Rackowe, 'Trial Marriage: Part One,' *Chatelaine*, October 1962, 34–5, and 'Trial Marriage: Part Two,' *Chatelaine*, November 1962, 54.
50 Rackowe, 'Trial Marriage: Part One,' 122.
51 Editorial commentary, 'The Last Word Is Yours,' *Chatelaine*, January 1963, 86.
52 Dr B.F. Nixon, Moose Jaw, Saskatchewan, to editors, ibid.
53 Name withheld, to editors, ibid.
54 AO, MHRS F-4-3-a, box 435, Mrs W. Hingston, Cawell, Saskatchewan, to Doris Anderson, 22 November 1962.
55 Ibid., Doris Anderson to Mrs W. Hingston, Cawell, Saskatchewan, 30 November 1962.
56 AO, MHRS F-4-4-b, box 445, Edmonton reader to Keith A. Knowlton, 15 September 1962.
57 The commentary on 'Sari' will be examined in the text, but space does not permit discussion of 'The Hutterites.' Readers interested in critical and praiseworthy letters received by the editors and published in the magazine

should see 'The Last Word Is Yours,' *Chatelaine*, January 1967, 72.

58 Russell, 'Sari in the Kitchen,' 37.

59 Mrs Janet Campbell, London, Ontario, to editors, 'The Last Word Is Yours,' *Chatelaine*, November 1962, 126.

60 AO, MHRS F-4-3-a, box 435, Mrs B. Larsen, Edmonton, to Doris Anderson, 29 October 1962.

61 Ibid., Doris Anderson to Mrs B. Larsen, Edmonton, 6 November 1962.

62 Louise Dickenson Rich, 'Vixen in the Snow,' *Chatelaine*, January 1950, 8.

63 See chapter 8 for an analysis of the article 'What Turns Women to Lesbianism?'

64 For a more sustained analysis of homosexual imagery, themes, and readings of *Chatelaine*, material, see V.J. Korinek, 'Don't Let Your Girlfriends Ruin Your Marriage,' *Journal of Canadian Studies* 33, 3 (1998).

65 Sheila MacKay Russell, 'Mr Nightingale,' *Chatelaine*, January 1968, 25.

66 B. Millway, Burnaby, BC, to editors, 'The Last Word Is Yours,' *Chatelaine*, April 1967, 128.

67 For a sample of this genre see Mignon G. Eberhart, 'Speak of Love & Murder,' May 1960, 44; Florence Ford, 'Death Comes to the Island,' *Chatelaine*, September 1960, 36; Forbes Rydell, 'If She Should Die' *Chatelaine*, January 1961, 18; Florence Ford, 'Claws of the Cat,' *Chatelaine*, September 1961, 44; Margaret Summeron, 'Nightingale at Noon,' *Chatelaine*, September 1962, 48; Taylor Caldwell, 'The Late Clara Beame,' *Chatelaine*, May 1963, 35; and Jacquelyn Humble, 'Ominous Stranger,' *Chatelaine*, May 1969, 28.

68 Eberhart, 'Speak of Love & Murder,' 44.

69 Humble, 'Ominous Stranger,' 28.

70 Cecile E. Leslie, to editor, 'Reader Takes Over,' *Chatelaine*, January 1952, 55.

Chapter 7: 'How to Live in the Suburbs': Editorials and Articles in the Fifties

1 (Mrs L.R.) Doris Gehman, Cultus Lake, BC, to editor, 'Reader Takes Over,' *Chatelaine*, August 1952, 3.

2 For accounts of housewife angst, upset, and the beginning of critical resistance to the status quo, see Wini Breines, *Young, White and Miserable: Growing Up Female in the Fifties* (Boston, 1992); Joanne Meyerowitz, ed., *Not June Cleaver: Women and Gender in Postwar America, 1945–1960* (Philadelphia, 1994); Melinda McCracken, *Memories Are Made of This* (Toronto: James Lorimer and Company, 1975); Joy Parr, ed., *A Diversity of Women* (Toronto, 1995).

3 Agnes L. Honey, Salmon Arm, BC, to editors, 'The Last Word Is Yours,' *Chatelaine*, September 1959, 144.

4 G.L. Galt, Ontario, to editors, 'Reader Takes Over,' *Chatelaine*, September 1951, 72.

5 The Fifties Editorials Database consists of all the editorials published in the January, May, and September issues of *Chatelaine*, from 1950 through 1959. Readers interested in a more detailed overview of this database – the categories of analysis and the results, should consult the appendix of my doctoral thesis, 'Roughing It in Suburbia: Reading *Chatelaine*, Magazine in the Fifties and Sixties' (University of Toronto, 1996).

6 In an interview with the author, Doris Anderson remarked that John Clare was a 'nice man but totally out of his depth! Didn't understand women, didn't want to understand women, and didn't want to be there.' Anderson interview, Toronto, 30 June 1994.

7 Byrne Hope Sanders, 'Goodbye and Good Luck,' *Chatelaine*, January 1952, 3.

8 Byrne Hope Sanders, 'Working Wives Outside the Home,' *Chatelaine*, July 1950, 3.

9 Byrne Hope Sanders, 'What Do You Think of Chatelaine Magazine?' *Chatelaine*, September 1951, 3.

10 Mrs W.R. Pringle, Headlingly, Manitoba, to the editor, 'Reader Takes Over,' *Chatelaine*, November 1951, 114.

11 Arthur Hanna, Montreal, to the editor, 'Reader Takes Over,' *Chatelaine*, November 1951, 4.

12 Ron de Armand, Vancouver, to the editor, ibid., 114.

13 Mrs N. Schurko, Gatehill, Ontario, to the editor, ibid., 4.

14 Mrs F.C. Knight, Burlington, Ontario, to editor, 'Reader Takes Over,' *Chatelaine*, July 1952, 6.

15 Lotta Dempsey, 'Chatelaine Centre,' *Chatelaine*, April 1952, 1.

16 Agnes Macphail, the first woman to sit in the House of Commons, was elected as the MP for Southeast Grey and held her seat from 1921 to 1940. After her federal defeat, she moved to the Ontario legislature and served as an MPP (York East) from 1943 to 1951.

17 Lotta Dempsey, '... she wouldn't have been elected dog-catcher ...,' *Chatelaine*, April 1952, 3.

18 Montreal subscriber, to editor, 'Reader Takes Over,' *Chatelaine*, June 1952, 2.

19 A former admirer, to editor, ibid.

20 Lotta Dempsey, 'Editorial,' *Chatelaine*, August 1952, 1.

21 Mrs N. Schurko, Gatehill, Ontario, to editor, 'Reader Takes Over,' *Chatelaine*, August 1952, 2.

22 John Clare, 'It's a Tough Time to Be in Love,' *Chatelaine*, May 1954, 1.

23 D.A. Robertson, Lethbridge, to the editor, 'Reader Takes Over,' *Chatelaine*, March 1953, 3.

24 '*Canadian Home Journal* ad' and '*Chatelaine* ad,' *Canadian Advertising: Canadian Media Authority*, January/February 1957, 121 and 127.

25 'New and improved' refers to their buyout of the *Canadian Home Journal* and the revamped style advocated by the Dichter Report.

26 Doris Anderson in Senate of Canada, *Proceedings of the Special Senate Committee on Mass Media*, The Honourable Keith Davey, chairman, Session No. 21 (Wednesday, 18 February 1970), 61.

27 Doris Anderson, 'We've Been Emerging Long Enough,' *Chatelaine*, October 1958, 16.

28 Doris Anderson, 'We Need More Women Scientists,' *Chatelaine*, April 1959, 16.

29 Doris Anderson, 'Clichés We Can Do Without,' *Chatelaine*, May 1959, 22.

30 Doris Anderson, 'Do Women Really Dominate Men?' *Chatelaine*, September 1959, 22.

31 Mrs H. McMaster, Orangeville, Ontario, to editors, 'Letters to Chatelaine,' *Chatelaine*, June 1956, 2.

32 Statistics taken from the 1950s Letters Database. All letters from the January, May, and September issues of *Chatelaine*, from January 1950 to September 1959 were entered into this database and classified by content and by the correspondant's region, gender, and tone of the letter.

33 'What's New,' *Chatelaine*, March 1958, 1.

34 Archives of Ontario (AO), Maclean Hunter Record Series (MHRS) F-4-4-a, box 438, Mrs P.J. Kennedy, East Chezzetcook, Halifax County, to editors.

35 Statistics compiled from the General Survey Database. Percentage based on the figures for total article pages and total magazine pages for the decade. The range throughout the decade is considerably different, from a low of 5.6 per cent in the November 1952 issue to a high in July 1953 of 31.3 per cent.

36 AO, MHRS, B-2-4–A-D, box 89, *Maclean Hunter Newsweekly*, 12 May 1950, 6.

37 Statistics taken from the 1950s Article database, which includes all articles published in the January, May, and September issues of *Chatelaine*, from January 1950 to September 1959.

38 Kate Aitken, Robert Thomas Allen, Doris McCubbin Anderson, Dr William E. Blatz, Max Braithwaite, Pearl S. Buck, June Callwood, Ellen Fairclough, Trent Frayne, Robert Fulford, Clyde Gilmour, Donald R. Gordon, Dr Marion Hilliard, Bruce Hutchison, Sidney Katz, Roger Lemelin, Jeanne Locke, Margaret Mead, C. Knowlton Nash, Hilda Neatby, Christina McCall

[Newman], Peter C. Newman, Phyllis Lee Peterson, Dorothy Sangster, Eric Sevareid, and Claire Wallace all contributed articles to *Chatelaine*, in the fifties.

39 Callwood interview, 1995.

40 The statistics on the article topics and themes were generated by the 1950s Article Database. A comparative graph for articles in both decades is included in chapter 8.

41 Beverley Grey, 'Housewives Are a Sorry Lot,' *Chatelaine*, March 1950, 26.

42 'Housewives Blast Business Girl,' *Chatelaine*, June 1950, 14.

43 'Who Is Beverley Grey?' *Chatelaine*, June 1950, 68.

44 Morgan Winters, 'The Common Law Wife,' *Chatelaine*, January 1952, 16.

45 M.F. Walpole, Hamilton, Ontario, to editors, 'Reader Takes Over,' *Chatelaine*, July 1952, 4.

46 Mrs L. Hosie, Regina, Saskatchewan, to editors, 'Reader Takes Over,' *Chatelaine*, April 1952, 104.

47 Mrs L.M., Winnipeg, Manitoba, to editors, ibid.

48 Blanche Gunton, 'We Drove the Kids to Alaska,' *Chatelaine*, January 1952, 8–9.

49 Mrs E.A. Scully, Lethbridge, Alberta, to editors, 'Reader Takes Over,' *Chatelaine*, April 1952, 104.

50 'Chatelaine Centre,' *Chatelaine*, April 1953, 1.

51 Marjorie Wilkins Campbell, 'One Big Happy Family,' *Chatelaine*, March 1952, 22.

52 Editor's note, 'Reader Takes Over,' *Chatelaine*, June 1952, 2.

53 M.M. Storey, Grandview, Manitoba, to editors, ibid.

54 Two anonymous American wives, 'Canadian Women Are Suckers,' *Chatelaine*, March 1952, 9.

55 'Reader Takes Over,' *Chatelaine*, March 1952, 2–3.

56 Mrs L.A. Pecker, Port Credit, Ontario, to editors, 'Reader Takes Over,' *Chatelaine*, March 1952, 2.

57 Fourteen Canadian Wives, Vets. Colony, Antigonish, NS, to editors, ibid., 88.

58 V.W., Vancouver, BC, to editors, ibid.

59 Mrs R. May, Strathcona, Manitoba, to editors, ' Reader Takes Over,' *Chatelaine*, July 1952, 4.

60 Gerald Anglin, 'The Pill That Could Shake the World,' *Chatelaine*, October 1953, 16–17.

61 Mrs Margaret Sorhus, Kindersley, Saskatchewan, to editors, 'Reader Takes Over,' *Chatelaine*, December 1953, 3.

62 Madeleine Waldron, Montreal, Quebec, to editors, ibid.

63 Jeannine Locke, 'Can the Hungarians Fit In?' *Chatelaine*, May 1957, 24.

64 Mrs M. Filwood, Toronto, to editors, 'Letters to Chatelaine,' *Chatelaine*, July 1957, 2.

65 Letter from a new reader, Halifax, NS, to editors, 'Letters to Chatelaine,' *Chatelaine*, August 1957, 3.

66 Rev. G. Simor, SJ, St. Elizabeth of Hungary Church, Toronto, to editors, ibid.

67 Yvonne Bobb and Jeannine Locke, 'Are Canadians Really Tolerant?' *Chatelaine*, September 1959, 27.

68 Ibid. Bobb claimed that many Canadians were smugly superior about their lack of racism, but her experiences convinced her otherwise. She labelled Canadians as hypocritical.

69 'The Last Word Is Yours,' *Chatelaine*, November 1959, 134.

70 Mrs Helen Ostapec, Thamesville, Ontario, to editors, ibid.

71 Mrs M. Ferrare, Toronto, to editors, ibid.

72 Helen Kent, Richmond Hill, to editors, ibid.

73 Sidney Margolius, 'We Sent an Expert to Help Make This Family Make Both Ends Meet,' *Chatelaine*, January 1954, 14.

74 Rev. W.B. Macodrum, Geraldton, Ontario, to editors, 'Reader Takes Over,' *Chatelaine*, March 1954, 3.

75 Mrs D. Milner, Winnipeg, to editors, 'Reader Takes Over,' ibid.

76 Mrs Lillian Tustin, Aldergrove, BC, to editors, 'Reader Takes Over,' *Chatelaine*, June 1954, 3.

77 Mrs W.J. Henley, Huntsville, Ontario, to editors, 'Reader Takes Over,' ibid.

78 'How to Live in THE SUBURBS: A Special Issue,' *Chatelaine*, March 1955.

79 'How *Chatelaine*, Went Calling in the Suburbs: Chatelaine Centre,' ibid., 1.

80 Doris Anderson, 'How to Live in a Suburb,' ibid., 12.

81 See Veronica Strong-Boag, 'Home Dreams: Women and the Suburban Experiment in Canada,' *Canadian Historical Review* 72, 4 (1991), for more details.

82 Anna Davies, Don Mills, to editors, 'You Were Asking Chatelaine,' *Chatelaine*, June 1955, 3.

83 Letter from Bunty Rutledge, Helen Selman, Margery E. Smith, Ruth Beedham, Dorothy Hunt, Barbara L. Duford, Rose Webber, and Helen Scott, Don Mills, Ontario, to editors, 'You Were Asking Chatelaine,' *Chatelaine*, May 1955, 3.

84 Davies letter, *Chatelaine*, June 1955, 3.

85 Kay Parley, to editors, 'You Were Asking Chatelaine,' *Chatelaine*, May 1955, 3.

86 Lorraine Porter, 'We Found Fun and Freedom on $2,100 a Year,' *Chatelaine*, September 1959, 43.

87 John Clare, 'Chatelaine Centre,' *Chatelaine*, January 1954, 1.

88 In an interview with the author, June Callwood stated that, among a select group, Dr Hilliard was candid and forthright about her lesbianism and, in particular, her partner and their relationship. Callwood now regrets that she 'omitted' references to same-sex sexuality because of her own naivety. See V.J. Korinek, '"Don't Let Your Girlfriends Ruin Your Marriage": Lesbian Imagery in *Chatelaine*, Magazine, 1950–1969,' *Journal of Canadian Studies* 33 3 (1998), for more detailed exploration of this topic in *Chatelaine*. For analysis of the thorny issue of 'naming,' see Estelle B. Freedman, '"The Burning of Letters Continues": Elusive Identities and the Historical Construction of Sexuality,' *Journal of Women's History* 9, 4 (1998).

89 Dr Marion Hilliard, 'Woman's Greatest Enemy Is Fatigue,' *Chatelaine*, January 1954, 13.

90 Betty Friedan, *The Feminine Mystique* (New York, 1963), 15.

91 Hilliard, 'Woman's Greatest Enemy Is Fatigue,' 58.

92 Mrs E.F. Hartwick, Arvida, Quebec, to editors, 'Reader Takes Over,' *Chatelaine*, April 1954, 3.

93 Mrs Louise Sandvold, Crystal Springs, Saskatchewan, to editors, ibid.

94 *Chatelaine* cover, January 1956.

95 Dr Marion Hilliard, 'Woman's Greatest Hazard – Sex,' *Chatelaine*, January 1956, 9.

96 Alfred C. Kinsey, *Sexual Behaviour in the Human Male* (Philadelphia, 1948), and A.C. Kinsey, *Sexual Behaviour in the Human Female* (Philadelphia, 1953).

97 Mrs John A. Brown, Toronto, to editors, 'You Were Asking Chatelaine,' *Chatelaine*, March 1956, 3.

98 E.M.K., Halifax, to editors, ibid.

99 R.H., Edmonton, to editors, ibid.

100 R.D., Campbellton, NB, to editors, ibid.

101 Owen J. Bennett, Abbotsford, BC, to editors, ibid.

102 Mrs Hilda Carscallen, Whitby, Ontario, to editors, 'You Were Asking Chatelaine,' *Chatelaine*, November 1955, 3.

103 Bonnie Lee McCubbins Adams, Fayetteville, Arkansas, to editors, 'You Were Asking Chatelaine,' *Chatelaine*, May 1956, 2.

104 Dr Marion Hilliard, 'Stop Being Just a Housewife,' *Chatelaine*, September 1956, 11.

105 Mrs Z.W. Dean, Calgary, to editors, 'Letters to Chatelaine,' *Chatelaine*, November 1956, 3.

106 A.B., Ontario, to editors, ibid.

107 Mrs R.B., Alberta, to editors, ibid.

108 Phyllis Lee Peterson, 'Don't Educate Your Daughters,' *Chatelaine*, September 1954, 18.

109 Letter from Joyce Fowler, BA, Mrs Marilyn Underhill, BA, Natalie Boyer, BA, Glenna Headley, BART, Barbara Scott, BA, Joyce Spani, BART, Saskatoon, to editors, 'Reader Takes Over,' *Chatelaine*, November 1954, 3.

110 Mrs Joan Arkett, Parry Sound, Ontario, to editors, ibid.

111 Mrs James French, Whalley, BC, to editors, ibid.

112 Mr and Mrs P. Grant, Agincourt, Ontario, to editors, ibid.

113 Anderson interview, 1994.

114 Dr Alastair MacLeod, 'The Sickness in Our Suburbs,' *Chatelaine*, October 1958, 22–3.

115 'What Our Readers Say about SUBURBIA,' *Chatelaine*, January 1959, 13.

116 Mrs Vera Fiddler, ibid., 50.

117 Mrs Irene Craig Neil, Port Stanley, Ontario, to editors, ibid.

118 In her articles, Veronica Strong-Boag has used this particular article and the feedback provided by the readers (primarily the statistical averages of negative and positive commentary) to indicate that there was 'diversity of opinion and experience.' However, the text is still the centrepiece of the analysis. That focus skews the portrait, as the inclusion of letters indicates not just that there was diversity of opinion, but that readers were openly critical of the expert and the magazine for publishing such an article. By shifting the analysis away from privileging the text, the readers' responses demonstrate that this material was contested terrain, that it was not uniformally accepted, and that readers were active in the process not only of making meaning from the messages in the magazine but of instructing other readers about how to critically evaluate the periodical's material. Strong-Boag, 'Home Dreams,' 501–2.

119 Cynthia Steers, 'How Much Are You Worth to Your Husband?' *Chatelaine*, April 1959, 34 and 35.

120 Mrs Anna Tennenhaus, Bathurst, NB, to editors, 'The Last Word Is Yours,' *Chatelaine*, June 1959, 110.

121 Tom Richardson, Kindersley, Saskatchewan, ibid.

122 Mrs D.T. Vanstone, Beaconsfield, Quebec, ibid.

123 Eileen Morris, 'How to Go to University at Home,' *Chatelaine*, August 1959, 8.

124 'Editorial Note,' *Chatelaine*, October 1959, 156.

125 AO, MHRS F-4-4-a, box 440, Doris Anderson to Eileen Morris, 17 August 1959.

126 AO, MHRS F-4-4-b, box 442, Mrs Phyllis Bentley, Montreal, to Anderson, 15 May 1962.

127 Joan Finnigan, 'Should Canada Change Its Abortion Law?' *Chatelaine*, August 1959, 17.
128 'The Last Word Is Yours,' *Chatelaine*, October 1959, 156.
129 Mrs H.C. Walshaw, Calgary, to editors, ibid.
130 V. Leclair, Ottawa, to editors, ibid.
131 Mrs R. S. Ricciotti, Wallaceburg, to editors, 'The Last Word Is Yours,' *Chatelaine*, November 1959, 134.
132 Mrs K. Kirkpatrick, Duncan, BC, to editors, ibid.
133 Betty Friedan, 'Introduction to the Tenth Anniversary Edition,' in Friedan, *The Feminine Mystique*, 6–7.

Chapter 8: 'Trying to Incite a Revolution': Editorials and Articles in the Sixties

1 Mrs Edith Sacker, Vancouver, to editor, 'The Last Word Is Yours,' *Chatelaine*, December 1961, 108.
2 Phyllis H. Meeks, Georgetown, Ontario, to editor, 'The Last Word Is Yours,' *Chatelaine*, March 1966, 112.
3 Archives of Ontario (AO), Maclean Hunter Record Series (MHRS) F-4-4-b, box 443, Dora Flagg, Wainfleet, Ontario, to Doris Anderson, 4 August 1962.
4 These results were taken from the Sixties Editorial Database, which includes all editorials published in the January, May, and September issues of *Chatelaine*, from January 1960 to September 1969.
5 Sixties Editorial Database.
6 AO, MHRS F-4-5–a, box 448, Starch readership figures, June 1970 Report, included in the Ted Hart Papers.
7 Ibid., box 449, Ted Hart Papers, 'Presentation Outline: Yardley Sales Meeting July 19–20, 1971' and 'Proctor and Gamble Introduction (1971).'
8 AO, MHRS F-4-4-b, box 445, Doris Anderson to reader, North Vancouver, 25 April 1962. The reader's letter is not extant (and it is clear from Anderson's letter that the letter writer requested anonymity), but it is possible to piece the situation together from Anderson's return letter.
9 Doris Anderson, 'We'll Do Our Own Censoring, Thank You Very Much,' *Chatelaine*, February 1960, 1.
10 'Do we Canadians need to have our television programs censored? Our February editorial on the CBC and Simone de Beauvoir said No. This month, readers take a stand of three to one for Yes ...' from the introductory header to 'The Last Word Is Yours,' *Chatelaine*, April 1960, 164.
11 Margaret Sluth, Ste-Therese, Quebec, to the editor, ibid.
12 Mr B.E. Field, Flesherton, Ontario, to the editor, ibid.

13 Doris Anderson, 'A Timid Defence of Feminists,' *Chatelaine*, March 1960, 1.

14 Doris Anderson, 'Women: A Chance for Change,' *Chatelaine*, October 1969, 1.

15 Mrs G. Baiton, Swift Current, Saskatchewan, to editor, 'The Last Word Is Yours,' *Chatelaine*, December 1969, 76.

16 Letter from Margee Hughes, London, Ontario, to editor, ibid.

17 Doris Anderson, ' Not Chattels – But Chattel-like Minds?' *Chatelaine*, May 1968, 1.

18 Mrs V. Musgrave, Willowdale, to editor, 'The Last Word Is Yours,' *Chatelaine*, October 1968, 120.

19 Mrs Leona A. Graham, Saint John, NB, to editor, ibid.

20 Doris Anderson, 'All Hair Combed and No Knotty Laces,' *Chatelaine*, April 1967, 1.

21 Doris Anderson, 'The Snail-like Battle for Progress,' *Chatelaine*, August 1967, 1.

22 Doris Anderson, June 1994.

23 Doris Anderson, 'We've Had All the Studies of Problems of Women We Need. Let's Have Action!' *Chatelaine*, June 1964, 1.

24 Doris Anderson, 'Let's Find Out What's Happening to Women,' *Chatelaine*, July 1966, 1.

25 Doris Anderson, 'Women 1967: Gains and Misses of 1966,' *Chatelaine*, February 1967, 1.

26 Doris Anderson, 'Can We Make This Royal Commission Count?' *Chatelaine*, March 1968, 1.

27 Naomi Black, 'Ripples in the Second Wave: Comparing the Contemporary Women's Movement in Canada and the United States,' and Monique Begin, 'The Royal Commission on the Status of Women in Canada: Twenty Years Later,' in Constance Backhouse and David H. Flaherty, eds., *Challenging Times: The Woman's Movement in Canada and the United States* (Montreal, 1992), both mention of the impact of editor Doris Anderson, and the role played by *Chatelaine*, on developments within the Canadian feminist movement in the sixties.

28 Doris Anderson, 'A Summer's Day Confession,' *Chatelaine*, August 1963, 1.

29 Murial Kerr, Ottawa, to editor, 'The Last Word Is Yours,' *Chatelaine*, October 1963, 114.

30 Doris Anderson, 'Here's Dirt in Your Eye House,' *Chatelaine*, June 1968, 1.

31 Mrs Margaret Reynolds, Edmonton, to editor, 'The Last Word Is Yours,' *Chatelaine*, August 1968, 72.

32 Phyllis M. Hodgson, Gibsons, BC, to editor, 'The Last Word is Yours,' *Chatelaine*, February 1961, 110.

33 Mrs Ilse Levi, Edmonton, to editors, 'The Last Word Is Yours,' *Chatelaine*, April 1961, 156.

34 Bernard E. Morin, Ottawa, to editor, 'The Last Word Is Yours,' *Chatelaine*, November 1969, 120.

35 Doris Anderson, 'A Funny Thing Happened on the Way to the Podium,' *Chatelaine*, November 1969, 1.

36 The statistics for articles are taken from the Chatelaine Articles Database for the 1960s, which includes 307 articles, the total of all the articles published in the January, May, and September issues of *Chatelaine*, from January 1960 to September 1969.

37 Women authors account for 83.4 per cent of all articles in the database. Statistics on nationality were not recorded because, with rare exceptions (e.g., Margaret Mead), almost all authors were Canadians. Canadian writers and locales, were the two key selling features that differentiated *Chatelaine*, from its American competition.

38 AO, MHRS F-4-1-a, box 427, Doris Anderson to Lloyd M. Hogkinson, re. Prices for Articles and Fiction in *Chatelaine*, 7 June 1960.

39 This is an omnibus category that includes all articles on these topics: family and the home; mothering; marriage; housewife syndrome (fatigue, ennui, etc.); children; family budgets; dating and relationship between the sexes; shopping; dieting; aging; sex; and new in this decade, the Mrs Chatelaine articles.

40 The statistics are taken from the Chatelaine Articles Database for the 1950s and the 1960s.

41 AO, MHRS F-4-5-a, box 448, Starch readership results taken from the June 1970 Report.

42 Bettie Hall, 'I Was a Working Mother When That Term was a Dirty Word: Mrs Chatelaine 1969,' *Chatelaine*, May 1969, 34.

43 AO, MHRS F-4-4-b, box 446, Mr H.C. Stratton, Windsor, Ontario, to Doris Anderson, 1 September 1962.

44 The Editors, 'What's New with Us,' *Chatelaine*, May 1962, 3.

45 Claude Bissell, 'The Intelligent Woman's Guide to Books,' *Chatelaine*, April 1961, 49. In a list headed by J. Conrad's *Nostromo* and completed with *Back to Methuselah* by G.B. Shaw, perhaps it is not surprising that Virgina Woolf, for one, does not make an appearance.

46 René Lévesque, 'Where Does Quebec Go from Here?' *Chatelaine*, April 1960, 14; Eric Sevareid, 'What Will Happen in 1960?' *Chatelaine*, January 1960, 14. Other famous journalists contributed columns, including Marjorie McEnaney 'The Quiet Revolution of Chinese Women' (September 1960), a five-page article on Chinese women; and Norman DePoe: 'De Gualle's

Dilemma: Algeria' (June 1960); 'How Independence Is Changing Africa' (August 1960); 'Where is Castro Leading Cuba?' (October 1960); and 'The Old Cold War Isn't What It Used to Be' (January 1961).

47 Christina McCall, 'Our Stubborn Stand on China,' *Chatelaine*, February 1961, 14; Christina McCall, 'Nuclear Weapons: Why Can't Canada Make Up Her Mind?' *Chatelaine*, March 1961, 12; Christina McCall, 'Our Troubled Dollar: What the Crisis Means,' *Chatelaine*, October 1962, 19.

48 The editors, 'What's New with Us,' *Chatelaine*, March 1961, 2.

49 AO, MHRS F-4-4-b, box 444, Miss Elizabeth Hardy, Welland, Ontario, to Anderson, 3 January 1962. The letter reads: 'I am a Grade 10 student at Welland High School and for a Geography report, we are to compile articles concerning the Common Market. In your December issue, I found an article about the above in "Your World Notebook." I used the picture for a previous Geography note and threw away the rest of the page. Since the article was interesting and informative, I would be very pleased if you could forward me the information in the article, and also, if possible, the sketch ... I used the November article, "The Canadian Senate," in my History Notebook.'

50 AO, MHRS F-4-3-a, box 435, Mrs D. Ross MacDonald, Hensall, Ontario, to Anderson, 25 September 1962.

51 Eileen Morris, 'Housework Is a Part-time Job,' *Chatelaine*, March 1960, 28–9. Housework was featured sporadically as a topic for the general feature articles. All writers shared a critique of the ways in which women's work in the home was organized and proposed changes in the amount, nature, and purpose of housework. However, they all presumed that women were responsible for housework. See Jean Yack, 'The Canadian Homemaker: What You Think of Your Job: A Special Chatelaine Report,' *Chatelaine*, March 1961, 54–5; Anna Davies, 'I Hate Housekeeping,' ibid., 56; Michael and Pam Cope, 'A Husband and Wife Change Jobs, ' *Chatelaine*, February 1965, 28–9; and Beverley Morin, 'How to Beat the Housework Rat Race,' *Chatelaine*, February 1966, 22.

52 Morris, 'Housework Is a Part-time Job,' 29.

53 The Editors, 'The Last Word Is Yours,' *Chatelaine*, May 1960, 158.

54 'The Last Word Is Yours,' *Chatelaine*, June 1960, 136.

55 Mrs Myrtle Gallup, of Danville, Quebec, to editors, 'The Last Word Is Yours,' *Chatelaine*, May 1960, 158.

56 Mrs J.B. Hughes, Calgary, to editors, ibid.

57 Mrs F. Weeks, London, Ontario, to editors, ibid.

58 Estelle Cooper, Red Deer, Alberta, to editors, ibid.

59 Mary Daniluk, Windsor, Ontario, to editors, ibid.

60 Christina McCall, 'Working Wives Are Here to Stay,' *Chatelaine*, September 1961, 31–5; 'All Canadians Are Equal – except Women,' *Chatelaine*, February 1962, 34–5; 'Why Can't We Treat Married Women like People?' *Chatelaine*, April 1962, 25–6.

61 Christina McCall, 'Booksbooksbooks,' *Chatelaine*, January 1966, 12.

62 McCall, 'Working Wives Are Here to Stay,' 31.

63 Mrs Mike Levin, Selkirk, Manitoba, to editors, 'The Last Word Is Yours,' *Chatelaine*, December 1961, 108.

64 Unfortunately, space restrictions do not permit detailed analysis of all the working women, particularly wives and mothers, articles that appeared during the decade. This list is a partial enumeration, to illustrate the variety of topics published, and provides interested readers with additional sources in the magazine: Sheila Ward, 'Going Back to Work,' *Chatelaine*, September 1960, 37; Jessie London, '76 Best Jobs with a Future for Girls,' *Chatelaine*, September 1962, 38–9, which was the 'beginning of a Special three-part Chatelaine report "The Revolution in Learning and Earning"'; Dorothy Sangster, 'How Good Are the New Nursery Schools?' *Chatelaine*, October 1962, 40–1; '70 Best Jobs for Homemakers Returning to Work,' *Chatelaine*, November 1963, 34–5, presented the results of a *Chatelaine*, national survey that 'pinpointed all likely job possibilities, the ways to train for and succeed in them'; Gwen Beattie, 'Special Section: The Working Mother,' *Chatelaine*, January 1965, 23; Cope, 'A Husband and Wife Change Jobs,' 28–9; Bonnie Buxton, 'Confessions of a Working Girl: I Want to Be Kept at Home!' *Chatelaine*, August 1966, 16; Barbara Pettit '87 Jobs Older Women Can Learn or Do, Right Now,' *Chatelaine*, April 1967 49; and, Mollie Gillen, 'Women at Work,' *Chatelaine*, February 1969, 38.

65 Christina McCall, 'All Canadians Are Equal – except Women,' 89.

66 Mrs Eldon Finell, Ponteix, Saskatchewan, to editor, 'The Last Word Is Yours,' *Chatelaine*, April 1962, 150.

67 Mrs Eugenie Ross, Don Mills, Ontario, to editors, ibid.

68 Mrs R. Berchtold, North Vancouver, to editors, ibid.

69 Christina McCall, 'Why Can't We Treat Married Women like People?' 26.

70 Mrs Maxine La Croix, Montreal, to editors, 'The Last Word Is Yours,' *Chatelaine*, July 1962, 76.

71 Mr. Fred W. Olsen, Cumberland, BC, to editors, ibid.

72 Mrs Helen Max-Duca, Vancouver, to editors, 'The Last Word Is Yours,' *Chatelaine*, June 1962, 126.

73 AO, MHRS F-4-4-b, box 443, Rabbi Abraham Feinberg, Holy Blossom Temple, Toronto, to Keith Knowlton, 8 December 1962.

74 Ibid., Jean Yack to Doris H. Anderson, 'Re this submission from Feinberg,' undated.

75 Ibid., Jean E. Yack to Doris H. Anderson, re. *Feminine Mystique,* no date.

76 Ibid., Keith A. Knowlton to Doris H. Anderson, re. *Feminine Mystique,* no date.

77 AO, MHRS F-4-4-b, box 443, Keith A. Knowlton to Almeda Glassey, 29 August 1962 .

78 Jack Batten, 'After Black Power, Woman Power,' *Chatelaine,* September 1969, 36–7; Articles with feminism as the topic were popular throughout the decade and appeared regularly in the magazine. A list of the more influential articles includes the following: Christina McCall, 'The Hypocrisy of Divorce Laws,' *Chatelaine,* April 1961, 35; Dorothy Sangster, 'The Remarkable Hospital Women Built,' *Chatelaine,* May 1961, 34; Eileen Morris, 'Why Can't This Girl Be a Minister?' ibid., 43; Anita Malik, 'Why Are Canadian Women So Backward?' *Chatelaine,* June 1961, 29; Dr Charlotte Whitton, 'Canadian Women Belong in Politics,' *Chatelaine,* October 1961, 44; Dorothy Sangster, 'Old Maids a Vanishing Breed?' *Chatelaine,* November 1963, 25; Catherine Sinclair, 'The Waste of Canada's Bright Girls,' *Chatelaine,* October 1964, 23; Mollie Gillen, 'Should You Have a Marriage Contract?' *Chatelaine,* November 1964, 27; Barbara Croft, 'The Struggle of Raising Children Alone,' *Chatelaine,* November 1965, 25; Sonja Sinclair, 'Can Canada Afford College Educated Housewives?' *Chatelaine,* November 1966, 20; Barbara Frum, 'Is There Prejudice against Women on Juries?' *Chatelaine,* April 1967, 96; Mollie Gillen, 'Royal Commission on the Status of Women: Will It Do Any Good?' *Chatelaine,* January 1968, 21; Mary Van Stolk, 'Canadian Women Are Masochists,' *Chatelaine,* September 1968, 27; and Mollie Gillen, 'Why Are We Still Brainwashing Girls about Marriage?' *Chatelaine,* December 1969, 23.

79 Lia Lafontaine, Ville de Laval, Quebec, to editors, 'The Last Word Is Yours,' *Chatelaine,* February 1967, 100.

80 Batten, 'After Black Power, Woman Power,' 37.

81 Marie Kiciuk, Winnipeg, to editors, 'The Last Word Is Yours,' *Chatelaine,* November 1969, 120.

82 Coleen Fitzpatrick, Burnaby, BC, to editors, 'The Last Word Is Yours,' *Chatelaine,* January 1970, 76.

83 Mrs Aileen Sivell, Oakville, Ontario, to editors, 'The Last Word Is Yours,' *Chatelaine,* November 1969, 120.

84 Mrs Hazel Vogan, Bath, Ontario, to editors, 'Last Word,' *Chatelaine,* January 1970, 76.

85 Marily Jones, Ottawa, to editors, ibid.

86 For an overview of the history of second-wave feminism in Canada and the difference between Canadian feminism and American feminism, see Constance Backhouse and David Flaherty, eds., *Challenging Times: The*

Women's Movement in Canada and the United States (Montreal and Kingston, 1992); Nancy Adamson, '"Feminists, Libbers, Lefties and Radicals": The Emergence of the Women's Liberation Movement,' in Joy Parr, ed., *A Diversity of Women* (Toronto, 1995); Nancy Adamson, Linda Briskin, and Margaret McPhail, *Feminist Organizing for Change: The Contemporary Women's Movement in Canada* (Toronto, 1988); and Ruth Roach Pierson, 'The Mainstream Women's Movement and the Politics of Difference,' in Ruth Roach Pierson, Marjorie Griffin Cohen, Paula Borne, and Philinda Masters, eds., *Canadian Women's Issues*, 1: *Strong Voices* (Toronto, 1993).

87 Marta Wasserman, as told to Christina McCall, 'How Mothers Mix Up Daughters for Love and Marriage,' *Chatelaine*, October 1962, 31.

88 Mrs D. Desmond, Vancouver, to editors, 'The Last Word Is Yours,' *Chatelaine*, December 1962, 84.

89 Mrs C. Munson, Terrace, BC, to editors, ibid.

90 Mrs Ellenmie Melcher, Rockyford, Alberta, to editors, ibid.

91 J.S. Cameron, Etobicoke, Ontario, to editors, ibid.

92 Mrs Jean Griffin, Ottawa, to editors, 'The Last Word Is Yours,' *Chatelaine*, February 1963, 80.

93 Readers interested in *Chatelaine*'s articles on birth control, abortion, sterilization, or other reproductive issues should consult Ron Kenyon, 'The Pill Nobody Talks About,' *Chatelaine*, November 1961, 31; Rev. Ray Goodall, 'Is Abortion Ever Right?' *Chatelaine*, March 1963, 40; Larry Ross, 'Vasectomy,' *Chatelaine*, May 1963, 42; Constance Mungall, 'Birth Control in Canada Today,' *Chatelaine*, April 1965, 18; Earl Damude, 'The Medical Discovery That Could Legalize Abortion,' *Chatelaine*, September 1966, 35; Constance Mungall, 'The Pill and Its Side Effects Today,' *Chatelaine*, November 1966, 33; Doris Anderson, 'The Pill and the Pope,' Editorial, *Chatelaine*, November 1968, 1; Joan O'Donnell, 'A Catholic Mother Answers the Pope,' Ibid., 26; Jack Batten, 'Is There a Male Conspiracy against the Pill?' *Chatelaine*, July 1969, 17; and Mollie Gillen, 'Our New Abortion Law: Already Outdated?' *Chatelaine*, November 1969, 29.

94 Elizabeth Donovan, 'Why Don't We Do Something about Sex Criminals?' *Chatelaine*, May 1960, 33; Eileen Morris, 'We're Telling Our Children Too Much about SEX,' *Chatelaine*, November 1960, 22; Dr John Eichenlaub, 'Sex, Your Child and You,' *Chatelaine*, August 1962, 15; Phyllis Parker as told to Patricia Young, 'Our Child Was Molested,' *Chatelaine*, January 1965, 17; Ruth Doehler, 'Incest: The Secret Crime against Children,' *Chatelaine*, March 1969, 20.

95 For a more detailed overview of the lesbian imagery in *Chatelaine*, magazine, see V.J. Korinek, '"Don't Let Your Girlfriends Ruin Your Marriage":

Lesbian Imagery in *Chatelaine* Magazine, 1950–1969,' *Journal of Canadian Studies* 33, 3 (1998).

96 Renate Wilson, 'What Turns Women to Lesbianism?' *Chatelaine*, October 1966, 33; June Callwood, 'Sex and the Married Woman,' *Chatelaine*, June 1968, 25. Although some readers were under the impression that articles about sexuality were rampant in the sixties version of *Chatelaine*, proportionately, the statistical information from the Articles Database does not indicate that. However, the larger number of articles meant that sexuality articles did appear with greater frequency. Interested readers should see Dr Sara B. Sheiner and Bob Allison, 'Modern Woman: Is She Really Losing Her Femininity?' *Chatelaine*, February 1961, 27, and Catherine Sinclair, 'What Is Sex Appeal?' *Chatelaine*, August 1963, 18–21. Many other articles about marriage or adjustment to marriage have a few paragraphs devoted to sexuality, although that was not the primary focus of the article.

97 Wilson, 'What Turns Women to Lesbianism?' 33.

98 Callwood, 'Sex and the Married Woman,' 25.

99 Mrs J. Barkaman, Steinbach, Manitoba, to editors, 'The Last Word Is Yours,' *Chatelaine*, August 1968, 72.

100 Mrs Audrey L. Wosley, Chilliwack, BC, to editors, 'The Last Word Is Yours,' *Chatelaine*, October 1968, 120.

101 Mrs P.A. Robinson, Regina, to editors, 'The Last Word Is Yours,' *Chatelaine*, December 1968, 94.

102 Mrs Barbara B. Duncan, Markam, Ontario, to editors, ibid.

103 As in the fifties, masculinity, while still a minor theme in the sixties, had a number of controversial articles devoted to it. See Robert Thomas Allen, 'Man the Next Best Sex, ' *Chatelaine*, August 1961, 29; Margaret Mead, 'What Makes a Man?' *Chatelaine*, July 1963, 17; Cope, 'A Husband and Wife Change Jobs,' 28–9; Eileen Morris, 'The Masculine Mystique – How to Raise Your Son to Be a Man,' *Chatelaine*, August 1965, 19; Mollie Gillen, 'Why Men Want Out of Marriage,' *Chatelaine*, March 1967, 28–9.

104 Cope, 'A Husband and Wife Change Jobs,' 63.

105 Mrs F.W. Barrett, Botwood, Newfoundland, to editors, 'The Last Word Is Yours,' *Chatelaine*, April 1965, 108.

106 Mrs Bonnie Heath, Stratford, Ontario, to editors, 'The Last Word Is Yours,' *Chatelaine*, May 1965, 104.

107 Mrs Carmen Bernard, Weston, Ontario, to editors, 'The Last Word Is Yours,' *Chatelaine*, April 1965, 108.

108 Gerald L. Morris, Stavely, Alberta, to editors, ibid.

109 Gillen, 'Why Men Want Out of Marriage,' 29 and 83.

110 Mrs Marion Schaffer, Sudbury, Ontario, to editors, 'The Last Word Is Yours,' *Chatelaine*, June 1967, 112.

111 Mrs Hazel Norrish, Thornhill, Ontario, to editors, ibid.

112 Unfortunately, space limitations do not permit a discussion of the articles on black Canadians or black Americans during the sixties, and I have opted instead to devote the space to articles on Aboriginal Canadians. Those interested in how the magazine dealt with blacks and interracial relationships (and they are very similar to the fifties' articles) should see Pat Carrington, as told to Lloyd M. Lockhart, 'The Marriage They Said Wouldn't Work,' *Chatelaine*, February 1964, 20–1; Florence Jones and Doreen Mowers, 'How Two Women Fought Race Prejudice,' *Chatelaine*, May 1965, 39; Thirza M. Lee, 'How We Adopted an Interracial Family,' *Chatelaine*, December 1966, 33.

113 For ethnicity in its various forms, see Frank Drea, 'Lucia's Trying Love Affair with Canada,' *Chatelaine*, April 1961, 40–1; Nicole Charest and Catherine Sinclair, 'How the Two Canadas Live,' *Chatelaine*, May 1964, 29; 'Christmas in Canada: A Festival of Many Traditions,' *Chatelaine*, December 1964; Edna Staebler, 'The Other Canadians,' *Chatelaine*, March 1965, 64–5; Renate Wilson, 'The Two Worlds of Lily Chow,' *Chatelaine*, November 1965, 32–3; and Sonja Sinclair, 'Exposé!' *Chatelaine*, October 1968, 50.

114 See Christina McCall, 'Canada's Eskimos: A People Trapped between Two Worlds,' *Chatelaine*, November 1960, 34–7; Frances McNab, 'The Forgotten Canadians,' *Chatelaine*, June 1962, 34–5; Sally Tootoo, 'Anguilik's Wife,' *Chatelaine*, April 1963, 32–3; Dorothy Keen and Martha McKeon, 'The Story of Pauline Johnson, Canada's Passionate Poet,' February 1966, 24–5; Mollie Gillen, 'The Story of Pauline Johnson,' *Chatelaine*, March 1966, 38–9; Barbara Frum, 'How Ottawa (and We) Slept,' part of the special feature – 'Canadian Indians, 1968,' *Chatelaine*, November 1968, 48–55.

115 The Editors, 'What's New with Us,' *Chatelaine*, June 1962, 3.

116 McNab, 'The Forgotten Canadians,' 34–5.

117 Special feature: 'Canadian Indians, 1968,' 48.

118 Frum, 'How Ottawa (and We) Slept,' 48.

119 Editorial subheading, 'The Last Word Is Yours,' *Chatelaine*, January 1969, 76.

120 W.J. Wacko, research and training officer, Community Development Branch, Province of Alberta (Edmonton), to editors, ibid.

121 Mrs B. Spence, Saskatoon, Saskatchewan, to editors, ibid.

122 David C. Ward, president and managing director of Team Products, Edmonton, to editors, ibid.

123 Kahn-Tineta Horn, Caughnawaga, Quebec, to the editors, ibid.

124 This topic was popular throughout the decade. See Christina McCall, 'The Dismal Failure of the Welfare System,' *Chatelaine*, November 1961, 34–7; Jessie London, 'Can Our Derelict Families Be Saved?' *Chatelaine*, June 1963, 26–7; Marie Smith, as told to Patricia Young, 'My Fight Back from Skid Row,' *Chatelaine*, October 1963, 27; Christina McCall Newman, 'The Poor in Canada,' *Chatelaine*, April 1965, 28–31; Sheila H. Keiran, 'What if Public Housing Came to Your Street,' *Chatelaine*, October 1967, 38; Mollie Gillen, 'THE POOR LIFE: We're Keeping Our Poor in GHETTOS,' *Chatelaine*, March 1969, 32–3; Ian Adams, 'The Real Poor in Canada Are Women,' *Chatelaine*, April 1969, 42–3; 'It's Hell on Welfare,' *Chatelaine*, May 1969, 30; 'We Can't Always Help the Poor,' ibid., 31; Ian Adams, 'Can Anything Be Done about the Poor? Conclusion,' *Chatelaine*, June 1969, 23.

125 Christina McCall, 'The Poor in Canada,' 28.

126 Bonnie Lee Morris, 100 Mile House, BC, to editors, 'The Last Word Is Yours,' *Chatelaine*, August 1965, 68.

127 Mrs Patricia Stitson, Gravenhurst, Ontario, to editors, 'The Last Word Is Yours,' *Chatelaine*, June 1965, 100.

128 Adams, 'The Real Poor in Canada Are Women,' 111.

129 Adams, 'It's Hell on Welfare,' 56.

130 Adams, 'Can Anything Be Done about the Poor?' 60.

131 Mrs K.M. McNeil, Mabou, NS, to editors, 'The Last Word Is Yours,' *Chatelaine*, June 1969, 72.

132 Nina Leclerc, West Hill, Ontario, to editors, ibid.

133 Miriam Hutton, Winnipeg, to editors, 'The Last Word Is Yours,' *Chatelaine*, July 1969, 64.

134 Mrs Gary W. Phillips, Creston, BC, to editors, ibid.

135 Mrs Joan Gagnon, Ottawa, to editors, 'The Last Word Is Yours,' *Chatelaine*, August 1969, 68.

136 Mrs D.C. Kerr, Chatham, Ontario, to editors, ibid.

137 See June Gibbs, as told to Cathie Breslin, 'We're Bushed and We Love It,' *Chatelaine*, March 1961, 38–40; Edna Staebler, 'The Village That Lives One Day at a Time,' *Chatelaine*, December 1961, 38–40; Edna Staebler, 'Miner's Wife,' *Chatelaine*, March 1962, 36–7; and beginning in April 1966, Cathie Breslin's 'The Women of Canada Series,' which profiled a different region or province every month. This feature was the first to include the Yukon and Northwest Territories (as the North, naturally) as part of the country worth examination.

138 Catherine Breslin, 'The Women of Canada: Nova Scotia,' *Chatelaine*, July 1966, 24–7.

139 Joyce E. McElroy, Calgary, to editors, 'The Last Word Is Yours,' *Chatelaine*, November 1966, 124.

140 Brenda Bravery, West Ewell, Surrey, England, to editors, ibid.

141 Marie Woodworth, Berwick, NS, to editors, 'The Last Word Is Yours,' *Chatelaine*, September 1966, 180.

142 What Breslin did depict are 'the folk,' so recently rehabilitated by Ian McKay's in *The Quest of the Folk* (Kingston and Montreal, 1995).

143 P. MacKenzie Campbell, Sydney, NS, to editors, *Chatelaine*, September 1966, 180.

144 Catherine Breslin, 'The Women of British Columbia,' *Chatelaine*, February 1968, 32–7.

145 Ethel Brant Monture, Middleport, Ontario, to editors, 'The Last Word Is Yours,' *Chatelaine*, April 1968, 126.

146 Miss Pearl Williams, B.C. Conference Indian Sub-Committee of the United Church of Canada, Vancouver, to editors, ibid.

147 Mrs Beatrice Carroll, Wisteria, BC, to editors, ibid.

148 The editors, ibid.

149 The historical articles will not be analyzed; interested readers should see Patricia Young, 'The Fabulous Dunsmuirs,' *Chatelaine*, September 1961, 38; Mary-Etta Macpherson, 'The Eaton's – Shopkeepers for a Nation,' *Chatelaine*, June 1962, 28–31; Catherine Breslin, 'Famous Families: The Molsons,' *Chatelaine*, June 1963; Audrey Y. Morris, 'The Amazing Strickland Girls,' *Chatelaine*, September 1966, 42. All of these articles were multipart series, and I have cited only the introductory article and issue.

150 Mordecai Richler, 'Why I Left Canada,' *Chatelaine*, March 1961, 21.

151 Donna E. Gerlach, Regina, to editors, 'The Last Word Is Yours,' *Chatelaine*, May 1961, 132.

152 Miss K.M. Graws, Sydney, NS, to editors, ibid.

153 Mrs K.A. Godenir, Ponteix, Saskatchewan, to editors, ibid.

154 Mrs A. Hanley, White Rock, BC, to editors, ibid.

155 Mrs R.E. Clubbe, Ottawa, to editors, ibid.

156 Mrs J. Wiszniowski, St Catharines, Ontario, to editors, ibid.

157 Mrs J.C. Bradley, Ottawa, to editors, and the retort from Jean Yack, associate editor, 'The Last Word Is Yours,' *Chatelaine*, May 1964, 86.

158 'What's New at *Chatelaine*,' *Chatelaine*, August 1969, 2.

159 Mildred Istona, 'The Good Life on $6,500 a Year,' *Chatelaine*, January 1968, 59.

160 Mrs Elizabeth Harding, Nipigon, Ontario, to editors, 'The Last Word Is Yours,' *Chatelaine*, March 1968, 96.

161 Mrs Etta L. van Nostrand, Gormley, Ontario, to editors, ibid.

162 Mrs Edward Heibert, Cloverdale, BC, to editors, ibid.

163 Editorial comment, ibid.

164 'Meet Mrs Chatelaine 1966,' *Chatelaine*, May 1966, 91.

165 Ethelyn Mosher, Middleton, NS, to editors, 'The Last Word Is Yours,' *Chatelaine*, August 1964, 62.

166 Mrs Marjorie E. Hallman of Pictou, NS, was one of the people who completed the author's questionnaire about reading the magazine in the fifties and sixties. Questionnaire dated 18 January 1994.

167 Marianne Fenton-Marr, to editors, 'The Last Word Is Yours,' *Chatelaine*, August 1964, 62.

168 Mrs G. Houston, Bowmanville, Ontario, to editors, ibid.

169 Mrs John Barrett, Hearts Delight, Newfoundland, to editors, 'The Last Word Is Yours,' *Chatelaine*, December 1964, 80.

170 Jas. I. Allen, Bechard, Saskatchewan, to editors, 'The Last Word Is Yours,' *Chatelaine*, March 1961, 154.

171 Mrs Henry MacArthur, Bonilla Island Light Station, Prince Rupert, BC, to editors, 'The Last Word Is Yours,' *Chatelaine*, April 1961, 156.

172 Mrs Dennis Bude, Alma, Saskatchewan, to editors, 'Last Word,' *Chatelaine*, March 1961, 154.

Chapter 9: 'Here in the Lodge': *Chatelaine*'s Legacy

1 'Producerly' is a term used by John Fiske. See also the introduction.

2 Under Mildred Istona, the magazine dropped the focus on feminism and became a much more traditional woman's magazine. The editorial commitment to feminist editorials was largely abandoned and more emphasis was placed on celebrities, a revamped and enlarged departmental section, attention to more affluent furnishings, clothing, and accessories, and a considerable decrease in the number of 'educational' articles or editorials. The emphasis was on affluence, entertainment, and consumption, although the magazine did, on occasion, still publish hard-hitting articles on women's social or political issues. Mildred Istona was editor from 1977 to 1994, when she was succeeded by Rona Maynard. The 'decline' of *Chatelaine*, has been noted by media commentators. See Janice Turner, 'Glossing Over the Issues,' *Toronto Star*, 24 October 1992, H1 and H3; Morris Wolfe, 'Magazines: Same Old Fluff in Modern Woman,' *Globe and Mail*, 2 March 1993; and Morris Wolfe, 'Magazines: Decline and Fall of *Chatelaine*' *Globe and Mail*, 11 May 1993.

3 June Callwood interview, 23 May 1995. See the commentary on *Chatelaine*'s role in chapter 2.

4 Mary Thom, *Inside Ms.: Twenty Five Years of the Magazine and the Feminist Movement* (New York, 1997).
5 Archives of Ontario, Maclean Hunter Record Series F-4-4-b, box 442, Grace A. Bontaine, Toronto, to Doris Anderson, 4 December 1962.
6 See chapter 2.

Select Bibliography

Primary Sources

Archives of Ontario, Maclean Hunter Record Series

'Brief of the Readers of *Chatelaine* Magazine to the Royal Commission on the Status of Women,' presented by Doris Anderson, editor, June 1968

Canada Year Book, 1950–73

Canada's Magazine Audience: A Study from the Magazine Advertising Bureau of Canada, 1: *Profile of the Readers* Originated by the Canadian Media Directors Council, Validated by the Canadian Advertising Research Foundation, Conducted by ORC International Limited. Ottawa: National Library of Canada, 1969

Canadian Advertising Rates and Data: The Media Authority, 1950–70

Canadian Consumer Publications Report. Montreal, Toronto, and New York: Gruneau Research Ltd., 1955

Canadian Consumer Publications Report. Montreal, Toronto, and New York: Gruneau Research Ltd., September 1957

Canadian Who's Who, 1975, 1981, 1984, 1993

Chatelaine, 1945–70

Dichter, Ernest. *A Motivational Research Study on Chatelaine Magazine*. Croton-on-Hudson, NY: Institute for Motivational Research Inc., for Maclean Hunter Publishing Co., Inc., April 1958

Report of the Royal Commission on the Status of Women in Canada. Ottawa: September 28, 1970

Report of the Special Senate Committee on Mass Media. The Uncertain Mirror: Volumes 1–3. Ottawa, 1970

Royal Commission on Publications. *Report of the Royal Commission on Publications*. Ottawa, 1961

Starch Readership Reports, 1949, 1950
Statistics Canada Census, 1951, 1956, 1961
Urban Family Expenditure, 1959. Ottawa: Dominion Bureau of Statistics, March
    1963
Urban Family Food Expenditure, 1957. Ottawa: Dominion Bureau of Statistics, 1960
Urban Retail Food Prices, 1914–1959. Ottawa: Dominion Bureau of Statistics,
    May 1960

Oral History and Questionnaire Respondents

Anderson, Doris. Interviewed in Toronto, 30 June 1994
'Anonymous' Questionnaires completed, 8 June, 2 July, 28 August, and
    28 December 1993
Baird, Bette-Jo. Questionnaire completed 22 July 1993
Baldwin, Jan. Questionnaire completed 22 August 1993
Callwood, June. Interviewed in Toronto, 23 May 1995
Ellis, June. Questionnaire completed 16 July 1993
Hallman, Marjorie E. Questionnaire completed 18 January 1994
Marlow, Dorothy. Questionnaire completed 29 June 1993
McLeod, Zena. Questionnaire completed 28 October 1993
Morris, Eileen. Interviewed in Toronto, 3 May 1996
Prophet, Marjorie. Questionnaire completed 6 June 1993
Wellspring, Barbara. Questionnaire completed 12 July 1992

Secondary Sources

Abrahamson, David, ed. *The American Magazine: Research Perspectives and
    Prospects*. Ames, Iowa: Iowa State University Press, 1995
Adams, Mary Louise. *The Trouble with Normal: Postwar Youth and the Making of
    Heterosexuality*. Toronto: University of Toronto Press, 1997
Adamson, Nancy, Linda Briskin, and Margaret McPhail. *Feminist Organizing
    for Change: The Contemporary Women's Movement in Canada*. Toronto: Oxford
    University Press, 1988
Anderson, Doris. *Rebel Daughter: An Autobiography*. Toronto: Key Porter, 1996
– *Rough Layout*. Toronto: McClelland & Stewart, 1981
– 'To My Readers: A Fond Farewell.' *Chatelaine*, September 1977
– *Two Women*. Toronto: Macmillan of Canada, 1978
– 'Women's Magazines in the 1970s.' *Canadian Woman Studies* 11, 2 (1980):
    15–16
Backhouse, Constance, and David H. Flaherty, eds. *Challenging Times: The*

Woman's Movement in Canada and the United States. Montreal and Kingston: McGill-Queen's University Press, 1992

Ballaster, Ros, Margaret Beetham, Elizabeth Fraser, and Sandra Hebron. *Women's Worlds: Ideology, Feminism and the Women's Magazine.* London: MacMillan Education, 1991

Barbour, Noel Robert. *Those Amazing People! The Story of the Canadian Magazine Industry, 1778–1967.* Toronto: Crucible Press, 1982

Barrel, Joan, and Brian Braithwaite. *The Business of Women's Magazines.* London: Kogan Page, 1988

Barthes, Roland. 'Myth Today.' *Mythologies.* London: Paladin, 1973

Bartos, Rena. *Marketing to Women around the World.* Boston: Harvard Business School Press, 1989

– *The Moving Target: What Every Marketer Should Know about Women.* New York: Free Press, 1982

Bartos, Rena, and Ar Pearson, 'The Founding Fathers of Advertising Research.' *Journal of Advertising Research* 17, 3 (1977): 1–8

Bashevkin, Sylvia. *Women on the Defensive: Living through Conservative Times.* Toronto: University of Toronto Press, 1998

Berger, John. *Ways of Seeing.* New York: Viking Press, 1973

Blashill, Lorraine. *Remembering the Fifties: Growing Up in Western Canada.* Vancouver: Orca Books, 1997

Bourdieu, Pierre. *Distinction: A Social Critique of the Judgement of Taste.* Translated by Richard Nice. London: Routledge & Kegan Paul, 1984

Bowlby, Rachel. '"The Problem with No Name": Rereading Friedan's *The Feminine Mystique.*' *Feminist Review* 27 (September 1987): 61–75

Boyd, Monica. *Canadian Attitudes toward Women: Thirty Years of Change.* Ottawa: Minister of Labour, Government of Canada, 1984

Braithwaite, Brian. *Women's Magazines: The First 300 Years.* London: Peter Owen, 1995

Breines, Wini. *Young, White and Miserable: Growing Up Female in the Fifties.* Boston: Beacon Press, 1992

Brown, Mary Ellen, ed. *Television and Women's Culture: The Politics of the Popular.* London: Sage Publications, 1990

Cawelti, John G. *Adventure, Mystery and Romance: Formula Stories as Art and Popular Culture.* Chicago: University of Chicago Press, 1976

Courtney, Alice E., and Sara Wernick Lockertz. 'A Woman's Place: An Analysis of the Roles Portrayed by Women in Magazine Advertising.' *Journal of Marketing Research* 8 (February 1971): 92–5

Courtney, Alice E., and Thomas W. Whipple. *Sex Stereotyping in Advertising.* Lexington, Mass.: D.C. Heath and Company, 1983

Cruz, Jon, and Justin Lewis, eds. *Viewing, Reading, Listening: Audiences and Cultural Reception*. Boulder, CO,: Westview Press, 1994

Currie, Dawn. *Girl Talk: Adolescent Magazines and Their Readers*. Toronto: University of Toronto Press, 1999

Damon-Moore, Helen. *Magazines for the Millions: Gender and Commerce in the Ladies' Home Journal and the Saturday Evening Post, 1880–1910*. Albany: State University of New York Press, 1994

Dancyger, Irene. *A World of Women: An Illustrated History of Women's Magazines*. Dublin: Gill & Macmillan, 1978

De Certeau, Michel. *The Practice of Everyday Life*. Translated by Steven F. Rendall. Berkley: University of California Press, 1984

Delaney, Janice, Mary Jane Lupton, and Emily Toth. *The Curse: A Cultural History of Menstruation*. Rev. ed. Urbana: University of Chicago Press, 1988

Dodd, Diane. 'Women in Advertising: The Role of Canadian Women in the Promotion of Domestic Electrical Technology in the Interwar Period.' In *Despite the Odds: Essays on Canadian Women and Science*, ed. Marianne Gosztonyi Ainley, 134–51. Montreal: Véhicule Press, 1990

Douglas, Susan J. *Where the Girls Are: Growing Up Female with the Mass Media*. New York: Times Books, 1994

Dyer, Gillian. *Advertising as Communication*. London: Methuen, 1982

Eco, Umberto. *Travels in Hyperreality*. New York: Harcourt Brace Jovanovich, 1987

Ehrenreich, Barbara. *The Hearts of Men: American Dreams and the Flight from Commitment*. New York: Anchor Press, Doubleday, 1983

– *Fear of Falling: The Inner Life of the Middle Class*. New York: Pantheon Books, 1989

Ehrenreich, Barbara, and Deirdre English. – *For Her Own Good: 150 Years of the Experts' Advice to Women*. New York, Doubleday, 1978

Faderman, Lillian. 'Lesbian Magazine Fiction in the Early Twentieth Century.' *Journal of Popular Culture* 11, 4 (1978): 800–17

– *Odd Girls and Twilight Lovers: A History of Lesbian Life in Twentieth-Century America*. New York: Columbia University Press, 1991

Faludi, Susan. *Backlash: The Undeclared War against American Women*. New York: Crown Publishers, 1991

Farrell, Amy Erdman. *Yours in Sisterhood: Ms. Magazine and the Promise of Popular Feminism*. Chapel Hill: University of North Carolina Press, 1998

Ferguson, Marjorie. *Forever Feminine: Women's Magazines and the Cult of Femininity*. London: Heinemann Educational Books, 1983

Fishburn, Katherine. *Women in Popular Culture: A Reference Guide*. Westport, CT: Greenwood Press, 1982

Fiske, John. *Power Plays, Power Works*. London: Verso, 1993
– *Reading the Popular*. Boston: Unwin Hyman, 1989
– *Understanding Popular Culture*. Boston: Unwin Hyman, 1989
Flaherty, David H., and Frank E. Manning, eds. *The Beaver Bites Back? American Popular Culture in Canada*. Montreal and Kingston: McGill-Queen's University Press, 1993
Foucault, Michel. *The History of Sexuality: An Introduction*, volume 1. Translated by Robert Hurley. New York: Vintage Books, 1990
– *Power/Knowledge: Selected Interviews and Other Writings, 1972–1977*. New York: Pantheon Books, 1980
Fox, Richard Wightman, and T.J. Jackson Lears, eds. *The Culture of Consumption: Critical Essays in American History, 1880–1980*. New York: Pantheon Books, 1983
Franklin, Sarah, Celia Lury, and Jackie Stacey, eds. *Off Centre: Feminism and Cultural Studies*. London: Harper Collins Academic, 1991
Freedman, Estelle B. '"The Burning of Letters Continues": Elusive Identities and the Historical Construction of Sexuality.' *Journal of Women's History* 9, 4 (1998): 181–200
Friedan, Betty. *The Feminine Mystique*. New York: Bantam Doubleday Dell, 1963
Galbraith, John Kenneth. *The Affluent Society*. 3rd rev. ed. London: André Deutsch, 1977
Gamman, Lorraine, and Margaret Marshment, eds. *The Female Gaze: Women as Viewers of Popular Culture*. London: Women's Press, 1988
Garvey, Ellen Gruber. *The Adman in the Parlor: Magazines and the Gendering of Consumer Culture, 1880s–1910s*. New York: Oxford University Press, 1996
Geise, L. Ann. 'The Female Role in Middle Class Women's Magazines from 1955 to 1976: A Content Analysis of Nonfiction.' *Sex Roles* 5 (1979): 51–62
Gleason, Mona. 'Psychology and the Construction of the "Normal Family" in Postwar Canada, 1945–1960.' *Canadian Historical Review* 78, 3 (1997): 442–77
Goffman, Erving. *Gender Advertisements*. New York: Harper, 1976
Golz, Annalee. 'Family Matters: The Canadian Family and the State in Postwar Canada,' *left history* 1, 2 (1993): 9–49
Grossberg, Lawrence. *We Gotta Get Out of This Place: Popular Conservatism and Postmodern Culture*. New York: Routledge, 1992
Grossberg, Lawrence, Cary Nelson, and Paula Treichler. *Cultural Studies*. New York: Routledge, 1992
Halberstam, David. *The Fifties*. New York: Villard Books, 1993
Hardt, Hanno. *Communication, History and Theory in America*. London: Routledge, 1992

Hartmann, Susan. *The Home Front and Beyond: American Women in the 1940s.* Boston: Twayne Publishers, 1982

Harvey, Brett. *The Fifties: A Woman's Oral History.* New York: HarperCollins, 1993

Heidenry, John. *Theirs Was the Kingdom: Lila and DeWitt Wallace and the Story of the Reader's Digest.* New York: W.W. Norton, 1993

Heilbrun, Carolyn G. *The Education of a Woman: The Life of Gloria Steinem.* New York: Dial Press, 1995

Hermes, Joke. *Reading Women's Magazines: An Analysis of Everyday Media Use.* Cambridge: Polity Press, 1995

Hershey, Lenore. *Between the Covers: The Lady's Own Journal.* New York: Coward McCann, 1983

Hilliard, Marion. *A Woman Doctor Looks at Love and Life.* New York: Doubleday, 1956

Hoggart, Richard. *The Uses of Literacy.* London: Pelican Books, 1958

Honey, Maureen. *Creating Rosie the Riveter: Class, Gender, and Propaganda during World War II.* Amherst: University of Massachusetts Press, 1984

– ed. *Breaking the Ties That Bind: Popular Stories of the New Woman, 1915–1930.* Norman and London: University of Oklahoma Press, 1992

Houlihan, Inez. 'The Image of Women in Chatelaine Editorials: March 1928– September 1977.' MA thesis, OISE, University of Toronto, 1984

Iacovetta, Franca, and Mariana Valverde, eds. *Gender Conflicts: New Essays in Women's History.* Toronto: University of Toronto Press, 1992

Jamieson, Kathleen Hall, and Karlyn Kohrs Campbell. *The Interplay of Influence: News, Advertising, Politics and the Mass Media.* Belmont, CA: Wadsworth Publishing, 1992

Jenkins, Henry. *Textual Poachers: Television Fans and Participatory Culture.* New York: Routledge, 1992

Jhally, Sut, and Justin Lewis. *Enlightened Racism: The Cosby Show, Audiences, and the Myth of the American Dream.* Boulder, CO: Westview Press, 1992

Jones, Deborah. 'Gossip: Notes on Women's Oral Culture.' *Women's Studies International Quarterly* 3 (1980): 193–8

Keller, Kathryn. *Mothers and Work in Popular American Magazines.* Westport, CT: Greenwood Press, 1994

Kelly, R. Gordon. 'Literature and the Historian.' *American Quarterly* 26 (May 1974): 141–59

Kennedy, Elizabeth Lapovsky, and Madeline D. Davis. *Boots of Leather, Slippers of Gold: The History of a Lesbian Community.* New York: Routledge, Chapman and Hall, 1993

Kent, Raymond, ed. *Measuring Media Audiences.* London: Routlege, 1994

Kome, Penney. 'Homemaker's.' *Canadian Woman Studies* 11, 2 (1980): 17

Kostash, Myrna. *Long Way from Home: The Story of the Sixties Generation in Canada*. Toronto: James Lorimer, 1980

Kuhn, Annette. *The Power of the Image: Essays on Representation and Sexuality*. London: Routledge, 1985

LaMarsh, Judy. *Memoirs of a Bird in a Gilded Cage*. Toronto: McClelland & Stewart, 1969

Leach, William R. 'Transformations in a Culture of Consumption: Women and Department Stores, 1890–1925.' *Journal of American History* 71 (September 1984): 319–42

Lears, Jackson. 'The Concept of Cultural Hegemony: Problems and Possibilities.' *American Historical Review* 90 (June 1985): 567–93

– *Fables of Abundance: A Cultural History of Advertising in America*. New York: Basic Books, HarperCollins, 1994

– 'A Matter of Taste: Corporate Cultural Hegemony in a Mass-Consumption Society.' In *The Culture of Consumption*, ed. Stephen Fox and Jackson Lears, 38–57

Lehman, Joy. '"The Advice of a Real Friend": Codes of Intimacy and Oppression in Women's Magazines, 1937–1955.' *Women's Studies International Quarterly* 3 (1980): 63–78

Leiss, William, Stephen Kline, and Sut Jhally. *Social Communication in Advertising: Persons, Products and Images of Well-Being*. Toronto: Methuen, 1986

Levenstein, Harvey. *Paradox of Plenty: A Social History of Eating in Modern America*. New York: Oxford University Press, 1993

Lewis, Lisa A., ed. *The Adoring Audience: Fan Culture and Popular Media*. London: Routledge, 1992

Light, Beth, and Ruth Roach Pierson, eds. *No Easy Road: Women in Canada, 1920s to 1960s; Documents in Canadian Women's History*, Volume 3. Toronto: New Hogtown Press, 1990

Litt, Paul. *The Muses, the Masses, and the Massey Commission*. Toronto: University of Toronto Press, 1992

Loewen, Candice. 'Mike Hears Voices: Voice of Women and Lester Pearson, 1960–1963.' *Atlantis* 12 (spring 1987): 24–30

Luxton, Meg, Harriet Rosenberg, and Sedef Arat Koç, eds. *Through the Kitchen Window: The Politics of Home and Family*. Toronto: Garamond Press, 1990

Mackenzie, David. *Arthur Irwin: A Biography*. Toronto: University of Toronto Press, 1993

Macpherson, Kay. *When in Doubt, Do Both: The Times of My Life*. Toronto: University of Toronto Press, 1994

Makaryk, Irena R., gen. ed. *Encyclopedia of Contemporary Literary Theory: Approaches, Scholars and Terms*. Toronto: University of Toronto Press, 1993

Marchand, Roland. *Advertising the American Dream: Making Way for Modernity, 1920–1940*. Berkeley: University of California Press, 1985

Marling, Karal Ann. *As Seen on TV: The Visual Culture of Everyday Life in the 1950s*. Cambridge: Harvard University Press, 1994

Maroney, Heather Jon, and Meg Luxton, eds. *Feminism and Political Economy: Women's Work, Women's Struggles*. Toronto: Methuen, 1987

Matheson, Gwen, ed. *Women in the Canadian Mosaic*. Toronto: Peter Martin, 1976

Mathews, Glenna. *'Just a Housewife': The Rise and Fall of Domesticity in America*. New York and Oxford: Oxford University Press, 1987

Mathews-Kline, Yvonne. 'How They Saw Us: Images of Women in National Film Board Films of the 1940s and 1950s.' *Atlantis* 14 (spring 1979): 20–33

May, Elaine Tyler. *Homeward Bound: American Families in the Cold War Era*. New York: Basic Books, 1988

Maynard, Fredelle Bruser. *The Tree of Life*. Toronto: Penguin Books, 1988

McCracken, Ellen. *Decoding Women's Magazines: From* Mademoiselle *to* Ms. London: Macmillan, 1993

McCracken, Grant. *Culture and Consumption: New Approaches to the Symbolic Character of Consumer Goods and Activities*. Bloomington: Indiana University Press, 1989

McCracken, Melinda. *Memories Are Made of This*. Toronto: James Lorimer, 1975

McLuhan, Marshall. *The Mechanical Bride: Folklore of Industrial Man*. Boston: Beacon Press, 1951

Meyerowitz, Joanne, ed. *Not June Cleaver: Women and Gender in Postwar America, 1945–1960*. Philadelphia: Temple University Press, 1994

Miller, Jane. *Seductions: Studies in Reading and Culture*. London: Virago Press, 1990

Millum, Trevor. *Images of Women: Advertising in Women's Magazines*. London: Chatto and Windus, 1975

Miron, John R., ed. *House, Home and Community: Progress in Housing Canadians, 1945–1986*. Montreal and Kingston: McGill-Queen's University Press, 1993

Modleski, Tanya, ed. *Studies in Entertainment: Critical Approaches to Mass Culture*. Bloomington: Indianna University Press, 1986

Moog, Carol. *'Are They Selling Her Lips?' Advertising and Identity*. New York: William Morrow, 1990

Nourie, Alan, and Barbara Nourie, eds. *American Mass Market Magazines*. New York: Greenwood Press, 1990

Nugent, Andrea. 'Canada's Silenced Communicators: A Report on Women in Journalism and Public Relations.' *Atlantis* 2 (spring 1982): 123–35

Oakley, Ann. *Housewife*. London: Penguin Books, 1974

O'Barr, William M. *Culture and the Ad: Exploring Otherness in the World of Advertising*. Boulder, CO, Westview Press, 1994

Ohmann, Richard. *Making and Selling Culture*. Hanover, NH: Wesleyan University Press, 1996

– *Selling Culture: Magazines, Markets, and Class at the Turn of the Century*. London: Verso, 1996

Owram, Doug. *Born at the Right Time: A History of the Baby Boom Generation*. Toronto: University of Toronto, 1996

Packard, Vance. *The Hidden Persuaders*. New York: David McKay, 1957

– *The Status Seekers*. New York: David McKay, 1959

Paglia, Camille. *Sex, Art and American Culture*. New York: Vintage Books, 1992

– *Sexual Personae: Art and Decadence from Nefertiti to Emily Dickenson*. New York: Vintage Books, 1991

Palmer, Jerry. *Potboilers: Methods, Concepts and Case Studies in Popular Fiction*. London: Routledge, 1991

Parr, Joy, ed. *A Diversity of Women: Ontario, 1945–1980*. Toronto: University of Toronto Press, 1995

Peirce, Kate. 'A Feminist Theoretical Perspective on the Socialization of Teenage Girls through *Seventeen* Magazine.' *Sex Roles* 23, 9/10 (1990): 491–500

Pierson, Ruth Roach. *'They're Still Women after All': The Second World War and Canadian Womanhood*. Toronto: McClelland & Stewart, 1986

Pierson, Ruth Roach, Marjorie Griffin Cohen, Paula Borne, and Philinda Masters, eds. *Canadian Women's Issues: Twenty-Five Years of Women's Activism in English Canada, 1: Strong Voices*. Toronto: James Lorimer, 1993

Pollay, Richard W. 'The Subsidizing Sizzle: A Descriptive History of Print Advertising, 1900–1980.' *Journal of Marketing* 49 (summer 1985): 24–37

Porter, John. *The Vertical Mosaic: An Analysis of Social Class and Power in Canada*. Toronto: University of Toronto Press, 1965

Prentice, Alison, et al. *Canadian Women: A History*. Toronto: Harcourt Brace Jovanovitch, 1988

Radford, Jean, ed. *The Progress of Romance: The Politics of Popular Fiction*. London: Routledge and Kegan Paul, 1986

Radway, Janice. *Reading the Romance: Women, Patriarchy, and Popular Literature*. Chapel Hill: University of North Carolina Press, 1991

Reed, David. *The Popular Magazine in Britain and the United States, 1880–1960*. Toronto: University of Toronto Press, 1997

Robinson, Daniel J. *The Measure of Democracy: Polling, Market Research, and Public Life, 1930–1945*. Toronto: University of Toronto Press, 1999

Robinson, Daniel J., and David Kimmel. 'The Queer Career of Homosexual Security Vetting in Cold War Canada.' *Canadian Historical Review* 75, 3 (1994): 319–45

Robinson, Gertrude Joch. 'The Media and Social Change: Thirty Years of Magazine Coverage of Women and Work, 1950–1977.' *Atlantis* 8, 2 (1983): 87–111

Roman, Leslie G., and Linda K. Christian-Smith, eds. *Becoming Feminine: The Politics of Popular Culture*. London: Falmer Press, 1988

Romanow, Walter I., and Walter C. Soderlund. *Media Canada: An Introductory Analysis*. Toronto: Copp Clark Pitman, 1992

Roskill, Mark, and David Carrier. *Truth and Falsehood in Visual Images*. Amherst: University of Massachusetts Press, 1983

Ross, Becki. *The House That Jill Built: Lesbian Nation in Formation*. Toronto: University of Toronto Press, 1995

Rubin, Nancy. *The New Suburban Woman: Beyond Myth and Motherhood*. New York: Coward, McCann & Geoghegan, 1982

Rupp, Leila J. '"Imagine My Surprise": Women's Relationships in Mid-Twentieth Century America.' In Martin Duberman, Martha Vicinus, and George Chauncey Jr., eds., *Hidden from History: Reclaiming the Gay and Lesbian Past*. New York: Meridian Publishing, 1990

Rupp, Leila J., and Verta Taylor. *Survival in the Doldrums: The American Women's Rights Movement, 1945–1960s*. New York: Oxford University Press, 1987

Rutherford, Paul. *The Making of the Canadian Media*. Toronto: McGraw-Hill Ryerson, 1978

– *The New Icons? The Art of Television Advertising*. Toronto: University of Toronto Press, 1994

– *When Television Was Young: Prime Time Canada, 1952–1967*. Toronto: University of Toronto Press, 1990

Rymell, Heather. 'Images of Women in the Magazines of the 30s and 40s.' *Canadian Woman Studies* 3 (1981): 96–9

Sangster, Joan. 'Canadian Working Women in the Twentieth Century.' In *Lectures in Canadian Labour and Working-Class History*, ed. W.J.C. Cherwinski and Gregory S. Kealey, 59–78. Newfoundland: Committee on Canadian Labour History and New Hogtown Press, 1985

– *Earning Respect: The Lives of Working Women in Small-Town Ontario, 1920–1960*. Toronto: University of Toronto Press, 1995

Scanlon, Jennifer. *Inarticulate Longings: The* Ladies' Home Journal, *Gender, and the Promises of Consumer Culture*. London: Routledge, 1995

Schiller, Herbert. *Culture, Inc.: The Corporate Takeover of Public Expression.* New York: Oxford University Press, 1989

Schmidt, Dorothy S. 'Magazines.' In M. Thomas Inge, ed., *Handbook of American Popular Culture*, 2nd ed., volume 2, 641–69. New York: Greenwood Press, 1989

Scholes, Robert. *Protocols of Reading.* New Haven and London: Yale University Press, 1989

Schwichtenberg, Cathy, ed. *The Madonna Connection: Representational Politics, Subcultural Identities, and Cultural Theory.* Boulder, CO: Westview Press, 1993

Spigel, Lynn, and Denise Mann, eds. *Private Screenings: Television and the Female Consumer.* Minneapolis: University of Minnesota Press, 1992

Spitz, Ellen Handler. *Art and Psyche: A Study in Psychoanalysis and Aesthetics.* New Haven: Yale University Press, 1985

Staebler, Edna, ed. *Haven't Any News: Ruby's Letters from the Fifties.* Waterloo, ON: Wilfrid Laurier University Press, 1995

Starch, Daniel. *Measuring Advertising Readership and Results.* New York: McGraw-Hill, 1966

Storrie, Kathleen, ed. *Women: Isolation and Bonding: The Ecology of Gender.* Toronto: Methuen, 1987

Strasser, Susan. *Satisfaction Guaranteed: The Making of the American Mass Market.* New York: Pantheon Books, 1989

Strong-Boag, Veronica. 'Canada's Wage-Earning Wives and the Construction of the Middle Class, 1945–1960.' *Journal of Canadian Studies* 29 (fall 1994): 5–25

– 'Home Dreams: Women and the Suburban Experiment in Canada.' *Canadian Historical Review* 72, 4 (1991): 471–504

Sutherland, Fraser. *The Monthly Epic: A History of Canadian Magazines.* Markham, ON: Fitzhenry & Whiteside, 1989

Task Force on Women and Advertising. *Women and Advertising: Today's Messages – Yesterday's Images.* Toronto: Canadian Advertising Advisory Board, 1977

Taylor, Helen. *Scarlett's Women: Gone With the Wind and Its Female Fans.* London: Virago Press, 1989

Tebbel, John, and Mary Ellen Zuckerman. *The Magazine in America, 1741–1990.* New York: Oxford University Press, 1991

Thom, Mary. *Inside Ms.: 25 Years of the Magazine and the Feminist Movement.* New York: Henry Holt, 1997

Tomlinson, Alan, ed. *Consumption, Identity and Style: Marketing, Meanings and the Packaging of Pleasure.* London: Routledge, 1990

Tompkins, Jane. *Sensational Designs: The Cultural Work of American Fiction, 1790–1860.* New York and Oxford: Oxford University Press, 1985

Tuchman, Gaye, Arlene Kaplan Daniels, and James Benet. *Hearth and Home: Images of Women in the Mass Media*. New York: Oxford University Press, 1978

Venkatesan, M., and Jean Losco. 'Women in Magazine Ads: 1959–1971.' *Journal of Advertising Research* 15 (October 1975): 49–54

Vinikas, Vincent. *Soft Soap, Hard Sell: American Hygiene in an Age of Advertisement*. Ames: Iowa State University Press, 1992

Vipond, Mary. 'The Image of Women in Mass Circulation Magazines in the 1920s.' In *The Neglected Majority: Essays in Canadian Women's History*, ed. Susan Mann Trofimenkoff and Alison Prentice, 116–24. Toronto: McClelland & Stewart, 1977

– *The Mass Media in Canada*. Toronto: James Lorimer, 1989

Weibel, Kathryn. *Mirror, Mirror: Images of Women Reflected in Popular Culture*. New York: Anchor Books, 1977

White, Cynthia L. *Women's Magazines, 1693–1968*. London: Michael Joseph, 1970

Williams, Raymond. 'Advertising: The Magic System.' In *Problems in Materialism and Culture*. London: Verso, 1980

– *Culture*. London: Fontana, 1981

– *Keywords: A Vocabulary of Culture and Society*. London: Croom Helm, 1976

Williamson, Judith. *Decoding Advertisements: Ideology and Meaning in Advertising*. London: Marion Boyars, 1978

Wilson, Susannh Jane Foster. 'The Relationship between Mass Media Content and Social Change in Canada: An Examination of the Image of Women in Mass Circulating Canadian Magazines, 1930–1970.' PhD dissertation, University of Toronto, 1977

Winship, Janice. *Inside Women's Magazines*. London: Pandora Press, 1987

Wolf, Naomi. *The Beauty Myth*. Toronto: Vintage Books, 1990

Wolfe, Morris. 'Magazines: Decline and Fall of Chatelaine.' *Globe and Mail*, 11 May 1993

– 'Magazines: Same Old Fluff in Modern Woman.' *Globe and Mail*, 2 March 1993

Wolfe, Susan J., and Julia Penelope. *Sexual Practice, Textual Theory: Lesbian Cultural Criticism*. Cambridge: Blackwell Publishers, 1993

Wood, James P. *Magazines in the United States*. New York: Ronald Press, 1971

Woodward, Helen. *The Lady Persuaders*. New York: Ivan Obolensky, 1960

Wright, Cynthia. '"The Most Prominent Rendezvous of the Feminine Toronto": Eaton's College Street and the Organization of Shopping in Toronto, 1920–1950.' PhD dissertation, Department of Education, University of Toronto, 1992

Zuckerman, Mary-Ellen. *Sources on the History of Women's Magazines, 1792–1960: An Annotated Bibliography*. New York: Greenwood Press, 1991

Index

Aboriginal, 34, 349
Aboriginal readers: articles, 347, 355; and cover art, 118
Aboriginal women: and articles (60s), 343–8, 354–6, 430n.14; and cover art, 346
abortion, 308–9, 370; in articles (50s), 306; in articles (60s), 336–7; *Chatelaine*'s impact on, 315
Abrahamson, Una, 197
Adams, Ian, 349
Adams, J.L., 88
Adams, Mary Louise, 15
advertisements: affluence and leisure in, 159–61; ageism in, 151, 153; alternate readings of, 135, 139, 148; children in, 152–3, 165–6; descriptions in, 42; diet dramas in, 147–9; difference between fifties and sixties, 159, 161; ethnic images in, 148, 150, 153, 161, 163; hetero-sexuality in, 151–2, 154, 176; home renovation in, 139–41, 157; home-maker fantasies in, 126–8, 144, 146; images of Canada in, 141, 163; images of men in, 139, 159–60, 163–5, 175–6; images of

romance in, 133–9; images of women in, 122, 141–3, 147–56, 174–5; importance of, 96; mecha-nized household in, 131–3; middle-class dreams in, 129; 'mothers' in, 127–8, 144, 146–7; overview of, 122–6, 174; people in ads, 124–5; processed foods in, 146–7; products in, 40, 122–4; purpose of, 106; racialized images in, 155–6, 165, 401n.34; ratio to editorial, 123; readers' responses to, 121–2, 167–73; sexist images in, 155–6, 159–62, 405n.79; Starch statistics in, 166–8; suburbia in, 139–41; working women in, 129–31, 147–8
advertising department at *Chatelaine*: advertisers' demands of, 168–9; appeals to youth, 201–2; CARD ads, 53–4; commercial imperative of, 71; departmental support for, 178–9; gendered images of, 120–1; goals of, 50, 52, 69; heterosexual sell in, 121; impact of *Chatelaine* ads, 37, 56; Magazine Advertising Bureau of Canada (MAB), 54;

market research of, 77–8, 368; masculine ethos of advertisers, 56; promotes feminism, 310; in sixties, 37; testimonials of, 55

affluence, myth of, 351

ageism: in beauty / fashion, 201–2; in cover art, 116; in departments, 184–5; inclusion in *Chatelaine*, 41; reader critique of, 358

Air Canada, 161–2

Alberta, 44. *See also* western Canada

Alexander, Shauna, 63

Aliman, Gene, 216

Aliman, Laura, 216

American magazines: Canadian circulation statistics, 66; compared with *Chatelaine*, 75–6, 78; competition with *Chatelaine*, 263; effect on Canadian market, 57–8

American women's magazines: *Chatelaine*'s competition with, 59–65, 222–3; comparison with *Chatelaine*, 64–5, 193, 214–19; declining fortunes of, 62; impact of editor's sex on, 388n.39

Anderson, Doris: and American magazines, 60–1; and articles (50s), 291, 293; biography of, 45–7; and *Chatelaine*'s impact, 314–17; and closet feminism, 365; comparison between *Maclean*'s and *Chatelaine*, 57; comparison of American and Canadian women's magazines, 64–5; and cover art, 110–11; and crafts, 215; and departments, 185; and editor's role, 101, 257, 269, 274, 370; editorial decisions of, 73, 79, 267, 344; editorial style of, 268–9; and editorials, 38, 258, 308–18; and

feminism, 46, 269–71; and fiction, 221–2, 226–8, 246; and food, 191; fostering community, 86; and gender division at Maclean Hunter, 49–51; and readers' letters, 79–80; and Maclean Hunter's goals, 52; memories of John Clare, 45, of B.H. Sanders, 44; and misreadings, 302; and Mrs Chatelaine contest, 90, 92; and paradoxes of editing *Chatelaine*, 97; and reader replies, 96–7, 318; *Rebel Daughter* (novel), 45; *Rough Layout* (novel), 47–8, 97, 316; and subversive editing, 52, 177, 317–18

Anglin, Gerald, 45, 283

anti–consumerism, 295, 358–61

anti–feminism: articles (60s), 301, 330–1; in *Chatelaine*, 27; letters, 328, 332, 334–6; reader response, 312–13

art directors, 108, 110

articles: abortion (50s), 306; anti-consumerism (50s), 281, 294–5, (60s), 358–61; Canadian history, 356; Canadiana, 282, 356–7; comparison of fifties and sixties, 319–21; consumer celebration, 285; conventional fare (60s), 335–6; editorial assignments, 274; fostering community, 282, 321–2; heterosexuality (60s), 338–40; humour, 300–2; impact, 289, 300; lesbianism, 337–8; marriage and women's issues (50s), 276–84; masculinity, 340–3; oppositional content, 332; oppositional meanings, 301, 324–6, 356–7; overview (50s), 272–5; overview (60s), 318–21; politics (60s), 323; poverty

(60s), 348–52; purpose of, 272, 306–7; race and ethnicity (50s), 284–7; reader response (50s), 276–7, 281–4, 286, 288–9, 297–8, 300–2; reader response (60s), 341–2, 347–8; suburbia, 279–80, 289–95, 302–6, 358–63; topics and themes (50s), 274–5; women's roles (60s), 324–6
Atlantic Canada, 19, 66, 82, 218, 353–4
Atlantic Canadian readers: on ads, 172–3; on articles, 273, 282–3, 286, 298, 341, 351, 354, 357, 362–3; on *Chatelaine*'s importance, 83–5; on children's department, 217; on cover art, 114; on departments, 185; on editorials, 314; on fashion/beauty, 199–201, 205; on food, 193; on homes, 210; on Mrs Chatelaine, 92
Atlantic Monthly, 227
Aunt Jemima, 139–40
Aylmer, 148–9, 161

Baird, Bette-Jo, 94
Barbour, Noel, 74–5
Barthes, Roland, 18
Batten, Jack, 308, 318, 331–2
Bell, Marilyn, 273
Bentzon, Johanne, 217
Better Homes and Gardens, 59
birth control: articles on (50s), 283–4, (60s), 309, 336–7, 370, 428n.93; letters about, 83
Bissell Carpet Sweepers, 135, 137
Bissell, Claude, 322
black Canadians: articles on, 286–9, 343, 353, 430n.112
Bobb, Yvonne, 286–8
Bombeck, Erma, 301

Boxer, Rosemary, 199
Branscombe, Keith, 110
Breines, Wini, 229
Brinton carpets, 159–60
British Columbia, 66, 80, 82. *See also* western Canada
Brown, Helen Gurley, 63
Brown, Marguerite W., 217
Buck, Pearl S., 222
Buckler, Ernest, 222
budgets, 358–60
Butler, Ron, 108

Callaghan, Morley, 222
Callwood, June, 3, 27, 308; Anderson's impact on, 50, 370; on Anderson's subversive editing, 73; on article composition, 274; articles of, 114, 338, 340; on cover art, 176; memories of John Clare, 45, of B.H. Sanders, 44; role in Marion Hilliard articles, 272, 296, 306, 337; on sexism at Maclean Hunter, 51
Campaigne, Alain, 207, 211
Campbell, Marjorie Wilkins, 280
Campbell's Soups, 131
Canadian Advertising Rates and Data (CARD): *Chatelaine* ads, 53–4, 120, 187, 374
Canadian celebrities, 109–10, 363–4
Canadian history, 356, 365, 432n.149
Canadian Home Journal, 33, 109, 184, 268; *Chatelaine* purchase of, 57, 75
Canadian Homes and Gardens, 33
Canadian nationalism, 107, 262–3
Canadian ways, 285
Canadian Westinghouse, 131–3
Cape Breton, 95
Carbine, Patricia, 63–4
Carter, John Mack, 63

Cawelti, John, 220, 224
CBC, 199, 311, 364
Centennial, 163, 319
Chalmers, Floyd, 44
Chalmers, Joan, 108, 400n.27, 111,116
Chatelaine: circulation statistics of, 35, 37, 59, 72, 268; community of readers, 8, 71, 282, 307, 321–2, 340, 366–7; community's importance to, 372–4; demographic profile of, 24, 36–7, 65–70, 120, 374; feminism in, 4, 9, 64, 70, 306–7, 369–71; feminist decline in, 4, 371–2; history of, 3, 9, 31, 33–5; history of production of, 25; impact of, 99, 279, 314–17, 323–4, 352; importance of, 26, 365–75; and *Maclean's*, 96; and modernization, 7; multiple messages of, 72; multiple readings of, 26; name of, 35; post-1977, 3–4, 371; sample issue description, 38–43; second-wave feminism in, 23–4, 65, 296; traditional images in, 106; traditional perspective in, 15, 381n.36; and U.S. women's magazines, 37, 59–65, 64–5, 70, 257–8, 283, 296, 299–300, 307, 311–12, 326–7, 364–5, 368–70. *See also* reading
Chatelaine Beauty Clinic, 202–4. *See also* fashion/beauty
Chatelaine Centre, 259, 266, 268. *See also* editorials
Chatelaine contests: Family Favourites, 182, 373; Memories, 359, 362
Chatelaine Cookbook, 182
Chatelaine Councillors. *See* Councillors, *Chatelaine*
Chatelaine Departments, 41. *See also* departmental fare

Chatelaine editors, 43–7
Chatelaine Expo Home, 211. *See also* homes features
Chatelaine fiction, 41. *See also* fiction
Chatelaine Institute, 181, 186, 191, 285, 318: and cover art, 109; reader response to, 91
Chatelaine letters, 42. *See also* letters
Chatelaine Seal of Approval, 170
Châtelaine, French-language edition, 35, 223
Chatty Chipmunk, 216–17
child abuse, 308–9, 315
Child Health Clinic, 216
children's departments, 216–17
Christie, Julie, 110
Clare, John: biography, 45; and *Chatelaine* Centre, 259–60; and cover art, 108, 113; and editorials, 267–8; impact on *Chatelaine*, 52, 57, 369
Clarkson, Adrienne, 110, 308, 324
class, analysis of, 24, 101; in ads, 129; in articles 278–81, 290; in departments, 184–5; in fiction, 240; issues of representation, 360–1; Mrs Slob case study, 92; poverty, 348–52; reader critique of, 192, 358; reader response to, 290–1, 348–9, 351–2; Sanders's editorials on, 261–2, 264
closet feminism, 269, 365, 369
Cold War, 5, 40, 171, 180, 267–8; editorials on, 269–70
Collett, Elaine, 186, 192–3, 197–8, 318
common law marriage, 277
consumption: gendering of, 53–6
Cosmopolitan, 4, 369
Councillors, *Chatelaine*: description of, 44, 87; editorial input of, 99, 374–5; food surveys among, 186–7; homemaker's survey, 1961, 97–8;

survey about Seal of Approval, 170; survey of U.S. magazines, 59

cover art: Canadian nationalism, 113, 118–19; contested terrain, 105–7; issues of representation, 113; overview of, 38–7, 108–10, 174; purpose of, 106–7, 120; racial diversity of, 113, 116–18; reader critique of, 109, 111; resistance to innovation, 111–13; sexual controversies, 113–16

Crack, Francis, 108

crafts: overview of, 214–16; reader response to, 215–16

cultural studies: British school of, 12; gender analysis of, 21–3, 384n.58; overview, 17–23

Currie, Dawn, 13

Curtis, Cyrus, 32

Curtis, Louisa Knapp, 32, 64

Damon Moore, Helen, 14, 32

Davis, Fred, 110

de Beauvoir, Simone, 258, 311–12

Dempsey, Lotta: biography, 44–5, 47, 369; and class analysis, 266; and cover art, 105–6, 108; and feminism, 265–6; and gardening, 213

departmental fare: and ads and advertisers, 168–70, 181; analysis of impact of, 217–19; crafts, 42; Homemaker's Diary, 42; homes, 41; Meals of the Month, 42; overview, 179; Your Child, 42, 216

depression, 295

Dichter publications, on advertising success, 171–2

Dichter, Ernest, 74

Dichter Study: on affluence, 210; on Canadian nationalism, 262; on

circulaton, 270; on cover art, 109; on fiction, 221; on food, 187; goals of, 395n.8; market research of Chatelaine, 52, 72, 74–9, 273; on reader agency, 100; as source of information, 395n.11

Dior, Christian, 141

discourse theory, 16,19

divorce, 308–9, 315

Dollery, Eveleen, 202–4, 206

Dominion Oilcloth and Linoleum Co., advertiser complaint, 169

Domtar, 158

Don Mills, 291, 293–4. See also suburbia

drug abuse, 308, 364

Dyer, Gillian, 126

editorial departments, at Chatelaine, 49, 51, 70; biographies, 43–7; editorial comments, 330–1; regional and class analysis, 46; subversive editing, 219

editorials: of Doris Anderson (50s), 268–71; anti–consumerism in, 266; of John Clare, 267–8; of Lotta Dempsey, 264–6; feminism in (50s), 269–71, (60s), 311–17; fostering community in, 315; goals of, 259, 306–7, 368; overview of (50s), 258–60, (60s), 309–11; parodying women's magazines in, 317–18; and reader response, 263–4, 308–9, 317–18; and Royal Commission on the Status of Women, 316–17; of B.H. Sanders, 260–4; sexism in (50s), 267–8, (60s), 313–14

Edmonton Bulletin, 44

Edmonton Journal, 44

equal work legislation, 309

ethnicity, 84, 86, 98, 107; learning
    Canadian ways, 94–5
ethnicity and race: in ads, 125; in
    articles (50s), 293, (60s), 343–8,
    359, 430n.113; and reader
    response, 308, 264, 286, 288–9,
    294; 'the other,' 285, 343
Everywoman's World, 33
Expo 67, 157. See also Centennial

family budgets, articles on (50s),
    289–90
Family Circle, 59–60, 369
Family Favourites, 186–7, 189–90,
    194, 373. See also food articles
Farnham, Emily, 14
Farrell, Amy Erdmann, 64, 98
fashion/beauty: advertiser support,
    204; age issues, 205–6; dieting,
    204–5; overview of, 198–207;
    reader response, 201, 205
Female Liberation Movement, 332.
    See also feminism
feminism: articles on (60s), 331–5,
    427n.78; Chatelaine's role in, 98–9,
    364–5, 369–71; closet feminism,
    365; editorials on (50s), 269–71,
    (60s), 311–17; effects of Chatelaine's
    content on, 97–9; first-wave, 269,
    312; in Marion Hilliard articles,
    299–300; liberal, 334–5; radical,
    332; and reproductive rights, 306,
    336–7; and unpaid household
    labour, 304–5; and working
    wives, 236. See also second-wave
    feminism
feminist analysis, of women's
    magazines, 332, 334
feminist readers: and articles (60s),
    332, 334, 343

fiction: alternate meaning in, 253–4;
    class and race in, 243–6; as 'com-
    mercial package,' 228–9, 243, 253;
    compared with U.S. fiction, 222–3;
    critique of consumption of, 239;
    editor, 222; editorial comments
    about, 226–8; female agency in,
    224–5, 232–3; gender relations in,
    225–6, 240–1; good provider in,
    232; heterosexuality in, 238;
    lesbianism in, 247–50; male angst
    in, 237–40; marriage in, 230–2;
    Martin stories, 85, 243–6; melo-
    drama in, 224; middle-class world
    in, 240; moral lessons in, 240–3;
    mystery, overview of, 251–2;
    overview of, 220–9; preferred
    meaning in, 252–3; reader re-
    sponse, 223, 228–9, 241–3, 245–6,
    251–3, 226–7; romance in, 223;
    suburban discontent in, 232–4;
    working wives in, 234–6
Fiske, John, 18, 20: methodology of,
    20–1; 'producerly text,' 20, 99, 367
Flare, 36, 216. See also Miss Chatelaine
food articles: advertiser promotions
    in, 191–2; Canadian fare in, 191,
    193–4; ethnicity in, 194; and
    Family Favourites, 182; overview
    of, 186–95; reader imput in,
    189–90; reader response, 178–9,
    190, 192, 276, 295; speed of
    preparation, 194; thrift in, 187–8,
    192–4
Foucault, Michel: discourse analysis,
    19–20; 'micropractices of power,'
    18–20, 100
Fournier, Roger, 222
Fraser, Catherine, 207
Fraser, John, 207

Friedan, Betty, 9, 296, 300; *Feminine Mystique*, 10–11, 15, 282, 307, 331, 370
Frum, Barbara, 308, 344–5, 347
Fulford, Robert, 273
Fuller, Bonnie, 63
Furnival, A. Stanley, 108

Galton, Lawrence, 40, 273, 323. *See also* Here's Health
gardening, 213–14
Gardner, A.B., 46
Garner, Hugh, 222, 238–9
gay men, as readers of *Chatelaine*, 95
gender, category of analysis, 24
General Electric, 133–5, 138
General Motors Canada, 165–6
George Weston Ltd., 126–31
Gillen, Mollie, 342
Glassey, Almeda, 222, 226–8, 331
Globe and Mail, 45, 95
Godey's Ladies Book, 32
Good Housekeeping, 33–4, 59, 93, 369: contents description, 60–2; fiction, 243
Gould, Beatrice, 59
Gould, Bruce, 59

Hallman, Mrs Marjorie E., 362
Harlequin, romances, 21–2
Hart, Ted: Maclean Hunter financial information, 57–8; promoting feminism, 310
Here's Health, 183, 273, 323
Hermes, Joke, 13, 73–4
Hershey, Lenore, 63–4
heterosexuality: in ads, 176; in articles (50s), 297–9, (60s), 308, 338–40
Hillard, Marion, 109, 268, 275;

articles of, 272, 295–300, 306, 337, 370; biography, 295, 420n.88; feminism of, 299–300; importance of, 296; popularity of, 76; reader response, 297–8, 300
Hodgkinson, Lloyd M: as *Chatelaine* publisher, 35–6, 46; and cover art, 110; and departmental fare, 180; and letters about ads, 168–9
Holmes, Marie, 186, 276
Homemaker's Diary, 96, 183, 197
Homemaker's magazine, 36–7
homes features: affluence in, 210, 211; *Chatelaine* departments, 141, 168; *Chatelaine* Expo Home, 211–12; *Chatelaine* Home Decorator Service, 212–13; overview of, 207–10; reader response, 210, 212–13
homosexuals, 337, 250. *See also* lesbianism, sexual orientation
Horn, Kahn-Tineta, 347–8
Hostess magazine, 36–7, 56
househusbands, 340–1
housekeeping features: article critique, 324–6; editorial critique, 318; overview of, 195–8; reader response, 197

illustrations, 228, 277
immigrants: articles on (50s), 284–6, 290, (60s), 344
incest, 308
interracial marriages, 308
Istona, Mildred, 3, 365, 371

Jobe, Kenneth, 110
Jukes, Mary, 274

Karsh, Yousef, 108

Kent, Raymond, 66
Khruschev, Nikita, 171
King, Annabelle, 207, 318
Kinsey, Dr A.C., 298, 338
Knowlton, Keith, 226, 331
Kraft, 131,147, 161

Ladies' Home Journal, 32, 62, 75, 222,
    369: compared with Chatelaine, 79;
    description of, 59–61; feminist sit–
    in at, 63–4
Laurence, Margaret, 222
Layton, Irving, 268
lesbianism, 251, 308, 370; and art
    director, 116, 400n.27; articles on
    (60s), 337–8; in fiction, 247–50; and
    Marion Hilliard, 295, 420n.88
letters: from Canadians abroad, 71,
    84–5; Chatelaine's prestige in, 87;
    from children, 91, 113–14; editorial
    closure of, 361; and ethnicity, 84,
    86; and fostering community, 83–4,
    86–7, 289; importance of, 372;
    from international readers, 80–1,
    83, 85–6, 179, 205, 215–16, 220,
    299, 362; methodology with, 79;
    'Mrs. Slob' collection, 88–92;
    overview of, 80–2; popularity of,
    79; reasons for reading, 81, 84;
    refute traditional analysis of,
    99–100; regional analysis of, 80;
    requests for assistance, 82–3; The
    Last Word Is Yours, 42–3
Lévesque, René, 323
Life magazine, 64
Light, Alison, 225
Listerine, 141
Locke, Jeannine, 284, 286
London, Jessie, 322
Look magazine, 64

MAB (Magazine Advertising Bu-
    reau), 170–1
Maclean Hunter, 3, 4, 8, 25, 33–7, 40,
    43, 51, 71, 78, 109, 368; advertising
    department, 48; advertising
    support, 168–71; Canadian con-
    tent policy, 25, 78; financial infor-
    mation, 56–7; gendered division of
    production, 69–70; goals for Chate-
    laine, 53, 181; production history,
    35, 37, 46, 49, 69; purpose of
    Chatelaine to, 48, 52, of Maclean's
    to, 49; selling Chatelaine, 107, 120;
    workplace culture, 31
Maclean's, 34, 40, 46, 93, 96, 267, 374;
    circulation statistics, 66; compared
    with Chatelaine, 51; editor Blair
    Fraser, 49; financial situation, 57
MacLennan, Barbara, 213
MacLennan, Hugh, 222
Macleod, Zena, 94
Macphail, Agnes, 265–6
Macpherson, Mary Etta, 43
magazine industry, history, 4, 31
magazine production (Chatelaine):
    circulation statistics, 368; commer-
    cial vs. editorial imperatives, 49–
    52, 71–2, 96–7, 107, 110, 120, 168–9,
    176–7, 187, 193, 211–13, 217–19,
    226–8, 257, 266, 280, 294–5, 310,
    317–18, 330–1, 367–8; gender of
    production personnel, 47–52;
    paradoxical content, 366; pay
    scale, 319; reader imput, 261, 263,
    273, 310–11, 372
magazine research: American
    magazines, 14, 378n.15; Canadian
    magazines, 14; history of, 12;
    methodology, 16; women's maga-
    zines, 13, 380nn.29, 33

Magic Baking Powder, 144, 146
Maitland, Mrs Beatrice (Mrs Slob), 88–92, 373
Marchand, Roland, 122, 176
Margolius, Sidney, 289–90
Maritimes, 199. *See also* Atlantic Canada
market research: Canada's Magazine Audience (1969), 65–9; impact of advertising, 50, 54–6
Marlow, Dorothy, 93
Martins of Alberta, 222, 243–6. *See also* fiction
Mary Maxim, 144–5
Massey Commission Report, 49
Masters and Johnson, 339
maternal feminism, 260, 264. *See also* Sanders, B.H.
maternalism, in ads, 127–9
maternity, 382n.39
Max Factor, 163
May, Edna, 273, 322
Mayes, Herbert R., 61–2
Mayfair, 33
Maynard, Rona, 3, 23, 371
McCall's magazine, 33, 64, 369; description, 59–61; fiction in, 243
McCall, Christina, 40, 273, 308, 323–4, 348; feminist articles of, 327–30, 370
McCracken, Ellen, 106, 129
McLaren, Angus, 83
McLaren, Arlene Tigar, 83
Mead, Margaret, 319
Meals of the Month, 96, 186; overview, 190–2. *See also* food articles
men: in ads, 127; in articles (50s), 318, 392n. 103, (60s), 340–3, 429n.103; in cover art, 113–14

menopause, 370
Messer, Don, 273, 363–4
methodology: content analysis, 16–17; cultural analysis, 17–23
Meyerowitz, Joanne, 10, 15; critique of Betty Friedan, 11, 15
micropractice, 31
Miss Chatelaine magazine: origins and history, 35–6, 216
Miss Clairol, 38, 151, 404n.74
Mitchell, Joni, 110, 120
Mitchell, W.O., 226
modernity, 76, 106, 354, 356, 361
Modleski, Tania, 21–3
Montgomery, Lucy Maud, 248
Morris, Eileen: articles, 199, 305, 319; 'in the lodge,' 374
Mrs Chatelaine Contest, 19, 315, 319–21, 361–2, 373; anti-contestants, 362–3; description of, 87–8; Maitland, Mrs Beatrice (Mrs Slob) 88–92, 373
Ms. magazine, 4, 369, 371; compared with *Chatelaine*, 98–9, 101; history of, 26, 63–4; liberal feminism in, 64
multiculturalism, 194, 286, 344
Munro, Alice, 222

National Action Committee on the Status of Women, 46
National Geographic, 281
National Organization for Women (NOW), 332
nationalism, 78
Nelles, Wanda, crafts editor, 214
New Brunswick, 45. *See also* Atlantic Canada
New Yorker, 227
Newfoundland. *See also* Atlantic Canada

Nichols, Wade H., 62
Nivea, 152–3
Nixon, Richard, 171
Nova Scotia. *See* Atlantic Canada
Nozema, 141

Oneida, 135–6
Ontario, 66, 80; readers: and ads,
    172–3; and articles, 271, 282, 286,
    278–9, 288–9, 290–1, 293–4, 303,
    309, 318, 321, 324, 326, 329, 334,
    340, 342, 349, 351–2, 357–8, 360–2,
    298, 300–2; and *Chatelaine*, 76,
    95–6; and cover art, 105, 107,109,
    113, 114, 116, 118; and editorials,
    259, 263–6, 312–14, 317; and
    fashion/beauty, 205; and fiction,
    221, 223, 245–6; and food, 182–3,
    189–91, 193, 195; and homes, 213;
    and housekeeping, 197; and Mrs.
    Chatelaine, 90; and questionnaire,
    95; and women's magazines, 60
O'Reilly, Helen, 213, 216
Osborne, Marg, 110

Packard, Vance, 74
paradoxical content, 24. *See also*
    reading
Pearson, Lester, 110, 316
Playboy magazine, 4, 369
Playtex, 141, 143
poststructuralism, 16,19. *See also*
    Michel Foucault
postwar Canada: affluent sixties,
    358–63; critique of, 356; economy
    in, 6–7, 290, 351; historical revi-
    sionism, 5, 25, 218, 258, 377n.6;
    and modernization of Canada, 82;
    North American culture in, 268;
    sexist society in, 329–30; society, 5,

374–5; women's role in workforce
    in, 129–31; women's roles in, 75–6,
    316
poverty, 348, 355, 364; articles on
    (60s), 348–52, 431n.124. *See also*
    class
Prairies, 19, 66, 80, 82, 218. *See also*
    western Canada
preferred meaning, 277, 373
prescriptive literature: analysis of,
    217–19; editorials on (60s), 314–16;
    editors' instructions about, 262,
    266; fiction critique of, 232–5; and
    reader agency, 55, 99–100, 198;
    reader interaction with, 179–80
Prince Edward Island, 46. *See also*
    Atlantic Canada
producerly text, 367. *See also* Fiske,
    John
prostitution, 355

Quebec readers, 66, 82, 84, 86; and
    ads, 121; and articles, 284, 297,
    304–6, 325–6, 330, 332, 347–8; and
    cover art, 116, 118; and editorials,
    265, 312; and feminism, 98; and
    food, 190, 192, 195; and homes,
    210; and Mrs Chatelaine, 91

race, 294. *See also* ethnicity and race
race analysis, 24, 101, 107; cover art
    representation, 116–18
racism, 116, 118, 288, 309, 355, 364.
    See also ethnicity and race
Radway, Janice, 21–3, 221
reader resistance: articles (50s), 303–
    5, (60s), 325–6, 332, 335–6, 342–3,
    363–4; editorials (60s), 312–13; to
    prescriptive literature, 180
reader response: and ads, 172–3; and

articles (50s), 257–9, 281–4, 303–6, 276–7, 286, 288–9, 293–4, (60s), 325–6, 328–30, 360–1, 341–3, 348–9, 351–2, 365, 353–5, 339–40; and departments., 182–5; and editorials (60s), 308–9, 312–13, 317–18; and fiction, 241–3, 220–1; and food, 190, 192; importance of, 367; and Mrs Slob, 90–2; to B.H. Sanders's editorials, 263–4

Reader Takes Over, 79. *See also* letters

Reader's Digest, 57, 65, 93, 263

readers: agency, 11, 21; Canadian reading preferences, 58; *Chatelaine* compared with U.S. magazines, 85; class background and tensions, 67–8, 82, 90–2; demographics, 8, 12; heterogenity, 24, 100; ideal, 107; international, 353–4; resistance, 27, 56, 258; role in *Chatelaine*'s success, 101; statistics, 66

reading: advertiser's instructions, 54–5; alternate meanings, 72–3, 100, 279, 343, 361; *Chatelaine* scrapbooks, 323–4, 425n.49; *Chatelaine*'s impact, 271–2, 305; close readers, 71, 173, 321–2; critics of *Chatelaine*, 95–7; Dichter study results, 75–9; editors' instructions, 246, 262; effects of *Chatelaine*, 97–9; fictional instructions, 234; fostering community, 77, 83–4, 93–4, 101, 324, 372–5, 362–3; gay male perspective, 95; instructions to readers, 317–18, 367; learning Canadian ways, 94–5; magazine parodies, 301, 315; misreadings, 72–3, 301–2; modifying the magazine, 116, 339; multi-

ple meanings, 93, 100, 233, 258; negotiating fiction fissures, 221, 229; negotiating paradoxes, 24, 151, 326, 352, 366; oppositional articles, 276–7, 293; oppositional reading, 72–3, 89–90, 100, 335–6; preferred meaning, 72, 92, 100; reader agency, 92, 99, 366–7; reader questionnaires, 93–5; sources and methodology, 72, 395n.3; suburbia case study, 303, 421n.118; surveys of reading habits, 69; ways and purpose, 43, 73, 76, 81, 94

Redbook, 59, 62, 369

regional analysis: articles, 280–1, 353–6, 363–4; and beauty, 199–201; category of analysis, 24, 101; and departments, 185; Mrs Chatelaine contest, 361–2

Report of the Special Senate Committee on Mass Media, 57

reproductive issues, 364. *See also* birth control

revolution, of women, 311–12

Reynolds, Barbara, 168, 207

Richler, Mordecai, 308, 356–7

Robinson, Elizabeth Chant, 42, 216. *See also* Your Child

Robinson, Gertrude Joch, 15

Roche, Mazo de la, 222

romance fiction, 220. *See also* fiction

Rowlands, June, 291

Roy, Gabrielle, 222

Royal Commission on Publications, 48

Royal Commission on the Status of Women: *Chatelaine*'s role in, 65, 98–9, 370; classist critique of, 349

Royal Family (Britain): articles on,

41, 272–3, 273, 275; cover art of, 109; critique of, 352

Rule, Jane, 222

Rumgay, Gordon, 46

rural: families, 290; life, 281; readers, 182–5, 189, 363–4; women, 322, 358–9

Russell, Sheila MacKay, 220, 222, 243, 248, 250, 253

Saint-Martin, Fernande: *Châtelaine* editor, 35

Sanders, Byrne Hope: Doris Anderson's memories of, 86; biography, 43–4, 47; and *Chatelaine* Councillors, 87; and cover art, 108; on editor's role, 262–3, 369; and editorials, 258–64; as maternal feminist, 260–1; and Second World War work, 43–4

Sangster, Joan, 7

Saskatchewan, 45, 91. *See also* western Canada

Saskatoon Star Phoenix, 45

Saturday Evening Post, 65

Savignac (artist), 111–13

Scott, Barbara Ann, 273

Scott, Keith, 108

Seal of Approval, 197

second-wave feminism, 9, 308–9, 364, 375. *See also* feminism; editorials

semiotics, 16–18. *See also* Barthes, Roland

Sevareid, Eric, 323

Seventeen magazine, 64

sex deviates, 271, 428n.94. *See also* sexual orientation

sexism: in ads, 175; in articles, 282; in Clare editorials, 267–8; in

editorials, 270–1, 309; at Maclean Hunter, 51; readers response, 105–6

sexual orientation, 297, 337, 364, 370; as category of analysis, 24–5, 101; and fiction analysis, 247–51

Shaw, George Bernard, 222

Shopping with *Chatelaine*, 197, 323

single mothers, 309

Smith, John Caulfield, 207

social feminism, 335. *See also* feminism

Souvaine, Mabel Hill, 59

Soviet Union, 269

Special Senate Committee on Mass Media, 269

Star Weekly, 46

Starch Reports: and ads, 166–8; and articles (50s), 275, (60s), 319; and departments, 181–2; and editorials, 310; market research on *Chatelaine*, 54; and readers statistics, 373

Stein, Robert, 62

Steinem, Gloria, 63–4

Strong-Boag, Veronica, 6, 23

suburbia, 5–6, 257–8, 366; in ads, 174, 127–9; articles on, 273, 275, 279–80, 289–95, 302–6; critique of, 293; and fictional discontent, 229, 232–4; and male experiences, 237–40

suffrage, 34

Sutherland, Fraser, 14

Swanson TV dinners, 146

Swift's Meats, 164–5

Sysak, Juliette, 110, 273

Taylor, Carol, 197

Taylor, Elizabeth, 110, 114–16

Tebbel, John, 62
Teen Tempo, 40, 216. *See also Miss Chatelaine*
television, 58
Texmade, 152–6
The Last Word Is Yours, 79. *See also* letters
Thériault, Yves, 222
Thistlewood, Doris, 207
Time magazine, 57, 65, 93, 263
Toronto Star, 45
traditional fare, 257
Trudeau, Pierre Elliott, 110
Tyrrell, H.V., 33–4, 368
Tyson, Ian and Sylvia, 110

United Church Observer, 93
United Church of Canada, 81, 355

Vanier, Madame, 118–19
Vipond, Mary, 15

Wabasso Cotton Company, 168
welfare, 348–50. *See also* class
western Canada, 90–2, 266, 344
western Canadian readers: and ads, 172–3; and articles, 257–9, 279–80, 281–4, 290–91, 297–8, 300–2, 304, 306, 318, 326, 332, 328–30, 334–5, 339–40, 341–2, 347, 352, 353, 355, 357, 361, 363–4; and *Chatelaine*, 81–82, 87, 178; and children's department, 217; and cover art, 105, 110–11, 113–14, 118, 120; and departments, 184–5; and editorials, 263, 268, 308, 310–13, 317–18; and fashion/beauty, 206–7; and fiction, 222, 232, 242–3, 246, 251–2; and food, 189–90, 192, 195; and gardening, 213–15; and homes,

210, 212; and magazines, 77, 87; and Mrs Chatelaine, 90–2
Western Home Monthly, 33
What's New, 40; overview (60s), 321–4
What's New in the Arts, 273, 322
Wilcox, Vivian, 199, 205–6; relations with advertisers, 169
Williams, Raymond, 16
Wilson, Anne Elizabeth, 43
Wilson, Barbara, 344, 346
Wilson, Ethel, 222
Wilson, Lois, 214
Wilson, Renate, 337
Winnipeg Ballet, 105
Winship, Janice, 12
Wolf, Naomi, 9
Woman's Day, 59, 75, 369; description, 59–60
women's culture, 23–4, 366, 375; departmental fare, 179–80; and editorials, 264; fostered by magazines, 101
women's magazines, 32–3; and construction of femininity, 11; as genre, 178–9, 220, 257; myths about, 9–12; reader response to, 97. *See also* American women's magazines
women's roles: 1961 Councillors' survey of, 97–8; in ads, 127–31; Doris Anderson's critique of (50s), 270–1; changes in (60s), 326, 329–30, 342, 364–5, 375; Dichter study finding about, 75–6; in fiction, 229, 232–3; in the home, 196–7, 324–6; in postwar Canada, 5–6, 100, 175–6, 366; traditional view of, 179; as working wives, 194–5, 235, 261

women's work; in articles (50s), 296–7, 282, 299–300, (60s), 340–1, 327–8, 426n.64; in editorials (50s), 308–9; in fiction, 230–1

working class: in articles (60s), 327–8, 348–9; critiques of, 24, 290–1, 325–6

Wright, Ouida: readership case study, 95–7

Wylie, Phillip, 270

Yack, Jean, 98, 358; and anti-feminists, 330–1; and crafts, 215

Yardley's, 141–2

You Were Asking *Chatelaine*, 79. *See also* letters

Your Child, 42, 216

Your World Notebook, 96, 273, 323, 424n.46

Zuckerman, Mary Ellen, 62

STUDIES IN GENDER AND HISTORY

General editors: Franca Iacovetta and Karen Dubinsky

1 Suzanne Morton, *Ideal Surroundings: Domestic Life in a Working-Class Suburb in the 1920s*

2 Joan Sangster, *Earning Respect: The Lives of Working Women in Small-Town Ontario, 1920–1960*

3 Carolyn Strange, *Toronto's Girl Problem: The Perils and Pleasures of the City, 1880–1930*

4 Sara Z. Burke, *Seeking the Highest Good: Social Service and Gender at the University of Toronto, 1888–1937*

5 Lynne Marks, *Revivals and Roller Rinks: Religion, Leisure, and Identity in Late-Nineteenth-Century Small-Town Ontario*

6 Cecilia Morgan, *Public Men and Virtuous Women: The Gendered Languages of Religion and Politics in Upper Canada, 1791–1850*

7 Mary Louise Adams, *The Trouble with Normal: Postwar Youth and the Making of Heterosexuality*

8 Linda Kealey, *Enlisting Women for the Cause: Women, Labour, and the Left in Canada, 1890–1920*

9 Christina Burr, *Spreading the Light: Work and Labour Reform in Late-Nineteenth-Century Toronto*

10 Mona Gleason, *Normalizing the Ideal: Psychology, Schooling, and the Family in Postwar Canada*

11 Deborah Gorham, *Vera Brittain: A Feminist Life*

12 Marlene Epp, *Women without Men: Mennonite Refugees of the Second World War*

13 Shirley Tillotson, *The Public at Play: Gender and the Politics of Recreation in Post-War Ontario*

14 Veronica Strong-Boag and Carole Gerson, *Paddling Her Own Canoe: The Times and Texts of E. Pauline Johnson (Tekahionwake)*

15 Stephen Heathorn, *For Home, Country, and Race: Constructing Gender, Class, and Englishness in the Elementary School, 1880–1914*

16 Valerie J. Korinek, *Roughing It in the Suburbs: Reading* Chatelaine *Magazine in the Fifties and Sixties*